DEEP SOUTH DYNASTY

DEEP SOUTH DYNASTY

THE BANKHEADS *of* ALABAMA

KARI FREDERICKSON

The University of Alabama Press
Tuscaloosa

The University of Alabama Press
Tuscaloosa, Alabama 35487-0380
uapress.ua.edu

Typeface: Adobe Caslon

Cover images: *Clockwise from upper left*, Speaker of the House Will Bankhead
wielding the gavel (courtesy of the Alabama Department of Archives and
History); John Hollis Bankhead with his sons, Henry, John Jr., and Will
(courtesy of the Alabama Department of Archives and History); portrait of
Tallulah Bankhead (Library of Congress, Prints & Photographs Division,
Carl Van Vechten Collection); Marie Bankhead Owen (courtesy of the
Alabama Department of Archives and History)
Cover design: Lori Lynch

Portions of chapters 5 and 6 appeared in "Brand New District, Same Old
Fight: The Bankhead-Hobson Campaign of 1916," in *Alabama Review* 70
(October 2016), 267–95; and "Manhood and Politics: The Hobson-Bankhead
Campaigns of 1904 and 1906," in *Alabama Review* 69 (April 2016), 99–131.

Cataloging-in-Publication data is available from the Library of Congress.
ISBN: 978-0-8173-2110-9
E-ISBN: 978-0-8173-9381-6

Contents

Acknowledgments

THIS BOOK BEGAN AS a conversation between a few members of the University of Alabama's Department of History and John T. Oliver Jr., Esq. A highly successful banker and businessman, former member of the University of Alabama's board of trustees, and chairman of the Bankhead Family Foundation (now the Walker Area Community Foundation), Mr. Oliver knew that within the family's history was an important story waiting to be told. I knew enough about the Bankhead family and its impact on the state of Alabama and the American South to take the bait. The foundation provided a generous grant that allowed me to hire several graduate students to undertake the early stages of the research for this book. The story of the Bankhead family from the end of the Civil War through the end of World War II turned out to be far richer and more complex than I had imagined; consequently, it also took much longer to research and write than the Bankhead family had hoped. I am grateful for the research support and for their patience. I hope they find the book worth the wait.

Several graduate students assisted with research for this book. Angela Jill Cooley, Charles Roberts, Matthew Downs, Daniel Menestres, Mills Barker, Charity Rakestraw, David McCray, and Joseph Pearson logged countless hours in the archives and on the tedious ride to and from the state archives in Montgomery. Talented historians all, several have since published their own books, and all have gone on to successful careers. Charles Roberts's feedback on the New Deal chapters was immensely helpful. His book on New Deal rural rehabilitation programs and Matthew Downs's book on federal development in the Tennessee Valley intersected with the Bankheads' story in significant ways. I am grateful for their insights.

I consider myself lucky to have spent my career at the University of Alabama. I have benefited from the support and keen historical insights of my colleagues here, as well as from historians around the state. George Rable and Larry Kohl remain valued friends and role models. Lesley Gordon joined our faculty late in the life of this project but quickly became a trusted confidant; she gamely read several chapters, as did Sam Webb and Rob Riser. I am grateful to Lisa Lindquist Dorr and Holly Grout for helping me make historical sense of Tallulah Bankhead. David Beito clued me in to available recordings of Tallulah Bankhead's radio program. Marty Olliff shared a draft of his fine book on Alabama road building. Our office staff—Ellen Pledger, Morta Riggs, and Marla Scott—provided critical administrative support and much-needed levity.

Every historian should be lucky enough to have Fitz Brundage and Wayne Flynt as their manuscript's reviewers. Their excellent feedback greatly improved this book. Fellow Tuscaloosans and historians Guy Hubbs and Cathy Randall made this a better book. Guy offered critical suggestions that strengthened the book's early chapters; Cathy read the entire manuscript and saved me from many embarrassing errors. David Ferrara read the final proofs, and Jessica Freeman prepared the index. My dear friend Ian Crawford joined me on a trip to visit various Bankhead sites. I benefited greatly from his knowledge of architecture and material culture.

Historians know that good archivists and editors are worth their weight in gold. Marina Klaric, Kate Matheny, Kevin Ray, and Donnelly Walton at W. S. Hoole Special Collections Library, University of Alabama, provided invaluable assistance at crucial moments in this project. Meredith McDonough at the Alabama Department of Archives and History was instrumental in helping me acquire this book's many images. Genealogists Nancy Peters and Nancy Bean helped me track the early Bankheads from South Carolina to Alabama. The fine folks at the University of Alabama Press, in particular editor in chief Daniel Waterman and senior acquisitions editor Claire Lewis Evans, remained enthusiastic and patient throughout the life of the project. Copyeditor Jessica Hinds-Bond improved the manuscript with her meticulous attention to detail. I am grateful for their help.

While I researched and wrote this book, my daughters, Olivia and Becca, became young women. There were times, especially toward the end, when it felt as though I was spending more time with someone else's family than with my own. They have been good sports throughout the life of this project, even as my research materials took over the kitchen table. They rolled their eyes (as only bored teenage girls can) when I pointed out to them contributions by one Bankhead or another as we drove across Alabama to volleyball matches and musical theater competitions. The satisfaction I feel in finishing this book pales in comparison to the pride I feel in their many accomplishments.

My biggest intellectual and personal debt goes to Jeff Melton. He lifted up my flagging spirits at critical moments and cooked more than his fair share of family meals. He listened patiently as I struggled to put my jumbled thoughts into words, and brought his editorial skills to bear on unwieldy sentences. His good humor and support mean more than I can say.

Abbreviations

ADAH	Alabama Department of Archives and History
ADAHP	Alabama Department of Archives and History Papers
JHB	John Hollis Bankhead
JHBP	John Hollis Bankhead Papers
JHBjr	John Hollis Bankhead Jr.
JHBjrP	John Hollis Bankhead Jr. Papers
JTH	James Thomas Heflin
JTHP	James Thomas Heflin Papers
MBO	Marie Bankhead Owen
MBOP	Marie Bankhead Owen Papers
RPH	Richmond Pearson Hobson
RPHP	Richmond Pearson Hobson Papers
TB	Tallulah Bankhead (b. 1902)
TBP	Tallulah Bankhead Papers
TMO	Thomas McAdory Owen
TMOP	Thomas McAdory Owen Papers
WBB	William Brockman Bankhead
WBBP	William Brockman Bankhead Papers

Introduction

Family Biography as Regional History

IN JUNE 1946, IN JASPER, ALABAMA, mourners laid a political dynasty to rest. Dignitaries and humble denizens gathered in this small town of five thousand souls to honor the life of the last member of one of the South's and nation's most powerful political families. US senator John Hollis Bankhead Jr. was buried in Oak Hill Cemetery near the graves of his father, Senator John Hollis Bankhead Sr.; and his brother William Brockman Bankhead, congressman and Speaker of the House. *Newsweek* magazine observed that, "It was not a man who died. It was a tradition. Congress would not be the same without a Bankhead."[1] This was not a statement of sentimentality. It was obvious. The Bankheads had served the state of Alabama in one capacity or another since 1865; a Bankhead had occupied a seat in Congress continuously since 1887. Their collective state and congressional service of eighty-one years encompassed some of the most transformative events in the history of Alabama, the South, and the nation. Yet today, the Bankheads are practically forgotten. If someone registers a flicker of recognition at the mention of the name, it is usually for Tallulah Bankhead, renowned stage and film actress. But even then, she is as often remembered more for her role as the Black Widow in the 1960s camp television show *Batman* as she is for her other, more illustrious, stage and film work. Even in the state of Alabama, the name "Bankhead" resonates mostly for its relation to places—Bankhead National Forest, Bankhead Lake, Bankhead Tunnel, Bankhead Highway—rather than for the accomplishments of their namesakes. Although the family has all but disappeared from public consciousness, at one time, its name was synonymous with dynastic power. The Bankheads are the South's most important, forgotten, political family.

This book traces the careers of five members of the Bankhead family over the course of three generations: John Hollis Bankhead (1842–1920); his sons John Hollis Bankhead Jr. (1872–1946) and William Brockman Bankhead (1874–1940);

his daughter Marie Bankhead Owen (1869–1958); and, to a lesser extent, his granddaughter Tallulah Brockman Bankhead (1902–68).[2] More than simply a reclamation project, this examination of a once-powerful but long-forgotten southern family provides a compelling way in which to tell the complicated story of the region during a critical period. From Reconstruction through the end of World War II, the Bankheads served as the principal architects of the political, economic, and cultural framework of Alabama and the South.

Much of the Bankheads' impact came in the form of public policy; thus politics serves as this book's narrative spine. Over the course of two generations, the Bankheads were instrumental in expanding the reach of the federal government to aid southern economic development. As a US congressman and later as US senator, John Hollis Bankhead, who became known as the "Father of Good Roads," was critical in securing federal money for southern infrastructure projects during the New South era, dramatically accelerating the integration of the South into the nation's economic life. Congressman William B. Bankhead and Senator John H. Bankhead Jr. became a formidable legislative team during the New Deal years. John Jr. was recognized as the foremost spokesperson for the cotton economy and became President Franklin D. Roosevelt's chief agricultural advocate in the Senate in the 1930s. He was instrumental in constructing an agricultural support system that cemented farmers' dependence on the federal government for the remainder of the twentieth century. He also authored one of the era's most radical endeavors to address the systemic problem of rural poverty. William (Will) Bankhead, elected to Congress in 1916, assumed a leadership role when the Democrats came to power in 1933. Serving first as the chair of the powerful Rules Committee, then as majority leader, and finally as Speaker of the House during Roosevelt's tempestuous second term, Will deployed his personal charisma and considerable political skills to keep the often unruly Democratic majority together and focused. That Roosevelt was able to accomplish any legislative victories during his second term—a period of disastrous political missteps by the president and a time when congressional interest in further New Deal legislation waned—was due largely to Will Bankhead's leadership. When *Newsweek* identified John Jr.'s passing as the end of a "tradition," the ability of southern Democrats to expand and direct the power of the federal government for the benefit of the South constitutes a key component of that tradition.

If harnessing the power and funds of the federal government for southern advantage was a critical component of the Bankheads' South, so too was the oppression of African Americans, as well as their exclusion from the benefits of federal intervention. The son of a slaveholder and soldier for the Confederate States of America, John Hollis Bankhead returned to his state in 1865 determined to limit the revolutionary potential of Reconstruction. The father's adherence to white supremacy was transmitted to the sons. In their various public positions, John Hollis Bankhead and his son John Jr. contributed significantly to the economic marginalization, social deprivation, and political disfranchisement of the state's black citizens. As members of the US Congress and the Senate, respectively, Will and John Jr. were instrumental in placing New Deal work and relief measures within what one historian has referred to as a "Southern Cage": as a powerful bloc within the Democratic majority, southern members of Congress designed New Deal programs and benefits in a way that blunted their revolutionary potential by ensuring that they were funneled primarily to white recipients.[3]

The Bankheads' rise to political power cannot be divorced from the creation of the one-party Democratic South. Fearful of a political coalition of black and white have-nots, the family was instrumental in the elimination of political challenges in the late nineteenth century; the family's home base of Walker County contained a fair number of Republican voters, so the possibility of a political challenge was, for a time, real. Although African American voters were the chief target of the turn-of-the-century disfranchisement campaign, elites like the Bankheads also remained suspicious of the political yearnings of poor white citizens. New Deal reforms that aided the have-nots in particular were valued as much for their ability to mute political challenges from disgruntled poor white southerners as they were for providing relief.

The Bankheads' political power was reinforced by their ability to shape southern culture. Convincing the coal miner, the textile worker, and the small farmer of the wisdom and legitimacy of the traditional white ruling class was a complex proposition that involved the dissemination of a particular set of ideas about race, class, and history that shored up the elite's claims to cultural and political hegemony. In both the political and cultural efforts to secure white supremacy and affirm the superiority of the traditional ruling class, of which the Bankheads were prominent members, the family played a critical role. Marie Bankhead Owen led this effort, first through her club and literary work, but more powerfully during her thirty-plus-year reign as director of the Alabama Department of Archives and History. Marie used her position as head of the state's most influential historical and cultural agency to promote a particular historical narrative that romanticized the antebellum era and rural life generally, legitimized secession, heralded the heroism of the Confederate soldier, minimized the contributions of poor white citizens, and all but erased African Americans entirely. Not surprisingly, her father and brothers play a central role in her historical narrative. For Marie, the history of the Bankheads *was* the history of Alabama and the South.

Because this is a book about the South, the movements of the most famous Bankhead—actress Tallulah—play a much smaller role than those of her elders. Tallulah Bankhead left Alabama in 1917 to chase fame and fortune in New York City at the tender age of fifteen; five years later, Tallulah booked passage to London, where she would remain until 1931. Tallulah's theatrical star rose in concert with the new cultural trends. Just as her grandfather, father, and uncle shaped the political world to bring economic benefits that helped craft a more modern South, Tallulah embodied the energy and possibilities of the New Woman. Although she returned to the United States in 1931, she never again lived in Alabama and rarely visited. Nevertheless, Alabamians claimed Tallulah Bankhead as their own, and she declared herself a "daughter of the South." Celebrity status provided Tallulah a voice and cultural capital distinct from the more traditional political power wielded by her family. Still, she did not shy away from converting her fame into other kinds of power when it suited her. Likewise, the Bankhead men leveraged Tallulah's stardom to confer on their dynastic political power a certain royal gloss. Coverage of Tallulah frequently referenced her political bloodlines, while stories about her father Will Bankhead highlighted the activities of his famous daughter. Unofficial guardian of the family legacy, Marie Bankhead Owen, kept close tabs on Tallulah, always looking for ways to mobilize her niece's public persona to the advantage of the Bankhead name; conversely, she also moved quickly to tamp down negative press on Tallulah. Although Tallulah resisted most of her aunt's efforts to direct her career, she strategically used particular southern tropes to the advantage of herself and her famous family.

When John H. Bankhead Jr. died in 1946, Alabama and the South stood at a crossroads. The one-party Democratic South dominated by the cotton economy and a tiny white elite—a South the Bankheads helped construct—was beginning to crumble. World War II unleashed powerful economic, social, and political forces that, over the course of the next twenty years, would render the Bankheads' South if not unrecognizable, at the very least profoundly altered. The death of the last Bankhead was not just the end of a political dynasty; it was the end of an era.

I

ASCENSION

1

❦

Becoming the Bankheads of Alabama

The Bankheads caught Alabama Fever. Drawn by the promise of agricultural wealth in the recently ceded lands of what in the early nineteenth century was called the Southwest, George and Jane Bankhead sold a sizable inheritance, packed up their four children and two enslaved workers, and left behind their life in South Carolina. They followed George's brothers and thousands of other migrants who poured into lands that eventually became the states of Louisiana, Mississippi, and Alabama.[1] It was not unusual for migrants to move several times before settling for good.[2] We cannot know exactly how the contagion entered the Bankhead household, but when the fever struck, it altered the family's fortunes dramatically. The story of the early Bankheads is woven into the story of early Alabama.

Settlers first took up land in the lush river valleys—the Tennessee, the Tombigbee, the Coosa—which combined rich soils with river transportation. As early as 1818, a thriving staple-crop economy had taken root. This farming for the market was centered in two places in Alabama: the Black Belt, a fertile crescent of rich, dark soil that stretched across the middle of the new territory and was thought at the time to be the world's best place to grow cotton; and, to a lesser degree, parts of the Tennessee Valley. The population in the new region expanded rapidly. The Territory of Alabama was created out of the eastern half of the Mississippi Territory in 1817. In 1819, Alabama became a state. By that time, a slave economy was firmly established.

The rush to pull up stakes in the old seaboard states in the 1810s worried one North Carolina planter. James Graham complained that "the Alabama Fever rages here with great violence and has carried off vast numbers of our Citizens. I am apprehensive, if it continues to spread as it has done, it will almost depopulate the country. There is no question that this fever is contagious, for as soon as one neighbor visits another who has just returned from Alabama, he immediately discovers the same symptoms which are exhibited by the person who has seen the allureing Alabama. Some of our oldest and most wealthy men are offering their possessions for sale and desirous of removing to this new country."[3] Nowhere was the population increase more frantic than in north Alabama's Tennessee River Valley.

It took a few years before George Bankhead and his family reached "allureing Alabama." Like many migrants from South Carolina, they stopped first in Tennessee, where they joined an ill-fated white settlement illegally located on Chickasaw land on the Elk River. The Bankheads and other settlers claimed they had innocently developed their homesteads "without any knoledg or intention of violating the laws of the government."[4] Unable to gain clear title to their property, the Bankheads pushed on. In 1816 George Bankhead purchased land in the Mississippi Territory. The land lay astride the "waters of Bear Creek," a tributary of the Tennessee River in what would become northwest Alabama, and close to General Andrew Jackson's Old Military Road, which ran from present-day Nashville to New Orleans.[5]

As of 1820, the Bankheads were living in what became Franklin County, in the new state of Alabama. The household had grown since George and Jane first left South Carolina, now numbering ten children ranging in age from infancy to eighteen years, and eight enslaved people. In Franklin County in 1820, there were 539 households. Of those, the majority—342—did not claim people as property.[6] Forty households enslaved ten or more people. George and Jane Bankhead were small farmers, determined to expand their acquisitions and move up the economic and social ladder. Like most new settlers, the family had to clear the land, fence in fields, plant corn, and construct a rough log house for the family and small cabins for the enslaved—all as quickly as possible. Frontier life was marked by grueling, constant labor, with men, women, children, and the enslaved tending the fields and the animals. Corn was a staple, and frontier families like the Bankheads used it to make ash cakes, corn pone, bread, and grits. They supplemented their diet with fish and wild game. Daily life was arduous and demanded much from everyone. The margins for success were thin.

But George Bankhead aspired to something more than mere subsistence. From 1820 until his death in 1847, he became fully invested in the economic and social life of the region by purchasing land and people to work that land. Bankhead bought 240 acres at the Huntsville land office in 1825 and an additional 240 in 1838—both parcels located in Marion County, immediately south of Franklin County in west Alabama. Marion County was not the most obvious place in which to become a successful planter. It was relatively isolated, and transportation networks were poor. Residents depended on "a much deteriorated Military Road and an only somewhat better Columbus and Moulton Road for trade and contact with the Tennessee and Tombigbee Valley plantation regions."[7] But just as the county's geography and soils were different from those of the Black Belt, so necessarily were its demographics. Marion County was predominantly white in 1830, with 3,452 white and 600 enslaved people. To work his ever-growing land parcels, Bankhead expanded his slaveholdings, which by 1830—either through purchase or natural increase—had risen to twenty-eight.[8] In addition to becoming a planter, George Bankhead aspired to be an entrepreneur. He built the county's first gristmill. He also owned and operated what was known as the Old Stagecoach Inn, near the town of Crews, a structure that remained intact until 1952.[9] Despite the county's agricultural limitations, George and Jane had built a respectable life for themselves.

Map 1.1. Map of Alabama with early roads.

NOTE: the official boundaries of Marion and Tuscaloosa Counties extended into Mississippi until December 18, 1820.

Over time, the Bankhead children set out to establish their own home-steads. George and Jane's second oldest son, James Greer, was twenty-eight years old when he married Susan Hollis in 1840, four years after his service in the Second Creek War. The Hollis family was from Darlington, South Caro-lina, and had come to Alabama in 1822, where Susan's parents had established a large plantation adjoining that of the Bankhead family.[10] James Greer and Su-san Hollis Bankhead first resided in a log house in the village of Moscow (later the town of Sulligent), located on the old Jackson Military Road. Their first child, John Hollis Bankhead, was born in 1842. An undated family photograph, most likely from that same year, depicts James, Susan, and infant John Hollis. In the style of the times, the couple is unsmiling. James is slight of build and wears his dark hair long, below his ears. His close-set eyes and asymmetrical eyebrows give him a somewhat haughty, quizzical look. His cross-legged pose is more relaxed than hers. Both James Greer and Susan are well dressed: he in a high-collared white shirt, vest, and jacket; she in a plaid dress with a lace collar. Susan has round, kind eyes and a high forehead, and she wears her hair in a rather severe style, pulled tightly back from her face. She is holding baby John Hollis in her lap.[11] Five years after the birth of grandson John Hollis, in 1847, George Bankhead died at the age of seventy-one.

By 1850, James Greer Bankhead had established himself firmly in Mar-ion County. The county was rugged and small, with fewer than five hundred households, five stores, a saloon, and a post office.[12] Farms in the region var-ied in size and value. The majority involved fifteen to fifty acres of improved land and were worth anywhere from $100 to $1,000.[13] As of 1850, James Greer Bankhead owned at least seven hundred acres of property and enslaved sev-enteen people ranging in age from nine months to fifty years old.[14] This put him in the top 4 percent of landowners in terms of the size of his holdings and their reported value.[15] In 1850, James Greer Bankhead moved his family into a newly constructed, two-story pioneer-style home, which they named Forest Home.[16] Perhaps it was pretentious to christen a relatively modest home with a name, but it was also unapologetically aspirational. The Bankheads had cho-sen to sink their roots in northwest Alabama, and Forest Home reflected that commitment and ambition. At the time of his death, in December 1860, James Greer Bankhead had amassed property valued at $5,000 and a personal estate—which included enslaved men, women, and children—valued at $45,475, includ-ing $1,592 in livestock (twelve cows, fourteen other cattle, and twenty sheep); his land produced fifty-five bushels of wheat, eight hundred bushels of corn, and eight bales of cotton. His cultivated acres totaled eight hundred.[17] He en-slaved thirty-six people, who resided in seven cabins on his property, making him the fourth-largest slaveholder in the county. William Greer Bankhead, James's older brother and John Hollis's uncle, was even more successful by the standards of the time. By 1853, he had moved to Noxubee County, Mississippi, where he amassed landholdings in excess of twelve hundred acres and worth roughly $18,000. He also enslaved fifty-one people. By 1861, his total landholdings had increased in taxable value to $28,000, and he owned seventy-one men, women, and children.[18]

As the second generation of Bankheads established themselves in Marion County, Alabama moved beyond its frontier conditions to construct a more complex society; but as it did so, the economy became increasingly dependent on cotton. This cotton kingdom was built on the labor of enslaved black workers, and slavery shaped every element of Alabama society.[19] The black population increased nearly tenfold, from 42,000 in 1820 to 343,000 by 1850, both from natural increase and purchase from other states. The state's largest slave-trade center was Mobile. While critical to cotton cultivation, slave labor was also used successfully in Alabama's early industries, such as textiles and coal. By 1860, the state's nearly 438,000 enslaved men, women, and children were kept by 33,730 slaveholders, or about a third of the state's white families. With a vast amount of capital invested in the slave labor system, commercial and industrial development lagged. Any available capital was invested in more land and slaves.

On the eve of the Civil War, Alabama had a highly stratified society. Only a few white people—a group that included James Greer Bankhead—were considered planters who owned the vast majority of the enslaved. The Bankheads were recognized members of this slaveholding elite. A biracial society of free black people living alongside free white people was simply inconceivable to the Bankheads and others like them. Alabama was a white man's country.

Having established themselves as rooted members of a growing aristocracy, the Bankheads, like most of the nation, faced an uncertain future in 1860.

Figure 1.1.
James Greer Bankhead completed Forest Home in 1850. This image is from the 1930s. Library of Congress Prints and Photographs Division.

Those in Alabama who were committed to expanding the power of slaveholders turned to William Lowndes Yancey, a newspaper editor and member of the Alabama General Assembly who had been advocating secession in defense of slaveholder rights since 1850.[20] By hitching its political and ideological wagon to Yancey, Alabama was moving closer to secession. Eighteen sixty was a presidential election year. Yancey controlled the Alabama delegation sent to the Democratic Party's national convention in Charleston in 1860 to nominate a presidential candidate and draw up a platform. Yancey took to the floor and insisted on a platform that demanded federal protection of slave property in the territories. But he did not have the votes. Thwarted by the convention, Yancey led the Alabama delegation out from the convention with other Deep South states closely behind. The convention adjourned without nominating a candidate.[21]

Ultimately, four candidates campaigned for the presidency in that fateful year of 1860. Stephen A. Douglas, the candidate favored by national Democrats, ran on a pledge to popular sovereignty; John C. Breckinridge, nominated by southern Democrats, ran on the Alabama platform; John Bell, nominated by a group of Whigs, ran on the Constitutional Union ticket with a compromise platform; and Abraham Lincoln, nominated by the Republican Party, ran on a platform that would prohibit slavery in the territories. Alabama was divided in its support, with five counties going for Douglas, five counties choosing Bell, and all the rest going for Breckinridge. Long before the Electoral College met, the governor called for elections for delegates to decide Alabama's future in or out of the Union. The state was divided among straight-out secessionists, who advocated immediate secession; cooperationists, who urged cooperation with other southern states, which they knew to be impossible, as a means of preventing secession; and other Unionists of various degrees. North Alabama, which included the counties in the Tennessee Valley and the hill counties such as James Greer Bankhead's home county of Marion, was dominated by cooperationists.[22]

White southerners were alarmed at the magnitude of Abraham Lincoln's victory in the North, where he captured more than 60 percent of the vote. This gave secessionists the opening they needed. They had to move quickly. On December 20, 1860, the South Carolina secession convention unanimously adopted an ordinance of secession. Mississippi and Florida soon followed South Carolina's lead, on January 9 and 10, 1861, respectively.

Yancey demanded Alabama secede immediately. The votes for convention delegates were largely divided by geography, with the counties lying within the Tennessee Valley and those in the northern hill country, including Marion, supporting the cooperationists, and south Alabama supporting immediate secession. To add to north Alabamians' concerns, Tennessee was still in the Union when the convention delegates met. North Alabamians did not want to find themselves trying to negotiate deals and trade with a state in a separate country.[23] A loyal Tennessee would also leave north Alabama vulnerable to federal invasion.

Delegates from north Alabama thus preached patience. The Bankheads, prominent landowners and slaveholders, resided amid a divided citizenry.

On January 11, 1861, the Alabama secession convention approved the ordinance of secession, 61–39. Alabama had left the Union. Both representatives from Marion County (Lang C. Allen and Winston Dilmus Stidham) voted against secession. By February 1, seven lower South states had left the Union. Montgomery was chosen as the provisional capital of the new nation. In north Alabama counties, the situation was chaotic. Marion County was divided; many small-scale nonslaveholding farmers supported the Union, while the larger slaveholders, the Bankheads included, rallied to the Confederacy.

As the new nation found its footing, the seceded states began rudimentary military preparations, although many still hoped to avoid war. Across the state of Alabama, the militia was reorganized and began to drill. Communities hastened to raise volunteer companies. Most men supplied their own weapons and horses. The Confederates' attack on and victory at Fort Sumter in April 1861 prompted President Lincoln's call for seventy-five thousand volunteers to put down the rebellion. By late April, in response to the southern victory at Fort Sumter in Charleston Harbor as much as to Lincoln's actions, the states of Arkansas, Virginia, North Carolina, and Tennessee had joined the Confederacy. Later that spring, the decision was made to relocate the capital to Richmond.

By the time of Lincoln's call for volunteers after the fall of Fort Sumter, the Confederacy's mobilization had already enlisted sixty thousand men.[24] Ultimately, a volunteer force would prove insufficient. The Confederacy needed more men. In April 1862, the Confederate government passed a conscription law requiring three years of military service for all able-bodied white men ages eighteen to thirty-five.[25] A fair number of men of conscription age in Marion County were Union supporters; some joined the Union forces, while others hid in the woods and hills to avoid military duty. As the war dragged on, layouts and an increasing number of deserters—many of whom were armed—banded together in the hills and hollows of the northern counties' farther reaches.[26] Some Alabama counties provided as many soldiers for the Union as for the Confederacy.[27]

Whether through volunteer service or conscription, few Alabama families remained untouched by the war. James Greer Bankhead did not live to see his home state secede or his oldest child march off to war. He died on December 31, 1860.[28] John Hollis Bankhead was eighteen years old when war broke out, old enough to serve in the conflict that would define the nation, the region, and his life.

John Hollis joined Company K, Sixteenth Regiment, Alabama Infantry, as a second lieutenant.[29] The sole photograph from his service years depicts an attractive young man—more adolescent than adult—with curly brown hair and blue eyes. The Sixteenth Regiment drew companies from Conecuh, Franklin, Lawrence, Marion, and Lauderdale Counties. The early mustering-in services across the new Confederate states were festive occasions.[30] Crowds of flag-waving and

Figure 1.2. Confederate soldier John Hollis Bankhead, 1861. Courtesy of the Alabama Department of Archives and History.

cheering civilians gathered to send off the troops to martial glory, confident that the war would be short.[31]

Bankhead's regiment, which was part of the Army of Tennessee and commanded by General Felix Zollicoffer, moved on to Knoxville. Colonel J. E. Saunders recalled, "From Courtland to Knoxville, the trip was one grand ovation. Confederate flags hung from almost every house top; at every cross-roads and town they were greeted with loud huzzas."[32] Corporal Westwood Wallace James recalled the march from Courtland to Knoxville. "After five days and nights on the road we finally reached the encampment of the regiment. . . . We are supplied plentifully with sugar, coffee, flour, mess pork and with beef once or twice a week. The men generally are pretty well satisfied. Some of them acknowledge they fare better here than they did at home, though myself and others find camp life pretty tough. Our field officers are inexperienced 'War Men' and have all yet to learn." He continued: "The life of a soldier, though sometimes pretty hard, is a very gay one. There is always something to amuse you if there were not so much vulgarity and profanity."[33]

From its initial position in Tennessee, the regiment moved into Kentucky. Corporal James observed: "The people are . . . Unionists. They fear the Southern army so much that they fly from their homes without taking any of their furniture with them. If there is any house [at all] inhabited it is owned by some poor widow old lady or some very old man. There is no open enemy anywhere about us. Don't know where any are. I am pretty sure I am eager to find them, for I am footsore and tired of hunting for them. I am eager to get into a regular fight."[34] Corporal James did not have to wait much longer, for shortly thereafter the regiment engaged the enemy at Mill Springs in January 1862. The Confederates were routed by Union forces. The Sixteenth Regiment lost sixty-four men. Following the battle, Bankhead was promoted to first lieutenant. As the men retreated, Colonel William B. Wood recalled, "The army, as it stretched along the road, looked like a great funeral procession, and indeed it was, for many a poor fellow, exhausted and crazed, fell by the wayside and perished. It was the most trying and most afflicting time of my experience as a soldier. My men were giving out and falling by the wayside, declaring that they could not go another step, and begging to be allowed to die where they were. I brought off nearly all of my regiment."[35] The festive atmosphere that surrounded the regiment in its early days had disappeared.

Following the defeat at Mill Springs, the Sixteenth Regiment was transferred to the brigade of General S. A. M. Wood, and it fought in the Battle of Shiloh in April 1862, the bloodiest battle of the war to date. Bankhead's regiment lost 162 men in the Confederate defeat. After Shiloh, John Hollis was promoted to captain. General Wood's brigade formed a part of the division of General Simon Bolivar Buckner, with which it moved into Perryville, where it was held in reserve. The regiment saw action at Triune and at Murfreesboro, where 168 men were lost.

At the Battle of Chickamauga, 244 men of the regiment were killed or wounded. Among the wounded was John Hollis Bankhead. A personal account in his papers describes the circumstances surrounding his injuries: "[Bankhead] led his regiment in a furious charge at Chickamauga, and was there severely wounded. The battle ground was an old sedge field, which, during hostilities, caught fire, which spread with great rapidity, to the dismay of many a wounded soldier. Although wounded himself and faint from the loss of blood, Captain Bankhead, before leaving the field, discovered private John Custer stretched out, severely wounded. Although his own life was in imminent peril, Captain Bankhead took him on his back, and managed to drag himself and his companion to a place of safety."[36] An unidentified newspaper account from 1915, written on the occasion of Bankhead's visit to that same battlefield, identifies the wounded soldier as "Champion." In this version, Bankhead "threw himself to the ground and thus gave Champion [his comrade] opportunity to roll upon his back. And thus burdened, he staggered again to his feet and carried the desperately wounded not only out of the range of the battle but out of the range of fire."[37] Discrepancies aside, Bankhead's wounds were severe enough to send him to the hospital for several months. He never again regained full use of his arm. The story of his battlefield heroics clearly marked him as a leader.[38]

Early 1864 found Bankhead back with his regiment. On January 20, he wrote to the secretary of war, asking "whether or not a company of infantry of 60 effective men strong would be allowed to reenlist for the war and mount themselves on good horses and report to Brig. Gen. John H. Morgan to serve in his command as mounted infantry." Bankhead's request was denied. Perhaps in response to this rebuke, Bankhead tendered his resignation from the Confederate Army. It was not accepted. He did, however, receive a twenty-five-day leave of absence on April 10, 1864. He returned to his regiment, which was engaged in the Atlanta campaign, and was again wounded in battle, although the specifics remain a mystery. July and August 1864 found him recuperating in a hospital.[39] While in Atlanta, Bankhead swapped an enslaved man who served his regiment for a barrel of persimmon brandy and a keg of chewing tobacco.[40]

Back home in Alabama, citizens' enthusiasm for the war quickly waned. Union troops occupied north Alabama in 1862. The city of Mobile was blockaded by the Union navy. Wartime shortages and hardships increased as the war dragged on into its second, third, and then fourth year. Citizens of the state grew ever more bitter about the burdensome taxes in kind, the relentless impressment of goods, and the constant foraging by Union and Confederate troops alike. Conscription became onerous, and increasing numbers of men evaded the conscription officers or deserted. Civil order rapidly deteriorated. Disillusionment with the war brought Unionist Whig and secession opponent Thomas Hill Watts to the governor's mansion, and moderates and cooperationists to both the General Assembly and the Confederate Congress, in 1863. When the end finally came, most residents welcomed it with a feeling of relief.[41]

On April 4, 1865, President Lincoln made his second inaugural address and asked the nation "to do all which may achieve and cherish a just and lasting peace." Less than a week later, General Robert E. Lee surrendered to General Ulysses S. Grant at Appomattox Court House, and in another six days Lincoln lay dead from an assassin's bullet. On April 26, General Joseph E. Johnston surrendered to General William T. Sherman in North Carolina, and on May 4, General E. R. S. Canby, at Citronelle, Alabama, accepted the surrender of the last Confederate forces east of the Mississippi. Jefferson Davis was captured by Union troops in Georgia on May 10. The war was over.[42]

Captain John Hollis Bankhead was discharged from the Confederate Army on June 16, 1865, at Decatur, Alabama.[43] Exhausted and war weary, and with his once-healthy body weakened by the enemies' bullets and by deprivations suffered over the course of four long years, Bankhead made his way back to his mother, sister, and younger brother at Forest Home.

As it would for most men of his generation, the Civil War would become the defining moment in young Bankhead's life. He remained close to his fellow soldiers well into old age, loyally attending Confederate reunions. Daughter Marie recalled that even as an elderly man, John Hollis "camp[ed] out with his old Confederate military company once a year." When his wife protested, "he said that as long as there were two men of them left he intended to meet with them and if he died at his camp fire it would be a very good way to pass on."[44] Defeated on the battlefield, Bankhead—like thousands of other Confederate veterans—returned to his community beleaguered yet anxious to regain the personal and economic power he had enjoyed before the war. He likewise was determined to define and shape the postwar South. This new struggle would take longer, and this time, white southerners would emerge the victors.

2

A SLAVEHOLDER'S SON IN THE POSTWAR SOUTH, 1865–1885

JOHN HOLLIS BANKHEAD survived the war. Like most Confederate veterans, he returned to a state that offered little material or spiritual comfort. Across the South, one in every ten white men had perished in the bloody conflict. The southern economy lay in shambles. Confederate bonds and currency were worthless; real estate values plummeted. Some of the most war-weary areas were in the Tennessee Valley and hill counties. Federal occupation of much of this region occurred early in the war. Union troops crisscrossing the state foraged from forests and farms, leaving the surrounding countryside destitute. Soldiers returned home to desolate farms, and exhausted wives and children. Many arrived too late in the year to plant a fall crop, and drought ravaged much of the crop that survived. In the counties of north Alabama, where Union supporters were plentiful and where conscription evasion and desertion from the Confederate Army were rife, guerilla fighters were slow to put down their arms, and the war lingered into the summer months. Starvation and violence stalked the land.[1]

Complicating the problem of statewide famine and continued hostilities was the abolition of slavery. White Alabamians worried about the freedmen in their midst, particularly whether they could be compelled to work. At the onset of the war, roughly half of Alabama's population was enslaved. The freeing of this population brought elation for the enslaved but consternation for white Alabamians. Questions abounded: What did freedom mean? Who would work the once-great plantations? What would be the social and political status of the freedmen in Alabama and southern society?

As men and women took up the challenges of peace and survival, it was not clear how exactly these questions were to be answered. Among those searching for solutions in the era known as Reconstruction was John Hollis Bankhead. Returning to the family homestead that was once worked by three dozen enslaved people, Bankhead was elected at the tender age of twenty-three to represent Marion County in the Alabama House of Representatives during the era of Presidential Reconstruction. Later, as that grand experiment came to a close, he would serve as state senator for the twelfth district. Bankhead was among those former slaveholders in whose hands the future of the state lay, and in whose hands the extent of the revolution in southern agriculture and politics was to be determined. As a state legislator, Bankhead rejected constitutional amendments establishing basic civil rights and protections for freedmen, and he voted in favor of state laws—collectively known as Black Codes—designed to place strict limits on the freedom of African Americans. There would be no revolution in Alabama. The political, social, and economic direction of the state would remain in the hands of conservative white men, many of whom had recently fought and lost a bloody war to preserve slavery and states' rights. Men like John Hollis Bankhead.

When the Reconstruction era came to an abrupt conclusion, the state turned its attention to industrial and infrastructure development. Hampered by a crushing debt and dedicated to keeping taxes low, the state put itself on the path to solvency by leasing convicts—mostly black men—to plantations, sawmills, railroading outfits, and coal mines. The relationship proved lucrative to both the state treasury and private industry, a potential that John Hollis Bankhead recognized. In 1881, Bankhead was appointed warden of the state penitentiary. He spoke eloquently and forcefully of the need to improve the dreadful conditions under which convicts labored, but he never questioned the system itself. Some of the changes he implemented resulted in improved conditions for the convicts, but his more significant contribution was to tether the financial health of the state to the leasing of convicts almost exclusively to coal mine operators. By the time he left office in 1885, the vast majority of state and county convicts—a majority of them African Americans caught in a legal dragnet that legislator Bankhead had helped create—labored under dismal conditions in the mines. Over the course of twenty years, from 1865 to 1885, as the state emerged from the wreckage of war to assume an important place in the industrializing New South, John Hollis Bankhead, son of a slaveholder, played a key role in crafting a conservative political culture, legal code, and industrial future that relied on and perpetuated white supremacy.

Until a postwar policy could be implemented, the US Army was the law in the South. The size of the territory to be policed and the number of mobile troops that could police it limited the troops' ability to maintain law and order. Communities descended into near anarchy. Hungry veterans straggling home took what they needed to survive, focusing particularly on "liberating" Confederate military stores. They joined bands of deserters and layouts who had preyed on communities during the war years. Alabama's provisional governor, Lewis E. Parsons, addressed the situation in July 1865, warning citizens that all vigilance committees and any unlawful means of punishing offenders were now strictly prohibited.[2] The governor's words went unheeded. Cotton and horse theft by large bands of armed and disguised men continued throughout the summer. Conditions continued to deteriorate, and the governor called on General C. R. Woods to send military force to one county.[3] As late as October 1865, six months after the conclusion of the war, outlaw bands in northern Alabama continued to threaten residents and confound Union officials.[4]

Human deprivation posed a real concern for the state's leaders. Speaking several months after Appomattox, Governor Parsons lamented the "untold sufferings [that] are still endured by thousands of our women and children and the aged and helpless of our land."[5] Officials estimated that as of November 1865, one quarter of the white population was destitute, many of them widows and orphans, who survived on meager state rations of meal and salt. State leaders estimated that if the same ratio of destitution existed among black people (in fact, the level of need was likely higher), the state had a quarter-million people in desperate straits. The level of need exceeded the state's ability to help. The governor reported that "the corn and small grain crops throughout the State are not more than one-fifth [of a normal harvest]." Basic survival was the order of the day and was about all the state and local communities could manage. The state's education system, although never robust, lay in shambles. School had been suspended during the course of the war. Governor Parsons noted that for the state's young people, the loss of education had been catastrophic: "Their education has been that of arms and strife; their training, that of the camp; their diplomas, mutilation and wounds."[6]

The task of addressing many of these problems awaited the reconstruction of state government and readmission into the Union. With Abraham Lincoln's assassination, the process by and conditions under which Alabama and the other rebellious states would reenter the Union were now in the hands of President Andrew Johnson of Tennessee. White southerners awaited his proclamations with unease and uncertainty.[7] Unionists in Alabama expected to take the lead in rehabilitating the state.[8] They believed they had a friend in Johnson. A Unionist who had at one time spoken of punishing Confederates as traitors, Johnson nursed a deep hatred of the planter class. Former Tennessee governor and Confederate Isham Harris once remarked that if "Johnson were a snake, he would lie in the grass to bite the heels of rich men's children."[9] Southern Unionists held their breath in anticipation of a harsh Reconstruction that would ultimately deliver the state into their eager—and, they believed, deserving—hands.

What they got from Johnson was a conservative policy that returned the state to its antebellum leaders. Johnson pursued a Reconstruction policy very similar to that proposed by the late president. Like Lincoln, he granted pardons to former Confederates, who, for twenty-five cents, could take an oath to sup-port the Constitution and the Union. When the number of oath takers equaled one-tenth of the voters of 1860, they were then free to hold elections, establish a government, abolish slavery, and receive presidential recognition of the state's return to the Union. In addition to the pardons established by Lincoln, Johnson required that wealthy and powerful individuals—those with taxable property over $20,000 and those who had held high political or military positions in the Confederacy—seek a pardon directly from him.[10] Among those who sought a presidential pardon was William Greer Bankhead of Noxubee County, Missis-sippi, John Hollis's uncle.[11]

The conservative thrust of Johnson's vision for a reconstructed South was evident in the provisional governors he appointed. The president failed to appoint a single Union loyalist. The majority of Johnson's appointees were drawn from those white southerners who had opposed secession but who eventually either supported their state in the new Confederacy or simply maintained public silence regarding the Confederacy.[12] Alabama's new governor was Lewis E. Parsons. A former Whig from Talladega, he had supported state funding for internal im-provements while serving as a member of Alabama's House of Representatives.[13] Parsons was a reluctant secessionist who, according to one historian, "aided the Confederacy materially but damned it spiritually."[14] During the war, Parsons practiced law in Talladega. Two of his sons fought for the Confederacy.[15] Parsons was returned to the Alabama House of Representatives in 1863, a year in which state voters chose a governor and legislature who advocated an end to the war.[16]

President Johnson's demands for readmission were modest. The state conven-tions were required to rewrite their state constitutions, officially abolish slavery, and nullify the 1861 secession ordinances.[17] Johnson said absolutely nothing about the status of the freedmen. Johnson's hatred of the planter class was exceeded only by his distaste for biracial democracy and his faith in states' rights; thus he left the fate of the freedpeople in the hands of white southerners. A smattering of radical Republicans in Congress recognized the implications of Johnson's conservative approach to Reconstruction, particularly his silence with regard to the rights of the freedmen, but they were powerless to challenge the policies.

All southern men not excluded by President Johnson's proclamation could take the amnesty oath and regain their citizenship. Newspapers across the state urged former Confederates not to "allow old prejudices to control our actions" and encouraged all eligible white men to take the oath, register, and vote for convention delegates.[18] Ultimately, 56,825 white Alabamians took the registra-tion oath, although not all of them voted for delegates.[19] The limits of Presi-dential Reconstruction were only too clear to Thomas Wilson, a farmer from Clarke County. Having arrived at the courthouse in Gainestown in August 1865 to take the oath of allegiance, he found it being administered by staunch south Alabama secessionist Lorenzo James. Three years earlier, James and a vigilance committee had broken into Wilson's home, assaulted Wilson and his elderly father, and imprisoned both in a Mobile jail for their "sinful, unionist ways."[20] The prospect of men such as James leading the state's postwar Reconstruction did not give strict Unionists much hope.

Alabama's constitutional convention opened on September 12, 1865. Any hopes that the convention might signal a new direction for the state were quickly dashed by one glance at the delegate roll call. Unionists within the state, not to mention newly freed men and women, were dismayed to discover that former Confederate leaders—recently pardoned by President Johnson—had been elected as convention delegates. Among the ninety-nine delegates were twenty-five former Confederate officers, soldiers, or government officials. Two delegates had signed the secession ordinance of 1861, while another five had attended the secession convention but had refused to sign the ordinance. In the end, these five had acquiesced in secession and were not vocal opponents. Only ten of the ninety-nine delegates had been open and consistent opponents of secession and of the Confederacy.[21] The delegates, nearly half of whom (forty-seven) had held government positions during the antebellum era, included two former governors, one US senator, one member of the US House of Representatives, and one foreign minister.[22] The convention delegates were also rather old, with almost half of them over the age of fifty. Only eighteen delegates were under forty.[23] According to one historian, "all delegates endorsed President Johnson's leadership. All sought readmission of Alabama with minimal preconditions."[24] The chances that this body would create a document that radically changed the contours of Alabama society were practically nil.

Despite an attempt by the Unionist minority, the delegates declared secession null and void but did not repudiate it. In other words, the delegates acknowledged the Confederacy's defeat on the battlefield, but they refused to admit that secession itself was wrong.[25] Ultimately, the convention crafted and then approved a constitution that abolished slavery, nullified secession, repudiated the Confederate debt, and reallocated representation in the state legislature based on the white population only. The delegates' fear of potential "negro domination" that could overwhelm the white citizens of the state was everywhere in evidence during the convention. One delegate worried that a strong denunciation of slavery would eventually allow the freedmen to "vote at the polls, sleep under our roof . . . mingle in our social intercourse and marry our daughters."[26] The delegates worried that were the freedmen counted for the purposes of apportioning representation, Congress would make the argument that freedmen should be allowed to vote as well.[27] Some delegates attempted to strike out the clause giving every citizen "the right to bear arms in defense of himself and state" because they feared it might be used to arm the freedmen. They failed.[28] A historian of the convention notes that "because of fear of the freedmen and despite the argument that it would be misconstrued in the North, the convention adopted an ordinance declaring that the abolition of slavery should not limit the power of the legislature to pass laws to regulate the freedmen."[29] The convention refused to incorporate positive provisions guaranteeing the freedmen's civil rights and instead passed that job along to the legislature.[30] Delegates voted unanimously to empower the legislature to "enact laws prohibiting the intermarriage of white persons with Negroes, or with persons of mixed blood, declaring such marriages null and void . . . , and making the parties to such marriages subject to criminal prosecutions."[31]

The constitutional convention adjourned on September 30, 1865. The convention refused to submit its handiwork to the citizens for approval. As one historian of the convention has written, no white Alabamian "considered that the loss of the war meant accepting a revolution."[32] This was an understatement, as the actions of the first postwar legislature would demonstrate.

The question of the status of the freedmen was on the minds of white and black Alabamians alike. The Civil War had shattered the institution of slavery but had left nothing in its place. The early postwar months were marked by turmoil and uncertainty as white and black people tested the possibilities—and the limits—of this new racial arrangement. The northern tier of the state had been under Union occupation since 1862. Enslaved people took advantage of this opportunity. Several thousand joined the Union Army; others worked on federal fortifications. Still others used the federal presence as an opportunity to escape their bondage. Elsewhere, the demise of slavery came at the barrel of a gun. For the majority of Alabama's enslaved population, freedom did not come until spring 1865 and the end of the Confederacy. Many celebrated their emancipation by leaving their former plantations—at least temporarily. During spring and summer 1865, thousands of freedmen and women migrated to Alabama's cities, despite the efforts of local, state, and federal officials to convince them to remain in the countryside. The *New York Herald* noted in July that "negroes from all quarters of the State have flocked to Montgomery to taste the sweets of freedom. They fill the streets and sidewalks, and are squatted about in all parts of the city."[33] One white citizen of Montgomery complained that "this city is crowded, crammed, packed with multitudes of lazy, worthless negroes. . . . Crimes multiply upon the accumulation of this mass of strong animal passions, and uncontrolled sensuality. . . . Nothing else need be expected from the packing together of these thousands of negroes with their idleness and filth, than crime and disease."[34] The *Montgomery Advertiser* regularly reported on the subsequent rural labor shortage and warned of aggressive labor recruitment plans pursued by other southern states.[35] Nevertheless, although the number of freedpeople in urban areas increased sharply, the bulk of the black population remained in rural areas.

Responsibility for navigating the transition from slavery to freedom fell to the Bureau of Refugees, Freedmen, and Abandoned Lands, more commonly known as the Freedmen's Bureau. Established by Congress in March 1865, the Freedmen's Bureau faced a monumental task during its seven-year life. The bureau was responsible for distributing rations to destitute white and black people, building hospitals and schools, overseeing labor contracts between freedmen and their employers, and protecting the legal, civil, and political rights of the freedmen. The bureau faced an uphill battle. Assistant commissioner C. W. Buckley reported in June 1865 to bureau chief General O. O. Howard about his experiences in Union Springs, in the southeast corner of the state. Upon his arrival, he wrote: "I found a disquieted and restless spirit among the colored people, which resulted from the fact that the planters had generally refused to enter into contracts with their hands, consequently the negroes did not know for whom they were working, or for what wages. They had nothing to gain by working, and it was very natural that they would be idle. The planters had circulated a report that President Johnson had revoked the Emancipation Proclamation, that their enslaved were not free, and they must do as they had always done. The result of this was much abuse and ill treatment."[36]

Buckley eventually called a meeting and demanded that the planters enter into labor contracts with their workers. He reported that since his meeting with the planters, some one hundred contracts per day were being brought to the office. Although clearly pleased with this progress, he nevertheless was overwhelmed. "If we do not do all you wish, if we do not do all we most earnestly desire to accomplish, it is because we have not sufficient help." Buckley remained impressed with the "patience and industry" exhibited by the freedmen. He concluded: "They act worthy of freedom."[37]

Ultimately, the Freedmen's Bureau in Alabama was overseen by thirty-year-old Ohio native Brigadier General Wager T. Swayne.[38] One of his primary duties was to secure labor contracts between white landowners and black freedmen. Rumors that confiscated land and stock would be divided among the freedmen circulated throughout the fall. In expectation of this windfall, black people balked at signing labor contracts. Aware of the rumors, and fearful of a general insurrection, the legislature took matters into its own hands.[39]

It was left to the new state legislature, elected in November 1865, and to the newly elected governor, Robert M. Patton (who had served as a constitutional convention delegate), to determine the shape and limitations of freedom. Like his predecessor, Patton had advocated industrial development and railroad construction during the antebellum period. In the postwar era, both governors pursued policies aimed at pacifying northern critics and maintaining good relations with the Republican Party. Both aggressively sought state and federal support for railroads and industrial enterprises. Patton spoke against punitive race legislation. He opposed laws that required freedmen to carry passes, laws that prevented freedmen from hiring themselves out for a period less than a month, and laws that prevented freedmen from having a light in their dwelling after any given hour. Such laws, he held, were inconsistent with liberty.[40] He maintained, however, that the state "must be guided and controlled by the superior intelligence of the white man," an assertion in which most white Alabamians took comfort.[41]

Historian J. Mills Thornton has argued that the most significant feature of the Alabama legislature of 1865–66 was the "marked decline in the wealth and social standing of the men elected."[42] On average, the men elected to the legislature during the era of Presidential Reconstruction "were poorer than they had been since the early antebellum years." This trend reflects a more general repudiation of the secession leadership—and the planter class—first seen in the elections of 1863. "The median legislative slaveholding for the legislators chosen in November 1865 (derived from the census of 1860) fell from seventeen to eight."[43] Still, as Thornton points out, the legislature boasted a significant number of wealthy men, including the chairman of the newly formed House Committee on Freedmen, Tristram B. Bethea, from Montgomery, who in 1860 had enslaved 221 people. Supporting Bethea in his unsuccessful bid for Speaker of the House was another legislator of means, young John Hollis Bankhead, elected to represent Marion County. In 1860—the date of the last federal census—Bankhead was eighteen years old and resided in his father's home, a fairly substantial plantation with thirty-six enslaved workers. But Marion County possessed divided sympathies. Also representing Marion County was Winston Steadham, a nonslaveholding yeomen farmer who had represented the county in the secession convention and had voted against secession. Residents in Marion and other hill counties were fairly evenly divided between Confederate and Union supporters, and their postwar representatives reflected this dichotomy. As for the state's representation in Washington, DC, five of the six congressional representatives had opposed secession, but some had ultimately served in the Confederacy. The legislature elected two Unionists to represent the state in the US Senate.[44]

The new legislature opened its session in Montgomery on November 23, 1865. One of the first orders of business was ratification of the Thirteenth Amendment, which abolished slavery. The governor urged the lawmakers to adopt the amendment unanimously. A racial paternalist, Governor Patton stressed that "I have come to the conclusion that our interest as a people, especially that of the white race, will be promoted by the passage of an act declaring that freemen shall have the same measure of protection which our laws secure to our non-voting white population."[45] Rather than approve the amendment straight up, the house amended the ratification resolution. Concerned that Congress intended to use the amendment to interfere in the rights of the state, Alabama lawmakers added a provision stating that they did so "with the understanding that it does not confer upon Congress the power to legislate upon the political status of Freedmen in this state." Representative Bankhead, son of a slaveholder, voted for the reservation. But when it came time to ratify the amendment, Bankhead was one of seventeen representatives who voted against ratifying the Thirteenth Amendment, putting him in a diverse group of legislators, according to one historian, "utterly unwilling to accept the outcome of the Civil War."[46]

The lawmakers then turned their attention to the activities of the freedmen. Both houses of the legislature created committees on freedmen chaired by former planters and populated by former slaveholders and members of plantation counties. The purpose of the committees was to "guard [the freedmen] and the State against the evils that may arise from their sudden emancipation." The first act pertaining to the freedmen that was passed was "an act to protect freedmen in their rights of person and property in this State." This act held that "all freedmen, free negroes and mulattoes, shall have the right to sue and be sued, plead and be impleaded in all the different and various courts of this State, to the same extent that white persons now have by law."[47] Even this limited grant of rights to the freedman was too much for John Hollis Bankhead. He voted no.

Having afforded the freedmen basic access to the courts, the lawmakers wasted little time proposing legislation designed to circumscribe their liberty. For bills in which the votes were recorded (rather than a voice vote), Bankhead voted against the extension of rights for African Americans. The legislature further approved a harsh vagrancy bill that amended the existing code to define vagrants as "any runaway, stubborn servant or child; a common drunkard, and any person, who, depending on his labor, habitually neglects his employment." Freedmen's Bureau official Swayne affirmed that the state's vagrancy law, although written in racially neutral language, applied only to freedpeople.[48] The legislature also approved an apprentice law that "provided that all orphans, or children whose parents refused to support them, could be put into custody of a suitable person. If the child had been a slave, the former master was awarded custody." An apprentice that ran away was considered a vagrant. Although freedmen were not prohibited from carrying firearms or knives, both were taxed at rates out of their reach.[49] Yet another act increased the penalty for grand larceny, arson, and burglary, establishing the minimum punishment at five years in prison and authorizing the death sentence at the discretion of the jury.[50] As Thornton has argued, Alabama's Black Codes were not nearly as harsh as those of other states, and more egregious bills were defeated.[51]

John Hollis Bankhead and his fellow legislators had accomplished what they set out to do, which was to deny equality to the freedmen and to control their labor. Confederates may have lost the war, but white men like Bankhead were determined to thwart any possible political or social revolution. In August 1866 those political leaders in the state determined to minimize the revolutionary potential of Reconstruction organized themselves into a new political party, known as the Democratic and Conservative Party.[52]

John Hollis Bankhead interrupted his political activities to wed Tallulah Brockman on November 13, 1866, just prior to the opening of the second session of the Presidential Reconstruction legislature.[53] Tallulah Brockman was born in 1844 in Greenville, South Carolina, to James Henry and Mary Elizabeth Stairley Brockman. James Henry Brockman was the son of Colonel Thomas Patterson Brockman.[54] Thomas Brockman, Tallulah's paternal grandfather, was a merchant and slaveholder in the Greenville district. A prominent Unionist before the Civil War, Brockman voted against nullification at South Carolina's nullification convention of 1832, and against secession at the 1852 Southern Rights state convention. He was a member of the South Carolina House and later the Senate. James Henry and Mary Elizabeth were married in 1843; it was a short-lived union. In 1844, twenty-two-year-old James Henry was making plans to move to Alabama when he died of an undocumented illness, leaving his young wife and daughter, Tallulah, alone. Mary Elizabeth married Lauchlin F. McAuley, also from South Carolina, and by 1850, she and six-year-old Tallulah were in Calhoun County, Alabama. The year that Tallulah Brockman married John Hollis, she was living with her mother and McAuley in Coosa County. Educated in private schools in Tuskegee and Montgomery, she was considered a "much admired belle." The couple married in Wetumpka and lived in Marion County. Tallulah's wedding photo shows an attractive young woman with dark brown hair, dark eyes, and delicate features. After fifty years of marriage, John Hollis noted that his "wife [was] as jolly as when we were married."[55]

While John Hollis Bankhead was courting his soon-to-be wife, the current of national politics began to move against southern conservatives. In Washington, Republican members of Congress had grown increasingly despondent over the course of Presidential Reconstruction. In December 1865, Congress refused to seat the southern representatives, including those from Alabama. In an obvious response to the Black Codes passed by the "reconstructed" southern states, Congress passed the Civil Rights Act of 1866 in April of that year over President Johnson's veto. The act declared all persons born in the United States to be citizens, granting them the right to give evidence in the courts, hold

Figure 2.1. John Hollis Bankhead, wedding photo, 1866. Courtesy of the Alabama Department of Archives and History.

property, and receive equal benefit of the laws. Uncertain that the act would survive a constitutional challenge or a later repeal attempt, Congress incorporated its major provisions into the newly crafted Fourteenth Amendment. The amendment conferred citizenship on all those born in the United States and guaranteed every citizen equal protection of the laws.[56]

At the opening of the 1866–67 legislative session, Governor Patton reported on the state of affairs. As to the freedmen, he stated, "let them be convinced that we are their friends, and that we feel an interest in their prosperity and welfare. They should be assured of our firm purpose to give them all their legal rights. We should advise them to let politics alone; and they should be especially taught the utter absurdity of expecting or aspiring to a condition of social equality with the white race. To do so, would be to struggle against a palpable and an inexorable decree of Providence." Patton also addressed the abject poverty in which many of the state's citizens still lived. "The amount of destitution in our State has been, and still is, not only distressing, but absolutely appalling."[57]

Figure 2.2.
Tallulah Brockman Bankhead, wedding photo, 1866. Courtesy of the Alabama Department of Archives and History.

The governor devoted a hefty portion of his address to the Fourteenth Amendment. By the time the Alabama legislature reconvened for its second session, in November 1866, the Fourteenth Amendment had been submitted formally to the states for ratification. Governor Patton initially urged legislators to reject the amendment.[58] Barely a month later, Patton changed his mind. By December 1866, it had become apparent that Alabama's readmission to the Union was contingent on its ratification of the Fourteenth Amendment. Hoping to remove Alabama from its current state of political limbo, Patton encouraged a cynical approach. Specifically, he urged the legislature to approve the amendment in order to regain membership in Congress. "Should you see proper to ratify [the amendment], and our full restoration follow," Patton wagered, "we may trust to time and the influence of our Representatives to mitigate its harshness." State legislators ignored his advice, choosing instead to follow President Johnson's advice. The Alabama legislature rejected the Fourteenth Amendment by overwhelming margins in both houses. Representative John Hollis Bankhead joined his colleagues in opposing the amendment.[59]

During his second session in the legislature, Bankhead continued his efforts to limit the revolutionary impact of Reconstruction, to establish his credentials as a conservative, and to secure a base of future political support. In addition to voting against the Fourteenth Amendment, he also was instrumental in carving out a new home county. Bankhead never sat entirely comfortably within Marion County, where his Confederate service and sympathies alienated half of the potential voters. He would never be able to create a secure political base there, as wartime allegiances and passions ran deep. Bankhead introduced a bill on January 21, 1867, to create a new county out of portions of Marion and Fayette Counties. The name he proposed for his new county? Stonewall, in honor of Confederate general Thomas Jonathan "Stonewall" Jackson. At 611 square miles, Stonewall would be one of the smaller counties in the state.[60] Although it was to be carved from Marion and Fayette and would technically be considered part of the hill country of north Alabama, the area that would become Stonewall boasted rich, productive land owned by large planters with Confederate sympathies. Union supporters in this area were few, and destruction by federal troops had been minimal.[61]

Bankhead's original bill to create the county of Stonewall failed. Perhaps naming the county for a Confederate hero was too provocative. He reintroduced the bill on January 29, this time proposing the new county be named Jones, in honor of Elliott P. Jones, a state legislator from Fayette County who had opposed the ordinance of secession.[62] This time, the bill passed. But nine months after the county's creation, the acreage used to create the new county was returned to its respective counties. In 1868, the state legislature created Sanford County, using the territory that had been Jones. In 1877, as Reconstruction drew to a close, Bankhead introduced a bill to change the county's name yet again, this time to Lamar, honoring Lucius Quintus Cincinnatus Lamar, the Georgia-born statesman who moved to Mississippi around 1845. Lamar had drafted Mississippi's ordinance of secession, served as a diplomat for the Confederate States of America, and later, after the war, represented the state of Mississippi in the US House of Representatives and the US Senate. The bill passed.[63]

While he was working with his colleagues to establish the conservative framework for a reconstructed Alabama, Bankhead also turned his attention to his expanding family, as well as farming and other economic pursuits. Children arrived in quick succession: Louise (b. 1867) and Marie (b. 1869) were born in Noxubee County, Mississippi; John Jr.(b. 1872), William (b. 1874), and Henry (b. 1877) were born near the town of Moscow, in what William remembered as "a very unpretentious house [with] low roofs and small bedrooms."[64] The Marion/Lamar County community to which John Hollis Bankhead had returned had to adjust to life without slavery. On the eve of the Civil War, James Greer Bankhead, John Hollis's father, had enslaved thirty-six people. The absence of probate records from the period make it difficult to trace whom exactly he owned and what might have happened to these individuals once freed. However, five years after the end of the war, the federal census listed thirteen households in the same township as John Hollis and his widowed mother, Susan, that are headed by "black" or "mulatto" men and women with the last name of Bankhead. Ages of the household members correspond roughly with the ages of James Greer Bankhead's enslaved workers listed in the 1860 federal slave schedules. These African American heads of households listed their occupations as either "farmer" or "farm worker." Those listing their occupations as "farmer" also listed real estate valued typically between $200 and $275, while the "farm workers" did not list any real estate holdings. It is likely that these black Bankheads were wage workers or sharecroppers working the land of their former slaveholder.

When not in Montgomery on legislative business, John Hollis Bankhead oversaw the administration of these farms.[65] He and Tallulah also lived part time in Macon, Mississippi, seat of Noxubee County, at Prairie Lawn, the home of his uncle William Greer Bankhead. Prior to emancipation, William Greer had enslaved seventy-one people. John Hollis's daughters, Louise and Marie, were both born while the family was at Prairie Lawn. During the fall and winter months, John Hollis also operated a cotton storage business in nearby Lowndes County, Mississippi. According to one account, most of his business came from farmers in Fayette, Lamar, and Pickens Counties in Alabama, men who "wore homespun jeans dyed with walnut stain."[66] Around 1877, the family moved in with John Hollis's mother at Forest Home.[67]

Although agriculture remained a critical element of his identity and livelihood, it was not John Hollis's only pursuit.[68] In 1870, he listed his employment as "clerk in a store." During this decade he apparently held a number of retail positions. In October 1877, the *Vernon Pioneer* announced Bankhead's new position with R. A. Honea & Son, seller of "family and fancy groceries," of Aberdeen, Mississippi, just west of Lamar County.[69] By 1879, Bankhead was working as a "commercial traveler"—a salesperson—for Culver, Page, & Hoyne, a Chicago firm that specialized in printing, bookbinding, and stationery.[70] His fourth child, William, born in 1874, recalled that his father built and operated some sort of mill when Will was young.[71] John Hollis's retail, sales, and cotton storage ventures allowed him to expand his circle of contacts beyond northwest Alabama and gave him experience in commercial transactions that would serve him well in the future. Like other men of his station, he was a joiner. He was active in the Masonic Grand Lodge of Alabama and was appointed senior grand warden in 1879. Also elected to a Masonic leadership position that year was Alabama governor Rufus W. Cobb of Shelby County. John Hollis's proximity to powerful men would prove useful in the future.[72]

In Washington, DC, the battle between Congress and President Johnson for control of Reconstruction had taken a decisive turn in fall 1866. Radical Republicans scored a resounding victory in the November congressional elections, securing a two-thirds majority over Johnson's supporters. Following the elections, the *Montgomery Advertiser* lamented that "the future is uncertain and gloomy and cheerless."[73] Reconstruction was now firmly in the hands of the radicals.

On March 2, 1867, Congress passed the first of four Reconstruction Acts, which put the fate of the southern states in new hands. Under Congressional Reconstruction, the ten "unreconstructed" southern states were divided into five military districts commanded by army generals. Alabama, along with Florida and Georgia, was in the Third Military District, commanded by Major General

John Pope (later replaced by General George G. Meade). The military would oversee the registration of all qualified voters, including black men, who would then vote for delegates to a new constitutional convention. The state constitution crafted under the Johnson plan was invalidated, and state legislatures were dismantled. John Hollis Bankhead quite suddenly found himself out of office.[74]

The election for delegates was held during the first week of October 1867, and this time, 71,630 African American men voted, compared to only 18,553 white voters.[75] The convention convened in Montgomery on November 5, 1867, and was dominated by the newly organized Republican Party. Among the one hundred delegates were nineteen African Americans.[76] The convention had to write the same suffrage requirements into the new constitution. When the document was approved, and when the Alabama legislature ratified the Fourteenth Amendment, Congress would decide whether the state was entitled to representation in Washington.

The onset of Congressional Reconstruction in Alabama brought radical change only in suffrage requirements. The 1868 constitution enfranchised black men and excluded many white men for a limited period. By 1870, most white men could vote.[77] Alabama politics during this period was controlled by native white Republicans, not African Americans or transplanted white northerners. The new constitution mandated that the legislature be reapportioned, with representation based on the whole population of the state, not just the white population as dictated by the 1865 constitution.[78] Although the delegates defeated amendments that would have established segregation in public spaces, the constitution did not make any affirmative statement on social equality for African Americans.[79]

The Republicans were unable to achieve unity, thus blunting the constitution's potential as a far-reaching, radical document. Nevertheless, conservative Democrats opposed the new document, regarding it as a blueprint for black domination. White Democrats tried to block ratification of the new constitution, and they encouraged white conservatives to register but to then refuse to vote. Their goal was to ensure that the vote cast fell short of the required one-half of registered voters. Ratification could come only if a majority of the registered voters participated. That did not happen. The boycott succeeded. Alabama was in limbo. On March 11, 1868, Congress passed the fourth Reconstruction Act. Ratification of a state constitution, it stated, "shall be decided by a majority of the votes actually cast." On June 25, 1868, Alabama rejoined the Union.[80]

At the same time that they voted to ratify the new constitution, Alabama voters also chose new state leaders and congressional representatives. Republicans were now in control, although it was a divided party. Neither of the state's two US senators was a native Alabamian. George E. Spencer was born in New York. A Union Army veteran, he moved to the state in 1865. Willard Warner was an Ohio native who moved to Alabama in 1867. Five of the state's six congressional representatives were Republicans; four had been agents of the Freedmen's

Bureau, and one was African American. Throughout the course of Reconstruction, three black men would represent the state in the national House of Representatives. In 1868, the state Senate was composed of thirty-two Republicans and one Democrat; the House had ninety-four Republicans (including twenty-six African Americans) and three Democrats. The new governor was William Hugh Smith. Smith had opposed secession and in 1862 crossed into federal lines. But he was no radical and had no sympathy for the freedmen.

A divided Republican Party and rising violence dampened the potential for more radical change to the political and social status quo in Alabama. The political scene was marked by chaos. Like many white men of his station, John Hollis Bankhead joined the Ku Klux Klan, which terrorized white and black Republicans, Freedmen's Bureau officials, and northern white teachers in its quest for a Democratic victory in 1870.[81] That year, with black voters avoiding the polls for fear of physical retaliation, Democrats secured the statehouse and elected a Democratic legislature. In 1872, with the Klan officially disbanded and with federal troops once again present, voters elected a Republican governor and gained a majority in the state legislature. Using fraud, violence, and racial hysteria, Democrats returned to power in 1874. As historian Samuel L. Webb has written, "restoring Democratic rule meant a return of white supremacy."[82] Firmly in control, the Democrats set about reversing Republican policies. For the third time in less than a decade, Alabama lawmakers rewrote the state's constitution. The majority of the delegates elected to the constitutional convention were Democrats, many of whom were Confederate veterans. The old state leadership had returned. John Hollis Bankhead ran for convention delegate from Lamar County but was defeated. The new constitution prohibited the use of state funds for internal improvements, and state taxation was set at an extremely low rate. Funds for education were slashed, and the state Board of Education abolished.

Although he failed in his bid to represent Lamar at the 1875 constitutional convention, John Hollis Bankhead returned to public office in 1876, as state senator from the twelfth district, and later, in 1881, as representative from Lamar County. By early 1880, he had moved from the village of Moscow to the county seat in Vernon.[83] He did not remain in the General Assembly for long, however. He sought a higher-profile post: warden of the state penitentiary at Wetumpka. Capitalizing on his professional experience, his military and political connections, and his slaveholder heritage as a man schooled in methods of racial control, Bankhead lobbied hard for the position, encouraging high-powered friends and associates from practically every county in the state to lobby the governor on his behalf. Luke Pryor, a wealthy planter and attorney from Athens who served as a state legislator, a US congressman, and a US senator, vouched for Bankhead as "capable, honest, faithful, friendly, and true." Other prominent Alabamians promoted his candidacy, including Edward A. O'Neal, Confederate veteran, lawyer, and Democratic Party stalwart from Florence; and William

Basil Wood, a circuit court judge in Florence who had also been a colonel in the Sixteenth Alabama Regiment, in which Bankhead had served. Wood wrote, "I had occasion to know [Bankhead], and opportunity to test him, in his early manhood." Wood called him "a gallant and faithful officer." Also offering support was S. A. M. Wood, a brigadier general in the Confederate Army, as well as groups of merchants and county commissioners from across the state.[84]

In 1881, bowing to public pressure, Democratic governor Rufus W. Cobb appointed the thirty-nine-year-old Bankhead warden of the state penitentiary in Wetumpka. Bankhead assumed his duties on March 1, 1881.[85] Known as the Walls, the state penitentiary was an overcrowded, run-down, frightful place, and its effective and efficient operation had long vexed state leaders. The Alabama legislature had approved the construction of a state penitentiary in 1839, and the first prisoner arrived in 1841. Hoping to make money from the operation—or at least to break even—the legislature in 1846 approved a six-year lease of prisoners to the highest bidder. Alabama was one of only two southern states that institutionalized the convict lease in the antebellum period. The other was Louisiana. Until the Reconstruction era, state convicts in Alabama worked within the prison walls.[86]

During Reconstruction, the legislature constructed a penal code designed to control the movements and financial activities of the African American population. The result was an explosion in the number of misdemeanants, who were in the custody of the county, and the creation of a unique two-tiered prison system in which felons were sent to the state penitentiary and misdemeanants remained in the hands of county officials. Many of these new county wards were ensnared by the state's broad vagrancy law—a law supported by legislator Bankhead. The minimum fine for vagrancy was fifty dollars (a princely sum for the newly freed) or a six-month prison term. Other statutes criminalized or discouraged independent economic activity by freedpeople. Black laundresses unable or unwilling to pay the required five-dollar license fee were arrested. Informal markets known as "deadfalls," where freedpeople would buy and sell goods, were also targeted by lawmakers. Unable to pay the fines, black people convicted of misdemeanors were sentenced to hard labor for the county. In addition to the levied fines, black defendants (and often black plaintiffs bringing suits) were charged court costs, which they paid for by serving additional time. For the counties, crime did pay. The county system operated—and profited from—this fee system. Abuse of the system was rampant.[87]

This county cash cow did not escape the notice of the governor and state lawmakers. Could the state penitentiary be converted into a profit-producing enterprise? In the first year following the war, the number of state convicts had increased, particularly the number of black inmates. In his 1866 address to the General Assembly, Governor Patton blamed this increase on the freedmen's irresponsible response to freedom. Following the end of the war, freedmen and women had flocked to the cities but, Patton noted, were "wholly unsuited" for urban life. "As a natural consequence, there was much demoralization and vagabondism among them; some of them became vagrants, and not a few resorted to larcenies." The expanding prison population made it difficult to profitably lease convicts for work within the prison walls. "But," he argued, "this labor might be made valuable and remunerative in mines, on railroads, and other works of internal improvements." The governor sought the authority to lease convicts to work in Alabama's fledgling industries. The leasing of convicts for work outside the prison would relieve the state of a burdensome expense. Also, the governor argued, "the convicts, by being employed in the manner recommended . . . *will contribute materially to the development of our mineral and other resources.*" Finally, the governor maintained that prison life was insufficiently harsh, noting, "it appears that many of the convicts, particularly of the colored race, do not regard their confinement as any punishment at all. The indolent life which they lead is rather enjoyed as a privilege. To them the penitentiary has no terrors. They feel none of its degradation. But such persons would keenly feel the severe hardships of enforced labor in iron and coal mines."[88] Doing time should hurt. And it should benefit the state.

The governor eventually took matters into his own hands, leasing 374 convicts to the firm of Smith and McMillen, a shadow company controlled by the Alabama and Chattanooga (A&C) Railroad, for a grand sum of five dollars.[89] The practice of leasing convicts accelerated as the state's fiscal crisis deepened. Determined to keep taxes low, lawmakers desperately sought new revenue streams. Convict leasing emerged as a solution for the insatiable labor needs of the state's expanding industrial base and as a quick fix for the state's fiscal woes.

Despite the fiercely partisan atmosphere of Reconstruction, economic development and railroad construction were issues on which Democrats and Republicans could agree. Both groups were anxious to develop transportation networks that could provide access to northern Alabama's rich mineral district, and both were willing to use the state's credit to build them. Democrats in charge during Presidential Reconstruction approved a general subsidy act for instate railroad construction. Under Governor William Hugh Smith's leadership, the Republican legislature expanded the government endorsement of company railroad bonds from $12,000 to $16,000 per mile. The state subsidy legislation also encouraged local grants to railroads, increasing not only the railroad mileage but the state's liability as well. The state debt ballooned, and bribes were the order of the day. The directors of the A&C gave generously to the governor and to several legislators. In return, the governor approved a $4 million direct-aid bill "primarily for the benefit of the Alabama and Chattanooga." Governor Smith's actions were highly suspect. He also endorsed bonds to the A&C in excess of the amount allowable by law. His frightening negligence and mishandling of the state's finances pushed the state into insolvency.[90] As of early 1871, the A&C

failed to pay the interest on its bonds and turned to the state for assistance. The new governor, Democrat Robert B. Lindsay, inherited this fiscal mess. He asked for a legislative inquiry, which revealed Smith's misdeeds. Speculation was rampant regarding the "state's ability to redeem other securities it had endorsed." Railroad construction came to a screeching halt. Some railroad companies went bankrupt during the Panic of 1873.[91] By the time Democratic governor George S. Houston took office, the state's indebtedness stood at $30 million. Houston and the newly elected Democratic legislature, of which Bankhead was a member, were determined not only to uphold white supremacy after what they termed the "debacle" of the biracial Reconstruction years, but also to follow the path of limited government and strict economy. Expansion of the convict lease under the penal code held the potential to allow the Democrats to uphold all three principles. John Hollis Bankhead would play a key role in this development.[92]

Appointed by Governor Houston, Warden J. G. Bass had, by 1876, expanded the lease of state convicts to eleven separate lessees, including those operating turpentine stills, lumber mills, coal mines, and plantations. The money started to roll in. In 1877, Warden Bass recorded that some 520 convicts brought in $14,000 in profit for the state; in 1878, it was $16,000.[93] According to one historian, "Alabama consistently ranked first among all states in revenue from convict labor." By 1883, profits from the labor of convicts constituted more than 10 percent of all state revenues.[94]

By the early 1880s, the growth of the state's coal mining industry relied increasingly on its access to convict labor, which was cheaper than free labor and not prone to staging strikes. New industrial enterprises hoping to exploit the mineral wealth in Jefferson, Shelby, and Talladega Counties—companies such as New Castle Coal Company, Alabama Furnace, Alabama Iron, Pratt Coal and Coke, and the Eureka Company—used prison labor. Two of the more dominant companies, Sloss-Sheffield and the Tennessee Coal, Iron and Railroad (TCI) company, used as many convicts as they could lay their hands on. Conditions in the convict mines were brutal. Prisoners endured whippings, torture, filth, and vermin. They were ill fed and ill housed. Mortality rates reached appalling levels.[95] In response to calls to reform the lease system—calls mostly from outside the South—the state decided to investigate. In 1881, a legislative committee investigated the prison system. The report was a whitewash. Investigators declared that the convicts were "kindly and humanely treated."[96] The exploitation continued.

John Hollis Bankhead assumed the office of warden of the state penitentiary on March 1, 1881. The move marked a significant change for the entire family. Bankhead's second son, Will, remembered the journey from their home in Lamar County to the site of the penitentiary in Wetumpka.

> We went from Vernon to Tuskaloosa in two, two[-]mule wagons, one of which Uncle Green drove and the other a negro. The trip took two days.

The first night we staid at Fayette at the Phillips Hotel, which was kept by Mr. H. D. Phillips whose dust now lies moulding in the village churchyard. The most vivid recollection I have of our sojourn here was the fact that all the jinger [ginger] cakes that mother had prepared to make part of our lunches had softened and run together in one yellow mass. We reached Tuskaloosa on the Northport side about dusk, and had to cross over the river on a ferry boat, the bridge having previously washed away. . . . We spent the night in Tuskaloosa at a boarding house. . . . The next morning we were hustled down to the station to take the train, and this was the first train I ever saw! People generally mark the epochs of their lives by reverses or successes; but one of mine was the mere fact of first seeing a full [illegible] live locomotive with its passenger coaches. And it moved off so easily and smoothly, so different to the rumbling of the wagons that had theretofore been my means of transit, that I much marveled and exclaimed with Nickodemus [sic], of whom I have since learned, "how can these things be?" My wonderment notwithstanding, the train flew on and we reached Wetumpka in due season.[97]

The new warden's annual salary was $2,000. The family stayed at the Campbell Hotel for about a month before moving into a large, comfortable home located on the prison grounds and staffed by prison labor. Son Will recalled fondly the family's "five happy years" at the penitentiary. "This, the penitentiary, is a beautiful place or was then, with its green trees, large gardens, and well kept hedges. . . . With my two brothers for playmates, and nothing save an occasional licking to hinder our mischievous inclinations, we romped, and sang, and were glad of the days, and weeks, and years. Happy memories cluster around those scenes, sweet and happy and sacred."[98] The idyllic experiences of the Bankhead children contrasted sharply with the terrors visited on the convicts.

One of John Hollis Bankhead's first acts as warden was to cancel the existing contracts. He regarded the language in the contracts as "conflicting" and "ambiguous." Contractors were instead given one-year agreements. John W. Comer, of Comer & McCurdy (which owned and operated the Eureka Company in Helena), sued the warden on behalf of the contractors but lost.[99] Aware of the complaints and news stories about conditions in the convict prisons, Bankhead authorized Dr. John Brown Gaston, president of the Alabama Medical Association, and Dr. Jerome Cochran, state health officer, to investigate the conditions of the mines and the convicts working within them. The doctors reported their findings to Warden Bankhead and also publicly lambasted the coal operators and the convict lease system for their atrocious and inhumane practices.[100]

State prison inspectors, in their biennial report to the governor, echoed the doctors' assessment of prison conditions. This report covered a two-year period, from September 1880 to September 1882, and offers a detailed glimpse into the state of the prison system when Bankhead assumed control. During the period covered by this report, the state prison population totaled 522 convicts, of which the majority were contracted to fourteen separate agricultural and industrial interests, including those involved in mining, railroading, lime rock excavation, and sawmilling. Work and living conditions for convicts were wretched. At New Castle Coal Company, the inspectors reported that "the beds and blankets were filthy." The prisons at New Castle were overcrowded and "infested with vermin." Convicts contracted to work on railroads were "in a worse condition. They were packed in small weather houses. The sick and well together. Their clothing and persons were infested with vermin. They seldom had vegetable diet." The death rate among these convicts alarmed the inspectors. They also reported excessive flogging of prisoners.[101]

Bankhead's first report to the governor echoed the findings of the inspectors, documenting the appalling conditions in which convicts served their sentences and building a case for a drastic change in the system: "[The convicts] were as filthy . . . as dirt could make them, and both prisons and prisoners were infested with vermin. The bedding was totally unfit for use. I found that convicts were excessively, and in some instances, cruelly punished; that they were poorly clothed and fed; that the sick were neglected, insomuch as no hospitals had been provided, they being confined in the cells with the well convicts. The use of dining room furniture, at some prisons, was unknown, the men having their meals spread on a bench, or a shelf, or given them by the cook in their hands. The prisons have no adequate water supply, and I verily believe there were men in them who had not washed their faces in twelve months."[102]

The report of the medical officer underscored the poor conditions endured by the convicts leased to various interests. According to the medical officer, the incidence of mortality of cases that came directly from within the Walls was 1 percent; mortality of patients sent from contractors was 25 percent. The hygiene of patients sent to the hospital by contractors was a particular issue. Noted the medical officer, "[the patients] looked like they had not washed themselves or their clothing in months. They were frequently covered with lice. Some of them had defecated on themselves, apparently for some time." In his report, the medical officer included accounts of those patients who had died at the prison hospital, among them a twenty-four-year-old white man named Luke Jernigan. Jernigan had been leased to a railroad contractor. According to the physician, Jernigan "had been sick for some time. Could give but an imperfect account of himself. The history was one of typhoid fever, complicated by sloughing ulcers on various parts of the body, some of which contained maggots. There was also thrombosis of the left femoral vein. Cause of death, exhaustion. This patient was hopeless from the time of his admission." For the relatively healthy convict, prison conditions were tremendously difficult. The lives of sick convicts were pure misery.[103]

Warden Bankhead took action against one contractor, a Dr. R. J. Thornton in Coaling. The prison's board of inspectors documented many abuses and reported to Bankhead that "Dr. Thornton was not a proper person to work convicts." In a letter to Thornton, Bankhead stated that "the most alarming feature in the whole business is the death rate at your place," a rate that hovered around 16 percent. "This is simply fearful and there can be no excuse for it. It must result from the grossest neglect and carelessness." Thornton's disregard for the treatment of convicts appalled Bankhead. "I am informed that the last man who died at your place was permitted to remain in the cell and in bed where he died all night and that well men slept by the side of him. I cannot believe this." Bankhead insisted that Thornton provide separate accommodations for sick prisoners and that he send to the Walls those convicts for whom he was unable to provide adequate care. He was tired of Thornton's excuses. "You have promised . . . to fix up better and have a place for your sick. You have failed to do it. Now I will demand it and no excuses will be taken." Despite having received many warnings, Thornton failed to improve conditions at his prison camp, and Bankhead canceled the contract in spring 1882.[104]

Dismal conditions such as those documented at the Thornton place made rehabilitation of the criminal impossible, Bankhead argued. "I am firmly of the opinion that our system makes men and women worse. They are more demoralized, and less fit to return to, or enter upon, their social duties than when convicted. Society is less secure after [the convict's] return than before his conviction." The system cried out for reform. In Bankhead's estimation, the current system "is a disgrace to the State, a reproach to the civilization and Christian sentiment of the age, and ought to be speedily abandoned."[105]

Despite his disgust at the dreadful conditions in which convicts labored, Bankhead did not advocate, as did some reformers, that the state abandon the convict lease system altogether. Nor, despite his criticism of conditions in the mines in particular, did he eschew the leasing of convicts to coal operators. The relationship simply was too lucrative to the state and too critical for the development of Alabama's industrial base. Indeed, Bankhead acknowledged that the "demand for convict labor has grown apace with the rapid progress made in the development of our natural resources, and with it an opportunity offers itself, which if taken advantage of by the State, will work a complete revolution [in] our convict system."[106] Bankhead proposed not to divorce the relationship between the state and industry but to intensify and solidify it on the backs of prisoners.

According to Warden Bankhead, the problem with the convict lease lay in its present design. The prisoners were too widely dispersed, making proper oversight difficult. "The trouble with the convict business," Bankhead argued, "is largely due to the fact that the prisons and their management must . . . be under the exclusive control of the contractor," who in turn entrusted the supervision of the convicts to "cheap men and reckless boys." He proposed a solution:

all convicts needed to be worked under the supervision of the warden. "This can only be done by a concentration of the convicts to one prison." But this could not be accomplished within the prison walls at Wetumpka. Bankhead's plan called for a new $18,000 prison to be built by a private company. The plan would cost the state nothing. The two-story prison would house six hundred male convicts and would include a "hospital, bath house . . . dining hall, guard quarters, bakery, [and] cook room." The warden's office would be moved from the Walls to the new prison, making supervision possible. "He can then prevent many of the abuses, if not all, that now make us ashamed of our convict system." In return for building the new prison, the contractor would receive all the convicts available.[107]

Under the Bankhead plan, prisoners would be racially segregated. Integrating the prisoners compromised their rehabilitation. By forcing white and black prisoners to share a cell, the state was "contaminat[ing] its [white] citizens . . . forcing them into associations that will demoralize and make them less fit for the duties of citizenship than before their conviction." White female convicts were particularly at risk, according to Bankhead: "White women who are sentenced to the penitentiary for living in adultery with negroes, must of necessity occupy the same cell with negro women, having them for their most intimate companions, and I suspect, frequently sleeping on the same bed with them. Do you expect that white woman to be reformed? Will she go out into the world, cured of her disease by the treatment administered to her by the State, or will she become a greater criminal and more abandoned than before her conviction?"[108]

Although agricultural and other interests cried foul at the clear labor advantage to be gained by some individual company, the state moved forward with Bankhead's plan, albeit with some revisions. Under the revised system, individual contractors would be required to lease a minimum of two hundred prisoners, a requirement that small industries and planters could not possibly meet. It also held that a single contractor could receive a maximum of two hundred prisoners (Bankhead had asked that all available prisoners be leased to one contractor). Bankhead had wanted ten-year contracts, but the legislature limited agreements to five years. The legislature also chose to continue operating the Walls in Wetumpka as well as the state farm.[109]

Bankhead advertised for bids for the new prison, and on April 1, 1883, the public learned that Pratt Coal and Coke Company would build the new prison and would receive two hundred convicts; coal operator Comer & McCurdy would likewise receive two hundred convicts. The remaining convicts would be leased to J. F. B. Jackson's lime quarry in Blount Springs. Prisoners who had been housed and worked at fourteen separate sites would now be concentrated at three sites. Those critical of the new arrangement pointed out that Pratt Coal and Comer & McCurdy were, in fact, the same company, as the company Comer & McCurdy was mining land owned by Pratt. Bankhead's plan solidified the relationship between the state and the development of the coal mining industry.[110]

As he had recommended in his plan, Bankhead moved his office and residence to the Pratt mines—to Slope No. 2 and the Shaft, to be specific—in Jefferson County in May 1883. He brought the penitentiary's physician with him. Wife Tallulah remained in Wetumpka and was kept busy with raising the couple's children and ministering to the spiritual needs of the prisoners. From his new on-site office, Bankhead supervised the construction of the new prisons to be paid for by Pratt. Construction began in June 1883.[111]

Along with implementing a modified Bankhead plan, the new governor, Edward A. O'Neal (who had recommended Bankhead for the position of warden), in 1883 appointed a new board of inspectors, led by Reginald H. Dawson. The new inspectors began their terms on March 1, 1883, and they determined that weekly inspections would allow them to correctly assess the conditions at the various prisons and to gain the trust of the convicts. The new inspectors filed their first report in fall 1884, a little more than a year after the Bankhead plan had been implemented.[112]

Throughout his tenure as chief inspector, Dawson consistently spoke out against the concentration of convicts in coal mining—the key component of the Bankhead plan. In their first report, the inspectors reported that "the health of the convicts has been unusually good, and the mortality has been very small, except at the mines." Fifty-three of sixty-three deaths were in the mines. Of those, forty resulted from disease, thirteen from accident. They also recorded "quite a number [who] have been seriously injured." The inspectors noted that "accidents sometimes occur among the free miners, but in nothing like the same proportion as among the convicts. We cannot give any reason for this. The convicts have sometimes told us, that they were forced to work in places so dangerous that free miners would not go into them."[113] In Bankhead's favor, the inspectors reported that "the health of the convicts at the mines has been much better since January 1884 than it was before that time; but there is still much more sickness there than at the places where the convicts labor in the open air."[114]

Bankhead presented a different view when it came to the dangers of work in the mines. Accidents occurred, but they were the fault of the convicts. "Men who are constantly exposed to danger soon become inured to it, and handle their lives as carelessly as a school boy handles his top. I am certain that every convict killed at the mines during the past two years was the result of carelessness on the part of the convict."[115] The inspectors regarded the mortality and illness rate as unacceptable. "The sickness at the mines, and the mortality there, both from disease and accident, are strong arguments against the employment of convicts in this kind of labor." The arrival of the physician (at the warden's behest) had a positive impact for the convicts. "Since the Physician of the Penitentiary took charge of the Hospital at Pratt Mines, the sick have been well cared for. . . . The convicts have been even more benefitted by his efforts to prevent sickness, by his attention to their diet and sanitary surroundings, and the care he has taken to keep men who have become broken down and weak from performing labor for which they were unfit."[116]

The inspectors visited the mines at Slope No. 2, operated by Comer & McCurdy, in May 1883, before the new prison was built. The conditions there were dismal: overcrowded, dirty, poorly ventilated, and infested with vermin. "At night, the heat, the stench from the privies, and the effluvia from the persons of the prisoners and from the filthy bed-clothing, made the cells almost unendurable."[117] However, conditions improved with implementation of the Bankhead plan and the construction of new prisons. "The Warden came here in May, and took charge of the proposed improvements," Dawson reported. "The Warden devot[ed] his whole time to supervising the construction . . . working as faithfully and energetically as if he were engaged in his own personal business. . . . The new prison affords ample room, and is well ventilated; the beds are comfortable, the water-closets decent, and the improvement in every respect very gratifying." The new hospital was constructed under the supervision of the prison physician and was regarded as "the best arranged and most comfortable convict Hospital in the State."[118]

The inspectors reported on the new prison constructed at the "Shaft" mine. This particular prison accommodated four hundred prisoners. The inspectors found it well ventilated and furnished with comfortable beds, but they also reported that the food was "insufficient in quantity, badly prepared, and lacking in variety."[119] In addition, the clothing worn by convicts at the "Shaft" was filthy and apparently had not been changed in weeks. The inspectors reported that after they complained, improvements were made by mine operators.

Despite noting improvements in the living conditions of the prisoners, Dawson's report also contained harsh words for the warden. According to Dawson, Bankhead was not nearly so responsive when it came to reports of what the inspector considered excessive punishment. The inspectors reported to the warden in August 1883 several cases of cruel punishment at Slope No. 2 but received no response from Bankhead regarding what, if any, action he planned to take. Two months later, the inspectors again discovered acts of cruelty and reported these to Bankhead. Again, the warden did not respond. The inspectors at that point went to Governor O'Neal and asked him to intervene, which he did.[120] Dawson and the other inspectors advocated the elimination of flogging as a punishment. Bankhead disagreed. Dawson noted, however, that "the Warden has endeavored to lodge the power of inflicting such punishment in the hands of discreet persons."[121] Dawson likewise criticized the warden's bookkeeping after the inspectors discovered state convicts at the Barbour County plantation of J. W. Comer, who did not have a contract for them (a situation that the warden did not rectify by removing the convicts).[122]

The inspectors made specific recommendations to the legislature. "With all of the convicts hired out, and only a few 'dead heads' remaining at the walls, there is nothing at all for the Warden to do at that place, and really very little for him to do anywhere else." They also did not like the fact that the warden had "the power to assign convicts to any contractor he pleases." This system was ripe for corruption. The inspectors remained opposed to convict work in mines, which was exceedingly more dangerous than work at sawmills or on farms.[123]

Dawson, while not necessarily an adversary, became a thorn in Bankhead's side. With the exception of contractor Thornton, Bankhead had not canceled a single contract, even in the face of the rankest abuse of prison labor. Bankhead's relative inaction was underscored by Dawson's actions on behalf of the prisoners. While the new prisons built with private money brought some improvement in conditions—at least temporarily—the long-term consequences were that Bankhead had cemented the relationship between the state and the coal industry. State convicts in Alabama would be sent to the mines for the next thirty years, and money from the lease would remain an important source of state revenue.[124] Access to cheap labor proved indispensable to the development of the coal industry in Alabama. Coal operators had John Hollis Bankhead to thank for that.

Ultimately, the legislature took Dawson's advice. On February 17, 1885, the state abolished the office of warden, transferring his authority to the board of inspectors. Bankhead relinquished his duties a month later.[125] At the age of forty-three, John Hollis Bankhead found himself out of a job but not out of prospects. He had accomplished much since returning from the war. Having failed to establish a slaveholders' republic as a young soldier in the Confederate Army, Bankhead had spent the next twenty years constructing a framework for the state's political, social, and economic development, one that consigned the state's black citizens to a second-class status and that relied on a captive black labor force. He now cast his eyes on a larger political prize: the US Congress.

3

"He Was a Getter, and He Got"

The Making of a New South Congressman

THE BANKHEADS LEFT THEIR HOME on the grounds of the state prison in Wetumpka and moved to the hill country town of Fayette, the county seat of Fayette County, in early 1886, where John Hollis Bankhead bought a five-hundred-acre farm. The trip back to their home region was less arduous than the trip to Wetumpka some six years earlier had been. Northwest Alabama had entered the age of rail. As son Will later recalled, "We pulled up stakes, took adieux galore of our recent scenes and went to Fayette, via Meridian, Miss., to Columbus, whence to Fayette the trip was made in a caboose of a freight train, as the Georgia Pacific road had not then been completed and no regular passenger trains had yet been put on."[1] By the time the Bankhead family arrived in Fayette, daughters Louise and Marie were young women of twenty and eighteen, respectively; John Jr. was fifteen, William was thirteen, and Henry was just ten years old. Also part of the household was Grandmother McAuley, Tallulah's mother. The Bankheads had at least two African American servants: Peter, who worked as a driver and handyman, whom Marie called "Old Pete—the faithful"; and Holiday, whom Marie referred to as her "faithful little servant." Most likely, given the family's size and status, they employed additional servants.[2]

In its early years, the town the Bankheads now called home was humorously called Frog Level after the "constant mournful croaking" that would burst forth from the frogs in the early spring.[3] By the late 1880s, with railroads pushing into the counties of Fayette and neighboring Walker (where the Bankheads would later live), the town began to shed its pastoral vestiges. Frog Level became Fayette. The bustling hill country town boasted wide boulevards and handsome homes, a general mercantile store, a saloon, a harness and saddle shop, two drugstores, two hotels, a post office, law offices, a Methodist church, a Baptist church, a two-story brick courthouse, and a two-story wooden jail.

The Bankheads moved into what originally was a relatively unadorned Federal-style house probably built in the 1830s. John Hollis Bankhead aggrandized it over time, adding an octagonal bracketed tower and replacing the fairly simple columns with bracketed latticework columns.[4] The Bankheads quickly settled into community life; they became active members of the Methodist Church and enrolled the boys in the Fayette Male and Female Institute at a cost of around ten dollars a month.[5]

Although he was no longer drawing an income from the state, Bankhead was far from destitute. Beginning in the early 1880s during his stint as warden of the state penitentiary, Bankhead began to pursue a number of economic opportunities. He invested in a lime and lumber manufacturing establishment at Blount Springs (an outfit to which he had leased convicts in 1883), helped organize the Birmingham Chain Works, and became a stockholder in Watts Coal and Coke Company, Birmingham Real Estate and Investment Company, and Sipsey River Coal Company.[6] Closer to home, he founded the Fayette Mercantile Company with neighbor Walter Worth Harkins, a partnership that lasted until 1898.[7] He took advantage of his knowledge of the coal industry acquired while expanding the convict lease and invested in several mines in neighboring Walker County, which he incorporated into Bankhead Coal Company in 1886. He made a point of hiring only free labor and succeeded in maintaining good labor relations.[8] In addition to the farm in Fayette, Bankhead acquired an orange grove in Lake County, Florida, that he leased to a local grower.[9]

Figure 3.1. The Bankhead home in Fayette, Alabama. John Hollis Bankhead is tending to his garden, c. 1895. Courtesy of the Alabama Department of Archives and History.

John Hollis Bankhead embodied the ambitions and energies of the industrializing New South. Although most southerners, white and black, would continue to scratch out meager livings in agriculture well into the next century, new economic forces had begun to penetrate the region. Rapidly expanding railroad lines threaded their way through the mountain passes, across pine barrens, over fall lines, and into swampy lowlands, hastening the exploitation of the region's rich natural resources and accelerating its integration into the national economy. In the closing decades of the nineteenth century, poor men and women abandoned failing farms to risk their lives in New South industries, ascending and felling trees for the lumber industry, descending mine shafts to extract coal, and surrendering themselves to the rhythm of machines in stifling cotton mills and iron forges. Southern industries shared certain characteristics; dedicated to the initial processing of raw materials, they relied on low-wage, low-skilled labor performing repetitive, exhausting, and often dangerous work. Railroads, industry, and an expanding cotton kingdom propelled the growth of interior cities like Birmingham, Charlotte, and Atlanta, which in turn became magnets for those seeking new opportunities. The New South was alive with movement and the thrum of the machine. John Hollis Bankhead's voice joined a rising chorus of New South boosters, mostly businessmen and newspaper publishers, who heralded industrial development as the key to regional progress.

Bankhead's return to elected office coincided with the national Democratic Party's return from the political wilderness. Democrat Grover Cleveland captured the presidency in 1884, becoming the first Democratic president in almost thirty years. His election reinvigorated southern Democrats, who feared that a Republican victory would lead to federal intervention in elections and who longed to move beyond the rancor of Reconstruction. As the American economy diversified, grew, and experienced periods of boom and bust, the two major parties crossed swords over tariffs and monetary policies. Cleveland and the Democrats criticized the high protective tariffs favored by the Republicans, arguing that such tariffs ultimately punished American consumers. Protective tariffs aided northern and eastern manufacturers while forcing the agricultural South to pay more for finished products and machinery. Farm incomes dropped precipitously throughout the late nineteenth century, while the price of manufactured goods did not. Southern Democrats were particularly critical of tariffs, regarding them as yet another federal tool to centralize power and wealth in the hands of northern industrialists. Democrats also criticized Republicans' currency and banking policies, which left southerners with insufficient supplies of money and credit. Locked into the cotton economy in an effort to meet its financial obligations to local banks and merchants, and plagued by inadequate transportation infrastructure, the South likewise did not receive its fair share of federal allocations for internal improvements.[10] Improved infrastructure, whether rail lines or navigable rivers, became the lifeblood of the New South.

The lack of capital available to southern farmers as well as a desire to bring his home state into the mainstream of the nation's economic life prompted Bankhead to return to elected office. Throughout his career, and despite his own increasingly diversified economic portfolio, Bankhead identified farming as his chief occupation and advocated for the interest of southern farmers when their political desires did not threaten the Democratic Party. A wealthy man by the late nineteenth century, John Hollis never tired of reminding his constituents of his rural roots and of promoting himself as a simple hill farmer. It was an effective political tool adopted by his family as well. Years later, second son William told a reporter that "I'm proud of what my father has done in a public way, but his achievement I'm proudest of is that mill-race over there." According to the reporter, "John H. Bankhead had dug that ditch, doing a good piece of amateur engineering in the way of turning a stream a mile out of its way to run a community grist mill, dug it with his own hands, aided by a few negro laborers, and it's a good mill-race today although put there forty years ago." William continued, "There's one of the fields over there, too, where he plowed. I remember the good crops he used to make. That's what I'm proudest of in my father."[11] Whatever else he would achieve, Bankhead forever regarded himself first and foremost a son of the soil.

Bankhead's lifelong identification as a farmer perhaps reflected his desire to appeal to as broad a constituency as possible within a diverse congressional district. Alabama's sprawling Sixth Congressional District had a complex physical and cultural geography that made representing the interests of its residents a challenge. Of the district's ten counties, five were majority white (Fayette, Lamar, Marion, Walker, and Winston); marked by a hilly terrain, these counties did not have a history of large slaveholding, and they were populated by small farmers and a growing number of coal miners. Walker County in particular possessed rich coal deposits that residents and investors were anxious to develop. Union sentiment had been strong in several of these counties, and the Republican Party enjoyed support there.[12] Three counties (Pickens, Sumter, and Greene) were predominantly agricultural and fell solidly within the Black Belt. Home to large plantations in the antebellum era, these counties boasted significant African American populations. White voters actively worked to keep power in white hands. The final two counties, Tuscaloosa and Jefferson, contained characteristics of each group and did not fit easily into either category. Jefferson County, home to the new city of Birmingham, was rapidly developing into the state's industrial center, adding yet another dimension to the district profile (Jefferson County would become part of the new Ninth Congressional District in 1892).

Throughout much of his career, John Hollis Bankhead performed as a fairly typical Bourbon, a southern Democrat interested in protecting the interests of large landowners and industrialists. Bankhead's district contained plenty of

Map 3.1.
Alabama's
congressional
districts,
c. 1880s.

each, but it also contained a fair number of small farmers and industrial work-ers—coal miners in particular—who did not always feel that their congressman was working in their best interest. Many of these men, especially in Walker County, voted Republican, while others participated in the farmers' revolt of the 1880s and 1890s. Congressman Bankhead kept his eye on these groups and did his best to appeal to the broadest constituency, but he ultimately advocated policies to disable grassroots political threats from the have-nots when they became too hot.

Bankhead threw his hat into the congressional ring in 1886 from the steps of the Fayette County courthouse, challenging incumbent one-term congressman John Mason Martin of Tuscaloosa County for the Democratic Party's nomination. The key issue in the contest was the Morrison tariff, a protectionist tariff opposed by most Democrats but supported by Martin. Bankhead ran as a self-professed "Conservative Democrat." Although he supported the Democrats' position on the tariff, Bankhead (like other lawmakers) sought exceptions for his home state's industries, in particular coal, iron ore, and lumber. He also supported federal aid to education, believing that "the very foundation of republican government rests upon an intelligent constituency."[13] In the era before primaries, party nominees were chosen in conventions that often stretched on for days as candidates and their point men cajoled, threatened, and horse-traded their way to a winning coalition. On September 13, 1886, after 154 ballots, Bankhead was nominated by the Democratic convention of the Sixth District of the State of Alabama to represent the district in Congress.[14] Bankhead and Republican Party candidate B. M. Long often traveled the district together, debating issues of the day before large gatherings of interested voters. Long criticized Bankhead's affiliation with the convict lease and won the support of Birmingham labor unions. He also supported the Republican Party's stance on protective tariffs, claiming they would help Alabama's iron industry. Despite the existence of scattered pockets of Republican voters throughout the district, no one expected Long to win. In the end, Bankhead emerged the victor with 64 percent of the vote and a 3,300-vote majority. Long captured the majority in Walker County.[15]

Formally taking his seat in Congress in March 1887, Bankhead would serve the citizens of Alabama—first as a congressman and later as a US senator—for thirty-three years. During that period, he would only twice encounter serious political challenges. His long tenure in Congress coincided with America's acquisition of an overseas empire and the country's involvement in the Great War in Europe. Bankhead often found himself at odds with the architects and promoters of the new American empire, criticizing overseas adventures and federal expenditures in the Philippines and elsewhere at a time when his region desperately needed federal investment. His interests and concerns were profoundly domestic, although not necessarily parochial. As much as any other legislator of his era, he dedicated himself to developing the tremendous natural resources of his region and the nation, in particular harnessing and improving the transportation and power potential of the region's many rivers and waterways, and extending federally financed roads into the South.

John Hollis Bankhead's life had taken an ironic turn. Having spent his early adulthood fighting to separate the southern states from the rest of the United States, he dedicated the second half of his life to the reunification of region and nation, fighting for Alabama's and the South's fair share of federal resources so that Alabama's citizens could participate in the mainstream of American economic life. Although a staunch state's rights Democrat, Bankhead ultimately was a pragmatist. Early in his career he jealously guarded the rights of the states to control the resources within their borders; over time, however, as American economic and cultural life grew more complex, Bankhead came to believe that development of the region could continue only through the increased regulatory authority of the federal government.

The new congressman arrived in the nation's capital as Washington, DC, was undergoing a period of tremendous expansion and modernization. The city's population of 177,624 had grown almost a third between 1870 and 1880. To accommodate these new residents, the capital refurbished its thoroughfares, constructed nearly eighty miles of sewer lines, laid improved water and gas mains, created numerous small parks, and planted hundreds of trees. Thousands of visitors poured into the city. One writer rejoiced in the transformation. "Washington . . . has clothed itself anew, thrown away its staff, and achieved a transformation bewildering to its old residents, but very grateful to the patriotic sense which had so long felt the stigma of a neglected and forlorn capital apparently without a destiny."[16] *Century Magazine* announced to its readers that "Washington has ceased to be a village."[17]

During Bankhead's decades-long tenure in Congress, he and his wife lived in various Washington hotels, as was the practice of legislators during that era. Very few maintained permanent residences in the district. For a time, the Bankheads lived in the Riggs House, located one block from the White House, which cost $200 per month.[18] They also lived in the New Ebbitt House, the New Willard Hotel, and the Farragut Hotel.[19] Often, the Bankheads hosted one or both of their daughters as guests. While in Washington, the Bankhead daughters enjoyed the capital city's vibrant social season, attending the many receptions hosted by daughters and wives of congressmen and senators.[20] On his frequent trips home to Alabama, Bankhead split his time between his homes in Fayette and later the town of Jasper (the county seat of Walker County) and the Florence Hotel in Birmingham. When in Fayette, he frequently could be found tending his garden, fishing, or hunting.[21]

Bankhead was forty-five years old when he entered Congress. Contemporary observers frequently commented on his commanding presence (granddaughter Tallulah put his height at six feet, three inches) and solid build. In 1897, a writer for the *Birmingham Age-Herald* noted that "Capt. Bankhead has a merry blue eye and the slight head covering left him is as black and curly as though crimped every night with curlers. His face betrays a jovial disposition and his physique commands attention."[22] He often was mistaken for Nebraska congressman and populist leader William Jennings Bryan. All described him as exuding a quiet competence. Bankhead was neither flashy nor outspoken as a legislator. He was not a gifted speaker and rarely spoke on the floor of the House or the Senate, preferring instead to do his best work in committee and behind the scenes. Although he rarely took to the floor, he held his own in debate, often using humor to defuse tension and to make his point. He was well liked by his colleagues. When asked to describe Bankhead, his colleague, friend, and New York congressman Amos Cummings declared, "There is a solidity about him that warrants confidence in his judgments."[23] The *Montgomery Journal* called him "one of the most astute politicians the state every produced—a man of wonderful resources, and who knows when to keep his tongue still and when to let it wag, when to talk in the open and when to keep quiet."[24] Republican senator Henry Cabot Lodge praised Bankhead's trustworthiness, kindliness, good sense, and abundance of personal charm.[25] John Hollis was well liked by most men regardless of political affiliation. He enjoyed bourbon and good cigars; he considered himself "a slave of the weed," once telling a friend that "many perplexing problems can be solved when viewed through the fragrant haze from a good cigar."[26] In all political matters, he was a strong party man.

The Congress that John Hollis Bankhead joined in 1887 bore little resemblance to that of antebellum America or even of the Reconstruction era. The issues that had dominated the contentious postwar years—the status of the freedmen, the relationship of the states to the federal government—gave way to concerns about the far-reaching economic and social impact of industrial and urban expansion. American life had grown more complex since the end of Reconstruction, and the congressional workload grew to reflect the diversity of interests. From 1871 to 1881, Congress considered some 37,409 bills; that number doubled between 1881 and 1891. To handle the increased volume of work, Congress regularized its procedures, and leading committee chairs and the speaker enhanced their power to control the course of legislation. The number of committees expanded, reflecting the growing challenges of governance. The character of congressional membership likewise changed. In 1875, roughly half the members of Congress were in their first term; by the mid-1890s, that percentage had dropped to roughly one-quarter. An increasingly complex nation demanded leadership possessing experience and expertise. The nation's political parties reflected many of these changes. By the late 1880s, parties had become highly organized and professional, and the men who carried their respective banners became the nation's first professional politicians.[27] John Hollis Bankhead was one of these men. But he was something else as well. Bankhead embodied the ambivalence of those men tasked with governing industrial America. Anxious to harness the power of the state for the purpose of industrial growth, many lawmakers nevertheless remained deeply rooted in parochial values. Although

Bankhead dedicated himself to more fully integrating the South into the lifeblood of the nation, he drew a bright line when it came to federal interference with race relations.

Bankhead's years in the House of Representatives, from 1887 to 1907, were spent mostly as a member of the minority party, a fact that at times hampered his overall effectiveness but taught him patience and diplomacy. During his twenty years in the House, he made two unsuccessful attempts at moving into party leadership, running for the position of minority leader in the Fifty-Fifth and Fifty-Sixth Congresses (1897–99 and 1899–1901).[28] He was appointed to the Committee on Public Buildings and Grounds (and would become the chairman during his third term) and the Committee on Pensions; in 1897, he joined the Committee on Rivers and Harbors, a fairly new committee created in 1883 that would become an important force in the development of southern industry. He used his position on the Committee on Public Buildings and Grounds and the Committee on Rivers and Harbors to win federal projects—court-

Figure 3.2. Representative John Hollis Bankhead, early 1890s. Courtesy of the Alabama Department of Archives and History.

houses, post offices, infrastructure—for his district and state. His ability to steer federal funds to Alabama helped Bankhead develop a strong patronage machine in his district in addition to support throughout the state.[29] Although a conservative states' rights Democrat in matters pertaining to race, he fervently believed that what power and resources the federal government possessed should be harnessed and exploited for the benefit of his constituents in Alabama. As one less-than-flattering contemporary article noted in 1907, "John Hollis has the reputation of being the greatest procurer of pork for his district and his State who ever strayed north of Mason and Dixon's Line. His skill at it is almost preternatural. He made no speeches. He indulged in no fancy gyrations to attract the attention of the proletariat." The key to Bankhead's political longevity and power was simple: "He was a getter, and he got."[30]

One area of Alabama that was ripe for commercial exploitation was the rich Warrior coal field, which reached into Bankhead's district.[31] But the region, which hosted a sparse population, was relatively remote. Inadequate transportation networks proved a major obstacle to industrial development. Much of the Warrior coal field sits firmly within the Black Warrior River Basin. By the late 1880s this region was fairly well served by railroads. Yet to be improved were the state's waterways, in particular the Black Warrior River, a 293-mile long tributary of the Tombigbee River. Since the early nineteenth century, state officials had struggled to address the Black Warrior's navigability. The river was narrow, crooked, and shallow, and cursed with numerous snags, logs, and other obstructions. Residents could ship goods down the river only during periods of "high water," when flat boats could pass over the rapids and shoals twenty-six miles above Tuscaloosa. Roughly one boat out of eight never made it to its destination. If properly improved, the Black Warrior River could provide a crucial link between Birmingham, the Warrior coal field, and the port at Mobile; Alabama's industrial future would be secure.[32] A deeper Black Warrior River would also serve a military purpose; the US Navy, stymied in the winter months by frozen rivers around the coal beds in Pennsylvania and West Virginia, was looking for an alternative source. Commissioned by the Army Corps of Engineers, state geologist Eugene Allen Smith conducted a survey of the shoals upriver from Tuscaloosa in 1880. To become a working river, the Black Warrior required a series of locks and dams. Initially, local leaders thought private investment could do the job, but the cost of the project quickly outpaced available resources.[33] Achieving navigation on the Black Warrior was critical to the development of the district and became a mission for new congressman John Hollis Bankhead.

Bankhead's work on the Committee on Rivers and Harbors, and particularly his ability to secure federal funds to improve Alabama's waterways, defined his years in the lower House and continued into his tenure as US senator. Much of his success was tied to his ability to build relationships with the majority party and with members from western states with similar interests. Bankhead developed a strong working relationship and personal friendship with the committee chair, Congressman (and later, senator) Theodore Burton of Ohio. Bankhead's service as the leading minority member on this committee coincided with a growing national significance of water issues, as a multipurpose approach to waterway development emerged in the late nineteenth century. Growth in the American West brought irrigation and the efficient use of spare water resources to the federal government's attention and spurred the growth of the conservation movement, while elsewhere citizens and political leaders expressed a new enthusiasm for the improvement of navigable streams.[34] Cheaper transportation routes fueled economic growth in communities across the country.[35] Alabama's 1875 constitution forbade the use of state money for infrastructure projects. Southern congresspeople like John Hollis Bankhead turned to federal appropriations to develop their region.[36]

Alabama's landscape was laced with rivers—according to Bankhead, some two thousand miles of "surveyed and improved" rivers—that were crucial to the state's development. Bankhead spoke eloquently of the nation's waterways, proclaiming that "they are nature's highways of commerce, which we are to use in making our country great."[37] Furthermore, river transport of industrial goods was cost effective and provided what he called a "safety valve for unjust and extortionate railroad charges."[38] One historian has called the period of 1883–1910, which encompasses Bankhead's years of service on the committee, "the most crucial in the entire history of rivers and harbors work."[39] Enhanced river transportation on the Black Warrior River above Tuscaloosa would aid the development of the Warrior coal field by drastically cutting the costs of coal mining interests in getting their product to Mobile and to points beyond.[40]

Work on improving the Black Warrior began while Bankhead was warden of the state prison. The River and Harbor Act of 1884 included an appropriation for the removal of obstructions from the river. Further appropriations were needed to make the Black Warrior a true working river. The construction of locks and dams began in 1888. The river between Tuscaloosa and Demopolis was exceedingly crooked, with a width of less than one hundred feet from bank to bank in some places. It was navigable only six months a year. Further locks and dams would be needed to make this section of the river navigable year round. Smaller appropriations were secured in the early 1890s.[41] Progress was slow.

In December 1897 (the year Bankhead was appointed to the committee), the city of Tuscaloosa kicked off the campaign for river improvement by hosting a rivers and harbors convention. Over three hundred men attended, including

Figure 3.3. Construction on Lock 17, Black Warrior River, c. 1914. Courtesy of the Alabama Department of Archives and History.

Congressman Bankhead; the governor; the mayors of Tuscaloosa, Mobile, and Demopolis; and area businessmen and industrialists, among them James Bowron, vice president of Tennessee Coal, Iron and Railroad (TCI) company. Attendees expressed enthusiastic support for securing federal funds to connect the mineral district of Birmingham with the Mobile harbor. In the convention's opening remarks, A. M. McGhee, president of the Tuscaloosa Business Association, stated that "this question of the development and expansion of the commercial interests of Alabama is the most important question our people have to consider at this time." Bankhead urged those in attendance to put aside local arguments and to instead make the development of the Black Warrior River an issue of national importance. "Give us an open waterway from Birmingham to Mobile," Bankhead stated, "and the rest of the United States can keep their local trade and we will take our chances with the world." Bowron of TCI echoed this sentiment. He argued that "if the export trade of Alabama is ever to assume larger proportions the people must have first-class merchant marine and a port to which foreign vessels will look for all kinds of business." New South industrialists kept their eyes on the international market, citing an enormous South American demand for coal.[42]

Bankhead's presence on the Committee on Rivers and Harbors transformed and sped up the work already begun on the Black Warrior and Tombigbee Rivers. He secured $15 million in appropriations required to complete the complex system. Ultimately, he was responsible for greatly enhancing the quality and speed with which the construction of locks and dams was undertaken. In total, the Corps of Engineers constructed a navigation system of seventeen locks and dams along the Black Warrior and Tombigbee Rivers. The final lock was described by one journalist as "a gigantic engineering structure" that possesses "even greater lift dimensions than Gatun and Miraflores locks of Panama." Writing in *Scientific American*, journalist Harry Chapin Plummer called Lock 17, with its sixty-three-foot lift, "the most signal engineering achievement." With the completion of the final lock in 1915, "the Southland's imperial dream of a navigable waterway 'from Birmingham to the Sea' was realized."[43] This single lock cost $3.5 million to construct. The total length of the improved Black Warrior River system covered over five hundred miles, making it the longest such system of locks, dams, and canals in the country.

The completion of the final lock was cause for celebration. The *Birmingham News* reported that "nearly a thousand Birmingham people steamed down the Warrior for about eighty miles, passing through seven locks. They found seven lakes or pools, long, deep, in much of the stretch a thousand feet long. Many of the visitors remembered the river as a continuous shoal, which could be forded everywhere. . . . The transformation was amazing to all, and especially to those who had known it before the engineer's magic hand touched it."[44] Bankhead and his second son, Will, attended the celebration. Asked to speak, Will

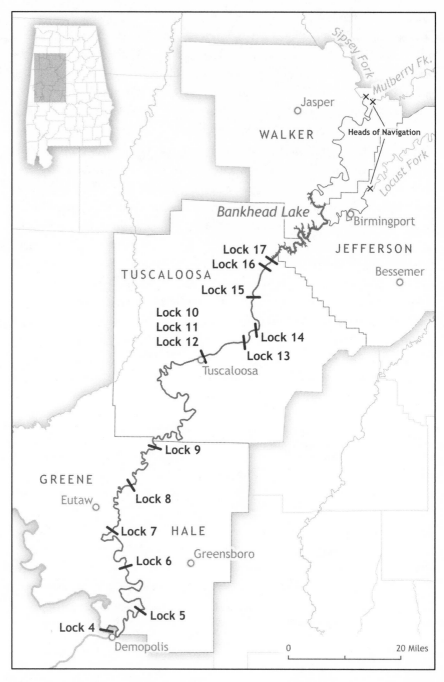

recounted how "until this day [residents of this section of the state] have suffered from inland isolation, but tomorrow even China is at our door!" He gave voice to the tension between excitement about Alabama's modern industrial future and its older traditions; those present at the speech knew that those older traditions meant white supremacy. Federal money would ensure industrial progress without disruption to the region's racial arrangement. Speaking specifically about the future of the city of Tuscaloosa, which bordered the banks of the Black Warrior, Will prophesized that, "In the years that are to come, when the cargoes of commerce shall congest these locks, freighted with products of Alabama's skill, and brain and initiative—when along this historic stream named for a stalwart brave, and across whose silent challenge the romantic De Soto led his cohorts in the quest for gold and empire, shall stand new towns, new homes, new hopes—in the midst of them—*holding fast to her ancient faiths, preserving her older and gentler ideals*, but recreated out of the materials of her seized opportunity, behold Tuscaloosa, a city of one hundred thousand souls."[45] In 1925, the lock and dam, as well as the reservoir that resulted from its construction, were named in honor of John Hollis Bankhead.

The economic benefit of improved waterways was readily apparent. Fellow Alabama congressman John McDuffie noted that in the course of a single year, "the Tombigbee River system carried almost a million tons of commerce, enough to fill 1,000 trainloads of 40 cars each, from the coal fields and along its banks down to the seaboard port of Mobile."[46] The deepening of Mobile harbor likewise brought impressive economic returns. Bankhead noted that in 1885, "4 steamships and 286 sailing vessels entered that port. During the first eleven months of 1905 1,320 steamships and 488 sailing vessels entered the harbor. As late as 1894 the exports for the year [through the port were] $2.8 million; the imports were $652,113. In the first eleven months of 1905 the exports [were] $18.4 million; the imports were $4.2 million."[47] The creation of the lock and dam system was critical to the development of Alabama industry. The Birmingham district alone produced some thirty-seven million tons of freight, which could be more economically transported via waterways than railroads. Even with these impressive gains, congressional allocations were meager and slow when compared to other outlays. Bankhead derided the fact that in 1906, Congress "appropriated 64 per cent of our revenue for preparation for and reparation of war, and 4 per cent to improve the rivers and harbors of the country to facilitate the transportation of our vast and rapidly increasing commerce."[48] Bankhead would continue to make comparisons between the cost of overseas ventures and the resources dedicated to the development of southern infrastructure throughout his career.

Bankhead's interest in the development of water resources extended beyond his congressional district. Through his work on the Committee on Rivers and Harbors, he acquired a broad view of the importance of improved navigation and the development of hydroelectric power, as well as the need for greater federal coordination, and he became a key player in the move toward greater regulation of transportation and the construction of hydroelectric dams.[49] Prior to the twentieth century, when power companies were less important, the US Department of the Interior awarded permits for prospective hydroelectric endeavors on a first come, first served basis. A group of progressives inside and outside of Congress agitated for greater regulation. The Rivers and Harbors Act of 1899, which Bankhead staunchly supported, began this process of regulation. Widely recognized as the nation's oldest environmental law, the act made it a misdemeanor to dump refuse of any kind into navigable waters without a permit. The act also made it illegal to dam navigable streams without a license from Congress; this included for the purposes of hydroelectric generation, at a time when the electric utility industry was expanding rapidly. Bankhead's stature on the committee rose to the point that—as one source reported—the committee chairman Theodore Burton, Republican congressman from Ohio, "began to rely on him for all the River and Harbor information in the South."[50]

Bankhead's dedication to the development of inland waterways impressed Republican president Theodore Roosevelt, who nevertheless disagreed with Bankhead on a number of issues related to the use of the nation's natural resources. Roosevelt's interest in conservation prompted him to become stingier when approving permits. The president's interest in the nation's waterways was also linked to the nation's transportation crisis. Despite the fact that moving goods by rail cost seven to ten times more than by water, railroads continued to carry the bulk of the nation's freight. Railroads were overwhelmed by the task, Roosevelt observed, "no longer able to move crops and manufactures rapidly enough to secure the proper transaction of the business of the Nation." In 1907, Roosevelt created the Inland Waterways Commission. Headed by Congressman Burton, the commission included John Bankhead. The commission was tasked with creating "a comprehensive plan for the improvement and control of the river systems of the United States." The commissioners looked specifically at the Mississippi and Missouri Rivers, and at the Great Lakes. They recommended the improvement of facilities for water transportation and the coordination of water power development. They also proposed that the federal government charge "for the privilege" of developing hydroelectric power in navigable streams.[51]

As a US senator, Bankhead continued to take intense interest in water issues. He supported the General Dam Acts of 1906 and 1910, which established uniform regulations for the development of hydroelectric dams. Although he fully supported federal funds for and control over navigation, Bankhead was cautious with regard to federal regulation of hydroelectric dams, in particular the insistence by conservationists that power companies continue to pay fees for the privilege of producing power. He was not alone, as Congress and President William Howard Taft, Roosevelt's successor, likewise struggled with the issue. In 1912, Congress was involved in a tense debate over a bill, promoted by Bankhead and private power interests in Alabama, to develop a dam and power station on the Coosa River. The bill did not provide for any charges to be paid by the company for the privilege of operating the dam. Bankhead was stunned when Taft reversed his position and vetoed the bill. When questioned by Bankhead, the president replied that he needed the support of the conservationist element of his party in the upcoming election: "I have not changed my opinion [regarding fees]," Taft explained. "I am too near the end of my administration to have a family row."[52] A month before Taft left office, in 1913, the Connecticut River Company agreed to accept a fifty-year permit with annual charges levied by the secretary of war for the privilege of developing water power. Congress debated whether it had the constitutional right to levy charges in addition to other regulations. Bankhead spoke out vigorously in opposition to these levies. Addressing the Senate in February 1913, Bankhead held that Congress's power over waterways was limited to regulating commerce and preserving navigability. "If the Government held absolute control and ownership in the waters of navigable rivers, it is easy to see how one of the richest assets of a State—the water power—might be absolutely destroyed and the property of the citizens virtually confiscated."[53] He opposed the fees not only because he saw them as a usurpation of the power of the states, but also because the burden of these fees would be passed on to the consumer. Conservationists saw water power as belonging to the people, and demanded that users of that privilege pay a fee. Bankhead offered an amendment that essentially killed the bill.[54]

The question of federal levies remained in stalemate for the next seven years, during which virtually no water power development projects were approved.[55] In 1920, Congress passed and the president signed the Federal Power Act, whose purpose was to more effectively coordinate hydroelectric projects in the country. The passage of the act represented a compromise between conservationists and private power interests that mandated charges and leases on the part of private power companies but also required the government pay fair market value for property upon taking possession of it. Bankhead served as the chair of the conference committee ultimately responsible for reconciling the House and Senate versions of the bill.[56]

While New South leaders like John Hollis Bankhead focused on developing the region's infrastructure and industrial capacity, the nation looked outward. In foreign affairs, most southern representatives' views in the late nineteenth century were shaped by their experiences during the Civil War and Reconstruction. With a few notable exceptions, southern Democrats' reflexive resistance to outside control, their abhorrence of federal power, and their support for white supremacy undergirded and directed their approach to foreign policy during the years 1865 to 1912.[57] They almost universally objected to the new imperialism and staunchly opposed the incorporation of nonwhite people into the country's body politic.

In his approach to foreign affairs, Bankhead differed very little from his southern colleagues in Congress. He supported the independence of Cuba but opposed US entrance into war with Spain in 1898 and the subsequent acquisition of the Philippines.[58] Speaking at the courthouse in Tuscaloosa, Bankhead stated that "the main question for the American people is whether this government shall be an empire, toward which it is tending under [President William] McKinley, or a republic, such as we have always had." Bankhead was particularly critical of the Republican president, whom he regarded as completely under the control of the Republican National Committee chairman.[59] Bankhead remained suspicious of those men desirous of building an overseas empire. His primary interests were much closer to home. In arguing for federal funds for the development of southern roads, for example, Bankhead regularly compared the outpouring of funds expended on places like Cuba and the Philippines with the lack of support for roads and infrastructure stateside.

While Bankhead was establishing himself in the House, daughters Louise and Marie were entering young adulthood, and sons John Jr. and William were coming of age. In their teen years, Louise and Marie were sent to Ward's Seminary for Young Ladies, located in the bustling New South city of Nashville.[60] Founded in 1865 by William E. and Elizabeth Hudson Ward, the seminary was a prestigious finishing school for young white southern women. While a student in Nashville, Marie made a trip to her birthplace, the plantation home Prairie Lawn, in Noxubee County, Mississippi.[61] She would forever maintain a close connection to the land, writing often and nostalgically of rural life and the southern landscape, and owning a number of farms throughout her life. In 1888, twenty-one-year-old Louise married William Perry, a congressman from South Carolina and son of that state's Reconstruction-era governor, in Fayette. Perry was nearly twenty-eight years her senior and three years older than her father. Louise would eventually have three children, two of whom survived infancy. She lived in Greenville, South Carolina, in Sans Souci, the Perry ancestral home. Perry remained in Congress until 1891, then returned to Greenville to practice law. By the turn of the century, Louise had established a girls' school at Sans Souci.[62]

Marie received her music certificate from Ward Seminary in 1886.[63] She spent the next several years teaching music and dividing her time between Fayette, Birmingham, and Washington, DC. After completing her schooling, she spent time in Washington with her parents, and then she made a grand tour of Europe, where she continued to study music, from April to October 1892.[64]

Sometime in the late 1880s or early 1890s, Marie began a courtship with Thomas McAdory Owen, whom she had met while attending a commencement ceremony at the University of Alabama. Three years her senior, Tom was the son of a physician, born and raised in the town of Jonesboro in Jefferson County. He graduated from the University of Alabama in 1887 with a law degree and a bachelor of arts degree. Tom began practicing law in Bessemer and served two years as chairman of the Jefferson County Democratic Executive Committee. In 1888, he became a justice of the peace; two years later he was Bessemer's city solicitor. In 1892, he was assistant solicitor of Jefferson

County.[65] In December of that year, Tom wrote to John Hollis Bankhead about his feelings for Marie:

> For a long time I have been a devoted admirer of your daughter, Miss Marie. This admiration, growing constantly, has ripened . . . into love. . . . She returns my affection and we are now engaged to be married. In view of this I have the honor, and it becomes my duty and pleasure as well, to solicit your hearty consent to a consummation devoutly wished for by us both. I am sure that I bear for her all of the tender regard and love that man should bear for the woman whom he fondly hopes to call his wife, and I have every reason to know, from my past and future prospects, that I can make her life a happy one. This will be my supreme pleasure—a life of pure devotion and ambitious effort for her. I desire, *if agreeable*, to meet you on your return home for the holidays, at which time, if necessary, we can speak together of the matter more fully. In the meantime, I beg to give you the following references.[66]

Tom closed the letter with a list of older established men in his community who could vouch for his character and prospects. The congressman gave his approval, and Marie and Tom were engaged on January 1, 1893. Shortly thereafter Tom bought a house in Bessemer.[67] During the four months of their engagement, Tom wrote Marie a letter every day.[68]

Twenty-four-year-old Marie kept a daily diary during the length of her engagement and into the early months of her marriage. Her entries reveal her to be a young woman very much in love and supremely conscious of the social expectations of a woman of her station. She frequently collected poems and nuggets of advice gleaned from popular periodicals. One clipping cautioned that women determined to maintain marital bliss should learn to "guard your tempers . . . learn to deny yourself and prefer others."[69] Perhaps she saved this particular pearl of wisdom because she struggled with true denial of self. Marie was an ambitious young woman living in a time when women's professional opportunities were distressingly limited. Tom Owen would become the vessel of her unrealized ambitions—a responsibility he did not always understand or appreciate. Marie had been raised in a thoroughly conventional fashion, taught to revere home and family, which brought her much fulfillment. Nevertheless, throughout her life she yearned for something more. Although she was excited about her impending wedding, the responsibilities of marriage and family sometimes weighed heavily on her. She was excited yet scared of the prospects of motherhood. In a single year, three of her close friends had died in childbirth.[70]

Marie was thrilled to have her father's blessing on her marriage: "He is a fine judge of men and that he should approve of my chosen one is a great comfort to me. Besides, he has been to me a generous, sacrificing, perfect father & I wish most earnestly to please him."[71] Conversely, mother Tallulah was skeptical about the match. Marie confided to her diary that "the financial state of Tom's affairs not being rose-hued [Mother] fears my future will be fraught with denial and hardships."[72] The idea of marrying someone below her station was risky and something for which she had criticized other women. She wrote in her diary of a local woman who "walks a mile [every day] to give seven music lessons. This is the sacrifice for love. Her husband is a carpenter and I dare say very much her inferior. She is of good blood . . . and was educated in England."[73] But Marie did not let their respective financial positions stand in the way. "I used to say I could not afford to marry a poor man," Marie admitted, "I am going to marry him despite the fact his brain, ambition, and energy are his only capital and risk the future."[74] Indeed, financial troubles would plague the couple throughout their marriage.

As was the practice of young women of her class, Marie spent the months before her marriage assembling her trousseau, practicing the piano, and visiting family and friends in Birmingham and elsewhere, even attending a reception at which popular southern author Thomas Nelson Page read from *Marse Chan*.[75] She purchased items for her trousseau in Birmingham and bought her wedding dress in Louisville.[76] An accomplished pianist, she desperately hoped that her parents would present her with a Steinway baby grand piano for a wedding gift.[77] When not preparing for her wedding and marriage, Marie spent her time doing what she referred to as "the little things that make a woman's world—with an hour or two at the piano, three hours serving, writing, reading the mail, housekeeping, and eating, and a little exercise the day is done—and then three hours to read, chat about the fireside and then 'sleep sweet sleep.'"[78]

Although her days were consumed with feminine domestic concerns, Marie was also keenly interested in politics, current events, and Tom's professional prospects. She was "deeply interested" in constitutional reform that would secure Democratic dominance and protect white supremacy.[79] She paid close attention to how her congressman father planned to distribute various patronage positions.[80] Tom seemed to appreciate her active mind and frequently sent her

Figure 3.4.
Thomas McAdory Owen, 1893. Courtesy of the Alabama Department of Archives and History.

reading material that they would then discuss on his visits.[81] The daughter of a congressman, Marie was schooled in the way of politics, and she did not hesitate to work her connections to help her betrothed advance in his career. During the state legislative session in early 1893, Tom was working on several bills related to the Bessemer court system. By mid-February they were on the governor's desk. Marie telegrammed a Montgomery contact, asking him, "Can't you help the Bessemer boys tomorrow with the Gov.?" She soon had second thoughts about her intervention. "I did this in my desire for the success of the bills—but I fear Tom will disapprove although I did not think of this until too late to recall." Still, she bristled at the thought that she should not do everything she could to help her fiancé. "If I have a 'friend at court' why not use his influence if I can command it?"[82] That same month (February 1893), Tom confided to Marie's brother John Jr. that the congressman from Alabama's Second Congressional District had approached him about running for US district attorney for the Northern Division of Alabama. Tom was flattered. "The proposition took me somewhat by surprise," Tom confided, "for although I have no doubt of my ability to fill it, I have always been modest in the estimate I've placed on my abilities and have ever been willing to rise gradually rather than by sudden leaps."[83] He was unsure whether to pursue the position, and he hoped that John Jr. might both give him advice and feel out Congressman Bankhead for support. But where Tom preferred to proceed with caution, Marie was anxious for him to take "sudden leaps." Unbeknown to Tom, Marie interceded with her father on his behalf. "I wrote to papa asking him to give his influence to Mr. Owen for the atty-ship."[84] Unfortunately, all the congresspeople were committed to other candidates.[85]

Figure 3.5. Marie Bankhead, perhaps in her wedding gown, 1893. Courtesy of the Alabama Department of Archives and History.

Tom was irritated when he learned of Marie's interference, and his disapproval left her deeply distressed. "An insinuation of his displeasure throws me into a bottomless abyss of despair," she wrote. "So enslaved am I to his will—and desire. I know I should resist such surrender of self."[86] Tom criticized her for having a "too politic manner," an accusation that "stung" her deeply.[87] But this would be a continuing pattern for Marie. Tom confided to his mother that his wife's "desire to further my ambitions [is] intense"—an intensity he did not always appreciate.[88] But Marie was determined to assist Tom in his work and, in doing so, perhaps satisfy in part her own thwarted ambition. About a month before her wedding she began learning shorthand "to assist Tom after we marry in his work. . . . I feel confident I can be a help meet to him in his literary and professional work."[89] Marie Bankhead and Thomas McAdory Owen were married on April 12, 1893, in Fayette. Musa Harkins, daughter of John Hollis's mercantile partner and girlfriend of younger brother John Jr., was

Marie's maid of honor. Following the ceremony the couple spent a week at Sans Souci with Marie's sister.[90]

Marriage and domestic life seemed to agree with the young couple. Two weeks after her wedding, Marie wrote, "I am a happy wife and have full joy in my home and its land." When not visiting friends or family, she was entertaining. Her life was made easier by the labor of two young African American servants. After an evening of entertaining, Marie wrote, "I was very proud of my dining and am surprised that Mollie, my cook a girl of 14 years of age, can do so well & Milton my little butler and her brother a boy of 10 (both light mulattoes) waited the table in good shape."[91] Tom likewise described "Mollie and Milt" as "treasures, the cooking of the former being palatable and satisfactory in every particular. And so for the latter he does a man's work, for he attends to the marketing, runs errands, waits on the table, cleans up my office, besides numbers of other small things."[92] But difficulty soon invaded their domestic bliss. About the time that she became pregnant with their first child, Marie contracted typhoid fever. Bedridden for three months, she convalesced at her mother's home and returned to Bessemer in November 1893. The couple's first child, Thomas Jr., was born in April 1894.[93]

Tom's vocation was the law, but his passion was history. He longed to write a history of the state of Alabama but found that he lacked access to the necessary primary materials. He took it on himself to assemble an archive. Passion soon became obsession. Shortly after graduating from the University of Alabama, Owen began acquiring books and primary documents related to the history of Alabama. His interest widened to include materials related to the histories of neighboring states.[94] He collected the annual reports of state agencies, copies of local newspapers, old maps. He bid on rare books at auctions and subscribed to countless newspapers, magazines, and journals.[95] Marie eventually came to share his passion and was a fervent supporter of his desire to write a history of the state. Evenings were devoted to reading. Tom told his mother that "in our home the library is the principal room."[96] A month into her marriage, Marie noted, "We are beginning our life long career of study together."[97]

Tom's collecting and research took precious time away from his law practice, and his purchase of historical documents drained the family's meager funds. Soon into their married life, the Owens owed money to a wide range of creditors, as well as to family members. In 1894, Tom borrowed $250 from Will to settle a debt. Asking his brother-in-law for money was "extremely mortifying," Tom confided. A year later this debt was still unpaid.[98] Tom searched for options. Through his father-in-law's political connections and the assistance of another Alabama congressman, Tom secured a position as chief clerk of the Division of Post Office Inspectors and Mail Depredations in Washington, DC.[99] The Owens made the move to Washington quickly and quietly in late summer 1894. Fearful that creditors might repossess their property in lieu of actual payment, Tom pleaded with his father to keep his new residence a secret. "Don't let anyone know any of our things are at Jonesboro. Neither let anyone know where our things are stored in Birmingham. In short don't let anything of our affairs be known."[100] Anxious for a fresh start and a more financially secure future, the Owens began their new life in the nation's capital.

Congressman Bankhead was determined that his sons receive the education denied him as a young man by the demands of war. John Jr., studious, methodical, and possessed of a solemn personality that some mistook for arrogance, entered the University of Alabama in 1887, the same year that Tom Owen graduated. Younger brother Will enrolled two years later. Will was John Jr.'s polar opposite in terms of temperament: affable and gregarious, he was a joiner who craved new experiences. He was a much beloved second son. His mother once told him, "In your babyhood you were a constant source of joy and we made so much over you as a little boy that strangers would ask the question, 'Is he the only child?'" Sister Marie remembered him as a prankster. She recalled a time when the family servant was away at church and company arrived unexpectedly, causing their mother to fret about who would serve their guests. Will put on one of his grandmother's dresses and played the role of "white servant," much to the delight of everyone.[101] Despite the differences in their personalities, the two brothers were devoted to each other as young men and remained extremely close throughout their lives. They later joked that they had engaged in only one fight as boys. "The cause of it was most important—a matter of principle, you might say," John Jr. later recalled. "It was a wad of chewing gum about the size of a hen egg. They called it wax in those days. Will came to bed with a cheekful of the stuff. I couldn't make him stop chewing it, so I could go to sleep. One word led to another, and the first thing either of us knew the argument had blossomed into a full blown fist fight. We might have had it out then and there if the confounded bed had not broken down. Sounded like somebody had dynamited the house. Next thing we heard was father, on the stairs, taking the steps two at a time. It was a matter of some 10 seconds or so for him to put a stop to our little show. From that day to this we have never quarreled."[102]

Located in the antebellum capital of Tuscaloosa, the University of Alabama, founded in 1831, consisted of a half-dozen buildings, twenty-five faculty members, and roughly 250 students in the late 1880s. Its curriculum resembled that of a preparatory school rather than a university. Tuition and board cost around $200 per year, low by national standards but out of reach for most white Alabamians. As a young man, Will recalled his first encounter with university cadets as the family traveled to its new home at the state penitentiary. "As we were going to embark for the [ferry boat], a couple of cadets on horseback rode up to

Figure 3.6. John Hollis Bankhead Jr. at the University of Alabama, 1888. Courtesy of the Alabama Department of Archives and History.

cross. They had been out on a ride, and in my youthful and uninitiated eyes, with their swelling chests and neat gray uniforms, cut a most romantic dash. Little did I think then, as a tow-headed, big-eyed child, that in a very few years, I would be a cadet like them, to live in the same scenes, to be filled with the same vanities, the same hopes, the same disappointments as they were. Veritably no man knoweth what a day will bring forth!"[103]

An 1888 photograph of John Jr. in his cadet's uniform shows a handsome young man with a prominent forehead, a strong jaw, and a shock of unruly dark hair. He pledged Sigma Alpha Epsilon fraternity and was elected president of his thirty-nine-member senior class. John graduated in 1891 with honors in English, Latin, and History.

Will was a good student, perhaps not as strong as his more studious older brother. Taller and better looking than John Jr., Will was active in track and was especially good at the long jump. He played right and center field for the university baseball team and, at 144 pounds, was the fullback and the field goal kicker on the university's first football team. He played in the first Iron Bowl, the annual football game between the University of Alabama and state rival the Agricultural and Mechanical College of Alabama (today's Auburn University). Will was orator of his class in his sophomore, junior, and senior years, and was awarded the Trustees' Prize for best oration. He was a member of the Shakespeare society and played triangle in the cadet orchestra. With a flair for drama, he dreamed of a career on the stage. His father disapproved but probably would have allowed it had Will's mother not stood firmly in opposition. Acting was not a respectable profession, even if it was Will's real love. Will abandoned this dream with much regret, believing it to be the one thing he was destined to succeed in.[104]

After graduation, John Jr. moved to Washington, where he worked for his father as a clerk on the House Committee on Post Offices and Post Roads. His annual salary was $1,500. He also assisted his father with his congressional correspondence, valuable early training in constituent service.[105] John Jr. enrolled in Georgetown University Law School in October 1891, rooming with some other young men from Alabama in a boardinghouse near the school. He worked several hours a week at the Capitol and attended classes in the evenings. Will once again followed his brother, arriving at Georgetown University in 1893. Brother-in-law Tom Owen wished Will well in his move to Washington, although he felt compelled to warn him against acquiring bad habits in the fast-paced urban environment. "Don't keep late hours," Tom advised. "Better a little bit of the hum-drum than an early death."[106] Will ignored this advice and immersed himself in big-city life, often to the irritation of his older brother. At Georgetown, John Jr. excelled in courses in contracts, evidence, and real estate, and did especially well in a moot court class. He was elected class president— the first student from the South to have achieved that distinction since the end of the Civil War—and graduated in 1893.[107]

Figure 3.7. William Brockman Bankhead at the University of Alabama, 1893. Courtesy of W. S. Hoole Special Collections Library, University of Alabama.

Although devoted to his older brother, Will was happy to now be on his own. He performed well at Georgetown. He was popular and, like his older brother, was elected class president. Also like John Jr., Will worked in the halls of Congress, serving as a clerk to the House Committee on Public Grounds and Buildings and as his father's private secretary.[108] He enjoyed Washington's lively social scene, going often to the theater, the racetrack, baseball games, saloons, pool halls, and the city's many art galleries. He watched children participating in the annual Easter Egg Roll on the White House lawn and attended church regularly, although not always the same church or even the same denomination. He also dated many young women from Forest Glen Seminary, a nearby women's boarding school. He wrote in his diary, "I certainly am a fortunate young man in my present surroundings. Drawing a comfortable salary, in the possession of a happy circle of friends, young, hopeful, healthy—laboring under no stress of conscience, nor in fear of any critics, in the most beautiful city in the land." A student of the law, Will also could be found at the police court, watching the proceedings, which he recorded in his diary: "Most of the unfortunates were young negroes, ranging in ages from twelve years up, many of them were sent down. It occurs to me that a revival of the whipping post or some other method of public castigation would have a more salutary effect upon these young boys, only charged with minor offense such as shooting craps and boisterous assembling, than sending them to jail to be associated in the impressionable years to the evil lairing and examples of hardened criminals with whom they are thrown. If the theory of punishment in the eye of the law is to prevent future crime, and not to avenge those already committed, then surely an improvement of the evil just suggested could be obtained."[109] Although Will's observation that jail time was probably too harsh a sentence for minor offenses was somewhat en-lightened, his prescription of public whipping of black teenagers for "boisterous assembly" revealed his adherence to an older code of racial control.

Following his graduation from Georgetown University Law School, John Jr. moved to Jasper, the seat of Walker County, and accepted a position as junior partner in the firm of Ezra W. Coleman, a friend and business associate of Congressman Bankhead. With a population of around three thousand in the early 1890s, Jasper boasted some thirty stores and was served by two railroads and twenty public roads leading into the town from all parts of the county.[110] Walker County lay astride the rich Warrior coal field. By the time John Jr. arrived, the county had four hundred coke ovens in operation, six coal mines within a few miles of the town, one foundry and machine shop, one brick works, two sand-stone quarries, thirty stores, four hotels, two banks, three school buildings, and three churches.[111] In addition to running his legal practice, John Jr. also assumed daily oversight of the family coal mines, located just outside Jasper. He taught Sunday school at the Methodist church, became a Mason, and was a founding member of the Jasper Debating Club.[112] He also served as his father's eyes on the ground, maintaining and nurturing important political and commercial contacts throughout Alabama's Sixth Congressional District. In all things, rock solid John H. Bankhead Jr. was deliberate and dependable, often serving as an anchor for his family and especially his more romantic and carefree younger brother.

In 1894, John Jr. married petite, dark-haired Musa Harkins, whom he had met at age fourteen, and who, family members remarked, was the first and only romance of his life.[113] Musa later recalled their first meeting: "I wore my hair plaited down my back and little short dresses, and the first gesture my future husband made toward me was his gallantry in offering to carry my books home from school."[114] John Jr. was determined to marry Musa. While he was still a teen, his father bought him a pig to raise. When the pig had a litter, John Jr. sold the piglets and bought a small diamond promise ring with the proceeds. Later, when he became a working attorney, John Jr. took the fees from his first legal case and presented Musa with a proper engagement ring. In the first six years of their married life, the couple would have three children: daughter Marion, born in 1896; son Walter William, born in 1898; and daughter Louise, born in 1900.[115] Perhaps wanting to be closer to John Jr. and his family, John Hollis and Tallulah Bankhead moved to Jasper in 1899.[116]

Congressman Bankhead was not keen for his sons to follow him into national politics. John Jr. recalled his father telling him, "There are two classes of men who should run for Congress: Those who have ample means to provide for their families, even if they get beaten in the election; and those who have no means at all, and who need the job to support themselves and educate their children."[117] For the time being, the sons listened to the father.

Financially, the Bankheads did very well in the tumultuous 1890s. Profits from the mines suffered as a result of the Panic of 1893, but production was back at regular levels by the end of the decade. The mines provided lucrative returns for the family. John Jr.'s law practice likewise prospered. The family was able to take advantage of the region's enhanced transportation infrastructure. Railroads, including the Louisville and Nashville, were among John Jr.'s many clients, and Bankhead Coal Company sold much of its product to the railroads.[118] John Jr. expanded his political activities, chairing the Executive Committee of the Walker County Democratic Party from 1889 until 1903.[119]

As his graduation from Georgetown drew near, Will began to consider his career options. Unlike his older brother, he did not have a plan. His first choice was to work for Constantine Buckley "Buck" Kilgore, former congressman from Texas who had been appointed by President Cleveland as a federal judge for the Southern District of Indian Territory (present-day Oklahoma). Will learned in May 1895 that "Judge Kilgore could not give me the position that I had in view out there. This changes my plans materially. I do not now know where I shall be at to begin active operation of my profession." He considered joining a Washington firm and met with an official from the US Navy. One day in May 1895, while meeting with his father, he ran into L. B. Musgrove, local Walker County, Alabama, political leader, coal operator, and publisher of the *Jasper Mountain Eagle*. Musgrove had advice for Will, which the younger man promptly recorded in his diary: "He suggested for me to go to New York to make my stand against the game of life. I don't know but that is the best thing to do. All the possibilities are in large cities. Fortune in politics, money, congenial associations, and personal comfort, are all there. What's the sense of going to some little one horse town or city to wait your life away upon its growth or brilliant prospects[?] There is no dearth of smart men anywhere I would consent to live. I might as well . . . fight them in a country that is a great country, rather than in one that *is going to be* a great country."[120] Nowhere in his diary does he talk of returning home to Alabama.

But with no prospects in Washington, DC, Will put aside dreams of big-city life and returned to Alabama. He was admitted to the bar and, in January 1896, moved to Huntsville with his dog, Joe. He confided to his diary, "I started out in the unequal struggle of life." He joined the law practice of Judge William Richardson, where he engaged in criminal and civil defense work, all minor cases.[121] Although he led an active social life in Huntsville (his diary shows him making daily calls on a variety of women, attending plays, joining clubs, playing whist, and singing in the church choir), he was not terribly happy. Quite simply, he was bored. Undated entries in his diary for February to June 1896 make plain his level of engagement with his work:

"Loafing in the Office"
"Clients like hen's teeth"

"Went hunting all day, then reading and loafing in the office"

"Nothing good is expected of Friday; but I did nothing bad."

"Same old routine in office . . ."

"General lassitude."

"Went bike riding; I went to the usual places and did usual things."

"ROUTINE."

"Reading the law, the endless law . . ."

"Doing same. It is always the same."

Not only was he bored, he was also broke. After eight months practicing law, he had earned a mere sixty-four dollars.[122] Itching for big-city life and the opportunities that hopefully beckoned, Will acted on L. B. Musgrove's advice and moved to New York City. He boarded with a few other southern men on East Fifteenth Street for $3.50 per week. He immersed himself in city politics, joining Tammany Hall's Anawanda Club and campaigning along the Bowery for mayoral candidate Robert Van Wyck. By October 1897, he was listed as a director and secretary of Admiralty Island, Alaska, Gold Mining and Development Company of Matawan, New Jersey. Writing to brother-in-law Tom Owen, Will admitted that although he had yet to find a position that fully engaged his talents, "I have no reason to regret my move to New York. I can make a good living here, even if I have to abandon the profession. I care nothing for the law, per se; but only as a means to an end. The profession here has not that prestige it possesses in the South."[123] While on the East Coast, he flirted for the last time with a career in theater. He learned that a theater company in Boston was looking to audition young men with southern accents. Bankhead rushed to Boston, auditioned, and won the role. The day before rehearsals were set to begin, he received a special delivery letter from his mother, pleading with him to abandon his hopes for an acting career. Her feelings about an actor's life had not changed since Will was in college. He later recalled that his mother told him that "if he sold his soul to hell by going on the stage the Bankheads were through with him." Unwilling to defy his mother, he relinquished the role and any serious thoughts of life as an actor. He returned to Alabama in June 1898 somewhat more determined to succeed at a conventional life.[124]

Although the Bankheads were generally prospering, many throughout the state and region were not. In the final three decades of the nineteenth century, black and white farmers in Alabama searched for the means to address serious economic problems. By 1880, close to half of all farmers were landless tenants.[125] Cotton prices dropped from thirty cents a pound in 1866 to seven cents by 1894. Plagued by unregulated and unfair railroad rates, inadequate access to credit, a deflationary money supply, and high interest rates, many small farmers in Alabama and across the South found themselves caught in an economic vice.[126] Manufactured goods, most of them produced in the Northeast and supported by protective tariffs, continued to increase in price. Small farmers and wage earners in the South further suffered from poorly funded public services. They regarded infrastructure projects (such as locks and dams) with suspicion, seeing such projects as boondoggles for industrialists and large producers. Political control of the state was in the hands of men dedicated to white supremacy and to fiscal austerity.[127]

In addition to their economic grievances, voters in the majority-white hill counties resented the control of the state party by Black Belt Democrats, who dominated state conventions. Convention delegates were apportioned by county and were based on the number of Democratic votes in state elections. Black Belt counties had an advantage because they manipulated black votes and intimidated black voters to rack up huge Democratic majorities.[128] Black Belt planters allied themselves with the railroad interests, mine operators, merchants, and other economic elites who had come to dominate economic life in the hill counties. This coalition feared an alliance of African American voters in the Black Belt and white voters in the hill country.[129]

Political reform by the have-nots was almost impossible to achieve. The state Democratic Party was tightly controlled. The party operatives kept a firm grip on the nomination process, with nominations awarded to safe and loyal candidates through the party caucus. Democrats registered the voters, kept the voting lists, conducted the elections, counted the ballots, and announced the winners. Furthermore, nominations and elections for state offices were held separate from those for national office in order to prevent federal intervention. White Alabamians physically threatened black voters to stay away from the polls or coerced them (both economically and physically) to support Democratic Party candidates.[130] Despite these efforts, African Americans continued to vote: roughly one hundred thousand remained eligible in the 1890s.[131]

Voting fraud was rampant across the South in the 1880s and 1890s. In his diary Will Bankhead described the machinations of a law school roommate who had been rewarded with a government job because of "the tact and courage he displayed as a juggler of the ballot box down in the 'black belt' of Conecuh County." The friend told Will "with great gusto how he would in the twinkling of an eye convert a Democratic minority vote into a startling majority. One of his methods was to place the Democratic tickets in the bottom of the ballot box, and cover them over so as to give it the appearance of being the bottom of the box. When the votes were to be counted, he would take up the paper cover off the tickets and count them as if voted, in the meantime having pocketed as many Republican votes as he had placed Democratic in the box."[132] Such tactics and worse were commonplace in Alabama politics, making reform practically impossible.

Frustrated with the conservative state Democratic Party's lack of response to their grievances, farmers and industrial workers in Alabama began to look to third parties and organizations, starting with the Greenback Labor Party in

1878, the Labor Party in 1888, and the Farmers' Alliance in 1889. By the end of the decade, the larger Farmers' Alliance and affiliated Colored Farmers' Alliance had absorbed the Labor Party and similar groups, claiming a combined 170,000 members. The alliance established a state exchange as well as a number of local cooperatives and warehouses. The organization soon began to think beyond community endeavors, supporting an inflationary monetary system provided by the free coinage of silver, the regulation of the railroads, and a government-subsidized credit program.

Antiestablishment fervor was running high in 1890. Working through the Democratic Party, the Alabama Farmers' Alliance rallied behind Reuben F. Kolb, commissioner of agriculture and candidate for governor. Kolb supported political rights for African Americans and better conditions for industrial workers. He also opposed the convict lease. After four days and thirty-four ballots, Kolb lost the nomination to Thomas Goode Jones, who became the compromise candidate of the anti-Kolb forces. Despite this setback, alliance-backed candidates won majorities in the lower house and made a strong showing in the Senate.

By 1892, seeing little movement in the legislature to address their concerns, individual county alliances advocated the creation of a third party. A third-party effort would transform black votes into a critical bloc, something that traditional Democrats feared. Kolb announced again for governor in 1892 but again was blocked by the Democrats. Undaunted, he ran as a Jeffersonian Democrat against the Democratic candidate Jones. Jones eked out a narrow eleven-thousand-vote victory in an election that is widely recognized as fraudulent.[133] Kolb ran as a Populist in 1894 and again was defeated, this time by conservative Democrat William C. Oates. As in the past, this election was marred by massive voter fraud. Historians believe that Democrats were able to disfranchise many potential voters in 1894 under the recently enacted Sayre Election Law of 1893, which enabled poll workers to fill out the ballots of illiterate voters.[134]

Although they sympathized with the plight of the farmer, conservative Democratic regulars such as John Hollis Bankhead found farmers' overall demands too radical, particularly the alliance's subtreasury plan. Under this plan, struggling farmers could store their commodities in government-funded warehouses and borrow up to 80 percent of the value interest free. Bankhead firmly believed that any split within the Democratic Party would grant undue influence to black voters and would ultimately threaten white supremacy. Conservative southern Democrats found common ground with disgruntled farmers on the currency issue. By the mid-1890s, many Democratic officeholders had split with President Cleveland over his currency position. The United States had been hit hard by the Panic of 1893. Cleveland was a firm supporter of the gold standard and believed that bimetallism had helped cause the recession. He forced the repeal of the Sherman Silver Purchase Act of 1890. Farmers, in contrast, supported the coinage of silver as a way to bring more money into circulation, allowing them to pay off debts with cheaper dollars. Sherman's act had required the government to purchase and coin large quantities of silver bullion, and its repeal outraged supporters of free silver. Cleveland's actions split the Democratic Party, with southerners and westerners embracing the cause of free silver.

Hoping to snuff out the rebellion, many Alabama Democrats (Bankhead included) came to support free silver as an inflationary measure that could help indebted farmers and possibly diffuse the rebellion.[135] Bankhead declared in the early 1890s: "I am heartily for free coinage [of silver]," which he believed would help "southerners who faced increasing debt and bankruptcy."[136] In January 1892, Bankhead introduced a bill "to prevent contraction, reduce taxation, and increase the volume of circulation." And it was on the issue of silver that Bankhead made his first speech to Congress, more than five years after becoming a congressman. Calling the current national banking system "oppressive," Bankhead criticized the unequal distribution of wealth in the country: "At present we have wealth and prosperity in one section and distress and bankruptcy in another section; yet both sections are governed by the same laws. It is the duty of the representatives of a people from all sections to discover the cause and apply a remedy."[137] Speaking in favor of his bill again in March 1892, he placed himself (at least rhetorically) squarely on the side of the oppressed farmer. "When the people can no longer stand the oppression, when they can no longer remain silent when the time comes, as I believe it will if they are not given relief, when the masses in this country rise up and demand justice at the hand of the lawmakers, I trust that I may be found on the side of the people and fighting with them for what I believe to be just."[138] The bill did not pass. The rebellion continued.

The Bankheads watched the growing political discontent with wary eyes. John Jr., active in Democratic Party politics in Walker County, was especially concerned with any third-party challenge to Democratic political control. He accurately noted that Walker County, home to the Republican Party's state organization, "has more Republicans in it than any county in the State." Any third party that drained votes from the Democrats threatened his father's political career and thus was greeted with scorn. Within Bankhead's congressional district, support for populist or alliance ideals was uneven. Many voters in his district—particularly those in the majority-white hill counties—had become disillusioned with the Democratic Party, which, they felt, catered to the elite, primarily large agriculture interests and industrialists. Drawing on an older political culture that cautioned against the concentration of wealth and power, they criticized the current Democratic Party as a closed system uninterested in their plight. Farm tenancy had increased in all hill counties between 1890 and 1900. As tenancy increased, farm owners became nervous and looked for political alternatives.[139] In the 1892 elections, the Jeffersonian Democratic candidate Kolb enjoyed considerable support statewide and in Bankhead's district, winning a majority of votes in Fayette, Lamar, Tuscaloosa, and Walker Counties, although in the presidential race of that year, only Fayette County supported the populist candidate, James B. Weaver.[140] Voters in Walker County gave Cleveland a slim hundred-vote majority. That year, Bankhead won reelection, although he lost in Fayette County and, like Cleveland, pulled out a slim victory in Walker County.

The Democratic nominating convention of 1894 gave Bankhead more trouble. Bankhead was challenged by three other candidates. After five days and more than five hundred votes in a hot and stuffy hall in Marion County, the convention remained deadlocked. Ultimately, the nominating convention voted to hold a primary. Bankhead's leading challenger, T. L. Long, protested the decision to hold a primary. In particular, he objected to the resolution that dictated that only qualified white voters be allowed to participate. Depriving black voters the opportunity to participate in the primary put him at a disadvantage, most likely because the decision prevented him from manipulating those votes.[141] Long held that although he was not "making any specialty of working the negro vote," the "convention's decision works a very great hardship on him and it is not fair." He argued that Sumter County, with a large African American population, "gave [the gubernatorial candidate W. C. Oates] as large a democratic majority as all of the balance of the seven counties in the district combined, yet the convention has so arranged it that Fayette, Mr. Bankhead's county, with less than half the population of Sumter and less than one-tenth the democratic vote, will have four times the strength in the selection of the nominee."[142] The matter was turned over to the state executive committee, which upheld the convention's decision to hold a primary in which only white Democratic voters could participate. Upon hearing of the committee's decision, Long withdrew from the race and threw his support to Bankhead, who prevailed in the primary.[143] Benjamin M. Long of Walker County was chosen by the Republicans to challenge Bankhead in the general election. Bankhead won that contest handily, although he lost both Fayette and Walker Counties.[144]

Bankhead's seat remained relatively secure during these tumultuous years, although he frequently lost Fayette County and eked out small margins of victory in Walker.[145] The *Walker County Record* questioned Bankhead's effectiveness, asking "what bill has Mr. Bankhead put through Congress having for its object present or future benefit or relief for the people of his district?" His defenders in the press pointed out his position as a Democratic congressman in a majority-Republican House: "of course no Democrat could accomplish anything." They also lauded his efforts to secure funds for the improvement of the Black Warrior River.[146] He easily won nomination and reelection in 1896.[147] But Bankhead had his eye on higher office. It was well known that Bankhead wanted to be considered for the US Senate that year.[148] He threw his hat in the ring but was not in the race for long. On November 16, 1896, supporters of candidate Edmund Pettus and Bankhead signed an agreement whereby Bankhead agreed to withdraw from the contest for US senator. In exchange for Bankhead supporters' backing Pettus, the latter's supporters would throw their backing to Bankhead should Senator John Tyler Morgan not survive his current term or choose to not run at the end of his term.[149] Morgan had been first elected to the US Senate in 1876 and was, as of 1896, seventy-two years old. Surely, the Bankhead forces wagered, retirement (or worse) was right around the corner. John Hollis Bankhead quite reasonably thought he had made a savvy political deal that would soon end up with him as Morgan's successor. But Morgan would hang on a lot longer than anyone could have predicted and showed no interest in stepping aside even as he entered his eighth decade. As for John Hollis Bankhead, Morgan's longevity would be the least of his problems as the turn of the new century brought him the most serious challenge of his political life.

Through fraud and intimidation, the Democratic Party in Alabama had withstood the challenge from Kolb and the Jeffersonian Democrats, as well as from the Republicans. Although they had emerged victorious, Democrats in Alabama and across the South were determined to put an end to political threats. As one historian has argued, Alabama Populists were hardly racial egalitarians. Nevertheless, many supported the right of black Alabamians to the franchise because black votes supported the economic interests of the underclass. Ultimately, "anyone who left the Democratic Party to vote for the Populists or Jeffersonians said, in effect, that white unity was less important than other issues."[150] Although beaten back in the bruising elections of the 1890s, such political apostasy needed to be eliminated. Throughout the region, white Democrats in every southern state took precautions to ensure that the Democratic Party—and by extension, white supremacy—would never again be challenged.

4

Establishing the New Order

The turn-of-the-century American South was dynamic and chaotic, alive with movement and taut with tension. Improved transportation networks—both rail and river—fostered industrialization and urbanization, which, in turn, produced exciting opportunities and achievements accompanied by tremendous challenges. Industrial expansion fostered the creation of a black and white working class whose needs often clashed with those of the political elite. At times in the 1880s and 1890s, industrial workers joined with the region's distressed farmers to challenge the political and cultural status quo. Although these political challenges were beaten back, Democratic leaders did not rest easy. They searched for a permanent means by which to defang the political opposition.

The white elite understood that achieving political dominance was not sufficient to secure what they considered a properly ordered society. Convincing the coal miner, the textile worker, and the small farmer of the wisdom and legitimacy of the traditional white ruling class was a complex proposition that involved the dissemination of a particular set of ideas about race, class, and history that shored up the elite's claims to cultural and political hegemony. In both the political and cultural efforts to secure white supremacy and affirm the superiority of the traditional ruling class, the Bankheads were intimately involved, playing key roles in designing the political, social, and cultural framework that would define Alabama society for the next sixty years.

The populist challenge of the 1890s and the constant fraud and manipulation of the votes of black citizens combined to convince the state's political leaders that a new constitution was needed, one that would ensure white supremacy and conservative Democratic governance into the new century. Alabama's Democrats were not alone in seeking to eliminate political threats. Across the South, beginning in Florida in the 1880s and concluding with Georgia in 1908, white

Democrats experimented with election laws and ultimately called conventions whose goal was to craft new constitutions that included barriers to black voting, such as poll taxes, property qualifications, and literacy tests. African American voters were not the only political targets. Such obstacles also had the potential to disfranchise poor white residents, thus eliminating the possibility of any political coalition of the have-nots.[1]

In Alabama white voters and political leaders in the Black Belt were the most enthusiastic about the proposed constitutional convention, while the strongest opposition came from the hill counties and those in the Wiregrass region in the southeast corner of the state. Although not in the forefront of the campaign, Congressman John Hollis Bankhead was a strong advocate of a constitutional convention with disfranchisement as its primary focus. He remained "firmly convinced" that the Fifteenth Amendment to the US Constitution had been a "grievous mistake." He described the political tensions of the 1890s in apocalyptic terms. He believed that "the two races are growing more restless. . . . It is possible, and many men believe it is inevitable, that there will be a race war." In order to protect against such a possibility, "many states have passed laws limiting the right of franchise by the property and education qualifications," and he expected Alabama to follow suit in short order.[2]

Support for a constitutional convention was mixed throughout Bankhead's district. Voters in majority-white Fayette and Marion Counties were staunchly against the convention, while white voters in majority-black Greene and Sumter Counties strongly supported it. Voters in Lamar, Pickens, Tuscaloosa, and Walker Counties supported the convention by slim margins.[3]

The Alabama constitutional convention was gaveled to order in Montgomery on May 21, 1901. Over the course of eighty-two sweltering days, the delegates crafted a document that would shape Alabama politics and society for the next century and beyond. Although the 155 delegates represented diverse political perspectives, the convention was dominated by a coalition of Black Belt planters and industrial leaders. No African American delegates were present, and only seven men who identified as Populist attended. The adoption of suffrage restrictions took center stage. Ultimately, multiple barriers were incorporated into the new document that took aim at both black and poor white voters struggling to find their economic footing in the New South. The convention adopted a residency requirement that stipulated that eligible registered voters must have lived two years in the state and one year in their particular county, a significant hurdle for transient tenants and workers trying to secure their place in the new industrial economy. The convention incorporated a poll tax of $1.50 per year to begin at the age of twenty-one. This tax was cumulative to a maximum of $36, a significant financial burden to poor white and black voters as the average tenant family lived on less than $100 per year and industrial workers suffered periodic unemployment. Finally, whereas most states adopted either the poll tax or the property requirement, Alabama adopted both. The state would require all registered voters to own forty acres of land or $300 worth of personal property. Potential voters also had to prove they had been employed for at least a year and had to pass a literacy test. They could also be eliminated if they had been convicted of a wide range of offenses, many of which touched those on society's margins, such as vagrancy. Sensing resistance from poor white voters, the convention adopted a loophole for them to slip through. For one year only, any adult white man who could prove that he understood the US Constitution and was also a veteran of any war or a descendant of a veteran would be exempted from all other requirements and could become a registered voter.[4]

Unlike in other states, the new Alabama constitution was put to the voters for ratification. Congressman Bankhead spoke almost daily in favor of the new constitution.[5] He admitted that although "it is not a perfect instrument, [the new constitution] is a great improvement over the old one."[6] Like other Democrats supporting the new constitution, Bankhead reassured suspicious poor white Alabamians that the disfranchisement of black men would not harm them. On the contrary, he promised, the removal of black voters would allow a competitive two-party system of white voters to flourish.[7] He vigorously supported ratification as the best means to secure white supremacy. "We are making a Constitution under which two distinct races must live: one vastly superior to the other; one created to rule and the other to be governed."[8] His feelings about African Americans had changed little since he was a young state legislator opposed to the Thirteenth and Fourteenth Amendments. He maintained, at best, a paternalistic attitude toward individual African Americans.[9] Believing African Americans wholly unfit to participate in electoral politics, Bankhead argued that "the most intelligent leaders of the [black] race in the South recognize the fact that their best help must come through their white neighbors."[10]

The new Alabama state constitution was ratified by a vote of 108,613 to 81,734, courtesy of massive fraud in the Black Belt. White-majority counties in the northern part of the state, with few exceptions, voted against it. If not for the Black Belt fraud, the constitution would have been defeated.[11] Within Bankhead's district, Fayette County voted against the constitution, 66 percent to 34 percent. Lamar voters rejected the new constitution by one vote. Marion County opposed the constitution and experienced the biggest swing within the district from those who supported the convention to those who opposed the constitution. Walker County supported ratification by only the slimmest of margins (51 percent in favor).[12]

Although not a member of the constitutional convention, John H. Bankhead Jr., in his own words, "advocated zealously" for the new constitution. He believed it had created "a new order of things," specifically, a political and economic order that assured the rule of the white elite for the foreseeable future. But the work was not quite finished. The new constitution required the legislature to pass laws providing for voter registration under what was known as the "permanent plan." John Jr. ran in 1902 to represent Walker County in the Alabama House of Representatives. His campaign was based on his advocacy of permanent disfranchisement of black men. He argued that "it is as important to provide proper methods to keep the negro from registering hereafter as it was to keep him from registering this year. The provisions of the new Constitution together with the aid of suitable registrars have kept him off the life roll of voters. The laws passed by the next legislature must keep him from registering in the years to come." He regarded the permanent disfranchisement of African American voters as "the matter of most general importance to the people." Like other white people, he believed that the removal of black voters was necessary to eliminate fraud and ensure honest elections. "As long as we keep the negro out there is no more excuse for dishonest elections." John Jr. promised, if sent to the state legislature, to "support all laws required to carry out the spirit of the Constitution."[13]

Figure 4.1. John Hollis Bankhead Jr., state legislator, 1903. Courtesy of the Alabama Department of Archives and History.

John H. Bankhead Jr. got his chance to play a critical role in securing white political supremacy when he was elected to represent Walker County in the state legislature. His inaugural session in the Alabama House was the first session after the adoption of the new constitution. The chief task of that legislature was to rewrite the election laws to conform to the franchise article in the new constitution. Although a first-term legislator, John Jr. was appointed chairman of the Committee on Elections and tasked with writing the new election law (called the "permanent plan") to conform to the registration and qualification requirements of the new constitution.[14] He introduced his bill in the Alabama House of Representatives on the sixth day of the new session, in January 1903, and in February the bill was approved and sent to the Senate, which did not take it up until the fall. After amendments and several conferences had been proposed between the two houses, the bill was approved in late September 1903.[15] With the passage of this legislation, John Jr. joined his father in crafting machinery to deprive black citizens of their rights for the next six decades.

Congressman Bankhead remained proud of his work in promoting the new constitution and its barriers to black voting. According to the congressman's local paper, the senior Bankhead was fond of telling a particular story about his own intimidation of black voters:

Mr. Bankhead was in Alabama right after the adoption of the new constitution. . . . He sauntered up to a registration booth and found the officials wrestling with a colored man of more than usual intelligence. One of the officials came over to where Mr. Bankhead was standing, evidently perturbed.

"This is a very smart negro," he whispered. "He has answered every question we can think of. Can't you suggest something?"

"Ask him to explain a writ of certiorari," said Mr. Bankhead with a grim smile.

This was done. The negro scratched his head for a moment.

"'Deed, boss," he said. "I reckon you'se done got me. I don't know what dat is, 'cept it is something to keep the nigger from votin'!"

All hands joined in the laughter that ensued and it was finally decided that the applicant was qualified to register as a voter.[16]

The impact of the new constitution and its enabling legislation, crafted by John Jr., was immediate and devastating, particularly in the state's black-majority counties. In 1900, some 79,311 African American voters appeared on the rolls in fourteen Black Belt counties. Once the constitution went into effect, barely over a thousand remained. Statewide, by 1908, Alabama counted a mere 3,742 registered black voters.[17] Although not quite as dramatic as the losses incurred by black voters, voter registration among poor white Alabamians suffered a decline that increased with the passage of time. By 1942, Alabama had only 440,291 registered voters but some six hundred thousand disfranchised white people. The strongest deterrent to white registration was the poll tax. With these voters essentially eliminated, the threat of political rebellion was snuffed out. The era of ballot stuffing came to an end, and the Democratic Party reigned supreme in Alabama and throughout the South for the next eighty years.[18]

The creation of a "new order of things," to borrow John Jr.'s words, was as much a cultural as a political battle. Having established their political hegemony through disfranchisement, the white elites had to legitimize their control. They accomplished this in part by creating a particular interpretation of the southern past and the southern present that made a virtue of elite rule, denigrated black culture, perpetuated a fear of black political participation, and taught reverence for the antebellum South and the Confederacy, as well as a distrust of northerners. Confederate heritage groups—the United Confederate Veterans, the Sons of Confederate Veterans, and the United Daughters of the Confederacy—led this endeavor, crusading for a particular patrician understanding of the past.[19] These groups commemorated the Confederacy through the erection of monuments, through public lectures and celebrations, and through the publication, circulation, and adoption in public schools of approved works of fiction and nonfiction. This effort was meant to inculcate not only opposition to black political activity but also a proper and deferential regard for elite leadership.[20] Any deviation from this time-tested social order threatened white supremacy. Southern women played a particularly important role in perpetuating this view of the southern past as a blueprint for the present.[21] While her father and eldest brother helped win the political battle for white supremacy, so too did Marie Bankhead Owen—along with her husband, Tom, who was driven by his obsession with the state's history—become a general in the cultural battle.

Tom Owen began his new job in the Division of Post Office Inspectors and Mail Depredations in late summer 1894.[22] Earning an annual salary of $2,000, Tom supervised some twenty-two other clerks.[23] He also acted as his father-in-law's eyes and ears on political developments in Washington while the congressman was back home.[24] For several weeks after their arrival, Marie was sick with what Tom referred to as "malarial fever," although it may have been morning sickness.[25] Marie became pregnant with their second child shortly after they settled in Washington. John Hollis Bankhead Owen was born in May 1895. Tom gleefully wrote to his mother that baby John was "large and fat, weighing ten pounds." Marie and her two sons spent much of summer and fall 1895 with Marie's older sister, Louise, in South Carolina and with her parents.[26]

Although relieved to have found steady employment, Tom was bored. He frequently confided to friends that his post office work was "congenial but exacting and confining."[27] The life of a government clerk was, he complained, "the most hum drum in the world. It is one eternal round, day after day, of office work."[28] Worse still, despite a steady income, Tom continued to struggle financially. He was late paying the couple's rent on their Washington residence.[29] He was slow to settle his debts. He admitted to his father, to whom he sent money to be distributed to creditors in Alabama, that "this matter has pushed me so much that I can't send you all anything for awhile. I am in a struggle now, but thanks to a good heavenly Father I'll soon see the light. . . . As soon as I can I'll go to paying up my other indebtedness."[30] He frequently sent creditors partial payments, often just covering the interest, and begged for more time to pay off the principal. He assured family members who had lent him money that he was being financially prudent. "Marie and I are living in a quiet, modest way—going out but little, and saving all we can." Despite his strained finances, Tom continued to purchase historical materials.[31]

If Tom found his work in the post office less than stimulating, his Washington location nevertheless was a boon to his historical research. "My chances for completing my collection of books necessary in my Alabama history work have been excellent, and I have made the most of them," he confided to a friend. "I am much better equipped now than ever, and am daily adding to my literary treasures."[32] Pursuing his historical work, he wrote, gave him "rare pleasure."[33] He became friendly with Dr. Ainsworth Rand Spofford, librarian of Congress, who became a mentor. With Marie and his sons frequently away visiting family, Owen spent his free time in the Library of Congress.[34] Tom began to think beyond his own historical project and began to work toward securing state support for the preservation of historical documents and records.[35]

Tom and Marie's time in Washington was short lived. With the election of a Republican president in 1896, Democratic Party patronage dried up. Tom was out of a job.[36] He longed for home and for a career that would allow him to pursue his passion for Alabama history. He sought, he confided to one friend, "a wider field of usefulness," and he believed that his education and training made him suited for "higher and better things than the routine of a Government clerkship."[37] Perhaps he could land a faculty position at the University of Alabama, he thought. Tom embarked on a furious letter-writing campaign to members of the university's board of trustees. "I do not . . . apply for any special place," Owen wrote to trustee William Richardson, "but will undertake any one of the chairs of History, English, Ancient or Modern Languages."[38] He asked brother-in-law John Jr. to intercede with members of the board of trustees on his behalf; John obliged but to no avail. No position was forthcoming. Tom was distraught. Writing to trustee Richardson, he acknowledged that he lacked the proper academic credentials, admitting, "I am not a PhD . . . nor have I been teaching recently." Nevertheless, Tom argued, "Is a man to be set aside on that account? Will my nativity, my high and honorable standing at the University, my work in any profession, my wide and favorable acquisitions, my capacity for success amount for nothing?"[39] The trustees were unmoved. Unsuccessful in this attempt, he also sought a position with the *Birmingham Age-Herald*.[40] Again, Tom was disappointed. Without a definite plan for the future, Tom and Marie returned to the state in fall 1897, along with their young sons, Thomas, age three, and John, age two.

Marie spent much of the fall with her parents in Fayette. Tom cast about for employment, finally entering into a law partnership in Carrollton, the county seat of Pickens County, located southwest of Fayette County on the Mississippi border. Brother-in-law Will Bankhead assured Tom that returning to Alabama was not a mistake. Pickens County "is certainly a good county and has a weak bar from all I hear."[41] Tom practiced law and kept tabs on local politics for his father-in-law, while Marie organized the town's first women's group—the Lavert Club, a literary club—and began writing short stories.[42] Grandmother McAuley, who was always close to Marie (Marie called her "a second mother"), was a regular house guest, assisting Marie with her young sons. By 1900, the Owens had moved again, this time to Birmingham.[43]

In October 1900, tragedy struck the Owen household. After a two-week illness, Marie and Tom's five-year-old son, John, died. Marie poured out her grief in a letter to younger brother Will. "Thursday night John ate his supper, quite heartily, but wakened before day nauseated and trying to vomit. I gave him calomel [a mercury-based compound used to treat a variety of illnesses in the nineteenth century], and in two days (Sunday morning) I sent for the Doctor as he remained so sick and pale. As soon as he looked at him he said, 'you've got a mighty sick boy, Mrs. Owen.'" She brought in two additional doctors. "They all agreed that his heart was so much involved that the usual measures could not be persued [sic]. His organs were all involved. His liver, kidneys, stomach, heart and nervous system. I believe the hand of death was on him from the beginning, for none of the remedies took effect *at any time*. He was sick for 13 days. He died . . . Thursday morning at 3am." A family friend let them place John's coffin in her family vault. This gesture brought Marie great comfort, as she could not bear the thought of her child lying in a grave. "I will not try to tell you how miserably I feel. Nothing on earth seems to hold a joy for me. His absence is all I feel. . . . I miss him every waking moment."[44] Tallulah, Marie's mother, tried to comfort her distraught daughter. "I trust time will in a measure heal your bruised and broken heart and life and joy and happiness will come again in your life. At present it seems that no such time will come, but trust and hope." She assured Marie that the family would build its own vault and move John's body there. Tallulah likewise took comfort in this. "It will not seem so cruel to die now if I can be by my angel John," she wrote.[45]

It was during this time that Tom's obsession with the preservation of the state's history really began to take hold. In 1898, Owen, along with several historians and other individuals interested in the state's history, revived the dormant Alabama Historical Society (AHS).[46] Tom worked hard to build up the membership, securing some three hundred new members within a few months.[47] He initially hoped that the society could establish and run a state history archive, but he was quickly disabused of that idea by Thomas C. McCorvey, a historian at the University of Alabama. McCorvey recommended that they seek to establish some sort of state bureau, perhaps through the secretary of state's office, that could be overseen by an archivist. "Let the state undertake the work of preserving her history," McCorvey suggested, "and the problem is solved."[48]

As secretary of the AHS, Owen crafted two bills that he submitted for consideration to the state legislature. The second of those bills, which called for establishing a commission to research and preserve Alabama's history, benefited from good timing: The state House of Representatives passed it one day before the unveiling of the state's Confederate monument on the north lawn of the capitol building. The bill sailed through the Senate with little opposition.[49]

In creating the Alabama History Commission, the state, led in its efforts by Tom Owen, was in the vanguard of a regionwide effort to use the power of the state to promote the study of the past.[50] The involvement of the state in the effort to collect, interpret, and disseminate an understanding of the region's past—heretofore the job of white hereditary societies, patriotic groups, and professional historians—marked an important turning point in the history of the South. The enthusiasm and support for official state historical agencies went hand in hand with political disfranchisement and was "an extension of the political ambitions of white elites." According to one historian, "State historical agencies provided the means to present the southern past in a manner consonant with the needs and goals of this ascendant white elite."[51] The elites determined whose materials were collected and preserved, whose stories were shared with the next generation, and whose were not.

Owen led the five-member commission's project to prepare a report that examined and documented sources, materials, buildings, and even battlefields and other sites of historical importance to Alabama. Many of these materials were held in archives or in private collections, or with benevolent institutions. The commission appealed to libraries and archives, foreign and domestic, as well as churches, colleges, and universities, to report on their holdings. Some of the most valuable material, the commission knew, lay in private hands. "Hid[den] away in old trunks, drawers, book-cases, and chests are numbers of manuscript treasures; private letters, letter books, diaries or journals, weather notes, manuscript maps, account books, surveyor's notes or field books" that provide valuable insight into the history of the state. Owen wrote that not only would the commission like to know the location, description, and condition of such collections, it also wanted their owners to donate them to the AHS.[52]

The commission's 447-page report, submitted to Governor William J. Samford in 1900, provided a detailed assessment of historical sites around the state (the vast majority were sites of white political, military, and cultural achievement), historical records and documents held in libraries and archives in Alabama and neighboring states, and manuscript collections in federal repositories. Also listed were collections held in private hands; the largest of those collections belonged to Owen himself. Since graduating from the university, Owen had amassed an impressive personal library whose "particular strength . . . lies in its practically complete collection of Alabama books and pamphlets." His collection included bound volumes of newspapers from around the state, maps, and the personal papers of prominent Alabamians.[53] The commission recommended that the state create a department whose purpose would be to preserve the state's historical resources and foster an interest in its history. Owen drafted a bill establishing a state department of archives and history "devoted exclusively to historical utilities, the further support of the State historical society, the purchase and marking of historic places, the publication of a Biennial State Register, the better regulation of the publication of State documents, and the better preservation of official records."[54] Should the state follow these recommendations, it would "place the State of Alabama in the front rank in respect to the permanent preservation of its records, archives and history."[55] State representative Richard Henry Clarke of Marengo County introduced the bill, which passed easily. Governor Samford signed the bill in February 1901 and appointed Thomas McAdory Owen the department's first director.[56] It was the first state archive of its kind in the nation, and it became a model for others to follow.[57] Three years after the archive's founding, the American Historical Association endorsed what it called the "Alabama plan" as the most efficient and effective records management system.[58] Mississippi, South Carolina, North Carolina, Virginia, and Tennessee followed Alabama's lead.[59] The founding of the Alabama Department of Archives and History (ADAH) preceded the creation of the National Archives by more than thirty years.[60]

The new ADAH was given a budget of $2,500 annually. Marie's son Tom Jr. later recalled, "I have often heard my father say that when he took charge of his office he had nothing but a few stamps, pen, ink, and besides a little stationery a determination to accomplish his purpose."[61] Tom worked tirelessly to develop and promote the archives, writing to over a thousand historians, collectors, and libraries across the country in his first six months of duty.[62] Tom reported through the press that the ADAH desired to "secure copies of all books and pamphlets written by Alabamians, or relating to the State, or published in the State, as well as general historical works. Also maps, prints, charts, manuscripts, historical pictures, photographs and old oil paintings, war records, school and college catalogues, all church literature, such as conventions, conference, or association minutes, and pamphlets or sermons or addresses."[63] He also appealed directly to the public for caches of letters or diaries they might possess.[64] Before long, Tom was overwhelmed with donations. Originally housed in the Senate cloakroom in the state capitol, the archives soon outgrew this space; in 1903 the state legislature appropriated $150,000 for the enlargement of the capitol building. The archives moved into one wing and into the basement.[65]

Under Owen's leadership, the ADAH became the state's premiere cultural institution.[66] As its director, Tom carefully balanced the department's three-part mission to serve as a cultural and educational institution; to manage and administer the state's historical resources; and to provide information, particularly to public officials.[67] As the archives flourished, Tom further established himself in the broader historical and cultural community, giving through his activities the imprimatur of the state to a particular interpretation of the southern past.[68] Tom founded the Alabama Library Association in 1904, served as the historian-general of the Sons of Confederate Veterans in 1907–17, and edited various historical publications, including *Transactions*, the official proceedings of the meetings of the AHS.[69]

Transactions provides an excellent illustration of the narrative of Alabama's past that was promulgated by professional historians and heritage groups at the turn of the twentieth century. Tom edited this annual publication and even provided documentation for many of the articles, giving them a slightly more scholarly heft. The bulk of the articles are historical reminiscences, verbatim publication of letters and other historical documents, and biographical sketches. Tom's father-in-law, Congressman Bankhead, even contributed a letter he received from the acting commissioner of the Department of the Interior that documents the history of the Alabama-Mississippi border.[70] Other articles are more interpretive, presenting a view of the past that promoted the values of the antebellum South as superior to those of the new. In an article titled "The Work of the South in Building the United States," Dr. William Robertson Garrett argues for the primacy of southern statesmen in promoting territorial expansion in the nineteenth century, without mentioning the role of slavery. He bemoans the economic and political setbacks brought about by the Civil War, but sees promise in the development of the New South, declaring that "we will have larger cities, more stately edifices, richer men, wealthier corporations, more varied interest, more widely diffused intelligence; but we will never have a higher social order, grander men, or more divine women than the men and women of the Old South."[71] In an article examining the forces that built Alabama, author William C. Ward considers the role of slavery, acknowledging that "it is doubtful if the great forests covering the fertile lands of Alabama, without the aid of negro slave labor, could have been cleared away. . . . In a large degree they created the wealth of the State and were the wealth of the State." He admits that "there were great and regrettable evils" associated with slavery, but nevertheless states that they would have been "corrected" had not the "fanatical" abolitionists intervened. Despite obvious abuses, slavery was "eminently respectable," creating "a dominant class and . . . the Southern aristocracy." Enslaved people, according to Ward, "shared the respectability as well as name of the master." Since the

Figure 4.2. Thomas McAdory Owen, director of the Alabama Department of Archives and History, at his desk. Courtesy of the Alabama Department of Archives and History.

demise of slavery, the influence of the African American in southern society "has tended to degrade both the white man and himself."[72]

The papers published in *Transactions* echo the interpretations offered by prominent professional historians. In his eight-hundred-page tome *Civil War and Reconstruction in Alabama*, published in 1905, historian Walter Lynwood Fleming presented Reconstruction as an era rife with corruption and damned by Radicals' insistence on racial egalitarianism. The Ku Klux Klan, Fleming argued, was a predictable and necessary response by humiliated white southerners. Fleming's work belonged to a school of historical scholarship that would dominate the profession until the 1960s. Interpretations offered by professional historians and archival institutions easily found their way into the broader culture. And the message was clear: the Old South, with its ruling white aristocracy, aspiring yet deferential small farmers, and enslaved black population, continued to serve as the model of a superior society.

Tom spent much of his spare time working on a multivolume history of the state of Alabama. Twenty years in the making, this was to be his magnum opus. But misfortune once again struck the Owen household in 1906, when a house fire destroyed much of the work for Tom's history of Alabama, along with Owen's own personal collection of historical documents and memorabilia. Marie confided to a friend that they lost many completed or nearly completed manuscripts in the fire, including two county histories, as well as an entire library of books that "we had nearly gone naked and hungry to buy." Fortunately, no one was hurt. The house burned while both were out, Tom at the archives and Marie at a poorhouse caring for Confederate veterans.[73]

While Tom was establishing a name for himself within the historical community and promoting a particular story of the state's past through his organizations, Marie pursued club activities, becoming an active member of both the Daughters of the American Revolution and the Alabama Division of the United Daughters of the Confederacy, both founded in the 1890s. Through these organizations, she joined other elite white women interested in shaping the history of their region and nation and, in particular, emphasizing women's contributions to that history. Through a variety of means, these groups actively promoted a historical narrative that presented slaveholders as benevolent, antebellum race relations as peaceful, and slavery as a benign and civilizing institution. The Civil War was more a result of a broad range of sectional differences, and white southern support for the war was overwhelming and unified. Reconstruction was vindictive and corrupt; the Redeemers were heroes.

In addition to her club work, Marie helped shape the discussion of the southern present and past first through her newspaper columns, short stories, plays, and a novel, and later through published works of history. In 1911, Marie was writing a column for the *Montgomery Advertiser* entitled Talks with Girls; she also wrote human-interest stories on prominent women and on women's issues, and eventually she became the editor of the women's section. While at the *Advertiser*, Marie received the nickname "Tiger Woman." Marie explained that old female tigers were called "man-eaters." When asked by a friend whether she resented the name, Marie responded, "No, indeed, honey, I'm tremendously proud of it."[74]

Talks with Girls was an advice column for young elite white women and girls. In constructing her columns, Marie made certain assumptions about her readership. For example, she assumed that most had domestic help, had "society obligations," and took vacations. A March 1911 column talks of the importance of keeping an orderly top bureau drawer. "Now of course a bureau top drawer is liable to get into a state of confusion. The housemaid is partially responsible and the hurry to dress for one's too many engagements does the rest."[75] Most of the advice she dispensed was rather conventional: Be a good friend. Do not gossip. Be punctual. Do not exaggerate. Often she would illustrate her point with a literary excerpt, a poem, or a vignette of the misfortune that had befallen a (probably) fictional young woman who chose not to embrace the particular character trait under discussion. On its face, the column is a rather banal example of the era's gender expectations for elite young white women. But a closer reading reveals a tension within the column, a tension that perhaps the author herself lived with as she struggled to satisfy her own intellectual curiosity and ambition within a set of stifling social expectations. Just as she had kept a reminder in her diary to live a life of sacrifice, so too in her column did Marie encourage women to learn to embrace self-sacrifice as if it were a "real joy to you."[76] Yet she also warned that putting others first was no excuse for ignorance, and she encouraged young women to become well versed in the issues of the day. She did not simply recommend that they read the latest literary and social commentary periodicals. She deplored the "Wretched un-Idea'd Girls" spoken of in James Boswell's *Life of Samuel Johnson* and urged women to move beyond sewing and reading circles to create what she called "walking clubs" that could educate young women on a variety of topics:

> It is not advisable to depend on books for all one's knowledge. Information gathered first hand is best assimilated and of greatest usefulness. What do you know about the chief industries of your community? Take cotton for instance. How is it cultivated? How marketed? How manufactured? What are its bi-products?
>
> Suppose your Walking Club maps out a month's program and has some subject as a source of interest and investigation. One day a field that is being plowed for the planting would be the objective. Any farmer would be flattered to have you visit for this purpose. Another time a visit to the Agricultural Department at the Capitol would make a delightful objective.

There the different kinds of cotton seeds and plants and the agricultural side of cotton would be taught.

Another day the club might visit the cotton factory at West End, and see the manufacturing side of our great staple as well as learn a great lesson about the lives of the people who make the thread and the cloth. The more ambitious members of the club might take up the study of sociology later, for the material [i.e., working-class girls] is at hand. Then there is the gin, the compress, the cotton seed oil plant all to be visited by this girls' walking club.

When you know all about cotton take up corn, then bee-keeping, then tree planting, lumber mills, boiler plants, etc.[77]

The suggestion that young elite women become conversant with the inner work-ings of the lumber industry was quite unusual and reflected Marie's own insa-tiable curiosity. As this column indicates, her interest in the lives of industrial workers was mostly confined to viewing them as objects worthy of sociological study rather than as a population with needs and desires, or as women with shared concerns. When her readers did come into contact with a member of the working class—"a girl behind a counter"—she advised that they speak words of encouragement. "Working girls don't want your pity. They don't need it. They want to be like other girls, and . . . you can help one forget for a little while that her lot is different from yours." If the counter girl was less than attentive and professional, perhaps it was because "she hasn't been taught the nice courte-sies of social relations and is careless out of ignorance."[78] The real struggles of the new industrial and urban working class (low wages, long hours, inadequate housing, substandard education) held no interest for Marie Bankhead Owen.

The majority of Marie's columns were aimed at girls in urban centers like Montgomery. Occasionally she addressed the concerns of rural girls. The ro-mantic and prosperous rural life she conjures in her column would be unrecog-nizable to most farm families in early twentieth-century Alabama. She laments the exodus of rural people to the cities. Were rural folks too materialistic, she wondered? Too focused on the labors of the farms and not enough on the plea-sures of the countryside? What could be done to keep them from abandoning the farm? The answer: more "picnics, house parties, evening gatherings, hay rides, cavalcades of equestrians, and the old fashioned tournament! What has become of that? Was not the masked knight of a generation ago as full of inter-est and mystery, as fascinating to the onlooking maiden, as he dashed down the course with his lance, gathering rings from a crane, as were the knights of old in the novels of Sir Walter Scott?"[79] For most rural Alabamians, this prescription for the myriad miseries they faced would have seemed ludicrous. Their chief problem was not a lack of entertainment options. By 1910, the majority of Ala-bama farmers were landless tenants and sharecroppers, the poorest of the poor. The labor of the entire family was required simply to keep everyone clothed and fed. And even then, there was never enough. The average farm family had no time for a week-long camping caravan, let alone a spare pair of mules or horses required for this activity that was "so popular among the smart set in England." Had she asked rural people why their children were leaving the farm, perhaps their answers would have surprised her: underfunded schools, no employment opportunities, grinding poverty, lack of modern sanitation, disease, poor medical care. But of course, these rural Alabamians were not her readers. For her urban readers, Marie's columns created a rural world that was more fantasy than reality. This idyllic rural world—a world that betrayed the real challenges faced by vast numbers of her fellow Alabamians—would eventually provide the backdrop to her only published novel.

Marie's writing career and her promotion of a set of elite cultural values extended beyond the *Montgomery Advertiser*. Marie published multiple short stories and one novel (she wrote a second but never published it), and she wrote several plays (there are indications that one was staged in New York). She had long been interested in literature and founded a number of literary groups as a young adult. Her stories follow fairly traditional conventions of southern writers of the time. Most of her work is set in the contemporary South, and her characters, settings, and themes are resonant of those who promoted the idea of the Lost Cause. This myth held that the antebellum South was a virtuous civilization of Christian men and women, and that slavery was not the cause of the Civil War. Further, the Lost Cause promoted the notion that slavery was a benign institution, race relations in the antebellum South were congenial, and black people were faithful servants; that southern generals such as Robert E. Lee were masculine paragons of Christian virtue; and that the Confederacy was defeated by the Union's superior resources and manpower. Authors and other producers of popular culture drew on these themes—what historian Karen L. Cox calls the "pastoral ideal"—that recalled a more romantic premodern America. Stock characters in this ideal were obedient and faithful black servants and slaves; stoic and honorable white southern gentlemen; and virtuous belles. Popular purveyors of this ideal were Joel Chandler Harris, whose Uncle Remus character in many ways came to define the genre, and Thomas Dixon Jr. Lost Cause fiction appealed to white people of both North and South who felt disoriented by the economic, political, and social upheavals of the late nineteenth century. Whereas disfranchisement established the political hegemony of the elite, literature and other forms of popular culture promoted a mythical, romanticized social order that legitimized white supremacy and elite rule.[80]

Marie's short stories, novel, and plays share some common themes. Like the readers of her column Talks with Girls, the female protagonists in her fiction are wealthy southern white women who are utterly devoted to domesticity but who often find ways to expand their horizons, if only slightly. Many of her works revolve around an impending marriage, as choosing a mate was likely the

most powerful act a woman could perform. In her stories, power relations between husband and wife are vastly unequal. Two of her works—her short story
"The Water Witch," published in *Uncle Remus's Magazine* in 1907, and her novel
Yvonne of Braithwaite: A Delta Romance, published in 1927—involve marriages in
which there is a significant age difference between husband and wife (not unlike the marriage between her sister and William Perry). In each of these works,
the husband meets his future wife when she is a child. In the case of *Yvonne*,
the husband even serves as his future wife's legal guardian (she is six years old
when they first meet). Even when a character purports to seek an independent
and unconventional life, she does not get very far. In Marie's unpublished no-
vella "The Masked Heart," the female protagonist sells everything she owns and
travels west, seeking adventure. She does not get far: Her first adventurous act
is to marry the dashing and mysterious Adrian within hours of meeting him.[81]
Should the husband's actions threaten the domestic ideal, it remained the responsibility of the wife to restore marital bliss. In her play *The Acting Governor*, female
protagonist Lester blames herself for the philandering of her husband, Dick. Her
friend Kate, a woman with a career, blames Lester as well. "You've spoiled Richard Forsythe. You did it yourself. Under the false system of adulation, approval,
flattery, deference—he's become a helpless, flabby mass. . . . He's a sick man.
You've made him sick." Lester's philandering husband likewise casts blame on
her, complaining that her passion for him had cooled, forcing him to seek affection elsewhere. "I want to be loved like a house afire," he whines. Her brother-
in-law calls Lester selfish for wanting a divorce. "Any woman can be a quitter! It
takes grit to stay by a bad situation and make it come out right. Grit. Character.
And by heaven, I once thought you had it!" Ultimately, Lester admits to Dick, "I
failed you." Properly chastened, a beaten-down Lester returns to her husband.[82]

Marie's stories, novels, and plays include African American characters. The
black characters are relatively interchangeable, so much so that she at times does
not even bother to come up with different names for the individual characters.
As was standard for southern fiction at the time, all black characters are utterly
devoted servants to the white protagonists. In *Yvonne of Braithwaite*, Mam Lou
and her husband, Ephrahim, remain on the Knox plantation in the Mississippi
delta. Mam Lou had been granted her freedom prior to the Civil War but chose
to remain with her former master. With the "liberal wages" paid by her former
master, Mam Lou purchased her husband. He was "her slave." When emancipation came, she refused to free him.[83] In this plantation story set at the turn of
the century, the only people still practicing slavery are black. In *The Acting Governor*, Lester and Dick have two servants, Elijah and Mam Tildy. Elijah calls
Dick "Marse" and goes to ridiculous lengths to protect him and Lester. In the
play's critical scene, Dick is shot by a character named Ashe, who is in love with
Lester. Ashe quickly exits the scene, leaving his gun behind. Lester enters the
scene and picks up the gun, at which point Dick's brother enters and sees Lester

with the gun. To protect Lester, Elijah confesses to having shot Dick. "I wanted ter be er 'big nigger' n' tote er gun." He offers to go to jail. Given the state of race relations and southern justice at the time, confessing to murdering a white man was a sure path to execution. In Marie's play, though, black characters value the lives of their white employers over their own lives. When it is discovered that the bullet had only grazed Dick, and that Elijah had taken the blame in order to protect Lester, the white characters are overcome. Turning to Elijah, Dick's brother declares, "You are a man of honor." But the most telling line belongs to Lester's friend Kate, who says to Elijah, "You're white!" Later, when Elijah learns that Lester is planning to leave Dick, he becomes upset because it means that Lester may have to work to support herself. "Don't you go an sile you han's wid common folks work. Me and Tildy can dress you in silks, des like you's al'as been dressed. We'll give you our wages." When Lester does finally leave, she takes Tildy with her. They are gone for a year. Although at some point Lester tries to get Tildy to return to Elijah and Dick (whom she calls "your master"), "she wouldn't come back." Tildy was more devoted to her white employer than to her husband.[84] In Marie's fictional world, domesticity and the marital bond was something only white people understood, craved, and honored.

Marie's only published novel, *Yvonne of Braithwaite*, provides the best opportunity to examine her ideas about gender, race relations, and southern development. Originally conceived as a play, the novel was published in 1927 by L. C. Page and Company, located in that most Yankee-fied of all northern cities, Boston. Other authors published by Page included Lucy Maud Montgomery, author of the *Anne of Green Gables* series; Eleanor Hodgman Porter, author of *Pollyanna*; and Annie Fellows Johnston, author of *The Little Colonel*, which later became a movie starring Shirley Temple. During this period, the majority of novels with southern themes were published by northern houses. This reflected not only the lack of southern publishing companies but also the interest of northern publishers and readers in southern fiction.[85]

Marie's novel is set mostly on the Knox plantation ("Braithwaite") in the Mississippi delta, where "peace and prosperity reign." The novel opens sometime in the late 1870s. George Knox is returning home to Braithwaite, his ancestral home, on a riverboat. On the boat he meets a Frenchman, Monsieur D'Aubigne, and his young daughter, Yvonne. A boiler on the boat explodes. D'Aubigne dies, and Knox saves Yvonne. Knox brings Yvonne to Braithwaite and raises her as his child. Upon his arrival he discovers that all of his family and most of those on neighboring plantations have died from yellow fever, which was brought to the region by a mysterious unnamed Spaniard. Knox also becomes guardian of Vance Walthall, a boy from the neighboring plantation Oakleigh. Knox has hopes that Vance and Yvonne will eventually marry. Vance and Yvonne flourish, with help from Knox's spinster cousin, Florrie Nichols, who acts as the children's governess; tutor Gibbs Warfield, a Confederate veteran; and a handful of faithful black servants. Vance ultimately falls in love with Frances ("Frank"), the daughter of a prominent Bostonian, while Yvonne and George develop feelings for each other. Meanwhile, a rakish young man from New Orleans named Decatur Tarbell is also pursuing Yvonne. Although George loves Yvonne, he wants her to experience the world away from the plantation. George also carries a dark secret and feels he cannot marry Yvonne until she knows who he truly is. She tells him it will make no difference; whatever he has done is in the past. George sends Yvonne off to New Orleans, where she once again runs into Decatur Tarbell, who wants to marry her. George sends a letter to Yvonne explaining his dark past. While a young man, he had traveled to Spain and met a woman, Juanita, who fell in love with him. Juan Noyan, a bullfighter, loved Juanita and made a pact with George: if, during his next fight, he felled a bull with one stab of his sword, Juanita would be his. This was fine with George, as he did not love her. Juan slays his bull, and George leaves town. But Juanita is obsessed with George and follows him to Italy. She refuses to return to Spain and ends up jumping into a volcano. George is worried that he will be charged with murder and so returns to Mississippi, only to find that the distraught Juan has gotten there ahead of him, spread yellow fever, and killed his entire family. Yvonne never reads the letter. George goes to New Orleans because he believes that Yvonne is going to marry Decatur, which is not true. George and Yvonne declare their love, return to Braithwaite, and marry. The story ends with the birth of their first child.

Marie intended for this fictional romance to nevertheless provide what she believed to be a truthful representation of the turn-of-the-century rural South. US senator John Sharp Williams of Mississippi contributed the book's foreword. He praised the book's "photographic accuracy," calling it "faithful to the cotton world of the late 19th–early 20th century."[86] The idyllic rural South that Marie conjured in her Talks with Girls column comes to fruition in *Yvonne of Braithwaite*. Perhaps her desire for a particular kind of rural life had its roots in personal nostalgia; Marie remembered fondly her time at her uncle George's Mississippi plantation, Prairie Lawn (Marie's birthplace), and the surname of her protagonist, George Knox, is borrowed from her cousin. Architecturally idiosyncratic, Braithwaite is not a white-columned mansion in the classical revival style so popular in the antebellum South but a refurbished hunting lodge that had been added onto over the years. It is expansive yet cozy and comfortable, its grounds lush and productive. Marie spends much time describing the flora and fauna in loving detail. The harsh realities of late nineteenth-century rural life barely touch Braithwaite and its residents.

The novel has much to say about the urban and industrial transformation of the American South, much of it negative. George Knox is a transitional figure, a man rooted in the soil yet nevertheless dedicated to using science and technology to his advantage. Knox initially welcomes the coming of the railroads, which he calls the "greatest land boomers in the world," and which also help him save "big money on transportation."[87] What he dislikes is the railroads' impact on race relations, as they literally offer a way out of the fields for many African Americans. In one scene, George and Yvonne are observing the comings and goings at the train station. "The [passenger] train came in and a half dozen negro men, that Knox recognized as among his least dependable hands, boarded it with noisy laughter and loud halloos to two slatternly black women who poked their heads out of the car windows. A frown of annoyance crossed his face. 'That's one of the evils of the railroad'—he said to his companion as they drove off: 'It is helping the more foolish of them one long step farther from their natural element, the soil. They ride out all their spare money, going as far as their cash will take them, and then they either walk back home or fail to return altogether, jumping their debts and leaving their crops in the fields. That's one type. There are others. The best negro in the world is the successful farmer. He has as near a moral sense as the race is capable of, and a commendable feeling of responsibility. . . . Some of them are approximately good citizens."[88] Echoing the paternalism of John Hollis Bankhead, the fictional George Knox exhibits a condescending attitude toward African Americans, believing he understands their nature and therefore knows what is best for them. "The negro's social, convivial nature is diametrically opposed to his plain interests," Knox tells Yvonne. "He loves amusement and a crowd." Industrialization and urbanization had created conditions that threatened African Americans' "plain interest." Knox continues:

> The ready money of the day laborers in the towns tempts him from the farm. . . . There he finds craps and keno for the three idle days his other three days' work affords him. That I furnish the land and the house free to him and his family, that he cuts my trees for his fires, that I supply him gratis his implements and mules and feed them, that I pay all the taxes upon everything, taxes that pay for the education of his children, he does not take into account. He's aggrieved when I want him to stick to his crops, and thinks I'm robbing him when I pay myself out of his share of the proceeds for the food he and his family have consumed during the year, and the clothes they have worn. He's a prodigal spendthrift as a rule, unless he feels a guiding, master hand over him. He is not capable of controlling his own destiny. His labor is his only capital, and when he turns it into coin it soon slips through his fingers.

Yvonne confirms that George is speaking of those African Americans born after emancipation, "and not those who got their training under white masters."[89] Knox fancies himself a progressive landowner who sometimes even spoils his tenants. Yvonne is incredulous that Knox replaced the old slave cabins with cottages. "'And you screened the cottages,' Yvonne declares. 'Think of screens for Delta negroes, will you!' She laughed a little." Providing decent housing for black laborers was borderline absurd. Knox also had a local doctor give his tenants "'a lecture on hygiene. . . . Half of them went away thinking that "hygiene" was a new kind of disease and those that only heard rumors of the talk took it for an advertising scheme for a new patent medicine: They're suspicious you know.' Yvonne laughs: 'Poor ignorant creatures!'"[90]

Marie's treatment of race relations and of African American characters is consistent with the southern fiction of the era. The novel's two main black characters—Mam Lou and Ephrahim—are loyal, obedient, superstitious, and childlike. Black children are described as "half-naked" and as if they are part of the landscape. In one scene, Vance and his northern companion go "for a ride through the cotton fields" and visit iconic southern scenes, such as the "great gloomy cypress brake," the Mississippi River, and "the little black pickaninnies playing about their door."[91] At one point, the tenants on the Knox plantation consider abandoning the plantation, urged on by "labor agitators and labor agents" working in the delta. Yvonne disguises herself and attends a meeting of black sharecroppers who are planning to leave. When she finally reveals herself, the sharecroppers are "completely amazed and scared numb," according to the plantation manager, who reports Yvonne's deed to Knox. "She talked to them in such a way, about their duty to you, who had advanced them their living for a half year, their duty to their families and to themselves, and all with such earnest simplicity, that the women went to shouting and the demoralized men caved in."[92] Through moral suasion and shaming, teenage Yvonne keeps the black families in their rightful place, the rural South. In reality, white landowners used much harsher methods to keep black people tied to the land.

The novel veers slightly closer to reality when it ventures into a discussion of discontent among the white farmers, noting that "debt was sapping their courage." But the cause of their troubles is "that they were ignorant of their trade." The answer to their problems is not political agitation but scientific methods, fertilizer, and higher education for the next generation. But not all farmers use these methods. "Ignorance, conservatism and doubt were valiant fighters, and under their banners were legions of men." They are misled by political leaders who "sowed discord, causing disruption for a while."[93] George Knox is among the group of progressive farmers who promotes diversified farming and talks glowingly about the "liberal education on farming" he received from the Department of Agriculture. Like John Hollis Bankhead, Knox sees an important role for the federal government in the region's economic development. "If our farmers would only study the material offered by the Department, they wouldn't be any body's meat. They'd quit depending on cotton alone. Diversify and live out of your own granary."[94]

Within the novel, Confederate veteran and tutor Gibbs Warfield and governess Florrie Nichols represent, respectively, the southern cult of honor and the feminine ideal. Gibbs had been engaged to Florrie before the war. She received word (false, as it turns out) that he had been killed in action. She marries a man named Nichols, who had intercepted letters between Warfield and Florrie, and in other ways deceived her. Warfield returns, learns of the deception, and kills Nichols in a duel. But Warfield and Florrie do not live happily ever after. They only see each other again as much older adults, when Warfield has been hired as a tutor. By this time, Warfield has lost his plantation, the Owl's Nest, to Reconstruction-era taxes. He also has been mistreated by the federal government. During the war, Warfield had invented some sort of projectile for rifles but had never been properly compensated for his patent by the government. Marie borrowed this element of Warfield's background from the real tale of Tuscaloosa physician John B. Read, who invented the "Read Rifle Shell." He patented it in 1856 and sold the manufacturing rights to West Point Foundry, which produced the shell for the Union during the war. Despite repeated attempts, Read was unable to recover royalties from the federal government.[95] Warfield and Florrie finally confess their love and marry at the end of the book, when Warfield is on his deathbed. He is the repository of southern honor and principle, denying himself her love until the very end. He feels unworthy because he killed her husband. They actually die as husband and wife, about a day apart. Florrie likewise denies herself Warfield's love, perfectly content to live at Braithwaite and raise Yvonne and Vance. She revels in her domestic duties and is often scandalized by the actions of the younger women in the novel.

The identification of the plantation South as home to a superior culture becomes clear when Bostonian Augustus Bridewell and his daughter "Frank" (Frances) come to visit Braithwaite. The brash Yankee father and daughter provide a striking contrast to the Mississippi Knoxes. The daughter's use of a man's nickname is not only confusing to the white southerners, it also establishes the young northern woman as less feminine than her southern counterpart, who is the ideal. Before meeting Frank, Yvonne asks, "Is she pretty?"[96] But Yvonne is not all artifice; although beautiful and refined, she is also intellectually curious, particularly about the cotton trade. Yvonne would have been the perfect participant for one of Marie Bankhead Owen's walking clubs. On the other hand, Frank knows how to roll a cigarette, attends a boarding school "where spoiled girls were given large margins of latitude," and makes the mistake of wearing trousers to go riding, much to the dismay of Florrie: "Think what the planters' families who might chance to meet you might think! Think of the negroes!"[97] During the visit, the Knoxes stage a week's worth of festivities in honor of their guests, very much like the pastoral pleasantries Marie had urged on the readers of Talks with Girls. Frank is ultimately won over by the southerners and "this arcadian paradise, where the very atmosphere was love and mutual sacrifice and helpfulness."[98]

Augustus Bridewell is the counterpart to Confederate veteran Warfield. At one point in the story, the Bostonian reveals that he had not fought in the Civil War but had hired a substitute. He was completely unaware that to an honorable people, this admission is a disgrace. "Yvonne blushed for him, but as he seemed not to realize the enormity of his offense she smiled kindly on his callous frankness . . . and tried to ignore what to her seemed a coward's deed of long ago."[99] Bridewell is impressed with Knox's knowledge of scientific farming methods and seems surprised when Knox tells him he's perfectly comfortable talking about states' rights or the race problem. "Those subjects are at the disposal of your pleasure, but I warn you beforehand that I think and feel about them just as my people feel. I'm a Deltan to my last drop of blood."[100] George Knox is eager to exploit new technological information and farming techniques, but the region's race relations and politics cannot be improved on. Knox considers any criticism of the southern way of life to be fighting words. Outside influences—like the diseased Spaniard bullfighter—are deadly. Just like the historians that Tom Owen published in the proceedings of the Alabama Historical Society, George Knox (and by extension, Marie Bankhead Owen) firmly believes that the white elite are the region's natural ruling class and that all others—especially African Americans—are forever to occupy subservient positions. To suggest otherwise is to threaten the stability of the southern way of life.

While older siblings John Jr. and Marie worked to solidify a new political and cultural order in Alabama, younger brother Will searched for professional and personal security. Having turned his back on a career in the theater and on big-city life, Will Bankhead returned to Alabama in 1897 with a renewed determination to make something of himself. He rejoined Judge Richardson's Huntsville law firm as a partner and became more actively involved in the life of the community. Although being the son of a congressman did not hurt, Will was popular in his own right. He was handsome, outgoing, and likable, possessed of a large degree of personal magnetism. Like other young men of his station, Will was a joiner. He helped found the Young Democrats Club in Huntsville, joined the Sons of Confederate Veterans, participated in community theater, and was active in the Knights of Pythias, the Elks, and the Woodmen of the World. Although not wedded to one denomination as a college student, once settled in Huntsville, Bankhead joined the Methodist Church.[101] Well known, talented, and popular, Bankhead was elected Huntsville's city attorney in 1898, and in 1900 he was elected to represent Madison County in the state legislature, where he focused his energies on education legislation. As the Madison County representative, Will was able to vote in favor of brother-in-law Tom's bill to create the state archives.[102]

That same year he established his own law office. Everything seemed to be coming together for Will, both professionally and personally. In 1899, Will met a young woman, Adelaide Eugenia Sledge, whom the Bankheads

Figure 4.3. The Bankhead siblings, late 1890s. *Left to right:* Will, Marie, John Jr., Louise, and Henry. Courtesy of the Alabama Department of Archives and History.

Figure 4.4. The Bankhead brothers, c. 1900. *Left to right:* John Jr., Henry, and Will. Courtesy of the Alabama Department of Archives and History.

called Gene. Gene was from a small town in Mississippi, although she spent a lot of time with family in Memphis, where she was "introduced" to society and attended debutante affairs.[103] A brief biography in a women's club publication described Gene as "a charming type of the beautiful and attractive womanhood for which the Tennessee Valley has long been famous." Gene was fairly well educated, having attended school in Memphis, at Salem College in

Winston-Salem, North Carolina, and at St. Catherine Convent in Louisville, Kentucky, where she graduated in 1898 as class valedictorian. She often made extended visits to her mother's childhood home near Courtland, Alabama. She had been to Paris and, like Will, was enamored of the stage.[104] Gene was engaged to a wealthy Virginia planter when Will met her in Huntsville. She was in town visiting one of her bridesmaids. Will wrote in his diary that it was love at first sight. Completely smitten, he began visiting her at her aunt's house in Courtland.[105] In late January 1900, Will burned the love letters he had received from other women.[106] He only had eyes for Gene. The few letters that survive between Will and Gene reveal the feelings of two people very much in love. Gene declared, "you can never guess what a pleasure your visits are to me but they only darken the rest of my days by comparison." She became heart-

Figure 4.5. Adelaide Eugenia Sledge, c. 1900. Courtesy of the Alabama Department of Archives and History.

broken when he had to cancel a visit. "I wish I could put you out of my mind and heart and my path in life would be plain. But you conflict with my every plan." She even threatened to return to Charlottesville, where her fiancé apparently attended the university.[107] Will's letters were equally sentimental. "I know that my letters are dull," he apologized, "because the field of observation is limited almost to the narration of my continued devotion." He wrote her every day between visits. He teased that he had never before written so many letters, and that the practice had become "a benediction to perform."[108] Years later, a friend recalled the first time she realized that Will and Gene were in love. "We were all in Belle Fuller's parlor down near the 'Big Spring' and somebody was sitting at a big squeeze piano singing 'I Don't Know Why I Love You But I Do,' & you turned such a lovestruck look toward Gene that everybody let out a roar of pure joy. I fear at the time that it was a mean trick, but you were so submerged you didn't even know we were laughing at you."[109]

Much to her family's dismay, Gene eventually broke off her engagement to the Virginia planter, and in front of seventy-five guests, she and Will were married in an Episcopal service in a private home in Memphis on January 31, 1900.[110] Unable to attend the wedding, Tallulah wrote to her son and his new

Figure 4.6. Will Bankhead with daughters Eugenia (*left*) and Tallulah, c. 1903. Courtesy of the Alabama Department of Archives and History.

wife from Washington the day after the wedding. She asked Gene to write her "and describe your presents. It will give me great pleasure. And tell me all about your wedding trousseau." She counseled them to "do your best and be good and grand in spirit and character, and help each other all you can."[111]

The local newspapers recorded the young couple's social activities. They participated in the May festival in Chattanooga, where Gene rode on a "charming float" while Will played the part of a knight, riding a horse alongside the float, and together they chaperoned a local dance for the sons and daughters of the local elite.[112] Gene soon became pregnant with the couple's first child. It was a difficult pregnancy, and Gene spent much of it with relatives in Memphis.[113] In 1901, daughter Evelyn Eugenia was born. A second daughter, Tallulah Brockman, was born exactly a year later, in 1902. Tallulah was a large baby, weighing thirteen pounds at birth according to Will's mother.[114] After Tallulah's birth, Will's maternal grandmother wrote to Gene with instructions not to change her clothes too often or to keep her room too warm. She also offered detailed suggestions on breastfeeding.[115] But Will's idyllic start to married life and fatherhood soon took a tragic turn. Shortly after giving birth to Tallulah, Gene contracted peri-

Figure 4.7. Tallulah (*left*) and Eugenia, c. 1904. Courtesy of the Alabama Department of Archives and History.

tonitis, an inflammation of the inner wall of the abdomen caused by an infection. What would today be readily treated with antibiotics was, in this earlier era, a death sentence. The infection most likely spread to the bloodstream, causing massive organ failure. Three weeks after Tallulah's birth, Gene died. She was only twenty-one years old. Will mourned this loss the rest of his life, recording in his diary nearly two decades later the anniversary of the death of "my sweet and beautiful little Gene, the mother of my children."[116]

Twenty-eight-year-old William

was now a widower with a toddler and a newborn to raise. His father wrote to him two weeks after Gene's death, encouraging him to stay in Huntsville and to take on a law partner. "You have the capacity to make a great lawyer." His father urged him to "get your old spunk back": "Don't worry over the future. We will take care of the children and be glad to do so until you are fully prepared to take them home."[117] During the early years of their childhoods, the girls lived alternately with their grandparents in Jasper and with Aunt Marie and Uncle Tom Owen in Montgomery, while Will worked in Huntsville. A year after Gene's death, the children were still with their grandparents. Will's mother reported that year-old Tallulah was "very fat" and that Eugenia had been sick. "We have rubbed [her] all over with a linament of lard and quinine and a little turpentine."[118] The family must have

Figure 4.8. Eugenia (*left*) and Tallulah, c. 1907. Courtesy of the Alabama Department of Archives and History.

wondered whether Will would ever be in a position to care for the girls properly.

The next few years were dark ones for Will, his only solace found at the bottom of a bottle.[119] He declined to seek reelection to the state legislature. The future did not look promising. In 1904, John Jr.'s law partner, Ezra Coleman, died; John convinced his brother to join his flourishing practice in Jasper. Surrounded by his supportive family, Will could begin to put his shattered life back together.

Will's tragedy was not the only one to befall the Bankheads. Eldest daughter Louise likewise suffered heartache at the turn of the century. Her husband, William Perry, died in 1902. Louise spent much of the next several years with her parents in Fayette and later when they had moved to Jasper. In 1912, at the age of forty-four, she married businessman and financier Arthur G. Lund of Boston in a Washington, DC, ceremony that counted President William Howard Taft among the guests. Shortly thereafter, the couple moved to Yonkers, New York.[120]

The turn of the new century brought new opportunities and new struggles—professional and personal—for John Jr., Marie, and Will. Of the three siblings,

John Jr.'s personal and professional life was the most stable. He took pride in having helped secure white supremacy in the political realm, but although his law practice flourished, he nevertheless was professionally unfulfilled. Steady, mature, and with a good head for business, John Jr. assumed primary responsibility for the family's financial security, watched over younger brother Will, and continued to serve as his father's closest political adviser. Still, he longed for something more. Marie and husband Tom suffered personal tragedy with the loss of their son John, but they found professional fulfillment as leaders in the battle to secure the cultural hegemony of the white elite. Will's wounds would take a long time to heal; he spent the next decade in a dark place, making some professional strides while battling personal demons. Through it all, his family was there to support him.

John Hollis Bankhead was surely proud of his children as they established themselves personally and professionally, and he supported their endeavors whenever he could. His children would get the opportunity to return the favor, as the congressman would soon encounter the toughest fight of his long political career. He would need all the help he could get.

5

POLITICAL CHALLENGES, 1904–1907

THE TURN OF THE NEW CENTURY brought fresh political challenges for John Hollis Bankhead. His first serious political contest came in 1904, the year of the state's first congressional primary.[1] For several years, conservatives and progressives alike had been demanding the institution of a primary for all political offices. They got their wish. The Democratic Party introduced the primary system, and the first primary—confined to races for state offices—was held in 1902. Two years later, to secure his tenth term in Congress, Bankhead would have to win the state's first-ever congressional primary.

The sixty-two-year-old Bankhead was the oldest Democrat serving in Congress.[2] The *Washington Post* noted that "he has earned the reputation of being a conservative and painstaking legislator, and no man from his section wields a greater influence."[3] His challenger was Richmond Pearson Hobson, a dashing naval captain almost thirty years Bankhead's junior. Whereas Hobson may have had youth and vigor on his side, Bankhead had a solid record, power, and connections. The campaign was exciting, entertaining, and full of personal insults. It was a campaign of opposites: the aging Confederate veteran dedicated to the development of his state's resources versus the hero of the Spanish-American War, committed to building a strong navy and expanding American power overseas. As veterans, both men benefited from the cultural link between manhood, military service, and political leadership. Nevertheless, campaign rhetoric and correspondence reveal interesting shifts in the changing standards by which masculinity was defined, standards that allowed a relative newcomer to challenge a nine-term incumbent. By most accounts, Hobson had set himself a huge task. Bankhead bested Hobson in 1904, but the naval hero never stopped campaigning, and he returned to challenge the senior congressman two years later, defeating him in 1906. To a greater degree than in the 1904 contest, Hobson took advantage of the surge of progressive politics across the state, aligning himself with a number of reform movements, in particular, the push for prohibition. In so doing, he benefited from a larger shift that saw evangelical men like himself making their own claims to the culture of honor, a culture that had been at odds with that of evangelical Protestants before the Civil War. These two hard-fought political races cemented in the arrogant and prickly Hobson a firm belief that John Hollis Bankhead was not just a political opponent but a personal nemesis determined to thwart the younger man's ambitions. Even after Hobson defeated Bankhead, this bitterness continued to fester in him, prompting him later to attempt to politically slay the son as he had the father. The outcome of that contest would be very different.

Born in 1870 in Greensboro, Alabama, Richmond Pearson Hobson attended private schools as a child, later enrolling at Methodist-affiliated Southern University (later Birmingham-Southern College) in Greensboro, and then, at age fifteen, the US Naval Academy. He was the youngest in his class. Even as a teen, Hobson possessed high ideals, a moral self-righteousness, and what one historian has called "an almost fanatical sense of duty."[4] He read his Bible daily and neither drank nor smoked. His classmates nicknamed him "Parson." He ran afoul of his peers when, while serving as cadet officer of the day, he reported infractions of several classmates. They retaliated by putting him "in Coventry," which meant that they refused to speak to him when not required by duty. This punishment lasted for two years. He endured this social ostracism until he graduated (at the top of his class) in 1889. He attended a naval design school in France. He worked in naval construction and repairs, served at sea as well as in naval yards in New York and in Newport News, Virginia, and taught courses at the US Naval Academy.[5] But Hobson yearned for action and the opportunity to prove himself.[6]

When the United States declared war against Spain in April 1898, Hobson was at sea with the North Atlantic squadron. He served as the fleet's constructor and was on the flagship USS *New York*. He participated in the blockade of Matanzas and the bombardment of San Juan de Puerto Rico in May. Spanish admiral Pascual Cervera y Topete had eluded the American navy thus far. Although his fleet was outnumbered and outgunned, if he could escape Santiago Harbor, he could prolong the war indefinitely.[7]

Hobson's most daring exploit, and for which he won national acclaim, was designing and carrying out a dangerous and quite possibly suicidal plan to bottle up Admiral Cervera y Topete's squadron in Santiago Harbor. In the early hours of June 3, under cover of darkness, Hobson and his crew of seven attempted to sink the USS *Merrimac* in the entrance of the harbor. Their objective was to create an obstruction that would trap the Spanish ships. As Hobson guided the *Merrimac* into the narrow part of the harbor's entrance, the Spanish opened fire, disabling the ship's steering. The ship began to drift. Hobson attempted to sink

it by exploding the vessel's five torpe-
does. Only two detonated. The *Merrimac* continued to drift, finally sinking
beyond the entrance to the harbor,
leaving the channel open. The Spanish captured Hobson and his crew and
held them as prisoners of war until
July 6.[8]

Though Hobson and his crew
failed to blockade Santiago Harbor
(the Spanish force would be defeated
soundly while fleeing the harbor on
July 3), they received a heroes' welcome for their courageous exploits
upon their return to the United States.
Hobson accepted the thanks of a
grateful Congress for his valiant work. He was promoted to the relative rank of
lieutenant and was commissioned inspector of Spanish wrecks in August 1898.[9]
Never shy about promoting his accomplishments, Hobson published an account
of his exploits in 1899.[10]

Figure 5.1.
Richmond Pearson
Hobson. Library
of Congress Prints
and Photographs
Division.

Almost overnight, this relatively obscure naval officer became a national
celebrity. The nation hailed his mission as one of the boldest—albeit not the
most successful—in modern history. Parents named their children in his honor.
He was included in children's books about American heroes. "Hobson's Choice,"
a new cigar, was created to celebrate him.[11] Songs and poems were written about
his heroism aboard the *Merrimac*:

> Hobson says, 'tis my belief
> 'Spite of every mine or gun
> Planted there, that I run
> The old collier, *Merrimac*,
> Up that channel's narrow throttle
> Like a cork into a bottle;
> Swing her round athwart the track;
> Blow her down and—run away,
> So's to fight another day.[12]

As one Hobson biographer astutely notes, the press "had labored hard to create a war, and now it labored equally hard to create a hero."[13] The tall, slim,
handsome bachelor fit the bill perfectly. Upon returning to the States in July
1898 following his release from captivity, Hobson met with President William
McKinley.

As inspector of Spanish wrecks, Hobson devised a method of salvaging them. The work was extremely hazardous and took a toll on the Cuban laborers and on Hobson himself. Hobson was later sent to Hong Kong to supervise the rebuilding of three Spanish gunboats. Setting off from New York in December 1898, he traveled across the United States by train to San Francisco, where he was to board a ship to Hong Kong.[14] He stopped along the route to deliver speeches at receptions sponsored by various patriotic, religious, and charitable groups, arriving first in Atlanta and next in Louisville. On December 18, 1898, he spoke at the Union League Club. The topic was the need for American naval supremacy. Following his speech, two distant cousins—who also happened to be daughters of a former governor of North Carolina—greeted Hobson, and each bestowed a discreet kiss on the naval officer. The bystanders cheered, and other women present, more than one hundred, demanded to kiss Hobson. A craze was born. Hobson was besieged by women as he traveled west, first in Kansas City and then by more than a thousand in Colorado. The press had a field day, renaming Hobson the "hero of the merry smack" and publishing stories with headlines such as "Hobson Is Kissing His Way to Manila." The twenty-eight-year-old lieutenant allegedly was mortified by this turn of events. When he arrived in Hong Kong, his fellow officers shunned him. The kissing craze was over, but the publicity—much of it exaggerated or completely fabricated—followed him for years.

While the young naval hero toured the country delivering speeches to adoring crowds, he kept his eye on Alabama politics. By early 1900, he was considering a political career. Never lacking for confidence, Hobson aimed high: the US Senate. He envisioned himself as the natural successor to Alabama senator John Tyler Morgan. Elected to the Senate in 1876, Morgan was an outspoken advocate of global imperialist expansion.[15] In 1900, the seventy-six-year-old Morgan was elected to his fifth term and showed no signs of retiring any time soon. Knowing that he never could dislodge the popular senator, Hobson recalibrated his considerable ambition. Back home in Greensboro, Hobson's father, James, kept him apprised of political affairs in the state. Although supportive of his son's ambitions, he advised patience: "Your hopes in regard to politics cannot be realized as early as you had hoped." Nevertheless, his father reminded Hobson that he had "plenty of time" to "gratify any aspiration you may entertain."[16]

But ambition alone could not overcome a failing body. Although Hobson was still a young man, his health had begun to decline. He suffered from "recurrent eye problems," an issue that may have traced back to his work inside Spanish wrecks in Santiago. Hobson himself blamed the noxious fumes seeping from decomposing bodies within the Spanish wrecks.[17] An eye specialist in Manila diagnosed him with congestion of the retina. Unless medical steps were immediately taken, warned the doctor, Hobson would eventually lose his eyesight. He underwent four operations in Manila and was sent to a navy hospital in Yokohama, Japan. A board of surgeons was convened, and Hobson was ordered back to the United States in September 1900. In late 1900, he was diagnosed with typhoid and was hospitalized for several months. His vision continued to deteriorate, and permanent blindness remained a real possibility.

With the prospects of progressing in his naval career growing slimmer, Hobson undertook a campaign for a medical discharge. In February 1901, a joint resolution of Congress (introduced in June 1898) was approved, formally thanking Hobson for his *Merrimac* exploit and authorizing his promotion. His title was changed from assistant naval constructor to naval constructor; he was advanced ten numbers on the seniority list in the Construction Corps; and he was promoted three grades from lieutenant to captain, making him the youngest man ever to achieve captain's rank in the US Navy.[18]

Capitalizing on his national popularity, Hobson began to speak out on the need for a superior navy. He wrote for national publications and became a recognized expert on developments in East Asia. By 1902, because of his declining eyesight, Hobson made the decision to retire from the navy. In January, he appeared before a Retiring Board of Surgeons, which was authorized to rule only on his current ability to perform his duties. Hobson admitted that he was at that time capable of work. But the work itself was debilitating. If he continued to work in the same capacity, his eyesight would continue to degenerate. The board held that its jurisdiction did not allow it to consider future developments. It declared Hobson fit for duty. He received orders to head up construction work at the Puget Sound Naval Shipyard in Washington. He was to report February 1903. Aware that the detailed mathematical and mechanical duties of a naval constructor would leave him completely blind, Hobson made the decision to apply for special legislative authority for retirement. His application was endorsed by the secretary of the navy, the chief naval constructor, and President Theodore Roosevelt, who also sent a special message to Congress endorsing Hobson's request. Hobson received no support from congressional Democrats, and Congress denied the application. His only option was to resign from the US Navy after eighteen years of service. His resignation was accepted on February 6, 1903.[19]

A week after his resignation was accepted, Park Benjamin, a former editor at *Scientific American* and *Appletons' Cyclopaedia of Applied Mechanics* who wrote frequently on naval affairs, published an article in the *Independent* in which he blamed the failure of Hobson's retirement bill on the congressman from his home district, John Hollis Bankhead. Benjamin noted that despite the fact that "the President . . . backed his appeal to Congress, . . . politics intervened, the pull of the 'district' statesman, whose well warmed place in the National Legislature, it was rumored Hobson might contest at the polls, worked powerfully, and [Hobson] was denied."[20]

Bankhead responded to this charge, although not directly. The *Montgomery Advertiser* published a letter from Bankhead's private secretary, Julien Walker.

Walker wrote that "he [Hobson] was not retired in the ordinary way because two different medical Boards of the Navy found that he was not physically qualified for retirement, that his eyes were quite good enough for the delicate and difficult work of the Naval Constructor. He was not retired by act of Congress for this reason, in part, because of the findings of the Medical Board, but mainly for the reason that a special act in his behalf would establish a precedent extremely dangerous to the well-being of the Navy, in that any young officer could with just as good excuse ask to be retired while the Navy is already gravely under-officered."[21] Hobson responded in kind. "I applied to Senator [Jacob H.] Gallinger [of New Hampshire], who introduced the required bill in the Senate and Mr. [Malcolm A.] Moody, of Oregon, who introduced it in the House of Representatives. I applied to Senator [John Tyler] Morgan to help me and take charge of the bill in the Senate. He consented and gave it cordial support and it was favorably reported upon by the Senate Naval Committee and placed upon the Senate calendar for passage. I applied to Mr. Bankhead for the same service in the House of Representatives. He refused, opposed the measure, and it was defeated in committee by his Democratic colleagues." Hobson continued: "A great injustice has been done me and I charge the responsibility directly and absolutely to J. H. Bankhead, who, in the apprehension of a political danger, grossly neglected this duty of his office." Hobson closed by calling Bankhead a scheming, unscrupulous coward.[22]

While waiting for Congress to act on his retirement, Hobson began his civilian career by embarking on a lecture tour that lasted from February to May 1903 and that took him to twenty-two states, sometimes with speaking engagements as often as six times a week.[23] Having by early 1903 set his sights on challenging Bankhead for his congressional seat, Hobson used these events to promote his ideas and to lay the groundwork for a political run, telling his fiancée that "the seed has been sown wide afield and in due time the harvest will surely appear." Although he wanted to use these events for political campaigning, he was advised to hold off. To begin campaigning for Bankhead's seat that early would give the congressman ammunition to charge that Hobson's request for retirement was merely a ploy to pursue a political career.[24] Hobson continued to accept speaking engagements in 1904, addressing Chautauquas and lyceums across the country.

On the lecture circuit and in letters to members of Congress, Hobson advocated America's role and responsibility as a world power. Hobson was a forceful spokesperson for what he called a "progressive naval program." American naval supremacy was of paramount importance. "If the United States fails to adopt now a naval program which would give this Government controlling influence on the sea," Hobson argued, "we will have to take the consequences of neglecting to use proper foresight in what are perhaps the [most vital] political questions of the day." He likewise talked about the importance of the Panama

Canal, and the "opening up" of China, as critical to American economic and military might. "In order to properly protect her interests, the U.S. must become the paramount power on the sea." He was particularly interested in the Far East. "The Orient is the battleground," he declared. "China is the objective."[25]

Hobson formally announced his candidacy for Congress in Alabama's Sixth District on January 11, 1904, and kicked off his campaign a few weeks later. This would be the state's first congressional primary. Hobson quickly ran into a significant procedural obstacle. As part of the new primary system, the State Democratic Executive Committee required all candidates to be themselves registered voters. Hobson was not registered. The registration books would not be open again until July 1904, three months after the primary. Hobson sought an exception, stating that his naval service had required him to be out of state at the time the books were last open. Bankhead informed the committee that he did not wish to bar Hobson from the ballot. To have done so would have created sympathy for Hobson, who quite possibly could have ridden this wave of sympathy to victory as a write-in candidate. Bankhead could not take that chance.[26] The State Democratic Executive Committee granted Hobson an exception.[27] Bankhead used the fact that Hobson had never been a registered voter in the district to his advantage throughout the campaign. Although Hobson was now a legitimate candidate, few gave him a fighting chance.

Hobson ran an aggressive campaign, speaking to enthusiastic gatherings in towns throughout the nine-county district. Hobson's major campaign theme was America's expanded role in the world and the need for a larger navy. But how would such an issue play in Alabama? Contemporary observers were skeptical and early on predicted an easy victory for Bankhead. Bankhead played the role of confident incumbent. He did not wish to engage his challenger face to face; to do so would only give Hobson's candidacy exposure and credibility. He politely declined Hobson's invitations to join him in debate (the eager and energetic Hobson suggested twenty such events), choosing instead to remain in Washington to attend to the nation's business. Bankhead responded to Hobson's request with feigned incredulity, stating that "I confess that I cannot quite understand what questions are open for discussion between two gentlemen both professing to believe in the principles and policies of the Democratic Party."[28] Privately, Bankhead confided to son-in-law Thomas McAdory Owen that it made no sense to leave his "important duties" in Washington "and go to Alabama and discuss imaginary questions with Captain Hobson."[29] The congressman preferred to leave any campaigning to his sons and his friends.

But the naval officer would not be put off so easily. Hobson continued to tour the district, attracting increasingly larger and more enthusiastic crowds. He cut a dashing figure, with dark hair and brooding eyes. Women and children were among his more boisterous supporters on the campaign trail. Hobson continued to repeat his accusations that Bankhead had sabotaged his retirement request. He also accused the congressman of securing an undue promotion in the army for his youngest son, Henry.[30] Hobson's rising popularity forced the incumbent's hand; by the end of February, John Hollis Bankhead was back campaigning in his home state, fighting for his political life.

Bankhead and Hobson met in several lively debates staged across the district. In Hamilton, the crowd sat through speeches given by twenty-four local candidates before Bankhead and Hobson took the stage. Their verbal jousting went on for an amazing four and a half hours.[31] Hobson promised that if elected, he would introduce a bill to finance the building of a larger navy. Specifically, his proposed bill called for an appropriation of $2.2 billion to fund the construction of new naval vessels for a period of twenty-two years. In an attempt to tie increased military spending to local needs, Hobson argued that a superior navy would aid Alabama cotton farmers. The current price of cotton, he pointed out, was being kept low because of the war between Russia and Japan. If the United States had possessed a large enough navy, it could have prevented the outbreak of that conflict. The current military conflict, Hobson argued, was also preventing the United States from selling cotton in the China market.[32] This argument was a bit of a stretch, and this part of his campaign agenda never gained much traction. Hobson also attacked Bankhead's record, calling him the "railroad Congressman" and an ally of corporations.[33]

When it was his turn, Bankhead downplayed the importance of the China market as well as US military involvement in Asia. His concerns were instead domestic and racial. He noted that "I have always voted to keep these Chinamen away from America and I will continue to do so. The 'black peril' here in Alabama is ten-fold worse than the much talked of 'yellow peril' in the Orient."[34] Seeking to diminish Hobson's military experience and status as a national hero—his challenger's strongest campaign asset—Bankhead characterized the Spanish-American War as a "little skirmish" that paled in comparison to the war of his youth. With tears rolling down his cheeks, and his voice breaking, Bankhead told the now-familiar story of how he had been wounded rescuing a fallen comrade. "In those days," he concluded, "we were all heroes."[35] Hobson's criticism of Bankhead's favorable relationship with the railroads was harder to counter: railroads were good customers of Bankhead Coal Company, purchasing more than half of the company's output.[36]

Both men benefited from the widely accepted notion that linked masculinity, military service, and political authority. However, in contrast to the acclaim for Civil War veterans, the praise for Spanish-American War veterans focused less on their noble purposes and more on their martial feats.[37] And no feat was more spectacular or better known than Hobson's. Still, even with the phenomenal publicity that surrounded the *Merrimac* escapade, the "heroic" nature of Hobson's sinking of the *Merrimac* was a subject of much interest and debate. Even before he had officially declared his candidacy for the Democratic nomination, there was discussion regarding his hero status. Writing in the *Jasper Mountain Eagle*, "Old Timer" told readers, "As a mere dangerous undertaking in defense of his country it [the sinking of the *Merrimac*] did not excel in this respect that of many a gallant men still remembered from this section of the state who stormed the belching cannons and destructive rifles from breastworks of the enemy. The one was as patriotic and heroic as the other." The paper regularly drew on Bankhead's own war service as a testament to his character, frequently recounting how during the Battle of Chickamauga, Bankhead, although severely injured himself, had dragged a wounded private from the field of fire. "His conduct towards those under him shows better than anything else what kind of a man he is," "Old Timer" asserted. "The fact that Capt. Bankhead is loved as a brother by the men who were under him shows that he has been tested and found true."[38] Hobson's self-promotion, such as the publication of his account of the *Merrimac*, rankled older soldiers, whose own acts of bravery went unheralded.

Privately, Bankhead mocked Hobson, even penning a poem that poked fun at the naval captain's ego and ambition:

> I am Hobson bold of the *Merrimac*
> I gave the girls a rousing smack
> I undertook the stump and take a crack
> At all of God's creation.
>
> The Navy was too small for me
> So I left it don't you see
> I should take charge you'll agree
> Of the whole American Nation.
>
> If I in Congress once could get
> I'd raise the duel there you bet
> And be the universal pet
> In two short weeks' duration
>
> The House would soon belong to me
> The Senate bend on lowly knee
> And Ted himself would quickly flee
> In utter consternation
>
> For I'm Hobson bold of the *Merrimac*
> I tote the world upon my back
> It would be no task for me to crack
> The world's entire foundation.[39]

The battle was joined; each successive debate appearance drew ever-greater crowds, and the rhetoric grew increasingly bitter and personal. The *Birmingham*

Age-Herald described the contest as "a political sensation."[40] The campaign was so demanding, the pace so grueling, that both candidates became ill during its course.

Some 650 citizens attended the debate at Jasper, county seat of Walker County, the most populous county in the district and Bankhead's new residence. Bankhead criticized Hobson's naval bill and questioned his standing as a Democrat, pointing out that the naval officer had never voted nor even registered to vote. "If you beat me," Bankhead pleaded, "for God's sake don't beat me with a man not of our party." Taking a jab at Hobson for the alleged "kissing craze," Bankhead continued: Hobson could have registered to vote while on leave of absence from the navy, but instead he was at "Atlantic City, or some other place up in New England" in a blue silk swimming suit. In contrast to the gallivanting Hobson, local Alabama farm boys dutifully left their plows to register when the books were open. Bankhead charged that Hobson spent his time up North dancing and having a good time with young women. The sixty-two-year-old congressman proceeded to prance up and down the debate hall, mocking his opponent. The audience shrieked with laughter. Attempting to paint Hobson as an outsider at odds with the cultural norms of the average Alabamian, Bankhead ridiculed the naval officer's pronunciation of the word "route" and essentially called him a hypocrite, accusing him of preaching in a church one day and leading a dancing party the next.[41]

Bankhead's withering mockery of Hobson revealed yet another dimension to the gender dynamics underlying this political contest. By poking fun at Hobson's dress, recreational choices, and speech, Bankhead emphasized what many already suspected: Hobson was a dude, someone more comfortable with his upper-class companions in the Northeast than with the sturdy citizens of the rural Sixth District. Could one be a dude and still lay claim to masculine prerogatives? Bankhead went further, though, when he criticized Hobson's role in the "kissing craze." Bankhead implied that such behavior demonstrated a distasteful and disqualifying lack of self-control. Here Bankhead drew on the older requirements of manhood that he himself embodied: the development of a strong character and control over impulse. Only by controlling oneself could a man control those weaker than himself.[42] The kissing craze revealed Hobson to be a man who could not control his passions and thus was unfit to lead others.

Clearly shaken by the congressman's attack on his character, Hobson struggled to gather himself for his reply. His voice trembling, he began by apologizing to the women and children who had been invited to attend the debate. Regarding Bankhead's attack, he declared that "the Scriptures have been repeated of the swine and his wallow, the dog that returns to his vomit." Sidestepping for the moment the issue of his own voter status, Hobson pointed out that the new election law, which had been framed by John H. Bankhead Jr., worked against young voters, a key component of Hobson's constituency. The registration books were closed from summer 1902 to summer 1904, and those men who had come of age during those eighteen months would be unable to vote in the primary.[43]

Just as Bankhead had attacked Hobson's reputation as a national naval hero, so too did Hobson take on Bankhead at his strongest, criticizing Bankhead's work on the Committee on Rivers and Harbors. In particular, he lambasted the congressman for the locks and dams constructed on the Black Warrior River. The Black Warrior River basin reached into all nine counties of the Sixth District and flowed into the Tombigbee River, which emptied into the Gulf of Mexico at Mobile. Once completed, it would become the longest canalized system in the country. Improved transportation would aid the area's farmers and industrial interests. Bankhead had been instrumental in guaranteeing federal funding for the project. The *Jasper Mountain Eagle* noted that "with the isthmian [Panama] canal and the Warrior opened to navigation we would have water communication with the world, and Walker County's inexhaustible coal supply would have cheap transportation to the leading markets of not only our own country, but to Central and South American ports."[44] Hobson criticized the project as a colossal waste of federal funds because the locks were too small and eventually would be obsolete. In making this charge, Hobson had made a serious misstep. Bankhead did not need to counter Hobson's charge; others did it for him. The *Birmingham Age-Herald* defended the Black Warrior River project, illustrating how the locks were comparable to those on the Monongahela River in Pennsylvania. Further, the paper published letters from interested parties and reports from local commercial concerns, defending the adequacy of the locks. Hobson backpedaled, stating that although the capacity of the locks was adequate for present traffic, they would prove to be too small once river traffic was enlarged. No one in Bankhead's camp bothered to engage this hypothetical charge, as Hobson's vision of an economically stunted future seemed improbable. Eventually, Hobson retreated almost entirely from his initial criticism of Bankhead's water transportation work, stating that if elected, he would work to finish the present lock system but would also advocate for its enlargement.[45]

Bankhead spent much time on the campaign circuit emphasizing Hobson's "outsider" status. He pointed out to the gathered crowds that his opponent had lived outside of the state since he was fourteen years old. He painted Hobson as a city slicker, a "national figger" as opposed to an Alabama man, who danced his way across the North. Although he himself had been in Washington for nearly twenty years and had amassed considerable wealth as a coal operator, Bankhead professed to be no more than a simple farmer, a plain "Alabama hill billy."[46] Hobson kept a grueling campaign schedule, delivering an average of three speeches a day. Although Bankhead met Hobson in a series of debates, the congressman did most of his politicking behind the scenes, meeting privately with local political leaders and groups.[47]

On the eve of the election, most astute observers were calling it a toss-up.

Hobson's aggressive campaign, national stature, personal magnetism, and superior oratorical abilities in the estimation of many gave him more than a fighting chance. But would it be enough to overcome twenty years of patronage and solid, productive work for the district? Hobson retired to his home in Greensboro, while Bankhead awaited the results in Jasper. On Monday, April 11, 1904, voters in Alabama's Sixth District nominated the incumbent John Hollis Bankhead by a fairly substantial margin. Hobson did best in his own county, Hale, winning by a large majority, but it was one of the smallest counties in the district. By contrast, Bankhead rolled up large majorities in Tuscaloosa and Walker Counties, the two most populous counties.[48] Although each side accused the other of Election Day "irregularities," no official charges were filed. Hobson announced a few days after the election that he would accept the results "without complaint" and gave Bankhead his support in the fall campaign.[49] Bankhead easily defeated his Republican challenger in the November general election.[50]

Hobson refused to go away and remained active in state politics. A month after his defeat, he was selected as a presidential elector-at-large at the Alabama Democratic Convention in Montgomery. At the convention, Hobson converted the delegates to the cause of a large navy—a position opposed by Democrats generally—in what one historian has called "a brilliant burst of forensic talent." He also announced his intention to run for the US Senate upon the retirement of either incumbent, both of whom were quite elderly.[51] Hobson remained active within the state party and campaigned for the party's presidential candidate.

Despite his defeat at the hands of Bankhead, Hobson felt confident that Bankhead's support had weakened considerably and that he remained vulnerable to a future challenge. It was a poorly kept secret that Bankhead had his eye on a seat in the upper chamber. Hobson wrote to his wife that "he will probably fail in any attempt to go to the Senate. His days of political life are numbered. His passing from political life will begin a new and happier era for Alabama politics."[52] Believing that Bankhead was behind the demise of his retirement bill, and having suffered defeat at the hands of the senior congressman in 1904, Hobson came to regard Bankhead as a political obstacle to his own personal ambition, someone who, in Hobson's words, wished to "check my rise in Alabama" politics.[53] Hobson's personalizing of his political fight with Bankhead—a fight that eventually would involve Bankhead sons John Jr. and Will—festered.

Throughout 1905, Hobson stayed in constant motion. He played around with the idea of running for governor of Alabama while he traveled around the state, delivering talks on the navy and US foreign relations.[54] Convinced that he could not best the popular Braxton Bragg "B. B." Comer, the president of the state railroad commission, Hobson hopped on the Comer bandwagon and once again challenged Bankhead for his seat as congressman from Alabama's Sixth Congressional District.[55] Hobson wagered that the political winds had shifted sufficiently so that his own progressive inclinations—in particular, his passionate support for statewide prohibition—would bring him victory at the polls in 1906.

The year 1906 brought with it complicated political questions. The Whitson Plan, approved by the State Democratic Executive Committee, set the gubernatorial primary for August but left individual congressional districts to set their own primaries. The committee, dominated by conservatives, wanted to thwart the popularity of the progressive Comer and to keep his influence out of congressional races. Also to be decided in the August primary were the two favored replacements for Alabama's US senators. Both senators were of advanced age and in poor health. In the likely event of a Comer governorship, the more conservative members of the executive committee did not want Comer to have any hand in choosing successors for the Senate seats. The Alabama Democratic Party scheduled a special election for August to choose their successors in case either or both could not complete their terms.[56] The two highest vote getters would become "alternate senators." Critics of the plan called it the "pall bearer's primary," the "graveyard election," or the "mortuary plan." One editor accused the plan's architects of staging a campaign for "dead men's shoes." Among the six men who declared for the "dead shoes" primary were two former governors, William C. Oates and Joseph F. Johnston.[57] Although he did not say so publicly, John Hollis Bankhead had his eye on this primary and was considered a front-runner by many political observers.

This second campaign between Bankhead and Hobson was as testy as the first. But the political ground in Alabama had shifted slightly in Hobson's favor, as fervor in support of a statewide prohibition amendment gathered steam. In the closing decades of the nineteenth century, the forces for temperance and prohibition had been relatively weak and scattered. The legislature experimented with a variety of measures to curb access to alcohol, including the licensing of saloons, mile laws, a local-option law, and the dispensary system, none of which were particularly effective. The push for outright prohibition took a major step forward with the arrival of the Anti-Saloon League (ASL) in Alabama in 1904. This organization succeeded in fusing the movement's disparate factions. Hobson would later become one of the ASL's most sought-after speakers.[58]

Hobson's attachment to the prohibition forces provided him with a strong cultural weapon in his campaign against Bankhead. As both the son of a slaveholder and a veteran of the Civil War, Bankhead was a product and beneficiary of the older southern code of honor. This code, with its emphasis on sociability (which included the consumption of alcohol), hierarchy, and prickly defensiveness, overshadowed the opposing evangelical culture during the antebellum period. The postwar surge in numbers of Baptists and Methodists, and the growing popularity of temperance and prohibition in the late nineteenth-century South, however, brought evangelicals new legitimacy and prompted a larger battle over who could claim to be a man of honor. As one historian illustrates, by the late nineteenth century, "times had changed . . . as had ideas about what constituted honor and how one went about achieving and maintaining it." Upper-class white men in the postwar era began abandoning some of the more violent aspects of honor, such as dueling, and evangelicals moved in, promoting a model of manhood based on pious Christianity. As evangelicals "attempted to redefine the code of honor in the South . . . they began to restate what it meant to be a man of honor—a manly man—along more Christian lines."[59] With his pious nature and his staunch support for prohibition (an inclination John Hollis Bankhead did not share), Hobson stood to benefit from this cultural shift, which legitimated evangelicals as men of honor and as political leaders.

As in 1904, Hobson undertook a rigorous campaign, speaking in small towns and crossroads across the congressional district during February and March 1906, often in difficult conditions and inclement weather. He delivered speeches in schoolhouses, churches, and courthouses. Unlike in 1904, Bankhead did not participate in joint appearances with his rival. Indeed, Bankhead's son Will dismissed the 1906 challenge, saying that Hobson had "fought his best fight last time."[60] Hobson poked fun at what he regarded as Bankhead's leisurely campaign pace. While Hobson sometimes delivered more than ten speeches in a single day, he noted that "Bankhead goes into the county this week, speaking at Ethelsville, Pickensville, Aliceville, one speech a day. This is his limit."[61] Hobson wrote to his wife, Grizelda, practically every day from the campaign trail. She, in turn, shared political news from across the state. At times, she campaigned with him. He regarded her as an important political asset.

Perhaps even more strongly than in 1904, Hobson made Bankhead's age and Confederate veteran status an issue. He wrote that Bankhead had served in Congress for twenty years and was long past the age when men retire. He did not believe the public would be well served by "men of a generation gone by." He continued, "Is it not time to make a change in our district and give the young men a chance?"[62] Hobson was not alone in his belief that Bankhead had outlived his usefulness. Bankhead's enemies privately referred to him as "Old Foggy."[63] Hobson claimed that Bankhead's effectiveness in Congress was further hampered by his status as a Confederate veteran, arguing that the prejudice against the South was too great for Bankhead to overcome. As a veteran of the Spanish-American War, Hobson would be free from such attacks.[64] The Bankhead forces made much of this statement, asking "has the time come for us to cease to honor our Confederate soldiers?"[65] Hobson privately mocked Bankhead's age and health, telling his wife that he did not believe that Bankhead could keep up the furious pace Hobson had set for the campaign.[66]

Hobson updated Grizelda regularly from the campaign trail, likening his campaign to a crusade against corrupt and entrenched forces. He spoke of "converting" voters and referred to his political struggle as a "holy fight." Such overheated language only heightened his feelings of personal grievance against

Bankhead. He called the city of Tuscaloosa a "ring hotbed" in the clutches of Bankhead men. He regarded Marion County as "a rough country" plagued by "ignorance and prejudice" but remained confident that he could win votes. He was irritated when "Bankhead men in the county called all men for road work" on the day that Hobson was in the town of Vernon for a speech.[67] He constantly feared that Bankhead would steal the election. "The air is full of rumors and tricks," he confided to Grizelda.[68] One "little incident" attributed to the Bankhead forces occurred in the town of Fernbank: "A reckless young man tried to disturb the [campaign] meeting. He had recently murdered a man in cold blood and was out on bond and to be tried in Vernon next week. The prosecuting attorney belongs to the [Bankhead] ring and evidently the young man thought that evidence of zeal in Bankhead's cause would get favor from the ring—and he seemed to have been drinking. His impertinent questions and remarks made me lose my temper for a time and the women and timid men went out. My friends, it seems, got ready and would have fired on the man if he had made a motion to draw his pistol as they expected."[69] As Election Day drew near, allegations of vote buying and other corrupt practices were hurled back and forth between the campaigns, as were allegations that the other was trying to win favor with African Americans in Alabama and therefore was not sufficiently dedicated to upholding white supremacy.[70]

Two additional years of campaigning, a more progressive political atmosphere, and a distracted incumbent brought about a different outcome for Richmond Pearson Hobson in 1906. In the congressional Democratic primary of April 23, 1906, Hobson defeated John Hollis Bankhead, albeit by a mere five hundred votes.[71] After twenty years of service on the part of Bankhead, his congressional career seemed to be over.

It did not take Bankhead long to recover his political sea legs, however, and by June—to the surprise of few—he was fully engaged in the primary for replacement US senator scheduled for August. The campaign posed obvious challenges for Bankhead. It was his first statewide campaign, his competitors had been campaigning for five months, and he was tired and financially strapped. Bankhead moved quickly. He established a campaign organization superior to that of any of the other six competitors. Still, Bankhead faced an uphill climb. Outside of the newspapers in his old district, only the *Birmingham Ledger* gave him support. But with the support of sons John Jr. and Will, as well as son-in-law Tom Owen, he waged a vigorous campaign. Bankhead spoke in cities and towns across the state, and his campaign sent out an average of fifteen thousand handbills and circulars per day. Bankhead focused on the importance of good roads and navigable rivers to the state's continued economic growth and prosperity. He reminded voters of his service in the Confederacy, his role in dispatching the "carpetbaggers," and his support for the 1901 state constitution, which cut "the cancer [African American voters] . . . from the body politic of Alabama."

Bankhead even instructed son-in-law Tom to ensure that his name appeared first on the ballot, because "IT WILL MEAN HUNDREDS OF VOTES" from uninformed and barely literate voters.[72] In August 1906, Alabama voters selected Bankhead as Senator John Tyler Morgan's successor, and Joseph F. Johnston as Edmund Pettus's. Bankhead led the field with 48,362 votes; Johnston received 36,107. Bankhead came in first in forty-one counties and second in thirteen counties. In a campaign to provide "alternates" for the state's two aging senators, the voters of Alabama had chosen the two oldest contenders.[73]

As if on cue, Senator Morgan died in June 1907. The newly elected governor, B. B. Comer, believing the conservative Bankhead unsuitable for the post, initially declared that he was not bound by the results of the primary. Comer further reflected on the hypocrisy of supporting the direct primary of US senators while simultaneously refusing to recognize the public's desire to elect Bankhead, however. Finding such actions inconsistent and politically risky, Comer

Figure 5.2. The Bankhead family, c. 1907. *Back, left to right:* Louise, John Hollis, Tallulah, unidentified girl, Musa, unidentified man, and Lula and Walter Harkins (John Jr.'s in-laws). *Middle:* William Perry (Louise's son), Marian (John Jr.'s daughter), and John Jr. *Front:* Will, Tallulah (Will's daughter), Louise (John Jr.'s daughter), Eugenia, Walter Will (John Jr.'s son). Courtesy of the Alabama Department of Archives and History.

eventually announced that he would not oppose Bankhead. Because US senators were still elected by state legislatures, the Bankheads swung into action, writing letters and meeting with reluctant legislators. The legislature voted in late August 1907. John Bankhead was now—officially and legally—a US senator.[74]

Richmond Pearson Hobson would go on to serve in the House of Representatives for four terms. His congressional career was spent largely in support of progressive causes, including women's suffrage, a graduated income tax, the direct election of US senators, and especially prohibition. The prohibition of alcohol and narcotics became a consuming crusade for Hobson, and it inspired utter devotion in his supporters. He campaigned on behalf of a state prohibition amendment in 1908 and was a high-profile member of the Anti-Saloon League. He declared that he had "consecrated [his] life to that cause."[75] Hobson was a popular speaker and spent much time during his congressional years on the lecture circuit, earning a healthy side income that left little time to devote to his constituents. Fellow congresspeople poked fun at Hobson's chronic absenteeism. In one instance in which Representative Hobson rose to address the House, a fellow congressman asked, "Who is this strange man who would address us?"[76] The nuts and bolts of legislating held no allure for the crusading Hobson.

Ever ambitious, Hobson kept his eye on higher office, hoping eventually to serve in the Senate. Despite defeating John Hollis Bankhead in 1906, Hobson remained suspicious that the senator would continue to block his political rise. Much to everyone's surprise, it was not the elder Bankhead but his second son, Will, who would eventually put the dagger in Hobson's political career.

6

ROADS AND REDEMPTION

JOHN HOLLIS BANKHEAD HAD LITTLE TIME to savor his victory in the primary race for US senator. He fell seriously ill with pneumonia while back home in Alabama in late fall 1907 and underwent surgery for a shoulder abscess that December. He spent part of his recuperation with family in Jasper; when he was back on his feet, he and Tallulah purchased "Sunset," a beautiful neoclassical home with fluted columns and a wraparound porch with double portico. The home sat at the top of a rise on an enormous lot that Bankhead landscaped with gardens, trellises, and footpaths. It was a home befitting a US senator.[1]

Taking his seat in the upper chamber in early 1908, Bankhead used his new position to advocate for internal improvements for the South. As a senator, Bankhead realized the most significant legislative accomplishment of his long career: the cosponsorship and passage of the Federal Road Act of 1916. This victory was made possible by the return of the Democrats to power. The election of President Wilson in 1912 and Democratic majorities in both houses of Congress gave southern legislators enhanced power and influence, which was exercised mostly in a progressive direction. Southern Democrats chaired twelve of the fourteen major standing committees in the Senate and eleven of the thirteen in the House.[2] Southerners in Congress generally embraced an activist government—very different from the Cleveland Democrats of an earlier era. Although not considered a progressive, Bankhead nevertheless contributed greatly to the expansion of the power of the state through his work on roads. The Federal Road Act of 1916 was a legislative watershed: it was the nation's first attempt to provide federal funding for the creation of roads and highways. The amount of money allocated dwarfed any previous federal grant-in-aid program to the states. Further, the act mandated unprecedented levels of federal oversight. Under Bankhead's leadership, road building became a federal priority. The passage of the act capped off a long career dedicated to securing funds for the economic development of the region.

As his father was reaching the pinnacle of his political career, William

Brockman Bankhead was just beginning his journey. Will's move to Jasper allowed him to begin rebuilding his shattered life under the watchful eye of his older brother. Despite his father's misgivings, Will stepped into the political ring. Although he was unsuccessful in his first race for Congress in 1914, family assistance at a critical juncture and a gift for campaigning secured victory for him in 1916. Will's victory was nothing short of political redemption for the entire family. His vanquished foe was none other than Richmond Pearson Hobson, the man who had beaten John Hollis in 1906. Will's political star was on the rise.

By the second decade of the twentieth century, John H. Bankhead Jr. was professionally successful yet personally unsatisfied. Even-keeled, he served as ballast for his more emotionally fragile younger brother. He continued to work diligently behind the scenes for his father's and brother's political success, waiting patiently for the day when his ambition for a federal judgeship might be realized. Unfortunately for John Jr., that day never came.

The creation of anything resembling a road "system" is a relatively modern development. American roads developed in a haphazard fashion, sometimes growing out of animal paths, or hunting and trade paths developed by Native Americans, pioneers, or the military.[3] Road development proceeded without much coordination. Consistent throughout the nation's history, though, was a demand by the citizens for better transportation routes to aid in development and growth. But road development suffered from a jurisdictional problem: who paid?

Figure 6.1. Sunset, home of Senator John Hollis and Tallulah Bankhead, in Jasper, county seat of Walker County. Library of Congress Prints and Photographs Division.

Since before the founding of the republic, roads had been local affairs. Interest in road construction and pressure for federal financing ebbed and flowed throughout American history as different forms of long distance transportation came to dominate American travel and commerce, and as military needs dictated. In the earliest days of the colonies, roads were maintained through statute labor compelled and overseen by local authorities. During the early national period, states chartered private turnpike companies that built and maintained roads, and charged tolls for their use. This proved a popular form of financing road construction, and by 1850, hundreds of companies had established turnpikes in every state in the nation. Federal support for roads came in the form of land grants to states given at the time of admission to statehood. States were directed to use 3 percent of proceeds from the sale of public lands to finance construction of roads, canals, river improvements, and schools.[4]

The expansion of transportation networks in the early national period received attention from national leaders. President Thomas Jefferson approved the creation of what eventually came to be called the National Road, although maintenance of this road was left to the states. In 1808, treasury secretary Albert Gallatin promoted a ten-year, $20 million road- and canal-building program, but the War of 1812 interrupted these plans. In 1816, Congress appropriated funds for what became known as Jackson's Military Road, connecting Nashville and New Orleans. It was on this road that John Hollis Bankhead's grandparents (and countless thousands of other settlers) made their way into Alabama from Tennessee. Ultimately, between 1807 and 1880, the military built more than one hundred roads. Although some leaders, such as Senators Henry Clay and John C. Calhoun, supported federal funds for internal improvements, others believed that such support violated the Constitution. The question appeared to have been settled by President Andrew Jackson's veto in 1830 of a bill to allow the federal government to purchase stock in a turnpike company. This particular turnpike would connect Lexington and Maysville, Kentucky. Supporters argued that the Maysville Road project was a continuation of the National Road, but Jackson regarded the bill as supporting an intrastate project and thus saw it as unconstitutional. Throughout the remainder of the nineteenth century, congressional appropriations for waterway improvement steadily increased, as did the granting of public lands to subsidize the expansion of railroads. With steamboats and railroads carrying the bulk of the nation's commerce, roads and turnpikes fell into disrepair.[5]

The interest in federal funding of roads revived in the late nineteenth century. The renewed push for federal funding of roads came from different sources: those seeking to expand rural free delivery to isolated farmers and to allow those farmers greater access to markets, and recreational bicyclists desiring access to picturesque rural reaches. Bicyclists organized themselves into the American Wheelmen, founded *Good Roads* magazine in 1892, and began lobbying for federal money for roads. Other good roads advocates followed suit. The first good roads association was founded in Missouri in 1891, and the first national conference on roads was held in 1894. The good roads movement even enjoyed support from the railroads, which did not regard improved roads as a threat to their status as the kings of interstate commerce. Quite the opposite: improved roads would only serve to expand their influence by making the railroads more accessible to producers in the hinterlands.[6] But progress was slow, particularly in the South. By the late nineteenth century, barely 4 percent of the roadways in the South could be classified as "improved," and most of those were in urban communities.[7] Rural southerners traveled over rough, rutted, poorly engineered dirt roads that became impassable when it rained. Poor roads amounted to real costs for the region's farmers. By 1904, the nation boasted 2.1 million miles of rural public roads, but only a little more than 150,000 miles had any kind of surfacing.[8] Personal ownership of cars was still quite rare at the turn of the century, with roughly 4,100 cars registered nationwide. Road construction and maintenance remained largely a local affair. By 1905, only fourteen states had highway departments.[9]

The first federal dollars for road building came through the Agricultural Appropriation Act of 1893, which directed $10,000 for the creation of the Office of Road Inquiry, which was housed in the Department of Agriculture. The office's purpose was to study best practices and make recommendations to the secretary of the Department of Agriculture, who would then disseminate that information through the agricultural colleges and experiment stations.[10] The Office of Road Inquiry also undertook a popular Object Lesson Road project designed to teach local road builders the latest engineering techniques and to educate the public on the benefits of improved roads. After the turn of the century, geologist and engineer Logan Waller Page took over the reins of what was now called the Office of Public Roads (OPR); he transformed the road-building movement by applying scientific principles to the creation of better roads. Under his leadership, the OPR expanded the Object Lesson Road program and undertook an extensive informational campaign, publishing articles on road construction and maintenance in county newspapers across the nation. Although quality surfacing materials were important to the creation of improved roads, Page advocated the use of local materials, which was welcomed by penurious southern communities in particular. More important, in his estimation, was the implementation of better road construction techniques. Expertise, not materials, was the most pressing need. Many roads were poorly located, improperly and too steeply graded, too curvy, and poorly drained. Nearly one-third of all money allocated for the construction of roads ended up being wasted because the roads themselves were so poorly constructed. To that end, the OPR hired a team of experienced road engineers and began sending them to counties as consultants. While on-site, engineers also made recommendations on how to modernize a particular state's road system and how to finance construction. It is difficult to overstate the popularity of this office and its programs. Communities inundated the OPR with requests for engineering assistance.[11]

Alabama's ability to build quality roads in sufficient quantities was hampered, according to one historian, by "poverty, indifference, and constitutional inhibitions."[12] The state's 1875 and 1901 constitutions prohibited the state from funding internal improvements. Thus the responsibility for road construction and maintenance fell to the counties. The state's mostly rural citizenry was unwilling to tax itself to pay for roads, preferring instead to rely on statute labor. The law required men ages eighteen to forty-five to work up to ten days per year on local roads. When the appointed time for roadwork came, many men simply did not show up. Those who did had neither the skill nor the motivation to create anything resembling adequate roads. The politics of road placement further compounded the problem. Where would new roads be built? Too often, powerful interests, not public need, determined the placement of roads.[13]

Alabama took a step closer to creating something resembling a road system when it created a state highway commission in 1911. The state contributed roughly $150,000 to the fund and provided matching grants up to $2,000 to counties for road projects. Still, counties balked at the cost.[14]

As automobile ownership expanded in the 1910s, so too did interest in improved highways. Of particular interest were long-distance roads, which brought tourists and auto enthusiasts into the road construction conversation. As of 1900, no automobiles were registered in Alabama. By 1913, this number had grown to over five thousand.[15] Pressure was building for a solution to the road problem.

John Hollis Bankhead was an early convert to the good roads campaign and eventually became one of its most influential voices. Bankhead served as an important bridge between tourist groups and organizations such as the American Automobile Association, who favored the creation of "national" or "main" roads, and rural citizens, who clamored for farm-to-market roads. He also was close with OPR director Logan Waller Page and frequently consulted with him on proposed legislation.[16] Bankhead helped found the North Alabama Good Roads Association and served as the vice president of both that organization and the National Good Roads Association.[17] Bankhead was a widely sought-after speaker at good roads events across the nation. In 1913, the seventy-one-year-old Bankhead donned a pair of seventy-five-cent overalls—"suspended by one gallus"—and participated in roadwork in Walker County. He even counseled one Alabama farmer on the use of the split-log drag to construct quality dirt roads. John Jr., always serving as his father's eyes and ears, urged his father to maintain leadership on the road issue. He criticized his father for not appreciating the political importance of self-promotion: "No man can succeed now in politics who does not keep [his] name before the voters. The old days have

Figure 6.2. John Hollis Bankhead doing roadwork, c. 1913. Courtesy of the Alabama Department of Archives and History.

passed. . . . Keep your name in the paper as doing something. I know you don't like this idea but you must conform to it."[18]

Bankhead argued that poor roads severely hampered small farmers and threatened rural life. Good roads, he claimed, would remove the disparities between urban and rural communities. According to one transportation analyst, "The rural economy was restricted by 18th century standards of mobility in an era when the urban population was reaping the direct benefits of modernized technology and organization."[19] Bankhead understood this issue and argued that "90 per cent of all of the commerce of the country is transported" over mostly inadequate roads at great cost, particularly to farmers. "The tax imposed on agricultural products between [the farm] and the railroad station or river landing by the miserable condition of these dirt roads is very much greater than the railroad or steamboat charges for carrying them to their ultimate destination." Improved roads, he argued, "save worry, waste, and energy."[20] Inadequate roads cost farmers $600 million a year in spoiled or damaged produce. He dismissed the constitutional opposition to good roads and criticized the amount of money spent on war preparation in comparison to that spent on "the building up of the American farm, home and roads and . . . the education of American boys and girls."[21] Alabama and the nation deserved modern roads. "The present system of road building is a relic of barbarism," Bankhead noted.[22]

The benefits of good roads were more than economic. Not only would improved roads drastically cut the cost of hauling goods to market, they would also improve social life in rural communities and staunch the drain of rural citizens to urban areas. Nothing less than the survival of rural life was at stake.[23] Bankhead held that "good roads will make farm life more cheerful and will contribute largely to the happiness and contentment of the farmer and his family, who will become better satisfied with life in the country."[24] Bankhead also noted the impact of bad roads on education. In states that contributed very little to road construction, school attendance averaged 59 percent, compared with 78 percent for residents of states with good roads. "The effect of bad roads on education, and consequently the standard of citizenship, is too obvious to be overlooked," Bankhead declared.[25] Finally, the anti-imperialist Bankhead chided Congress for allocating federal funds for the building, repair, and maintenance of public roads in the Philippines, Puerto Rico, and Cuba, while American farmers struggled with poor roads.[26] A self-professed supporter of farmers and rural life, Bankhead nevertheless upbraided rural citizens for failing to tax themselves to pay for roads. "The Government will help. Good roads are a military necessity. All are ready to help: the railroads, the Government, the States, the businessmen, all are ready to help when the farmer shows he is willing to do his part."[27]

The interest in federal funding for roads reached a fever pitch during the first decade and a half of the twentieth century, and every session of Congress from 1903 to 1916 considered a bill proposing some type of federal aid for road construction; sixty-two bills were introduced in 1912 alone. All major groups that advocated for improved roads supported federal aid of some kind. The key was to craft legislation that gave enough to all parties. Also in question was what the funding mechanism would look like. Bills foundered for a number of reasons: inadequate funding formulas, too heavy a focus on rural roads, too heavy a focus on national roads, lax federal supervision. Still, the constitutionally based opposition to federal funding for roads remained a formidable obstacle.

Supporters found their opening in article 1, section 8, paragraph 7 of the Constitution, which gave Congress the power to "establish Post Offices and post Roads." The creation of rural free delivery provided leverage for those seeking federal funding for roads. Good roads supporters such as John Hollis Bankhead, a member of the Committee on Post Offices and Post Roads, recognized that Rural Free Delivery (RFD) could become a "powerful force for road improvement."[28] The nation's first experimental rural delivery routes were established in West Virginia in 1896; the experiment proved a success, and by 1903, some five million Americans were receiving mail at home.[29] As the demand for RFD grew, so too did the demand for improved roads. With RFD, Bankhead saw his opening. In 1912 the Democrats became the majority party in Congress, and Bankhead became the chair of the Committee on Post Offices and Post Roads. Bankhead successfully inserted an amendment to the Post Office

Appropriation Bill of 1913 authorizing a $500,000 appropriation for experimental roads. The funds were to be spent by the secretary of agriculture (through the OPR), in cooperation with the postmaster general, "to improve the condition of certain selected post roads, and thereafter, to determine 'the increase in the territory which could be served by each carrier as a result of such improvement.'"[30] In order to receive federal funding, state or county governments needed to cover two-thirds of the total cost. Although rates of participation were somewhat disappointing, the program provided valuable experience that was reflected in later decisions on federal aid. The most important result was the realization that federal aid should go only to the states, not to the counties. OPR was too small to work with three thousand counties, each with its own public works mechanism.

Legislative success for advocates of federal funding for roads came in 1916. Working with Missouri congressman Dorsey Shackleford in the House, and with OPR's Page and the National Association of Highway Engineers, John Hollis Bankhead introduced a bill in the Senate that would provide federal funding for road construction. The bill provided $75 million in federal 50/50 matching funds to the states over a five-year period. Under the act, federal funding was provided for rural post roads on the condition that they be open to the public at no charge. Funding was to be distributed to the states based on a formula incorporating each state's geographic area, population, and existing road network. To obtain the funding, states were required to create state highway departments and to submit project plans, surveys, specifications, and estimates to the secretary of agriculture. The legislation did not require any specific type of road surface; a proposed dirt road could qualify for funding provided that road was "substantial in character."[31] The US Good Roads Association endorsed the bill, stating quite clearly that it wanted Congress to appropriate money for roads before addressing war preparations as war engulfed Europe. Good roads advocates regarded war preparation and road building as mutually exclusive.[32]

Opposition to military preparedness was fierce in the rural South as war raged in Europe. Rural southerners—those most in need of quality roads—remained some of the strongest supporters of neutrality and would have been repelled by any attempt to tie the need for good rural roads to what they termed "militarism." For many, road building and war preparation were competitors for federal dollars. In introducing his bill, Bankhead clearly stated that the goal of improved roads was to "promote agriculture, afford better facilities for rural transportation and marketing for farm products and encourage the development of a general system of improved highways." The role of the bill in constructing roads that might facilitate interstate commerce or aid in the movement of military supplies was secondary.[33] Other members of Congress were more direct in placing military preparedness and road building in opposition. Congressman Edward Saunders of Virginia caustically observed that a bill "to expend a thousand millions of dollars on a needless increase in our military establishment is hailed with delight, while a bill to expend a meager twenty-five millions on farmers' roads is denounced as a pork barrel. Well the fellows that have been enjoying the fat sides and plump hams of the past, ought not to begrudge the farmers a few spareribs and backbones. . . . The men who are advocating a billion-dollar military program begrudge them this pittance."[34] Representative James Aswell of Louisiana questioned the definition of preparedness, arguing that internal improvements—not armies and navies—were the source of national strength. "We are to be called upon to expend extra millions for the Army and Navy in preparedness. When is a nation prepared? That nation is best prepared when it equips itself within for stalwart growth, prosperity, and power. Internal stagnation means national weakness. It is understood that preparedness means an adequate Army and Navy, with ample coast defense and an efficient merchant marine, but it also means good roads, good schools, rural mail routes, improved waterways and drainage, scientific agriculture, rural credits, and adequate public buildings for the conduct of the public business." Aswell concluded, "As we grow strong within we become more truly the leading world power."[35] Bankhead's bill passed both houses of Congress, and President Wilson, an advocate of good roads, signed the legislation on July 11, 1916.

Within a year, some twenty-six states had applied for federal aid to construct close to one thousand miles of roads. By 1918, more than 99 percent of the nearly six hundred road projects proposed had been approved. Most roads proposed were to be constructed from macadam, gravel, sand and clay, or other relatively permanent materials; only a minority of projects were for dirt roads. To protect against haphazard road building, the renamed Office of Public Roads and Rural Engineering required states to create highway commissions and submit a comprehensive road-building plan. The act further required that states build "substantial roads," thus ensuring a certain national minimum standard while still granting initiative and autonomy to states. The requirement of coordination with the secretary of agriculture rescued road building from the petty machinations of local politicians that had long plagued it.[36] Even with these requirements, several years would pass before any individual state—let alone, the nation—possessed anything resembling a "road system." The act further required that repairs and maintenance of these roads be a direct responsibility of the states. States that failed to fulfill this obligation would lose their federal allotments. Federal oversight and the ability to compel compliance were strengthened in subsequent acts and were instrumental to the program's success.[37]

With this act, John Hollis Bankhead had engineered the largest transfer of federal funds to the states in the nation's history. It certainly was not the first federal subsidy program. Federal land grants to the states had long required that a portion of that land be set aside for public schools. The first and second Morrill Acts (1862 and 1890) provided for the endowment of land-grant colleges. The 1887 Hatch Act provided for the establishment and maintenance of experiment stations connected to agricultural colleges established under the first Morrill Act. However, land grants for education gave the money to the states with no oversight or restrictions except that the money be provided for education. The Morrill Act had no restrictions other than that the money be used to teach agriculture and mechanic arts. Other acts provided federal funds for fire protection and for the creation of the National Guard, and the 1914 Smith-Lever Act provided for cooperative agricultural extension work.[38] But the 1916 Federal Aid Road Act exceeded these former acts in terms of funds allotted and degree of federal supervision and oversight required. In advocating for extensive federal oversight, Senator Bankhead recognized the importance of uniformity and expertise, and the individual states' inability to achieve anything resembling quality roads. Although he had not wholly abandoned a states' rights philosophy, his leadership on this issue indicated a significant modification of it.

Alabama moved quickly to claim its portion of the federal allocation, but generally states were a little slow to act. Many states, particularly in the South, had created weak highway departments that lacked the power to initiate road projects. In addition, some state legislatures dictated that federal funds be apportioned in a way that led to the development of "bits and pieces of roads" rather than a system.[39] It was also difficult to get states to coordinate their own systems with those of their neighbors; the individual states were interested in state systems, not national systems. Federal aid projects were too widely scattered to create anything like a workable national system. This deficiency would be fixed in later acts.

American involvement in the war in Europe in 1917 severely curtailed the impact of the 1916 act while simultaneously underscoring the importance of quality roads. For the duration of America's involvement in the war, priority in road construction using federal funds was given to projects that served the greatest economic or military use.[40] Most rural road projects were put on hold, while skilled road construction engineers and road-building equipment were diverted to the war effort. According to one federal study of the history of roads in the United States, "the highway construction industry collapsed" during the war.[41]

The nation's railroad system was unprepared for the demands of wartime. A shortage of railroad cars and congestion at terminals threatened the nation's war effort and prompted the birth of the trucking industry. The use of heavy trucks put stress on the nation's roads. Road maintenance was considered nonessential work, and materials that might have been used for road repair were funneled to other needs. The damage done to the roads during wartime was such that annual appropriations designated by the 1916 act would be inadequate.

To jump-start stalled road-building projects following the conclusion of the war, John Hollis Bankhead once again came up with a solution. He successfully inserted a provision into the Post Office Appropriation Bill for 1920 (40 Stat. 1252) that authorized the transfer to the secretary of agriculture "all available war material, equipment, and supplies not needed for the purposes of the War Department, but suitable for use in the improvement of highways, and that the same be distributed among the highway departments of the several states to be used on roads constructed in whole or in part by federal aid."[42] Congress eventually passed four acts to secure the transfer of surplus equipment from the military to the states for use in road construction. By April 1920, Alabama had received 340 vehicles from the Department of War.[43]

Despite the shortcomings of the 1916 act, the road-funding logjam had broken. Congress approved a $200 million post office appropriation for roadwork in 1919. In this appropriation bill, the term "rural post road" was reconfigured to mean "any public road a major portion of which is now used or can be used, or forms a connecting link not to exceed ten miles in length of any road or roads now or hereafter used for the transportation of the United States mail." Opponents howled that this description could refer to any road, and they were right. That was exactly the point. No longer would the federal government be confined to developing post roads. Other deficiencies of the 1916 act were corrected in a revised act passed in 1921. And the appropriations continued to grow. In 1912, four years before the act's passage, the total of the payments from the federal treasury to the states (this includes all programs) was approximately $8 million. By 1925 it had risen to $147 million. By 1927, 60 percent of all federal aid to the states was for road construction, an outlay that dwarfed all federal spending prior to the New Deal.[44] In addition, some $224 million worth of surplus war material was delivered to state highway departments. Despite the deficiencies of the Federal Aid Road Act of 1916, and despite the damper on construction caused by the war, the act established road building as a federal priority, a commitment that continued to grow throughout the twentieth century. It was the crowning achievement of John Hollis Bankhead's long career.

Several months after President Wilson signed the legislation, good roads advocates gathered in Birmingham to inaugurate the Bankhead Highway project: a transcontinental highway named in honor of the "father of good roads" that would stretch from Washington, DC, to San Diego. Initially a connected series of county roads, the Bankhead Highway had grown by 1920 to become an integral part of several state highway systems, and more than three-fourths of the highway was being improved under the direct inspection of the federal government. In June 1920, a highly publicized US military motor convoy set off on its goal to drive the length of the highway. The convoy included forty-four trucks, four of which were ten-ton size, seven cars, and four motorcycles. Personnel included twenty officers and 160 enlisted men. They set off early in the morning from the zero milestone on the Ellipse in Washington, DC, to the triumphant strains of the Marine band. President Wilson was on hand to witness the impressive historic event. The purpose of the trip, explained General Charles B. Drake, chief of the Motor Transport Corps, "was to assist in

Map 6.1. The Bankhead Highway.

the development of a system of national highways by bringing before the public in an educational way the necessity for such a system; to provide extended field service in connection with training of officers and men in motor transportation. To recruit personnel for the various branches of the army. To secure data on road conditions throughout the territory in the immediate vicinity of the highway along which the convoy will operate."[45] It was the second such convoy undertaken by the US military, the first having been made in 1919 over the Lincoln Highway. Among those participating in the first convoy was a young lieutenant colonel named Dwight D. Eisenhower, who decades later would make his own contribution to the development of the country's highway system.

As the 1920 convoy snaked its way through small towns across the South and Southwest, residents celebrated its arrival with banquets, barbecues, and chicken dinners. From Washington, DC, to Atlanta, the convoy averaged around fifty to sixty miles per hour. But as it began its journey through the Deep South, the going got worse, with a combination of heavy rains, flooding, and inadequate roads cutting the average speed of the convoy in half.[46] This part of the journey, more than any other, convinced many that the federal government needed to expand its support for roads beyond the commitment secured by the

1916 act. Ironically, while many in Congress had seen the First World War as a threat to federal funds for roads, many now agreed with secretary of war Newton D. Baker's assessment that World War I had been "a war of motor transport," and that good roads were a key component of national defense. Some four thousand miles and 111 days after the convoy left Washington, in early October 1920, the dusty convoy arrived at its California destination.[47] The trip was a resounding success. The difficulties encountered by the Motor Transport Corps convoy along its southern route underscored the need for further federal investment and generated support for what eventually became the Federal Aid Highway Act of 1921. The trip and the 1921 act, which improved on some of the deficiencies of the 1916 act, were a final flourish to John Hollis Bankhead's long and distinguished career.

With the support and encouragement of his family, Will Bankhead began to put his life back together. Will's parents and his sister Marie, who was still grieving the loss of her son, assisted with the care of his young daughters, while emotionally stoic brother John remained a constant source of support for his distraught brother. In a letter to their father, John Jr. noted that he spent a lot of time "working to get Will's mind off of sad things."[48] John Jr.'s knowledge of the law combined with Will's genial relationship with clients made the brothers a good legal team. Their law practice prospered and counted among its clients the Southern, Frisco, and Louisville and Nashville Railroads; John Jr. in particular gained a reputation as an able corporate attorney. A skilled political manager and adviser, John Jr. lacked the charisma and warmth that came so naturally to his father and brother. For the time being, his political ambitions took a back seat to those of his brother. In addition to his legal work, John Jr. was responsible for the family's financial health. He managed and developed the family's coal mines. A loan from the J. P. Morgan Company allowed him to expand production and to modernize equipment. The results were somewhat disappointing. The daily output of the mines was about three thousand tons of coal a day—about a third of their capacity. Roughly half the coal was sold to the railroads.[49] John Jr. was also charged with investing family profits in the stock market. Although the family owned several coal mines, farms, and a hotel in Fayette, it often lacked liquid assets.[50]

By all objective measures, John Jr. was a success. He had married his childhood sweetheart, was financially secure, and was a respected leader in his community. Yet he remained professionally unfulfilled. He desired a federal judgeship—something his senator father could potentially deliver, although the chances were slim so long as the Republicans controlled the White House. In 1907, the Department of Justice created an additional seat in the Northern District of Alabama. Although John Hollis supported his son, he warned him that his chances of being appointed by a Republican president were slim. John Hollis also felt that at age thirty-five, John Jr. was perhaps too young for the position. "If you decide to go in I will make the best effort of my life for you but I want you to be very careful and to be well satisfied that your chances are at least even with that of other applicants. You don't want to enter this contest without the hope of success. You are yet young with a very bright future before you and I have serious doubts about the wisdom of giving up your practice and being compelled to neglect your private interests to go on the bench at your age."[51] John Jr. ultimately decided not to seek the appointment. He did not give a reason.[52] Still, he continued to hope for a shot at the bench. He confided to Congressman Oscar Underwood, a close family friend, that "my only personal political ambition has been to be a Federal Judge. [However], I am not sure that I will ever be an applicant. I know that I will never be if it embarrasses in any way my good Father."[53]

Despite this disappointment, John Jr. remained a dedicated foot soldier, managing his father's 1910 reelection campaign. John Hollis was opposed in the primary by Anniston businessman Frank S. White, a staunch prohibitionist. White attacked Bankhead's lukewarm support for prohibition, while Bankhead criticized White for opposing the poll tax and the grandfather clause while a delegate to the 1901 constitutional convention. A gifted orator, Will stumped for his father throughout the northern part of the state, while son-in-law Tom Owen kept busy reminding acquaintances across the state of Bankhead's reliable record. Bankhead easily won the nomination.[54]

Will Bankhead's heart was not in the practice of law. He focused on civic engagement, and on the building of social and political networks, although his father was not keen for either of his sons to follow him into national politics. For the time being, the sons listened to the father, focusing on state and local politics. In 1908, Will was unanimously elected chairman of the Walker County Democratic Executive Committee. He served as the solicitor of the Fourteenth Judicial Circuit from 1910 to 1914.[55]

Will Bankhead received unexpected exposure to the national political scene when he was selected in 1912 to make the nominating speech for Alabama representative Oscar Underwood for the Democratic Party's nomination for president. The able and popular Underwood had served in Congress since 1899 and was chairman of the Committee on Ways and Means. Senator Bankhead managed Underwood's campaign, and Tom Owen served as the campaign's secretary; John Jr. and Will were charged with building support for Underwood within the Alabama delegation. The Underwood forces arrived at the Democratic National Convention in Baltimore with the pledged support of four state delegations: Alabama, Florida, Georgia, and Mississippi, and they held the balance of power as the convention split between New Jersey governor Woodrow Wilson and Champ Clark, Missouri congressman and Speaker of the House of Representatives. Will Bankhead was a curious choice as the nominating speaker, as he was just a local political figure.[56] Still, he was a gifted orator and delivered a stirring address.[57] But the rousing speech did little to win new delegates for

Figure 6.4. Will Bankhead was crowned the king of the Jasper Cotton Ball in 1914. Courtesy of the Alabama Department of Archives and History.

Underwood. Slowly, the convention momentum began to turn toward Wilson. John Hollis maintained a firm grip on the Underwood delegates through the forty-fifth vote, at which point he removed Underwood's name from nomination and released the delegates, who overwhelmingly threw their support to Wilson, assuring a Wilson victory.[58] John Jr. later wrote to Underwood that "Father realized that it was up to him to gracefully withdraw you or let you be destroyed by the Alabama delegation."[59] Wilson went on to win the White House over a divided Republican field. Democrats also captured majorities in the Senate and the House of Representatives, making Senator Bankhead a member of the majority for the first time since 1893, when he was in the House.

While Will was taking the first tentative steps onto the national stage, daughters Eugenia and Tallulah were entering their teen years. They had spent their first ten years living primarily with grandparents John Hollis and Tallulah, alternating between homes in Jasper and in Washington, DC; they also spent time with their Aunt Marie Bankhead Owen in Montgomery, where they crossed paths with Zelda Sayre and Sara Mayfield, two Montgomery residents who were destined to make their own marks on American culture. Existing report cards from 1910 have both girls attending the Jasper Public School. They were good students, each earning a spot in the "first rank." Their lowest marks were for deportment, but even that grade was a ninety-five.[60] Eugenia was rather frail, having contracted both whooping cough and measles as a child. As a result, her vision was temporarily impaired, and she required treatment in Birmingham and Washington. Poor health would continue to plague her as an adult. Tallulah was a large and boisterous child, given to impersonations and mimicry, often to win her father's attention. Both girls tried the patience of their grandparents, their primary caregivers. Years later, when both girls were in their twenties, their grandmother would remark to their Aunt Marie how proud she was of both "Gene" and "Tally." "How I love those children," she wrote. "They have been a great source of anxiety but are proving o.k."[61] Tallulah and Eugenia returned the affection. Tallulah later wrote that "until her death, Grandmother was Mama to me."[62] Will's troubles with alcohol persisted once he returned to Jasper. It was not unusual for him, after a night of drinking, to wake up young Tallulah and have her impersonate performers they had seen in Birmingham.[63] Eugenia recalled later that he often became morose when drunk, brandishing a pistol and threatening suicide.[64] Tallulah always felt that Will favored Eugenia, and as children they competed for his attention. Despite the security provided by their grandparents, both girls suffered greatly from the loss of their mother and the unpredictability of their troubled father.

In 1912, the girls (ages ten and eleven) left the security of their grandparents' care and were sent to Convent of the Sacred Heart on New York City's Upper East Side, the first of five boarding schools they would ultimately attend over the next four years. Eugenia was an attentive student, while Tallulah was distracted and incurred frequent disciplinary problems. Although the girls were far from their father and grandparents, newly remarried Aunt Louise and her husband were nearby in Yonkers. The next year, they attended Mary Baldwin Seminary in Staunton, Virginia, along with their older cousin (and John Jr.'s daughter) Marion. They only lasted half a year at Mary Baldwin. By January, they were attending the Convent of the Visitation in Georgetown. In fall 1915, for reasons that are unclear, fourteen-year-old Eugenia was sent to a boarding school in Montgomery, while thirteen-year-old Tallulah was shipped off to Holy Cross Academy in Maryland. Desperately lonely, Tallulah sank into despair and stopped eating. Eugenia was promptly sent north to be with her sister.

Figure 6.5.
Fourteen-year-old
Tallulah Bankhead,
c. 1916. Courtesy
of the Alabama
Department of
Archives and
History.

The following fall, the girls were in yet another school, Fairmont Seminary in Washington, DC.[65] Will sent them spending money regularly, but the girls longed for the taste of home. "Daddy," Eugenia wrote, "we get very hungry once in awhile. I wish you . . . would send us a real home box soon."[66] Along with homesickness, the girls also dealt with the trials of puberty, which for Tallulah meant extra unwanted pounds and acne. Because they changed schools every year, the sisters were denied even the community of boarding school. Despite their grandparents' best efforts, the lack of consistency in their upbringing, in addition to the tragic loss of their mother and the relative absence of their father, would have serious consequences for them as adults.

Several months after his political coming-out party at the Democratic National Convention, Will Bankhead turned his attention to elective office. He set his sights on the seat in the Sixth Congressional District—the same seat held by his father, John Hollis, for twenty years before he was defeated by Richmond Pearson Hobson in 1906. Hobson had taken his seat in Congress as the representative of Alabama's Sixth Congressional District when that body convened in December 1907. For the next seven years, Hobson proved himself to be a staunch advocate of a strong navy. He spoke frequently of his concern about Japan's growing power and urged his fellow congressional representatives to support generous naval appropriations and general military preparedness. Hobson also became a reliable advocate of progressive reforms. He opposed protective tariffs, which he believed hurt rural folks and promoted "an abnormal growth of city life," and he supported additional federal aid for education, constitutional amendments instituting the graduated income tax and the direct election of US senators, and the Clayton Antitrust and Federal Trade Commission Acts. Though popular with his constituents, Hobson was not well liked by his fellow congresspeople, particularly those from his own state. While in Congress, he developed a reputation as something of a maverick and was not considered a reliable southern Democrat. For example, Hobson supported New Jersey governor Woodrow Wilson for the Democratic Party's nomination for president in 1912, breaking with Alabama's congressional delegation, which supported favorite-son candidate Underwood.[67]

Hobson stood apart from his southern colleagues on a number of critical issues. Viewing women as natural allies in the progressive reform battle, Hobson was one of the few southern representatives to actively support women's suffrage. Of the value of women's political participation, Hobson argued, "We find ample provisions of law for dealing with cholera in hogs or foot-and-mouth disease in cattle, but there is nothing to reach infant mortality and little to reach child labor, debauchery, and moral obliquity." Giving women the vote would make it more likely that political solutions would be found for these problems. When the National American Woman Suffrage Association staged the first suffrage parade in Washington, DC, in 1913, it named Congressman Hobson as a parade leader. Some political observers spoke of his potential as a vice presidential and perhaps even presidential candidate.[68]

More conspicuous than his support for women's suffrage was his response to what became known as the Brownsville affair. In late 1906, President Theodore Roosevelt ordered a dishonorable discharge of 167 African American soldiers of the Twenty-Fifth Infantry Regiment, stationed at Fort Brown in Texas. The presence of the black troops had exacerbated racial tensions in the nearby town of Brownsville, and following the shooting deaths of a white bartender and a Hispanic police officer, as well as an alleged attack on a white woman, townspeople accused the soldiers. Suspicion ultimately focused on twelve soldiers, but local authorities were unable to secure a grand jury indictment. The US inspector general concluded that a "conspiracy of silence" existed among the black troops.

On November 5, 1906, President Theodore Roosevelt discharged "without honor" all 167 men garrisoned at the fort. The discharged soldiers, many of whom had served in the Spanish-American War, lost their pensions and any possibility of future work in a civil service capacity. African American leaders were outraged and demanded justice for the discharged men. Led by Senator Joseph Foraker of Ohio, a Senate Committee on Military Affairs investigated the incident. Congress ultimately voted in favor of establishing a board of inquiry with the power to reinstate the soldiers. Hobson was the only Alabama congressman to vote in favor of the board of inquiry and the reinstatement of the African American soldiers, whom Senator Bankhead called "murderers and midnight assassins."[69] Hobson couched his defense of the soldiers in white supremacy and paternalism, proclaiming that "the white man is supreme in this country; he will remain supreme. That makes it only the more sacred that he should give absolute justice to the black man who is in our midst." The president's treatment of the soldiers offended him. "When these crimes were committed at Brownsville, the President could have ordered all officers and [enlisted] men to remain within barracks and could have ordered a court of inquiry, followed by a court martial, which, held on the spot, without delay, would no doubt have established the guilt or innocence of all of the men, and would have given a regular, legal opportunity to every innocent man to establish the fact of his innocence. If, under duly administered oath, any man had refused to tell the whole truth or had been found to have abetted or concealed the guilty, he could have been punished accordingly." By refusing to follow established procedure, President Roosevelt had committed a grave injustice. These men were soldiers, Hobson declared, and deserved to be treated accordingly. "I saw black men carrying our flag on San Juan Hill; I have seen them before Manila. . . . We are standing here on the field of eternal justice, where all men are the same. It is justice that links men to the divine. Whether the heavens fall or the earth melt away, while we live let us be just."[70] Despite the fact that Hobson held fairly orthodox southern views on race, his vote on the Brownsville inquiry left him politically vulnerable on this issue.

Hobson's consuming passion was prohibition. A devout Methodist and a dry, he first became aware of the dangers of alcohol while at Annapolis. Alcohol destroyed men both physically and morally, Hobson declared. It was the nation's number-one public health crisis, responsible for more than 3.5 million white male deaths every year. Hobson argued that alcohol made the host more susceptible to diseases such as tuberculosis and typhoid. Further, alcohol "has an affinity, a deadly attack, for the top part of the brain, the line of evolution. . . . In this top part of the brain of humanity resides will power. Every time a man drinks, he takes that much away from his manhood; will power declines."[71] He delivered countless speeches against what he believed was the nation's top social evil. In 1911, Hobson became the first congressman to introduce for consideration a constitutional amendment for prohibition. Although the amendment received a majority, it ultimately failed to receive the necessary two-thirds votes.[72] Securing a prohibition amendment became his overriding political goal.

After serving four terms in the House, Hobson decided to challenge incumbent US senator Oscar Underwood for his seat in 1914, leaving his congressional seat in the Sixth District up for grabs. Will Bankhead had already declared his candidacy in December 1912, more than a year before the primary.[73] Unlike older brother John Jr., Will was less likely to heed his father's advice to stay out of national politics. John Jr. later recalled, "Brother Will was always politically minded and he took a notion to run [for Congress]. So he slipped off and went over to announce it without telling father. Father didn't know it for several days, though they were living in the same house in Jasper."[74] Will's challenger for the Democratic Party's nomination was William Bacon "Buck" Oliver, dean of the law school at the University of Alabama, former solicitor of the Sixth Judicial Circuit, a staunch prohibitionist, and a well-known figure in Tuscaloosa County.[75] Oliver did not announce his candidacy until April 1913.[76] Local editors predicted a close race, as both contenders were "men of ability, high character, eloquent orators, and of great personal popularity."[77] Will confided to sister Louise that he expected "a very hard fight . . . but promise to make it hot for my opponent."[78] Brother John likewise expected a "hard fight," acknowledging that "no other man in the District could give Will much trouble." Perhaps they could get rid of Oliver before the race even began. He asked his father, John Hollis, whether "it would be possible to get a high [diplomatic appointment] for Buck Oliver and thereby dispose of him? He is a type that should appeal to Wilson. . . . [He] is polished and scholarly."[79] No such appointment was forthcoming, and the campaign proceeded apace.

Will Bankhead supported the creation of a national department of health, federal aid for roads, improvements for the Tombigbee River, and advocated on behalf of agriculture.[80] Although Oliver's campaign was generally civil, he criticized Bankhead's conviction rate while solicitor of the Fourteenth Judicial

Circuit. He claimed that this rate compared unfavorably with his own, particularly in terms of convictions for prohibition violations.[81] As one Bankhead supporter noted, however, the majority of those prosecuted in Bankhead's section were white, whereas most of Oliver's defendants were African American, who were far more likely to be convicted by all-white juries.[82]

The Bankheads called in favors and dispensed patronage in their energetic effort to win the district for Will. They sought federal government positions for those men who, in Will's words, could "be of considerable service" in the campaign, or sought to neutralize particularly troublesome opposition.[83] John Jr. wrote letters to his father recommending various men for federal posts in return for their support in the campaign.[84] Senator Bankhead's position as chair of the Senate Committee on Post Offices and Post Roads was particularly useful in promising positions in return for electoral support for Will. John Jr. was aggressive in the patronage game, in one instance writing to his father about postmasters in the towns of Covin and Fernbank, who refused to allow the Bankhead campaign to put up notices of Will's speaking engagements: he wanted the men fired. "Can't you arrange to have a Post Office Inspector sent to Covin and Fernbank with instructions to find grounds for the removal of these Postmasters[?] I am informed that they are obnoxious and exceedingly officious in their opposition to Will. Of course I would not want them removed on political grounds but if some other ground growing out of the conduct of their office can be found it will be well to have them removed."[85]

The Bankheads wrote to sheriffs and judges on Will's behalf, reminding them of favors that John Hollis had done for them.[86] No position was too humble to hold out in exchange for support, and Senator Bankhead promised positions for elevator operator and stenographer to potential Will Bankhead supporters.[87] They even sought parole for a convicted murderer with "a large number of relatives and friends in Pickens and Tuscaloosa Counties." Will asked his father to ask the governor to parole this prisoner: "I want to get this man out if possible so that he can do some work before the Primary."[88] For his part, John Hollis urged Will to play up his rural roots while on the campaign trail: "Don't forget that you are a gardener and a chicken raiser as well as a candidate for Congress."[89] John Hollis mostly worked behind the scenes. He provided funds for the race—several infusions of $1,000—but did not make any personal appearances on Will's behalf.[90]

Will had to answer charges of, if not nepotism, then something akin to Bankhead fatigue. To potential supporters, he wrote: "It has been urged against me that my father is in the United States Senate and that is enough for one family. I submit to you that it is not fair to close the door of hope in my native State because my father has lived an honorable life and has been promoted as a worthy public servant. If that rule should be invoked there would be little encouragement for a father to leave his children an honored name." In fact, Bankhead noted, his father's position in the Senate would work to the advantage of the residents of the Sixth Congressional District. "Whatever measures for the benefit of our district I may be able to get through the House will certainly have proper attention through the co-operation of my father in the Senate."[91]

The senatorial vacancy and Richmond Pearson Hobson's candidacy provided extra drama during the campaign season. It was no secret that the Bankheads supported Oscar Underwood for the Senate seat, having been active in his 1912 campaign for the Democratic Party's presidential nomination. Aware of Hobson's prickly antipathy toward John Hollis, as well as his tendency to personalize political struggles, however, the Bankhead forces were careful not to antagonize Hobson or his supporters in the Sixth Congressional District. The editor of the *Marion County News*, G. J. Wilson, confided to John Jr. that "I cannot explain why the people go crazy over Hobson, but it is a fact that they do."[92] John Jr. urged his father to "please handle this Senatorial matter the best you can to avoid the appearance of a fight against Hobson. The situation is very critical in this district. You know how sensitive the H[obson] fools are about him." Antagonizing the Hobson voters would hurt Will's campaign. John Jr. wrote to his father that "if [the Hobson people] are stirred to a fight against [Will] he had just as well quit."[93] John Jr. reported that "the Senatorial vacancy matter is seriously affecting Will's race. A lot of the extreme Hobson men are holding off and some are talking of supporting Oliver." Oliver and Hobson had combined forces, encouraging their followers to support the other candidate as well. Limiting the damage from Hobson's campaign was crucial. "Unless we can maintain neutrality with Hobson Will might as well quit."[94]

John Hollis and John Jr. kept up the pressure on supporters throughout the district, while Will did what he did best: campaign. John Hollis's advice was to "keep Will in the field, tell him to go to the country and stay there."[95] Finally, primary day arrived. Despite the best efforts of Will, John Hollis, and John Jr., Bankhead lost the primary to Oliver by just under six hundred votes.[96] Underwood defeated Hobson quite handily in the race for the US Senate, winning 62 percent of the total vote. Hobson carried only five counties, all of them in his home congressional district. Underwood captured Hobson's home county, Hale, by a slight majority. With Hobson thumped soundly by Underwood, his political career appeared to be over. Most observers expected that he would return to his lucrative work with the Anti-Saloon League (ASL).[97]

Once again, Will's family was there to pick him up when he had fallen. Determined that Will should have a political career, but understanding that he probably could not beat the popular Oliver, the Bankheads decided to create a congressional district for him. Alabama's population growth as confirmed by the 1910 census had earned it an additional congressional representative. For the 1912 and 1914 legislative sessions, a stopgap measure had been instituted, and the seat had been filled by election of a congressman-at-large. A permanent redistricting of the state needed to be undertaken. It was in this proposed redistricting that the Bankheads literally mapped out Will's future.[98]

The Bankheads' plan involved dividing the existing Sixth Congressional District, separating Tuscaloosa and Jasper Counties, thus removing any conflict between the political ambitions of Will Bankhead and Buck Oliver, whose home county was Tuscaloosa. John Jr. drafted the initial legislation creating the new Tenth District. Comprising Fayette, Franklin, Lamar, Marion, Pickens, Walker, and Winston, the Tenth would take four counties from the Sixth, two from the Seventh, and one from the Ninth. The new district would not include the home county of any existing congressman. With one minor change, the Bankhead plan was introduced in the 1915 session of the Alabama legislature by Bankhead supporters from Etowah County.[99]

Backlash against the plan was immediate. Opponents leveled accusations of nepotism. They also charged that the new plan violated the state constitution, which required that population serve as the basis for redistricting. The proposed district had fifty thousand fewer residents than the next smallest district.[100] The bill's supporters did not dispute the population charge but answered this critique with a political response, pointing out that the creation of the new district would help Democratic candidates in the Seventh Congressional District by siphoning off some Republican voters. The bill to create the new Tenth District would divide this Republican strength and thus make all Alabama congressional districts safely Democratic, which would protect white supremacy. Despite these appealing partisan arguments, the bill remained controversial; after four hours of heated debate, the bill passed on the final day of the legislative session by a razor-thin margin of five votes. The bill passed the Senate easily. Shortly thereafter, Will Bankhead dutifully and predictably announced his candidacy for the Democratic nomination for congressman for the newly minted Tenth District.[101]

This nifty piece of political maneuvering was interrupted by a romantic interlude when Will married Florence McGuire on January 16, 1915. Will was forty years old; Florence was twenty-five, making her closer in age to Eugenia than to Will. Florence's late father was a well-known attorney in Jasper, Alabama. Florence had attended Judson College, a women's college in Marion, Alabama, in the Black Belt, where she was a member of Kappa Delta sorority and also played basketball. Florence had applied to the Bankhead and Bankhead law office for a job as a stenographer. The local Jasper newspaper reported Will and Florence attending the same social events as early as 1908.[102] In a human-interest piece on the couple published years later, the *Chicago Daily News* wrote that Will "tried to ignore the flaming, wavy hair and to determine whether the girl knew anything about office work. She did, to his surprise, so he hired her. Florence followed orders well and had a sweet smile. He proposed. She accepted."[103] Florence made an ideal political wife. She was attractive and sociable, and utterly devoted to taking care of her husband. Although comfortable at political events, Florence was a small-town girl at heart and often spoke of her love of fishing. "I really am good at rod and reel fishing," she told one reporter, "and I'd rather get into my hip boots and fish for black bass than anything in the world." She even spoke of entering Mobile's "fish rodeo." Florence had interests beyond the natural world, specifically astrology.[104] It is difficult to know how Will's daughters felt about his marriage. Florence appears to have provided

Map 6.2.
Alabama's congressional districts, c. 1916.

much needed stability to Will's life; still, she also was competition for his attention and affection.[105]

Back in the political world, a bombshell: former congressman and recently defeated senatorial candidate Richmond Pearson Hobson announced that he would oppose Bankhead for the Democratic nomination of the newly created Tenth Congressional District. Hobson's announcement stunned Alabama voters and opinion leaders. Hobson had never lived in any part of the new district (his home county of Hale remained firmly in the Sixth District), although as congressman from the Sixth District he had represented part of what was now the Tenth District.[106] Also, Hobson had seemed determined to retire from politics following his defeat by Underwood in 1914. With the death of his father in 1905, the family's Hale County home of Magnolia Grove, along with the two sisters and a brother who resided there, had become his financial responsibility. His speaking fees from the ASL provided a more lucrative salary than that earned by a member of the House.[107] His reasons for challenging Bankhead seemed profoundly personal. The state's political commentators anticipated a contentious campaign. As the *Birmingham News* noted, the race for the Tenth would be between "two persons who have been enemies for a lifetime."[108] Everyone anticipated a fiery contest.

Will wasted no time attacking Hobson. He charged that during a single two-year congressional period, Hobson had visited the Sixth District one time, and that his family had been absent from the district for eight years, echoing a theme hammered home by the Underwood campaign in 1914.[109] More serious, though, was the residency question. During his tenure as congressman, Hobson had claimed Greensboro as his residence, although he spent much time in Tuxedo Park, New York, a wealthy village of fewer than one thousand residents some forty-five miles from New York City. Tuxedo Park was home to such notables as financier J. P. Morgan and the heir to the Colgate-Palmolive fortune, and it featured homes designed by the renowned architectural firm of McKim, Mead & White. In fact, it was from his tony New York home that Hobson had notified both the probate judge in Walker County and the mayor of Jasper that his legal residence was now in Jasper. He revealed that he and his wife had made the decision to move to Jasper several years earlier. He wrote: "For forty-five years I lived in Greensboro; for the next forty-five I intend to live in Jasper." Waxing nostalgic, Hobson wrote, "I want my barefoot children to play in the Jasper sands with your barefoot children, and with them to grow into a sober and industrious manhood."[110] Hobson later told an audience that he was in the process of purchasing a lot in Jasper and planned to build a home. He desired that his children attend school in Jasper "so that they might be free from the evil influence of a city."[111]

Hobson claimed that he had received much pressure and encouragement from residents of the new district to throw his hat in the ring.[112] Never lacking for confidence, Hobson believed he could win the race without stepping foot in the district. "I know that the people of the new Tenth District will understand my motives. I know these people and trust them and believe they know me and trust me. So complete is my confidence in them that my present intention is to continue in the field of the National Anti-Saloon League as regularly laid out in its present important stage without going into the district to campaign for myself."[113] Hobson had no plans to visit the state for the duration of the campaign.

There is no evidence that the citizens of the new Tenth District urged him to enter the race. Rather, he and the ASL wanted him back in Congress to provide an effective and persuasive spokesperson for prohibition and a sponsor for another try at a constitutional amendment. After the loss to Underwood in 1914, Hobson's wife, Grizelda, had no desire to participate in another campaign. She felt that his talents were wasted in Congress. Perhaps more politically astute than her ambitious husband, she believed that voters would regard their arrival in the new district as a cynical political move.[114]

Both Richmond and Grizelda were concerned about the cost—financial and physical—of undertaking yet another political campaign. They met with national and state officials of the ASL in early February 1916 to discuss the prospect of a Hobson candidacy. At that meeting, Hobson suggested not only that the cost of the campaign be borne by the ASL, but that he continue his speaking engagements for the ASL at full salary. He could trust "the [campaign] work in the district to friends of the cause and personal friends to conduct." Hobson's campaign manager, L. B. Musgrove, publisher of the *Jasper Mountain Eagle*, assured the candidate that he would solidify the details with the ASL. Grizelda was satisfied as this arrangement did not require her to campaign with her husband and limited his travel away from home to ASL speaking engagements.[115]

Still, if Hobson wished to return to Congress, why not run in his old district, the Sixth? Perhaps it was because, in his 1914 race for the US Senate, challenger and ultimate victor Oscar Underwood had defeated Hobson in the Sixth District by a wide margin. Hobson did not believe that he could defeat the popular sitting congressman Buck Oliver. Equally as likely was that the prospect of besting the son of his former adversary was simply too good to pass up. Newspapers throughout the state turned a skeptical eye to Hobson's candidacy. The *Birmingham News* accused him of "overweening vanity" and called his candidacy "a most unusual bit of audacity." The *Sheffield Standard* wrote that Hobson's "intense dislike of the Bankheads, no doubt, caused him to enter the race in a district other than that of his legal residence," while the *Alabama Democrat* compared Hobson's run to "carpetbaggery."[116] In a letter to Hobson, Walker County tax assessor C. W. Stubblefield echoed these concerns. "On account of your having had some tilts with the Bankheads heretofore others will construe [your candidacy] as a little spite work." Despite denying the accusation that this political contest was personal, Hobson accused Stubblefield and others of regarding the new district "to be a chattle of the Bankheads."[117]

Hobson's decision not to campaign in the district only made the criticisms regarding his speedy change of residence that much more pointed. To counter accusations that he was a carpetbagger, Hobson quickly abandoned his plan to leave campaigning to his supporters. Much to Grizelda's dismay, March 1916 found Hobson back in Alabama and running hard. Hobson was desperate for his wife to join him, promising her a "nice reservation at the Tutwiler [Hotel]" and "nice quarters" at Jasper.[118] Grizelda refused. Hobson's decision to make a personal canvass of the district and her refusal to join him caused a serious rift in their marriage. She had had her fill of southern politics and small-town life during her husband's previous campaigns; she found the weather insufferable and the travel accommodations and dining options of the campaign trail decidedly lacking. She preferred life in New York, where "citizenship is of a higher order" than that found in Alabama. Believing politics in Alabama to be hopelessly corrupt, she quite pointedly wrote, "You are going to be defeated, no power can help with that." Hobson's attorney and his campaign manager pleaded with Grizelda to reconsider. She refused. Her husband's work for the ASL already kept him away from home for months at a time; while he was working for the league, she and Hobson had agreed that she "must not be left alone and unprotected and that it was his own idea that for whatever period he should be in the field I should be located in Tuxedo under the protection of my parents and of my life-long friends." She was not coming to Alabama. "Am I not due some consideration?" she asked. "Is there no limit to the sacrifices that I must make?" More seriously, she feared for the safety of her children. She had received an anonymous threat (Hobson suspected the "liquor interests") that she and the children would be "dynamited" were Hobson to make another run for Congress.[119]

Upset by his wife's lack of support, Hobson pressed on. His campaign events were well attended, with his speeches lasting several hours. He made it clear that his race for Congress was a means to achieve a prohibition amendment. "I am not a seeker after public office," he declared, "but my thoughts are on the greater thing, national prohibition."[120] Most predicted a close race.[121]

Hobson wasted no time going on the offensive, attacking the Bankhead family's role in the redistricting bill—a role, incidentally, that the Bankheads had not tried to hide. Will Bankhead confronted the accusations of high-handedness by admitting that he had gone to Montgomery to lobby for the redistricting bill, stating, "I am proud of the fact, proud of the new district, and have no apologies to make for the connection I had with it."[122] He continued to insist that the new district was gerrymandered to make all congressional districts safely Democratic, thereby further strengthening the forces against any federal legislation that tinkered with white supremacy. Privately, Hobson complained about Bankhead campaign tactics, grousing that their "money was scattered all over [Lamar County]" and that "there is more coercion and intimidation from the competition than I have ever seen before."[123] Hobson reminded voters of the family's role in placing convicts in coal mines, a labor practice that had become a target of progressive reformers, and the Bankheads' opposition to a bill challenging the convict lease, so "that the poor convicts might be kept perfectly in the bowels of the earth against their consent." He also poked fun at what he referred to as Will Bankhead's "eleventh hour conversion" to prohibition.[124] Hobson's campaign events often included a speaker from the ASL.[125]

The prohibition issue gave Will some trouble, as it had in his 1914 campaign against Oliver. Although at heart a supporter of local option, Bankhead recognized the change in the political landscape on this issue. He could not hope to beat Hobson on this issue; Hobson's credentials as a staunch prohibitionist were well established. The best he could hope to do was to neutralize it. Bankhead pledged that "if elected to Congress I shall vote to submit to the states a Constitutional Amendment providing for National Prohibition." Two Hobson supporters told the *Carbon Hill Journal* that Bankhead's willingness to support the submission of a constitutional amendment for prohibition would most likely eliminate it as a divisive campaign issue.[126] Bankhead's cause was helped immeasurably when the ASL announced that because both candidates had pledged support for a constitutional amendment, the league would endorse neither man. Hobson was furious. To Grizelda, he wrote that the ASL's failure to back him "is not only stupidity but treachery."[127]

Just as the contest between Hobson and the elder Bankhead had often turned on older and newer definitions of manhood and masculinity, gender conventions played a part in the 1916 campaign. Whereas Hobson had consistently ridiculed—both in public and especially in private—the stamina of John Hollis, only four years separated Hobson and Will Bankhead. Now himself the older of the two candidates, Hobson tried to infantilize Will by creating an image of him as helpless and dependent on the intervention of his family. He made personal attacks on Bankhead, calling him "Little Willie," the "Cub," and the "weaker brother."[128] Bankhead's alleged weakness was intimately tied, in Hobson's mind, to Will's past problems with alcohol. Numerous times, Hobson stated that he hoped Will "had quit his drinking." Although Hobson was still interested in military preparedness, this issue took a back seat for him. Hobson challenged Bankhead to a debate, but Bankhead declined, stating that his opponent "would cause the debate to degenerate into offensive personalities to the disgust of the public."[129] Of the two, Hobson was the more persistent mudslinger, consistently questioning Bankhead's toughness and virility. Bankhead's failure to meet him in debate, Hobson argued, revealed his craven nature. Hobson promised one crowd that if Bankhead met him in debate, he (Hobson) would go with one hand tied behind his back and gave his word not to harm a hair on Will's head.[130]

Whereas questions of virility as a prerequisite for political leadership might have hindered the elder Bankhead in his 1906 contest with Hobson, Will Bankhead could himself draw on and benefit from notions of masculinity that had come to the forefront during the Progressive Era. By the turn of the twentieth century, the athletic male body had become the ideal masculine form. Furthermore, strenuous exercise and team sports had come to be seen as crucial to the development of powerful manhood. Theodore Roosevelt was the "quintessential symbol of turn-of-the-century manliness." A hunting and sports enthusiast, Roosevelt promoted the "strenuous life" as key to revitalizing American manhood and advancing the cause of American imperialism.[131] While Hobson's publicized desire about his barefoot children growing into manhood in the sands of Walker County tied him to this "primitive masculinity," so too did Will Bankhead's sports history. Will's college sports career became a regular feature in Bankhead press releases and other campaign material. As Gail Bederman has argued, physical capacity had become a hallmark not just of a vital citizenry but of capable leaders as well. So when Hobson joked about going easy on Will Bankhead in debate, he attempted to present himself as the more physically imposing of the two candidates and therefore the better equipped to lead. But the blows did not quite land on Will Bankhead, who held equal claim to the same gender conventions.

Will Bankhead leveled several charges at his opponent, among them the issue of Hobson's residence, claiming that not only was Hobson not a resident of the district, he was not a registered voter in any county of the district, nor had he paid any taxes in the district. In a campaign circular, Bankhead charged, "You have no place of abode in the 10th District and contribute nothing in this district to the support of the Government. You cannot vote for anybody. You can't even vote for yourself in the primary."[132] Indeed, Hobson's family had not moved to Jasper but had remained in Tuxedo Park. Hobson addressed this criticism by claiming that it did not matter where in Alabama he lived because "the Bankheads might decide to change the county lines and leave me in some other county. They might even want to get rid of me so much that they would change my residence over into Mississippi." Will criticized Hobson's inconsistencies, including his change from his initial announcement that he would forgo campaigning in person, his flip-flop on the issue of women's suffrage, and his opposition to President Wilson's policies related to Germany and the war in Europe.[133]

Despite these attacks, Hobson remained confident—so confident, in fact, that he left the campaign for a week to deliver some prohibition lectures in Texas. It was, perhaps, a decisive blunder. The race was closer than most had predicted. Voters went to the polls on May 9, 1916, and chose Will Bankhead as the Democratic nominee of Alabama's Tenth Congressional District by a slim margin of fifty-one votes.[134] Although both camps complained about voting irregularities, no official charges were filed. Bankhead faced a Republican challenger in the November general election, besting him by a vote of 8,091 to 6,813.[135]

With Hobson having been defeated in 1914 in his race for US Senate and in 1916 in his race for the House, it appeared that his political career was finally over. The *Montgomery Advertiser* declared that Hobson had been beaten in a fair fight and would no longer be a factor in Alabama politics. The *Birmingham News* was not so certain, warning that Hobson was unpredictable and his ambition unquenchable.[136]

In fact, the *Advertiser* was correct. Shortly after the primary, Hobson moved to Evanston, Illinois, and then to Los Angeles, ultimately spending his final years in New York City. Hobson's dream of a constitutional amendment prohibiting the manufacture, sale, and distribution of alcohol came to pass, but the victory must have been bittersweet; having been the first in Congress to propose such a resolution, he was unable to cast a vote on the successful amendment. Hobson spent the next twenty years speaking and writing about the evils of alcohol and narcotics use. In 1933, he was awarded the Congressional Medal of Honor for his heroism aboard the *Merrimac* some thirty-five years earlier.[137] The following year, the US Congress reconsidered Hobson's resignation from the US Navy. Hobson always believed that then-congressman John Hollis Bankhead had blocked his retirement, forcing him instead to resign. In 1934, Hobson was reinstated, advanced to naval constructor with a rank of rear admiral, and retired at that rank with a pension. Among those supporting this action was none other than Congressman William Brockman Bankhead. Hobson suffered a heart attack and died in 1937.[138] Will confided his thoughts about Hobson's passing to his diary: "Twenty years ago I would have received the news of his death with complaisance in view of the sharp and bitter contest which we waged in the old Tenth District . . . but the aspirates and bitterness of political contests should be, and often are, softened by the passage of time, and I very sincerely regret his death."[139]

If the 1916 campaign spelled the end of Hobson's political career, Will Bankhead's star was on the rise. The 1916 victory was the first of many for him, the beginning of an illustrious political career that would carry him to the pinnacle of congressional power as Speaker of the House of Representatives and place him within sight of the White House. John H. Bankhead Jr., meanwhile, felt his ambitions thwarted. It seemed unlikely that Alabama voters would tolerate yet another Bankhead in office. He kept his attention on his law practice and the coal business. Once more, in 1916, Senator Bankhead sought a federal judgeship for his oldest son. Unfortunately, the Department of Justice insisted that all candidates have judicial experience, a qualification that he lacked. John Jr. was profoundly disappointed, writing to his father that it was "the only job I ever wanted and it was a little hard to abandon hope for it but I promptly settled it and began figuring on some way to make it to your advantage." He suggested that his father nominate his former political opponent Frank S. White, effectively removing him from state politics. Bankhead took his son's advice, but White was not interested. Bankhead refused to nominate either Alabamian favored by the Department of Justice.

❦

The year 1916 concluded on a happy and nostalgic note. On November 13, 1916, John Hollis Bankhead and Tallulah Brockman Bankhead celebrated their fiftieth wedding anniversary at Sunset, their home in Jasper. It was an elaborate affair. The yard was festooned with Japanese lanterns and fancy floral arrangements, and the house was filled with dignitaries and beloved family and friends. The party included the recitation of a poem written by a guest, Minnie Reynolds

Saffold of Montgomery. Entitled "The Golden Wedding," the poem was written in "negro dialect" and celebrated the union of "Mars John and Miss Talluh." According to a local reporter, Saffold performed the poem "with an exquisite combination of pathos and humor." Not every family member attended: absent from the celebration were Tom Owen Jr., and Eugenia and Tallulah Bankhead. Tallulah, writing from Fairmont Seminary, sent a congratulatory note.[140]

Together, John Hollis and Tallulah Bankhead had traveled far in fifty years, from the ravages of the postwar South to the chamber of the US Senate. Their personal journey in many ways mirrored the trajectory of the region, from vanquished foe to leading voice of the Democratic Party. Over those fifty years, parents and siblings remained extremely close, visiting one another frequently and corresponding often. Although the family had suffered its share of personal tragedy, John Hollis and Tallulah must have taken great comfort in the fact that their children—now adults—were personally and financially secure, if not entirely satisfied.

7

Party Men, City Women

The second session of the Sixty-Fourth Congress, which opened in March 1917, featured a political novelty. For only the second time in the nation's history, a father and son were serving together in the same Congress.[1] In its "Washington Scenes and People" montage, the *Washington Post* featured a photograph of Senator Bankhead and Representative Bankhead. Dressed for the cool early March weather, father and son walk arm in arm, faithful party men poised to do battle for the Democratic majority as the nation edged closer to war.[2]

Father and son struggled with what America's role should be in the raging conflict in Europe. The election of Woodrow Wilson as president in 1912 transformed how southern Democrats approached foreign policy. Eager to support the Democratic president, Senator John Hollis Bankhead and Representative William Brockman Bankhead threw their weight behind the internationalist Wilson, joining the majority of their southern colleagues in Congress in abandoning the region's fifty-year-long opposition to a strong military and to an activist foreign policy. Their willingness to support enhanced executive, federal, and military power would have enormous consequences for southern economic development and for American foreign policy in the decades to come.[3]

The disruptions of wartime and the collapse of European markets as a result of the British blockade brought hard times for the South's cotton farmers. The 1914 cotton crop was the largest on record—some sixteen million bales—and southern cotton farmers relied on exports, which accounted for 60 percent of the crop. In a mere three weeks in July and August 1914, cotton prices had plummeted from thirteen cents a pound to eight cents. Many feared they would continue to fall. Southern cotton growers faced financial ruin. Alabama was the third-leading cotton-producing state in the United States behind Texas and Georgia; such a precipitous drop in prices sent farmers in that state in desperate search for solutions. Losses in 1914 totaled $500 million, roughly half the value of the crop.[4] A prolonged wartime blockade meant economic devastation. It also held potential negative consequences for US-Anglo relations. If cotton prices continued to drop, representatives of the cotton-producing states could pressure the White House to challenge Britain's blockade.[5]

Cotton farmers in Alabama and across the South begged political leaders for help in securing federal aid, but those pleas fell on deaf ears. The Wilson administration opposed any direct relief to American farmers; instead, secretary of the treasury William Gibbs McAdoo issued $68 million in emergency funds to national banks in the South to be used for short-term loans. But this was a temporary solution; the allocation was too small to be of much consequence in meeting the farmers' needs. As one farmer commented to Alabama congressman Oscar Underwood, this round of federal aid "amounts to about two drops in one bucket of water." Farmers remained skeptical that banks receiving federal funds would act in their interest.[6]

As summer turned into fall, it became clear that McAdoo's efforts had provided very little relief for the state's farmers. Adding insult to injury, southern states did not possess adequate warehouses to store the record crop while farmers waited for prices to rise. Farmers' patience was running thin. By mid-October 1914, cotton hovered at around six cents per pound.[7] With a southerner in the White House and Democrats in control of Congress, farmers demanded action. The president of the Talladega Chamber of Commerce put it bluntly in

Figure 7.1. Senator John Hollis Bankhead (*left*) and Representative William Brockman Bankhead, March 1917. Courtesy of the Alabama Department of Archives and History.

a letter to Senator Bankhead: "The South is now in the saddle from the President down, why don't Congress carry out some of the promises made us for the past forty years[?]"[8] Another farmer, Jackson M. Young, reminded Bankhead that the senator owed his long political career to the support of farmers such as himself, and that the cotton economy and political system relied on a certain amount of coercion and control of the have-nots, control that was becoming harder to maintain as cotton prices plummeted and Washington dithered. Young told Bankhead of a tenant farmer on his property named Henry Stone. He described Stone as "a good man" and noted that he personally had taken tenant Stone to the polls "to get his vote in right." Stone made a measly eight dollars on a five-hundred-pound bale of cotton. According to Young, the tenant farmer "went away swearing that he would see the whole lot of you in h_ll before he would ever again quit his work and vote a Democratic ticket." Farmers like Young were nearing the breaking point: "we are going to stampede sooner or later, if help comes too tardily." Young feared a "strike of the lower stratum."[9] Three Alabama congresspeople introduced bills in August 1914, all designed to provide financial assistance; all three failed. Governor Emmet O'Neal also tried to find a solution, but he was not able to bring the other cotton-growing states (in particular, Texas) along with him.[10]

The situation for cotton growers grew more desperate throughout the early fall. Prices continued to drop, and loans came due. Looking for a temporary fix, Alabama farmers adopted the "Buy-A-Bale" movement that was sweeping the cotton states. Buyers purchased bales for ten cents a pound and agreed to store the cotton until the market improved. Response to the movement in Alabama was enthusiastic; buyers in Montgomery, Mobile, and Birmingham absorbed thousands of bales, with the proceeds going directly to needy farmers. Senator Bankhead himself purchased a bale. But the movement faded as quickly as it had arrived. It was not a long-term solution.[11]

The elder Bankhead watched the unfolding drama with a growing sense of unease. Although he praised Governor O'Neal for trying to get out in front of the problem, in the end the cotton-state governors were unwilling to consider alternatives beyond federal assistance. Although sympathetic to the farmers' plight, Bankhead articulated the political realities of federal intervention on behalf of cotton growers: "The cotton growing States have 20 senators out of 96 and 98 Congressmen out of 435. The people of the other States who consume cotton are interested in the low price of cotton just as our people are interested in cheap flour. The producers of many other articles are in distress as a result of the great war. When it is proposed that the Government buy or lend cotton, the suggestion is promptly made to add copper, tobacco, naval stores, salmon and various other things produced by other sections of the country."[12] Bankhead proposed a bold yet simple plan that required state intervention. He prodded the legislature in his home state of Alabama to seek a constitutional amendment authorizing the state to issue bonds in the sum of $40 million with which it would purchase some eight hundred thousand bales of cotton at ten cents per pound, roughly half the crop of each producer. The legislature would provide a warehouse system; the farmer would take his cotton to the warehouse and receive a warrant, which would then be exchanged for bonds. Such bonds would be accepted by merchants and banks in lieu of cash.[13]

Bankhead's plan was far from perfect. Calling the legislature into session, amending the constitution, and issuing bonds would take time. Even if these items were accomplished in a timely fashion, the state did not possess adequate storage facilities for eight hundred thousand bales of cotton. Furthermore, considerable opposition arose to Bankhead's plan, which some believed would set a dangerous precedent of state interference to rescue a failing industry. Bankers and businessmen considered Bankhead's plan to be radical and fiscally unsound.

To build support for his plan, the senator initiated a grassroots campaign, much of it directed by John Jr. His plan—advertised as an "Appeal to the People of Alabama"—appeared in newspapers across the state in early October. He encouraged farmers to meet and send petitions to the governor demanding a special session to consider amending the state constitution. If the state's newspapers were mixed in their responses to the senator's plan, cotton farmers were decidedly enthusiastic. They gathered outside their local courthouses across the state to hear Bankhead's appeal read aloud. They added their names to petitions and demanded the governor take action. With cotton prices at six cents a pound and threatening to drop even further, and with a quarter of all producers unable to cover their debts, farmers were desperate for action. John Jr., while encouraged by the action of farmers, was discouraged by the lack of support from media outlets. Many failed to carry reports of mass meetings, and in John Jr.'s opinion, publicity was necessary if such a movement was to carry weight with the governor. Senator Bankhead stepped up the pressure, addressing Congress on October 8, 1914, and sending letters and copies of his address to southern governors and prominent politicians, urging them to call special legislative sessions to discuss his relief proposal. Bankhead spoke in Montgomery and urged citizens to demand a special session; he later traveled the state promoting his plan.[14]

Bankhead's plan was never considered by the Alabama state legislature, primarily because events had taken a turn for the better for cotton farmers. On October 24, Secretary McAdoo announced the "cotton-pool" plan, which established a subscribed fund of $135 million to be administered by the Federal Reserve Board and private bankers and distributed to banks in the cotton states. Cotton farmers also received help from across the Atlantic. Complaints about the restraint of trade and the ensuing economic hardship reached the ears of British officials, who worried about the implications for Anglo-American relations. American leaders pressured Great Britain to make its policy toward cotton clear. Understanding the power of southern Democrats in the US Congress, the British took steps to pacify their American friends. British foreign secretary Sir Edward Grey assured American leaders that the British would not regard cotton as contraband, thereby reopening the European market. The British promised that they would not interfere with the movement of cotton, even those shipments bound for Germany. With a firm commitment from the British, President Wilson declared the "cotton crisis" over.[15] When legislators were finally polled about holding a special session to consider Bankhead's plan, only twenty-seven supported the call. Although his plan ultimately failed, some of his ideas would be resurrected during crises of the 1930s.

Almost as quickly as cotton prices fell, they began to rise. Less than a year after prices had hit rock bottom, they rose to eleven cents, then to nearly twenty, then to thirty-six. From 1917 to 1919, cotton prices averaged twenty-seven cents.[16] The crisis had been averted, but not for long. Fluctuating prices would return in the 1920s, and by the end of the decade the bottom had dropped out of the cotton economy. Addressing the problem of the Cotton Belt would become John Jr.'s overriding concern in the 1930s.

As war engulfed Europe, John Hollis Bankhead kept relatively quiet about American involvement. Like many southern leaders, he was suspicious of calls for military preparedness, noting that this call was led by northeastern Republicans, such as Theodore Roosevelt. Likewise, throughout late 1914, Wilson rejected demands for preparedness because American safety was not threatened. Wilson soon changed course, though, with Germany's declaration of submarine warfare in February 1915 and the sinking of the British ocean liner the *Lusitania* in May. In December 1915, the president presented his preparedness program to Congress. He proposed the construction of ten battleships, six battle cruisers, ten cruisers, fifty destroyers, and one hundred submarines over five years and the recruitment and maintenance of a regular army force of nearly 142,000 and a reserve force, the so-called Continental Army, of 400,000.[17]

Senator Bankhead was skeptical of calls to increase military appropriations, which would require a tax increase, telling one constituent in late 1915 that he was "inclined to be conservative on the question of National Preparedness."[18] But Bankhead was fiercely loyal to President Wilson. While North Carolina congressman and Democratic majority leader Claude Kitchin led a group of antipreparedness congresspeople, some twenty of whom were from the South, Bankhead kept his own counsel. Privately he pledged to "stand by the President in his policy of National Preparedness, provided he does not go beyond the length of my cable tow."[19] He felt that "all this cry about 'Preparedness' is the result of a propaganda started by the munition manufacturers who are now reaping a rich harvest from the sale of our products abroad."[20] He supported additional appropriations for the navy and an expansion of the National Guard, but he balked at an expansion of the army. Just as he had argued twenty years earlier, Bankhead much preferred "to spend large sums of money building national highways and factories for the purpose of manufacturing explosives and arms when we reach the point where they will be needed." He remained firmly convinced that war would not come.[21] Writing to one constituent in late 1915, he confided, "I do not believe this Government is in danger of an attack from any outside source within the next 25 or 50 years, if ever, and I do not see any use of going crazy over the subject."[22] He confided to another constituent that "I am not [in] favor of 'peace at any price,' but I am not willing to take any position with reference to our foreign relations that would bring on a fight between the United States and the Allies or with Germany and her Associates until we have exhausted every means known to diplomacy."[23] Despite some serious misgivings, Bankhead stood with the president and ultimately supported what became known as the National Defense Act of 1916.[24] By April 1917, Senator Bankhead felt that war was inevitable and that the nation must fight, writing to one constituent that "there are things that a nation, the same as an individual, cannot ignore."[25]

Forty-two-year-old Will Bankhead was sworn in as representative of the Tenth Congressional District of Alabama on March 4, 1917. Will later recalled that his father advised him to "learn the rules" of Congress.[26] Will did as he was told, in the process becoming a good student of parliamentary procedure; he also was a conscientious legislator, present for 404 of 447 roll calls in his first session.[27] Like his father, Will was first and foremost a party man. Unlike his father, though, Will was a gifted speaker, skilled in the art of debate. His biographer has observed that he was "cautious without being timid; vigorous without being foolhardy. He was willing to compromise when the situation warranted, for he preferred partial success to crusading for lost causes."[28] On top of that, he was likable. He had the type of personality that attracted friends easily. In an interview in 1950, sister Marie Bankhead Owen described her three brothers in the following way: "If I were out to see the world and have a good time, I'd want Henry (an army officer) for a companion. If I needed sound advice on some business problem, I'd turn to John. But if I were in Hell and needed someone to talk my way out, I'd turn my case over to brother Will in perfect confidence."[29] These traits would serve him well in his long legislative career.

When President Wilson asked Congress in April 1917 for a declaration of war, Will in the House of Representatives voted yes, while Senator Bankhead did not vote. His fellow Alabama senator, Oscar Underwood, announced from the floor during the vote that Bankhead was "unavoidably detained in Alabama," but had he been present, Underwood continued, he would have voted for war.[30] Twenty years later, in 1937, Will Bankhead recalled this momentous vote, writing in his diary, "I shall never forget the mental torture that I endured in undertaking as a new congressman to make up my mind what my duty was in voting on the war resolution. I so thoroughly abominate and despise war as an institution that it was a spiritual crucifixion for me to reach the conclusion that it was my duty to my country under all circumstances then presented to vote for the resolution." He looked back on the vote with regret. "Looking back upon the whole transaction now I greatly fear that my vote was wrong and that we really accomplished nothing for civilization by our vast expenditure of life and treasure."[31] Like it did many southern families, the war touched the Bankheads personally: Major Henry Bankhead, the senator's youngest son, commanded a group of volunteers in the Quartermaster Corps who were posted to France in summer 1918. Marie and Tom Owen's son, Tom Jr., was drafted as a first lieutenant; John Jr.'s son, Walter Will, was inducted on October 30, 1918; neither served overseas.[32]

After the United States declared war on Germany, President Wilson directed the armed forces to expand to a million members. It soon became evident

Figure 7.2. Senator John Hollis Bankhead (*seated*) with sons (*left to right*) Henry, John Jr., and Will, c. 1915. Courtesy of the Alabama Department of Archives and History.

that volunteers alone could not fill the ranks. A draft was needed. Like most of their southern colleagues, both Senator and Congressman Bankhead initially opposed conscription. This opposition was rooted in the states' rights orientation and a fear of policy initiatives that enhanced central political and military powers.[33] Will, worried about the opposition to the draft in his own district, was reluctant to support Wilson's plans to increase the inadequate army of two hundred thousand men through selective service. John Jr. urged his brother to accept conscription, telling him that the people of Jasper favored it and "the country people" could be convinced of its necessity. John Jr. believed that only conscription "will raise [an] efficient army. . . . I believe bold actions will be appreciated by your constituents."[34] With assurance provided by John Jr., Will grew more enthusiastic in his support for Wilson's war program. Following Congress's declaration of war, Senator Bankhead remained concerned about conscription. He received letters from constituents urging him to vote against the proposed Selective Service Act. Writing to a constituent, he admitted that "I have not yet brought myself around to the belief that we should send an army to the trenches in Continental Europe, nor am I convinced that any form of conscription is the proper method to secure an army at this time."[35] However, by late April, roughly three weeks after war had been declared, Senator Bankhead was on board with conscription, telling one constituent that "I do not believe in any other manner can we raise an effective army. Conscription lays its hand equally upon all alike."[36]

Correspondence from constituents was staunchly in favor of conscription. One constituent argued that conscription was "more of a moral than an efficiency question." He wrote: "I do not think that we should kill or invalid the very cream of our citizenship and leave the slackers for the second or third calls, which may never come."[37] Whereas his father had waited more than five years to address the House, Will made his first speech in Congress on April 25, 1917, a mere month after being sworn in. He spoke in support of the conscription act. In a twenty-minute address that was interrupted eleven times for applause, he declared his belief that compulsory military service was part of American civic life, like taxes or jury duty. He referred to the "universal obligations of service and burden [that are] inextricably interwoven in all our political and civil relations to the state."[38] He emphasized the equity of the draft. The draft "is the only way in which every man of military age may secure a fair and square chance to serve upon terms of equality with his neighbor. The rich and poor are on the same simple level of responsibility and mutual liability to service. This is the only way to keep this from being 'a rich man's war and a poor man's fight.'"[39] Will worried about the reception of the speech, although brother John Jr. assured him, "I don't think there is any occasion whatever for feeling any uneasiness about the correctness of your position." Conscription was "democratic and will raise an efficient army with expedition. . . . If I were in Congress I would support whatever Wilson asked for."[40] John Jr. expressed great pride at his younger brother's maiden speech and wanted to share the moment with him, even if he could not be physically present. The day following Will's speech, John Jr. wrote: "I would like for you to write me your own impressions about your speech. Did it frighten or excite you to start the speech, and what impression do you feel you made on the House?"[41] Congress ultimately passed the Selective Service Act, which President Wilson signed into law on May 18, 1917. More than a million men from the South would enter the armed forces. The war claimed more than 6,200 casualties from Alabama.

As with most sweeping pieces of federal legislation, white southerners remained sensitive to the impact of the draft on white supremacy. Some feared that not enough black men were being drafted. One constituent from Houston County reported to Senator Bankhead that the draft was a "Yankee" plot "to put the Southern white man in the trenches and save the negro."[42] Senator Bankhead referred this question to secretary of war Newton D. Baker, who denied that African Americans would be exempt from the draft. "As a matter of fact," Newton continued, "the colored men will not apply for exemption, as the soldier's career seems peculiarly to appeal to them."[43] Another constituent opposed "our government taking all the able-bodied White men to the army and leaving the negroes here to commit all kinds of crime among our old men, women, and children." This constituent asked that "if you cannot use the negroes for soldiers, I say pass a law to take all guns of any kind away from all negroes and forbid the sale of any kind of ammunition or guns to negroes for the duration of the war."[44] Still others feared that too many black men were being drafted and asked the senator whether black men could be conscripted for farmwork.[45] Employers of farm labor were concerned by the loss of agricultural labor to military service and to higher-paying industrial work.[46] White southerners remained ever vigilant against any development that threatened the racial status quo.

The critical questions of war facing the nation coincided with more personal dilemmas facing the Bankhead grandchildren Eugenia and Tallulah, who were enrolled at Fairmont Seminary as the nation girded itself for war. Their matriculation at Fairmont offered them some semblance of a normal, secure life. Because the school was located in Washington, DC, the girls could live with family—Eugenia with Will and Florence, and Tallulah with her grandparents. They could partake of Washington's active social scene. Although not as cosmopolitan as New York City, Washington, DC, was worlds away from tiny Jasper, Alabama. Like many teenage girls of the era, Tallulah was enamored of the movies and the stage, and the options for escape to the grand movie halls and theaters were at her doorstep. Father Will had taken his daughters to the theater a number of times. One particularly exhilarating performance got both girls so wound up that they wet their pants. The play was "a tremendous emotional dose" for Tallulah; she recalled, "I didn't sleep for two nights running."[47] One does not soon forget so visceral a thrill. When she wasn't attending performances, Tallulah immersed herself in tabloids and magazines that described the fashionable lives of the stars of stage and screen. Movie magazines were like catnip to Tallulah, providing simultaneously an accelerant to and an escape from teen insecurity.

By 1916, the motion picture industry had moved beyond its infancy. Directors like D. W. Griffith were pioneering new techniques, and plotlines evolved as well. Tried-and-true stories of men and women upholding Victorian virtues gave way to tales that glorified "pleasure, excitement, physical comedy, athleticism, and luxury—that is, to the consumer ethos that was coming by and by to dominate American culture."[48] By 1920, the country had over twenty thousand movie theaters. If she wanted to, Tallulah could see a different movie every day of the week. Popular screen idol Mary Pickford alone made fifty-two films in 1916. Young women and teens like Tallulah lost themselves at the movies. Captivated by the on-screen drama of lovely Mary Pickford and handsome Douglas Fairbanks, teens and young women could likewise immerse themselves in the behind-the-scenes stories of the Pickford-Fairbanks romance and their glamorous lifestyle as covered by the industry's many magazines.

Like her father, Tallulah dreamed of a life on the stage and screen. With stepmother Florence's help, she entered her photograph in a beauty contest sponsored by *Picture Play* magazine in June 1917. The winner would be given a role in an upcoming film produced by Frank Powell. Now fifteen years old, Tallulah had shed much of her baby fat. Her wavy, dark blonde hair tumbled down her back, a style no doubt influenced by the enormous popularity of Pickford. The photographs of the twelve winners were announced in the September issue. Among them: Tallulah Bankhead. But Tallulah had neglected to write her name on the back of her photo. Underneath her picture ran the caption: "WHO IS SHE?" Tallulah and her father quickly confirmed her identity.[49] This origin story would become a key element of Tallulah's later celebrity. The "discovery" of Tallulah became part of her appeal. If this teenager from small-town Alabama could rise to stardom, surely anyone could make it. What the myth conveniently ignored, though, was the role her family's influence and wealth played in her ability to leverage this once-in-a-lifetime contest win into a successful career.

The entire family weighed in on what to do. Should young Tallulah be allowed to travel to New York and pursue an acting career, an opportunity that had been denied her father? She was, after all, only fifteen years old. Her grandmother, who had threatened to disown Will were he to pursue a career on the stage, was surprisingly supportive, as was her grandfather. Years later, Tallulah's Aunt Marie recalled that John Hollis—not Tallulah's father, Will—cast the deciding vote in favor of allowing Tallulah to travel to New York to seek her fortune, dramatically declaring, "Tallulah shall have her chance." Grandfather

John Hollis provided the financial backing for the venture. It was decided that Aunt Louise, already living in New York, would serve as her chaperone, later to be replaced by Marie.[50] And with that, fifteen-year-old Tallulah was off to New York, never again to live in Alabama.

Tallulah and Louise rented a small apartment in the theater district. Joining them was Ola, the fiancée of Louise's late son, William. Eighteen-year-old William had died of typhoid fever in 1915; Louise believed she could contact him through one of the many spiritualists who operated in the city. Perhaps ready to move on with her life, Ola returned to Alabama after a few months. Louise and Tallulah next took up residence in the Algonquin Hotel, long favored by actors and writers. As promised, Tallulah received a small part in *Who Loved Him Best?* Produced by the Mutual Film Corporation, the film was released in February 1918. For her labors, Tallulah received twenty dollars per day. Tallulah reveled in her residence at the Algonquin, where she was able to rub elbows with theatrical celebrities. Older actors were slightly bemused by the antics of the brash young woman from Alabama. Although her first film had been forgettable, she had made an impression on at least one young man in the wartime trenches in Europe. A sergeant with the American Expeditionary Forces wrote to Tallulah shortly before the Armistice to let her know that he had found a picture of her "in a captured German dugout."[51]

Following her film debut, Tallulah struggled to find work, finally landing a nonspeaking role in *The Squab Farm*, a new play that opened in March 1918 but closed after a four-week run. Her stage debut was followed by roles in two forgettable films, *When Men Betray* and *Thirty a Week*. This was not the career launch she had hoped for. In the closing months of World War I, Louise traveled to Europe to serve as a nurse's aide in the Red Cross. Marie Bankhead Owen stepped in as Tallulah's chaperone but soon returned to Alabama. By early 1919, seventeen-year-old Tallulah was on her own in New York City.[52]

Military preparedness and then entry into the war had a profound effect on the nation's and the South's economy. Southern states and industries were eager recipients of military installations and defense contracts. Naval stations and shipyards from Hampton Roads, Virginia, to the Texas coast hummed with activity.[53] War likewise was a boon for coal operators, and the Bankheads prospered by selling more and more coal to the railroads. Wartime prosperity prompted John Jr. to expand the family enterprise. After repaying a small loan from the J. P. Morgan Company, the Bankhead Coal Company extended its holdings, buying competing mines and acquiring new, undeveloped property. When a tax was imposed in 1916 on war profits, John Jr. devised a plan to save money by converting the corporation into a partnership with himself and his father as owners, a legal fiction because all members of the family shared in the profits. By the end of the war, the corporation and its subsidiaries were realizing profits of several thousand dollars annually.[54] John Jr. was employed by the Coal Operators' Association to lobby on operators' behalf in Washington during the war.[55]

To ensure that sufficient men and material were available for the war effort, and to guarantee that both men and goods secured easy passage to the East Coast, Wilson nationalized the railroads. He seriously considered nationalizing the coal industry as well. The industry was plagued by angry strikers and profiteering owners. Wilson pleaded with management and labor to settle their differences. Cooperating with Wilson, Senator Bankhead arranged a series of conferences between government officials, coal operators, and union leaders to try to quell the strife. His contribution may have been small, but Bankhead was pleased when the president decided to permit the coal industry to remain in private hands.[56]

Senator John Hollis Bankhead had spent his long career securing federal funds to develop Alabama's infrastructure, and the country's involvement in World War I provided a golden opportunity to continue this effort. With war raging in Europe, the president and others focused on the nation's munitions supply. The country was almost completely dependent on Chilean sources for nitrogen compounds necessary to the manufacture of explosives. This South American source put the United States at some risk were Germans to disrupt the shipping lines. Elsewhere, other nations were rapidly developing domestic synthetic nitrogen facilities. To address this shortfall, Senator Ellison DuRant "Cotton Ed" Smith of South Carolina introduced a bill in 1916 that provided for the production of synthetic nitrogen on a large scale in the United States. The Smith bill was eventually incorporated into the National Defense Act of 1916, which, among other things, "authorized the President to ascertain the most feasible method of synthetic nitrogen production and to construct and operate such plants, hydroelectric dams, and other facilities as the President might deem necessary for the production of nitrates."[57] The act also allowed for the peacetime use of the nitrate plants for the production of fertilizer. These plants would be operated by the federal government. John Hollis Bankhead was keenly interested in the continued production of fertilizer in the postwar era as a way to rehabilitate Alabama's worn-out soil. Writing to one constituent three months after the country entered World War I, the Alabama senator revealed that "the real purpose of the law was to make a complete fertilizer for delivery to the farmer at a cost of about half of what he has been paying."[58]

Senators Bankhead and Underwood wanted the new plant for the Muscle Shoals region in northern Alabama. A shallow zone in the Tennessee River, the Muscle Shoals site was ideal for producing power.[59] The sixth-largest river in the United States, the Tennessee River drains some forty-four thousand square miles in seven states. State leaders had tried for years to develop that region. In order to improve the commercial capacity of the Tennessee River, obstructions at the Shoals region had to be removed and other impediments to navigation addressed. At the turn of the twentieth century, the privately owned Muscle Shoals Hydro-Electric Power Company (MSHEPC) had purchased the land around the shoals and planned to construct a hydroelectric dam at the site. The dam would generate power for a nearby nitrate factory. Much of the promotion of the development of Muscle Shoals was orchestrated by J. W. Worthington, a Sheffield, Alabama, banker and one of the founders of MSHEPC. MSHEPC was eventually bought out by Alabama Traction, Light & Power, which was a holding company that included the statewide utility Alabama Power. Worthington began working with Bankhead and Underwood to lobby Congress for the rights to build a dam at Muscle Shoals. Bankhead gave testimony in 1910 regarding the need to develop the site, and Underwood signed on as well. The plan stalled until the war changed everything.[60]

Once Wilson signed the National Defense Act, the prospect of some sort of industrial project at Muscle Shoals brightened considerably. The government investigated a site on the Black Warrior River as well but concluded that the Warrior site could not supply sufficient power. Bankhead noted, "What I want is a nitrogen plant, one with power sufficient to make nitrogen in quantities that will supply the farmers at a cost of not more than one half [of what] they are paying at the present time. This bill was not passed to benefit any particular locality. It is not local in its nature, and was not intended to be. It is national in its character, intended to serve the whole country where fertilizers are used."[61] The Department of War also considered a site in West Virginia.

Real estate in and around Florence, Alabama, was quickly snapped up as residents and speculators anticipated a boost in economic activity related to the proposed federal project. All suspicion was put to rest when, on September 28, 1917, President Wilson chose nearby Sheffield, Alabama, as the site of the plant, which became known as nitrate plant no. 1. The community eagerly awaited the arrival of thousands of construction workers, as well as the permanent staff that would operate the facilities.[62] Bankhead traveled to Sheffield on November 9, 1917, to meet with the secretary of war about the project. Wilson soon thereafter authorized the creation of a second plant and a dam (eventually known as Wilson

Dam) at Muscle Shoals to provide power. The second plant, which used a different manufacturing process than that used for plant 1, was capable of producing forty thousand tons of nitrogen a year. Construction of the site began in early 1918 and involved some eighteen thousand workers. Sufficient housing was not available for the workforce, so the government constructed some 185 residential units, twenty-three mess halls, a hospital, three barbershops, and a school that could accommodate 850 students. The war ended before the project was finished. Plant No. 1, which cost approximately $12 million, was never entirely successful; activities at the plant were suspended in January 1919. Plant No. 2 cost $68 million and was ready for operation by October 1918. Wilson Dam was completed in 1921.[63]

Just as quickly as wartime excitement hit Alabama, it was over. The cessation of hostilities in Europe in November 1918 left the Muscle Shoals project in limbo. What was to be done with it? Would it continue as planned—as a government-run project—or would it be sold to be operated as a privately owned company? Farmers in the region were particularly interested in the production of cheap fertilizer. Farmers in the Tennessee Valley produced soil-depleting crops; fertilizer would improve productivity.[64] Although farmers had experienced a brief period of peak cotton prices from 1916 to 1919, prices dropped steeply beginning in 1920. The region's tenants and sharecroppers were hit particularly hard. The Muscle Shoals question would vex Congress for the next decade and in the process lay the groundwork for a much larger regional planning project, the Tennessee Valley Authority. Congressman Will Bankhead became actively involved in the Muscle Shoals project in the postwar era. Through his involvement, his ideas about the role of government in regional development underwent a transformation that would ultimately shape his approach to policy during the Great Depression.

The Muscle Shoals project likewise had ramifications for John Jr.'s career. One of his clients was the Alabama Power Company, one of the most vilified corporations in the state. John Jr. crossed an ethical line in trying to use his father's Washington connections for personal benefit and the benefit of his client. At the time that the government had become interested in Muscle Shoals, John Jr. went looking for inside information. He wrote to his father that the company would profit greatly from knowledge of the amount of acreage the government intended to buy and the kind of dam it contemplated. Senator Bankhead was appalled by the request. He was well aware of the utility's unpopularity and urged his son to renounce his association with it. Ignoring his father's advice for one of the few times in his life, John Jr. kept Alabama Power as a client and used his position to acquire land that was later sold to the government at a considerable profit. The dam was to become extremely controversial during the next decade.[65] John Jr.'s involvement with Alabama Power, which was admittedly quite limited, would continue to haunt him for that same stretch of time.

The war in Europe was over much sooner than most had anticipated. With the fighting quelled, the nation turned to the construction of peace. In a highly controversial move, President Wilson traveled to Paris to negotiate the peace treaty that would officially conclude the bloodiest conflict in the history of mankind. Even before the American entrance into the war, Wilson had hoped that the outcome of the conflict would bring about a new kind of world order. In particular, Wilson hoped to create a League of Nations that would arbitrate world conflicts. Senator Bankhead remained relatively quiet about the Treaty of Versailles and the creation of a League of Nations prior to the president's return in February 1919, as did most southerners in Congress.[66] To those constituents writing to him to either support or reject the league, Bankhead noted, "This is perhaps the most important question that has been presented to the people of this country since the beginning of the World War. I have never at any time, and do not intend to express an opinion on the subject until I am fully advised as to what the provisions of the League are to be."[67] Bankhead kept quiet.

Wilson's hope for achieving a transformed postwar world became even more challenging following the midterm elections of 1918. The Republicans gained control of the Senate; the fate of the Treaty of Versailles and especially the League of Nations was in their hands. Southern senators were generally supportive of the president and his policies, although some were uncomfortable with individual aspects of the league. Senator Bankhead kept quiet about the league, although many of his colleagues began speaking out once Wilson returned in late February 1919. As of March 1919, Bankhead supported the proposed League of Nations, telling one constituent that "I have enough confidence in President Wilson to believe that nothing will be submitted that does not take care of the United States and protect its interests."[68] As of June 1919, he declared himself to be "entirely in sympathy with the principle and purpose of the League of Nations."[69] Leading the fight against Wilson's league was Senator Henry Cabot Lodge, chairman of the Senate Committee on Foreign Relations. Lodge supported American entrance into the league only if the Senate adopted a long list of reservations. Wilson would not budge, and neither would the majority of southern senators. Ultimately, only four southern senators publicly criticized the league. Southern senators followed Wilson's directive and rejected reservations proposed by Henry Cabot Lodge, thus dooming any version of the treaty to defeat.[70] The United States did not ratify the Treaty of Versailles.

Despite its short duration (in terms of American involvement), the war spurred social change. The war gave tremendous impetus to the women's suffrage movement. Within the state, the effort to win the ballot for women was led by the Alabama Equal Suffrage Association, founded in 1912. John Hollis Bankhead staunchly opposed a women's suffrage amendment to the Constitution, vowing to do "everything I can toward its defeat." He believed the extension of the franchise to be a right reserved to the states. To one constituent, he noted, "I have no objection in the world to women of Alabama having suffrage, but I want the State to extend it."[71] Anti-suffrage activists were strong in the state. The Alabama Association Opposed to Woman Suffrage urged Senator Bankhead to oppose the amendment because it threatened white supremacy. The anti-suffragists argued that the amendment's adoption "means enforcement of [the] fifteenth amendment bringing unrest, strife, and discord throughout the South, particularly in the hundreds of counties with large negro populations."[72] Although Senator Bankhead called Alabama's congressional delegation together on December 12, 1917, to meet with a group of Alabama women working for suffrage, he ultimately voted against the amendment, as did Congressman Bankhead.[73] Nevertheless, Congress approved the amendment and dispatched it to the states for ratification.

Senator Bankhead clearly was no friend of women's suffrage; however, the most prominent anti-suffragist in the Bankhead family was Marie Bankhead Owen. Like her father, Marie saw women's suffrage as a backdoor assault on white supremacy. If passed, the amendment would open the polling booth to African American women. Marie served as the legislative chair of the Women's Anti-Suffrage League. Once the amendment was approved by Congress in 1919 and sent to the states for ratification, the Women's Anti-Suffrage League swung into action, leading the fight to defeat it in the Alabama state legislature. The league based its fight on an appeal to states' rights, southern manhood, and white supremacy. It reached out to every member of the state legislature, arguing that "women would exert more influence by maintaining supremacy in the home, rather than by extending it into the political sphere." The anti-suffragists viewed the amendment as a threat to both states' rights and white political hegemony.

The Women's Anti-Suffrage League held weekly meetings and rallies during summer 1919. It received positive coverage in the anti-suffrage *Montgomery Advertiser*. The league claimed that the majority of voters and "most of the white women of middle Alabama" were opposed to ratification. The state legislature convened in July to consider the amendment. The league sent each legislator a letter, urging them to reject the amendment. The letter read, in part, "[we] earnestly beg that you, as true men of the South, decline to ratify this Amendment which violates the time honored question of States Rights and which dishonors the principle for which the Confederate soldier shed his blood." The league also submitted a petition to the legislature, stating that "adoption [of the amendment] would forever forfeit the right of the state to regulate its own election laws, and transfer this power to a government not in sympathy with our social order. The Fifteenth Amendment is not dead. It merely sleepeth. Why arouse it from its slumber?" The state legislature rejected the amendment overwhelmingly.[74]

Marie's anti-suffrage campaign centered on protecting white supremacy and Democratic hegemony. This same goal of racial supremacy animated her historical work. In 1919, Alabama celebrated its hundredth year of statehood. In recognition, the legislature created the Alabama Centennial Commission

Figure 7.4. The Owen family, c. 1918. *Left to right:* Tom, Marie, Mabel (Tom Jr.'s wife), and Tom Jr. Courtesy of the Alabama Department of Archives and History.

in February 1919 to coordinate activities to commemorate the event. As the state archivist, Tom Owen was appointed to serve on the commission; joining him were the state auditor, the state superintendent of education, University of Alabama history professor Thomas McCorvey, and Alabama Polytechnic Institute professor and former football coach George Petrie. Marie was appointed the commission's secretary.[75] The organization commissioned Marie to write historical plays to commemorate the occasion. Communities were encouraged to perform these plays during the state's centennial year.

Marie wrote a total of six plays, three for children and three for high school students and adults (although evidence suggests that she had originally planned on five plays for adults). The plays commemorate three events in Alabama's history: the Battle of Mabila, between Hernando de Soto's Spanish warriors and Chief Tuskaloosa's forces; the creation of the French colony at Mobile; and the coming of statehood in 1819. No play touches on historical issues post-1819. The children's plays are more simplistic versions of the adult plays. Taken together, the plays present the history of the founding of the state of Alabama as the inexorable and inevitable march of European civilization. In the children's and adult plays about the Battle of Mabila, Marie incorporates certain historical inaccuracies common to contemporary historical scholarship, such as incorrectly identifying De Soto as the first European to visit Alabama, grossly overstating the size of the Spanish expedition, and definitively identifying the location of Mabila. More troubling, though, is her interpretation and representation of Native American culture. Although the characters refer to the Spanish as "a bloody lot" and are critical of some of their methods, such as the use of vicious dogs, the entire Native American way of life is called into question with the frequent use of the word "savage" to describe the people and their culture. The children's play on De Soto ends dramatically, with the children heralding the victory of the white men and—by extension—European culture ("The Spaniards beat! The white men beat!" cries one child). The adult play ends on a darker note, with Chief Tuskaloosa's widow placing a curse on De Soto and foretelling his death. Apparently, the plays focusing on De Soto and Tuskaloosa had been based on an earlier story Marie had written about the event. In 1914, she tried to interest a New Jersey production company in making films based on her stories that focus on Native Americans and De Soto. Nothing came of this venture.[76]

Both the second and third children's plays (about the French colony and the establishment of statehood, respectively) incorporate African American characters. The children's version of the Mobile play includes two enslaved characters—Good Times and Muscadine—while the children's play about statehood features a slave character named Lucy, "a negro Mammy." Slavery as an institution is discussed briefly in the third adult play, about the coming of statehood. One character, an innkeeper, directly asks another (who happens to be a preacher) how he feels about slavery. The preacher replies, "Slavery? It is God's way of putting the poor heathen in reach of the gospel and of salvation. They were mostly slaves already in their native country. Their heathen masters were more capable of cruelties towards them than the meanest white man ever made can be." The innkeeper then notes the positive impact that slavery will have on white folks, stating that the presence of enslaved Africans "will develop a fine quality of self-esteem in the mind of the superior race."[77] The adult play thus becomes a clumsy vehicle with which to defend the institution of slavery rather than an opportunity to explore its critical importance in the development of the state.

The children's play actually handles the issue of slavery with more subtlety than does the adult play. The children's statehood play is based in Huntsville in 1819. The setting is a collection of rented rooms above a tavern. The play's action is quite simple: a group of children from different places of origin are staying in the rooms. They become friends, thus illustrating the "peopling" of Alabama by migrants from South Carolina, Tennessee, Georgia, and elsewhere. They have all decided to make Alabama their home. In the play, the children are brought together by Lucy, an enslaved woman. By incorporating this device, whether the author intended it to or not, the play has something profound to say about slavery: just as Lucy facilitates the common connections among the children, so too did the institution of slavery bind together white Alabamians.

Although the adult play about the Battle at Mabila contains action and a plot, the other two plays are notable for their almost complete lack of action. They must have made for pretty dull theater. But entertainment or dramatic tension was not the point: the point of the plays was to instruct the audience in Alabama's "proper" history as the state marked its hundredth year. Mostly the plays are tedious exercises in character exposition: different historical figures appear onstage and "explain" an event that is taking or has just taken place. The third adult play focuses on the role of the Creek War of 1813–14 in the creation of

Alabama statehood. Andrew Jackson occupies a prominent role in the play and is presented as a near-mythic figure, with one character declaring that "nothing is impossible with God and Andy Jackson." Although the characters denounce various acts of violence on behalf of the Creek, such as the attack on Fort Mims, some attempt is made to explain the Creek position. Upon his surrender to General Jackson, Red Stick leader William Weatherford laments that "we [the Creek] gave the white man a bridle path through our nation and soon it became a wagon road filled from end to end with white families coming to take our hunting grounds and to stay. We gave him a field and he took a Nation." The Andrew Jackson character replies: "It is the law of nature, Weatherford, that the fittest shall survive. We have met you on your own ground and the victory is ours. The end of your day has come."[78] Taken together, these plays commemorate the arrival, extension, and ultimate superiority of European culture. The creation of the state of Alabama, as Marie's Andrew Jackson declares, was inevitable.

In early 1920, John Hollis Bankhead fell ill with the flu. Daughter Marie traveled to Washington, DC, to care for him. The family expected him to make a full recovery.[79] By mid-February, the local Jasper newspaper reported that the senator was walking around his room and that "his condition was rapidly improving."[80] He never recovered. John Hollis Bankhead, seventy-seven years old and the last remaining Confederate soldier to serve in the US Senate, died of heart failure at one o'clock in the afternoon on March 1, 1920. Condolences poured in to the senator's office and to his home. President Warren G. Harding told Marie, "I have never known a man in public life who attracted my confidence more quickly, or for whom I had a more genuinely affectionate regard. He was a really big, courageous and most honorable man."[81]

A special funeral train was dispatched to bring the senator's body home to Jasper. Traveling with their fallen colleague was a delegation of dignitaries from Washington, DC. Among those attending the funeral were fellow Alabama senator Oscar Underwood as well as senators from the states of Ohio, Nevada, Michigan, Arizona, Mississippi, Tennessee, and Minnesota. It was the most distinguished group of public figures ever to visit the small Alabama town. The train arrived in Jasper amid "the worst wind and rain storm seen in Jasper in many a year," recorded the *Jasper Mountain Eagle*. "The very elements seemed to be in the general grief of his home people." The paper reported that the inclement weather kept away thousands of mourners. Local businesses closed for the day.

The funeral was held in the newly built First United Methodist Church, a beautiful Beaux-Arts structure. Floral tributes lined the chancel of the church, and the casket was draped with both the US and the Confederate flags. When the service was over, the white funeral mourners filed past the casket; black mourners who wished to pay their last respects were allowed to view the senator separately. Following the funeral, the body was interred in the family vault.

Several months later, on December 9, 1920, John Hollis Bankhead's fellow senators delivered memorial addresses; former colleagues in the House of Representatives followed suit on January 30, 1921. Will noted in his diary that the memorial service in the House was "of course an occasion for very sad memories, yet it was filled with sweet consolations too, in the fact that my sire had made such a profound impress upon his times and his associates in public life. . . . It is a renewed inspiration to me, to know that he wrote indelibly upon the scroll of his day and generation."[82] Wife Tallulah remembered her husband simply as a "superb man."[83] Two months after John Hollis's death, widow Tallulah Bankhead was visiting her daughter Marie in Montgomery. Her late husband was on her mind, and being in the capital city gave her comfort. She felt peace, she wrote to her son in Washington, "when I look at the capitol Dome here and know that your father served under it—in his youth after 4 years of hard war service, then after, served 33 years under the Dome [in Washington]. He was great."[84]

John Hollis Bankhead left his family well provided for. His will dictated that each of his five children receive $10,000, equivalent to roughly $120,000 today. His stock in the Bankhead Coal Company was also divided among the children. He bequeathed his home, Sunset, to John Jr., "with the understanding that he convey to my son William his home place." He estimated that his home was worth roughly $15,000 ($183,000 today). Will also received additional stocks in the Caledonia Coal Company, while son Henry received additional bonds in the company.[85]

As the local Jasper newspaper declared, John Hollis Bankhead had lived "a long and useful life." He had left his mark on the state of Alabama and the nation. He dedicated his public life to the development of Alabama's natural resources, its fledgling industries, and the success of its farmers. By closely aligning the state's convict lease system with the coal industry, securing funds for the development of Black Warrior River and the facilities at Muscle Shoals, and, most importantly, ensuring the passage of the Federal Aid Road Act of 1916, he made it possible for the state and many of its citizens to participate more fully in the economic life of the nation. He would forever be remembered as the "Father of Good Roads."

But his career was not unblemished. John Hollis Bankhead's tenure in office was also defined by complete opposition to the creation of a biracial democracy in the aftermath of the Civil War. As a state legislator, he supported the Black Codes and opposed the Thirteenth and Fourteenth Amendments. During his tenure as warden of the state penitentiary, his advocacy of the convict lease doomed black men caught up in the state's legal dragnet to a miserable existence in the state's coal mines. As a congressman and senator, he feared that the coalition of poor black and white farmers who made up the populist movement foreshadowed a race war; in response, he did his part to support the creation of a state constitution that stripped African Americans and many poor white voters of their political rights.

John Hollis Bankhead's vision for the reconstructed and New South was ultimately a cramped one predicated on the mistaken belief that full economic prosperity, as well as political and cultural integration into the life of the nation, could only be realized by denying basic rights and opportunities to African American citizens. This, too, was his legacy. Many years would pass before southern politicians would embrace a different vision.

II
SUCCESSION

8

New Directions

THE YEAR 1920 MARKED a sad turning point for the Bankhead family. The death of John Hollis Bankhead on March 1, 1920, was followed three weeks later by the unexpected and tragic death of Marie's husband, Thomas McAdory Owen. The cause of death was heart failure.[1] He was fifty-three years old. Marie believed that his death was hastened by overwork. She recorded Tom's last moments in her diary several months later: "He got up, went into the bath room, undressed for his tub, and I heard a crash. He had fallen, catching upon the seat, and I eased him to the floor, screaming for help. [Son] Thomas and [daughter-in-law] Mabel came. But he was dead. He had dropped dead, only gasping a few times, then gone! I don't think he had a moment's consciousness." Reflecting on their life together, Marie wrote, "We had always had a financial struggle, but he never failed to gratify my pride in him."[2] Marie vowed to complete Tom's magnum opus: a history of the state of Alabama. "When that is done I pray you Lord," a heartbroken Marie begged, "take me out of this world of mine."[3]

Tom's death was followed by other personal losses. In February 1921, the family learned that sister Louise, the eldest of the Bankhead siblings, had died. Will wrote in his diary that "my precious sister Louise had dropped dead today [February 19] about 2pm in a curio shop in Miami, Florida, where she was visiting friends." Will was distraught. "I can not try to express now my profound sorrow and shock. I cannot realize it—She was so intimately a part of our family. So . . . affectionate, so capable." Will was particularly worried about the impact on his mother, who had come to rely on Louise since the death of John Hollis. "It is awful—awful! God help us!" Louise's body was returned to Jasper, and her casket was set up in John Jr.'s home. Mother Tallulah, who had been visiting Will and Florence in Washington, stayed away from the funeral under doctor's orders. Will described the "sad and heartbreaking trip to Alabama to lay away the mortal remains of our darling Louise. What an unexpected journey of desolate hearts."[4] Those "desolate hearts" had barely begun to heal when another tragedy struck the family. A little more than a year after the death of her

daughter Louise, mother Tallulah died in May 1922. She had been in poor health for some time, although she continued to travel to spend time with her children.[5]

The new decade brought new professional challenges and opportunities for the Bankheads, and saw politics within the state head in unexpected directions. The return of the Republican Party to majority status in both houses of Congress with the 1918 midterm elections dramatically changed the fortunes of congressional rising star Will Bankhead. Although often frustrated by the Republican majority, Will used his decade in the minority party as extended training in legislative maneuvering. Despite his junior status in the minority party, Will became adept at reaching across the aisle for cosponsors and at learning the rules of the House. He continued his father's work on developing the state and nation's infrastructure and became engaged in the decade-long struggle to determine the fate of the Muscle Shoals project, a struggle that led the young congressman to rethink how he viewed the role of the federal government in regional development. Hard work in the congressional trenches as a member of the minority party would pay off when the Democrats came roaring back to political life with the election of Franklin D. Roosevelt in 1932.

The death of his father, as well as the return of the Republican majority, effectively killed John Jr.'s dream of a federal judgeship. He trained his sights on a political future. He ran for the US Senate in 1926 but was steamrolled by a relative newcomer to the political realm, a young attorney named Hugo L. Black. The victory of the liberal Black stunned the traditional political establishment and made it clear that new actors—in particular, the reborn Ku Klux

Klan—were now wielding political influence. Uncharacteristically, John Jr. and Will misread the political landscape and were caught flat-footed by the Klan issue in 1926; however, only four years later, the political terrain had shifted yet again. By 1930, the Klan's violent excesses and subsequent crackdown by law enforcement had greatly diminished that group's influence. Further, the crisis in the rural economy brought yet new issues to the forefront, prompting John Jr. once again to throw his hat into the ring, this time against bombastic incumbent US senator James Thomas Heflin, and with a very different result.

Officially taking his seat in spring 1917, Will Bankhead hit the ground running. He proved to be a more active initiator of legislation than his father, who, admittedly, served during prolonged periods of Republican dominance and so had less opportunity to make his mark. Denied a chairmanship because of party control, John Hollis had conducted most of his work within committees, biding his time until the Democratic majority gave him more power. With the Democrats gaining power during the Wilson years, Will Bankhead spent the first few years of his career as a member of the majority party. Unlike his father, he frequently spoke on the floor and quickly developed a reputation as a gifted orator and debater. Whereas John Hollis had primarily been interested in developing the South's infrastructure with federal money, Will broadened his focus to people as well as place. And when he did turn his attention to resource development, he moved beyond state and sectional concerns to partner with members of Congress from the West and elsewhere to create meaningful legislation. Early on, the affable Will was cultivating relationships and learning to think nationally.

Will's initial legislative efforts targeted adult literacy. He was disturbed to learn that a disproportionately large number of young men from his state had been rejected during the military draft because of poor health or illiteracy.[6] Bankhead spent four years in an ultimately unsuccessful effort to acquire federal funding to fight this latter problem.[7] Despite his best efforts to illustrate that it was in the nation's best interest that her citizens (both native- and foreign-born) be able to read and write English, most members of Congress considered adult illiteracy an issue best handled by the states.

Bankhead found legislative success advocating for vocational rehabilitation. His efforts in this area piggybacked on a series of acts aimed at assisting disabled soldiers. In 1919 Bankhead introduced a bill that would extend the rehabilitation program to persons disabled in industry. Arguing the merits of the bill on the floor of the House, Bankhead estimated that there were three hundred thousand disabled workers "for whom no concerted action was being taken by the state, municipal, county, or federal governments." He compared the workers' service to the nation to that rendered by soldiers. "When our soldiers went to the front there was no man here who said we did not owe a duty to retrain those who came back disabled, because they were serving their Government in a great national crisis. But you take these men and women covered by this bill, were they rendering any service to the Government? Why, they are composed of people of every element of our citizenship, of men who are injured upon the railroads carrying on the transportation facilities of the country absolutely necessary for its economic and industrial life; men injured down in the bowels of the earth, working in the coal mines to produce fuel which will sustain the life of the Nation against the rigors of winter; and women, if you please, all over the country, working in shops to earn an honest living for themselves and their families. . . . What is the result when they are disabled?" Bankhead estimated that workers disabled on the job lost $100 million in earning capacity annually. Appealing to sentiment, Bankhead painted a picture of the broken and desperate: "You have seen beggars with little tin cups in the hands on the streets, or selling pencils, or in the poorhouse. You have seen these people maimed and handicapped." For those concerned about federal overreach, Bankhead reminded them of the critical importance of federal aid in building good roads, establishing land-grant colleges, and creating the agricultural extension system.[8] The substance of Bankhead's bill was ultimately incorporated into a new bill with a smaller appropriation by Republican congressman Simeon D. Fess of Ohio and became law as the Civilian Vocational Rehabilitation Act in 1920. The act was extremely popular, and within a few years, thirty-six states chose to participate. In arguing for the bill's renewed appropriation in 1924, to the applause of his fellow congresspeople, Bankhead again spoke eloquently of "the man in overalls, the woman in gingham, the bread earners, the heads of families, who go out in pursuit of a livelihood and are mangled in the machinery of factories or mines or railroads and become so much human wreckage in the society of our Nation." These individuals deserved a chance to "go back into the earning life of the Nation with self-respect, with some dignity of purpose, and a capacity to earn a livelihood for themselves and their families."[9] In 1932, with the appropriation once again up for renewal, Congressman Bankhead spoke of the law's success in helping those injured on the job pursue gainful employment. "When I close my eyes . . . [I] see the more than 50,000 American citizens, crippled and maimed and disheartened and discouraged, who under the beneficent provisions and operation of this bill have been placed back in gainful employment in a self-respecting way, earning a livelihood [and] taken off the human scrap heap." The House erupted in applause.[10] Will Bankhead understood the power of oratory. For his efforts on behalf of disabled workers, Bankhead received support from the American Federation of Labor.[11]

It was difficult for a young Democratic congressman to make a name for himself in the Republican 1920s. As he embarked on his third term in 1921,

Bankhead wondered "if the game is worth the candle. I am spending now the very vigor of my manhood in public service. It has some compensations, but few rewards."[12] Determined not to be done in by the challenges of crafting successful legislation as a member of the minority party, Bankhead used this time as a training period. He drew on the advice he had received from his father when he first entered Congress: "Learn the rules."[13] As a member of the Committee on Rules, he improved his knowledge of parliamentary procedures. Gifted with a flair for the dramatic, the one-time aspiring thespian became an effective floor advocate for the Democrats, speaking often and eloquently, and established important relationships with minority leadership. And he learned the importance of reaching across the aisle. Finally, as the decade wore on, he illustrated that he was more political pragmatist than ideologue, becoming more comfortable with the notion that the federal government must play an active role in addressing social and economic issues, with the exception, of course, of race.

During the decade, Will Bankhead worked hard for reclamation of what he called "the waste places of America," among which he would place arid western lands as well as the exhausted and oft-flooded lands of the Tennessee Valley.[14] He confided in his diary that "I am determined to make *this* a big thing in my career."[15] He was particularly interested in uniting South and West in a program of land reclamation. In 1921, he and Senator William E. Borah of Idaho jointly authored a cooperative reclamation act.[16] This bill called for $500 million appropriated over eleven years to reclaim private land in cooperation with local organizations.[17] Republican president Warren Harding gave the bill tepid support, noting that his focus was on international affairs such as disarmament. Undeterred, Bankhead promoted his bill wherever possible. Speaking on behalf of his bill in North Carolina, Bankhead declared that "the great, outstanding menace to government is the over-industrialization of the civilized states of the World." He noted that projected population growth would necessitate an additional 130 million acres over the next twenty years to support this expanding population. These new lands could be reclaimed from the arid regions of the West and the cutover lands of the South. "These are the last frontier."[18] Private capital was insufficient to bring about reclamation. In advocating for government-funded land projects, Bankhead revealed his pragmatism. To those who cited "constitutional objections," Bankhead declared, "I am a 'strict constructionist,' but as time progresses and conditions change and where the general good is to be accomplished, I waive that."[19] Although his bill did not pass, he continued to urge the cooperation of southerners and westerners and showed himself willing to support western projects, such as the construction of Boulder Dam in the Colorado River Basin.[20]

One of the most contentious and significant political issues of the 1920s concerned the fate of the Muscle Shoals property and Wilson Dam. Will Bankhead took great interest in the project. He regarded the justification for the

Muscle Shoals project and for soil reclamation as roughly synonymous, as both addressed the problem of cultivating additional acreage to meet the needs of a rapidly expanding population.[21] But on the two issues, Bankhead advocated two different positions: private operation for Muscle Shoals, and government funding for land reclamation. Bankhead's position on Muscle Shoals was pragmatic, not ideological; he simply believed that private operation was most expedient. Over the course of the decade, however, as the potential for private lease of the Muscle Shoals property encountered increasingly strong resistance, Bankhead (and a majority of southern lawmakers) came to support public operation and ownership.

The war had ended before sufficient use could be made of the nitrate plants, and as of 1920, the dam remained unfinished. The future of Muscle Shoals occupied Congress for the entire decade and encompassed many questions: Was it primarily a fertilizer project or a water power project? Should it be operated as a public, government-run project, or should it be leased to a private concern? Would leasing the project violate provisions of the recently approved Federal Water Power Act, a piece of legislation shepherded by John Hollis Bankhead that represented a compromise between private power forces and conservationists and had taken years to craft? Congress struggled mightily with these questions.

The congressional Republican majority hoped to mothball the project and win political points by painting it as a Democratic boondoggle plagued by waste and corruption. Unable to prove any mishandling of funds, the Republicans nevertheless thwarted the project's completion and operation in the postwar era, at least in the early part of the decade. Democrats, led by Alabama senators Oscar Underwood and James Thomas Heflin and congressmen Edward Almon and Will Bankhead, argued for the completion of the dam and the production of much-needed fertilizer as stipulated by the National Defense Act of 1916. Addressing the House in late December 1920, Bankhead compared the need for fertilizer to reclamation projects in western states, which received federal support. He appealed to representatives from western states with the claim that the principle was the same, that "the proposition at Muscle Shoals is but a replica of the irrigation projects of the West." Although he argued that farmers as a group were not "entitled to any special legislation," he held that "Providence has created, and human ingenuity has harnessed there at Muscle Shoals, a great proposition of potential power for their benefit and for the benefit of other people."[22] For Bankhead, the dam was simply the latest in a series of important technological developments, and he believed it was almost his destiny to continue to fight for the project's completion. Writing in his diary, Bankhead mused, "I have lived in a wonderful era of inventive development—Electricity, flying machine, phono-graph, moving pictures, wireless telegraph. . . . We are going to finish that dam!" Despite Will's best efforts to "*make* Congress realize the value of fertilizer as the only practical labor saving device," Republicans feared that government-produced fertilizer would unfairly hinder private firms and voted against any funding either to complete the dam or to operate the plants.[23] By the early 1920s, the project was stalled.

The Muscle Shoals project received new life when the Harding administration announced that it would consider leasing the project to a private concern. In July 1922, secretary of war John W. Weeks received a bid from none other than automobile manufacturer Henry Ford, who offered the government $5 million for the nitrate plants. The nitrate plants had cost the government some $106 million to construct. Ford proposed that the government complete Wilson Dam and then lease it to him for a period of one hundred years, absolutely free of government regulation. Ford would use the facilities thus obtained partly for making fertilizer at a profit to himself not to exceed 8 percent, with no restrictions on the other use of the property.[24] His initial proposal guaranteed neither cheap power nor cheap fertilizer, although he later modified it to include stronger assurances for the production of fertilizer.

Both John Jr. and Will enthusiastically supported Ford's plan. Will's district stood to benefit from the investment. John H. Bankhead Jr. severed his connection with the Alabama Power Company and announced his support for the Ford plan.[25] Some Ford supporters declared that his proposal also included an aim to provide cheap power to southerners and would develop the Muscle Shoals area into a gigantic industrial center with additional sites for the extraction of potash and the production of aluminum. Supporters proclaimed that the Muscle Shoals area would become the "new Detroit." The Alabama delegation fed these dreams, with one representative declaring that Ford's industries would provide jobs for up to one million men. Many people supported his proposal because they had tremendous faith in Ford himself.[26]

While the administration was considering Ford's proposal, Will did what he could to ensure acceptance of the industrialist's plan. He met with Secretary Weeks in October 1921 and with Ford in January 1922.[27] The entire Alabama congressional delegation was united behind the automobile manufacturer's proposal, seeing it as the surest and quickest means of harnessing Muscle Shoals' power for the production of inexpensive fertilizer.[28] Not everyone was thrilled with Ford's plan. Some of the strongest opposition to the Ford proposal came from Alabama Power Company, American Cyanamid Company, and other corporations, which feared a future monopoly of power by Ford. Secretary Weeks wanted the Alabama Power Company to take over at Muscle Shoals and sent its bid to Congress, where it met stiff opposition from the Alabama delegation. With mounting opposition, Secretary Weeks turned the issue over to Congress, where battle lines were already being drawn. Some opposed Ford's proposal because acceptance of it would be in violation of the Federal Water Power Act of 1920. He would have access to cheap power, giving him an advantage over other manufacturers. The opposition to the Ford offer was led by Senator George W. Norris, progressive Republican from Nebraska and chairman of the

Senate Committee on Agriculture. He wanted Muscle Shoals to remain under government control.

Congress wrangled with the Ford offer for three years. Bankhead spoke often on the floor of the House, reminding his colleagues of the importance of this project to the area's farmers. He noted that the major farm advocacy groups—the National Grange, the American Farm Bureau Federation, and the National Farmers Union—supported the Ford plan.[29] Bankhead supported Ford's proposal because he believed that it contained the greatest potential to manufacture cheap fertilizer.[30] He urged his fellow congresspeople to regard the issue of Muscle Shoals not merely as a sectional issue but as one of national importance. "The question of preservation of soil fertility and the reclamation of our abandoned farm lands is not a sectional question but a national one that we cannot afford to ignore." He urged his colleagues to not pass up "an opportunity to emancipate the American farmers from this thralldom they have so long endured . . . so they may continue to occupy the soil."[31] In 1924, the House voted to accept the Ford offer. The Senate added amendments, the bill went to conference, and a report returned to the two houses on February 6, 1925, six days before Congress adjourned. Neither house took action. Henry Ford had had enough. He withdrew his offer.[32]

Senator Oscar Underwood of Alabama made a final attempt to secure the site for private industry. He introduced a proposal in December 1924 that gave the president the authority to grant a fifty-year lease of the nitrate plants and power facilities to a private entity for the manufacture of fertilizer. The bill passed the Senate and came to the House in early 1925. President Calvin Coolidge supported the bill, as did the majority of the Alabama delegation, Bankhead included. But support for some sort of public option as favored by Senator Norris was strong in the House, and the bill failed. A group of southern and western congresspeople then passed a joint resolution favoring government operation of Muscle Shoals, but Coolidge killed the bill with a pocket veto in 1928.[33] Most southern Democrats had originally supported private leasing but by the late 1920s saw Norris's plan as the only feasible solution.[34] Chief among the supporters of Norris's plan was Senator James Thomas Heflin of Alabama. Ultimately, the House and the Senate passed the Norris plan. Will Bankhead voted yes.[35] A delegation of southern congresspeople met with President Herbert Hoover to encourage him to sign the bill, to no avail.[36] Hoover vetoed the bill on March 3, 1931. The Muscle Shoals project remained in limbo until the election of Franklin D. Roosevelt gave it renewed life.

The decade of the 1920s was a period of growth for Congressman Will Bankhead. Despite losing on a number of issues, he could take pride in the knowledge that he had fought hard for Alabama's farmers. He had learned when to dig in, when to concede, and how to compromise. In so eloquently stating his party's case on the floor of the House, he proved his value to Democratic leaders. When the Democrats regained the majority in 1932, the polished and genial Will Bankhead was ready to reap the rewards of a decade spent in the trenches.

Will and Florence Bankhead quickly settled into life in Washington, DC, frequently attending cultural events and going for long drives in Rock Creek Park. Will, forty-six years old in 1920, clearly felt like he had won a second lease on life. He adored Florence, privately referring to her as the "prettiest woman in Washington." On her birthday in 1921, he wrote in his diary: "I renew to her on her natal day the pledge of my tender love, loyalty and faith. She deserves it, for she has been a treasure to my life."[37] Although they enjoyed life in the nation's capital, they always looked forward to returning to Jasper. In 1925, Will and Florence built a house in Jasper on land Will had acquired in 1916. The two-story brick Colonial Revival home and its extensive gardens would be a refuge for the couple over the course of Will's political career.

As 1920 dawned, Tallulah, now eighteen years old, was mostly on her own in New York. Father Will provided her with a weekly allowance of fifty dollars and tried (but failed) to enforce a midnight curfew. He also enlisted the help of the Algonquin Hotel's manager in a desperate attempt to keep Tallulah on a short leash. He failed. Without a chaperone, Tallulah gravitated toward older actresses, who served as surrogate guardians. Now on her own, Tallulah reveled in outlandish behavior; always a mimic, she amused her new friends with her impersonations of established stage actors and actresses. She craved attention yet struggled with shyness. In her memoir, Tallulah noted that "I was consumed by a fever to be famous, even infamous." She possessed a "scorching eagerness to be a somebody."[38]

What better place for an ambitious teenager from small-town Alabama to become "a somebody" than New York City in 1920? Postwar New York City was the epicenter of the emerging consumer culture and birthplace of the New Woman. Cities across the country became magnets for young people, especially young women, offering greater employment opportunities as well as a greater degree of social freedom. Dance halls, theaters, and clubs, once considered off-limits for the single woman, offered an escape from adult supervision that was thrilling.[39] An army of shop girls and clerks in New York and elsewhere spent any disposable income in the pursuit of fashion and amusement. New entertainment possibilities transformed traditional social conventions; the practice of a young man "calling on" a young woman at her home with guardians nearby was replaced by the "date." The proliferation of the automobile only enhanced young women's social mobility. This new freedom and sociability was not reserved for America's urban centers but was enjoyed by women on college campuses. One coed at the University of Alabama—in Tallulah's home state—went on dates with fifty-three different men in one year alone.[40] The New Woman was gainfully employed and free from family surveillance, an eager participant in the new consumer culture that celebrated indulgence and pleasure.[41]

The rise of celebrity culture accompanied the expansion of consumer culture, making it easier to become a "somebody." Magazines such as the *Saturday Evening Post* and *Collier's* spent as much or more space on celebrity profiles as they did on features of political or business leaders. And Tallulah was in the thick of it, surrounded not only by her stage and screen idols but also by the men and women responsible for the amplification and dissemination of celebrity culture. She became friendly with Frank Crowninshield, editor of *Vanity Fair*. Impressed by her ebullience and her natural acting chops, "Crownie" took a shine to the young actress and introduced her to important people in the theater industry.[42]

While Tallulah was finding her footing in New York, another young woman from Alabama was turning heads around the city and being heralded as the quintessential New Woman and flapper. Celebrated Montgomery belle Zelda Sayre married novelist F. Scott Fitzgerald in spring 1920. Scott wrote about the flapper, while Zelda embodied her. The couple spent the first year of their marriage in and around New York City. Their drunken exploits became the stuff of legend. They were, as one historian has noted, "the golden couple of the moment . . . young and beautiful, with cash to burn."[43] But it was so much style over substance. The slightly younger Tallulah Bankhead better fit the definition of "modern." Unlike Tallulah, Zelda never achieved the independence that was the true hallmark of the modern woman. Although she acquired more freedom than she could have enjoyed as a married woman in Montgomery, Zelda was ultimately dependent on her husband for her lavish lifestyle. Tallulah Bankhead, on the other hand, was struggling to make her own way.

Tallulah spent a few weeks with a theater company in Massachusetts before returning to New York, where she began work on a new film, *The Trap*, which opened in 1919 to mediocre reviews. Although Will tried to encourage her to pursue more roles in motion pictures, Tallulah's heart was on the stage, and she informed her father, "I am giving up pictures to go on the legitimate stage as that means so much more to me." Ten years would pass before she appeared in another film.

Tallulah's persistence paid off, and she won a speaking part in the touring company of *39 East*, written and directed by prominent playwright Rachel Crothers. Tallulah had impressed Crothers when she had filled in for the lead actress while the play was on the New York stage. Tallulah wrote jubilantly, "I am going to make good with a bang!!! Wait and see. Then you will be proud of your bad little girl with her bad little temper." Following a burst appendix and a prolonged hospital stay, Tallulah prepared for the scheduled eight-month tour of *39 East*. Suddenly fearful that to leave New York would mean the end of her career, she procured a doctor's note stating that she was not yet well enough to travel, a move she later noted was "shockingly unprofessional."[44] She departed for Washington, DC, where she lived with Will and Florence for several months before returning to New York.

Tallulah remained in constant fear of disappointing her family and being forced to return to Alabama. For Tallulah, a life in Alabama meant only one thing: failure. She kept her family at arm's length. At one point, uncle Henry Bankhead, Will's younger brother, was dispatched to check up on his niece in New York City after word reached the family that Tallulah had been fired from a play. "She will not tell me the truth about anything," an exasperated Henry wrote. "I can depend on nothing she says. She seems to resent being asked any questions about her work or prospects." Tallulah lived briefly with Henry and his family on nearby Governors Island. In January 1920, Will, in New York on business, likewise checked in on his daughter, using his political contacts to spark interest in Tallulah. He advised his daughter, "If you can't get what you want take what you can get. Idleness around the hotel is not to be desired." He need not have worried; for the next two years Tallulah found steady employment. She landed her first lead in the play *Everyday*, another Rachel Crothers production, and received strong reviews.[45]

Always eager for intriguing story lines, the press in New York and elsewhere latched onto the story of the young thespian from a prominent southern political family. Her political bloodlines gave her a certain gravitas that the teenager had not yet earned, while her rising stardom lent a touch of glamour to the political Bankheads. The press reveled in her southernness, calling her "the Alabama Beauty," "the blond 'Bama bombshell," and later, the "Diabolical Lady of Dixie." At times, reporters likened Tallulah's extroverted personality and penchant for exhibitionism to the region's sometimes turbulent weather, referring to her as "Alabam's stormiest daughter" and "the cyclone called Tallulah." Tallulah's own relationship with her native region was decidedly ambivalent, if not borderline hostile. As a young woman trying to make her way in the New York theater world, she was desperate to appear worldly and sophisticated. She lived in fear of being called back to tiny Jasper. Certainly her class status and political connections helped smooth her path; financial support from her family allowed her to stay in New York much longer than a girl from a less wealthy family. She was better connected than most actresses just starting out, and, as actor Douglas Fairbanks Jr. later remarked, Tallulah "was very consciously upper class in a world that was drawn mostly from either lower or middle."[46] Much later, when she had established herself on the stage and the threat of a life confined to Alabama was no longer hanging over her head, Tallulah would leverage her southern roots more confidently and strategically. Like her father and grandfather, she referred to herself on occasion as "a hillbilly" and played up her

Figure 8.2. Tallulah Bankhead, age twenty-one, in 1923. Courtesy of the Alabama Department of Archives and History.

rural roots and ancestral ties to the Confederacy for effect.[47]

Tallulah fell in love for the first time while in New York, falling for twenty-five-year-old Napier Alington, a charming British aristocrat. He was not her first affair, however; that distinction belonged to British Norwegian actress Eva Le Gallienne, who was several years older than Tallulah. According to one biographer, Tallulah had affairs with women throughout the course of her life.[48]

Five years after arriving in New York, Tallulah was working steadily and making a name for herself in the theater world. The future looked promising. Thanks to Frank Crowninshield, word of her talent reached the theater community in London, and in late 1922, she received a telegram offering her the lead in *The Dancers*, a new play by one of the most prominent actors and theater managers in England, Sir Gerald du Maurier. Tallulah hastened to arrange travel. A second telegram soon followed. Du Maurier had had a change of heart and had secured a more established actress for the role. Undeterred, Tallulah fired back a cable: "I'M COMING ANYWAY." And so she did. In January 1923, Tallulah Bankhead, twenty years old, set sail for London, where she would establish herself as one of the brightest stars of the stage. Although she visited the States later in the decade, Tallulah Bankhead would not return to live in the United States until 1931.[49]

During the 1920s, Eugenia and Tallulah entered adulthood. But truthfully, Will's daughters had been on their own since they were ages eleven and ten, respectively. Their grandfather and grandmother, along with Aunt Marie, had been the most constant adult presence in their lives. Marie was, in 1920, grieving the sudden death of husband Tom, which had so soon followed the death of father John Hollis. The girls' father had a new wife and an all-consuming political career. The girls truly were on their own. Grandmother Tallulah confirmed as much in a letter to daughter Marie. Writing while on a visit to Will and Florence in Washington in 1921, Tallulah lamented the absence of Will's daughters. She wished they could live "at home," but she confided that "there is no love for them here but it can't be helped." She did not elaborate.[50] Perhaps there was tension with their new stepmother. Will indicated as much in a letter to the younger Tallulah in 1919 in which he complained that Eugenia and Florence "have had another row" but that he hoped "it will be patched up soon. Old

Daddy really gets the worst of these affairs."[51] By 1922 Grandmother Tallulah was also gone.

Eldest daughter Eugenia spent the new decade chasing romantic fulfillment. In August 1920, Eugenia, who often went by the name Jeanne and was described by the *Washington Post* as "one of the popular young members of the congressional circle in Washington," married Morton Michael Hoyt following a year-long engagement. Hoyt was the son of the late Henry M. Hoyt, who served as President William Howard Taft's solicitor general. The young couple resided first in New York City. Theirs was a tumultuous relationship that would end in divorce in 1927. By 1932, Eugenia had married and divorced five more times; three of those marriages and divorces were to Hoyt. Records of their 1928 divorce in Reno, Nevada, cite Eugenia's "extreme cruelty and extravagance" as the cause of the marital discord. Hoyt specifically charged that "Eugenia gambled and would not pay her debts." In December 1929 Eugenia married Wilson Lawson Butt, a football star at the University of Nevada who also worked as a soda jerk. This marriage was annulled when it was discovered that Butt's divorce from his first wife was not final. Her fifth marriage was to Howard Lee, an aviator and sportsman from Dallas. She married Lee in July 1930 and divorced him in August 1930. Marriage number six was to Edward Ennis White, a stockbroker described as "the scion of a socially prominent New York family." They married in June 1931; the ink on their marriage license was barely dry before they divorced three months later, in September.[52] Eugenia, who had been a sickly child, continued to face health troubles. Childhood problems with her eyesight returned, and she underwent an operation in early 1921. As Will noted in his diary, "The dear child has been grievously afflicted with her eyes."[53] Like her younger sister, Eugenia eventually moved to Europe, where she would remain well into the next decade.

How does one attempt to explain such a peripatetic personal life? Eugenia declared that when it came to marriage, she was simply "an incurable optimist."[54] That is certainly one way to look at it. Another was that she sought the male attention and security that she failed to receive as a young girl. Despite the loving attention of her grandparents and aunts, what Eugenia and Tallulah never received was adequate, consistent attention from their father, and nothing could take the place of their deceased mother. That both women would spend their lives seeking security and attention was the sad consequence of their even sadder early circumstances.

With the death of his father, John H. Bankhead Jr. assumed the role of family patriarch. John Jr. maintained his law practice and oversaw the family assets. He remained active in state politics, participating in state Democratic Party

conventions and serving as chairman of the state convention in 1922.[55] As he had with his father, John continued to advise brother Will, acting as his unofficial eyes and ears in the district. Despite their physical distance, the brothers remained close, visiting each other whenever their schedules permitted. Will confided to his diary, "I am always delighted in my heart when I can be with John. He is a remarkable man in many respects. Sound in his judgment, logical in his deductions, fair in his conclusions. He has won great success at the bar, and is regarded as one of the very best lawyers in Alabama, which he undoubtedly is. He has been to me a wonderful brother—just, helpful, tolerant and loving! I owe much gratitude for his unfailing affection."[56]

John also stepped in to advise his newly widowed sister, Marie. On April 1, 1920, only a week after Tom's death, the board of trustees of the Alabama Department of Archives and History elected Marie as its director. She was fifty years old and only the second woman in state history to run a state agency. She would serve as the director for the next thirty-five years, stepping down in 1955 at the age of eighty-five.[57] The position provided her with an all-too-crucial salary—"a meal ticket," as she described it to John Jr., himself a member of the department's board of trustees—but Marie would continue to struggle financially throughout her life, forcing her to reach out to family members for support. John stepped in often to help, assuming a debt of almost $1,300 in 1920. Exasperated, he reminded her that his ability to assist her financially had limits and strongly urged her to sell some of the land she had inherited from their father. "Please do not lead the banks to understand that I am going to become endorser on the balance of your notes as they fall due," he cautioned.[58]

Despite her grief, or perhaps because of it, Marie buried herself in her club work and her new job. She was constantly on the road, procuring collections of letters hidden for years in old attic trunks, or advising club women interested in creating a local library. She sold part of Tom's personal library—some five thousand items—to the state for $500. She attended seminars dedicated to the proper care and handling of archival material. She proudly reported to the archive's board of trustees that thirteen states had adopted the "Alabama Model" for state archive creation.[59]

Under her direction, the archive's collections continued to grow. People donated specimens for the natural history exhibits, heirlooms for the museum, oil paintings for the portrait collection, and letters and diaries for the original manu-

Figure 8.4. Marie Bankhead Owen, 1920. Courtesy of the Alabama Department of Archives and History.

script holdings; and valuable military records were found quite by accident under the state capitol, "where the boxes containing them had been enclosed and bricked up and only discovered when a portion of the floor collapsed." Added to these was the regular receipt of documents from state agencies that needed to be cataloged and housed. This embarrassment of riches presented Marie with an enormous problem: where to store it all? Many collections remained unprocessed and inaccessible to researchers and to the staff because of the lack of space. "Precious relics" that might otherwise have been displayed were stuffed into closets and cabinets throughout the Capitol building. Multiple years' worth of newspapers sat "arranged in piles in the basement, which is already in a very overcrowded condition," because they lacked a proper storage facility. The museum's collection of birds and "small fur animals" was stored at the nearby White House of the Confederacy; when the Alabama Federation of Women's Clubs needed more space for its headquarters, this collection, along with archival documents, was moved to the vestibule of the recently purchased Adams Street Baptist Church, while yet more records were stored in a neighboring frame house. Security for these materials was nonexistent. Marie received reports of "small boys [climbing] in the windows at night to prowl through the collections housed there." She also noted with alarm that "great quantities of burnt matches were found strewn about the floor," an obvious fire hazard. With collections and historical objects spread throughout the state capitol and several downtown Montgomery buildings, the need for a dedicated archival and museum space was critical. The Alabama Memorial Commission had initiated a campaign for the creation of a World War Memorial Building to be constructed near the state capitol that would ultimately serve as a permanent home for the archives. The land had been acquired, but nowhere near the half-million dollars necessary to build the structure had been raised. The lack of space remained Marie's biggest challenge throughout the decade.[60]

In addition to attending to her duties related to the Department of Archives and History, Marie, in her capacity as director, also served on the Workmen's Compensation Bureau as the workmen's compensation commissioner, a position for which she received no additional pay. This position required a good deal of record keeping, correspondence, and reporting. In 1920 alone, 7,200 accidents were reported. She was relieved of those duties in 1922 when the legislature transferred the administration of the workmen's compensation law to a different state agency. Incredibly, despite this mountain of work, Marie managed to finish Tom Owen's multivolume *History of Alabama and Dictionary of Alabama Biography*, which she published in 1921.[61]

Like many other Americans in the 1920s, John H. Bankhead Jr., hearing of the fabulous profits being made in Florida real estate, became seduced by the prospect of sudden wealth and the possibility of retiring at a relatively early age. The usually conservative businessman and lawyer sold over half his interest in the mines and hurried off to Palm Beach in February 1925. There he met up with his nephew Thomas Owen Jr., who was selling lots for a local real estate firm. Buying several lots in West Palm Beach from young Owen, who realized a "nice commission," Bankhead quickly resold his acreage, doubling his money in the transaction. One of the more fortunate speculators, Bankhead made several thousand dollars within a few weeks and returned to Alabama.[62] Marie Bankhead Owen, hoping to improve her financial situation, mortgaged her house in Montgomery, sold a farm, took a leave from her position at the archives, and hastened to Palm Beach to join her son. Operating on Will's capital as well as her own, she bought and sold hundreds of lots within a few weeks. John Jr., looking to duplicate his earlier success, commissioned his sister to invest $32,000 (or nearly $500,000 in 2020) in a development near Palm Beach. The Bankheads' good fortune eventually ran out. The real estate bubble burst early in 1926. Will lost over $8,000; John Jr. recouped a few thousand dollars on his last gamble; Marie lost almost everything she had invested.[63] She returned to her position as director of the archives; by the end of the decade, Tom Jr. had returned from Florida and was working as Marie's assistant at the state archives.[64]

John Hollis's death in 1920 prompted questions over whether John Jr. would enter the race to complete his father's term. Although encouraged by the support of his friends and associates, John worried that by entering the political ring he might hurt Will's prospects.[65] After much thought, he decided against running; Representative James Thomas Heflin won nomination for Bankhead's seat in the Senate. John Jr. had not completely ruled out a run for office, however. He saw his chance when senator and longtime Bankhead family friend Oscar Underwood announced his retirement, putting his seat up for grabs in 1926.

Economically, the state was in better shape in the 1920s than it had been in previous decades, and it enjoyed relatively responsible and efficient state leadership. But the war and accompanying rise of cultural issues dramatically shifted the political terrain. As one historian has observed, "the war had accelerated forces of bigotry, nativism, and exclusion."[66] The prohibition amendment and the women's suffrage amendment had both been added to the US Constitution, and the revived Ku Klux Klan had become a powerful political actor in Alabama public life. The Klan that came of political age in the 1920s looked quite different from its Reconstruction-era predecessor. Although physical terror remained an important element, the second Klan (as it has come to be known) took on issues such as prohibition enforcement, the defense of Protestant cultural values and traditional gender roles for women, and immigration restriction, in addition to its founding purpose of maintaining white supremacy. The Red Scare of 1919–20 ratcheted up citizens' concerns about radicalism, which they identified with immigrants. "Taken all together," observes one historian, "the resentments represented a potent political force waiting for an organizer."[67] The Klan would play this role. In Alabama the Klan also had an anticorporation slant; for many working-class Alabamians, it seemed the only effective organization working against the corporations and industrialists who controlled much of the political life in the state. By 1924, the Klan had eighteen thousand members in Birmingham alone. In 1925, the organization elected its entire slate to the city commission. By mid-decade, the hooded organization boasted an estimated ninety-five thousand members across the state.[68]

No one quite knew what to make of this political upstart, and at least initially, the state's entrenched political leadership was not overly concerned about either the organization's violence or its political potential. Men like Senator Oscar Underwood and publisher Victor Hansen (of the *Birmingham News*, the *Birmingham Ledger*, and the *Montgomery Advertiser*) welcomed the Klan. They equated the 1920s Klan with the Klan of their fathers, which had stood for white supremacy and had helped bring an end to the dreaded Radical Reconstruction. But the 1920s Klan saw itself as an agent of change, a political mouthpiece for those white Alabamians who felt ignored by the entrenched planter and industrialist elite.

The rising influence of the Klan in Alabama politics played an important role in Oscar Underwood's decision to not run for another term as US senator. His resignation signaled a turning point in state politics. Underwood had put himself forward as a presidential candidate in 1924 and tried to get a strong anti-Klan statement into the Democratic Party platform. He had little support beyond his home state because of his opposition to both the Klan and to prohibition. He succeeded in deadlocking the convention; after ten days and 103 votes, the convention nominated compromise candidate John W. Davis of West Virginia. The defeat had a decisive impact on Underwood's political future. Increasingly out of step with Alabama voters, he quietly left the political stage.[69]

The Klan was at the peak of its influence in 1926, a year in which both the governorship and a seat in the Senate were at stake.[70] And so it was in this chaotic atmosphere that John Jr. decided to enter the contest for US Senate. Also seeking the Democratic Party's nomination was former governor Thomas E. Kilby, a business progressive and prohibition supporter. During his time in office, Kilby decreased the state's bonded indebtedness, failed to end the convict lease but succeeded in improving the conditions of convict labor camps, expanded mental health services, created the Child Welfare Department, and increased spending on education.[71] Rounding out the field was L. Breckenridge "L. B." Musgrove, a Jasper coal operator who, although at one time a family friend, was now a Bankhead opponent; James J. Mayfield, a former state supreme court justice; and Hugo L. Black, a brilliant but little-known attorney and police judge from Birmingham. The *Birmingham News* threw its support behind Bankhead, characterizing his platform as "conservative . . . and yet progressive, in that it is forward looking without radicalism."[72] John Jr. started his campaign with a speaking tour in the southeastern part of the state. He wrote to Will in January 1926 that "nearly everybody seems to recognize that I am in the lead.[73] Always measured, never impetuous, John hoped to avoid the Klan issue.

Hugo Black was the dark horse in the race. Born into relatively humble circumstances in Clay County in east central Alabama in 1886, he attended Ashland College (a combination high school and junior college) and briefly attended Birmingham Medical College before enrolling in the law school at the University of Alabama. After trying his hand at a solo practice in Ashland, Black headed to Birmingham in 1907. In his first verdict, he won a $150 judgment for an African American plaintiff who, as a convict, had been leased to a steel company. The plaintiff, Willie Morris, charged that the company forced him to work twenty-two days beyond his prison sentence. Black was hired to represent a carpenters' union and played a minor legal role for the United Mine Workers union in 1908. In 1911, the twenty-five-year-old Black was appointed judge of the police court at an annual salary of $1,500. According to his biographer, "From his bench each morning, Judge Black viewed a motley collection of drunks, petty thieves, crapshooters, dope peddlers, loafers, prostitutes, and those who the night before had been hot-tempered or careless with fists, razors, and switchblades. Minor offenders were the clientele of police court, where the dregs of a city famed for violence got their reprimands and sentences."[74] In 1914, he was elected Jefferson County solicitor; one of his first acts as solicitor was to dismiss the cases of five hundred offenders who, he declared, were victims of the prison fee system. In 1915, the Jefferson County grand jury investigated police brutality in Bessemer at Black's instigation.[75] Although he was exempt from conscription by the time the United States entered the war in 1917, already being thirty-one years old, Black resigned his post as county solicitor and volunteered for the US Army. He never saw action overseas. He returned to private practice following the war, representing workers injured on the job. He received national attention for defending accused murderer Edwin R. Stephenson. Stephenson was accused of murdering James E. Coyle, a Catholic priest. The prosecution alleged that Stephenson killed Coyle because the priest had performed a marriage ceremony between Stephenson's eighteen-year-old daughter Ruth and Pedro Gussman, a middle-aged Puerto Rican. In his defense of Stephenson, Black portrayed Gussman as African American, playing to the racial fears of the white male jury. Black was helped by the fact that the jury foreman was a member of the Klan. Part of Black's fee for defending Stephenson was paid for by the Klan. Stephenson was acquitted.[76]

Black campaigned for the nomination as a political outsider. He attacked the other candidates' wealth, history of officeholding, and ties to corporations, a charge that fell heavily on John Jr. Bankhead complained to brother Will about Black's "demagogic appeal against corporations" and surmised that Black was "the man I will finally have to deal with."[77] The Klan issue was critical during the campaign. Hugo Black had joined the Klan in 1923 but resigned in 1925.[78] Although he was no longer a member, Black aggressively courted Klan support. His anticorporation stance and advocacy on behalf of organized labor was attractive to a certain segment of Klan members. He was also a staunch prohibitionist and a devout Baptist.[79] Hustling for votes, Black campaigned at every single Klan outpost in the state, 148 "klaverns" in all.[80]

The Klan issue worried Will. He begged John Jr. to denounce the organization, which by late spring had thrown its support to Black. John Jr. hoped to avoid the issue. "It's a two-edge sword, and for present, I am going to let it rest," he wrote to his brother regarding the Klan.[81] Black remained on the offensive, attacking Bankhead's long association with the Alabama Power Company and charging (incorrectly) that John Jr. and Will had opposed Ford's offer to develop Muscle Shoals.[82] Black received broad support from Baptist and Methodist clergy for his continued prohibitionist stance.

John H. Bankhead Jr. ran a campaign typical of a political insider and conventional conservative Democrat, hoping that his connections with the establishment could help him weather the grassroots maelstrom. He touted his business experience, his positive relations with labor, and his 1922 split with Alabama Power Company. He promised to continue his father's efforts to improve roads and waterways. He took special care to emphasize his interest in the state's farmers, advocating the creation of a national cooperative to oversee the buying and selling of cotton. The cooperative would be invested with the power to withhold cotton from the market until a good price could be realized.[83] Many of John's speeches were drafted by brother Will; just as John often provided sound political advice, so did Will lend his brother his flair for the dramatic.[84] But Black outworked all other candidates combined. According to one historian, "Six months before the primary, [Black] had visited fifty-seven counties, making multiple speeches daily."[85]

Drawing on a coalition that included organized labor, small farmers, and the Ku Klux Klan, Black won an upset victory in the August 1926 primary.[86] Will noted that John "was up against an impossible situation with three conservative candidates running against one radical and Ku Klux [Black]."[87] Also victorious in 1926 was gubernatorial candidate Bibb Graves, a political progressive and supporter of former governor B. B. Comer. Like Black, Graves had joined the Klan and benefited greatly from its electoral support. He ran on a strong labor platform, pledging to abolish the convict lease, improve public services, lengthen the school year to seven months, and increase funding for public schools.[88] Although a substantial number of people voted for either Graves or Black but not for both, it's difficult to determine the power of any single group (such as the Klan or supporters of prohibition) in this election cycle. What can be said, though, is that for the time being, the political trend in Alabama posed a distinct challenge to traditional conservative leadership and John H. Bankhead Jr.'s political future.[89]

Following his defeat, John returned to his law practice. In 1927, he sold his remaining interest in the family coal mines to a Birmingham syndicate for over $200,000 (nearly $2.8 million in today's dollars).[90] He remained interested in public affairs and kept a keen eye on political developments. Chief among them was the fate of the Klan. The organization became increasingly violent in 1926 and 1927, going on a flogging spree and committing outrageous acts of violence. Many of the victims were white women accused of violating local mores.[91] The state attorney general's office received reports of seventy cases of mob violence in the course of a matter of days. The attorney general, a Klan member, resigned publicly from the organization and set out to prosecute the floggers.[92] The new governor, Bibb Graves, declined to denounce the organization. As a result of the spike in vigilante violence and growing protests against the Klan, membership in the organization began to dwindle, from a total of nearly ninety-five thousand members in 1926 to just ten thousand by the end of 1927.[93] Leading the fight against the Klan was Grover C. Hall, editor of the *Montgomery Advertiser*. A close friend of H. L. Mencken, Hall was awarded the Pulitzer Prize for Editorial Writing in 1928 for his columns against the hooded order. Sensing an opportunity and a turning of the political tide, John Jr. attacked the organization in a widely publicized letter to the *Birmingham News*. He identified those candidates who had benefited from Klan support in the 1926 elections, only a few of whom had repudiated it in light of its recent actions. He demanded that the organization disband.[94]

With the Klan in decline, John H. Bankhead Jr.'s electoral prospects brightened considerably. His political fortunes became tied to the 1928 presidential election. The leading contender for the Democratic Party's nomination was New York governor Alfred E. Smith. Smith had unsuccessfully sought the party's nomination in 1924. He was an Irish Catholic and a foe of prohibition, and his potential candidacy was anathema to southern Democrats. Protestant leaders across the region expressed fear that Smith would take orders from the Pope. Other opponents were convinced that the New York governor possessed little knowledge or understanding of the problems of the farmer. Still others vowed to oppose him because he favored repeal of the Eighteenth Amendment, prohibition. Southern Democrats found themselves in a bind: the Democratic Party had been the instrument through which they had defended white supremacy. Would religious and cultural concerns trump race in 1928? Would white southern voters abandon the Democratic candidate and support the hated Republicans?

Will Bankhead and the rest of the state's delegation in the House of Representatives opposed Smith's nomination but declared that they would support him if he was nominated. The state's US senators—Hugo L. Black and James Thomas Heflin—gave no such assurances. John H. Bankhead Jr., a member of the State Democratic Executive Committee, declared his opposition to Smith's candidacy; however, should the party nominate Smith, the elder Bankhead brother would support him. He urged party unity.

At the Democratic Party's national convention in Houston in late June, no real strategy emerged for fighting Smith's candidacy. The Alabama delegation lamely pledged its support to various favorite sons. With no organized opposition, Smith easily won nomination on the first ballot. For many white southerners, however, the fight against Smith and what he represented had only just begun. Smith's candidacy was of special concern to Will. Any split among Democrats posed a serious threat to his reelection in the Tenth District because of the great number of Republicans living there. Writing to brother John, Will confessed: "I am going to have trouble if Smith is nominated[.] [A]ltho I believe I can win in the District, a vigorous Republican opponent would require a very energetic and possibly an expensive campaign which of course I want to avoid." Will asked John to talk to some prominent Republicans in the area to see whether he could convince them to not put up a candidate for Congress in 1928. "In the event they are not willing to do that," he added, "see if they are not willing to nominate some weak man who would not be able to make an intelligent campaign." John Jr. did as his brother asked, reminding Republicans in the Tenth District of Will's generous patronage, and reminding them that Will had "never known a Republican from a Democrat in looking after their interests."[95] The Republicans refused to be played for suckers. Witnessing division within the Democratic ranks, the Republicans smelled real opportunity for victory and nominated a candidate to challenge Will.

The anti-Smith forces in Alabama were led by Senator Heflin. Nicknamed "Cotton Tom" for his advocacy on behalf of cotton farmers, Heflin was one of the more colorful politicians of that or any time. Elected to Congress in 1904, Heflin served eight terms in the House and won election to the US Senate in 1920, upon the death of John Hollis Bankhead. Heflin was not a terribly effective legislator. He supported the rights of organized labor, worked hard for the development of the Muscle Shoals property, and was a staunch prohibitionist. He was best known for his strident anti-Catholicism and virulent white supremacy. Cotton Tom's passionate speeches on the floor of the Senate delighted gallery crowds only slightly more than did his eccentric style of dress. The *New York Times* gleefully described his typical outfit, which included "a cream-colored double-breasted waistcoat, a Byronic cravat and a long coat with flowing skirts that [resembled] a combination of a morning coat, an old-fashioned Prince Albert, and a dressing gown."[96] He gladly welcomed the rise and support of the Ku Klux Klan, wholeheartedly embracing the organization's racism, anti-Catholicism, and support for prohibition.

In the presidential election of 1928, Heflin's fellow recipients of Klan support, US senator Hugo L. Black and Governor Bibb Graves, announced that they would support Smith but would not campaign for him. Heflin would have none of it and embarked on a full-fledged political revolt. Along with Birmingham attorney Hugh A. Locke, Heflin campaigned to swing the state to Republican nominee Herbert Hoover.[97] Joining Heflin in denouncing Smith was the Klan, the Anti-Saloon League, and the Women's Christian Temperance Union.[98] Heflin saw papal conspiracies everywhere. Writing to the mayor of Montgomery, Heflin tried to convince him that "the Al Smith bunch were smuggling Roman Catholics in from foreign countries and increasing the Catholic population in certain states until they had become strong enough to dominate the party and control those states."[99] Following the nomination of Al Smith, Heflin declared that Jesuit hit men, with "murder in their hearts and mean looks on their faces," planned to assassinate him.[100]

Alarmed by Heflin's campaign against the Democratic Party's presidential candidate, the state's Democratic organization countered with a strong campaign of its own, staging rallies and meetings throughout the state. John and Will Bankhead, while not entirely comfortable with Smith's Catholicism, argued that he was a superior candidate to Hoover and appealed to party loyalty. Sister Marie went one step further, creating flyers that declared Hoover a supporter of racial equality. Will Bankhead actively stumped for Smith. One friend, concerned that Will's support for Smith would cost him votes, cautioned, "Bill, for God's sake, don't make any more speeches for the party. Let Al Smith tote his own skillet."[101] Will focused on the theme of party loyalty. At one stop, he was egged by members of the Klan. Turning to the organizers of the event, the always-gracious Bankhead remarked, "Sir—I have been treated discourteously," before continuing on with his speech.[102] Sidelined by illness, John H. Bankhead Jr. kept a low profile during the campaign. He spent much of the year recovering from a variety of upper-respiratory ailments, finally receiving treatment at the Mayo Clinic.[103]

Smith's Catholicism, ties to Tammany Hall, and opposition to prohibition provided ammunition for those fighting him in Alabama. But the strongest weapon against Smith was the charge that he would undermine white supremacy. The use of racial fear to oppose a Democratic candidate was fairly novel, as the Democratic Party had long ago established itself as the party of white supremacy. Calling the New York governor a "Negro Bootlicker," anti-Smith forces charged that Smith favored interracial marriage; had appointed African Americans to government jobs in New York, giving them supervisory power over white female employees; and was actively seeking support from black voters. Sometimes anti-Smith speakers combined concerns about race with concerns about Smith's opposition to prohibition.[104] The *Alabama Christian Advocate* speculated breathlessly on the chaos that would ensue were prohibition repealed: "There are ten million Negroes living in the South. To give these ten million Negroes free access to liquor—to place this passion-inflamer in the hands of the child race not far removed from their savage haunts in the jungles of Africa— would be to court tragedy unspeakable."[105] Speaking in the city of Dothan in October, Heflin painted Smith as the harbinger of a racial apocalypse, claiming that "he is in favor of appointing negroes to office where they will be in authority over white people" and declaring that "there are now dance halls in New York City . . . where every night negro men dance with white women and white men dance with negro women."[106] Democratic loyalists struck back, reminding white Democrats of the tragedy of Reconstruction, when carpetbaggers invaded the South and freedmen served in the legislature. A vote for Herbert Hoover, they cried, meant a return to black domination.

The turnout for the 1928 presidential election was one of the largest in Alabama history, with some 250,000 of 300,000 eligible voters coming out to cast their ballots. Ultimately, party loyalty and the Democrats' history of protecting white supremacy trumped religious bigotry and fear of revocation of the Eighteenth Amendment, but just barely. Al Smith carried Alabama by a mere seven thousand votes, the margin of victory coming in the Black Belt counties with their heavily Democratic majorities. Still, roughly one hundred thousand Alabama Democrats had voted for Herbert Hoover.[107] For many, it was their first time supporting a Republican. Cotton Tom Heflin and the Klan had failed in their bid to disrupt the election. Never again would the Klan wield significant political influence in the state. In the Tenth District, Will Bankhead won his seventh term, besting his Republican opponent 15,133–10,862.[108]

Following the presidential election, John and Will Bankhead looked toward the future and John's next shot at the Senate. Confident in the knowledge that Senator Heflin would pay a political price for abandoning the Democratic Party in the 1928 presidential election, John H. Bankhead Jr. officially announced his intention to challenge Heflin in the 1930 Democratic primary.[109] John retired from the practice of law and severed all ties to clients in order to focus on the campaign.[110] Not everyone was thrilled with this announcement. Congressman John McDuffie believed that John Jr.'s early declaration was a mistake. Writing to one confidant, McDuffie noted, "Frankly and confidentially, he has hurt himself a great deal by rushing out and taking the front of the stage before more consultations with some of those who bore the brunt of our last National campaign. Please do not misunderstand me. I shall give him my hearty support, and especially so if no other candidate announces. Personally I believe his brother Will can make a better race than he can, but of course Will will not give up his present position." McDuffie also acknowledged that some in the state were suffering from something akin to "Bankhead fatigue": "a good many people . . . suggest that the State has been good to the Bankhead family and that one Bankhead is now in Congress, and his sister is holding a State job."[111] With so many Alabama citizens hurting as the economy tanked, would they tolerate yet another Bankhead in public office?

Whether Senator Heflin would even be allowed to participate in the 1930 Democratic primary was up for debate. The bruising 1928 election and defection of prominent Democrats like Heflin left the political situation within the Alabama Democratic Party muddled. Party loyalty in the South was a serious matter; what was to be done with those officeholders and voters who had bolted the party in 1928? Will and John Bankhead counseled amnesty, as it was in their political interests to be magnanimous toward the bolters. Despite the Bankheads' efforts in 1915 to create a congressional district for Will that would simultaneously dilute Republican strength across several congressional districts, the fact remained that a tradition of Republicanism stubbornly persisted in that part of the state. If treated too harshly for abandoning Smith for Hoover in 1928, anti-Smith Democrats might make common cause with these Republicans, which could spell trouble for Will. Writing to fellow congressman Miles Allgood of the Fifth District, Will said that barring Heflin and other Democratic bolters was a bad idea. "It would be especially hazardous in your District and mine in the next general election . . . to have a divided party." Allgood concurred, and he urged Will to have John Jr. use his influence in state politics to work against a purge.[112] As for John, who had already announced his intention to challenge Heflin for his Senate seat in 1930, it would be much better to fight Heflin within the Democratic primary. Congressman George Huddleston agreed. "If [Heflin] can't be beaten in a primary in which Republicans can't take part," Huddleston argued, "he certainly can't be beaten in a general election with all the

Republicans voting for him."[113] Senator Black reminded the State Democratic Executive Committee that supporters of the Populists in the 1890s had not been driven from the Democratic Party. Although Heflin had not voted in the 1928 presidential election, he had publicly disavowed the Democratic candidate.[114] For his part, Will Bankhead wrote to fellow congresspeople and members of the Democratic State Executive Committee that it was best to let bygones be bygones. He also called on the chairman of the National Democratic Executive Committee to put pressure on his state counterpart, again making the case that barring voters who had supported Hoover would put those running in 1930 in political jeopardy.[115]

In December 1929, the forty-eight-member State Democratic Executive Committee voted 27–21 to allow Democratic voters to participate in the 1930 Democratic primary without any repercussions; however, candidates for state, district, federal, or circuit offices who "either voted a Republican presidential ticket in November 1928 or openly and publicly opposed the election of the Democratic nominees" would be barred. Senator Heflin could not run for reelection as a Democrat in 1930. The *Birmingham News* and *Montgomery Advertiser* applauded the party's decision, calling it a victory for party unity. "Year-round and life-round," the Birmingham paper observed, "party fidelity marks the breed that has saved the South and this commonwealth more than once from domination by the enemy." Others, such as the *Tuscaloosa News*, were more direct: in excluding Heflin from running for reelection in 1930 as a Democrat, "the party washes its hands of a man whose rewards from the party have far outweighed his services to it." The *Dothan Eagle* predicted that the decision meant the end of Heflin's political career, and that "after the primary of next August the patient people of this State will be pestered by him no more."[116] Heflin called his dismissal from the party "punitive, vindictive, inexcusable and indefensible." He claimed that the committee "got some of the members drunk in order to influence them," while other committee members had been bought off.[117] After failing to secure a court injunction against the ruling, Heflin and Locke declared themselves candidates for the US Senate and governor, respectively, under the banner of "Jeffersonian Democrats."[118]

The year 1930 was shaping up to be a historic election year in the state. John H. Bankhead Jr. had declared his intention to challenge Senator Heflin in the Democratic Party primary. With Heflin effectively barred from the primary, the political road appeared relatively smooth for John. But even the casual observer knew that Heflin was not going to go quietly.

9

Senator from Alabama

With Senator James Thomas Heflin barred from participating in the 1930 Democratic primary, the path to a seat in the US Senate seemed clear for John H. Bankhead Jr. But no sooner had the state party read Heflin out of the primary than Representative Lister Hill, a popular young congressman from Montgomery, threw a monkey wrench into John Jr.'s plans. Hugo L. Black's dark-horse victory in 1926 had fueled Hill's ambition.[1] Hill let it be known in January 1930 that he might want to make the race for Senate. Many of Hill's advisers considered the race against Bankhead a toss-up.[2] Hill's father, a Montgomery physician, queried his colleagues around the state regarding Lister's chances. Most replied that Hill had a fifty-fifty chance against Bankhead, although none of them indicated any strong opposition to Bankhead. Hill's chances were based more on a lack of enthusiasm for the other candidate.[3] Congressman John McDuffie preferred Bankhead over Hill, "not as a man[,] because I am very fond of Lister, but I believe as between the two [Bankhead] would more quickly stand up and be counted in the face of danger."[4] Hill's prospective candidacy worried the Bankheads. The congressman was popular and wealthy. The Bankheads did what they could to discourage Hill, using their influence to delay the confirmation of Hill's uncle to a federal judgeship to demonstrate their political power.[5] Hill ultimately decided against making the race.

With Hill out of the race, John Jr. once again thought he would run unopposed in the primary. Again, he was wrong. Frederick I. Thompson, a wealthy Mobile newspaper publisher, threw his hat into the ring. Bankhead sought the assistance of Congressman McDuffie for help in discrediting Thompson; he was looking for "anything that can help put a cloud on that bird."[6] McDuffie encouraged Bankhead to keep the heat on Thompson and to "puncture his pompous hide."[7] Thompson echoed Hugo Black's attacks on Bankhead during the 1926 campaign and painted Bankhead as a corporate tool, citing his past association with Alabama Power and declaring that he had opposed government development of the Muscle Shoals project. Alabama Power had garnered a lot of negative publicity as a result of a congressional investigation of utilities undertaken by Senator Black in 1929. The committee's report, made public in early 1930, mentioned Bankhead among the prominent attorneys for the company. Bankhead remarked to Will that it was "nasty" of Black to identify him in that way.[8] Bankhead's platform called for a revision of the tariff, continued development of the federal road system, and several measures to aid the state's farmers.[9] He did not shy away from attacking Thompson, calling him a "master fuss maker and creator of discord."[10] Black remained relatively quiet until very late in the primary campaign, when he urged party loyalty, effectively supporting neither Thompson nor Bankhead, but signaling to Heflin supporters that they should participate in the Democratic primary and forgo a wasted vote for Heflin.

John H. Bankhead Jr. bested Thompson by a sizable majority, although the number of voters participating in the US Senate primary was 25 percent smaller than those voting for governor.[11] Bankhead now turned to face Heflin in the November general election. Would the coalition of disgruntled Democrats that had rejected Al Smith two years earlier be sufficient to propel Heflin to victory? For his part, Heflin was excited by the prospect of taking on the scion of one of the state's most illustrious political families. "For God's sake, let me in there with old John," Heflin cried. "Why, John hasn't got any more chance to go to the United States Senate than a mouse-colored mule has to operate an airplane. You can bet I'll feast on his bones in November."[12] Heflin's supporters urged on his worst political instincts, confirming his anti-Catholic paranoia by claiming that "the Rum Tammany Rascob alcoholic bunch . . . will steal the election" and by declaring the election "a fundamental fight of Romanism vs. Americanism."[13] Although Heflin's virulent anti-Catholicism and staunch support for prohibition had convinced many Democratic voters in the state to turn against New York governor and prohibition opponent Al Smith in 1928, Heflin's ravings were less effective against the Methodist Bankhead.[14] More effective and closer to home were Heflin's criticisms of Bankhead as an opponent of government control of Muscle Shoals and as a tool of the Alabama Power Company.[15] Heflin got a boost when the state Republican Party, which had gained strength as a result of the Democratic Party schism during the 1928 election, decided against nominating a candidate of its own. Alabama Republicans urged their voters to support Heflin. The *New York Times* estimated that this endorsement was worth about fifty thousand to sixty thousand votes.[16] Republican support for Heflin potentially could cause trouble for John H. Bankhead Jr.

As Election Day drew closer, tensions between the candidates grew more intense. Bankhead, preferring to discuss the issues, bristled at Heflin's attacks on his character. But he gave as good as he got. In a radio address on the eve of the election—indeed, his final speech in the campaign—Bankhead addressed what he referred to as Heflin's "appeal to ignorance and prejudice." He declared that Heflin and his supporters "stopped at nothing short of physical murder" in their efforts to undermine and defeat the Democratic Party nominees. Bankhead surmised that Heflin was mentally ill and prone to paranoia and delusions of grandeur, his "crazy imaginations" emanating from "feverish and scrambled brain cells." Heflin possessed a "constant fear of being poisoned or otherwise injured," Bankhead charged, and was in the habit of carrying a pistol for protection. Bankhead likened Heflin's infirmities to those of a mentally ill woman confined to the state mental hospital in Tuscaloosa. This patient "imagined she was Queen Victoria. To please her crazy whims, the authorities built a throne for her in the women's sitting room. Crazy ladies in waiting thought she was Queen Victoria. She has passed on, and her throne is empty. Move the throne to the men's sitting room and Heflin is eligible to ascend it." He declared: "I brand Heflin as a character assassin, a creature more detestable and despicable than a man-killer. The only extenuating circumstance is the unfortunate state of his mind. It is impossible to doubt that he is a crazy man. . . . It is impossible for Heflin to be mean and vicious enough to manufacture [these lies] with a cool brain. . . . His mind is wobbly, the people of Alabama will not send to the United States Senate a traitor to his party . . . a traitor to his people, a character assassin, or a demented man."[17]

Would the coalition of prohibition supporters and Klansmen be strong enough to defeat John H. Bankhead Jr. as they had done in 1926? Realizing that the moment had arrived to begin to forge a new coalition, Senator Black took to the stump, not necessarily for Bankhead, but for party unity. Black addressed the economic depression, placing full responsibility for the Depression squarely on Herbert Hoover and thus making Heflin—who had campaigned for the Republican president and was trolling for Republican votes—guilty by association.[18] Heflin claimed the support of organized labor, although the executive board of the Birmingham Trades Council, the central labor body that was affiliated with the American Federation of Labor, issued a report favorable to Bankhead: "His [Bankhead's] attitude toward the miners at the mines owned by him was fair at all times. In fact, he was very valuable to the individual member and to the local and to the national organization of the Mine Workers of America." The group noted that "Mr. Bankhead for 11 years operated a coal mine with union labor, and never had a strike at his mines. For the operation of his mines he signed the 'Blue Book Contract,' which provided a wage scale and working conditions agreeable to the United Mine Workers of America. While operating his mines he furnished a hall as a place of meeting free of cost to the union mine workers at a place near his mine. He was of great direct benefit to the United Mine Workers organization in helping to obtain the Garfield Agreement, which applied to the mine workers throughout the United States and was satisfactory to their organization."[19] The votes of working-class men and women could go either way.

Bankhead's campaign not only drew on party loyalty but tried to present a picture of John H. Bankhead Jr. that made him more sympathetic to the average Alabama voter. Bankhead promoted himself as a "staunch Prohibitionist." To counter the accusation that he was a tool of the "trusts" because he had built his career as a corporation attorney, he highlighted his good relationship with organized labor. He also took a page out of his father's political playbook and emphasized that he "was born on a farm, of a farming ancestry and is in full sympathy with the farmer's problems." Campaign material likewise downplayed Bankhead's wealth, stating that he had "accumu-

Figure 9.1. John Hollis Bankhead Jr., candidate for the US Senate, c. 1930. Courtesy of the Alabama Department of Archives and History.

lated only a modest estate, and *that* by hard work and conservative living habits." Finally, his campaign emphasized that the Democratic Party was the "white man's party."[20] A vote for Heflin imperiled white supremacy.

Bankhead emphasized several issues during the course of his campaign, including his long support for good roads and the critical role of continued federal support. He noted that since the passage of the 1916 legislation, Alabama had received approximately $9 million in federal aid. The continued development of Muscle Shoals remained an important issue. He reminded voters that his father, Senator John Hollis Bankhead, had secured the first federal appropriation for the development of Muscle Shoals for both navigation and power. He declared that his father "was governed by the conviction that Muscle Shoals could be made a direct asset to the South by the production of plant food which could be distributed to the farmers more cheaply and to better advantage than they now secure [from] commercial fertilizers. I embrace his views." He believed that the farmers' problem was one of yield per acre. "It is entirely and needlessly too low. The problem is not how to raise more cotton on the present planted acreage, but how to raise as much on a smaller acreage, thereby securing the same yield with less labor and securing the excess acreage for corn and other by-product crops." The passage of legislation that would ensure cheaper fertilizer via the Muscle Shoals facilities would advance "the upward and onward march of progress which typifies our generation." He did not at this time indicate whether he preferred government ownership or private ownership. He supported the continued development of the Port of Mobile, as well as efforts to improve the navigability of the Alabama and Coosa Rivers. River development was tied closely to power. "We are entering an electric age," he optimistically declared. And electricity meant more creature comforts for Alabama's rural poor, who lived in conditions little changed since the nineteenth century. Bankhead promised a more modern future. "I have a vision of the comforts and conveniences of electricity being made available to people upon the farms. I hope to see the day when every well ordered farm house will be electrically lighted; when electric pumps, and churns, and irons and washing machines and stoves will contribute their part toward making the lot of the farmer's wife more in consonance with the daily life of the town woman. Who thought 25 years ago that telephone lines would serve so many country homes today? Who thought 25 years ago of the automobile and good roads development of today? Who dreamed five years ago of the radio sets now bringing concerts, lectures, and music into millions of homes, both urban and rural?" Bankhead specifically addressed low cotton prices. He advocated a national cooperative marketing arrangement whereby "cotton could be put into a pool[;] the owners could fix a reasonable price and hold the cotton until that price was paid." He acknowledged that such an arrangement might require national legislation. Bankhead also complained about the growth of the federal government during World War I and criticized Congress for its slow pace in eliminating the numerous bureaus he believed were not needed during peacetime. He concluded his address with an appeal to white supremacy, stating that "I will support no measure which will enable the people of the North to interfere for political purposes with our local control of white and colored schools." The technological advances that heralded a bright, new future, Bankhead promised, would leave racial practices untouched.[21]

On the eve of the election, a college friend of Bankhead's who had relocated to Denver wrote to John Jr. to share his personal thoughts about the campaign. The friend noted that Heflin "tells an anecdote well" and would be popular "among a class of citizens who like to be amused but who do not think very deeply about political principles." But such a man was not a serious political player. "He cannot have any influence in Washington and out here we regard him more as a monkey than a man."[22] John Jr. hoped that the majority of Alabama voters shared his friend's sentiments.

Although John H. Bankhead Jr. was the Democratic Party's nominee in 1930, Heflin ran as if it were still 1928, with Catholic Al Smith on the ballot. As the economy continued its downward spiral, Heflin continued to lash out against the wet, Catholic menace. Heflin's ravings about a Catholic conspiracy that was destined to threaten prohibition and white supremacy turned fewer heads in 1930 than in 1928. The ground had shifted in two short years. Even Alabama's white voters, who rarely missed an opportunity to vote their bigotry and racial grievance, had other things on their minds. By 1930, the cotton economy was in the ninth year of a steep decline, falling from a high of thirty-five cents per pound in 1921 to around five cents per pound by 1930. The world built by the cotton economy was collapsing. Men who had once owned their own farms fell into debt and tenancy; over the course of the decade, the number of landowners in the state fell from around ninety-six thousand to seventy-five thousand. The average farm decreased in size, while the number of tenant farmers and sharecroppers increased. One-third of all sharecroppers were functionally illiterate, and most were constantly on the move. White sharecroppers moved an average of once every 2.6 years; black families moved once every 5.1 years. Although industrial workers felt the grip of the Depression later than those on the farm, by 1930, mills and mines across the state were starting to lay off employees. Contemplating shadowy papal conspiracies was a luxury most Alabamians could ill afford. And John H. Bankhead Jr. was no Al Smith.[23]

On November 4, Bankhead defeated Heflin by some fifty thousand votes. Bankhead won fifty-seven counties to Heflin's ten. Heflin won mostly traditional Republican counties, such as Winston, Shelby, DeKalb, and Chilton, as well as some Democratic counties that went for Hoover in 1928, including Clay, Chambers, Henry, and Escambia.[24] One historian notes that

Figure 9.2. US Senator James Thomas "Cotton Tom" Heflin. Courtesy of the Alabama Department of Archives and History.

the 1930 primary election "was a stunning victory for the party regulars who had managed to hold their state in the Democratic column by a bare 7,000 votes two years earlier. The coalition of Klan, prohibition, and labor, joined for expediency by Republicans, had been decisively defeated."[25] But Heflin would not go away quietly. He declared the election to be "one of the most fraudulent and corrupt ever held in Alabama" and threatened to seek a Senate investigation. The *Birmingham News* counseled Heflin to "take his beating like a man."[26]

Heflin refused to concede. Believing he had bested Bankhead by "between fifty and a hundred thousand" votes, he was determined to fight on.[27] He continued to make claims about the size of his victory, something that made his attorney, Horace C. Wilkinson, extremely uncomfortable. "In my opinion," Wilkinson advised, "you are doing yourself a grave injustice by dealing so liberally in figures. . . . I would content myself with the claim that I was elected, without specifying the size of the majority."[28] Heflin complained about voter intimidation, writing to one confidant that "captains of industry in several places intimidated their employees and threatened them with the loss of their jobs if they did not vote the Tammanycratic ticket."[29] Heflin's supporters rallied to his cause. Some believed that his loss was the work of a Catholic conspiracy that foreshadowed a religious and racial apocalypse. "I can foresee a huge religious war in the next eight years," one South Alabama man wrote. "Rome will gain control of America. The people will degenerate back two million years by marriage and mingling with negroes."[30] Others simply thanked him for fighting the good fight. "Thank God you ar another Stone Wall Jackson an[d] ar standing like a mountain far jestuice," wrote J. S. Daw. "An far God sake don't flinch we ar with you tell Death."[31] Not all Alabama voters were thrilled with Heflin's actions, however. One particularly irate voter from Selma told Heflin, "You are dead forever in this state. . . . I want [the Senate] to vindicate the good people of Alabama and for you [to] take the KKK and Independent-Republican Party . . . and stick it up your [a]ss."[32] Tempers were running hot.

Shortly after the election, Heflin met with Gerald P. Nye, chair of the Senate Committee on Privileges and Elections, and demanded a full investigation into alleged violations. Based on Heflin's initial complaints, Nye sent preliminary investigators to Alabama. John H. Bankhead Jr. complained to both brother Will and Senator Nye that the investigators were not working impartially. Although he stated quite clearly that he had every confidence that Heflin's charges of fraud and intimidation had no validity, Bankhead questioned whether the investigation was being conducted properly. He complained that the investigators were passing confidential information to Heflin, and that one investigator in particular was acting in a less-than-impartial manner. The *Montgomery Advertiser* reported that an investigator by the name of Aarhus revealed that there was no reason to investigate anything except facts that might prevent Bankhead from being seated. "I am not sure that I understand the objective of the investigation," Bankhead wrote to Nye. "Is it to discover evidence to aid in a contest, or to ascertain whether illegal and improper methods and practices were used? Is that inquiry confined to [the actions of] one political party?"[33] The investigators submitted a report to Nye in late December 1930.

Addressing his colleagues in the Senate in late February 1931, Heflin declared that the election "reeked with fraud, intimidation, and corruption."[34] Heflin accused the Bankhead forces of buying votes, paying poll taxes, bribing election officials, and exceeding the legal limit for campaign expenditures. Based on the preliminary report of Nye's investigators, the Senate approved a full investigation in February 1931. Nye appointed a subcommittee headed by Republican senator Daniel O. Hastings of Delaware. The subcommittee was authorized to seize ballot boxes in select counties as part of its investigation.[35]

The outcome of the subcommittee's investigation had implications that extended beyond the state of Alabama. Whoever won the contest would have a critical impact on the party balance in the Senate. The Democrats had gained ten seats in the Senate in 1930, winning open seats and defeating Republican incumbents—the first of a series of four elections in which Democrats would make remarkable gains. With the outcome of the Alabama race up in the air, the Senate was split, forty-six Democrats to forty-eight Republicans and one Independent. Although Heflin considered himself a Democrat, his support of Hoover in 1928 made it likely that he would vote with the Republicans on some issues.

The Hastings subcommittee investigation dragged on for more than a year and cost taxpayers close to $100,000. Hoping to uncover voting irregularities, Heflin traveled the state, urging supporters "to bring every item they can gather of the conduct of the last primary and the general election"[36] Although he had no choice but to cooperate with the investigation, John H. Bankhead Jr. called the challenge "a willful waste of thousands of dollars of public funds and an effort to set aside the duly expressed will of the people." Throughout summer and fall 1931, attorneys for Heflin and Bankhead filed briefs and arguments with the subcommittee in support of their particular positions. Heflin argued that the state illegally prescribed qualifications for electors in the primary, that the qualifications for voters were different than those for candidates, and that the State Democratic Executive Committee prevented voters from writing in names on the ballots, all of which rendered the primary illegal. Finally, because Bankhead approved of these alleged "abridgements of the freedom of voting," he was morally unfit for office.[37] Heflin's attorneys also purported that Bankhead disqualified himself as a senatorial candidate by excessive expenditures in violation of state statute, which set the limit for the primary and general election at $10,000. Heflin claimed that Bankhead spent $1,531.58 more than the law allowed.[38]

The subcommittee held hearings in Washington in April 1931 and heard testimony from the attorneys for Bankhead and Heflin. Bankhead's attorney, Robert B. Evins, argued that even if fraud had occurred, there was no proof that it had affected the election's outcome. Regarding Heflin's charges that Bankhead had exceeded the amount allowed for campaign expenditures, Evins countered that the Alabama statute allowed for expenditures of $10,000 each for the primary and for the general election. Also, he contended that even if one accepted the interpretation that the statute allowed for $10,000 for both elections together, then Bankhead still came under that threshold if one deducted certain expenses not required according to federal guidelines. He also argued that the Senate did not have the power to look into state primaries.[39]

In addition to conducting hearings, the subcommittee set about the business of a ten-county recount. Sealed ballot boxes were sent to Washington, DC. They were stacked high against the walls of the Caucus Room of the Senate Office Building, where thirty men and women recounted the ballots. The recount began on April 20, 1931. Ballot counters received six dollars a day, each working four days per week "in order to spread work among the unemployed."[40] Senate investigators identified a number of irregularities and evidence of ballot tampering. Not all ballot boxes were sealed as required under Alabama law, some poll lists were not certified, and some lists of qualified voters contained additions that were not properly certified.[41] Ballots from Bibb and Houston Counties had been burned at the order of the sheriffs. The sheriffs insisted that the burning of the ballots had been based on "a misunderstanding of the law."[42]

In the ten-county recount, Bankhead lost 6 percent of his votes, while Heflin lost 8 percent. Although the subcommittee initially intended to count the ballots of only those ten counties, after the review, and under prodding from Heflin, the subcommittee recommended recounting the ballots in every county in the state.[43] Bankhead initially opposed broadening the investigation but eventually withdrew his protest.[44] Altogether, some 2,043 ballot boxes were packed up and sent to Washington.

The contest dragged on through the summer. On December 7, 1931, even though the dispute had not yet been adjudicated, John H. Bankhead Jr. took the oath of office as US senator from the state of Alabama. He took his seat with the understanding that he might be unseated later should Heflin's challenge reveal gross irregularities. The election challenge cast a shadow over what should have been the highlight of an already successful career. In his matter-of-fact way, Bankhead recorded the bittersweet moment in his journal: "At 12 o'clock the Senate was called to order. I was in my seat. [Wife] Musa, [sister-in-law] Florence and [daughter] Marion were in the gallery. Heflin was in the Senate chamber. Eight new senators in alphabetical order were called to take the oath. I was . . . escorted to the front by Senator Hugo Black, my colleague. After we had gathered in front of the Vice President—Curtis—and were ready to take the oath, [Republican senator Samuel] Shortridge interrupted and read his statement relating to the contest against me and also to a contest against Senator Bailey of N.C. He read slowly for 15 or 20 minutes. Then we were sworn in."[45] The question remained: would he keep his seat?

The election challenge ground on. Following the recount, Bankhead held a 47,706-vote lead. Hearings on the election challenge were held in Birmingham in January 1932. Heflin presented over two hundred witnesses claiming fraud or irregularities. No subcommittee members attended these hearings, although a record was created of the testimony.[46] Finally, in February 1932, the subcommittee was ready to present its findings and vote. Unable to reach a consensus, the subcommittee filed a majority and a minority report. In the majority report, Senator Hastings discounted three of the main charges urged as grounds for unseating Bankhead. The subcommittee reviewed over three thousand pages of testimony from the Birmingham hearings but ultimately held that "it does not appear that the purchase of votes was carried on to such an extent as to seriously affect the election." Heflin charged that Alabama Power Company coerced its employees into voting for Bankhead. Hastings noted that although seventeen witnesses testified that certain corporations had used influence to have their employees support Bankhead, officers of these companies denied the charges. The committee addressed voting irregularities. Among those irregularities was a charge by a witness for Heflin that on Election Day, "an election officer became intoxicated at Liberty Hall, in Walker County, started to disrobe and finally attempted to drive his horse into the polling place, a church vestibule." Hastings also charged that 67,688 votes could not be confirmed because 569 qualified lists could not be located. The minority report, submitted by Senator Walter George of Georgia and Senator Sam Bratton of New Mexico disputed this conclusion, noting that the 569 lists were not missing; rather they were in the hands of election supervisors instead of inside the ballot boxes. The minority report asserted that only thirteen qualified lists were actually missing, and that those missing lists involved 1,016 votes. Regarding technical irregularities, the minority held that "irregularities were of the same general character and quantity in counties where election machinery was controlled by friends of Heflin as in counties controlled by Bankhead's supporters." This report further noted that these irregularities were minor and included ballots that were folded or rolled by election officials; failure to number the ballots; and failure to number them in pen and not pencil. The minority report further argued that "oral testimony of voting irregularities, although numerous, were [not] evidence of fraud." The Senate subcommittee voted 3–2 to unseat Bankhead. The full Senate committee, by a one-vote margin, recommended that Bankhead keep his seat.[47]

The vote of the subcommittee may well have been influenced by the fate of two Republican senators in 1926 who were denied their seats because of fraud and corruption. Democratic leader in the Senate Joseph T. Robinson accused Hastings of meeting secretly with Republican senators before submitting his report on the Bankhead-Heflin contest. Hastings did not deny the accusation but said that there was "nothing improper" in meeting with his colleagues.[48] Will Bankhead confided to one political supporter that he was concerned that the Senate's Republican majority might vacate the Senate seat. There was a backup plan. Will had received assurances from Governor Benjamin M. Miller that, should this happen, he would reappoint John to the seat immediately.[49]

Following the vote of the subcommittee and committee, the fight then went to the Senate floor, where Bankhead was defended by Senators Black, George, and Robinson. In a rare move, the Senate voted to allow Heflin the privilege of addressing the body. He took full advantage of this opportunity, presenting his case in what one Birmingham paper called "a five-hour harangue." Reporters noted that although Bankhead was not present when Heflin began his speech, he arrived later "and sat in the rear row on the same side of the aisle." Senator Heflin wore his "traditional costume—a long, square-tailed coat, black vest edged with white, and spectacles dangling from a long ribbon. The Senate galleries and the floor were crowded as they haven't been crowded since the stirring days of the World War." Heflin's remarks were aimed mostly at the Republicans. As the *Birmingham News* reported, "that is where his votes must come if he is to bust Bankhead from the seat he held so long."[50]

Heflin spent much of his time challenging the validity of the primary and his removal from it. He repeated the accusations of fraud, corruption, and "general skullduggery" that had fueled his election challenge. He painted himself as the victim of a dastardly attempt by the state party to deny the people of Alabama their rights. "The State Committee had ordained that [Bankhead] must be nominated; they manipulated it and fixed it. They ordained then that everybody should be whipped into line and I must be crushed."[51] To Senator Black's accusation that his election challenge reflected poorly on the state of Alabama, Heflin was incredulous: "I would give my life to protect [Alabama's] good name and its honor. I am fighting for my State. I am fighting for the humble factory girl who stands all day at the loom and weaves, who was intimidated by the bosses of the mill to vote for Bankhead against me. I am fighting for the boys who wear lamps on their caps and go down in the bowels of the earth to dig coal and iron. I am fighting for the farmer in the furrowed field, the merchant, the clerk. I am fighting for the school-teachers, who were browbeaten in wholesale fashion, telling them they got their jobs from the Democrats, and if they did not vote for Bankhead they would lose them. I am fighting for a fair deal for these people all down the line."[52] He accused Alabama Power of putting undue influence on its employees to vote for Bankhead. Stylistically, this speech was Heflin at his best: cajoling, incredulous, often imploring his colleagues to grasp the grave ramifications of his case. "Oh God, Senators!" "Just think of it, Senators!" No reference was too hyperbolic, no story too maudlin for him to employ. He referred to the state party's decision to bar him from participating in the Democratic primary as "political assassination." He peppered his speech with folksy tales and jokes, and frequently his colleagues and spectators in the galleries erupted in laughter. He discussed the importance of investigating every ballot box in the state and lambasted the "awful condition of the ballots" and the resistance of Bankhead's supporters to having all boxes examined. Their alleged hesitancy, Heflin mused, "reminded me of the story of an old negro down in Arkansas":

> He had stolen a pig weighing about 70 pounds from Mr. Jones. He dressed the pig nicely and took him home. They searched for that pig high and low and could not find him. They thought of old Sam's house out in the middle of the field. The sheriff and the deputy went out looking for the pig. They went in, and old Sam was sitting there rocking a cradle, with quilts tucked in at the head and foot and sides, rocking the cradle, singing "Doan' you cry little baby; you'll be an angel by and by." The sheriff and deputy said, "Sam, we are looking for that stolen pig of Mr. Jones." Sam threw up his hands in holy horror. Just like you have seen here. He said, "Dar you go, white folks! You 'cusing me of stealing. Dat's the way it is:

Old nigger sitting here, and his baby nearly dead with the pneumonia, and you 'cusing him of stealing a pig! Dat's it—Lawd have mercy!" They looked around the closet and under the bed, and they could not find the pig. They came back and said, "Sam, what have you got in that cradle?" He said, "It's my baby, and he's got pneumonia." They said, "Well we will look in there." He said, "No sah! If de light hits him, he's gone." "Well," they said, "we are going to look in there anyhow"; and Sam said, "Well, you let me get out. I doan' want to see my baby die"; and that nigger fled across the field with the speed of the wind and when they pulled the quilts back, there lay Mr. Jones's pig. [Laughter] That is the way it is here. They closed this case while I was gone. They did not want me to pull the quilt off their contestee's baby, "cause the light and the air would kill it." He had machine politics "pneumonia." [Laughter][53]

At the conclusion of his speech, the Senate gallery erupted in applause. Although overly long, his presentation had been entertaining. Alabama congressman John McDuffie called Heflin's accusations of fraud "the wild vaporings of a defeated candidate."[54] *Time* magazine reported that Heflin's speech filled twenty-seven pages of the Congressional Record and cost the government $1,000 to print.[55]

Although he had not planned to speak, Bankhead did not want to let Heflin's accusations go unanswered. On April 27, 1932, he likewise addressed the Senate, stating his case in two hours.[56] Bankhead's address was concise and sober; there were no homespun tales, racist anecdotes, or rhetorical flourishes. He spoke of his respect for the Constitution and for the Senate's prerogative to determine the outcome of the contest. "I have engaged in no buttonholing of Senators; I have engaged in no electioneering with them; I have not in any way pressed my claims in this case. . . . I have made no appeal to friends upon this side of the Chamber."[57] He disputed Heflin's claim that he had had a hand in the decision of the State

Figure 9.3. Senator John Hollis Bankhead Jr. with daughter Louise and grandchildren. Courtesy of the Alabama Department of Archives and History.

Democratic Executive Committee to bar Heflin from the primary, when, in fact, he counseled leniency. He challenged Heflin's accusation that he was a tool of the Alabama Power Company, telling the chamber that "eight or ten years ago I had a small retainer from that company. When agitation over Muscle Shoals came up, I was not in accord with the Alabama Power Co. having Muscle Shoals, and on that account, so that I could have complete liberty of action without embarrassment either to myself or to my client, I tendered my resignation as local attorney from that company."[58] Ultimately, he argued, "every line of investigation in this case leads to the conclusion that there has been no fraud in the Alabama election."[59] It was time for the full Senate to vote.

The Senate agreed with John H. Bankhead Jr. On April 28, 1932, a year and a half after Alabamians had gone to the polls, the Senate voted 65–18 to recognize Bankhead as the victor in the 1930 election for US senator.[60] One reporter wrote that Heflin remained in the chamber for the roll call vote, "his face flushed as the names and votes rang out." When the voting concluded, Heflin walked quietly out of the chamber unnoticed, while Bankhead received warm congratulations from his new colleagues.[61]

After decades spent promoting first his father's political career and then his younger brother's, John H. Bankhead Jr., sixty years old, was a US senator. The diligent levelheadedness that had made him a successful attorney and trusted political adviser would serve him and the South well as he turned his attention to legislating. And not a moment too soon. With the dark days of the Great Depression descending on the country, America needed problem solvers.

10

❦

Burning Bridges, Taking Chances

THE BANKHEAD FAMILY'S FOCUS on John H. Bankhead Jr.'s contested US Senate seat was interrupted by a near tragedy. In January 1931, the small house that Will and Florence Bankhead had leased for the remainder of the congressional session caught fire. They had only been in the house for two days, Will reported, when a fire that began in a neighboring house spread to theirs. They awoke at 1:30 a.m. to discover the lower floor engulfed in flames and the house quickly filling with smoke. Escaping down the stairs was impossible. "Florence hit the fire alarm," Will told his brother, and the couple waited anxiously on the second floor for firefighters to arrive. They ultimately made their escape through a second-floor window into thirteen-degree weather "clad only in their nightclothes." Will reported no property loss "except a second-hand hat" that was on the first floor of the house.[1]

America's economic house was similarly on fire in 1931. Commodity prices continued to plummet, while industrial unemployment skyrocketed. Destitute and desperate Americans on farms and in cities looked for relief that did not come. The Bankhead brothers, members of the minority Democratic Party in their respective houses of Congress, battled gamely (but ultimately unsuccessfully) with the Republican majority and president in 1930 and 1931 for more aggressive economic intervention. The inauguration of Franklin D. Roosevelt in 1932 and the installation of a powerful Democratic majority in both houses of Congress altered the political landscape dramatically and provided unique opportunities for each brother. For Will, the New Deal years were bittersweet. His time spent toiling as a relatively effective member of the minority party in the 1920s, coupled with his seniority secured as a member of the important southern caucus within the party, paid off in increasingly powerful leadership positions. Political observers universally praised the leadership style of the suave, affable Alabamian. Described by one New York journalist as "a sizable man, broad-shouldered, his gray hair topping a large, well-shaped head," Will was the House of Representatives' most skilled parliamentarian and had few enemies.[2] But a failing body tragically denied him the ability to utilize that power to its full potential during Roosevelt's first term. Freshman US senator John H. Bankhead Jr. excelled in his new role. Determined to bring relief to the region's struggling cotton farmers, Bankhead dedicated himself to understanding the problems of the rural economy. He quickly became a key adviser to President Roosevelt, and an important contributor to and supporter of the administration's signature farm legislation. Together, the brothers made a formidable team within the powerful southern Democratic bloc that played a critical role in shaping New Deal legislation and America's future.

The Bankheads suffered personal economic reversals as a result of the Depression, although they were far better off than most Americans. Well-connected men, John and Will became lifelines for their family. In 1932, brother-in-law and widower Arthur Lund confided to Will, "I find myself in the most desperate need of funds," and asked to borrow $100. Will could not spare it as he was deeply in debt. His failed Florida real estate venture had put him in a deep financial hole, and the stock market crash, he lamented, had "taken every dollar that I once owned." He had to cancel a life insurance policy because he could not afford the premium.[3] Although he was unable to send money to Lund, he did contact New York City mayor Fiorello LaGuardia about a job for his brother-in-law.[4] Will likewise promised his niece Maude (brother Henry's daughter) that he and brother John would try to find a position in Washington for her son.[5] Will cosigned a loan for nephew Tom Owen Jr. but grew impatient when Tom fell behind on the payments. "When I endorsed this note for you the last time, you assured me that you would take care of the monthly installments. I am not in a position to bear this burden at this time."[6] Will also supported his daughter Eugenia throughout the decade. Even a woman who had worked as a domestic for John Hollis when he and Tallulah had lived at the Riggs Hotel wrote to Will, asking for any old clothes they might be able to spare.[7] Despite these setbacks, Will managed to establish a small dairy operation on his farm in Walker County. Called Blackwater Meadows Dairy, the operation promoted itself as an "absolutely new, modern dairy to supply a part of the milk requirements of Jasper."[8] Beset by too many financial obligations, however, Will considered changing professions. He wrote to Democratic National Committee chairman John J. Raskob in May 1929 seeking a position with Raskob's investment firm. "If I could secure an association with your concern—say as manager or executive officer for the enterprise in the State of Alabama, I would give very serious consideration to the retirement from public life to return to the field of business."[9] It is not known whether Raskob replied. Whatever his response, Will remained in his position as a member of Congress, although his financial situation did not improve greatly during the decade.

Marie Bankhead Owen continued in her role as director of the Alabama Department of Archives and History, which paid her an annual salary of $4,000 until the Depression hit; under the direction of Governor Benjamin Miller, her salary was sliced to $2,700 in 1931. As unpleasant as this reduction must have been, she was fortunate to still be employed. Dedicated to getting the state's fiscal house in order during lean times, Miller commissioned the Brookings Institution to undertake an examination of state government, including the Department of Archives and History. The report was not favorable, and its authors recommended abolishing the department. Although this drastic step was not taken, the outlook for the immediate future was dim. Marie confided to niece Tallulah that "we are now deeply in debt as a State and the Legislature is cutting down on all kinds of expenses." With the archives already operating on a stingy budget, Marie's relation-

Figure 10.1. Marie Bankhead Owen, director of the Alabama Department of Archives and History, late 1930s. Courtesy of the Alabama Department of Archives and History.

ship with Governor Miller rapidly deteriorated after he ordered her to furlough four clerks, including her son Tom. When the governor later discovered that Tom continued to work at the archives (Marie claimed to one board member that Tom had taken over the work of an ill colleague with the governor's approval), he apparently "humiliated" her at a board of trustees meeting with accusations of nepotism. Marie was embarrassed and enraged, telling one board member she was "spoiling for a fight" with the governor. She was blunter with brother John, also a member of the board. "I hope that I conducted myself as a lady [when accused by the governor] but also with the courage that our father would have expected [of] one who had sprung from his loins. If I would follow my instincts at the present moment I would cut his G—D throat."10

Lack of space for the archives' ever-expanding collections remained a problem. Marie was desperate for funds for a new building. Every year since becoming director, Marie brought the issue to the attention of the department's board of trustees with little success. Unprocessed records from state agencies continued to pile up because there were not enough hours in the day for a skeleton staff that was already stretched thin; acquisition of new collections had dwindled because potential donors were aware of the lack of funds and space. Why donate a historically significant family heirloom if it could not be properly displayed? With the deepening Depression, plans for a permanent archives building remained on hold. In the meantime, to economize, she discontinued the traveling library program and the legislative reference library. Marie's spirits were low. She complained to niece Tallulah that she was ready to call it quits. "If I were thirty instead of sixty this sort of program might appeal to my patriotism, but realizing that I am now at the very pinnacle of my power and energy I do not want to mark time. I want to be in the midst of progressive things and for that reason I am determined to find something else to do that will pay me a living wage and a surplus that will meet my obligations so that I can save my property to have something to fall back on when my earning power is at nill."[11] During the 1930s, Marie owned both a home in Montgomery and a six-hundred-acre farm, Glen Owen, in Elmore County. The two-story, ten-room farm home at Glen Owen dated back to 1810 and was in constant need of repair, which required money that Marie did not have.[12] She had few options.

Among the Bankheads, only Tallulah had a relatively rosy fortune as the nation slid into depression. Her gambit to travel to England in 1923 without any prospects had paid off. She quickly became the darling of the London stage, receiving strong reviews (with one or two exceptions) even when the plays themselves left something to be desired. Theatergoers and critics marveled at her unique beauty, her long, wavy, golden hair (that is, until she got it bobbed in the style of the times), and her low, throaty voice. She worked steadily throughout the 1920s, performing in sixteen plays in eight years, and put forth honest effort to hone her craft. Some reviewers criticized her lack of technique, but others reveled in what they regarded as her quintessentially American style, so different from the cool reserve of British actors. One critic wrote that Tallulah could "discharge more emotion and give more of herself in one undisciplined half-minute than almost any English actress can contrive in three acts of polite disturbance." Tallulah was unrestrained and unpredictable. Although she worked hard on any given part, much of her acting was simply instinctive. Audiences loved it. Writing for the *New York World*, playwright and critic Saint John Ervine observed that, whatever one thought of her technique, no one could deny that "she seizes and holds and keeps her audience."[13] Before long, Tallulah had groupies, packs of young working-class women (and some young men) who waited in line for hours to purchase tickets for her plays. They screamed her name from the gallery; they huddled outside the stage door hoping to catch a glimpse of their heroine before she was whisked away to an after-hours party. According to her biographer, "even by the norms of the gallery, its adulation [for Tallulah] bordered on the hysterical."[14] Tallulah herself referred to them as fanatics.[15] Tallulah Bankhead had become a celebrity.

Tallulah spent money as quickly as she earned it. She bought a house and a Bentley automobile. She employed a staff of three. She traveled to continental

Europe and spoiled her friends. She was big hearted and generous to a fault. Making her own money and feeling the adoration of young theatergoers, Tallulah became increasingly audacious and reckless in her behavior. She experimented with narcotics, both cocaine and heroin, and continued to use cocaine throughout her career. She engaged in countless casual affairs with men and women throughout the decade. By one account, she had four abortions before she was thirty years old. She became almost as well known for her exhibitionism as she was for her stage performances. She created a per-

Figure 10.2. Tallulah with fiancé Anthony de Bosdari, 1928. Courtesy of the Alabama Department of Archives and History.

sona, telling one New York reporter that, "Over here they like me to 'Tallulah.' You know—dance and sing and romp and fluff my hair and play reckless parts."[16] And she complied. Often.

Despite her freewheeling lifestyle, Tallulah privately craved the stability denied her as a child. "I was not as free of inhibitions as the casual observer might believe," she admitted. "On the surface all confidence, all swagger and strut, inside I churned with doubt. Any minute the clock might strike twelve and I'd be back in a hall bedroom at the Algonquin, or, worse yet, in Grandfather's yard at Jasper."[17] For Tallulah, a return to Alabama meant failure.

Just as her father was a distant figure during her formative years, so too did Tallulah seek romantic commitment from men who were in various ways unavailable to her. She hoped that her arrival in England might rekindle her relationship with Napier Alington. The British lord was impulsive, unreliable, and self-destructive, given to prolonged bouts of drinking and gambling. Tallulah was enthralled. "When he was in London I was with him constantly," she revealed in her memoirs, "fascinated by his rakishness, his pranks, his indifference to fame and fortune. Then he'd disappear for months and I'd not hear a word from him. When he bobbed up without warning, again I'd be hypnotized, though inwardly ravaged by my inability to break off a relationship that was part ecstasy, part torture." The relationship eventually ended when Alington married a high-born British woman. In 1928, Tallulah was engaged briefly to Count Anthony de Bosdari, "an Anglo-Italian venture capitalist"; she called off the wedding after she discovered that England did not recognize Bosdari's American divorce. Technically, he was still married. By the end of the

Figure 10.3. Tallulah (*center*) with Florence and Will, 1931. Courtesy of the Alabama Department of Archives and History.

decade, Tallulah was ready to return to the United States. She decided to pursue a future in films and signed a contract with Paramount Pictures that paid her $5,000 per week. She arrived in New York in January 1931.[18]

The Bankheads were thrilled with Tallulah's success and her return stateside. With Tallulah back in the country, Marie recognized an opportunity. Shortly after Tallulah's return, she wrote to her niece to inquire whether the star might hire Marie as her personal secretary. Marie touted her credentials. Her experience working for the *Montgomery Advertiser* had made her "a first rate 'publicity man'; my social experience has civilized me and my love for you would warrant me in becoming a shock absorber between you and the clamorous public. I think the reason some of the American film stars have gone on the rocks with their reputations is because they did not have wise buffers between them and the public."[19] Could she be Tallulah's "wise buffer"? Marie also contacted the public relations department at Paramount Pictures about a possible position. No job was forthcoming.[20] Undeterred, she reached out to other contacts with the New York advertising firm of Batten, Barton, Durstine & Osborn, the Universal Radio Service in Hollywood, and the National Broadcasting Company.[21] Still no luck. Marie quietly resigned herself to remaining in her position with the Department of Archives and History. Although she never secured a position for her aunt, Tallulah sent Marie money throughout the decade.[22]

Tallulah Bankhead had spent the better part of her twenties away from family, in one of the most cosmopolitan cities in the world. She had encountered diverse ideas and practices, and engaged with people completely unlike the denizens of tiny Jasper, Alabama. Although she would maintain many of the class pretensions of the southern elite, she had shed much of their provincialism. In this way, she was part of a small sorority of white southern women that included contemporaries Virginia Foster Durr of Birmingham and Katharine Du Pre Lumpkin from Georgia: white women who left the South for extended periods of time and who became vocal critics of white supremacy and supporters of the struggles of the white rural and urban poor. Although not as overtly political as Durr or as introspective as Lumpkin, Tallulah quietly moved away from the more overtly racist expressions of her family's heritage. Her correspondence reveals that she still clung to racial paternalism, but unlike sister Eugenia, she did not use crude racial epithets. Throughout the 1930s and 1940s, she evolved into a fairly conventional liberal anticommunist, a position that sometimes put her at odds with the more left-wing members of the acting community. When civil rights became a political issue that engaged both major parties, Tallulah publicly rebuked those standing in the way of equality, her own family included.

The country's increasingly dire economic circumstances consumed President Herbert Hoover and Congress. The Republicans maintained a razor-thin majority following the 1930 elections; subsequent elections held in 1931 to fill vacancies caused by death gave the Democrats in the House a four-vote majority during the last year of Hoover's presidency. After spending more than a decade as a member of the minority party, Will Bankhead would move up the leadership ladder in the critical 1930s. He was patient and humble. Writing to fellow congressman and friend Sam Rayburn of Texas regarding his chances to become majority leader, Bankhead admitted that although he would be flattered to be considered for the post, "I will not take the initiative in pressing my claims. I think that would be highly improper and indeed an evidence of vanity and personal ambition rather than looking after the real interest of the party in Congress."[23] Content to wait his turn, Bankhead instead worked to advance the prospects of friend and fellow Alabama congressman John McDuffie for Speaker.[24] Ultimately, House minority leader John Nance Garner of Texas was the unanimous choice for Speaker, while Congressman Henry T. Rainey of Illinois was chosen floor leader by a single vote over Bankhead. Bankhead remained on the powerful Committee on Rules as the second-highest-ranking member. The chairman of that committee, Edward W. Pou, was plagued by illness, effectively surrendering leadership of the committee to Bankhead.[25]

Now in control of the House, the Democrats wasted little time in beginning their attack on President Hoover's handling of the Depression. On December 8, 1931, Hoover delivered his annual address to Congress; the next day, December 9, the Democrats went on the offensive, criticizing the president's speech and his failure to adequately address the needs of suffering Americans. Floor leadership made a critical error, allowing Alabama congressman George Huddleston the first shot at responding to the president's message. Huddleston, a progressive Democrat, was far more liberal than the rest of the state's delegation. Huddleston painted a bleak picture of the country. "In millions of American homes the shadow of starvation and despair looms darker than even a year ago." To alleviate this need, Huddleston proposed an appropriation of $100 million in direct relief, the first such legislation in history. He pointed out that Hoover was staunchly opposed to any direct relief to citizens.[26] Huddleston's address prompted an uproar. Republicans seized an opportunity to put the Democrats on the defensive. One Republican congressman pointed out that by allowing Huddleston to speak first, "the majority party in the House of Representatives today would commit the government to the principle of a dole." To hearty applause from the minority, yet another Republican declared that "this great Democratic party has abandoned entirely the principles of Jefferson for the principles of Karl Marx." Will Bankhead hustled onto the floor and spoke up to defend Huddleston from the "concentrated fire" he was receiving from the Republicans.[27] With grace and wit, he was able to diffuse the testy nature of the opening exchange. Frequently interrupted by laughter and applause, Bankhead simultaneously defended Huddleston while also assuring his Republican counterparts and the American people that the Democrats "are going to undertake nothing intemperately or hurriedly or ill-advisedly; . . . we are not going to attempt a panacea program for all the ills from which the country is suffering, but we do expect to bring in . . . a policy and a program that will bring some sane and substantial remedial legislation to bring the country out of its present morass of destitution." But while he was willing to assure the Republicans that his party was going to act responsibly, he also reminded them that they now inhabited the minority role because of their "ineptitude and lack of leadership."[28] His extemporaneous address redirected the discussion of the House, and the small crisis was averted. Bankhead's skill in this particular instance did not go unnoticed by the press in attendance. A reporter from the *Washington Herald* criticized Speaker Garner for allowing Huddleston the opening spot in the new session. That honor should have gone to "Mr. Bankhead, Tallulah's dad." He continued: "That gentleman subsequently got the Democrats out of their hole. . . . That man knows words and the power of speech. . . . It was around him that the scattered Democratic host rallied Wednesday. It was around him that they cheered and whooped. It was he who responded so quickly to the Republican interpolators that they looked like fools, and who aroused the Democrats to such a pitch that they laughed and cheered lustily at his every retort, whether it was good or not. And most of them were good."[29] It would not be the last time that the suave Alabamian saved the House Democrats from self-inflicted wounds.

John H. Bankhead Jr. began the work of a US senator even before his election dispute with James Thomas Heflin had concluded. He became consumed with the problems of rural America, particularly the cotton economy—the lifeblood of a majority of his constituents—and began publicly advocating for more stringent production controls as a way to increase farm income.[30] Later in his career, John Jr. reminisced about his early years as a senator and the way that he came to focus on rural problems. He spoke of sitting in his law office in Jasper, looking at his father's papers, which he kept in a safe. He came across a cartoon that illustrated the importance of good roads for farmers.

> As I looked at it, my memory went back to the period of my father's dedication of himself to the cause of good roads, to the long struggle he made to secure the accomplishment of his heart's desire, and to the wonderful developments throughout the country as a result of his pioneering work in behalf of good roads. I asked myself: Is there anything that I can do during my public service that will be helpful to the plain people in a way comparable to what my father did? As I stood in front of that old safe, looking at that road cartoon, the thought came to me—Cotton farmers are nearly all poor. Cotton is their chief cash crop. The price of producing it is not sufficient to cover the cost of production. . . . What a difference it would make in the welfare and happiness of millions of people if, when the farmer drove along a good road going to town to sell his cotton, in his mind's eye he could see written on the side of each bale of cotton, the words 20 or 25 cents a pound. Would it be possible for me to bring about such a wonderful reality? I made up my mind then and there to do my very best to find a legal and economic solution of the problem.[31]

This commitment was not entirely altruistic. John's laser focus on the cotton problem would also help people forget his former association with the Alabama Power Company and his presidency of a coal company, affiliations he did not see as particularly helpful to achieving his political goals. After securing his Senate seat in December 1931, John H. Bankhead Jr. was appointed to the Committees on Agriculture and Appropriations. He kept a low profile until his final confirmation in April 1932.[32]

Bankhead had his work cut out for him. Farmers across rural America were struggling in the early 1930s, but the situation for cotton farmers was especially dire. The Cotton Belt, secretary of agriculture William M. Jardine remarked, was the "black spot" of the country's agricultural sector.[33] Since World War I, cotton prices had fluctuated wildly. With a few exceptions, cotton farmers responded to each new crisis by expanding production, hoping to make up for lost income by cultivating additional acreage.[34] By 1926, the price of cotton had fallen below the cost of production. There was simply too much cotton. Voluntary restriction of acreage had proved unsuccessful over the years, and mandatory restriction was difficult to achieve. The Alabama Farm Bureau supported reductions, and the governor of Alabama declared the week of October 30, 1926, to be "Cotton Reduction Week." All cotton producers were encouraged to sign a pledge to reduce their production by 25 percent. Although reduction had broad regional support, not all states were on board. In particular, Texas's governor refused to urge reductions for the state's cotton growers. Despite the enthusiasm, voluntary reduction did not work. Prices continued to fluctuate. In 1927 and 1928, cotton was bringing twenty cents a pound. Farmers again responded by expanding production. Despite the onset of the Great Depression and steadily dropping prices between 1928 and 1932, farm output changed very little.[35] Overproduction was not the only problem facing farmers. They also faced a shrinking overseas market, in which American cotton was undersold by cotton grown in Brazil, Egypt, and India. In addition, manufacturers were substituting other products, notably rayon, for a number of products.[36]

Cotton farmers' dire situation was compounded by the fact that the prices of nonfarm commodities did not fall as fast or as far as those of agricultural products. This disparity between farm income and the price of the industrial goods that farm families purchased became the focus of farm advocates like John H. Bankhead Jr. The aim of farm groups was to give farm families the same purchasing power they had enjoyed between 1909 and 1914, a period during which the relationship between farm income and the cost of nonfarm goods was considered fair. That farm-price sweet spot—in which farmers' commodities had fair exchange value in relation to the goods they had to purchase—came to be known as the parity price.[37]

Farmers, particularly those tied to the cotton economy, also suffered from a lack of adequate credit. Farmers' income was irregular and uncertain. They needed reliable, long-term credit at low interest rates to cover operating and daily living expenses. With shrinking deposits, banks set loan rates relatively high and kept the loan period short: three to six or nine to twelve months. Farmers usually had to repay the loan before they sold the crops or livestock that the loan had enabled them to acquire and cultivate.[38]

Farmers had a range of grievances, and from 1920 to 1933 they sought government assistance to reduce surpluses, raise agricultural prices, and achieve parity.[39] Hoover eventually signed the Agricultural Marketing Act in June 1929. This act established a Federal Farm Board, which was empowered to purchase surpluses to uphold prices. What the act did not do was establish production controls.[40] Understanding that the government would purchase their surplus, farmers expanded production. The Farm Board was overwhelmed; surpluses soared. Prices plunged to their lowest level since 1894. By 1932, cotton was selling at five cents a pound.[41] Bold action would have to await the new president.

President Hoover remained at odds with the Democratic House, and Will Bankhead stayed on the offensive against the Republican president, criticizing him for failing to address the needs of the "8,000,000 or 10,000,000 hungry, starving, hopeless and disillusioned men and women in America today without employment." He called the president's farm relief bill a "major debacle" and ridiculed the "disastrous results" of the 1930 Smoot-Hawley Tariff Act. Bankhead demanded congressional action and criticized a Republican senator who had wondered aloud whether the country needed "a Mussolini." This lawmaker was not alone in wondering whether this particular liberal democracy could properly address the economic crisis. Bankhead, incredulous, responded, "Has democracy failed in America? Has representative government, framed and fashioned by our fathers, collapsed?"[42] Proving the efficacy of liberal democracy was a challenge Will Bankhead was eager to take on.

Bankhead used his position as acting chair of the Committee on Rules to assist passage of Democratic legislation. In May 1932, Speaker Garner introduced a $2.3 billion bill in which half the funds would be used for a federal public works program and another billion dollars would go toward increasing the capitalization of Hoover's Reconstruction Finance Corporation. Hoover lashed out at the bill, calling it the "greatest pork-barrel scheme conceivable."[43] Not all Democrats supported the bill. Missouri congressman Clarence Cannon declared it a "raid on the already depleted Treasury." He instead called for retrenchment and a balanced budget. "You cannot put out a fire by drenching it with gasoline. You cannot cure a deficit by spending more money." Bankhead, as acting head of the Committee on Rules, pushed forward a strong rule strictly regulating debate and forbidding any amendments to Garner's bill. He offered no apologies. He admitted that the rule proposed was drastic, but desperate times called for desperate measures. "The number of unemployed men and women is constantly increasing," and he feared that Congress would soon adjourn without having passed "any . . . bold or courageous legislation . . . to meet this desperate unemployment situation."[44] The House and Senate passed the bill, which the president promptly vetoed on July 11, 1932. Congress passed a substitute bill over the president's veto.[45]

As the presidential campaign of 1932 began to heat up, Will Bankhead, one of the party's best spokesmen, moved confidently into the forefront to parry Republican thrusts. In a radio address run-up to his keynote address at the upcoming Republican National Convention, Senator Lester J. Dickinson of Iowa attacked the Democrats, accusing them of "a congenital incapacity for government." A proud party man, Bankhead could not let the insult go unanswered. He took to the floor of the House to deliver an hour-long response. He proceeded to instruct his colleagues on the accomplishments of the Democratic Party, highlighting legislation such as the Underwood Tariff Act, the Smith-Lever Act, the National Defense Act of 1916, and the Federal Water Power Act. He emphasized the Democratic Party's focus on labor, "the men and women of America who toil, the man in overalls, the woman in gingham." Republican prescriptions had only brought more misery. The time for change had arrived. To meet the demands of the current crisis, "We are going to have to burn some of our bridges behind us in our preconceived notions of economic policy." Nothing less than the survival of liberal democracy was at stake. The extraordinary circumstances called for new approaches, in particular unprecedented spending so that "people do not actually starve and shiver to death . . . and also to provide work for our hordes of idle workers." The country demanded bold action. "New developments, new conditions, social and economic and financial, are going to call upon us as a challenge to exercise our genius for legislation and our constructive leadership to meet the new conditions, and we may not expect to rely absolutely upon the old, archaic, and unstable policies of the past that are not sufficient to meet the conditions with which we are now confronted." Bankhead's call to action was greeted by boisterous applause from the Democrats.[46] Congress adjourned in July 1932. A novel approach would have to await a new administration.

John and Will turned their attention to the upcoming presidential election. Both were favorably impressed with New York governor Franklin D. Roosevelt. John traveled to Roosevelt's home in Hyde Park, New York, in early 1932 to celebrate Roosevelt's fiftieth birthday. Roosevelt was impressed with Bankhead's assessment of the farm crisis.[47] Eager to line up delegates for the National Democratic Convention in Chicago, Roosevelt invited the brothers to Warm Springs, Georgia, for a visit. Not quite ready to commit, they tactfully declined.[48]

As spring turned into summer, both John and Will Bankhead became enthusiastic supporters of Roosevelt, preferring him over the other contenders for the ticket, Al Smith and Speaker Garner. Roosevelt courted the brothers and other southerners. John H. Bankhead Jr. locked down the support of the Kentucky and Tennessee delegations for Roosevelt, who was nominated on the fourth ballot. The brothers campaigned for Roosevelt, speaking at party rallies in Kentucky, Indiana, and Missouri.[49] A veteran of some extremely close political campaigns early in his career and never one to underestimate the power of the opposition, Will remained cautious about Roosevelt's chances, confiding to Texas congressman Sam Rayburn in late October that "I think Roosevelt reached the peak of his strength thirty days ago and I feel that Hoover is now gaining ground." Nevertheless, Will did "not believe that [Hoover] can overcome Roosevelt's margin."[50] Roosevelt did much better than Will Bankhead anticipated, winning 472 Electoral College votes to Hoover's 59. Hoover won a meager five states.

The election was also a crushing defeat for Republicans in Congress; Democrats picked up seats in both houses and looked forward to commanding majorities in the upcoming session of Congress. New senator John H. Bankhead Jr. impressed Democratic majority leader Joseph T. Robinson of Arkansas and other party leaders, and later in November 1932, after the Democratic victory, Bankhead joined Robinson on a visit to Roosevelt's vacation home in Warm Springs, Georgia, to meet with the new president and the future secretary of agriculture Henry A. Wallace of Iowa. John Jr. was appointed to a special committee to develop a plan for agriculture, an unusual honor for a freshman senator.[51]

Despite a lame-duck Republican majority in the Senate (the new Democratic-controlled Senate would not be seated until 1933), John H. Bankhead Jr. moved forward on the farm problem. Like his brother, John Jr. demonstrated his own willingness to burn ideological bridges by adopting more experimental legislation to bring relief and recovery. In particular, he advocated stronger federal measures to control cotton production and restore commodity prices.[52] In December 1932, before Roosevelt's inauguration, he introduced a bill that would regulate the production of cotton and wheat through restrictions on the shipment of these commodities in interstate and foreign commerce. Will introduced the same bill in the House.[53] Debate on the bill was contentious, with conservatives on both sides of the aisle denouncing its unbridled interference in the marketplace. John H. Bankhead Jr. admitted that the bill's approach to the farm problem represented a new tactic for him. Unlike in the previous decade, when he believed that private interests could best assist in something like Muscle Shoals, the current economic situation demanded a new direction. He declared that he had reached "the point where . . . former theories of mine shall not control my action on this great question so long as it appears to me . . . that the plan is workable and will bring about the desired result."[54] With a Republican majority in the Senate, a lame-duck Hoover still in the White House, and strong opposition from conservative Democrats, no one was surprised when the bill failed. Bankhead was not deterred; this was the opening skirmish in what promised to be a long war. He was destined to become an important and pragmatic voice for agriculture during the Roosevelt years.[55]

Following Roosevelt's election, the farm situation reached a critical point. Edward O'Neal of Alabama, president of the American Farm Bureau Federation, predicted that unless farmers were given relief, "we will have a revolution in the country-side in less than 12 months."[56] By 1933, farm prices had dropped to 64 percent of parity.[57] The average annual income per farm in 1932 Alabama was $200, down from $700 in the immediate postwar era.[58] The agricultural crisis fell most heavily on those least able to weather the storm: tenants and sharecroppers, who made up the majority of southern farmers.

During the Roosevelt era, both Bankheads became staunch supporters and effective champions of the New Deal, their support driven in part by party loyalty. But their enthusiasm for Roosevelt's legislative program also sprang from an evolution in their political thinking, particularly with regard to the appropriate role of the state. They demonstrated a new willingness to experiment, to take bold action to provide relief for destitute Americans. To those who preferred to move slowly and to rely on old theories, Will replied, "It is the solemn duty of Congress to take some chances, to experiment a little bit, if you please, to pioneer a little bit, with some courageous legislation, even if it may be a mistake in some detail, in order to find relief."[59] With the election of Franklin

D. Roosevelt and strong Democratic majorities in both houses of Congress, the time for action had arrived.

President Roosevelt called Congress into special session on March 9, 1933. Speaker Garner had been elected as Roosevelt's vice president, opening up a leadership challenge in the House. Although Garner supported Alabama congressman John McDuffie for his former post, a split among southern Democrats allowed Henry T. Rainey of Illinois to win the race for Speaker. Will Bankhead remained on the Committee on Rules, serving as de facto chair in place of the ailing Congressman Pou. Although the legislation introduced during the dramatic first hundred days of Roosevelt's first term bypassed traditional congressional procedures, the Committee on Rules, under Bankhead's leadership, was soon front and center, establishing fairly drastic rules that limited debate and the ability to offer amendments to New Deal bills. One congressman from Massachusetts remarked that because of the limitations on debate established by the Committee on Rules, "many new members [of the House] may never find out how the House considers bills," to which Bankhead replied that nearly everything he knew about gag rules he had learned in the 1920s from the Republicans.

Finally, after a decade as a member of the minority, Will found himself in an enviable position to help guide legislation at a critical moment. But something was wrong. Will confessed to daughter Tallulah in March that "I have not been at all well for a week."[60] The fact is that Will had not been well for some time. In February 1933, daughter Eugenia wrote, "I had no idea you had had another serious heart attack."[61] Another? Her wording implies at least two episodes as of February. The public record reveals no health issues for Bankhead prior to this time, and save for this letter, his private papers likewise reveal nothing. Although physically weakened, Will continued to advocate vigorously for the administration's agenda. But the furious pace of the first hundred days was taking a physical toll on him.

In April 1933, Congress was deep in debate on the administration's agriculture bill. The *New York Times* described action on the House floor as "tempestuous" and full of "fireworks."[62] On April 11, after delivering a rousing speech on the floor in support of the rather harsh rules governing debate approved by the Committee on Rules, Will left the chamber to join Congressman McDuffie for lunch. While in the House cloakroom, Will was stricken by chest pains. Alarmed, McDuffie and several other congresspeople rushed him to the office of Dr. George W. Calver, attending physician of Congress. Dr. Calver's initial diagnosis was that Congressman Bankhead had suffered a heart attack; he soon changed his mind and announced that the congressman had suffered from an attack of "acute indigestion" and that Bankhead was "resting easily and will be able to go home very shortly."[63] Will likewise told his brother-in-law Arthur Lund that he had suffered from indigestion.[64] Brother John informed his own family "that Will's condition was not serious and that he would be back in Congress after a few day's rest."[65] At best, this was wishful thinking. At worst, it was a lie. Tallulah wired Eugenia that the April 1933 event had been a heart attack. Eugenia, lamenting to her father, expressed what Will no doubt was also thinking: "I do think it is darn tough luck on you to be laid up just now with your party in control for the first time in so many years."[66] The recovery took longer than anyone anticipated. When Will returned to the House a month later, "the entire membership of the House stood and applauded [his] return." Will made occasional appearances in the House in May but still had not returned to work full time by the time Congress adjourned in June.[67]

As his brother recovered, Senator John H. Bankhead Jr. developed into a highly effective legislator and trusted New Deal adviser for President Roosevelt. He even looked like a southern senator. Often wearing a rumpled seersucker suit, he was a bit portly as he entered his sixth decade. Like his father at his age, John Jr. was bald and favored rimless glasses. One reporter noted that "the Senator lacks the suavity of his younger brother. He is inclined to be pompous, bombastic in speech, old-fashioned in oratory. His Phi Beta Kappa key dances and gleams as he enforces his points with earnest and vigorous gestures."[68] John H. Bankhead Jr. had come to believe that control of production was the key to raising farm prices, and he supported secretary of agriculture Henry A. Wallace's idea to offer subsidies to farmers who limited output.[69] Bankhead kept

Figure 10.4. Will Bankhead (*right*) with President Franklin D. Roosevelt (*center*) and Vice President John Nance Garner, c. 1933. Courtesy of the Alabama Department of Archives and History.

in daily contact with the president, and he and Senate majority leader Joseph T. Robinson of Arkansas became the leading spokesmen in the Senate for the administration's agriculture plan.

Farmers and farm organizations were not of one mind when it came to the farm problem. Most who wrote to the secretary of agriculture and the president demanded some sort of federal action, but they differed on what shape that action should take. Many farmers expressed strong faith in Secretary Wallace and supported strong executive action to meet the emergency. Through the debates of the 1920s, farmers had come to believe that parity prices were a right. Based on the correspondence received by the secretary, the most unpopular element of the new legislation would be the production controls.[70]

The Agricultural Adjustment Act (AAA), the administration's plan for saving farmers, became law on May 12, 1933. The act's goal was to restore farm purchasing power as it existed in the pre–World War I era. To achieve this, the secretary of agriculture was given broad powers to raise farm prices by reducing output and bringing production into line with effective demand. To reduce output, farmers were offered cash benefit payments. Funds for these cash payments would come through taxes on packers, millers, and other processors of farm commodities. The act did not require farmers to take land out of production; rather, the administration hoped that the enticement of government payments would encourage farmers to comply.[71] The administration hoped that the increase in farm income would also increase farmers' purchasing power, thus stimulating industrial recovery.[72] John H. Bankhead Jr.'s unsuccessful December 1932 bill was folded into the AAA, and he became one of its most forceful advocates.[73] John Jr.'s role in the creation of New Deal agricultural policy was so prominent, and his advocacy on behalf of the idea of establishing parity for farm products so consistent, that he earned the nickname "Parity John."

By the time the bill became law, the 1933 crop was already in the ground. Farmers were paid for plowing up a quarter of their fields, an idea for which Bankhead took credit.[74] Ultimately, some 10.5 million acres were plowed up.[75] During the bill's inaugural year, approximately three million farmers in forty-eight states signed production-control contracts. The commodities affected included wheat, cotton, corn, hogs, and tobacco. In June 1934, AAA administrator Chester D. Davis announced that the program had enjoyed a "good beginning," noting that "the march of 3,000,000 farmers to joining their county production control associations in a voluntary experiment of such scope is a dramatic and historic thing."[76] Despite its obvious problems (critics lambasted the decision to destroy cotton and hogs at a time when so many people were cold and hungry), the AAA represented an improvement over what Davis derided as "the tooth-and-fang individualism of the Old Deal days." Individualism "means exposure of the farmer to a one-handed contest with the blind forces of nature, with which his trade forces him always to match his strength. It means misery and starvation somewhere for some farmers every year."[77] In fall 1933, hundreds of thousands of farmers received checks from the federal government. For many, it would be the first meaningful income they had received in years. With the AAA, one historian has noted, "the federal government now had a new relationship with farmers."[78] By the end of the decade, farmers would regard federal financial assistance as an entitlement. Senator Bankhead was a key architect of this new relationship between agriculture and the state.

Despite some early promising signs, the AAA's voluntary control measures did not achieve the crop reductions necessary to improve cotton prices appreciably. Furthermore, a severe drought curtailed reduction plans on other crops in the Plains states. In the South, either farmers refused to participate or they reneged later on agreements to cut back on production. Still other farmers intensified their use of fertilizers to make their allotted acres more productive. John Jr. and his son, Walter Will, traveled through Alabama, Georgia, and the Carolinas to observe the cotton situation firsthand. The senator was discouraged and complained to the president that more drastic steps needed to be taken to curtail future production.[79] The 1933 cotton crop was even larger than the 1932 crop.[80] Prices for cotton dropped. John Jr. used this state of affairs to push for mandatory controls.

Convinced that parity could not be achieved without mandatory reductions, Senator Bankhead aggressively pursued his plan to institute strict quotas for the ginning of cotton in an effort to control production and raise prices. He appealed to Secretary Wallace. If cotton prices continued to drop, farmers would have less money to spend. Bankhead speculated, "how will the industrial east and north dispose of the products of their factories with millions of the customers eliminated as buyers?"[81] Bankhead held meetings in Birmingham, Memphis, and Atlanta with commercial growers, ginners, and manufacturers to discuss his plans for stricter controls. Originally skeptical of mandatory controls, Wallace threw his support behind Bankhead's plan after a survey of forty thousand cotton growers indicated that 98 percent favored compulsory controls.[82]

The overwhelming support expressed for mandatory controls convinced Bankhead and Congress that something stronger was required. On the first day of the new session, John Jr. introduced what would become known as the Bankhead Cotton Control Act in the Senate, while Will introduced an identical measure in the House. The purpose of the act was to address deficiencies in the Agricultural Adjustment Act. The Bankhead Act focused on baleage and not acreage reduction. Each farmer was allotted a production quota 40 percent below his average. Under the Bankhead Cotton Control Act, each state had an allotted quota of cotton; within each state, each grower received a quota of allocated market tags.[83] The Bankhead plan instituted a severe cash penalty for each bale of cotton that was ginned over a farmer's allotment.[84] Although not a huge proponent of mandatory controls, the president signed the act on April 21, 1934.[85] The provisions were to be effective only for the 1934–35 crop year. Thomas L. Stokes of the *New York World-Telegram* noted that John Jr.'s "success with the compulsory cotton bill is a tribute to his persistence and tenacity. He took it to the floor of Congress, enlisting support here, there and everywhere by continuous missionary work on its behalf. And the Bankhead boys scored again."[86] Journalists made much of the legislative power of the "Bankhead boys." Despite Will Bankhead's recent heart attack, one journalist equated his legislative prowess with physical dominance, writing that Will "still has the carriage of the fullback he once was. His broad shoulders are stooped now; he carries a cane. But if you dressed him in moleskins and put a helmet on his head, he would, in appearance, at least, be a threatening backfield man."[87] New Deal legislation was in capable hands.

Criticism of and skepticism about the bill were widespread. Declaring that the "Bankhead boys" had stirred up "a rumpus" with the bill, one New York paper reported that Republicans "bewailed the 'Russianizing' of American agriculture." The US Chamber of Commerce assailed the bill, predicting it "would subordinate the free American citizen to the dictation and tyranny of the government."[88] The *Saturday Evening Post* called the Bankhead act "a piece of tyranny."[89] Cotton farmers themselves were cautiously optimistic.

In its first year, the act succeeded in holding production below the desired national quota of 10,466,000 bales, and some cotton producers and representatives from cotton states advocated terminating the law. Others regarded the policy as a "failure" because it hurt small producers, tenants, and day laborers and favored wealthier farmers. Sociologist Rupert B. Vance noted that sharecroppers and tenants were "expected to bear the brunt of reduced acreage in dismissals comparable to the lay-off of idle factory hands. It is they who stand to receive but a fraction of the benefit paid the landowner for retiring part of the acreage they cultivate." Vance observed that sharecroppers and tenants were responsible for 60 percent of average cotton production yet received only one-ninth of the benefit payments.[90] John H. Bankhead Jr. himself favored a suspension of the law that bore his name. Ultimately, the administration decided that the controls would be continued through 1934, although the quota for small producers would be increased 10 percent to "iron out inequities."[91]

A 1936 report issued by the Department of Agriculture noted that because of mandatory controls, the price of cotton had risen from 6.3 cents per pound in March 1933 to 11.3 cents per pound in December 1935. The cotton crop and seed therefrom yielded a cash return of $35,535 in 1932; the cash return in 1934 was $71,013. The report also noted that the "farmer's money goes to town" and helps drive the industrial sector and thus "puts people to work."[92] Several months after the publication of this report, in an October 1936 ceremony at Senator Bankhead's Jasper home, Alabama Polytechnic Institute (now Auburn University) conferred on John Jr. an honorary Doctor of Laws "in partial recognition of his splendid service to the farmers of America and especially to the cotton farmers of the South."[93]

But which cotton farmers? What the Department of Agriculture report failed to mention but sociologist Vance and others already knew was that landlords, and not tenants, received the lion's share of the benefits; among land owners, large producers did better than small. Only landlords were allowed to sign contracts. For the 1934–35 season, the government issued two types of payment. Landlords received rental payments for land taken out of production. Parity payments were based on quotas and production, with the payment split between the landlord and the tenant based on their division of the crop produced. The landlord was entrusted with the parity payment distribution. Some were honest. Others were not and kept the entire payment. Landlords were allowed to determine the status of their tenants for payment purposes. Landlords lied about their tenants' status, downgrading rental tenants to sharecroppers, sharecroppers to wage workers. Some landlords simply evicted their tenants rather than share any payment whatsoever. Abuse of the system was rampant; tenant complaints were turned over to a dispute committee, which was dominated by landowners.[94] As one historian has noted, "The benefits [of the AAA and later acts] were programmed to go to farmers with acreage and production; others would have to look elsewhere for help."[95]

In his 1936 plea for the plight of sharecroppers and those trapped by the cotton economy, Howard Kester, a Christian socialist and activist dedicated to helping the South's dispossessed, had harsh words for the AAA, which he referred to as an "economic monstrosity and bastard child of a decadent capitalism and a youthful Fascism."[96] He cited the "calamitous and devastating effect" of the AAA "on the masses of people, white and colored." He noted that "not only were cotton tenants eliminated from the land by the reduction program, but those who remained on the land had their already miserable standard of living lowered and received practically none of the benefits which were due them under the government contracts."[97] Designed to address the problem of overproduction, the AAA and the Bankhead Control Act had initiated a massive upheaval in the tenant system that compounded the misery of an already suffering class of people.

Amid the social dislocation taking place in the cotton fields and the real pain being felt by the families of sharecroppers and tenants, Senator Bankhead pursued a very different program that rested on a more romantic vision of farm life. John H. Bankhead Jr. embodied the contradictions of the New Deal's approach to rural America. On the one hand, he recognized the dire straits in which cotton farmers in particular existed, and he had a key role in developing the AAA; simultaneously, though, he (and the president) viewed rural America as an Edenic refuge capable of absorbing unemployed urban workers.

John H. Bankhead Jr.'s interest in rural America extended beyond issues of supply and demand. Like his father, with his quest for good roads, John Jr. eyed a larger prize: the rehabilitation of rural life. In his estimation, the country had suffered an imbalance as a result of decades of industrialization and urbanization. The Great Depression was an inevitable result of that imbalance. Not too far from the senator's Jasper home, the city of Birmingham was object lesson number one on the failures of industrial life. Steel production in 1932 fell to a quarter of its 1929 level. Unemployment skyrocketed, and many destitute fled the city to return to the countryside. The number of farms in Jefferson County nearly doubled between 1930 and 1935. In Bankhead's home county of Walker, coal mining jobs were rapidly disappearing.[98] What would happen to these people?

With no future in sight for the urban and industrial unemployed and underemployed, Bankhead envisioned a different and better life for them back on the farm. He devised a relief plan for the millions of destitute Americans walking the unemployment line. Bankhead quite rightly pointed out that private charity could no longer meet the needs of the destitute. He supported the idea of large public works projects, although he doubted whether Congress would sufficiently finance something on a scale commensurate with the need. Even before Roosevelt's election, Senator Bankhead had introduced a plan to resettle millions of unemployed and underemployed industrial workers on subsistence farms. "If 1,000,000 men now unemployed could be financed under a back-to-the-soil program," he argued, "an improvement in business conditions would more quickly afford work for the other unemployed, and would remove several million people from the ranks of the very large number who are anxiously thinking of food for tomorrow." The program would be funded by taking $400 million from the Reconstruction Finance Corporation funds, to be administered under the secretary of the interior through state and local agencies. The bill offered loans at an interest rate of 4 percent, with the stipulation that no more than $1,000 would be advanced to any family. Homeowners would have twenty years to repay the loan.[99] For skeptics who questioned whether the urban unemployed would really be better off in the equally devastated countryside, Bankhead painted a rosy picture of rural life, noting that "rural life has in recent years been vastly changed. With good roads, rural mail delivery, improved school facilities, consolidated schools with free bus service, free transportation to high schools, rural telephones, and many other advantages, country life from a social standpoint is in large measure comparable to suburban opportunities."[100]

Franklin D. Roosevelt shared Bankhead's affinity for moving the urban and industrial unemployed back to the farm. While still governor, Roosevelt had announced a plan to resettle New York State's unemployed to semirural subsistence homesteads. Like Bankhead, Roosevelt held a romantic view of rural life and the prospects for the poor, proclaiming, "They may secure through the good earth the permanent jobs they have lost in overcrowded industrial cities and towns."[101] In his inaugural address, Roosevelt acknowledged an "overbalance of population in our industrial centers" and supported the idea of population "redistribution."[102] Despite evidence to the contrary, Roosevelt, Bankhead, and others saw farms and farmers as more secure than urban industrial populations. The senator's and then-governor's descriptions of farm life did not match the reality, particularly in the South, where the majority of farm families anxiously awaited the basic amenities of modern life. Most southern farm families lived without electricity. As of 1930, only 14 percent of all southern homes had a telephone, compared to a national average of 34 percent. In Bankhead's home state of Alabama, fewer than 5 percent of all farm owners enjoyed running water. In 1934, the majority of southern farms still used privies. Southern rural schools were inadequate. A single study of one thousand farm families found one-third of the adults to be functionally illiterate.[103]

Early New Deal initiatives resulted in programs that, in many regards, reflected the idealized notions of rural life held by the president and Senator Bankhead, and failed to grasp the realities of rural poverty. In fact, roughly 1.7 million farm families across the South were on some type of relief by early 1934, most of it administered by the Federal Emergency Relief Administration (FERA). For many tenant families, relief payments were a godsend, providing them a higher standard of living than had been possible under farming. But direct relief was expensive, so FERA turned its attention to what it called "rehabilitation," basically providing loans, seed, tools, and supervision to assist impoverished rural families, allowing them once again to become self-sufficient producers. The rehabilitation division of FERA also undertook resettlement projects.[104]

John H. Bankhead Jr. doggedly pursued his own plans for resettlement. In March 1933, he introduced a bill seeking a $400 million loan from the Reconstruction Finance Corporation to move unemployed industrial workers to subsistence homesteads. Will introduced a similar bill in the House. After this bill failed to make it out of committee, John Jr. introduced a second, more modest bill, in April 1933. This bill, too, failed.[105] Just as his father had forged an unorthodox path to break the resistance to federal financing of roads, so too did John Jr. succeed through an unconventional route. In May 1933, Congress debated Roosevelt's plan for industrial recovery. Passed by Congress and signed by the president in early June 1933, the National Industrial Recovery Act authorized codes of competition designed to foster industrial recovery, established protections for workers, and created the Public Works Administration (PWA). Embedded within the act's Title II, establishing the PWA, was section 208, entitled "Subsistence Homesteads." The act authorized $25 million to aid "the redistribution of the overbalance of population in industrial centers" by "making loans for and otherwise aiding in the purchase of subsistence homesteads."[106] Bankhead noted that the small acreage intended under the subsistence homestead program would not create additional commercial farmers; rather, "it provides means of earning from the soil the necessities for keeping body and soul together and for retaining inviolate the family circle and for the development of family spirit. Such a life instills self-respect, and with proper diligence gives assurance that hunger will not molest the family."[107] Bankhead's subsistence homestead project would be housed in the Department of the Interior's Division of Subsistence Homesteads. It would be the first of several bureaucratic homes for the program.

During the course of the New Deal and beyond, the homestead program was hampered by a number of difficulties, among them any substantive agreement as to what a homestead should be. Was it designed for short-term relief, or was it a long-term program? Many advocates, Bankhead included, leaned toward the latter. They believed that the current economic dislocation would not be remedied for years, perhaps decades; they remained skeptical as to whether the industrial economy would ever again be able to absorb all the unemployed. A return to the land was the only recourse. The focus, therefore, was not merely on rescuing individual homesteaders but on creating a new type of community.

Five homestead communities were created around Birmingham and John H. Bankhead Jr.'s hometown of Jasper: Palmerdale, Mount Olive, Greenwood, Cahaba, and Bankhead Farms. Initially, the homestead effort was highly decentralized, which reflected director M. L. Wilson's focus on creating these communities as laboratories in democracy. Local corporations designed to oversee the projects were created in Jefferson and Walker Counties, and potential homestead sites were chosen by committees made up of local citizens. Within a year, the local homestead corporations were dissolved and operation of the homesteads became centralized in Washington, DC. The homesteads' administrative home remained in flux throughout the New Deal years. In 1935, the homesteads fell under the direction of the recently created Resettlement Administration. This bureaucratic movement created multiple lines of authority, which fostered confusion and slowed work on the homesteads.

Birmingham-area homesteads encountered a host of problems. Decisions had to be made quickly, but construction of the homesteads proceeded slowly. Resettlement administrators had high hopes for the Palmerdale homesteads. The land was ideal for farming. What they did not count on was how long it would take to remove existing property owners from the tract. In July 1934, more than a year after the act was passed, a large dairy operation still had not relocated. Bankhead Farms, located five miles north of Jasper, planned for one hundred homesteads. John H. Bankhead Jr. was particularly invested in this project. He suggested to the director of the Homestead Division that the homesteaders market tomato juice and passed along the name of a local man who had developed a type of tomato that would be perfect for the venture.[108] Funds were allotted for the Bankhead Farms project in January 1934, but construction did not begin until the end of January 1935. In February 1935, John expressed disappointment in these delays, observing that the program "has been made bureaucratic and has been so centralized that it is practically broken down from my view."[109]

Although Palmerdale and Bankhead Farms lay on promising land, the same could not be said for the other projects. Land in the Greenwood homesteads was severely eroded and could be used only as pasture. Much of the Mount Olive property was hilly and dry, while other areas were sandy and prone to leaching nutrients. Even land that was ideal for cultivation required extensive terracing and the construction of outlet ditches. All this took time, thus delaying construction of the houses.

The first homes—twenty-four at Bankhead Farms and sixty at Palmerdale—were officially opened on September 1, 1935, more than two years after the projects were authorized. The cost of each house was around $2,000, which was considered a good deal. But the houses were poorly constructed. They were insufficiently weatherproofed, leading to frozen pipes, water-damaged walls, and cold floors. In a letter to Rexford Tugwell, head of the Resettlement Administration, Senator Bankhead expressed his embarrassment and frustration with the slow pace of progress of the Birmingham-area homesteads. He accused the Resettlement Administration of favoring suburban resettlement programs in the East and of giving preference to "colored housing projects" over those for white residents: "Frankly speaking, the people of Birmingham and this mineral district feel like this section is the stepchild of this Administration."[110] Ultimately, because of construction delays and other problems, houses in Greenwood, Mount Olive, and Palmerdale averaged a sale price of around $6,500 each, while the larger Bankhead Farm homes were about $7,200 each. These communities experienced a great deal of flux and turnover in the early years, during which time the homesteads were rented to tenants, and it took almost five years before the process for selling the homes to the residents began.

The projects failed to meet their objectives when it came to selecting residents. They were designed with unemployed industrial workers in mind, so the number of white-collar occupants was meant to be kept to a minimum. That rule was not always followed. The size of the Bankhead Farms homesteads averaged twenty acres and was planned for irregularly employed coal miners. But coal miners disliked the location and complained about the high rents. Eventually, middle-class families moved in. Few used their property to establish subsistence farms. Those who established effective farms did so by hiring labor, not an original goal of the program. The homestead projects also embodied the racial limitations of most New Deal initiatives. Not only were the projects designed exclusively for white residents, but existing black residents were often removed from properties slated for homestead construction.

The other homestead communities experienced similar problems. Despite the fact that a knowledge of farming was a prerequisite for residency, a majority of homesteaders in Greenwood—many of them unemployed workers from the Tennessee Coal, Iron and Railroad (TCI) company—knew little to nothing about agriculture. The average resident of Cahaba was a white-collar employee with a salary sufficient to make cultivating a garden unnecessary. The sites chosen for the resettlement communities were not convenient for working-class people. They were too far from the industrial work sites in Birmingham, many residents did not own cars, and public transportation was either inadequate or nonexistent. Residents were never wholly committed to the goals of the project. Many ultimately hired black laborers to work their fields. Those homeowners who did possess experience in agriculture were typically familiar with cotton cultivation, not subsistence farming. Cooperative farm services, stores, and filling stations initiated on the individual homesteads were largely unsuccessful.[111]

The homesteads employed a resident selection process, but that did not stop the Bankheads from using their influence to help individual applicants. In fact, individuals involved in resident selection made it clear that a letter of recommendation from the congressman or senator would ensure them a home in one of the projects. Will Bankhead wrote to the resident selection supervisor for Bankhead Farms on behalf of an applicant named John Swindle. Bankhead wrote, "I have known this young man for a number of years, and know him to be a man of good character, and also that he will keep his payments up and meet all his obligations."[112] Will recommended another family because they were "good people, active in church work," and another because "his father worked for us [for] many years when we operated the coal mine at Bankhead, and they are good people."[113] He wrote on behalf of people who were employed, including a man who worked for the Walker County Department of Public Welfare, one who was employed by the *Birmingham News*, a gentleman who was the owner of a "high class Café," a man who was employed as a school principal and who had a "$1200–$1500 annual income," as well as men working as station agents and section foremen for the Northern Alabama Railway.[114] When it came to accessing New Deal benefits, it paid to be white; it also paid to know a Bankhead.

The indefatigable Marie Bankhead Owen shared John's affinity for a certain type of rural life and worked hard to use her considerable connections to develop a subsistence homestead community in Elmore County, where she owned a farm. Writing to her brother, she admitted that "for many years I have been interested in the idea of small farms grouped about a community center, such as they have in certain sections of the old world." John's bill seemed to be the perfect vehicle with which to achieve this. "In such a center could be located recreational programs, a library, room for club meetings of women and of men, and a room for exchanging products, or where visitors could purchase surplus products which could be put in a common store room for sale, a school room probably for small children, a place where the community could assemble for singing, lectures, etc." Not just anyone could settle in Marie's ideal community, however. "Such a community should be organized in a selective way so that there would be congeniality," she advised. Her ideal residents were "what you would call 'white collar' men and women"—people like Marie Bankhead Owen. What about the underemployed working-class family for whom the subsistence homestead project was originally designed? Marie noted that "other colonies of a different class of people who would be congenial could be assembled by an interested party."[115] The needs of the grubby underclass—people desperately in need of federal assistance—held no interest for her. Brother John was encouraging, telling Marie that her ideas were basically "sound." Marie located an available property, roughly eight hundred acres near a train station. Close by were "good schools and churches." The property also contained a gravel deposit and stands of timber that held profitable potential. She considered the property to be a good location for a glass manufacturer and met with a representative of Alabama Power about recruiting potential industry. Marie was unconcerned that several black families currently lived on the property. They lay wholly outside her definition of "congenial" members of the community. She informed John Jr. that their homes "could be repaired or removed for white families if they are not properly located." She spoke of a Catholic priest who desired to create a subsistence homestead community for African Americans. John Jr. advised her to encourage the priest to locate it near Tuskegee Institute, where college administrators could "keep the settlers under their influence." She assured her brother that the priest in question "has a genuine interest in the Negro from *our point of view*." Marie tried for months to establish her "congenial" rural hamlet; despite her best efforts, no subsistence homestead project was established in Elmore County.[116]

Administration of the projects was transferred to the Farm Security Administration in 1937 and finally to the Federal Public Housing Authority during World War II. The coming of World War II eliminated the need for the homestead program. By 1944, most residents were employed full time. There was not sufficient labor to make the farms productive. By August 1944, the homestead communities had lost all contact with federal supervision.

Although the Birmingham-area homesteads failed to meet most of their goals as envisioned by Senator Bankhead and others, the residents of these communities were largely satisfied with their situation. Most experienced a better standard of living, and they expressed pride in the communities they had built. Mrs. H. N. McLean, a resident of Bankhead Farms, wrote to Senator Bankhead in 1937 to let him know how thrilled she was with her homestead. "For the first time, we have been able to have fresh vegetables from our garden and fryers [chickens] we have raised." She was grateful to be able to get her children "things they have always wanted and could not have had if it had not been for your wonderful mind and love of your fellow man."[117] They also considered themselves part of an important and successful social experiment, a positive example of what government should do to help citizens.[118]

The death of Speaker Rainey, congressman from Illinois, in August 1934 after a bout of pneumonia set off a leadership struggle among the Democrats that lasted throughout the fall. With Rainey gone, southern representatives were the primary figures in the line of succession, which did not sit well with Democrats from other parts of the country. Majority leader Joseph Byrns, representative from Tennessee, expected to be elected to the post. Alabama congressman John McDuffie, who a few years earlier had contemplated the Speaker's post, announced that he would not seek the position but would instead throw his support to Will Bankhead. Roosevelt indicated that he would prefer a Democrat who would shore up his newly won support in the West. On August 25, speaking from his home in Jasper, Bankhead announced his candidacy for the position of Speaker of the House. He lobbied hard for it throughout the fall.[119] Also interested in the speakership was Congressman Sam Rayburn of Texas; Rayburn and Bankhead were both determined to prevent Byrns's election as Speaker and shared information. "Although we are trying to beat each other," Bankhead wrote to Rayburn, "I feel that a candid and frank interchange of information upon this subject might be helpful to both of us regardless of what the ultimate outcome may be." Bankhead was confident that "Byrns can be stopped."[120] In mid-November, one congressional colleague assured him that if the decision for Speaker "rest[ed] on the basis of merit and personal popularity, there could be no question of your election."[121] By December, Byrns's candidacy had gained strength, leaving Bankhead discouraged. Northern Democrats were urging Bankhead to remove himself from the race for Speaker and instead make himself available as majority leader, sometimes referred to as the floor leader. According to the *New York Times*, northern Democrats considered Bankhead to be the body's best parliamentarian, "popular and resourceful," and that those traits would be needed in a floor leader for the upcoming legislative session. "It is more important to have a suave pacifier as floor leader than an experienced legislator as Speaker," the *Times* noted.[122] Acknowledging that it appeared that Byrns could not be beaten, Bankhead mused to a reporter, "You know I went fishing this summer with Joe Byrns down in the Gulf. I managed to catch a 125-pound shark one day. I now find I made a mistake in not throwing Joe overboard and feeding him to the shark."[123] By late December, Bankhead had the inside track as floor leader, with the Democratic caucus planned for early January.[124]

Ray Tucker, writing for *Collier's*, offered a colorful assessment of the "surplus of strong men" vying for the role of Speaker. "Lanky, drawling" majority leader Byrns was the recognized front-runner, but although many of his fellow House members "love this homely, grizzled old-timer from Tennessee," he was considered by many to be "too good-natured and easy-going" to effectively lead. Sam Rayburn of Texas provided a striking contrast to Byrns. Described by Tucker as "a bald, stocky, rugged farmer-lawyer from the red clay country of Texas," Rayburn was "unspectacular and undemonstrative, even unimpressive." A serious man, Rayburn had a legislative style vastly unlike that of Byrns. "Rayburn never budges or gives an inch on the floor. He prefers to outfight and outargue the other fellow." Will Bankhead, Tucker wrote, "has nothing in common with Byrns or Rayburn—except an ambition." In contrast to Rayburn and Byrns with their more folksy manner, Bankhead "is polished, cultured, gracious. He dresses well and has a distinguished presence. He is, without a doubt, the finest natural orator in the House, and one of the most compelling on Capitol Hill. Unlike most congressional spellbinders, he gets on his feet only when he has something to say. He speaks seldom, but when he does, the House listens and pays heed." Tucker observed that whoever was elected the next Speaker would have his work cut out for him, as House Democrats in the new session would require more "leading and guidance than a brawling nursery at bedtime." The upcoming session promised to be contentious. "This Congress must pass upon legislation more fateful than the batch of revolutionary measures which its predecessor ground out. That body accepted and enacted an admittedly emergency and experimental program because there was nothing else to do. The next Congress must end or prolong or modify many basic experiments which so deeply affect our social, economic, and political life. It must lay a firmer and more permanent foundation under the shifting structure of the New Deal." The performance of the next Congress likewise would strengthen or weaken President Roosevelt's prospects for reelection in 1936.[125]

With Will Bankhead poised to climb the next rung on the Democratic leadership ladder, tragedy struck yet again: Bankhead suffered a massive heart attack on New Year's Day 1935. Worried that knowledge of his illness would jeopardize his chance at being elected majority leader, those closest to the congressman kept the event a secret. Brother John discussed the situation with members of the Alabama delegation, who were determined to make Will majority leader. They kept their mouths shut. Will's secretary announced at the Democratic caucus at which party leaders would be chosen that the congressman had a "bad cold" and could not attend. Will's wife, Florence, likewise confirmed that his condition was "not serious," while fellow Alabama congressman William Oliver attributed his absence to "a cold and indigestion." Although some members of the party caucus objected to electing someone not physically present, Bankhead was elected majority leader on the second ballot, on January 2, 1935.[126] His election was notable for its lack of sectionalism. It was the first time since the Civil War that Democrats had not chosen to split the top two positions between the North and the South. Newly elected Speaker of the House Joseph Byrns administered the oath of office to Bankhead while Will lay in a bed at the Naval Hospital. The *New York Times* praised his election and leadership; referring to him as one of the "New Deal Shepherds," it noted his parliamentary skills and his conciliatory nature. "Often, when tempers flare, and voices rise, [Bankhead] walks quietly, gracefully, down the middle aisle and says, 'Let's examine this situation.' Then he states the predicament and presents the solution so lucidly and so eloquently that he often saves the day—and the Democrats."[127]

An accurate accounting of Bankhead's health remained a closely guarded secret. In its January 14, 1935, issue, *Time* magazine included a story on Bankhead's election as majority leader and subsequent hospitalization. It repeated the bogus diagnosis of "a cold and indigestion." The breezy story recounted how "daughter Tallulah flew to the Capital, and ran to his bedside [at the Naval Hospital]." Upon leaving her father, she told reporters, "Daddy will be all right. I talked a blue streak and it may not have helped him any. . . . Daddy just won't take care of himself!"[128] Apparently no one at *Time* questioned why Tallulah hastened to the hospital if her father was suffering from a simple head cold or indigestion. Other newspaper accounts reported that he was "suffering from phlebitis," while brother John told one reporter that Will's problem was "a stomach disorder." But as winter turned into spring, and with no sight of the new majority leader as the new session got underway, journalists began to speculate. Hearst journalist George Rothwell Brown noted in his Washington Sideshow column that "Will Bankhead . . . is a much sicker man than has been let on," although he noted that Bankhead was yet "an abler one sick than most of his colleagues in full possession of blooming health." Brown derided "the political ineptitude of the unwieldy democratic majority of the House" in Bankhead's absence. Bankhead's ability to use his skills to the advantage of the New Deal agenda would be severely limited. He was discharged from the Naval Hospital in late February 1935 but continued to be treated at Johns Hopkins University Hospital, where Tallulah had engaged a cardiac specialist to oversee his recovery. Once the weather improved, his doctor allowed him to leave his apartment for daily automobile rides. During the course of his rides Bankhead would order the car to halt in front of the House Office Building. His stenographer would greet the majority leader and take dictation in the car. In June 1935, he returned to Jasper, which he considered "the ideal place for me to be."[129]

Recovery was slow. Will confided to brother John that he was "trying to get along with a minimum effort."[130] As of June, five months following the incident, he still could not climb stairs. He informed his doctor that "I am sleeping down stairs in my home but as there is no bath on the first floor I have to be carried upstairs in a chair for the purpose, and I would like for you to let me know how soon you think it would be safe for me to walk up stairs by slow stages." The following month, July 1935, he reported to his physician that he weighed 158 pounds and was taking a heart tonic.[131] Despite his fragile health, Will underwent what he described as "some rather severe treatment on my gums for pyorrhea" in August.[132] Now called periodontitis, this common gum disease is understood to be linked to heart disease. Neither Will nor his doctors could have known at the time, but it is quite possible that this disease and the "severe treatment" further compromised his ailing heart.

Despite his confinement, Will Bankhead remained involved in shepherding critical New Deal legislation, working the phones regularly, and providing direction to the acting majority leader, Representative Edward T. Taylor of Colorado, a seventy-eight-year-old lukewarm New Dealer.[133] The first session of the Seventy-Fourth Congress was momentous, as Roosevelt and his allies attempted to address harsh criticism from the political left. The session witnessed the passage of landmark legislation, including the Emergency Relief Appropriation Act, which at $5 billion was the largest single appropriation in the nation's history; the Social Security Act, which created a national system of old-age insurance; and the National Labor Relations Act, commonly referred to as the Wagner Act, which protected workers' right to bargain collectively. But trouble was brewing for the New Deal. The administration suffered a tremendous setback when, on May 27, 1935, the US Supreme Court ruled the National Industrial Recovery Act unconstitutional, declaring that Congress had exceeded its authority under the commerce clause of the Constitution when it ceded code-making authority to the executive branch. The court's decision not only dismantled the president's primary plan for economic revitalization; it also threatened other New Deal programs, including the AAA and the Bankhead Cotton Control Act. The price of cotton dropped two cents a pound when the court's decision was announced.

Will had to watch all this from afar. When Congress adjourned in August 1935, Will Bankhead was still in Jasper. Bankhead's absence prompted discussion among other congresspeople of dividing his leadership duties for the upcoming session. Representative Patrick J. Boland of Pennsylvania informed Will of rumors "that you were contemplating to resign as Floor Leader before the coming session." All schemes were abandoned when Bankhead announced in December 1935 that he was fully recovered and prepared to resume his duties at the start of the new session in January 1936.[134]

President Roosevelt's first term and the early years of the New Deal were dramatic for the nation and for the Bankheads. John Jr. and Will took pride in their support for the administration and the work they did to help make possible the federal relief and jobs programs that rescued so many families in Alabama and across the nation. Senator John H. Bankhead Jr. had, in a few short years, established himself as a trusted presidential adviser and as a serious legislator, although his two major accomplishments did not turn out entirely as he had planned and had, in the case of the AAA and the Bankhead Cotton Control Act, compounded the misery of many tenants and sharecroppers. Although Will Bankhead found tremendous gratification in his election as majority leader and in the accomplishments of Congress, his body failed him at critical moments. Frustrated and disappointed, Will had no choice but to remain patient, convalesce, and hope that he could return to fight another day.

11

❧

Mr. Speaker

After a difficult recovery from his heart attack in January 1935, Will Bankhead returned to his position as majority leader in January 1936. "My long and desperate illness last year took a good deal out of me," Will confided to daughter Eugenia; "I cannot expect to be as strong and vigorous as I was before. . . . I am doing everything possible to take care of myself."[1] Will had high hopes for the upcoming legislative session, telling reporters that the session would be "snappy, although probably not short."[2] He did not anticipate any monumental legislation in this election year, which was fortuitous because some disgruntlement was starting to bubble up within the Democratic majority. Party unity was beginning to fray.

The 1935 session had been tumultuous and momentous. By the latter part of that year, nearly all of what is now recognized as landmark New Deal programs, including the Wagner Act and the Social Security Act, had been enacted. President Roosevelt told one confidant that he was looking forward to a "breathing spell" in 1936. It was an election year, and he wanted to keep potentially divisive legislative fights to a minimum. Nineteen thirty-six would be, in the words of historian William Leuchtenburg, "a time of healing, when [Roosevelt] would unite the party by salving the wounds of his opponents and avoid new conflicts with Congress until he had won re-election."[3] Roosevelt delivered his annual message to Congress in early January 1936, essentially repeating Bankhead's predictions for the upcoming session.

No sooner had the words left his mouth than the Supreme Court dropped a bombshell: in a 6–3 decision, the court invalidated the Agricultural Adjustment Act (AAA), the president's signature farm legislation. The court's major objection was to the subsidies paid to farmers, which were generated by a tax on food processors. The court ruled it unfair to tax one group (processors) to benefit another (farmers). The justices further argued that the AAA invaded the rights of states. Will Bankhead called the decision "distressing and disappointing." His brother John H. Bankhead Jr., senator and prominent architect of the legislation, told the *New York Times* that "people [in the cotton-growing states] are in better shape than they have been in ten years, and they will bitterly resent the decision." The senator was hopeful, however, that Congress could craft new legislation that would pass constitutional muster.[4] During the period in which the AAA had been in effect, farmers had enjoyed a "striking increase" in income. Bankhead and others would have to go back to the drawing board.[5] Without the processing tax, the cotton control program was immediately discontinued. Congress repealed the Bankhead Cotton Control Act on February 6, 1936.[6] Farm prices dropped sharply.

The president headed into his reelection year with his signature programs for industry and agriculture dismantled. The Supreme Court continued its assault on the New Deal throughout the 1936 session. Roosevelt fumed but kept his public comments short as he formulated a plan. As early as 1935, Roosevelt was considering some sort of move against the court, preferring some form of legislation over a constitutional amendment. Such an action would no doubt be controversial and so would have to wait until after the 1936 election. First things first.

In the early months of the 1936 congressional session, the administration moved quickly to address the farm situation. After meeting with agricultural committee leaders, including Senator Bankhead, the administration drafted the Soil Conservation and Domestic Allotment Act as a replacement for the stricken AAA. Approved in February 1936, the act directed the government to pay farmers bonuses for planting soil-enriching grasses and legumes in place of soil-depleting commercial crops.[7] The administration was determined that farmers continue to receive support, especially in an election year.

Other than the uproar over the Supreme Court's decision on the AAA, the congressional session was relatively quiet. By early June 1936, Congress was winding down. Members were anxious to return to their home districts for rest and a little politicking. Then tragedy struck. The date was June 4, 1936. At eleven o'clock in the morning, the House of Representatives was ready to convene, but the Speaker's chair stood empty. The clerk of the House, South Trimble, rapped the gavel. "It is my sad painful duty," intoned clerk Trimble, "to inform the House of the death of the Speaker." Joseph Byrns had died the previous night of a cerebral hemorrhage. Members sat in shocked silence. Representative John J. O'Connor of New York, chair of the Committee on Rules, rose to present a resolution nominating William B. Bankhead of Alabama, majority leader, as the new Speaker. "It is necessary," O'Connor said, "for the machinery of government to go on." "Are there any nays?" asked clerk Trimble. The House was silent. Clad in a white linen suit, Congressman Bankhead, head bowed, marched down the aisle to the dais, where he was sworn in. Bankhead raised his gavel and rapped slowly twice.[8] By circumstances outside his control and not of his making, Will Bankhead had just been elected Speaker of the House of Representatives.

Assuming the role of Speaker—third in line to the presidency—was a mixed blessing for Will Bankhead. On the one hand, it was the achievement of a lifetime, validation of two decades of hard work and party loyalty. In his scrapbook, beneath photographs celebrating his election as Speaker, Will included a copy of Rudyard Kipling's poem "If." This most-beloved poem is a compendium of virtues that make a man: humility, patience, rationality, dependability, truthfulness, perseverance. It is viewed by scholars as the quintessential expression of Victorian reserve and stoicism. In his typically dramatic fashion, Bankhead was reminding himself that although he had just realized a profound achievement, the burdens of leadership—of true manhood—were demanding. Bankhead would need these virtues to succeed in his new role, for his time in the Speaker's chair coincided with a significant slowdown—some would say collapse—of the New Deal. Serious political missteps by the president, coupled with a recession and an invigorated and confrontational labor movement, emboldened the Republican minority as well as detractors within the president's own party.

In this increasingly fractious environment, achieving additional significant legislation would be an uphill battle. These political challenges put considerable stress on Will, and he constantly worried that he might not be physically strong enough to do the job. But there were some bright spots during Roosevelt's second term, and one of them came at the hands of the Speaker's brother, Senator Bankhead. John Jr. had spent the better part of three years working to address the problem of farm tenancy, the escalation of which many tied to the senator's earlier efforts to control farm production. The Bankhead-Jones Farm Tenant Act, signed by the president in July 1937 and considered by some historians as the one of the most radical agricultural programs of the New Deal, was an important step toward providing security for some of the country's poorest citizens.

Celebration in the nation's capital of Will Bankhead's election to the Speaker's chair was muted out of respect for the deceased Byrns. Bankhead's home state was a different matter. The *Birmingham Age-Herald* published a photograph of Tallulah telephoning her congratulations to her father. In winning the speakership, as she told reporters, he had "realized a life-long ambition." When asked his opinion about Will's new position, John Jr. quipped, "I don't know what I can say appropriately about my brother. I'm the oldest and for many years we were law partners, and I was boss. Now he's been promoted to the most powerful position in the government next to the president, and now I'll have to take orders from him. From now on, I'll sit at the foot of the table."[9] Privately, the Bankheads rejoiced. Tallulah sent a telegram to her "precious daddy" letting him know that "this is really the happiest day of my life."[10] Will's congressional district staged a huge homecoming celebration in late June in Jasper. Will

Figure 11.1.
Speaker of the
House Will
Bankhead wielding
the gavel, c.
1936. Courtesy
of the Alabama
Department of
Archives and
History.

and Florence were met at the train station by a thirty-two-piece marching band from the Alabama Boys Industrial School and escorted by highway patrolmen to the center of town, along a mile-long parade route festooned with bunting. Thousands of citizens and local dignitaries lined the route and crowded the town square for "Bankhead Day." Missing was brother John, confined to his home by illness. It was a glorious celebration of a difficult climb. Alabama was justifiably proud.

Now third in line to the presidency, Will Bankhead remained humble. Perhaps no better illustration of this humility was his love of telling a story about his Jasper homecoming, a story he retold throughout his years as Speaker. As the story goes, the celebration in Jasper was reaching its climax when a farmer rode in from the tiny community of Bull Flats. Seeing the bunting and the flags and hearing the bands, he asked:

"What's all this fuss fer?"

"Why," replied a bystander, "Billy Bankhead has just arrived back home!"

"Billy Bankhead's back home?" gasped the Bull Flats farmer in amazement, adding: "Why, where's he bin?"

Bankhead liked to tell his amused listeners that after that, he could never get "swelled up."[11]

Will's ascension first to majority leader and ultimately to the speakership brought significantly more attention to Will and to his wife, Florence. The number of visitors—official and casual—to his Capitol Hill office expanded tremendously. Will welcomed them with grace, even on Saturdays, noting in his diary, "A great many persons from all sections do me the honor to ask for an interview and greeting, which I am very glad to bestow."[12] Local and national papers and popular periodicals did puff pieces on "the third lady of the land" and the Bankheads' home life. Readers learned that the Speaker and his wife owned a spacious home in Jasper and had four servants. They owned a beloved wire-haired terrier named Zip, who accompanied the couple everywhere. On Christmas Day 1936, Will wrote a letter from the Mayflower Hotel in Washington, DC, to Zip, who remained under the care of the Bankheads' domestic workers in Jasper. The letter included all sorts of advice; he warned Zip to "be prudent as to vehicles—nothing faster than a wheel barrow!" He concluded the letter by noting, "[I] sat behind the President at church today—He likes dogs too, but not as much as I like my dog."[13] News stories described Florence as "langorous and soft-voiced," and "not even remotely politically minded." But that did not mean she was not politically savvy. Florence demurred when questioned about New Deal legislation; however, after a reporter for the *Birmingham Age-Herald* asked her to name the "most attractive woman in Washington society," Florence remarked, "Unquestionably . . . I'd say that Mrs. Roosevelt has more charm and personality than anyone in official life."[14] She understood the world of Washington wives.

Florence insisted that she was "a small town girl" who loved her Jasper home. A Birmingham paper found Florence's personal touches "reflected in the delightful informality of her home. The colonial living room . . . , for all of its exquisite furnishings, has a lived-in atmosphere. An open book by this deep-cushioned chair. A bowl of roses by that. A Beethoven sonata on the grand piano. A ball of wool zephyr and knitting needles where Mrs. Bankhead had left them when her husband summoned her to the turnip patch." Florence did not revel in the socializing that was part of being the Speaker's wife. "Billy and

I go out very little in Washington," she told the reporter. "Only to affairs which are expected of us."[15] Although Will Bankhead was regarded as one of the more polished and cultured members of Congress, at heart he was relatively unpretentious. Following a breakfast with several naval officers, Bankhead wrote in his diary, "To one of my country rearing, the idea of having a meal at 12:30 and calling it breakfast is somewhat ludicrous."[16] *Life* magazine published a photo spread on the Speaker in late December 1936. Declaring the speakership "a killing job," the article took pains to illustrate that Will "is stronger now, having rested up for six months at his lovely home in Jasper." The spread emphasized the Speaker's southern roots and reinforced racist assumptions about black southerners. One photo featured the Speaker, in white shirt and tie, giving instruction to a young African American man holding a rake. The young man, readers are told, is "Doc." His "job is to tend the Bankhead zinnias and keep an eye on the Bankhead birdhouse, which is occupied by a family of cardinals. 'Doc' and the House of Representatives are similar in one respect. Both work better when ruled with a firm hand. That hand is Mr. Bankhead's." Another photograph features the Jasper train depot, with an African American man sleeping on the platform. The caption reads, "Jasper, home of the Bankheads, is a Deep South town of 5,313 inhabitants. On the platform of its little railroad station, darkies doze in the Alabama sunshine." Eugenia wrote from Europe to congratulate her father on the *Life* piece. "The house looks lovely and you look so well. The sight of the nigger on the station of Jasper made me very homesick."[17] Florence's hobbies, readers learned, included flowers and reading; an observant reporter for the *Birmingham Age-Herald* noted that an open copy of *Gone with the Wind* lay on a table in the Bankheads' living room. Will's hobbies included collecting gavels from past Speakers. Florence loved fishing, and Will loved golf, although he admitted that he rarely played since suffering a heart attack the year before. After artist Howard Chandler Christy painted the Speaker's portrait, the artist gifted Will with a paint set. Will gave it to Florence, who became quite the enthusiast. She later took up sculpture. Many stories in national publications made much of daughter Tallulah and her career, often mentioning Will's own flair for the dramatic as well as his aborted acting career. Poor Eugenia was often a footnote in these stories, dismissed by one writer as "the woman of many marriages known to Sunday supplements."[18]

Florence was excited about Will's election as Speaker, but, she cautioned, "my first concern is for his health. I am going to take him to Canada on a fishing trip later this summer. I shall devote myself to seeing that he does not work too hard."[19] Florence kept a careful eye on the Speaker. She traveled to the Capitol twice a day to check on Will. She joined him for lunch, made sure he was eating properly, and stood watch as he took an afternoon nap as prescribed by his doctor. She possessed an interest in astrology, telling friends and family that Will's heart attack was prophesied by his horoscope, although his history of cardiac episodes, stressful job, and love of cigarettes were much more reliable predictors.[20] He continued to smoke following his heart attack; newspapers in the capital regularly published photographs of him strategizing with Vice President John Nance Garner, cigarette in hand.

By his own account, Will's relations with the president were warm and cordial. He chalked up the president's "great personal popularity" to "his absolute human qualities." Taken aback when the president apologized profusely for phoning the Speaker on a Sunday afternoon, Bankhead mused, "I imagine that [neither] Hitler, Mussolini nor Stalin would make any such gesture in communicating with one of their subordinates, but it signifies the consideration that the President shows everyone in his dealings with them."[21] He and the other party leaders met weekly with Roosevelt while Congress was in session. Regarding these meetings, Will noted, "I find President Roosevelt most amenable with practical suggestions with reference to legislation. He has never exhibited at these conferences any disposition to be arbitrary or intolerant of our views, but, upon the contrary, has shown a most earnest disposition to cooperate in the most practical fashion with the suggestions made by the Vice President, Senator Barkley, [Majority Leader] Rayburn and myself."[22] Despite an increasingly divided Democratic caucus in Congress, Will continued to enjoy his colleagues and valued their friendship. He frequently noted that as leader, he was "a conciliator, not a combatant." He wrote in his diary that "the only real compensation that a man gets out of his service in Congress is based upon his intimate and agreeable associations with his comrades in this service."[23] Political observers frequently commented that his brilliance as Speaker differed from that of his more tyrannical predecessors, such as Republican Speakers Joseph Gurney Cannon (1903–11) or Nicholas Longworth (1925–31). *Time* magazine observed that "partly from bent, partly of necessity, [Bankhead] used the gentler arts of persuasion, parliamentary device, friendship." Previous Speakers enjoyed the power of patronage. However, Roosevelt had assumed most of the Speaker's patronage power, "Leaving William Bankhead with no club to hold, no favors to give." Bankhead's success would lie in his "unquestioned reputation for integrity, a thorough knowledge of parliamentary rules, [and] a commanding presence."[24]

Despite the passage of important legislation, agriculture remained a sore spot in the nation's economy. Although controlling production and achieving parity remained the number one concern of Senator John H. Bankhead Jr. and other legislators from rural regions, the nation's focus during the mid-1930s began to center on the most destitute and desperate of the agricultural poor: tenants and sharecroppers. Early New Deal antipoverty programs employed a wide range of ideas to deal with tenants and sharecroppers. They did not have much ideological coherence, and they were all over the place administratively, what one historian calls "an institutional mess."[25] The AAA and the Bankhead Cotton Control Act addressed the problem of parity while creating another problem, which was the eviction of tenants, sharecroppers, and wage laborers from the land.[26] With the deepening of the Depression, the problems of tenants and sharecroppers—the poorest of the rural poor—began receiving more attention from social scientists and others. Sociologist Rupert B. Vance observed that although "the Bankhead Act may [have] aid[ed] in solving a temporary problem of overproduction, it has no solution to offer for cotton tenancy."[27] In fact, according to many observers, it made the problem worse.

Farm tenancy was widespread in the Cotton Belt, ensnaring more than 1.7 million farmers, whom Vance called the "homeless wanderers on the face of the earth." In some places, it included over 60 percent of all farms.[28] Political activist Howard Kester, one of the founders of the Southern Tenant Farmers Union, referred to sharecroppers as "the most exploited agricultural worker in America."[29] Tenancy created its own "cultural landscape," marked by the "miserable panorama of unpainted shacks, rain-gullied fields, straggling fences, rattletrap Fords, dirt, poverty, disease, drudgery, and monotony that stretches for a thousand miles across the Cotton Belt."[30] Vance noted that "the common complaint of landlords is of houses allowed to go to ruin, fences torn down, and land lacerated by erosion." But such developments were baked into the system, which "gives the tenant no interest in his tenancy. A tenure of twenty years gives the renter no more right to remain than a tenure of twenty days. . . . In addition the law gives the tenant no claim for improvements made. The tenant then does not look forward to a future but only to a present use of the farm. . . . To fix fences, clear land, stop gullies from washing, to repair a shed, or shingle a roof is from his viewpoint a foolish waste of time and energy."[31]

Tenants were highly mobile, which, Vance argued, promoted "a lack of attachment to the farms which they have cultivated." White sharecroppers moved more often than did black. Their average period of occupancy ranged from four months to a year and a half. Most moved within a single county. The ebb and flow of the cotton economy exacerbated the tenants' already precarious standard of living. Cotton growers' income was cyclical, which gave them a "shifting standard of living" and prevented them from "acquiring habits of thrift." Lacking a reliable income, families found it impossible to live according to a budget. Their consumption of goods tended to run in cycles. Luxuries were bought on the spur of the moment during a good season; those same luxuries were paid for by deprivation the next year. Landowners frequently complained about "the phonographs, sewing-machines, organs, player pianos, [and] automobiles that their tenants buy during seasons of prosperity" and regarded such purchases "as evidences of inherent lack of judgment and extravagance of Negroes and poor white people," rather than as a result of the cyclical nature of cotton farming.[32] The plight of sharecroppers and tenants was dramatized by novelist Erskine Caldwell in *Tobacco Road*, which told the story of Georgia sharecropper Jeeter Lester and his family. Admittedly, Caldwell was less optimistic than were New

Dealers about the ability of the federal government to improve the lot of the landless. The book was published in 1932, and in 1933 it was made into a Broadway play that would run for the next seven years.[33]

For southern Democrats, the impoverished tenant or sharecropper was not only an economic and social problem. He was a political problem as well. New Deal administrator Will Alexander noted that the expansion of tenancy in the 1920s and 1930s posed a threat to democratic institutions because "the masses of southern tenants do not develop initiative, self-reliance, and independence of thought."[34] Their poverty made them susceptible to radical political ideologies. Those interested in improving the lives of tenants were concerned as much with maintaining political stability as they were with alleviating the daily misery that was the lot of the South's landless class.

Early New Deal programs attempted to attack the source of poverty. The Resettlement Administration's rural rehabilitation division ran a loan and grant program for small farmers, tenants, and sharecroppers who struggled to borrow money in the credit-poor region. Within its first year, it served nearly eight hundred thousand farmers.[35] The Resettlement Administration came under attack for being overly bureaucratic and borderline socialistic in its focus on planning. To counter bad publicity, its chief, Rexford Tugwell, sent out a team of talented photographers to document successful New Deal projects and capture images of the tremendous need that still existed. As tenants and sharecroppers moved into the national limelight, New Deal politicians began to take notice.

Among those legislators were Senator John H. Bankhead Jr. and Representative John Marvin Jones of Texas, who began focusing on the problems of tenancy in early 1935. Jones took a conservative legislative approach. He was interested in helping only the most successful tenants achieve landownership. Bankhead had bigger plans. He envisioned a bold, ambitious, and expensive federal program that would attack the system at its roots. After meeting with officials of the Department of Agriculture, economists, and lawyers, Bankhead introduced a bill in February 1935. Entitled the Farm Tenant Home Act, Bankhead's program called for a $1 billion budget and the creation of a government corporation (called the Farmers' Home Corporation) to purchase land and re-sell it to tenants, sharecroppers, and wage workers. Bankhead's bill drew heavily from a plan devised by a group of academics, including a young researcher named Frank Tannenbaum, who proposed that the United States establish a land-purchasing system similar to that pursued by Mexican reformers. John Jr. laid out the case for his bill in an article in the *New York Times*. The goal of the bill, he wrote, was to help "thousands and thousands of worthy tenants to establish themselves on pieces of land they can call 'home.'" It will "slow down the annual rate of movement of our tenants. It will transfer many from the gypsy type to home owners."[36] Tannenbaum spoke out in favor of the bill, declaring in the *New Republic* that it would "make possible the break-up of the plantation system in the South."[37] The bill was taken up by the Senate Committee on Agriculture, which John Jr. chaired.

Key to the success of this legislation was the task of convincing Congress of the worthiness of the potential recipients of government aid. As envisioned by the bill's authors, the deserving poor were white. Over and over again, Bankhead and supporters of the bill took pains to point out that tenancy was "not a Negro problem," noting that tenancy rates among African Americans had actually declined, while white tenancy was increasing.[38] Even social scientist Rupert B. Vance felt it necessary to write that "while one may not be surprised to note that over half of the Negro tenants are croppers, it is startling to learn that over one-third of the white tenants are in the same poverty-stricken class."[39] Poor black tenants and sharecroppers were a given, a fixture of the South's impoverished rural landscape; destitute white folks, on the other hand, constituted a national disgrace and therefore a problem that demanded government attention. Crafting legislation to attack this problem with racial precision would be tricky. Southern politicians and voters remained on alert for New Deal programs armed with the potential to undermine the region's racial arrangement. Providing thousands of black farmers the opportunity to become independent landowners would deny white landowners easy access to cheap labor, long a staple of the southern economy. By pointing out that tenancy was a white problem, the bill's author and supporters made clear that the effort to turn poor southerners into independent landowners was focused primarily on white farmers.

Hearings on the Farm Tenant Home Act were held in March 1935.[40] Numerous witnesses, including secretary of agriculture Henry A. Wallace, highlighted the degree to which tenancy and sharecropping were a white problem. Wallace also admitted that the reduction program of the AAA had contributed to the problem.[41] Secretary Wallace and L. C. Gray (chief of the Land Policy Division of the Agricultural Adjustment Administration) noted that tenancy was likewise a political problem. "The present conditions, particularly in the South," Wallace warned, "provide fertile soil for Communist and Socialist agitators."[42] Wallace also observed that communities in which there was a high degree of tenancy were socially unstable. "It is almost impossible for tenant families who move from place to place every 2 or 3 years, to participate in the activities of schools, churches, and other similar rural institutions."[43] Tenants lacked an attachment to community life. The 1930 census demonstrated that over half of all tenants had been on their farms for fewer than two years.[44]

The issue of tenancy also amplified the need for relief. In the cotton states, 23 percent of all tenants, sharecroppers, and wage laborers were on relief. The assistant administrator of the Federal Emergency Relief Administration (FERA) in charge of rural rehabilitation testified that relief needs were lower in areas that had greater farm ownership.[45] Rates of tenancy were high across the Cotton Belt. In Bankhead's home state of Alabama, 64.7 percent of all farms were worked by tenants; in Mississippi, the number was 72 percent. Nothing less than the survival of rural America was at stake as impoverished and landless farmers fled the farm for the city. One citizen complained to Bankhead that "our farm populations are living mean, pinched, and disillusioned lives." He was concerned that "the best examples of the farm populations select themselves for city life, the culls remain on the farms." This rural migration to urban centers would have disastrous consequences. "Whenever the rural-urban migration continues for a long time selective in favor of urban life, the gradual effect on the national character must be the same effect as we would have in a breeding stable from which we selected each generation the best examples . . . and sent them away to be raced, breeding only from the culls left behind. After a while there wouldn't be any race horses worth looking at."[46] Culls made for poor citizens. Clarence Poe, editor of the *Progressive Farmer*, agreed, writing, "Not until general home ownership replaces tenancy can we build a great rural civilization in the South."[47] S. H. Hobbs Jr. of the University of North Carolina chimed in, writing that "the South cannot develop a high type of rural civilization with an overwhelming mass of tenants, especially of the cropper type." Landless folk were unreliable citizens. In advocating for his legislation, John H. Bankhead Jr. stressed that "the root of the tenant trouble in this country is the 'system,'" not the Depression, bad landlords, or shiftless tenants.[48]

Senator Bankhead and Congressman Jones reached a compromise, and the bill came to be known as the Bankhead-Jones Farm Tenant Act. Simultaneous with the introduction of the tenant bill was the publication of *The Collapse of Cotton Tenancy*, inspired again by Frank Tannenbaum's research and written by a group of social scientists. The book examined the devastation wrought to tenants and sharecroppers by the AAA and recommended a comprehensive land distribution policy along the lines of Bankhead's bill. The book sold thousands of copies, bringing much-needed attention to the problem.[49] Accompanying *The Collapse of Cotton Tenancy* was the publication of a host of academic studies by noted social scientists who offered withering criticism of the tenant and sharecropping systems. The issue was gaining momentum. Debate on the bill was vigorous and continued for nearly two weeks. The Senate passed the bill in late June 1935; the bill stalled in a House committee and died when Congress adjourned in August 1935.[50]

By 1936, the drive to alleviate the scourge of tenancy had received broad support. In the South, a good portion of support to move tenants to landownership was driven by fear that displaced tenants were falling prey to communist organizers. In 1934, black and white sharecroppers in Arkansas organized the Southern Tenant Farmers Union. By 1936, the union claimed some ten thousand members in Arkansas, Mississippi, Tennessee, Missouri, Oklahoma, Alabama, and Texas. They staged strikes and lobbied Washington officials to get their fair share of AAA payments. Local officials responded with violence. The *Nation* laid the responsibility for tenant displacement at the feet of John H. Bankhead Jr., claiming that crop reductions under the AAA and the Bankhead Cotton Control Act had led to wholesale evictions; those who had not been evicted were forced into cheap day labor. They also complained that planters kept the tenants' share of the AAA benefits. The *Birmingham News* referred to tenancy as "a Breeder of Revolution in the South," noting that Bankhead's new bill would staunch the defection of black southerners to the Communist Party.[51] Not all Bankheads disagreed with the goals of the union. Tallulah Bankhead lent her support to National Sharecroppers Week, something her father found particularly embarrassing. Although he typically did not interfere in her life, in this case, he asked her to remove her support. "I dislike to make the suggestion to you," he wrote, "but it is my opinion that this organization is composed quite largely of Reds and Communists, and while it purports to be organized in the interest of the white and colored tenant farmers, its leaders are subject to very grave suspicion, and they are not entitled to be sponsored by your name." Tallulah followed her father's advice. She wrote to the organizers of National Sharecroppers Week that "information that has come to me from unimpeachable sources" has revealed "that many of the heads of your organization are Reds and Communists." She asked that her name be removed as a sponsor. Though she professed to "feel deeply for the plight of the sharecroppers," she wrote, "I feel that the sharecroppers will suffer . . . if this set-up [communist leadership] is not removed."[52] Addressing the communist threat, Secretary Wallace argued that "the cure [for tenancy] is not violence or oppressive legislation to curb these activities but rather to give these dispossessed people a stake in the social system."[53] *Newsweek* made the connection between these local power struggles and Senator Bankhead's new tenant legislation, stating that his proposal would "turn restless 'croppers into contented landholders."[54]

John H. Bankhead Jr. and John Marvin Jones met with the president in early 1936 to strategize for the upcoming session. Secretary Wallace and Will W. Alexander (who had replaced Rexford Tugwell as the head of the Resettlement Administration) recommended the budget be slashed to $50 million (John Jr. had requested $1 billion) and urged the elimination of the Farmers' Home Corporation, to which John Jr. reluctantly agreed.[55] In all iterations of the bill, Bankhead emphasized the goal of moving tenants from submarginal land, putting that land into conservation, and establishing family farms, thus removing these tenants from the cash-crop economy.[56]

Jones and Bankhead introduced their bill again in 1936, but the bill again made no progress. Will applied pressure where he could. In May 1936, Will pressed Congressman Jones to take "some definite action" on the bill, although he confided to John that he had "discussed it personally with other members of the [House Agriculture] Committee and am very much disgusted to have to tell you that I do not believe that it is going to be possible to get the bill voted out of the Committee at this session." He saw no sense in forcing a committee vote during an election year. Will remained frustrated in his inability to assist his brother: "The whole situation has displeased me very much and I regret that I have been powerless . . . to force favorable action."[57] Will met with Jones during the fall and was assured he would introduce the bill in early 1937; Will recommended that John Jr. do the same. Despite the lack of success on passing the legislation, the issue continued to garner public attention and to gain political traction. The *Philadelphia Record* lauded John H. Bankhead Jr. as its "Man of the Week" in September 1936, declaring that "the Senator from Alabama Intends to Put Jeeter Lester Back on His Feet."[58] Although the president had been fairly quiet with regard to the proposed tenant legislation, the increased public attention on tenancy and general support for some sort of legislation got his attention. In September 1936, Roosevelt publicly endorsed Bankhead's bill.

The tenant bill got bogged down in 1936 in part because illness kept John away from Washington for the majority of the session. He contracted what many believed was the flu, and he spent February and March in the Bethesda Naval Hospital.[59] Then, under the advice of doctors, he traveled to Daytona, Florida; Will reminded John that the doctor was "emphatic in his belief that it would not be wise . . . to leave Florida until your cough and its results were better in hand." Will was anxious that John "make no mistake" with his health.[60] After several months of cough and intermittent fever, doctors determined that his illness was due to a lung abscess, which was treated in the early fall. By the second week of October 1936, son-in-law Charles B. Crow was telling friends that the senator was "well advanced on the road to recovery." The doctors had eliminated the abscess. "The process . . . entailed absorption of a great deal of the poisons from the abscess by the rest of his body. Now, he must eliminate the poison."[61] After John Jr. returned to Congress following his prolonged illness, he and wife Musa rented an apartment adjoining Will and Florence's in the Mayflower. Will was delighted to have his brother so close by.[62] But by December 1936, the senator was still not fully recovered, although his staff expected that he would be ready for the January session.[63] The president remained concerned about John's health and was glad to hear that John planned to be at the January 1937 session.[64]

John was not the only Bankhead to suffer illness during this period. Will reported to Eugenia that Florence underwent a serious operation in early 1936 to remove, in his words, "a large tumor from her stomach, also her appendix and some of the other works."[65] Eugenia herself was not in the best physical condition. In 1933 Eugenia, once again divorced, was living abroad, first residing in England and then moving back and forth between France and Italy. She was briefly engaged to the son of a Scottish coal magnate, but just as quickly the engagement was called off.[66] She complained to Will of her multiple health issues, writing, "I developed an abscess in my ear, then all my teeth went wrong. I have been in a most deplorable state." She also suffered from "one of those chronic female troubles that must be constantly watched and treated." In 1936 she contracted tuberculosis while visiting Corsica. She moved to a small mountain town in northern Italy to recover. She assured her father that "there is absolutely no pain or suffering whatsoever. I feel fine and eat like a nigger." The $150 a month that Will sent her, already a burden for him, was insufficient to cover her mounting medical bills. Tallulah likewise had been sending Eugenia money, but she had recently cut her contribution by half. Having to resort to begging for money, Eugenia became increasingly despondent, ashamed of what her life had become. She referred to herself as "the perfectly useless member of the family." She continued, "I know I haven't given you much happiness in my life, but I do love you so dearly that I pray there will always be a place in your heart for me in spite of all the stupid things I have done. . . . I am getting old and I feel my life has been of little use to anyone."

Financially strapped, Will counseled Eugenia to look to religion for aid and comfort. "I have always felt that there were deep wells of spirituality in your nature that if properly touched would make a great difference in your outlook on life," Will wrote. "It may seem rather a strange request, but I wish you would go to a church or Cathedral occasionally and by yourself commune with our Heavenly Father for guidance and comfort."[67] It is unclear whether Eugenia sought divine intervention for her many troubles.

Tallulah's financial security, made possible by her contract with Paramount Studios, gave Will one less thing to worry about. She was able to settle many of her debts, support a staff of four, and even build up some savings. She was earning a commendable salary, yet critical success in film eluded her. In the two years since she had returned from England, Tallulah had made four films for Paramount and one for Metro-Goldwyn-Mayer Studios (MGM). Although she often received strong reviews, the films themselves were forgettable. Both Paramount and MGM wanted to keep her under contract albeit at a lower salary. Dismayed by her lack of success in film, Tallulah decided to return to the world she knew best: the stage.

Now in her thirties and more savvy about the theater industry, Tallulah decided to bankroll her own play. *Forsaking All Others* opened in January 1933. The Depression put a damper on theater ticket sales, and the play closed in June. Tallulah alleged that she lost $40,000 in her production venture.[68] She began rehearsals for her next play, *Jezebel*, in August. But something was wrong. Tallulah checked into New York's Doctors Hospital in late August with "severe abdominal trouble."[69] She thought it was the flu. The play was scheduled to open on Broadway on September 25. Three days before the opening, Tallulah was still in the hospital. Not yet fully recovered from his April 1933 heart attack, Will was

Figure 11.2. Tallulah Bankhead, 1930. Courtesy of the Alabama Department of Archives and History.

"extremely anxious" and begged Tallulah or her assistant to "write to me immediately [to relieve] my anxiety."[70] Tallulah left the hospital briefly in mid-October but soon returned, this time to Lenox Hill Hospital, with a raging fever. Doctors finally reached a diagnosis: gonorrhea. Tallulah's condition was life threatening. She underwent a radical hysterectomy on November 3, which newspapers around the country reported as a "slight" operation.[71] Tallulah's prolonged illness had taken its toll on her physically and emotionally; when she left the hospital in late November, she weighed a mere seventy-five pounds. After resting in her New York hotel, she traveled to Jasper, Alabama, to spend the Christmas holidays with Will and Florence. It was the first time in seventeen years that she had been back in Alabama. Thin, haggard, and exhausted, she nevertheless was the toast of that small town and consented to brief public appearances to standing-room-only crowds at the town's two small theaters. "Whatever the verdict of Hollywood and Vine, whatever the judgments of the screen critics," Tallulah recalled, "in Jasper I was a screen star." She dressed like she suspected the locals expected of a Hollywood star—black dress and signature bright-red lipstick, her neck and wrists dripping with jewels—and delighted the crowd. Spending time with her family was restorative for Tallulah, and she entered the new year determined to recapture the momentum of her stalled career.[72]

The stress of the session, coupled with John's absence and Florence's illness, as well as the ever-present financial strain of Eugenia, took a toll on Will. He worried that he might not be strong enough to carry on. He confided to nephew James Knox Julian in early spring 1936 that "I am upset about these matters, but I am trying to take it all calmly, as I certainly cannot afford to crack up again."[73] Will wrote to Julian again in mid-June 1936 and mentioned that he remained "under . . . tremendous pressure."[74] Concerns about family and his own health would continue to weigh heavily on the new Speaker.

While John's tenant bill worked its way through committee, the Bankhead brothers turned their attention to the upcoming election. Confident Democrats gathered in Philadelphia in June 1936 to nominate Franklin D. Roosevelt for a second term. Although chosen as a convention delegate, John was too ill to attend. Will was concerned about Roosevelt's reelection, but the concern turned out to be completely misplaced. The president cruised to an easy victory over Republican candidate Alf Landon of Kansas. The Democrats also won overwhelming majorities in both houses of Congress. Will confided to his nephew that "I am really worried about having such an overwhelming Democratic majority in the House. I am afraid it will be very difficult to keep them in hand."[75] Roosevelt's 1936 victory heralded the arrival of a new and rather unwieldy political coalition comprising northern urban dwellers, white southerners, African Americans, and organized labor. Labor, in particular the newly organized Congress of Industrial Organizations (CIO), led by John L. Lewis of the United Mine Workers, became an important financial backer of the Democratic Party. The United Mine Workers constituted the single-largest contributor to the president's reelection campaign.[76] For its critical support of the president, labor would expect continued protection of the rights of working people. Republicans and conservative Democrats kept a wary eye on the CIO.

Neither brother spent much time on his own reelection campaign. John's health continued to keep him from being very active. It did not matter. Both brothers enjoyed relatively easy victories in their 1936 reelection bids, receiving the endorsement of organized labor. The *Jasper Mountain Eagle*, their hometown paper, noted that while President Roosevelt received 237,200 votes from Alabama voters, Senator Bankhead received 239,532 votes, an impressive tally given the popularity of the president. Clearly Senator Bankhead's efforts on behalf of the state's farmers had paid off. Will bested his opponent by 15,000 votes.[77]

The Democratic Party increased its presence in both houses of Congress as a result of the 1936 elections. The Democrats picked up ten seats in the Senate, giving them a 69–25 majority over the Republicans. In the House, the Democrats gained eleven seats, giving them a gaudy 322–103 majority. This overwhelming majority gave pause to Will, who was determined to carry out the president's agenda. He confided to his diary that "I have been apprehensive that because of the tremendous Democratic majority in the House that at times by the formation of special groups and blocs they might get out of hand as far as the Party program is concerned."[78] In an interview with *New York Times Magazine*, Will got more specific: "the party in power can best carry out its plans when its majority does not exceed fifty or sixty. . . . With a comparatively small majority and a strong, efficient opposition, the members of the controlling party feel the necessity of hanging together and of working in harmony. When the minority shrinks to a feeble number, then the majority no longer feels the same obligation to act in concert and is likely to divide into small groups, each opposing the other rather than presenting an unbroken front to their political adversaries."[79] Unlike other members of the majority, Will opposed the gag rule as a way to prevent organized minority groups within the majority from jeopardizing legislation. Ever the conciliator, he told the *New York Times* that the best hope of keeping the House in order "lay in moral suasion."[80]

Organization and discipline also helped. Will returned to Washington in December 1936—"long, lean, and in the best of health" according to one columnist—to meet with his leadership team prior to the new session.[81] He organized the Democratic membership into geographic zones, each overseen by an assistant whip. Whips were instructed to prevent all blocs and to use every means at their disposal to keep the majority in line.[82] For Democratic Party whip Congressman Patrick J. Boland of Pennsylvania, organization and discipline in the House were matters of life and death. "There is no question in the minds of many of us," Boland told a reporter, "that the hub-bub and confusion which prevails on the House floor contributed to the deaths of Speakers Rainey and Byrns. And it will have its effect upon the health of Speaker Bankhead unless something is done to remedy the situation."[83] Plagued by worry over his fragile heart, Speaker Bankhead steadied himself for the next session and Roosevelt's second term. It would prove to be the most tumultuous period of the New Deal era.

Thwarted in her attempts to secure employment in the entertainment sector, Marie Bankhead Owen continued her work as director of the Department of Archives and History. The passage of New Deal work and relief programs brought her much-needed assistance. Through funds provided by the Reconstruction Finance Corporation, the Civil Works Administration, the Federal Emergency Relief Administration, and the Works Progress Administration, Marie was able to employ numerous white-collar men and women who otherwise would have been on relief rolls.[84] She benefited as well from the election of Governor Bibb Graves in 1934. A progressive and enthusiastic supporter of the New Deal, Graves was a welcome change over the penny-pinching Governor Miller. Graves restored some of Marie's salary, and she was once again able to employ her son Tom.[85] Most important, though, were what Graves referred to as his "plum-tree-shaking expeditions" to Washington to acquire funds for his state. It was through Graves's efforts that the state was finally able to complete the construction of the World War Memorial Building, which Thomas McAdory Owen had initiated before his death and for which Marie had been fighting ever since she took over the departmental reins in 1920. Graves arranged a meeting in Washington, DC, for himself and Marie with Harry Hopkins, close aide to President Roosevelt and supervisor of the Works Progress Administration. As Marie pleaded for funds for the archives building, Hopkins remained noncommittal. After Marie had departed, leaving Graves and Hopkins alone, Hopkins dismissed her request, remarking to the governor that "the government did not have the money to construct a building for every little old lady who wanted an archive."[86] Graves tactfully pointed out that Marie's brothers were Senator John H. Bankhead Jr. and Speaker of the House Will Bankhead. Hopkins's face fell. He quickly summoned Marie back into the room and solicitously inquired where she intended to build her new archive. Marie was understandably thrilled. Whenever she spoke of the archives' new permanent home, she gave all credit to Governor Graves.

By the late 1930s, all archival records were under a single roof in the twenty-thousand-square-foot marble building. But years of stingy budgets, inadequate infrastructure, and overworked staff would not be rectified overnight. Records continued to pile up, hampering the ability of the archives to fulfill its administrative function. The Department of Archives and History would continue to struggle with this particular responsibility.[87]

Not all blame for the archives' continuing struggle to fulfill its mission can be placed on years of inadequate funding. Marie's own interests and particular vision for the agency had a powerful influence on the direction of the archives in the 1930s and 1940s.[88] Marie Bankhead Owen reveled in her role as the director of the state's most powerful historical and cultural institution, and she pursued every opportunity to shape the dominant historical narrative of Alabama and the South. Time that could have been spent organizing records was instead spent traveling, presenting her particular version of Alabama history to clubs and at community celebrations throughout the state. At times, she had three speaking engagements per week. Son Tom likewise participated in this function of the agency, presenting a weekly program, *Romantic Passages*

Figure 11.3.
Alabama Department of Archives and History building. Courtesy of the Alabama Department of Archives and History.

in Alabama History, over the radio. Marie filled in occasionally. Distressed that Alabama history was no longer taught in state schools, Marie published four books during the 1930s on Alabama history, including one specifically for junior high school students, two for younger children, and one for the general public. She dedicated one of the children's book to the memory of her son John Hollis—"greatly loved and lost awhile"—who had died thirty-five years earlier. Her authorial voice reached an audience beyond the state through scripts prepared for nationally syndicated historically themed radio programs. All this activity took precious time away from records management.[89]

Through her books, public addresses, and media appearances, Marie continued to promote a historical narrative that acknowledged the state's rich natural resources as the source of its prosperity, lauded the philosophy of states' rights and the doomed efforts of the Confederacy, vilified Reconstruction, privileged the singular genius and accomplishments of the white elite in general and her family in particular, and marginalized African Americans. She defended the legality of secession and identified President Lincoln's call for volunteers following the firing on Fort Sumter as the start of the Civil War, which she called the War between the States. She defended slavery as a civilizing institution and praised the enslaved men and women for remaining "true to their masters, faithfully keeping guardianship over their material possessions and the more sacred charge of wife and children while the head of the family was far away fighting with the Confederate Army."[90] Although slavery had continued to be profitable on the eve of the Civil War, and although stopping the expansion of slavery into the new western territories was a primary concern for Lincoln and the Republican Party, Marie parroted a staple of Lost Cause mythology, arguing that "many of the great Southern families had freed their slaves [before the war]. It was only a question of time when the slave holders of the South would have freed their slaves, probably by the gradual process of time limits, or by compensation by Congressional action. But both slave and nonslaveholders resented the threat by compulsion."[91]

If the Confederacy was a noble cause, Reconstruction was a travesty, a great injury inflicted on southern whites by "carpetbaggers and Negroes." Among its many missteps, according to Marie, was providing education for the freedmen at public expense. The Freedmen's Bureau "attempted to arouse bad feeling between the races and its agents enriched themselves in every possible way in both money and land." In response to such outrages, the Ku Klux Klan provided white Alabamians "some little protection."[92]

Although she singled out the state's rich natural resources as the source of its postwar prosperity, she acknowledged that Alabama's development in the post–Civil War era was due in large part to the existence of low-paid (often incarcerated, thanks to the convict lease promoted by her father) labor of the state's black citizens. In a radio script for *Southern Radio News*, Marie wrote that "the great number of negroes in the State, most of them unskilled laborers and domestic servants, afford cheap and ample labor for farm, forest and mines." She stated emphatically that despite the fact that African Americans made up a third of the state's population, "There is no race problem," primarily because of "the law abiding character of the Negro population and inviolable laws forbidding intermarriage of the races."[93] Like other elites, Marie insisted that Alabama's white citizens were politically unified, conveniently ignoring the fact that the majority of poor white citizens remained disfranchised.[94] Whenever possible, she wedded her family's history to the history of the state and region, frequently lauding the contributions of her father and brothers, in particular the Federal Aid Road Act of 1916 and the subsistence homestead program.

Marie used her influence within the United Daughters of the Confederacy (UDC) to ensure that the state's schoolchildren were taught what she felt was "appropriate" history. Elected historian of the Alabama UDC in 1936, Marie received a report from one member that a junior high teacher in Montgomery was teaching students that Jefferson Davis was a traitor. Marie mobilized members across the state, urging them to interview their local superintendents to determine what was being taught. "In case any [teacher] is so ill informed as to be teaching this false history," she advised, "the truth of the matter should be placed in their hands." Students should be taught "that what the South fought for was the same kind of independence as our Revolutionary fathers fought for when they felt their interests, both social and economic, were being jeopardized by their mother country. Whether secession were wise or unwise, it was Constitutional."[95] In addition to "investigating" teachers, Marie urged members to "contact their newspapers, school teachers and public officials" and demand they use the term War between the States as opposed to Civil War. UDC members should take time to explain "the difference between a civil war and a war between two definitely organized governments." The power and reach of Marie and the UDC should not be underestimated. In 1936 alone, the organization delivered 457 historical talks to nearly one hundred thousand students, and twenty-seven radio addresses on "southern heroes" to audiences across the state. Members of the organization also published eleven pamphlets and presented three plays.[96] Through their impressive numbers and public presence, Marie and the women of the UDC attempted to smother competing historical narratives.

Perhaps Marie's greatest victory in her quest to cement her particular historical perspective onto the state of Alabama came in her campaign to change the state seal and the state motto. She began this crusade in the early 1920s. The original state seal, designed during the territorial period and adopted in 1819 after Alabama became a state, consisted of a drawing of the state with its rivers prominently featured. This seal was replaced in 1868 by the legislature elected under Radical Reconstruction. This legislature also adopted the motto Here We Rest, which at the time was considered a proper translation of the

Figure 11.4. Alabama state seal, 1868. Courtesy of the Alabama Department of Archives and History.

Figure 11.5. Alabama state seal, 1939. Courtesy of the Alabama Department of Archives and History.

name "Alabama." Just as her father and brother worked to undo any revolutionary potential stemming from the Civil War and Reconstruction—in particular, the extension of the franchise to African Americans—so too was Marie determined to erase any vestige of the Reconstruction era from anything within her control. The seal adopted in 1868 was circular in shape and featured an eagle alighting on a US shield. In the eagle's beak is a ribbon emblazoned with the state motto. According to Marie, the seal was, quite simply, "a monstrosity."[97] Its provenance, she argued, was politically illegitimate. "The Carpetbag Legislature, made up of men who were strangers to our traditions, and in the main of local renegades and negroes," discarded the "beautiful old seal." In creating the new seal, these "out-of-state men . . . desired to brand the people of Alabama who had so lately been in arms against the Union with a United States emblem." Marie found unacceptable this apparent capitulation to national unity. She likewise attacked the state motto, complaining that "it brings ridicule upon us by persons of other parts of the country indicating inertion and lack of energy."[98] Marie advocated a return to the old seal that highlighted the state's waterways and lobbied for a new motto, one of her own making. She drew inspiration from an eighteenth-century poem by Sir William Jones whose first line, "What Makes a State?" was followed by an attack on monarchical rule and corruption.

> Men, who their duties know,
>   But know their rights, and, knowing, dare maintain,
> Prevent the long-aimed blow,
>   And crush the tyrant while they rend the chain:
> These constitute a State . . .

Marie refashioned these sentiments into a new motto for the state of Alabama: We Dare Defend Our Rights. Given her profound dislike of the nationalist sentiments embodied in the 1868 seal, it is difficult to see her preferred motto as anything other than a states' rights declaration. But whose rights, exactly? Probably as much as any family, the Bankheads had contributed to the expanded reach of the federal government. Indeed, Marie herself pursued her states' rights campaign while ensconced in a magnificent new archival building made possible by federal funds. But like most southern politicians, the Bankheads drew a bright line when it came to any federal power used to advance rights or protections for black citizens. Given that the object of her attack was the Reconstruction-era seal and motto, it is safe to assume that her motto was a declaration that any federal encroachment on race relations in the South would be met by white Alabamians with fierce determination.

Supported by the UDC, Marie hoped to make her attack on the Reconstruction-era seal a regionwide battle. She struggled to enlist other states of the former Confederacy in her campaign to purge all signs and symbols of Reconstruction from the body politic. Response from around the region was lukewarm. Undeterred, she lobbied state legislators and fellow clubwomen, many of whom disagreed with her and instead expressed preference for Here We Rest. She ignored them. Marie finally secured a sponsor for the legislation establishing the new seal and motto. Not everyone was thrilled with the proposed seal. One critic thought it looked like "a side of beef." Marie was not amused. To those who criticized the new seal and motto, she countered with the full cultural weight of Lost Cause apologists, declaring "10,000 United Daughters of the Confederacy can't be wrong!"[99] The Alabama legislature and Governor Frank M. Dixon agreed, and in December 1939, the state adopted the new seal and motto. They remain Alabama state symbols even eighty years later.

Much of Marie's legacy lay in her ability to craft and disseminate a self-serving historical narrative that protected the privilege she and other elite white southerners enjoyed. She was less successful in her attempts to craft niece Tallulah's public image. Tallulah on more than one occasion declined Marie's offer of her professional services. Interested in tying Tallulah's celebrity to a larger Lost Cause narrative, Marie implored her famous niece to attend the state's Confederate reunion in spring 1931. "It would make good national publicity as you would be featured as a southern celebrity coming home to honor the memory of your grandfather who was a distinguished Confederate soldier."[100] Tallulah stayed away. Even now that she was back in the United States, she kept her family at a distance; she visited infrequently and was a poor correspondent. Will despaired that he hardly ever heard from her. Lack of communication did not stop Marie from trying to exert some influence over her niece. No doubt privy to at least some of the stories of Tallulah's unorthodox behavior, Marie took pains to stress to Tallulah the importance of "good conduct," going so far as to remind the younger woman that the spirits of her beloved deceased grandparents were watching.[101] She worried about the film roles Tallulah was given. Too often she portrayed morally ambiguous women; the suicidal cabaret singer, gambling addict, and unfaithful wife that Tallulah portrayed in her Paramount movies were so unlike the virtuous women in Marie's own fiction.

Upon hearing that Tallulah was slated to play the female lead in the screen adaptation of *Thunder Below*, a 1931 novel by Thomas Rourke, Marie read the book. It was, she lamented, an "obscene story." She continued, "I was in hopes that your producers would select for you something of a nobler character for your next production." Will likewise expressed hope that "your management will ultimately find for you a picture that will give you a real opportunity to produce a real masterpiece, which they so far have not done."[102]

If Marie was unable to influence Tallulah's decisions in the types of parts she accepted, she could at least try to minimize damage to Tallulah's reputation (and the Bankhead name) wherever possible. Marie had her work cut out for her following the publication of "Has Hollywood Cold-Shouldered Tallulah?" by Gladys Hall in the September 1932 issue of *Motion Picture Magazine*. Hall's gossipy feature investigates the rumor that Tallulah had been socially blackballed by Hollywood hostesses uncomfortable with her brash nature. In the piece, Hall alleges that Hollywood's elites were particularly uncomfortable with Tallulah's propensity to talk frankly about her "love affairs," including her partner's "abilities or his disabilities, his prowess or his lack of prowess." According to Hall, "No good hostess . . . could dream of exposing her guests to such ribaldries." Tallulah told Hall that reports of her social blackballing were "absurd and untrue." The actress dismissed accusations that she was promiscuous and superficial. She had no problem with Hollywood; Hollywood had no problem with her. If she did have a problem, Tallulah admitted, it was her lack of romantic attachment. "I WANT A MAN!" she declared to Hall. "I haven't had an *affaire* for six months. . . . Six months! Too long. . . . Six months is a long, long time. *I want a man!*"[103]

The backlash to this interview was swift. By referencing sexual activity, Tallulah, Hall, and *Motion Picture Magazine* had stepped afoul of Will H. Hays, chairman of the Motion Picture Producers and Distributors of America (MPPDA). Hays had instituted a production code, a set of moral guidelines applied to motion pictures. Tallulah had also upset Marie, who worried about the repercussions that discussions of sexuality could have on Tallulah's reputation as well as the Bankhead name. Marie dashed off a blistering letter to her niece, warning her that "I'm afraid [what I have to say] won't be very pleasant." Marie was as upset about what Tallulah had said as she was about how she came to find out about the interview. Marie's friend told her that a "manicurist in a Beauty Parlor here was snickering" about Tallulah's interview. A working-class woman laughing at a Bankhead was intolerable. "I was so humiliated, so grieved," Marie wrote, "that I lay [awake] all night in tears." Not only had Tallulah damaged her own reputation, but she had "done . . . all those who have pride in you a great injury." Did Gladys Hall misquote her? If so, "your lawyer ought to put 'Motion Picture' magazine up against the wall and blast it to pieces with a machine gun." That Hall had put Tallulah "in this denuded position of indecent exposure before the public is criminal." Regardless of who was at fault, the story had done great damage. Tallulah's reputation had already suffered because of the "poor stories they have given you to play. This disgusting statement will lop off a good many more [fans]. A heroine must arouse enthusiasm not revulsion. You have been left no more privacy than a crossroads sign board." Hall made Tallulah sound like "the yapping of a hot canine locked up in a kennel." Marie signed off "with love and grief."[104]

Tallulah responded quickly with a telegram to "Darling Aunt Marie" expressing regret that the article had upset her and assuring her that the "article is a tissue of lies and misquotations from beginning to end." She promised to "refuse all [future] interviewers."[105] Marie shared Tallulah's telegram with Will, encouraging him to contact Hays at the MPPDA; she also arranged for Tallulah's denunciation to be published in the *Montgomery Advertiser* and the *Birmingham Age-Herald*. Father Will sent a letter to Tallulah assuring her that "the very ugly situation arising out of that infamous interview . . . will not permanently impair your standing with the public."[106] Will appealed to Hays and to Adolph Zukor, head of Paramount Pictures, to denounce Gladys Hall, which they did.

Marie was not finished in her campaign to clear the Bankhead name. She appealed to Alabama's governor, William W. Brandon, asking that he write to noted humorist Will Rogers, with whom the governor was acquainted, and ask that Rogers use his *New York Times* column to denounce "this conspiracy" against Tallulah. Brandon demurred, telling Marie that he was not close to Rogers and therefore would be uncomfortable making such a request.[107] And there the matter concluded. Crisis averted this time, Marie Bankhead Owen would continue to struggle with Tallulah's celebrity, taking every opportunity to push stories for public consumption that promoted her niece's career and the Bankhead name while remaining ever watchful for stories that threatened their collective reputations.

Was Tallulah as regretful of the candid interview as she led "Darling Aunt Marie" to believe? Probably not. Tallulah had spent the 1920s cultivating not only her craft but her celebrity. She became as famous for her personality as she was for her theatrical performances. She embodied the modern woman: financially independent and sexually liberated, she knew that her fans craved stories that celebrated those qualities. While she was in England, her family was spared what they would consider some of the more unsavory details of her freewheeling lifestyle. Now back in the United States and a woman in her thirties, Tallulah found her every move publicized. She had come of age as both countries embraced consumer culture, and she (like other movie stars) became a product to be consumed. Tallulah's success depended on her cultivation—through celebrity magazines and gossip columns—of the cult of personality. Despite the financial strain of the Depression, celebrity magazines continued to fly off the shelves, a cheap diversion from the drab grind of everyday life.[108] Consumer culture's emphasis on personality collided with Marie's Victorian values, which prized character and restraint. Yet there was no denying that Tallulah's celebrity lent the Bankheads a modern cultural appeal that they did not entirely deserve. Marie's quest to control the Bankhead legacy and name was complicated both by her continued financial reliance on Tallulah and by her own stifled ambitions. She envied Tallulah's independence and earning power. Tallulah's cultural power and persona at times conflicted with the political aims of the Bankheads; when she feared that something she had said or some action she had taken threatened her father in particular, Tallulah abided by his wishes and took steps to rectify her misstep; Marie's concerns were often ignored.

With the presidential election behind him, in mid-November 1936, Roosevelt turned his attention to the problem of tenancy, establishing a special committee populated with prominent social scientists and agricultural experts, and chaired by secretary of agriculture Henry A. Wallace to study the problem and to recommend a long-term program of action.[109] The committee held a series of regional meetings across the country, including in the Bankheads' home state of Alabama. The president's committee likewise solicited input from other groups, including the Southern Policy Association, which delivered its recommendations to Secretary Wallace in mid-December 1936. Although generally supportive of the Bankhead-Jones bill, the Southern Policy Association considered its suggested appropriation too small to make much of a dent in the problem. The association urged bold action. Members called for minimum wage guarantees for farm laborers, as well as the inclusion of farm laborers in the provisions for social security. Also recommended were protections against land speculation. The southern research group paid special attention to the implications of the proposed recommendations for southern race relations. Member Rupert B. Vance noted that "the Black Belts offer an especially difficult problem. In areas of seventy to ninety percent Negroes, the shift of this group from tenure to ownership status will mean—if it could be carried through—the practical evacuation of the areas by the white population. Now this may be a good thing, but at least we should realize the possibility. The white landlords here are something like the British colonial servants. They remain in a fairly alien environment simply because they exercise the function of social control and economic direction. Remove that function and they will retire, leaving the Black Belts to govern themselves or to be governed from the State Capitol."[110] The message was clear: any tenant legislation was going to have to contend with the racial fears of white southerners.

Following the winter break, Will conferred with the president about the upcoming session. Will told reporters that solving the problem of tenancy was the "paramount challenge to the next Congress."[111] In his address to Congress on January 7, 1937, the president echoed the Speaker's concerns. Despite the progress that had been made toward economic recovery, the country still had far to go. "Many millions of Americans still live in habitations which not only fail to provide the physical benefits of modern civilization, but breed disease and impair the health of future generations. The menace exists not only in the slum areas of the very large cities, but in many smaller cities as well. It exists on tens of thousands of farms, in varying degrees, in every party of the country." Tenant farming, he declared, was "un-American."[112]

The president's committee on tenancy published its report in February 1937. In his message to Congress announcing the report, the president highlighted the increase in tenancy over the preceding decade. For these Americans, Roosevelt stated, "the agricultural ladder . . . has become a treadmill."[113] The report noted that the problem of tenancy was particularly bad in the South, where the majority of tenants and sharecroppers lived. Once again, race entered the policy conversation. "The problem there," the president explained, painfully aware of the concerns of southern politicians, "is not a race problem, for of southern tenants and croppers two-thirds are whites and only one-third are Negroes."[114] The report on tenancy highlighted the various causes of tenancy, or what it called "insecurity," including the decades-long drop in cotton prices, the Depression, and inadequate credit, as well as the consequences of insecurity, among them both soil erosion and "erosion of our society," marked by "shifting citizens." The report noted that in 1935, one-third of all tenants had occupied their present farms for a single year. Constant movement meant low rates of social participation, interrupted education for children, and led to mental insecurity.[115] It also meant political instability. Cognizant of the committee and president's focus on white farmers, committee member Charles S. Johnson, in a statement tucked into the end of the report, urged that any tenant legislation include "safeguards to insure the full inclusion in the benefits of these programs of Negro tenants and sharecroppers. For, while it is true that only one-third of the sharecroppers and tenants in the South are Negroes, four-fifths of all Negro farm operators are tenants and sharecroppers."[116]

The recommendations of the president's committee veered close to John H. Bankhead Jr.'s original bill and included the creation of a "farm security corporation" that would purchase suitable farmland and sell it to tenants, a key provision from the senator's original bill that had subsequently been dropped. Qualified tenants would purchase these plots with low-interest long-term loans from the corporation. The goal was to create family-sized farms.[117] Armed with the recommendations of the president's committee, the backing of the president, and the tide of popular opinion, Bankhead had the wind at his back as he headed into the new congressional session.

At the dawn of 1937, John's health remained precarious. The senator and his staff were most worried about how concerns regarding his health might affect the prospects of his farm tenancy bill, which he introduced again in early January 1937. His staff worked to get positive news stories about his improved condition into the paper.[118] Although the senator missed only one roll call in January, he still was not at full health. He met with very few people in his office and tired easily, regularly taking naps in the afternoon. Will encouraged him to travel to Arizona until the danger had passed. The senator reluctantly agreed, only after receiving approval from the president, who promised to "protect me on my Farm Tenant Bill during my absence."[119] The senator left for Arizona in late January and did not return until late March. While in Arizona, he met with a new team of doctors who determined that he probably never had an abscess; rather, his problems were the result of allergies.[120]

Before John H. Bankhead Jr. left for Arizona, he and Congressman Jones introduced their nearly identical bills once again. The proposed tenant program was more limited than that requested by Bankhead in 1935 and less comprehensive than the recommendations of the president's farm tenancy committee. The appropriation requested was half of what Bankhead had proposed in 1935. For critics, even this request was too large. By May 1937, Roosevelt recommended that the appropriation be reduced to $10 million. Bankhead commented that he would prefer "the proposal fail than have it become only a 'gesture.'"[121]

Despite the bill's much-reduced appropriation request, opponents speculated what the bill would mean for the future of government intervention, especially what this intervention might mean for race relations. The program called for the government purchase of tracts and supervision of clients, something Tennessee congressman John Mitchell saw as un-American. "I do not think that the Government agents should be dictating how [the client] is to do everything. That is how this country was developed and made great. Our granddaddies built it up with individual initiative."[122] Others felt the program would impede efforts to raise farm prices, while still others felt that the best solution to the farm problem would be to provide easier credit to only the very best tenant farmers. The American Farm Bureau Federation was uncharacteristically silent during the debate, focusing its energies on keeping commodity prices up. Concerns about how government-assisted farm purchases might affect race relations remained close to the surface of any conversation about the bill. J. L. Edwards, a white cotton farmer in Selma, warned Senator Bankhead that tenancy "is a very dangerous question, especially for we fellows in the Black Belt. We took care of our negroes through the depression to the point we all liked to have gone broke in fact we have always taken care of them regardless." He was worried because African Americans in the region outnumbered white residents nine to one and remained a source of cheap labor. Bankhead tried to allay Edwards's fears that his bill would disrupt racial arrangements in the Black Belt, writing, "our primary interest is in the white tenants, and it may surprise you to know that a majority of the farm tenants in Alabama are white." He emphasized that "local committees will be appointed to pass upon tenants who are applying for aid in purchasing farms. Surely the white people in the Black Belt who constitute these local committees can handle that end of it for their own protection."[123] Local control of federal funds would prevent even the most progressive of New Deal measures from disrupting racial arrangements.

In addition to his own health problems and the racial concerns of his congressional colleagues, John saw the progress of his bill affected by the actions of a newly aggressive and powerful labor movement and the president's surprise assault on the Supreme Court, two developments that energized a nascent conservative block of Democrats and Republicans in Congress eager to stem to the radical potential of future New Deal programs. Conservatives were particularly concerned about the growing political influence of organized labor. New protections for unions embodied in the 1935 Wagner Act had led to the creation the following year of the CIO, led by John L. Lewis. The CIO was instrumental in Roosevelt's reelection, and labor quite naturally regarded the president as a friend of the working man. Although Lewis had his sights set on organizing the steel industry, events soon took on a life of their own. The union movement had been reborn among auto workers and their CIO-affiliated union, the United Auto Workers, particularly those working for General Motors. Workers at the Cleveland Fisher Body factory initiated a sit-down strike on December 28, 1936, followed two days later by strikes at Fisher Body No. 1 and No. 2 in Flint, Michigan. These three plants produced bodies and parts for roughly three-quarters of all General Motors production. The strike quickly spread to the company's plants in Detroit as well as Indiana, Ohio, and Wisconsin. A shortage of materials forced General Motors to shut down other plants not already out on strike. General Motors was not going to give in easily, and it became clear early that the workers were in for a protracted fight.

The sit-down strikes captured the nation's attention. Although not an entirely new strategy, the sit-down strike was viewed by the business community and a certain segment of the population as "a much greater threat than any ordinary walkout because it involved the seizure of private property and rendered useless many of the weapons employers had traditionally used against conventional strikes."[124] Lewis and the CIO moved quickly to demand the president's help to bring General Motors to the negotiating table. Secretary of labor Frances Perkins tried to broker a meeting between the two sides; Lewis quickly agreed to a meeting, while the president of General Motors, Alfred P. Sloan, rebuffed her offer. Perkins tried another tactic to bring the two sides together. In late January 1937, Perkins sent Speaker Bankhead a message urging the introduction and passage of legislation that would grant the secretary of labor "the extraordinary powers not now possessed by that office to subpoena witnesses, records and documents and to have hearings upon pending disputes between labor and employers with reference to making recommendations for the adjustment and settlement of such controversies." The *New York Times* reported that congressional leaders were "taken aback" by the request and did not make any public comment.[125]

Privately, Will noted that he was "amazed" to have received such a message from a cabinet officer, especially given the current conflict between the CIO and General Motors. "I shall certainly take no steps in the matter until and unless the President makes a strong recommendation in favor of it. I am utterly unwilling to concede the right of any Cabinet officer to propose legislation to the Congress." He promptly contacted the White House about Perkins's request. Later that evening, the president's son James came to Will's apartment at the Mayflower to let him know that the president "was unaware of [Perkins's] letter, that it was not done at his suggestion or with his approval and requested that I take no steps to carry out the Secretary's suggestions at this time." Bankhead concluded his entry by stating his opinion that Perkins "is totally unfitted for the very responsible position now held by her," and he expressed his hope that she would not last for the entire term.[126]

A deal was finally reached with General Motors in late February 1937, but by then the sit-down strikes were escalating, spreading to other industries.[127] By March, some 160,000 workers were on strike. The sit-down strike, the *Detroit News* mused, "has replaced baseball as a national pastime."[128] The pace of sit-downs quickened in March, involving electrical workers in Saint Louis, Missouri, and casket workers in Springfield, Ohio. But the major battleground remained Michigan and the auto industry. As turbulence spread, so too did criticism in the US Senate and elsewhere. Vice President Garner was uncomfortable with the sit-down strikes, declaring them a threat to "our entire theory of property ownership and government."[129] Will Bankhead noted in his diary that "the so-called new method of sit-down strikes continues to grow in the country and I am very deeply concerned and distressed with reference to the possibilities of this new order of labor activity. It seems to me that it violates every fundamental principle of property rights and I think that the labor leaders who give encouragement to such methods are making a grave mistake and run the risk of forfeiting in large measure favorable public opinion for their cause."[130]

As industrial America roiled, Roosevelt—emboldened by his electoral landslide—decided the time was right for an attack on the judiciary that had dismantled much of the early New Deal. On the morning of February 5, 1937, Speaker Bankhead received a telephone call from one of the president's private secretaries, summoning him to the cabinet room at ten o'clock to discuss a "highly confidential" matter. Assembled at the appointed hour were Senate majority leader Joseph T. Robinson of Arkansas, Speaker of the House Bankhead, House majority leader Sam Rayburn of Texas, the chairmen of the House and Senate Committees on the Judiciary, all members of the president's cabinet, and Vice President Garner. Roosevelt had planned the meeting as a means to launch what he believed would be "the greatest triumph of his presidency." He had deliberately kept party leaders in the dark, confident that he could gain advantage from surprise. The president hurried into the room while aides passed around copies of his plan to revise the court. As those in the room frantically tried to absorb the plan, the president stated that he would have little time to discuss it as he had a press conference scheduled in half an hour. As Bankhead later recalled, "Practically no discussion of the message was invited as it was apparent that the President had formulated his policy and was putting it up to Congress to adopt or reject it."[131]

The party leaders were, to put it mildly, stunned, both by the plan itself and by its hasty delivery. The president's plan was sweeping: it would allow him to increase the number of judges on the Supreme Court to as many as fifteen if judges failed to retire at the age of seventy; add a total of not more than fifty judges to federal courts; and send appeals from lower-court decisions on constitutional matters directly to the Supreme Court. At the time of his announcement, six judges were age seventy or older. Roosevelt justified his plan by arguing that it would improve court efficiency. During his noon press conference, he declared that the federal courts needed reorganizing, and he focused on "the complexities, the delays and the expense of litigation in the United States." The US Supreme Court in particular, he declared, "is laboring under a heavy burden," and his plan was designed to relieve "present congestion" by "enlarging the capacity of all the federal courts." Compounding the problem of backlog, the president noted the advanced age of many of the judges, pointing out that the court needed "younger blood." Finally, he noted, reform was needed "to adapt our legal forms and judicial interpretation to the actual present needs of the largest progressive democracy in the world."[132]

Ever the party loyalist, Speaker Bankhead, who earlier had expressed a desire to deal with the court issue through constitutional amendment, told the New York Times that he thought the president's proposal was based on "a sound principle of judicial reform." He later confided in his diary that "it was patent to me that many of the more prudent and thoughtful Members of the House were disturbed, if not alarmed, by the recommendations made."[133] Conservative Democrats and Republicans were taken aback by the president's proposal; once they had gathered their collective wits they began accusing the president of trying to wreck the judiciary. Former president Herbert Hoover accused Roosevelt of attempting to "pack the court" to win favorable judicial decisions.[134] Although congressional leadership followed Bankhead's lead and was fairly tight-lipped regarding the proposal, Texas congressman Hatton W. Sumners, chair of the House Committee on the Judiciary, which would receive the president's proposal, expressed his displeasure with the plan privately to his colleagues as they left the White House. "Boys," he declared, "here's where I cash in my chips."[135] The president could not expect support from Sumners. Congressional leaders girded themselves for a fight. Bankhead was worried: "I greatly fear that the reaction in the country to this proposal will be adverse and harmful to our Party."[136]

The press, both liberal and conservative, attacked the president's court plan. Liberal columnist Dorothy Thompson of the *New York Herald Tribune* compared Roosevelt's plan to the machinations of totalitarian dictators in Europe. Mail received by congressional offices, some of it engineered by right-wing opponents but much of it authentic, was running nine to one against the plan.[137] Only a few days after the president's announcement, a bill from Congressman Sumners that addressed the issue of elderly justices passed the House, taking some of the wind out of the president's sails. The bill would allow justices to retire with full pay and continue to receive tax immunity.[138] Sumners had also lined up opposition to the president's plan within his committee, should it get the opportunity to consider the proposal. The president was caught completely off guard by the ferocity of the political backlash. The response to his plan was so strong and so negative that it threatened to derail his second term and his legacy.

A few days after the announcement, Will reported to John, who was still in Arizona seeking medical attention, that the president's proposal "has raised a lot of trouble and sentiment, which has not as yet sufficiently crystalized to determine what Congress is going to do about it. There is a tremendous amount of opposition among conservative Democrats against that feature proposing to make possible fifteen members on the Supreme Court." Will confided that although "personally I do not like the idea . . . , I presume that in a quiet way I will go along with the President."[139] To a fellow House member, Will expressed his irritation at having been kept out of the loop. "Wouldn't you have thought that the President would have told his own party leaders what he was going to do[?] He didn't because he knew that all hell would break loose."[140] In his diary, Will confided, "I am frankly very profoundly disturbed by this situation, which could have been avoided in large measure if the President had seen fit to take into his confidence some of the Members of Congress who are his real friends."[141] A week later, Will reported to John that the court reform issue had "caused more consternation and concern among Members of Congress than anything that has been done during his administration. There is a very great opposition to his proposal as a whole among Members of the House and Senate. Frankly, I doubt very much if a vote were taken today that the Bill would pass either branch. It has given me a very great deal of personal concern but I have already reached the conclusion that there is nothing left for me to do except to go ahead with my full endorsement and support of his program. It is absolutely possible that if the Senate will pass the [Sumners] Bill which the House passed a few days ago giving the privilege of retirement at full pay to Justices over seventy years of age, that at least two and possibly three of the Justices will take advantage of it." According to Will, Congressman Sumners "privately informs me that he is confident" that the bill would prompt some justices to retire, but Will was not so sure.[142] John was critical of the president's plan but had made no definite announcement about how he would vote if the plan made it to the floor of the

Senate. By March, Will was expressing his deep concern about John's "apparent attitude on the Supreme Court matter," but also noted that "I am happy to know that you will reach no definite conclusion about it until you return to Washington. There are several angles of the problem that I wish to discuss with you when you return. The more I undertake to analyze his objective the less worry I have about supporting it."[143] Because Will had come out in support of the president's plan, he felt that "it might be a matter of some embarrassment [should John] take the opposing side."[144] Still, Will predicted that by sticking with the president, "I will assume heavy political liabilities."[145]

The president's court bill was sent to the Senate Committee on the Judiciary. Will noted in his diary that "I have been able by some strategic movements to place the burden upon the Senate of acting upon this proposition."[146] As he predicted, the hearings did not proceed smoothly, with supporters of the administration's plan immediately put on the defensive. Witnesses who supported the plan did a poor job defending it. Opponents of the plan scored a major victory when Senator Burton K. Wheeler of Montana, serving as a witness in the hearings, read a searing letter from Chief Justice Charles Evans Hughes affirming the court's opposition to the plan and demolishing the president's claim that the court was overworked and justice delayed. The president's plan was in deep trouble. In early May, the Senate Committee on the Judiciary voted 10–8 to reject the president's bill, calling it "a needless, futile, and utterly dangerous abandonment of constitutional principle. . . . It is a measure which should be so emphatically rejected that its parallel will never again be presented to the free representatives of the free people of America."[147] The president's plan was also losing by winning: in the spring, the Supreme Court returned affirmative verdicts on the Wagner Act and the Social Security Act, two key pieces of New Deal legislation. In his diary, Will noted that the decisions "will no doubt constitute a milestone in the progress of a more liberal construction of the Constitution as far as the powers of Congress are concerned on interstate and labor legislation."[148] The Supreme Court's decisions were made, incidentally, on Will's sixty-third birthday. President Roosevelt called the Speaker to share his best wishes, adding "it's a pretty good day for all of us."[149] Although Roosevelt was pleased that these acts had passed constitutional muster, these victories made it more difficult to argue that the court was out of step with the needs of a progressive democracy.

By May, Will was reporting to John that "everyone here now seems to think that the Court program is licked in the Senate." Significant developments had severely compromised the president's chances for success. With his salary secured by the actions of Congressman Sumners, Justice Willis Van Devanter announced his decision to step down from the bench. With one of the elderly justices retiring, the need for Roosevelt's plan was less clear. Will confided to John that "Van Devanter's resignation has had quite a jarring effect on the President's original program." Regarding Van Devanter's replacement, Will revealed that "personally, I would like to see [Senate majority leader] Joe Robinson get the vacancy and I imagine that he has a good chance for it."[150] Roosevelt had long ago promised the first Supreme Court vacancy to Robinson. But the majority leader was sixty-five years old; his appointment would contradict Roosevelt's professed interest in bringing new blood to the court. Roosevelt also worried about Robinson's conservative leanings. And the president was still wedded to his court plan, although he was willing to compromise.

In June, Roosevelt directed Senator Robinson to work out some kind of compromise. If Robinson could come up with a plan that would allow Roosevelt to appoint additional judges, one of those judges would be Robinson himself. Robinson went to work, ultimately crafting an amended plan that would allow the president to appoint one extra justice for each sitting justice over the age of seventy-five. Furthermore, the plan would limit the president to one additional justice per calendar year. Under this arrangement, Roosevelt would be able to nominate three new justices to the court. Unfortunately for the president, public opinion was running hot against this plan, with 62 percent of respondents to a Gallup poll firmly opposed.[151] At a June meeting with Roosevelt, Will told the president that the compromise bill stood little chance of making it out of the Committee on the Judiciary. When Roosevelt suggested the use of a discharge petition to bring the bill to the floor, Will was not encouraging, telling the president "it is my candid judgment that it would be extremely difficult, if not impossible, to secure the signatures of a majority of the Members of the House for such petition."[152] Will was not anxious for the House to consider the new plan. Robinson's compromise bill went first to the Senate. As Will noted in his diary, "The first two days['] debate has developed a considerable amount of personal bitterness and recrimination upon the part of Democratic Senators and I very greatly fear that before the conclusion of the debate many irreparable wounds will be inflicted."[153]

In the midst of a torrid Washington, DC, summer, Robinson waged a brutal, desperate battle for the president's compromise plan and for his own place on the Supreme Court. The cost was high: on Tuesday, July 13, Robinson dropped dead of a heart attack in his Washington apartment. The news came to the Speaker's house the next morning while he was in the bath. He was "most profoundly grieved and distressed" at receiving the news. Will noted that "Senator Robinson and I had in the last year or so formed for each other quite a close and affectionate mutual regard." What, he wondered, would his death mean for the court plan? The court issue "has reached such a volcanic stage in the Senate and which threatens such disaster to our Party solidarity. This Court question has given me more concern and apprehension than any issue that has arisen during my public service and I yet hope that there may be some points of providential direction that will enable us to solve it without the absolute disruption of our Party."[154]

Later that day, Bankhead, House majority leader Rayburn, and Democratic whip Boland were summoned to the White House. Bankhead noted that Roosevelt "impressed me as being in rather low spirit" because of the "tragic death of his right hand man." The president was also, Bankhead wrote, "no doubt hurt by the public implications that by his insistence upon pressing the Court issue in the Senate he had directly contributed to Senator Robinson's death." Should the public blame the president for putting undo strain on Robinson, Roosevelt suggested a counter-narrative be pushed out to the press, namely that "those who had started the filibuster in the Senate were responsible for the situation."[155]

The compromise plan that Robinson had devised and fought vigorously for died with him. In August, both houses passed a much watered-down judicial reform bill that bore almost no resemblance to the president's initial plan. It was Franklin D. Roosevelt's first major legislative defeat.[156] In his diary, Will wrote that "this court proposition [has been] the most serious thing from a Party standpoint that has been presented during this administration."[157] Having to support such an unpopular proposition placed the Speaker under great strain.

As Congress wrangled and fought over the president's court plan, the tenant bill remained bogged down in the House. Criticism of the bill ran the political gamut. The chairman of the advisory board of the Works Progress Administration spoke out against Bankhead's bill, which he argued would fail because sharecroppers and tenants lacked the training to become independent farmers, and because they had a "generally bad physical condition." He argued, "In the South they have lived for generations in mosquito-infested and unsanitary surroundings, on an improper diet, and with totally inadequate medical care. A large proportion of them are afflicted with insidious, energy-sapping diseases. The prevalence of malaria, pellagra, hernia, bad teeth, and deceased tonsils is without question a major cause of the shiftlessness and indolence with which these people are so often reproached."[158] Some New Dealers felt the government should not be selling to individual landowners but rather should create a communal or collective system. Others felt that the current proposal was too modest and would not develop farm ownership on a large-enough scale to be effective.[159] Still others believed that "advances in technology and mechanization have already made the family-sized farm [the goal of Bankhead-Jones] an inefficient unit. . . . The large-scale cooperative farm [was] the logical alternative."[160]

In late May 1937, Will met with the president. He tried to push the president on expanding the original appropriation for John Jr.'s bill but was unsuccessful, telling his brother that the president "still seems . . . of the opinion that not more than ten million dollars should be available as a starter."[161] The constant delays and bickering in Congress exasperated and discouraged John. In June, desperate to save John's bill, Will Bankhead left the Speaker's chair to speak on behalf of the bill as the representative of Alabama's Tenth Congressional District. He painted a picture of those he called the "forgotten men" of agriculture: "And there stands a desolate, hopeless, dejected man, working some other man's property, pillaging it, despoiling its rich resources by virtue of the fact that it is not his, but some other man's and at the end of the year, when they cast up the account, this man who has worked in season and out of season during the whole crop season finds himself with no profit with which to go through the winter, with nothing with which to buy magazines, medicines, or comforts, for his family. It is a rather pathetic picture, and as a man representing that section of the country I am ashamed, almost, to describe it here before my colleagues, but God's truth is the God's truth wherever we stand face to face with it." The Speaker concluded his remarks by reciting Edwin Markham's poem "The Man with Hoe," which asks:

> Who made him dead to rapture and despair,
> A thing that grieves not and that never hopes.
> Stolid and stunned, a brother to the ox?
> Who loosened and let down this brutal jaw?
> Whose was the hand that slanted back this brow?
> Whose breath blew out the light within this brain?

He acknowledged criticism of the act as containing too small an appropriation to make much of a dent in the problem. He urged his colleagues not to let the perfect be the enemy of the good. "A great many other useful things that have taken deep root in our governmental enterprises started as experiments," he noted. "I very well recall when my honorable father was pioneering here in Congress for Federal aid for the improvement of our national highways. It was regarded as a dream, as unconstitutional, and never possible of accomplishment. . . . And you see the result." This bill gave farmers a chance "to put off the sackcloth and ashes that they have worn for so many years with an inferiority complex and stand up and look into the face of the sun and their Creator and say, 'By the generous grace of a sympathetic Government I am being given another opportunity to prove the mettle of my pasture.'"[162]

After years of wrangling and delay, the Bankhead-Jones Tenant Farm Act finally passed the House at the end of June. Bankhead's bill passed the Senate effectively unopposed; the compromise Bankhead-Jones Farm Tenant Act, with some slight changes, easily passed both houses of Congress in July 1937.[163] Roosevelt signed the act on July 22.[164] The *Montgomery Advertiser* attributed the passage of the bill to the "Bankhead Boys" and their intimate knowledge of farming, emphasizing their connection to the land, which had been a political staple for father and sons since 1865: "They know what it is to open the earth to make a warm bed for precious seeds. They know what it is to be anxious for the fortune of a crop that is the helpless pawn of the weather and the confusion of man. Many people think of them today as two ruddy-cheeked, pampered sons of a great family who never knew what it was to toil and sacrifice. But the truth is that John and Will Bankhead are old plowboys and hoe hands."[165]

In reality, the passage of the Bankhead-Jones Farm Tenant Act in July 1937 was bittersweet. The appropriation was a mere fraction of what John had originally proposed, a billion-dollar corporation carrying out a comprehensive farm security program. The plan as approved was more modest. The tenant purchase program would be administered by the newly created Farm Security Administration, which was placed under the auspices of the Department of Agriculture. Title I of the act authorized making loans for the purchase and improvement of land. Only farm tenants, sharecroppers, agricultural laborers, and others who made their living from farming were eligible. The tenant purchase program received funding for three years at an amount of $10 million, $25 million, and $50 million, respectively.[166]

Despite the act's shortcomings, one historian has called the Farm Security Administration, "one of the New Deal's most aggressively redistributionist agencies."[167] It was a key agency in the "agrarian New Deal," a collection "of often-dissonant programs that targeted culture, environment, poverty, land tenure, and the fostering of rural democracy."[168] Another scholar has noted that "for all its shortcomings and all their disappointment, however, supporters recognized the [Bankhead-Jones bill] as a big step, or at least a first one."[169] Credit and close supervision were the program's main tools. By June 1941, the tenant purchase program had authorized nearly $120 million in loans to twenty-one

Figure 11.6.
The Bankhead
brothers, late
1930s. *Left to right:*
John Jr., Will, and
Henry. Courtesy
of the Alabama
Department of
Archives and
History.

thousand clients.[170] Seen as something of an upstart, the Farm Security Administration was constantly under siege.

With its rather small budget (in comparison to Bankhead's original request) as a result of congressional opposition, the program adopted a cautious and conservative approach. The tenant purchase program had a relatively small number of carefully selected clients, who received more money than those in the rural rehabilitation program and much more supervision. The program needed clients to succeed to keep the program politically viable. If clients failed, congressional opponents would pounce, declare the program a failure, and kill it. The program chose its clients carefully; by June 30, 1943, the Farm Security Administration boasted a 98.4 percent return rate on loans.[171]

The first tenant purchase loan was made on February 12, 1938, to Wiley J. Langley of Jasper, Alabama, hometown of John H. Bankhead Jr. Langley was a sharecropper with twelve children. He received a $3,800 loan to purchase a 180-acre farm. A farmer from Pickens County named Bankhead Jones was also approved for a loan under the program.[172] Demand for loans was high, but administrators were cautious. In its first year alone, the tenant purchase division received 38,000 applications but approved only 1,879 loans. In its first three years of operation, the program received more than 280,000 applications and approved 12,234 loans. By 1949, the federal government had approved roughly 62,000 tenant purchase loans. Of those, about 15 percent had been foreclosed, sold, transferred, or repossessed by the government. Of that 15 percent, roughly one-third resulted from accidents, death, illness, or old age, or by a switch in occupation by the borrower. Criticisms of the program centered on the small size of the appropriation, which resulted in fewer loans. The application process was fairly rigorous. Loans went not to the poorest farmers, but rather to those that the tenant purchase division regarded as the safest credit risks. Applicants for loans were assessed on their farming skill, their willingness and ability to cooperate with farm and home supervisors, their character, and their reputation in their community. Ultimately, as historian Charles Kenneth Roberts has illustrated, the tenant purchase program "was the most successful on the balance sheets and most politically popular of the [Farm Security Administration's] programs; it also was the most cautious and conservative."[173]

For the new farm owners themselves, the program was a godsend. When asked about the difference between owning and renting, successful client John H. McCullough responded, "Why, there's all the difference in the world. When a man's got his own land he feels like working it and building it up, because he knows he's going to get the benefit of it. And a man's his own boss when he's working his own place." Such successes were common in the program; unfortunately, the program was far too modest to seriously overhaul the tenant system. A larger appropriation might have accomplished that. But, as Roberts points out, although a larger appropriation would have meant more loans, close supervision was critical to the process, and this may not have been achieved with additional clients.[174]

Throughout the New Deal, southern congresspeople and senators remained on alert for programs that had the potential to upset race relations in the South. As a group, they were resoundingly successful in excluding black southerners from the benefits and protections of New Deal programs. The Bankhead-Jones Farm Tenant Act was no exception. The bill's success hinged largely on the fact that tenancy was presented as a white problem; hence, most agents and clients were white. "In many cases," Roberts notes, "African American farmers were ignored or even pushed off their land in favor of white clients." The Farm Security Administration took care to avoid violating southern racial norms.[175] In Will Bankhead's congressional district, documentation reveals that 219 white farmers and fourteen black farmers received loans with which to purchase farms.[176]

President Roosevelt spent part of summer 1937 on a cross-country tour, where he was greeted regularly by enthusiastic crowds. The outpouring of support convinced the president that if Congress were called into special session, he stood a good chance of passing legislation that had failed to pass during the regular session. But the state of the economy was making it more difficult for the president to achieve additional legislation. In fall 1937, the economy slipped into a recession that would stretch into 1938. Unemployment rose from 14.3 percent in 1937 to 19.0 percent in 1938. Business interests blamed what they regarded as the New Deal's "anti-business" outlook, while others claimed that the government needed to increase spending. Will was "deeply concerned over the financial and economic condition of the country," in particular, "the recession in business and the alarming growth of unemployment." He feared the political repercussions should the economy not stabilize before the midterm elections. "It has been my observation that it is almost impossible for the dominant political Party to survive a panic." He predicted that Republicans would "gain a very large number of seats in the next House of Representatives" if the state of the economy did not improve.[177]

On October 12, 1937, Roosevelt called for Congress to convene on November 15. Will was not surprised that the president called a special session; the president had mentioned it in August, and, Will wrote in his diary, "I have long since found that the President very rarely abandons an idea once fixed in his mind."[178] Will met with the president shortly before the start of the session. Among the key items the president wanted passed was the Black-Connery bill, which established wage and hour standards for American workers. A law that established a minimum wage and a standard work week while also eliminating child labor abuses had long been the desire of secretary of labor Frances Perkins and the broader labor movement. But she and Roosevelt both feared that such a law would not survive review by the Supreme Court. In March 1937, in a 5–4 decision, the court validated Washington State's minimum wage law, giving hope to those seeking additional protections for American workers. Perkins and Roosevelt sensed their opening. In May 1937, the president sent his bill to Congress, with the accompanying message that a country as wealthy as America should be able to give "all our able-bodied working men and women a fair day's pay for a fair day's work." Furthermore, "a self-supporting and self-respecting democracy can plead no justification for the existence of child labor, no economic reason for chiseling worker's wages or stretching workers' hours." Alabama senator Hugo L. Black sponsored the bill in the Senate, while Representative William P. Connery Jr. of Massachusetts introduced a comparable bill in the House.

Public support was strong, and most expected smooth sailing for the bill. But opponents, many of them from the South, came out swinging, charging that the bill would establish a tyrannical industrial dictatorship. Both Bankhead and Rayburn were in favor of some sort of bill but not terribly enthusiastic. A weakened bill passed the Senate in July 1937, but a coalition of Republicans and southern Democrats kept the House bill bottled up in the Committee on Rules. In August 1937, Will wrote to John about problems with the Black-Connery bill. It was causing him a lot of stress. "The House leadership is . . . in a bad jam with reference to the Black Connery Bill. For the first time since I have been Speaker, the Rules Committee has absolutely balked on granting a rule for the consideration of this bill, although I as Party Leader have urged upon the Democrats of the Committee the very unfortunate situation in which the organization will be placed if no rule is granted." A self-professed conciliator, Will found even his considerable skills of persuasion stretched to their limits. "I have been unable even by personal appeal to southern Democrats on the Committee to blast them out of their determination against granting a rule." Will was sympathetic with the position of southern employers, whom he believed would be put at a disadvantage by the bill, but he believed that in his role as Speaker, his job was to take all steps necessary to bring the bill to a vote. His leadership role required him to rise above sectional interests. The burdens of the office were weighing heavily on him. "I am extremely anxious to get away," he told John, "but I am conserving my strength and nerves in every way possible and am determined not to crack up because of the heavy responsibilities now upon me in the closing days of the session."[179] Congress adjourned with no action on the bill.

When Roosevelt called Congress back into session in November, passage of the Black-Connery bill was high on his agenda. The bill had been passed by the Senate but was bottled up in the House Committee on Rules by five committeemen from the South. Amid the struggle over the bill, *Time* magazine published an issue with Will Bankhead on the cover, observing that "by the time [the special session] adjourns, Speaker Bankhead will have had his abilities as leader, parliamentarian and politician thoroughly tested."[180] Will confided to his diary that the bill "has caused me a great deal of concern." He noted that these southern obstructionists "regard the Bill as so disastrous to southern industries in its application that they feel in conscience justified in refusing to go along with the House leadership in reporting out the Bill." He noted that "some sort of show down" was planned.[181] The leadership, including Speaker Bankhead, decided to force release of the bill from committee by petition, which required 218 signatures. One pundit called the struggle for signatures "one of the hardest and hottest behind-the-scenes battles the membership has witnessed in years."[182] A Washington columnist observed:

> It has been virtually raining fruit, candy, and nuts in the House since Thanksgiving Day when the bountiful Speaker Bankhead and Leader Sam Rayburn pulled on their white whiskers and decided to make everybody happy—that is, everybody who would sign the petition to get up the wages and hours bill. . . . One Florida member is supposed to have secured a promise to consider the Florida ship canal. Another Florida member is supposed to have bought a promise not to take up the Florida ship canal. . . . Many (12 to 20) Southern (and a few Western) farm belt men were openly bought with promises of left wing labor support on the farm bill. . . . But there was one other delectable donation, which is being accredited to Bankhead alone. . . . It was arranged for the mileage allowance to be voted with a minimum of discussion, and without a record vote, so no one could even tell who voted for it and who did not.[183]

Martin Dies Jr. of Texas, one of the obstructionist members of the Committee on Rules, complained, "They have swapped everything today but the Capitol."[184]

Despite a successful petition, the bill did not pass during the special session but was recommitted to the Committee on Labor. Of the 133 House Democrats opposing the legislation, over half were from the South. For many southern opponents, race was the key issue. Representative J. Mark Wilcox of Florida ranted, "the [federal] Government knows no color line. I warn you that you cannot go into the South and prescribe the same wage rates for the black man as for the white man." Representative Maury Maverick of Texas, a bill supporter, replied, "It's that attitude that has kept the white man's wages down in the South." Furthermore, Maverick continued, the South had benefited greatly from New Deal programs. "When you take Uncle Sam's money, you have to take his laws, too."[185] Bankhead found the southern opposition "quite embarrassing . . . but in view of my position of leadership and of the great interest of the President in the bill I did what I could to secure its consideration."[186] Opponents of the measure proposed that the bill be recommitted to the Committee on Labor. Bankhead seldom voted as Speaker, but in this instance, he took the opportunity to vote against recommitment, which in reality was a vote to kill the bill for that session. William Mitch, president of United Mine Workers District 20, made note of Bankhead's vote against commitment. "I want you to know you spoke the sentiment of the workers in this section."[187]

The bill continued to give Will "a great deal of concern." He remained committed to passing it. His brother, on the other hand, kept quiet about the bill, refusing to take a public stand one way or the other. He hoped that the House would kill the bill, thus saving him the choice of having to support workers at the expense of industrialists who were his friends. When the special session finally concluded, Congress had not passed a single bill the President requested.[188] Bankhead tried to soften the blow by stating, quite accurately, that "important spade work" had been undertaken for bills that would be considered during the regular session to begin in January. Although true, this was hardly a ringing endorsement for Congress or the president.[189]

A revised wages and hours bill was introduced in January 1938. Once again, the Committee on Rules bottled it up. A petition to discharge the bill from the committee was placed on the Speaker's desk; within two and half hours, the petition had 218 signatures and the bill went to the House floor. Discussion of the bill was brutal. Finally, the House approved a compromise bill in June 1938, with the Senate approving shortly thereafter. Roosevelt signed the Fair Labor Standards Act on June 25, 1938. The law established a minimum wage (twenty-five cents per hour, soon to rise to between thirty and forty cents per hour), a standardized forty-four-hour work week (which would later drop to forty hours), a requirement to pay extra for overtime work, and a prohibition on certain types of child labor.[190] Senator John H. Bankhead Jr. ultimately did not vote on the bill.[191]

The Fair Labor Standards Act was one of the final legislative accomplishments of the New Deal. After six dramatic, exhilarating, and exhausting years of domestic reform, the New Deal was losing steam. Any further legislation proposed by the president would have to confront an increasingly hostile alliance of conservative Democrats and Republicans. Throughout the president's second term, Speaker Bankhead used every tool at his disposal to keep the majority together and focused on passing the president's agenda. The effort took a physical and psychological toll on Will, and he worried constantly that he might not be up to the task.

As the decade drew to a close, events in Europe quickly overtook domestic concerns. Although the 1930s were marked by an isolationist foreign policy born of dismay over the conclusion of World War I, the rise of totalitarian regimes and the threat they posed to liberal democracies were proving ever more worrisome to the American president and Congress. Any further domestic legislative reform would soon take a back seat to international developments.

12

"A Good Soldier in Politics"

The Last Campaign

THE COURT-PACKING DEBACLE, the sit-down strikes, the 1937 recession, and the prolonged struggle to pass the wages and hours legislation combined to embolden the Republicans and conservative Democrats in Congress. By 1938, the president, one historian has written, "seemed nothing more than a lame duck politician who had lost his grip, facing the dead end of his career."[1] The fight for his agenda in Congress grew increasingly more difficult. Expectations that Franklin D. Roosevelt would be able to achieve additional reform measures following the bruising battle for the wages and hours legislation decreased by the day. The slowdown of the president's domestic reform agenda coincided with the increased threat posed by the fascist dictatorships in Europe. As war clouds gathered, isolationist sentiment in the nation remained strong, and neutrality legislation severely constrained the president's ability to act. The outbreak of war in Europe in August 1939 focused the nation's attention on security. As the German war machine rolled across the European continent, Roosevelt struggled with Congress and public opinion to take steps to guarantee the nation's military preparedness. Speaker of the House Will Bankhead worked closely with the administration in its attempt to beat back restrictions on the president's ability to respond to increasingly hostile developments overseas and in its effort to ensure that if and when war came, America would be ready. During this period, Will served as an effective and eloquent spokesperson for the responsibility of democratic nations threatened by autocratic nations.

As Will became more expansive in his political and policy outlook and interests, brother John remained fixated on sectional issues, mainly the price of cotton, to the exclusion of almost everything else. The senator felt that fears about impending war were overblown and continued to support a position of neutrality. However, he kept his distance from the Senate's most-outspoken isolationists, believing that the president deserved greater latitude of action to confront the escalating crises in Europe and the Far East.

Along with the rest of the country, the Bankhead brothers looked for signs of Roosevelt's political plans as his second term drew to a close. Would the president run for an unprecedented third term? The president kept his plans a secret, leaving even his closest advisers in the dark. As the convention drew near, and with no statement by the president, possible presidential nominees began to emerge—among them, Will Bankhead. Ever loyal to the president, though, Bankhead kept calls for his candidacy at bay but quietly harbored thoughts of higher office.

As the decade wore on, the sense of urgency that had defined the Roosevelt administration's early years had dissipated considerably, although the Depression was by no means over. The president held out hope for additional New Deal legislation, but he understood that his chances for legislative success required a more liberal Senate. Frustrated by conservative southern senators in particular, Roosevelt undertook a campaign during the 1938 spring and summer primaries to purge the body of Democrats he considered to be obstructionist. In the president's crosshairs were Senators Walter F. George of Georgia, Ellison DuRant "Cotton Ed" Smith of South Carolina, and Millard Tydings of Maryland. Will Bankhead steered clear of the president's purge tour but paid close attention to the reelection bid of Representative John J. O'Connor of New York. As chairman of the House Committee on Rules, O'Connor regularly opposed the administration's agenda. He also hungered for a leadership position. House majority leader Sam Rayburn of Texas reminded the Speaker of the problems caused by O'Connor and the Committee on Rules in passing the wages and hours bill. But, Rayburn warned, "Our trouble of last session with him would be a small affair compared to what we would have next session if he should lose the Democratic nomination and be nominated by the Republicans."[2] Rayburn was anxious to know Bankhead's plans: "If our friend in New York is renominated what are you going to do[?] If you congratulate him, what will you say?" Bankhead was simply going to wait and see and not do anything.[3] Bankhead's cautious approach was prudent; O'Connor was the only Democrat on the president's purge list who was defeated in the Democratic primary. He ultimately ran in the general election as an anti–New Deal, anti-Roosevelt Republican but was again defeated. With the exception of O'Connor's loss, the president's actions ultimately backfired: not a single senator targeted by Roosevelt for removal lost his race.

The midterm elections of 1938, while not a complete rebuke of the New Deal, certainly were a body blow to the president. The Republicans increased their presence in Congress, picking up eighty-one seats in the House and eight in the Senate.[4] Congress became increasingly obstreperous. The president's opponents feared him less than they did during his first term because they expected him to be gone in a little over a year. No one expected Roosevelt to run for an unprecedented third term.

Even the most ardent New Dealers found their attention drawn increasingly to foreign affairs as the decade came to a close. Concern over international developments and interest in the country's foreign policy had taken a back seat during most of Roosevelt's presidency as Congress and the president focused on the economy. Although himself an internationalist who advocated active engagement with other nations, Roosevelt was keenly aware of the isolationist sentiment in the country. For many Americans, the country's entrance into the First World War had been a colossal mistake. They believed that bankers and munitions manufacturers had severely compromised US neutrality by lending money and selling munitions to the Allies, thus implicating the country in the Allies' victory and bringing the nation into the war. This belief was supported and amplified by a growing and increasingly vocal isolationist movement that was determined to keep the country out of the next major conflict. With each new international crisis—the Japanese attack on Manchuria in 1931–32, the German rearmament in 1935 and occupation of the Rhineland in 1936, the Italian invasion of Ethiopia in 1935, and the Spanish Civil War in 1936—the isolationist block in Congress grew more determined. In the mid-1930s, Congress passed and Roosevelt signed a series of neutrality laws. These acts "forbade Americans to export arms or extend loans to belligerents, to travel in a war zone aboard ships of belligerent countries, or to arm merchant ships trading with belligerents." Roosevelt did not originally support neutrality legislation, but in the face of strong support in Congress and the public, he did not oppose it.[5]

With only a few exceptions, southerners in Congress followed the president's lead and did not challenge the isolationists. John H. Bankhead Jr. was one of two senators who voted against the first Neutrality Act, although he kept his opposition quiet in deference to the administration. Speaker Bankhead remained uncomfortable with the neutrality legislation, believing that "the President should be clothed with quite a large discretion in such matters and should not be restricted in the exercise of that discretion by iron-clad mandatory provisions in the law."[6]

Events continued to escalate in Europe and in Asia. Japan invaded China in July 1937. In December 1937, the Japanese bombed the American gunboat *Panay* while it was anchored in the Yangtze River near Nanjing. The crew of the *Panay* was evacuating Americans from the city. Fearful that the incident might escalate into full-scale conflict, Congress took up the Ludlow Amendment two days later. Proposed by Representative Louis Ludlow of Indiana, this constitutional amendment provided that after Congress had passed a declaration of war against any foreign government, before such a declaration should become effective, a majority of the people of the United States through a referendum should ratify such action by Congress. Will was staunchly opposed to the resolution, regarding it as "a most dangerous movement, especially in view of our present international situation." During a press conference, Bankhead declared that the resolution would not diminish the likelihood of war. He added: "I think it is reasonable to assume that there are forces in this country—alien influences—that are aiding and abetting the 'war referendum' to let certain countries in the world believe that this democracy is not standing behind its constitutional rights in national defense."[7] The administration hoped to keep the amendment bottled up in the House Committee on the Judiciary. Despite the Speaker's best efforts, a discharge petition was signed by the required 218 House members, moving the amendment to the floor. The president asked Bankhead to speak against it on the floor, which he did on January 10, 1938. "I was here when we went through the World War," he began, acknowledging the feelings of the isolationists, "and I know the reactions upon its miseries and its exactions; but I am unwilling, my colleagues, to abandon . . . the wisdom and judgment of the framers of our Constitution who established the fundamental law, our Constitution, and depart from it in times like these, and say that no longer are the people of this country willing to trust their chosen Representatives in the Congress of the United States to reflect their views, or to protect the security of the Republic." Roosevelt opposed the amendment, noting that it "would cripple any President in his conduct of our foreign relations, and it would encourage other nations to believe that they could violate American rights with impunity."[8] The Ludlow Amendment was defeated in the House 209–188, with "southern congressmen proving the decisive margin by opposing the measure 88 to 20."[9] The most important address against the amendment, the *London Times* argued, was the address by Speaker Bankhead.[10]

The situation in Europe and the Far East worsened. The Germans annexed Austria in March 1938 and invaded Czechoslovakia seven months later. In December 1938, the Empire of Japan ominously proclaimed a "New Order in East Asia." Senator John Bankhead felt that fears of impending war were entirely overblown, complaining to sister Marie in April 1939 of a "hysterical fear of war in the air."[11] Roosevelt, anxious to acquire greater latitude to deal with international crises, met with congressional leaders, including Speaker Bankhead, in May 1939, to discuss a revision of the neutrality law in a way that would allow him some flexibility of response. Bankhead promised to take up the bill desired by the president, telling reporters, "speaking for myself, I never did favor the principles of the existing law." When the bill came before the House, Bankhead again took the floor to support the administration's position. Congress had, he declared, "made a supreme and colossal mistake in policy . . . when we departed a few years ago from the time-honored and time-tested constitutional principle of leaving the management of our foreign and diplomatic affairs in the hands of the President of the United States and of the State Department of this country." He urged his colleagues in the House to decide the question, "this great, imperious, paramount question affecting the safety and security of the United States of America, on the basis of logic and on the basis of past experience."[12]

Bankhead also spoke out publicly. In an address at the Washington Cathedral, he discussed American security more broadly. Attempting to walk a fine line between interventionists and isolationists, he called for military preparation "to meet any attack on the continental United States or anywhere in the Western hemisphere"; the use of "moral persuasion" to preserve world peace; and a plan to "reassure" Americans that the United States had no intention to use aggression or go to war in Europe or Asia.[13] An amended bill, which only slightly revised the Neutrality Act and certainly was not all the administration had hoped for, passed the House by a vote of 201 to 187 but died by filibuster in the Senate in July.[14]

When war broke out in Europe in August 1939 with the German invasion of Poland, the president called Congress into special session and again tried to revise the neutrality legislation, something that Senator John H. Bankhead Jr. supported.[15] Despite favoring revision, Senator Bankhead ignored the summons to return to Washington, telling secretary of agriculture Henry A. Wallace, that he had no interest "in hearing a long drawn-out debate in the Senate on the Administration's neutrality program."[16] Speaker Bankhead, on the other hand, fought hard for the revision, which Congress eventually approved. The Neutrality Act of 1939 lifted the arms embargo and allowed for trade with belligerent nations under the terms of "cash and carry." Secretary of state Cordell Hull thanked the Speaker for "the exceedingly able and highly valuable service you have rendered in advancing this legislative program to a splendid conclusion."[17]

While Will Bankhead led the fight in the House to win greater freedom of movement for the president in meeting the fascist threat, Senator John H. Bankhead Jr. continued to focus on the problems plaguing the southern cotton economy. As the country slid into recession in 1937, cotton dropped to nine cents and the year's crop promised to be bountiful. Bankhead continued to support strong compulsory controls; without controls, he warned Secretary Wallace, "the small farmer would be reduced to 'peonage' because the larger farmers would store their excess fibre until the price rose."[18] John Jr. regularly butted heads with Wallace, who remained opposed to controls. Although Bankhead did not always agree with the president and secretary, he remained on cordial terms, endeavored to be a supporter of their interests, and favored granting the president greater flexibility to address international developments. Even so, he opposed additional funds for defense if they came at the expense of the unemployed and farmers. Instead, he encouraged additional taxes to pay for increased defense.[19] John Jr. hoped that the outbreak of war in Europe would stimulate American exports, but exports declined. He encouraged appropriations to raise farm prices to 75 percent of parity, arguing that such a policy increased farmers' purchasing power, which aided the broader economy.

As the decade, and Roosevelt's second term, drew to a close, Will Bankhead remained one of the party's most sought-after speakers and reliable spokespersons for the impact and legacy of the New Deal, as well as for military preparedness. He welcomed these opportunities to display his considerable oratorical talents. After the annual Jackson Day dinner at the Mayflower Hotel in 1938, First Lady Eleanor Roosevelt praised Bankhead's address in her newspaper column, saying that on the way to the event, she had warned the president that "the speeches would have to be very good or I would fall asleep." She found Bankhead's speech to be "extremely humorous and [it] managed also to summarize the achievements of the last five years in a way which I thought really masterly."[20] As the president increasingly turned his attention to foreign affairs, he could count on the eloquent and persuasive Speaker of the House to make a compelling case for preparedness and greater flexibility of response.

As 1940 dawned, Roosevelt focused on military preparedness, including increased production of military transports and hardware. The country was not involved in the war in Europe, so Roosevelt was less excited about instituting a program of compulsory military training. Senator Bankhead pledged himself to resist any attempt to build a large army. "I cannot see those exhausted and crippled nations landing an army on the shores of America," he declared. "I am not going to vote for any national plan to send an army to foreign nations."[21] Roosevelt addressed Congress on May 16, 1940, and requested new military appropriations. He spoke of developments in Europe. As countries toppled in the wake of the German blitzkrieg, America's regular army and National Guard numbered around half a million. In late May, Roosevelt appointed a defense commission to help implement and oversee the government's expanded defense program.[22] Despite congressional testimony from army officials that the country's armed forces were woefully short on numbers, the president refused to commit to a peacetime draft. Roosevelt was hesitant to move out in front of public opinion, which still contained a strong isolationist bent.[23]

Members of Congress concerned about the country's state of readiness were unwilling to wait on the president. In June, two days after the fall of France to the Nazis, Senator Edward R. Burke of Nebraska, a Democrat and interventionist, introduced a selective service training bill on the Senate floor; the next day, Republican James Wolcott Wadsworth Jr. of New York introduced the identical bill in the House. Neither man was a strong Roosevelt ally. The bill's most effective advocate was US Army chief of staff George C. Marshall, who testified at fifteen separate hearings before the Senate and House Committees on Military Affairs. The need for a peacetime draft was "hardly debatable," he argued. "I think it is a time of peril."[24] Still, Roosevelt refused to commit. He first needed to secure the nomination for the 1940 presidential race.

Five years after returning to the United States, Tallulah Bankhead still had not landed the proper vehicle to match her star power, although she was consistently employed and continued to deliver strong performances and receive good reviews, with some notable exceptions. Her family was increasingly anxious that Tallulah secure a role that was worthy of her and that would also reflect well on the Bankhead name. In the late 1930s, the perfect solution presented itself: what better boost to Tallulah's career and the Bankhead name was there than landing the role of Scarlett O'Hara in the film version of Margaret Mitchell's best-selling novel *Gone with the Wind*? Published in 1936, *Gone with the Wind* quickly rose to the top of the best-seller list, and by the end of the year, Selznick International Pictures had acquired the film rights and begun casting the movie. Nearly every stage and screen actress coveted the role of Scarlett. Finding the right actress proved incredibly difficult, as the role demanded that the actress portray a character who was equal parts naive and brazen, demure and crafty. The part also required the actress be convincing as a teenage Scarlett and as a mature woman.

Tallulah Bankhead was at the top of the list for most betting people. She certainly was near the top of producer David O. Selznick's list. He regarded Tallulah as one of the top two established actresses vying for the role. He had seen her in *Reflected Glory* at the play's opening in Los Angeles and was impressed. He scheduled Tallulah for a screen test, which she undertook in December 1936. For Tallulah to land the role would be more than Marie Bankhead Owen could ask for. What better means by which to forever enshrine the Bankhead name than for Tallulah to play Scarlett? Marie promptly initiated a letter-writing campaign on Tallulah's behalf. Selznick's staff admitted that letters in support of Tallulah far outnumbered those for other actresses.

Tallulah herself felt she was perfect for the part. In her memoirs, Tallulah wrote, "I felt I had qualifications beyond any of the hundreds of candidates. I had the looks, the Southern background and breeding, the proper accent. . . . I knew I could play the pants off Scarlett." Sister Eugenia agreed, writing to Tallulah from Italy that "there is only one person to play Scarlett in America. Who but you who were born and bred in that briar patch?"[25] Tallulah felt the same, later writing, "I looked upon myself as a symbol of the South, the fine flower of its darkest hours."[26] She arrived for her screen test in Hollywood a few days before Christmas. She underwent three tests, the last in color. She recalled that the third test "frightened me stiff. I looked a fright. My heart went into my boots. If I tangled with Scarlett in the spectrum, I might touch off another war between the states. But in black and white, in that second test, I was something to cheer up the Confederacy."[27] Selznick wrote to Tallulah two days after the screen test that he was "worried about the first part of the story, and frankly if I had to give you an answer now it would be no, but if we can leave it open I can say to you very honestly that I think there is a strong possibility."[28] Meanwhile, although Tallulah was regarded by many to be among the leading contenders for the role, Selznick had undertaken a nationwide talent search for the perfect Scarlett. Months passed with no word from Selznick. By September 1937, even though others were holding out hope, Tallulah herself knew she had no chance. Eventually, after a two-year search, the role was awarded to twenty-four-year-old British actress Vivien Leigh. Tallulah later wrote that "I'll go to my grave convinced that I could have drawn the cheers of Longstreet and Beauregard and Robert E. Lee had I been permitted to wrestle with Rhett Butler."[29] Selznick's earlier letter to Tallulah revealed the main reason she had not been cast: at age thirty-four, Tallulah was simply too old to play teenage Scarlett. Selznick offered her the small but significant role of Atlanta madam Belle Watling. She turned it down. Marie, at least, must have breathed a sigh of relief knowing that her niece avoided yet another role in which she would have portrayed a woman of questionable character.

As Tallulah waited for word from Selznick, she took a step toward establishing a slightly more conventional life: she got married. Tallulah met John Emery, a handsome and well-regarded stage actor from a theatrical family, in Los Angeles in 1936; the following year, while spending the summer on an island in Long Island Sound, she encountered Emery yet again when he was performing in a play in nearby Westport, Connecticut. Not interested in a long engagement, Tallulah and John (whom she and other close friends called Ted) were married in late August in Jasper at her father's home. Tallulah was thirty-four years old; John was thirty-two. Tallulah presented her new husband with the wedding ring worn by her grandfather John Hollis Bankhead. A crowd gathered outside the Bankhead home, hoping for a glimpse of Tallulah and John. Will Bankhead, Tallulah, and John Emery greeted the well-wishers. "Isn't it ridiculous?" Tallulah exclaimed. "I have never married before—and I never shall again."[30] Marie Bankhead Owen was unable to attend but visited with the newlyweds the following day in Birmingham before they returned to the East Coast, where they would begin rehearsals for their next play, *Antony and Cleopatra*.

Neither the play nor the marriage lasted long. Most, but not all, critics panned Tallulah's Cleopatra, while generally praising Emery's Octavius Caesar. The *New York Times* called Tallulah's Cleopatra "cataclysmic."[31] The *Chicago Tribune* despised the modern touches Tallulah brought to the role, griping that "Tallulah's Queen of the Nile belonged in a night club rather than a palace."[32] Once on Broadway, the play closed after five performances. The stress of performing in an unsuccessful play took its toll on both Tallulah and John. Both drank heavily and engaged in extramarital affairs during the length of their brief marriage. In recounting her marriage in her memoir, Tallulah commented, "it wasn't John's fault our marriage failed. My interests and enthusiasms are too random for sustained devotion, if you know what I mean. . . . After twenty years of unbridled freedom, of acting on whim, I couldn't discipline myself to the degree necessary for a satisfactory union. I had roamed the range too long to be haltered."[33] The marriage lasted barely four years; the couple divorced in spring 1941.[34]

Tallulah's next play provided some salve for her wounded ego. She received strong reviews for her performance in W. Somerset Maugham's comedy *The Circle*, which opened in New York in April 1938 and ran for seventy-eight performances. She followed with *I Am Different*, a "flimsy vehicle" that opened on the West Coast and never even made it to Broadway. Tallulah was now thirty-six years old, and true artistic and commercial success continued to elude her. Recalling those dark days, she wrote, "I was fed up. I had scorned that easy Hollywood swag because I was discontented, frustrated by the tripe in which I was obliged to appear." At least in the theater, she could choose her plays. Unfortunately, she did not always choose well, leaving theatrical greatness just beyond her reach. "You needn't be an Einstein to figure out that since I fled Paramount I had averaged nine weeks a year on the New York stage. Over that span I had spent almost as much time in the hospitals."[35] When would she land a role worthy of her talent?

Tallulah's fortunes changed in late 1938, when she was cast as Regina Hubbard Giddens in Lillian Hellman's play *The Little Foxes*. Set in a small southern town in the early twentieth century, the play is a taut family drama, a story of

Figure 12.1. Tallulah and husband John Emery (*left*) celebrate their wedding with Will and Florence Bankhead, 1937. Courtesy of the Alabama Department of Archives and History.

greed, deceit, and ambition. Tallulah described Regina as "a rapacious bitch, cruel and callous." She found few redeeming qualities in her character. "She was soulless and sadistic, an unmitigated murderess. For profit she would have slit her mother's throat, but not before so staging the crime that the guilt would be pinned on another." It was, she wrote, "the best role I ever had in the theatre."[36]

The Little Foxes was a sensation, and Tallulah's performance was hailed as the best of her career. The play ran for 410 performances, and *Variety* named her the best actress of 1938–39. Tallulah reveled in the affirmation she had craved for so long. *The Little Foxes*, she wrote, "established me as a dramatic star, an emotional actress worthy of the critical halos voted me." In addition to professional respect, her performance also earned her a lot of money, allowing her to wipe out her debts.[37] Six years after leaving Hollywood, twenty-one years after leaving Alabama, Tallulah Bankhead finally had achieved artistic and commercial success.

By the end of the 1930s, both Bankhead brothers enjoyed national stature. Columnists Drew Pearson and Robert S. Allen, who wrote the column Washington Merry-Go-Round, named Will Bankhead "Congressman of the Year" for 1937. Senator Bankhead was the recognized leader of the farm bloc. Several news outlets identified both Will and John as potential successors to Roosevelt.[38] They constituted a formidable political team. The *Boston Globe* called them "the No. 1 Brother Act of American Politics." Just as they had as young men, they remained as established politicians a study in opposites: "Orator Will is tall, intense, bespectacled, a man who can twist an audience around his little finger any time he bears down. Plugger John is medium height, stockier, balder, a logician who holds a Phi Beta Kappa key. They're like [the] hare and tortoise in politics, but contrary to the story book, they're romping toward the finish line together."[39] But where, exactly, was the finish line?

Nineteen forty was a presidential election year. Before Franklin D. Roosevelt was halfway through his second term, the question was being asked: would he seek an unprecedented third term? The president kept his plans under wraps. A third term was unheard of in American political history, but America had never experienced a political leader like Roosevelt. Although he had suffered some setbacks in 1937 and 1938, he remained extremely popular. Early in Roosevelt's second term, following a conversation with the president, Will commented in his diary about Roosevelt's prospects for a third term, writing, "There has been some talk that he might have in mind running for a third term but this conversation convinced me that he has no such idea in his mind."[40] In June 1938, John H. Bankhead Jr. told the *Birmingham News* that he did not think the president would seek a third term, but he would not venture to guess who the Democratic Party candidate might be.[41]

Perhaps it would be his brother Will. Certainly folks in Alabama thought so. The Bankhead-for-president draft began in fall 1937. A circuit court judge from Anniston suggested it to Bankhead and to Birmingham columnist John Temple Graves II, who endorsed the move in his column on October 13, 1937. The movement chugged along in local political circles. Widely popular in Alabama, Will Bankhead garnered support from liberals and conservatives, Big Mule industrialists, and organized labor. Support outside Alabama was scattered; not surprisingly it was strongest in the South. Will was flattered by the attention but refused to make any active campaign so far in advance of the nominating convention. Bankhead was smart enough to know that Roosevelt held all the cards; if the president desired to run for a third term, the nomination would be his.

Lister Hill, who had joined John H. Bankhead Jr. in the Senate following fellow Alabamian Hugo L. Black's nomination to the US Supreme Court, became a vocal advocate of Bankhead's candidacy, offering a "spirited endorsement" of the Speaker at a meeting of public officials, industrialists, and business leaders in Birmingham in September 1938 and again in August 1939 at the Alabama Polytechnic Institute at Auburn.[42] Hill told "dear Billy" that he stood ready "to do everything in [my] power to bring about your nomination." In Hill's estimation, Bankhead's stewardship of New Deal legislation made him more than qualified to succeed Roosevelt. The cause of the New Deal, Hill noted, was "the cause of the South. To this cause you have given your heart's devotion and the very best of your great ability. Robert E. Lee had no finer or more faithful lieutenant in Stonewall Jackson than President Roosevelt has had in you."[43] Always eager to promote her family's interests, sister Marie urged Will to approach Grover C. Hall of the *Montgomery Advertiser* for an endorsement; Will thought it much too early for that sort of positioning.[44] Marie's son Tom encouraged Uncle Will to throw his hat in the ring. "It would be swell to be kin to a president," he mused.[45]

Calls for a Bankhead candidacy came from outside the state's borders as well. *Newsweek* called him the "best-loved man in Congress" and noted that "with an increasing number of Democratic 'dark horses' riding high in the news, it seems likely that the 1940 convention may result in a series of deadlocks. In such a case, the smiling Alabamian, one of the youngest of the proposed candidates, might fill the bill for both factions."[46]

Bankhead's potential candidacy hinged on Roosevelt's plans. It also was tied up in state politics, in which conservatives and New Dealers were wrangling over the composition and disposition of the state's delegation to the convention. The continued support of the New Deal was the key issue. In August 1939, Bankhead was invited to address the state legislature. On the eve of the address, Bankhead issued a statement declaring his willingness to have a delegation pledged to his candidacy "if a majority of voters in the primary sincerely favor it."[47] Addressing the legislature, Bankhead took the opportunity to review the accomplishments of the New Deal. Bankhead was proud of the achievements of the past six and a half years. "I stand here before the representatives of my fellow citizens of Alabama, not to apologize for the record of the present Democratic administration as a whole, but on the contrary to proclaim, praise, and justify it."[48] Support for Bankhead's candidacy continued to build. In April 1940, prominent businessmen from across the state of Alabama pledged themselves to raise funds for a vigorous campaign for Will.[49] Textile magnate Donald Comer took the lead in the campaign, recognizing Bankhead's candidacy as an opportunity for the South to offer a candidate for the presidency who was more than a regional candidate.[50] By early June, the "Bankhead for President Fund" had raised close to $10,000; many contributions were for $1 and $5.[51] Alabama chose its delegates for the Democratic National Convention in the May 1940 primary. The twenty-two chosen were dedicated to nominating Will Bankhead for president; even brother John's old political nemesis, James Thomas Heflin, declared his support for Will.[52] Despite his gratitude at this show of support, Bankhead made clear that his candidacy was not in opposition to a third term for Roosevelt.[53]

Franklin D. Roosevelt kept uncharacteristically quiet. He stated several times in 1939 that he was not interested in serving a third term. Pundits understood that such pronouncements left the president some wiggle room. The outbreak of war in Europe in August 1939 encouraged those who wished to see the president run in 1940. Many wanted an experienced hand at the wheel. Henry A. Wallace took the lead and urged Roosevelt to run for a third term. Others close to the president wagered that he would not run again. Vice President John Nance Garner, staunchly opposed to a third term for Roosevelt, announced his own candidacy in December 1939, and postmaster general James A. Farley, chairman of the Democratic National Committee and campaign manager for the president's 1932 and 1936 campaigns, entered the Massachusetts primary for the purpose of blocking a third term.[54] In February 1940, John H. Bankhead Jr. publicly asked the president to state whether he intended to run for a third term or not.[55] The president ignored the question.

By keeping his plans for a possible third term secret, Roosevelt had successfully frozen all competitors in place. The real race, most serious observers believed, was for the vice presidency, and Will was wholly engaged in that race. The *New York Times* noted that there was a "large field of the willing" and that "new candidates appear hourly." Among those mentioned as possible candidates for the vice presidency included Senator Paul V. McNutt of Indiana, Senator James F. Byrnes of South Carolina, Senator Alben W. Barkley of Kentucky, Representative Sam Rayburn of Texas, federal loan administrator Jesse Jones, secretary of agriculture Henry A. Wallace, and, of course, Speaker of the House Will Bankhead.[56] Support for Bankhead emerged from around the country.

Congressman John Dingell of Michigan, whose son would go on to become the longest-serving member of Congress, told Lister Hill that he would be proud to support Bankhead for the second spot. "He has poise, personality, intellectual development to the highest degree and withal broad tolerance and consideration for his fellow man."[57]

Common themes emerged from those pushing Bankhead's candidacy. Supporters heralded his New Deal record, his fidelity to the Roosevelt program, his magnetism, his oratory, his grace, his comity, his charm, and his leadership. Among members of Congress, he was beloved. They also focused on his rural roots and his "common man" qualities. The *Montgomery Advertiser* took issue with an Associated Press story that noted that "the speaker carries a brown leather case to the capitol every working day" that contained "his lunch, packed for him by Mrs. Bankhead." The *Advertiser* quipped that the story was edited by "city slickers" and that the "briefcase" was actually a "shoe box . . . customarily packed with fried chicken (or pork sausage), 2-story biscuits that when hot melted the butter on them, a bottle of sorghum syrup—Bankhead is a North Alabama sorghum-sopper—1 or 2 cold sweet potatoes and a slice of fruit pie, plus a little package of bicarbonate of soda. That's what they fed him on when he was going to school that's what he took with him on the train whenever he went to Birmingham to see the state fair. . . . In fact that's the style to which Alabama farm boys traditionally have been accustomed. . . . What the Associated Press tactfully describes as a brief case is in truth a shoe box with vittles that mean something to an honest working man. . . . We will never believe that Speaker Bankhead's lunch consists of caviar and frog legs."[58] Like his father, Will Bankhead reveled in and benefited from homey coverage that emphasized his country roots.

Will Bankhead was honored and gratified by the enthusiasm he was receiving from Alabamians and from supporters across the country. The idea of becoming vice president held great appeal. The stress of the Speaker's job was exacting a high physical toll. Quite simply, his body was wearing out. In early spring 1940, Will was sidelined with a case of the flu and was ordered by his physician to take a break from the rigors of his job in order to recover. He confided to brother John in May that he was "trying to take things as easily as possible and seek every opportunity to stay out of the [Speaker's] chair and to rest in my private office." He was concerned that he still had not put on much weight since his illness but believed that once Congress adjourned, "I will speedily get back to normal."[59] Bankhead's desire for the vice presidency had very much to do with the rigors of the speakership.

As the convention neared, John and Will Bankhead wagered that Roosevelt would run for a third term, so they channeled their energy into securing the vice presidential nomination for Will. After the Alabama primary, in which delegates had been chosen to support Will as a "favorite son" candidate, Alabama congressman Henry B. Steagall and Senator Lister Hill met with

Roosevelt to feel him out about Bankhead as a potential running mate. Roosevelt told the delegation that he wished for Bankhead to deliver the convention keynote. He also expressed some apprehension about the state of the Speaker's health.[60] Simply put, Roosevelt felt Bankhead was too sick and too old for the second spot. Having been asked by the president to deliver the keynote, the Speaker, some believed, was faced with a conundrum. Columnist Drew Pearson noted that "the keynote customarily is made by a dignitary who is not a candidate. For [Bankhead] to accept the role, therefore, would be an admission that he was out of the running. And Bankhead is anything but that. He is very much in the vice-presidential race."[61] The *Montgomery Advertiser* disagreed, instead arguing that Bankhead's selection to deliver the keynote indicated "that his chances for high party honors, either as the standard bearer (in the event President Roosevelt will not accept a nomination) or as the second man on the ticket in the event he does have been highly improved."[62] Everyone was trying to read the political tea leaves.

Will Bankhead found himself on the horns of a dilemma. At a luncheon with the Alabama congressional delegation in late June, Bankhead told the group that he would not deliver the keynote, refusing to do so for fear that it would give the impression that he was withdrawing as a candidate. His colleagues countered that they were relying on his keynote speech to gin up more support for his candidacy among the delegates. "After a long argument," the *Birmingham News* reported, Will called Democratic National Committee chairman James A. Farley and accepted the keynote position.[63] Feeling angry about how Roosevelt had treated Will, and watching his brother struggle with how to address the keynote issue, John Jr. grew increasingly irritated with the president. He wondered "if we are going to be as anxious to please F.R. *after* Chicago as we are *before*. Personally I think he is the most selfish [man] of all who have risen to the Presidency. It is all F. D. R. with him or nothing doing."[64] Even though both men were now in their sixties, John remained protective of his younger brother.

Roosevelt kept his plans hidden from even his closest advisers. In early July, with the convention only two weeks away, secretary of the interior Harold L. Ickes asked the president about his plans for the convention. Was there a strategy? Who would serve as floor leader? Who would place his name in nomination? The president told Ickes that he had no suggestions. Ickes was dumbfounded. Even as delegates began arriving in Chicago, the president still had not given clear directions to his team. As one historian has observed, "By keeping his intentions a secret, he had neutralized the other presidential hopefuls. . . . None could campaign energetically for the nomination without seeming to go against the president." The men interested in the nomination universally stated that the nomination was Roosevelt's if he wanted it.[65]

By late June, the Bankheads were strategizing for the convention and the vice presidential nomination. John Jr. advised his brother to "select the man to put you in nomination and notify him so he will have ample time to prepare his speech." He recommended Congressman Steagall for this honor. "He is the dean of our delegation, your co-manager and your friend. Lister [Hill] is the other choice. He is a good orator, but gets excited and sometimes speaks too fast and too loud." He suggested that Will also think of four or five people to second his nomination; in making his choice, he should consider "speaking qualities, geographical locations, and personal following. [A] big eastern state should be considered if suitable speakers are available." He also asked Will to send him a draft of his keynote speech. "I might be able to make some helpful suggestions." He urged Will to "put some strong sentiment in it at the close. It would not hurt if you make them cry!"[66] Will was pleased that Steagall and others in the state delegation were "stirring up considerable enthusiasm among Members of the House [for his VP nomination]," reporting, "I have really been very much pleased at the generous response."[67]

As the convention neared, the pressure on Will mounted. He confided to his brother that "I have been absolutely overwhelmed not only with my duties as Speaker and constant calls from Members about all sorts of things, but also in an effort to draft the keynote speech which I found to be quite a difficult under-taking."[68] Two days later, he wrote again, confiding to his brother that he was struggling to write the speech, "under all the circumstances." He was endeavor-ing to incorporate some "spiritual fervor" into the text.[69] His task was tricky: he had to deliver stirring oratory that excited the convention delegates but that did not give too much attention to Roosevelt, in the event that the president decided not to run. He had to celebrate Democratic accomplishments while acknowl-edging the war that had engulfed the European continent. Given Roosevelt's recent dismissal of Bankhead's vice presidential candidacy, the Speaker may also have been feeling not terribly charitable toward the president. The *Birming-ham News* reported on the eve of the convention that Bankhead had "author's jitters" and had rewritten the speech five times.[70] John Jr. remained skeptical of the president's plans for the convention. He speculated that "I don't think you can expect any help from R." The best Will could hope for was a neutral posi-tion from the president. "If he does not help any other one," John predicted, "I think you have a good chance."[71] Would Roosevelt put his thumb on the vice presidential scale?

Delegates streamed into Chicago, the site of the convention, in mid-July. With Roosevelt all but ensured of the nomination, the convention carried lit-tle suspense. The hot, humid weather only compounded the delegates' lethargy. Harold L. Ickes noted that the convention was "dead and cold. Everything was dull and bogged down."[72] Delegates were listless and apathetic. The location of the convention did little to inspire the delegates. The cavernous Chicago Stadium was described by one reporter as "massive, utilitarian, and ugly as the underside of a railroad bridge. Girders are exposed and the floor space seems big enough for a football game." Spectators seated in the galleries were "lost in a blue haze, and looking up at the roof it resembles the underside of the Brooklyn Bridge as you pass beneath it on the 5 o'clock ferry."[73] Another reporter likened the hall, when filled with delegates, to "a beehive, magnified a million times, and human masses cling to the walls in two complete encircling galleries, like black clusters."[74] The Democrats did their level best to transform the hulk of a space, which was decked out with 612 American flags and three thousand yards of bunting. The stifling air and sweltering delegates and visitors—some twenty thousand in all—were kept cool by 2,400 tons of ice that were hoisted to the rafters and placed in thirteen hoppers. Huge fans drew air over the ice and down into the stadium, where the cooled air did battle with the million-watt battery of lights that would illuminate the proceedings. The Democrats chose not to televise the proceedings, as the apparatus to make that possible would only compound the heat. The three-ton amplification system was suspended above the speaker's platform. Gigantic portraits of President Roosevelt and Vice President Garner hung from opposite ends of the stadium. The speaker's rostrum was fronted by an impressive golden eagle with a six-foot wingspan. Four hundred college-aged men, each dressed in blue and gold, stood ready to usher participants to their seats.[75]

When the convention opened on Monday morning, July 15, 1940, the delegates were uncharacteristically subdued and perhaps, conjectured *New York Times* reporter Sydney M. Shalett, "a bit jaded." Entirely lacking at the morning session, Shalett noted, "was the electrical spontaneity, the willingness to cheer at the drop of a hat that is traditionally associated with Democratic conventions." The atmosphere changed considerably by the evening for the keynote address. The nearly twenty-one thousand in attendance were boisterous; the massive stadium organ pounded out state songs. Each convention speaker and personality got his own theme song. Democratic National Committee and Convention chair James A. Farley was serenaded with "Take Me Out to the Ball Game," a nod to his impending association with the New York Yankees, while national committee secretary R. L. Robert Jr., an alumnus of Georgia Institute of Technology, got "I'm a Rambling Wreck from Georgia Tech." A moment of confusion arose when the organist began playing "Dixie" as New York governor Herbert H. Lehman ascended the stage. The error was quickly rectified. Absent from organist Al Melgard's playlist for the evening was the Democrats' 1932 and 1936 anthem, "Happy Days Are Here Again." When asked about it, the nine-fingered Melgard replied, "there are no happy days with so many people suffering the horrors of war."[76]

By nine o'clock in the evening, stadium attendance was near capacity. Delegates and spectators swayed and danced to the convention's forty-piece band. Speaker of the House Will Bankhead strode to the stage amid thundering applause. Bankhead's oratorical skills were legendary; everyone expected a rousing address to breathe life into the moribund affair. Those hoping for a ripsnorting stem-winder were uncharacteristically disappointed. According to one reporter, the address was "quieter than expected" and set a somber tone. Bankhead took some jabs at the Republicans, which received the requisite applause, but he focused greatly on the European war.[77] His speech highlighted the accomplishments of Democrats and the New Deal. He never mentioned Wendell Willkie, the Republican nominee.[78] He spoke of "this Democratic Administration" thirteen times but mentioned "the president" only twice. Never did he identify the president by name.[79] More than past Democratic party keynotes, he spent a fair amount of time on foreign policy. He noted that Americans were living in "terrible times." The administration had done everything possible "within the bounds of reason" to assure peace in Europe. His coverage of the administration's foreign policy was meant to keep party isolationists happy, although it misrepresented the president's lack of comfort with the neutrality legislation.[80] He emphasized political unity and stressed that the country would "resist to the death" any compromise with "malignant" dictators. He proposed to support every assistance, short of war, to aid Great Britain, which "alone stands against the hurricane of the Blitzkrieg." Bankhead was interrupted numerous times by applause, but at no time was there extended demonstration. The *New York Times* observed that "the great bursts of enthusiasm often associated with a keynote speech were absent."[81] Bankhead celebrated the New Deal accomplishments but warned Americans of dark days ahead: "Already this juggernaut of physical force and brutal power has laid its blighting hand upon the freedom and sovereignty of eight small and defenseless nations." Journalists covering the convention found the speech uncharacteristically underwhelming. Sister Marie, on the other hand, was quick to offer praise. Listening to the speech back home in Alabama, she was overwhelmed by pride and by loss. "I was alone in the house at the farm and was so overwhelmed with the memories of the [1912] Baltimore Convention when you put Underwood in nomination that I could hardly stand it. I could see Pap, Tom, Sister, Mama and [niece] Louise Holloway, all now dead and just burst into tears."[82] Marie's emotional response aside, most observers criticized the convention for lacking "sparkle" and "spontaneity." The *Los Angeles Times* said that Bankhead's speech "fell considerably short of the high forensic marks" set by the Speaker on other occasions.[83]

The convention ground on, uninspired. A group of young women, many of them the wives and daughters of delegates, sought to bring a little color and levity to the second day of the proceedings. Decked out in pastel-colored crepe-paper dresses, they were scheduled to perform on the center stage. The women were shocked when they were prevented from entering the convention hall by the fire chief. Motioning to the many floor delegates holding cigarettes and cigars, he declared the women in their paper dresses to be fire hazards. After much discussion, the women were allowed to perform, escorted to and from the stage by the fire chief.[84] This brief interlude of excitement did little to change the overall trajectory of the moribund affair. Ickes sent Roosevelt an urgent telegram: "THIS CONVENTION IS BLEEDING TO DEATH." He pleaded desperately with Roosevelt to come to Chicago to provide leadership and inspiration. The president refused to budge.[85] The *Christian Science Monitor* reported that "the vast majority" of delegates believed that Roosevelt would be nominated and that he would accept the nomination. They waited "impatiently minute by minute for the explosion of excitement that will break out" when word of Roosevelt's acceptance finally arrived. Until then, "to the faint ticking of the time clock of impending events this dullest of conventions fidgets through another day."[86] The *Los Angeles Times* called the situation "ridiculous."[87] Back in Washington, the president gave a press conference to some two hundred assembled reporters and cameramen. He refused to reveal his plans, stating instead that they would be revealed that evening by convention chairman and Senate majority leader Alben W. Barkley.[88]

Senator Barkley ascended the convention stage around ten o'clock in the evening. He delivered a crowd-pleasing romp that poked fun at the delegates and at the Republicans. In the midst of his address, Barkley suddenly departed from his prepared text and spoke three words: Franklin Delano Roosevelt. The pro-Roosevelt delegates went wild, confetti rained down from the rafters, and the massive pipe organ played "Happy Days Are Here Again" (apparently any misgivings the organist may have had about this song had been allayed). Delegates chanted "We Want Roosevelt!" and paraded around the cavernous Chicago Stadium. When order was restored, Barkley announced that he had a message from the president. He reminded the delegates that many had "long known that he has no wish to be a candidate again. The president has never had, and has not today, any desire or purpose to continue in the office of the President, to be a candidate for that office, or to be nominated by the convention for that office. He wishes in all earnestness and sincerity to make it clear that all of the delegates to this convention are free to vote for any candidate." The president did not say, however, that he would decline the nomination if the convention nominated him. It was a brilliant move designed to manufacture a "draft." Almost on cue, a voice from nowhere began chanting: "New Jersey wants Roosevelt! Illinois wants Roosevelt! The world needs Roosevelt." On and on it went, the same voice. Delegates looked around. The voice was coming from below. The *Christian Science Monitor* quipped that "the same voice poured its phrases into the microphone . . . until they sounded like a professional soundtrack which has accompanied some New Deal films such as 'The Plow that Broke the Plains.'"[89] The disembodied voice actually belonged to the City of Chicago's superintendent of sewers, whom Mayor Edward J. Kelly had stowed away in a basement room with a microphone.[90] Delegates resumed their cheering and dancing for another hour. Although the delegates were relieved to have something to celebrate, the press corps was decidedly more jaded. The *Baltimore Sun* called the statement by Roosevelt "hollow and meaningless."[91] James F. Byrnes, one of the leaders of the "draft Roosevelt" movement, called for the convention to convene until noon the following day when the delegates could adopt the platform and "finish the job which we came here to do by renominating Franklin D. Roosevelt."[92]

The next evening, July 17, delegates and spectators returned to the Chicago Stadium, ready to get down to business. Barkley gaveled the session to order a little after eight o'clock, and the roll call of the states and the nominating process began. First up: the state of Alabama. Senator Lister Hill stepped to the microphone. The *Christian Science Monitor* reported what happened next: "In a voice with the tremolo stops pulled a little too far out, he launches forth." There was one technical glitch. "The tremolo in his voice reaches a pitch that is too much for the unemotional acoustic system and it blows out a fuse or something with a banshee squawk that brings forth laughter and dampens the oration." A columnist sitting in the press section asked, "who is he nominating?" It was not altogether clear until the final sentence. "This is no time for untried hands to pilot the ship. . . . I place in nomination for President of the United States, Franklin Delano Roosevelt!"[93] The delegates jumped to their feet, dancing, marching, and cheering in the aisles. Not everyone was thrilled with Senator Hill. Never one to keep her own counsel, Marie Bankhead Owen later groused to Will: "I did really and truly want to take hold of Lister Hill when he nominated the President, pull his coat tail and tell him for God's sake realize he was not imitating an old fashioned vaudeville actor. I was really repelled by his artificiality in the way of delivering his speech that I could not put my thoughts on what he was saying. Everyone who has talked to me has just roared with laughter about his 'dramatics.' Isn't it a pity that everyone cannot have a proper sense of proportion[?]" Will concurred.[94]

The nomination of Roosevelt was seconded by Arizona. The choice of Roosevelt was not unanimous. The elderly senator from Virginia, Carter Glass, whom one reporter described as "a little bantam cock of a man," staunchly opposed a third term—for Roosevelt or for anyone. "The falcon faced frail little man stands there at the microphone and dares the audience to howl him down" as he nominated James A. Farley, Roosevelt's former campaign chairman and friend. Maryland nominated favorite son Millard Tydings. Texas put Vice President Garner's name into contention, a move that almost caused a fist fight between Roosevelt supporter and young congressman Lyndon B. Johnson and a Garner supporter. At 1:20 a.m., the roll call of states concluded. One reporter called it "one of the most tedious roll calls on record. As exciting as a race with only one horse."[95] On the first ballot, Roosevelt had 946½ votes; the next highest vote getter, Farley, received 72½. A loyal Democrat, Farley moved that the rules be suspended and that Roosevelt be nominated by acclamation. By two o'clock it was over: Franklin D. Roosevelt had been nominated for an unprecedented third term as president of the United States.[96]

The delegates arrived for the final day of the convention decidedly testy and annoyed. Many felt that they had been used, like props, by the president. At least, they thought, they could nominate a vice presidential candidate of their choice. There was no shortage of candidates. Roosevelt's first choice was secretary of state Cordell Hull, but Hull was not interested. His second choice was secretary of agriculture Henry A. Wallace. Wallace would help him secure the farm vote; equally important to the president, Wallace was not an isolationist and understood the escalating crises in Europe and Asia. Should the president not survive a third term, he felt confident that Wallace would carry on as he would have. He confided his desires to secretary of labor Frances Perkins, who was at the convention. "[Wallace] knows a lot, you can trust his information," the president told Perkins. "He digs to the bottom of things and gets the facts. He is honest as the day is long. He thinks right. He has the general ideas we have. He is the kind of man who can do something in politics. He can help the people with their political thinking."[97] The delegates would not have free rein to choose a vice presidential nominee. The president was adamant: he would not come to Chicago until Wallace's nomination for vice president was secured. Presidential adviser Harry Hopkins was worried, telling another aide that there were ten candidates who had more support at the convention than Wallace.

The president's floor managers got to work. Hopkins and James F. Byrnes spread the word of Roosevelt's demand. They tried to persuade all others to withdraw from the vice presidential contest. Will Bankhead refused. The president himself called Bankhead at the Stevens Hotel, where the Speaker was staying, and tried to persuade him to withdraw. Bankhead held firm, telling the president that he had "bowed to the White House" during the presidential nomination process but "could not afford to back down on the No. 2 spot."[98] After seven loyal years of service on behalf of the administration, after having stood by the president during even his most egregious political missteps, Will Bankhead stood his ground. Convinced that he could garner sufficient votes to win despite Roosevelt's opposition, Bankhead stubbornly remained in the race.

Roosevelt's demand put delegates in a bitter, rebellious mood; many delegates showed their frustration by attacking the secretary of agriculture, taunting him by crying "we want a Democrat," a reference to Wallace's earlier Republican allegiance. Although many delegates had concerns about Wallace—he was not a great campaigner, he had once been a Republican—the greater part of their opposition was aimed at Roosevelt and his heavy-handed tactics in choosing his own running mate. Once again, they felt, they had been steamrolled by the president. Roosevelt floor lieutenants Hopkins and Byrnes warned delegates that Roosevelt might refuse to run if Wallace was not chosen. Perhaps the only people who were happy that night were reporters, who finally had something dramatic to cover. A *Los Angeles Times* reporter wrote of the "roaring insubordination" and "riotous rebellion" of the delegates, irate that yet again their choice was being dictated to them.[99] Aware that the convention might spin out of control, the president dispatched his wife to Chicago to speak to the delegates. Wearing a blue dress and matching hat, and carrying a bouquet of red and white flowers, Eleanor Roosevelt claimed the podium. She encouraged calm and urged the delegates to concede to the president's wishes. The delegates received her words respectfully, but soon after she left the stage, the uproar over the president's "edict" began anew.[100]

The roll call began. It was 10:40 p.m. The heat in the stadium was oppressive. Up first: Alabama. Henry B. Steagall nominated Will Bankhead for vice president. "Our party is going before the country upon the record of the present Democratic administration," Steagall declared. "Every great measure was submitted to his enlightened judgment and entrusted to his skillful leadership. Surely no nomination for vice president could be more logical or give greater assurance of harmonious and successful administration than that of the Speaker of the House!"[101] The Alabama delegates erupted in applause but for a few lonely minutes were alone in their demonstration; the organist struck up "I'm Bound for Alabama" and "Oh Suzanna." The Alabama delegation was soon joined by the delegations of South Carolina, Louisiana, and Wisconsin. "The noise rose as Texas and Maryland joined in, along with North Carolina. Bankhead pictures and placards were liberally sprinkled throughout the hall." The demonstration was swept along by the convention band but was also fueled by the resentment of the delegates over the White House's dictation of the vice presidential spot. "We Don't Want Wallace!" the Washington delegation bellowed. "The rebel yells grew in intensity," the *New York Times* reported, "and there seemed to be a determination, coming out of nowhere, to demonstrate for anybody not picked by the White House."[102] Barkley finally succeeded in gaveling the sweaty, red-faced delegates back to order. The roll call rambled on for more than two hours. Indignant state delegations shouted defiance. Roosevelt's floor managers scurried around the stadium, desperate to keep delegates in line. Chairman Barkley wielded his gavel liberally to tamp down prolonged demonstrations. "For more than two hours, while recalcitrant state delegations shouted defiance, while indignant emissaries sped here and there," the *Los Angeles Times* reported, "wild disorder prevailed."[103] The anti-administration vote rallied around Bankhead.

Will Bankhead followed the action at the convention over the radio in his suite at the Stevens Hotel.[104] In the end, the delegates' ire at the president's heavy-handed tactics was insufficient to win the day for Bankhead. Wallace won on the first ballot, garnering more than the required 551 votes. Bankhead came in second with 329 votes.[105] The venerable H. L Mencken concluded, "The [Roosevelt] steam-roller had worked, but certainly not smoothly. It heaved and pitched, in fact, all evening, and more than once it appeared on the verge of disaster."[106] At 12:15 a.m., John H. Bankhead Jr., bitterly disappointed but determined to unify the party, mounted the rostrum to ask that Wallace's nomination be unanimous. The unrepentant delegates jeered and booed; Secretary Wallace departed the speaker's platform without making his acceptance speech.[107] Wallace later thanked John Jr., telling him he had never "witnessed a more gracious and sportsmanlike act than your motion. . . . It was consistent with the traditional statesmanship of the Bankhead family."[108] Will promptly wired his congratulations to Wallace.[109] Following the convention, a poll revealed that 92 percent of Democrats remained confident in Roosevelt's leadership and supported his candidacy.[110]

Alabama citizens were disgusted by the treatment of their favorite son. The editorial staff of the conservative political magazine *Alabama* blamed Senator Hill, whom, they claimed, "used [Bankhead] as a stalking horse for Roosevelt." Not fans of Roosevelt, they wrote that "the president dropped on Will Bankhead's neck, and on his sensitive appreciation of loyalty and magnanimity, the guillotine of that most selfish and ruthless living American."[111] Calling out Roosevelt's "dictatorial tactics," the *Tuscaloosa News* drew on the familiar theme of southern victimization to explain Bankhead's fate. "Once again the Solid South was roundly slapped on the cheek for the reason that the political machinists thought it inexpedient to select a man from this section of the [country]. Once again a great son of Alabama was sacrificed on the altar which we have built ourselves through the years by fealty to Democracy."[112]

Supporters from across the state and region sent letters to Bankhead, some on engraved stationery, others on cheap lined paper. At times, in their zeal to let the Speaker know how incensed they were at Roosevelt's betrayal, they may have made Bankhead feel somehow worse. S. W. Williams of the rural community of Gordo in Tuscaloosa County was angry that the party leaders "dragged you to the barnyard and threw you on the dump." He despaired that "the Bankheads' good name has been set down on, spit on, and kicked around like a football."[113] Mostly, though, supporters of the Speaker were broken hearted. "From the start to the finish of last night's session I sat by my radio, pencil and pad by my side, so that I might not miss a single vote for *my* candidate," one woman wrote. "The suspense and excitement of it all was so very great that had I had a weak heart I would have doubted my ability to live through it. I was sick from disappointment over the outcome of the final tabulation."[114] Will graciously responded to each letter. To several, he noted that although he was disappointed, he fully intended to support the Democratic Party in November, calling himself "a good soldier in politics."[115] Although he personally had lost a battle, he was suited up to fight for the Democrats in the November general election.

Will was, in truth, deeply hurt by the president's refusal to accept him on the national ticket.[116] It was hard for him or John Jr. to deny that Roosevelt's intervention had cost him the nomination. But the brothers shared their feelings only with each other. In public, they delivered the party line. John Jr. stated at several public events that although he would have preferred his brother Will in the second spot, he was perfectly happy with Secretary Wallace and considered him a good friend to farmers.[117] To anyone who complained about the president's high-handed actions at the convention, Will dismissed the event as "just politics," affirmed his party loyalty, and repeated his pledge to support the Democratic ticket in November. Marie Bankhead Owen, never content to hold her tongue, was seething with indignation at the way the president had treated her brother. She spoke of how excited she was to hear the roll call of states during the nomination for the vice president. "Even my two negro servants stayed up . . . until past one o'clock and were so excited about your increasing delegates as the roll call went along that we all almost had fits."[118] Hoping for a little gossip, she was dying to know "what you think about President Roosevelt switching over to Wallace." Ultimately, though, she thought perhaps that "from the standpoint of health it is probably best that you are spared from the active campaign you would have had to make if you had been nominated."[119] Will wrote to Marie: "Except for the President's intervention I might have been nominated, but, frankly, I had no assurance of it and I am well content with the whole result."[120] Both men soldiered on. John H. Bankhead Jr. was chosen to direct the southern regional campaign for Roosevelt's reelection, while Will prepared to hit the road for the party ticket.[121] Despite the loss, the *Birmingham Post* found a silver lining for the region. Noting that Bankhead received support throughout the nation, the paper declared, "It's no longer a sin to come from Dixie, even though it may be bad manners to run against the White House favorite."[122]

With the nominating conventions over, attention in Washington and the nation once again turned to the war and to conscription. Antidraft organizations from the political left and right had spent the summer lobbying against the Burke-Wadsworth Act. Labor leader John L. Lewis opposed the draft, as did leading isolationist figure Charles Lindbergh. Opponents of a peacetime draft flooded Congress with letters and telegrams. Roosevelt finally came out in favor of the bill on August 2. At a press conference, he stated, "You cannot get a sufficiently trained force by just passing an Act of Congress when war breaks out, and you cannot get it by the mere volunteer system." By August 11, some 71 percent of Americans supported conscription. Still, Roosevelt worried that his support of the bill could hurt him come November. But he believed he would be "derelict in my duty if I did not tell the American people of the real danger which confronts them at the present time."[123]

Debate on the bill in the Senate began in early August. Opponents of the bill argued that "the United States faced no threat from abroad; compulsory military service would destroy American democracy; and a voluntary system was efficient."[124] Senators Burton K. Wheeler, Arthur H. Vandenberg, Robert A. Taft, and Pat McCarran declared a peacetime draft a threat to democracy that would lead to totalitarianism. Debate dragged on for three weeks. Although it became clear that the bill had enough votes to pass, isolationists sought to delay its passage by offering countless amendments in the hope that they could win some concessions. Supporters of the bill received a huge boost when Republican presidential candidate Wendell Willkie announced on August 16 that he would not make conscription an issue in the election. Following their candidate, Republican lawmakers reported that the party would not issue a position on conscription and that members would be free to vote their consciences. Although Willkie's proclamation fell short of a full endorsement, it effectively took the wind out of the sails of the opponents. The Senate passed the bill on August 28.[125]

Consideration of the bill then moved to the House. The antidraft movement showed no signs of quitting. On September 5, some fifteen hundred young men and women protested the draft bill on the steps of the Capitol.[126] Twenty-five opponents of conscription picketed outside the Mayflower Hotel, where Will and Florence resided.[127] Antidraft organizations unleashed a letter-writing campaign to the Speaker. One opponent of the bill from Pittsburgh reminded Speaker Bankhead that "Honest Abe Lincoln freed the slaves of the South a good many years ago, and it surely will be too bad if you men in Washington vote to enslave not only the South but the whole country."[128] Closer to home a Birmingham businessman wrote that "we businessmen feel that we have virtually a dictator in Washington now, and should he be re-elected with conscription laws on the books, he would be a dictator." He also warned that the president's support for conscription would surely hurt him in November. To these opponents, the Speaker's secretary sent cursory responses.[129] Frank Dixon, a leader of conservative forces in the state of Alabama, wrote a letter of support, telling the Speaker that "the nearly unanimous opinion of the people of Alabama is favorable to the immediate passage of a selective service act." Dixon believed it important "for us to proceed at once to train the manpower of this nation for the defense of our way of life and all that implies. Delay and divided counsels will leave us where France found herself: helpless in the face of a powerful enemy."[130] A professor from the state teachers college in Jacksonville, Alabama, sent Bankhead a resolution signed by 272 students supporting the bill. They wanted to let the Speaker know that "behind your efforts is a public opinion as active, aggressive and determined as that small number of short-sighted and sometimes traitorous people who are trying to prevent the passage of the bill." Furthermore, they wanted to demonstrate that "those most affected are willing to go; the number of signatures would have been considerably increased had not a large contingent of National Guard left . . . for camp." To this letter and resolution, Bankhead responded personally, congratulating the professor and students "upon this fine display of your real patriotism."[131]

As Congress debated the conscription bill, the Battle of Britain raged on and Roosevelt turned to aid for the British. Here, Roosevelt acted unilaterally. In mid-August, Roosevelt cemented the bases-for-destroyers deal, in which the United States would furnish to Great Britain some fifty aging destroyers and other war material in exchange for ninety-nine-year leases on naval and air bases in Newfoundland, Bermuda, and the Caribbean. Opponents of conscription were livid. "If Mr. Roosevelt can do what he wants with our destroyers without consulting Congress, and we give him our boys," Congresswoman Frances P. Bolton of Ohio declared on the floor of the House, "God knows what he will do with them."[132] Antidraft groups continued to agitate, staging prayer vigils on the steps of the Capitol and lobbying members of Congress. The bill passed the House on September 8; President Roosevelt signed the bill on September 16, 1940.

The conscription bill well in hand, John Jr. and Will turned their attention to the 1940 campaign. Although he was desperate to escape the Washington heat, Will, ever the "good soldier in politics," readily agreed to campaign for the president. Will's involvement in the campaign was against his doctor's orders as well as the desires of his wife and his secretary. The Speaker was not physically strong, suffering from overexertion and weariness.[133] Washington's hot, sticky weather only compounded his physical ailments. He longed to escape the heat, even if only for a few days, but he had already accepted an invitation to open the campaign of the Maryland Democrats on September 10. After that speech, he could retreat to his beloved Jasper; although no less hot and humid than Washington, it was far less stressful.

With his doctor accompanying him, Bankhead traveled the short train ride from Washington, DC, to Baltimore. He checked into the stately Emerson Hotel and looked over the speech that he was to deliver later that evening at the Lyric Theatre. By early evening, "the large theater was packed to the doors and the enthusiasm of a typical Southern political meeting had risen to white heat as the crowd sang and yelled while they waited for Mr. Bankhead's appearance on the platform." Where was he? Then word came. The Speaker had collapsed in his hotel room. Worried murmurs traveled around the theater. Sometime on the evening of Tuesday, September 10, Bankhead had passed out. He was found by Dr. George W. Calver, attending physician of Congress, who had accompanied the Speaker. Dr. Calver told reporters that the illness was "an excruciatingly painful attack of sciatica." Bankhead was resting in his hotel room. Someone retrieved the speech from the Speaker's suit coat pocket. Maryland governor Herbert R. O'Conor delivered an edited version of the speech, which was also broadcast over the radio.[134]

After consultation with Baltimore physicians, Dr. Calver reported that the diagnosis was "serious."[135] Bankhead was transported to the Naval Hospital. Florence was with him, and daughters Tallulah and Eugenia arrived on a chartered flight from New York. Tallulah appeared upbeat, telling the assembled press, "I was happy to find my father's condition no worse than it is. I see no cause for alarm. He is resting comfortably."[136] In reality, the situation was worse than she implied. The Speaker had suffered a ruptured abdominal aortic aneurysm. Dr. Calver withheld the true diagnosis because Bankhead was still conscious, talking with family and friends and reading newspapers, and he did not wish the Speaker to learn how seriously ill he was. On September 12, the *Birmingham News* reported that the Speaker was expected to come home to Jasper to recover. Brother John reported that the doctor had said that his brother's heart was fine and there was "no reason for alarm and no reason to fly east to be at his bedside."[137] On Saturday, September 14, the *Birmingham News* reported that Bankhead's condition was "not satisfactory." The Speaker "had spent a fitful night. . . . He has developed a slight fever and at times complains of considerable pain in his lower left back and left leg."[138] He continued to decline. Bankhead suffered a second rupture Saturday evening. He fell unconscious around nine o'clock and died four hours later, at 1:35 a.m. on Sunday, September 15, 1940. Florence, Eugenia, and brother John were with him. Tallulah was in Princeton for a performance of *The Little Foxes* and did not make it back in time. William Bankhead was sixty-six years old.[139]

Condolences poured in to the surviving Bankheads. Henry A. Wallace, who had defeated Bankhead in the nomination for the vice presidency just a few weeks earlier, wrote to say that he was "inexpressibly grieved at the loss of one of the finest men I knew and one of the truest gentlemen in all of our history. He gave his all to his party and his country."[140] Columnist John Temple Graves II penned a eulogy for the *Birmingham Age-Herald*. "The nation has lost a ranking officer, Alabama her most distinguished son, John Bankhead his beloved brother and coworker, thousands of us a warm and loyal friend." He described a man who had come "within whispering distance of the White House" but "who had an ear for everybody, who brought glory to a great family name without ever becoming too famous to be befriended, too important to be loved." It was, Graves wrote, "a life of rare distinction and service, full of drama, bounded in grace, uninterrupted in great advancement, allowed with no cheapness or falterings, rich always in dignity and love."[141] President Roosevelt delivered his tribute to the Speaker over the radio aboard the USS *Potomac*. With Bankhead's death, the president lamented, "Every American loses a tried and proven friend of our system of government. His experience, his fairness and his personality had endeared him to his colleagues and to all who knew him." Roosevelt closed by saying he "personally [felt] the loss deeply."[142] The First Lady recalled the Speaker fondly in her My Day column, calling him a "kindly, tolerant, and high-minded human being."[143] Hugh Gladney Grant, American minister to Thailand and fellow Alabamian, commented on the circumstances of the Speaker's death, noting that he "literally died like a soldier in the trenches in defense of his country."[144]

Services for William Brockman Bankhead were held in the House of Representatives the day after his death. Beautiful floral arrangements surrounded his casket and filled the chamber, the largest of which was a wreath of white and pink lilies from his fellow members of the House. Mourners packed the galleries, and a heavy police presence surrounded the Capitol. Wife Florence, brothers John and Henry, and daughters Tallulah and Eugenia were ushered in, followed by members of the Senate, cabinet officers, and several foreign dignitaries. The president was last to enter. "The President's face seemed gray and careworn," a reporter noted. "He sat directly in front of the casket." House chaplain James Shera Montgomery opened with a prayer. Newly elected Speaker and longtime friend Sam Rayburn and Alabama congressman Henry B. Steagall, their voices choked with emotion, struggled to hold back tears as they spoke of their admiration and love for Will Bankhead. Overwhelmed by the loss of his friend, Steagall said, "I know of no words to do justice to his great record and great public service." A benediction concluded the brief service. As a quartet sang the hymn "Be Still My Soul," mourners quietly filed out, remembering Will Bankhead—colleague, friend, brother, father, husband, Alabamian.

> Be still my soul when dearest friends depart
> And all is darkened in the vale of tears
> Then shalt thou better know His love His heart
> Who comes to soothe thy sorrow and thy fears

The House recessed for three days to allow members to attend the funeral of their beloved Speaker. A special funeral train carrying members of the family, the sixty-member House delegation, and two dozen senators left for Jasper in the late afternoon on September 16 and arrived the following morning at eleven o'clock. President Roosevelt, members of his cabinet, and other administration officials followed on a separate train. Tallulah could not be present but sent a beautiful spray of lilies with the inscription, "Good night, sweet prince, and flights of angels sing thee to thy rest," a poignant remembrance of her playing Juliet as a child opposite her father's Romeo. Fifty thousand people—"president and pauper, industrialist and laborer, rich man and poor man, Negro and white"—poured into Jasper to pay their respects to "Mr. Will."[145] Local merchants shuttered their shops for the day. In the early afternoon, mourners began filing into the First United Methodist Church, where two decades earlier they had grieved the passing of John Hollis Bankhead. Among them were the Speaker's seven black servants, who were seated in their own separate pew.[146] Reverend T. L. McDonald opened the service at half past two with the story of a working-class mechanic who had been in the church the day before. The man said he was from New Orleans. He was unable to attend the funeral but wanted to come a day early and pay his respects. "Will Bankhead was a friend of mine

Figure 12.2. Services for Speaker of the House William Brockman Bankhead, September 1940. President Franklin D. Roosevelt sits in the aisle, directly in front of the casket. To his left are Senator John Hollis Bankhead Jr., Florence Bankhead, and Tallulah Bankhead. Courtesy of the Alabama Department of Archives and History.

and a friend of my father," the man told Reverend McDonald. "He was responsible for the bread in my house." The unnamed man asked to sit near where the casket would be. He sat silently for an hour, his head bowed. Occupying that same seat at the funeral was the president of the United States. Will Bankhead was beloved by the high and the humble. This summed up the man, the reverend remarked.[147]

William Brockman Bankhead, representative from Alabama, and forty-seventh Speaker of the US House of Representatives, was laid to rest in Oak Hill Cemetery near the graves of his parents.

13

At the Crossroads

In fall 1944, twenty-five hundred curious people flocked to the Hopson farm two miles outside of Clarksdale, Mississippi, to catch a glimpse of the future. Under the delta sun, eight fire-engine red mechanical cotton pickers made their way through four thousand acres of the white fiber. Working together, these voracious machines did the work of nearly five hundred laborers. They harvested one thousand pounds of cotton an hour, compared to the fifteen pounds picked by the average man. Mechanization on the Hopson place was not confined to harvesting. Employing both military and industrial metaphors, a reporter sent to cover the event for *Collier's* noted that the Hopson plantation was "as mechanized as an armored division" and operated "like a Detroit assembly line." Tractors were used for planting and cultivation, flamethrowers destroyed the weeds, and airplanes dusted the cotton with insecticides. Before the machines arrived, 130 tenant families—some seven hundred men, women, and children—had called the Hopson plantation home. With mechanization, the Hopsons ran their operation using the labor of forty skilled workers.[1] Other popular periodicals likewise heralded the "revolution in cotton" that transpired during the war years. Although such declarations were premature (it would take a decade or so before most farms were at least partially mechanized), the forces that would ultimately change the South were underway by the end of World War II. The future had not quite yet arrived, but it was clearly visible.

By the 1940s, the South that the Bankheads had a significant role in creating over the past seven and a half decades teetered on the cusp of change. The war unleashed forces that shook the cotton economy and undermined traditional race relations, two critical features of the South that had defined John H. Bankhead Jr.'s political career. Bankhead began his legislative career in 1903 by crafting the legislation that disfranchised a generation of black voters and consigned them to second-class status. He spent the bulk of his senatorial career obsessed with the cotton economy, which relied on low-wage captive labor. But the war's insatiable demand for manpower and John Jr.'s own legislative handiwork in the service of cotton farmers set in motion the dismantling of the old cotton economy. The war drained off much of the excess farm labor, accelerating changes in both the cotton economy and race relations to the point that, when peace finally came, the South—and John H. Bankhead Jr.—found themselves at a crossroads.

Throughout late 1940 and 1941, John H. Bankhead Jr. remained a reliable and vocal supporter of President Roosevelt's foreign policy, including the contentious Lend-Lease Act, which authorized the president to provide military aid to any nation whose defense he deemed vital to the protection of the United States. In a nationally broadcast radio address in March 1941, Bankhead called for national unity behind Roosevelt's preparedness program. Although he recognized the importance of stopping the advance of the Germans in spring 1941, Bankhead considered Japan a "greater menace in the long run than Hitler will be." He disputed those who criticized the defense program as unnecessary and provocative. "We are not engaging in a great national-defense program because we want to fight," he argued. But failing to prepare would be "tragic beyond expression."[2] In private, Bankhead complained about the size of defense appropriations and interpreted foreign policy initiatives through the lens of the cotton economy. When secretary of agriculture Claude R. Wickard authorized the purchase of soybean oil and lard, both of which were competitive with cottonseed oil, to deliver to the British under provisions of Lend-Lease, John railed at the secretary about disadvantaging cotton. Wickard reminded Bankhead that Lend-Lease was "part of the general defense program [designed to] help do the things most necessary to protect this country." It was not, he pointed out, concerned with domestic production and price issues.[3]

After the Germans sank US destroyer *Reuben James* in October 1941, the administration sought yet again to revise the neutrality legislation by allowing merchant ships to arm themselves and enter European territorial waters. Senator Bankhead hoped that the entire Neutrality Act of 1935 would be repealed. "Don't get the idea . . . that I am in favor of war or anything of that kind," he warned reporters. "But I do not favor taking dictation from Hitler as to where we shall trade or when. I believed when the neutrality act was passed (in 1935) it would come nearer bringing us to war than its defeat would have done. Now, of course, thinking Americans everywhere see the thing as I and one other senator saw it long ago."[4] He believed in preserving freedom of the seas for American ships and commerce. "If [our ships] are liable to encounter assault or attack from any hostile source, they ought to be equipped immediately for protection of the ships and the lives of men on them."[5] Following the attack on Pearl Harbor, Bankhead joined his colleagues in supporting the president's request for a declaration of war.[6]

Even before the United States joined the war against the Germans and the Japanese, the increased industrial demand from Great Britain and her allies was beginning to pull the country out of its decade-long depression. American entrance into the war and the intensification of industrial production accelerated the nation's economic recovery. The economic benefits to the southern states were particularly notable. The wartime investments and expenditures in the region dwarfed those from the New Deal. The government invested about $7 billion in military bases and industrial facilities. One-quarter of the region's income payments, which rose 25 percent during the war years, came from the federal government. Industrial output grew by 40 percent, and the region became more urban. Bankhead paid close attention to the awarding of defense contracts and advocated on behalf of his state. By January 12, 1941, Alabama had received more than $245 million worth of defense projects, not counting shipbuilding contracts and other contracts for aluminum and textiles.[7] He complained to the Maritime Commission that Alabama was not receiving its fair share of shipbuilding contracts, which instead were going to firms on the West and East Coasts.[8] By February 1941, even before the Lend-Lease Act was approved, the federal government's defense expenditures and aid to Britain ballooned to over $40 billion.

Senator Bankhead's primary preoccupation during the war remained what it had always been throughout his career: farm income, in particular, the price of cotton. Because of New Deal legislation Bankhead had helped craft, land planted to cotton declined from 37.8 million acres in 1929 to about 20 million in 1939; nevertheless, in September 1939, when war broke out, prices remained low. Cotton was bringing about 9.9 cents a pound, which was 66 percent of parity.[9] Huge surpluses filled government warehouses. America's share of the international market likewise had dropped since the 1920s as nations such as Russia, Brazil, Egypt, and Mexico expanded production. Bankhead hoped that war in Europe would stimulate cotton exports; he was dismayed when they declined.[10] In 1940, exports to Britain and other European countries dried up. The export market would remain depressed for the duration of the war. Adding insult to injury, the 1940 cotton crop was bountiful, not what Bankhead had hoped for in an already glutted market.[11]

The outlook for cotton improved with the American entrance into the war. Demand from American mills increased, and farmers were encouraged to expand production. Acreage allotments were removed in 1943, and cotton prices rebounded. By 1943, prices averaged around twenty cents per pound, double the price in 1939 and 1940. Despite this encouragement, though, farmers, beset by labor shortages, reduced their acreage in cotton and planted more profitable alternative crops.[12] But even with the reduction in acreage and an uptick in demand, surpluses remained. Bankhead often found himself at odds with the architects of the defense effort, who, he claimed, hoped "to drive down agricultural prices" to benefit consumers at the expense of producers. Ignoring the fact that his constituents were consumers as well as producers, John remained fixated on cotton prices.

The ramping up of industrial production to meet war needs was accompanied by concerns about inflation as workers' wages rose and the availability of consumer goods declined. The Roosevelt administration created the Office of Price Administration (OPA) in 1941, which was tasked with establishing and administering a system of rationing and price controls. The creation of the OPA empowered consumers and gave them a sense of entitlement to what they considered fair prices, which often put them and their congressional advocates at odds with producers and their allies. The OPA was staffed with economists and others who believed that underconsumption had caused the Great Depression. To avoid a future recession, they argued, wage earners required adequate disposable income to consume the goods pumped out by the nation's manufacturing sector. The ability to generate mass consumption relied on a high-wage, low-price economy. The OPA's reach through price control and rationing was extensive.[13]

Bankhead and other agriculture advocates chafed against the efforts of the OPA to maintain a hold on commodity prices as a way to control inflation.[14] With the acceleration of the defense program, and with workers earning more, Bankhead wanted farmers to enjoy their fair share of wartime prosperity.[15] During the war, Bankhead emerged as a recognized leader of the farm bloc, an alliance of Democratic and Republican representatives and senators from

Figure 13.1.
Senator John Hollis Bankhead Jr. on the porch of Sunset, c. 1940s. Courtesy of the Alabama Department of Archives and History.

agricultural states dedicated to protecting agricultural interests. The farm bloc often crossed swords with the administration over parity prices, consumer subsidies, and surplus commodities.[16] The administration prioritized keeping inflation in check. Senator Bankhead firmly believed that for farmers to share in wartime prosperity, wages as well as commodity prices should be controlled.[17] Just as working-class advocates and consumer advocates had done, farmers, as represented by the farm bloc, were asserting their right to an "American standard of living."[18]

Senator Bankhead moved quickly and aggressively to protect farm interests. With exports and thus farm incomes on the decline, Bankhead introduced a bill in early 1941 that would assure growers of "basic crops," which included cotton, loans at 85 percent of parity, arguing that farmers across the country were not benefiting from a recovering economy. The loans would artificially inflate farm prices. In order for cotton farmers to achieve what was considered to be equitable purchasing power, cotton would need to sell at about 15.82 cents per pound.[19] More than simply a price-boosting measure, the bill would also mandate controls in production, which would address the surplus problem. Only those farmers who participated in the soil conservation program would be eligible. In advocating for help for farmers, Bankhead argued that "as a result of the expenditure of billions of dollars by the Federal Government in its national preparedness program, prices of industrial commodities are getting higher." The pay of industrial workers was likewise increasing. It was only fair, Bankhead argued, that agricultural commodity prices keep pace. The president was skeptical, worried that creating a price floor for commodities would encourage inflation.[20] Senators raised objections that the cost of such a bill would be passed on to consumers; reports in newspapers across the country estimated that prices for food and other goods might increase between 10 and 20 percent. Such "brazen and absurd" arguments, Bankhead stated, were promoted by "professional economists . . . who never in their lives produced a single commodity." The purpose of his bill, he argued, was to obtain some measure of justice for the farmer. "The laundryman who washes [a cotton] shirt gets 5 to 10 times as much every time he launders the shirts as the farmer who toils to produce the cotton gets for the raw materials in the shirt." The increase in the cost of cotton to the manufacturer, Bankhead argued, would not be so significant as to require a rise in the cost of the manufactured product to the consumer.[21] Roosevelt, skeptical of the new appropriation and fearful of ever-growing surpluses, hinted at a veto but ultimately signed the bill at the end of May 1941.[22] The *Wall Street Journal* called the bill the "biggest farm grab in history" and criticized farm advocates of selfishly putting self-interest before the good of the country. The act set a precedent of mandatory loans for basic crops, a policy that continued throughout World War II.[23]

President Roosevelt's skepticism over the farm bill was just one indication of a growing wartime rift between the president and the farm bloc. After the attack on Pearl Harbor, the administration and the OPA moved more aggressively to combat inflation, which had worsened following American entrance into the war. A price control bill was introduced in fall 1941, discussed in hearings of the Senate Committee on Banking and Currency in December 1941, and taken up by the full Senate in early 1942.[24] The debate over the Emergency Price Control Act was acrimonious, the first serious wartime challenge to Roosevelt. Farm advocates swung into action and insisted that the bill prohibit farm prices from falling below 110 percent of parity.[25] Although Roosevelt wanted the OPA to have control over commodity prices, Bankhead successfully added an amendment to the bill demanding that any ceiling on commodities would require the prior consent of the Department of Agriculture. Bankhead justified the amendment as "effective security . . . against any harsh and unfair orders that might be made by the price administrator."[26] The *Washington Post* called the approval of the amendment a "unity shattering revolt."[27] Those who supported the amendment trusted the secretary of agriculture and his advisers—"men who have worked with this program for 30 and 40 years"—to protect farm interests. Senator Walter F. George of Georgia scoffed at the experts within the OPA, whose understanding of farm issues was, in his words, "theoretical," asking his colleagues whether they were willing to leave farm problems in the hands of "the most estimable men of Harvard."[28] It was a significant victory for farmers but not what the president wanted. Roosevelt vehemently opposed the amendment, which gave the secretary of agriculture a virtual veto over recommended farm price ceilings. He threatened to veto the bill but ultimately signed it at the end of January 1942.[29]

Farmers were further protected through an amendment offered by Alabama congressman Henry B. Steagall to the Stabilization Act of 1942, which required the government to make loans on commodities at 90 percent of parity for two years after the war. The amendment was a critical win for the farm bloc. It established the principle of protection and helped remove the fear that postwar deflation would wreak havoc on farmers as it did following the First World War. But the policy also guaranteed that farmers would count on high support prices, which encouraged surpluses.[30]

John H. Bankhead Jr. faced an easy reelection in 1942. The *Birmingham News* opined that Bankhead "is the recognized leader of the agricultural forces in Congress. He has long since become known the country over as America's foremost agricultural statesman. There has hardly been a piece of agricultural legislation of any consequence in the last 10 years of which he was not either the author, the coauthor, or a leading proponent on the floor of the Senate."[31] One citizen critical of Bankhead complained to the *Birmingham News* that with his fixation on the cotton economy, the senator was "just a little out of step. It seems he is thinking more of other things than he is the war."[32]

While Bankhead cruised to victory in 1942, other Democrats were not so fortunate. Republicans increased their presence in both houses of Congress that year, gaining fifty seats in the House and eight in the Senate.[33] Republicans gained seats in large part because soldiers, who tended to vote Democrat, had been unable to vote. Most of the Democratic Party's losses were in nonsouthern races, thus giving southern Democrats stronger control over their party. The coalition of conservative Democrats and Republicans that emerged during Roosevelt's second term grew stronger under wartime pressures, as white southern Democrats' fears of federal intervention aligned with Republican Party's small-government philosophy in the fight over a host of issues.[34]

Conservative Democrats and Republicans joined together to attack New Deal programs they considered to be unrelated to the wartime emergency. The Works Progress Administration, Civilian Conservation Corps, and National Youth Administration, all of them work-relief programs, were abolished in 1943. Conservatives in Congress likewise took aim at the Farm Security Administration, which had been created by the Bankhead-Jones Farm Tenant Act of 1937. Although not always in favor of some of the Farm Security Administration's programs, Bankhead nevertheless remained a defender of the agency and fought off those who sought to cut its appropriations. He defended the agency's administrator, whom congressional critics labeled a communist and who was criticized for what some regarded as "subversive practices," like cooperative farming.[35] Bankhead was on the losing end of this battle. Conservatives succeeded in slashing the agency's funds in 1943, mortally wounding it. They abolished the Farm Security Administration altogether in 1946.[36]

Following his reelection, Bankhead moved further away from the president, taking whatever action he deemed necessary to support agriculture. John confided to sister Marie that although "there is not unkind feeling between us that I know anything about," he acknowledged that their differences had created a distance between the two men. Unlike during the New Deal years, the president rarely conferred with Bankhead.[37] Bankhead introduced a bill in fall 1943 that would virtually wipe out the government's food subsidy program. Subsidies were paid to farmers to encourage production while holding down food prices for consumers, and they constituted a critical component of the administration's overall price control structure.[38] Opponents such as Bankhead saw subsidies as hidden wage increases for workers and preferred that prices for agricultural commodities be adjusted upward and subsidies eliminated.[39] The president regarded subsidies as critical to holding down inflation.[40] He also declared that farmers enjoyed "favorable prices and incomes," as well as postwar government price supports (thanks to the Steagall amendment), "a guarantee against postwar disaster afforded to no other group." Bankhead and others argued that consumers, enjoying higher wages, were entirely capable of paying higher prices for food and should do so.[41] Although Bankhead never succeeded in killing government food subsidies, he and the farm bloc would continue to challenge the Roosevelt administration on farm prices and consumer subsidies throughout the duration of the war.[42]

During the war years, Tallulah finally achieved the critical success that had escaped her grasp for so long. Following her remarkable run in *The Little Foxes*, Tallulah was determined to consider only quality roles that befit a true theatrical star. In late December 1941, she went against type and played a working-class housewife in Clifford Odets's *Clash by Night*. She received mostly excellent reviews, and the show ran for seven weeks.[43] She followed this performance with her role as Lily Sabina in Thornton Wilder's *The Skin of Our Teeth*, an absurdist comedy directed by relative newcomer Elia Kazan. It was a challenging play. "Flouting formula," Tallulah recalled, "Mr. Wilder scrambled both time and circumstance. He thought nothing of having a dinosaur frolicking on the lawn while the [main characters] were bemused by a radio commentator."[44] Tallulah loved the brilliant, controversial play. Audiences were not so sure. "The theater has always been the foe of change, of progress, of innovation," Tallulah remarked when recalling the reception of Thornton's play. "I'm surprised it ever conceded the electric light."[45]

The Skin of Our Teeth opened in November 1942. Some critics loved it; others hated it; audiences were confused by it. Tallulah's performance earned her honors from *Variety*, and she was given the New York Drama Critics Best Actress Award. "If I had been validated by Regina Giddens," Tallulah declared, "I was canonized by Sabina."[46] With the success of *The Little Foxes* and *The Skin of Our Teeth*, Tallulah was able to purchase an eighteen-acre estate in Westchester, New York, which she named Windows. It was the first home she had had since leaving London in 1931.[47] Tallulah had always loved dogs, particularly Pekingese, and she had owned several since her time in England. Back in the United States, she owned a rotating menagerie of dogs and cats, as well as a monkey and a lion cub she named Winston Churchill. She filled Windows with pets both furred and feathered.[48]

Tallulah left *The Skin of Our Teeth* in June 1943 and was immediately sought out by director Alfred Hitchcock for his new film, *Lifeboat*. For $75,000, Tallulah portrayed foreign correspondent Constance Porter. She adored Hitchcock. The film premiered in January 1944. Tallulah received the New York Film Critics Circle Best Actress Award for her performance.[49] Like her success in *The Little Foxes*, her role in *Lifeboat* was a personal victory. "At last I had licked the screen," she proclaimed, "the screen which had six times betrayed me." She did not, however, win an Academy Award for her performance. She blamed Hollywood politics for the slight. She explained: "The people who vote in that free-for-all know on which side their *crêpes Suzette* are buttered. I wasn't under contract to any of the major studios, hence was thought an outlaw."[50]

As Tallulah reached the heights of her profession, sister Eugenia settled into a slightly more conventional life. She married yet again, this time to William Sprouse, a sergeant in the Marine Corps. In 1942, Eugenia and William adopted a child, whom they called Billy. While William served overseas, Eugenia and Billy moved into Marie's farmhouse in Elmore County, which Eugenia converted into a boardinghouse for servicemen and their wives.[51] Tallulah had a fondness for children and was always solicitous of the young actors with whom she worked. She lavished attention on Billy, which helped smooth over some of the rough edges in her relationship with Eugenia.

While Senator John H. Bankhead Jr. and the farm bloc battled the administration for what they believed was the farmers' fair share of wartime prosperity, they faced another, more difficult challenge: a labor shortage. The traditional cotton economy had always relied on low-paid surplus labor. Although cotton prices inched up during the war, they never reached a point to provide agricultural workers what most considered an acceptable "American standard of living."[52] Even at the peak of wartime demand, sharecroppers and tenants made a little over $200 a year. One contemporary observer noted that in the South, cotton farming was "a world in which survival depended on raw courage, a courage born out of desperation and sustained by a lack of alternatives."[53] Although New Deal programs, many of them devised by Senator Bankhead, had begun to disrupt the traditional system of farming in the South, the problem of too many people and not enough opportunity remained.[54] World War II brought the alternatives that had long eluded the southern rural poor. This frightened rural white landowners, who feared not only the loss of cheap labor but also the loss of the social control that accompanied it.

The expansion of war production brought an increased demand for manpower. The War Manpower Commission and the US Employment Service intensified labor recruitment for the defense industry, identifying the traditional surplus labor in the rural South as a particularly rich vein to tap. According to one historian, the southern labor surplus was "absolutely integral to an Allied victory."[55] As demands for manpower increased, rural workers—black and white—exercised that quintessential American right of mobility. The results were dramatic. In the state of Texas alone, cotton growers lost a hundred thousand farmworkers in 1942. Altogether, across the South, some two million farmers left agriculture that year.[56] For these workers, wartime mobility carried with it the promise of economic security that had long eluded them.

Plans to recruit southern agricultural laborers for work on the West Coast or in the industrial Midwest did not go over well with southern growers.[57] Land-owners and political leaders went to great lengths to hold these workers on the land. Congress attached an amendment, authored by Senator Millard Tydings of Maryland, to a military draft bill, giving power to local draft boards to defer or draft farmworkers. Various states issued work-or-fight proclamations and ordered local sheriffs to arrest vagrants and put them to work in the fields.[58] Bank-head and other members of the farm bloc not only sought to stem the flow of rural workers to industrial centers; they also questioned the military's voracious manpower needs. In early 1943, the armed forces announced they would need eleven million men in the armed forces by the end of the year. Bankhead and the farm bloc were incredulous.[59] To continue to induct farmworkers would bring the country, Bankhead warned, "to the brink of starvation." He advocated keeping Americans home to raise food and make weapons while leaving the British, Chinese, and Soviets to do the fighting.[60] He encouraged farmers to decrease their production of cotton and increase production of food. Speaking to a gathering of farmers in South Carolina, he told his listeners that "it is wasteful in wartime to continue to grow a surplus of things not needed. We have plenty of cotton for clothing; we do not have too much food."[61] Bankhead took to the radio in late February to press his case that more men were needed in production and farm labor. "The time has arrived," he declared, "when some decision should be reached on whether the United States is in a position to raise armed forces as large as any country in the world, except Russia, and at the same time provide both an abundant arsenal and overflowing granary for our allies. Can that be done without destroying the morale of our people?" Bankhead feared that military manpower needs would result in serious shortages on the home front, "placing a burden on our people they are unable to carry. It might result sooner or later in a negotiated peace without requiring unconditional surrender from our enemies."[62] Secretary of agriculture Claude R. Wickard agreed with Bank-head that the country could not meet its food production needs, which included civilian and military needs, as well as demands of the Lend-Lease and foreign aid programs.[63]

With pressure increasing on local growers to acquire adequate labor from a shrinking supply, Bankhead emerged as the "spearhead" of the "food-over-soldiers" effort. He remained strongly in favor of providing enough labor to run America's farms, even if it meant limiting the size of the nation's military.[64] Bankhead sponsored legislation that would order the deferment of farm laborers provided they stayed at their jobs. They would not be allowed to leave their post for military service or a higher-paying industrial job without permission from the draft board. According to the Selective Service System, roughly 60 percent of agricultural workers who left farmwork did so to pursue industrial employment. One senator remarked that freezing farmworkers at their jobs was akin to involuntary servitude.[65] A second bill demanded the furlough of men stationed in the United States who, previous to their induction, had worked in agriculture. They would be required to return to agricultural employment.[66] Bankhead also chaired a Senate appropriations subcommittee charged with investigating industrial and military manpower needs. The subcommittee held closed-door hearings with military leaders to assess the validity of military needs. Bankhead joined with other senators in declaring that it might be necessary to withhold appropriations for increases in the size of the US Army unless something was done to address the farm labor problem. Roosevelt rebuked Bankhead, dismissing the notion that there would be any downward revision in the army's estimated needs. The Department of War, Selective Service System, and Office of Economic Stabilization opposed the bill, which the House did not consider.[67]

In mid-March 1943, Bankhead introduced substitute legislation that deferred those workers producing "essential" crops, which the Senate approved.[68] African American activists strenuously objected to this bill, calling it a "back-to-slavery bill" and pointing out that "it would put four and a half million Negro adults in 12 southern states at the disposal of the 1,641 local draft boards in these states, not one of which has a single Negro member."[69] Responding to the pressure, the War Manpower Commission issued an order to Selective Service boards to defer "essential" farm labor.[70] Hoping to thwart congressional action, the president issued an order in early April 1943 to "Hold the Line," which incorporated a demand that workers in essential industries be prevented from transferring to a job in a nonessential industry.[71]

Despite the best efforts of Bankhead and others, workers continued to leave the South for better-paying jobs elsewhere. The largest decline of black farmers—almost all of them sharecroppers—occurred in Alabama, Mississippi, Arkansas, Louisiana, and Texas. Industrial jobs paid some workers more for an hour's work than farmworkers made in a day.[72] Those who remained in rural areas saw their wages rise; in some areas, wage rates more than tripled between 1940 and 1945, although they were still low by national standards. Bankhead frequently argued that labor costs be considered when calculating parity prices for farm commodities.[73]

While many farmers demanded help from elected officials to keep rural workers in their place, an increasing number of landowners took a different route. Recognizing that these workers were unlikely to return to the farm at war's end, and that the cotton economy was changing, some farmers diversified, leaving cotton behind for other crops, such as soybeans, and purchasing livestock. Still others turned to mechanization. Southern farms had been slow to mechanize prior to the war. With a ready supply of cheap labor, mechanization did not make economic sense. Also, most southern farms were too small and the fields too irregular to implement machinery effectively and efficiently. More importantly, no reliable machine could weed and pick cotton.[74] If mechanization was going to succeed, southern farms had to be organized differently.

Some farmers began to mechanize during the 1930s, when federal farm credit programs encouraged mechanization. But the real push came with the war. According to one historian, "Wartime prosperity made it possible for farmers to reduce their debts and increase capital expenditures. Some bought more and better machinery to replace the departing workers, others purchased additional land and enlarged their farms," making mechanization a better, more rational, choice. As mechanization took hold, cotton production moved west to Arizona and California, where single landholdings were larger and more conducive to mechanization, and thus better able to expand and produce more efficiently as the need for labor was not as great.[75]

The demands for manpower and the exodus of labor—particularly black workers—from the southern countryside had broader political implications for the South and the nation. As one historian notes, in plantation regions, "farm workers' dependency undergirded local economic and social power."[76] Out-migration placed enormous pressure on southern political and social institutions. Some one million African Americans left southern farms for northern and western cities, where many became registered voters eager to support the president. African Americans used their newfound industrial muscle to push for economic and political reforms.

Conservative and liberal southern congressional representatives and senators spoke with one voice in opposing legislation and executive orders that touched on race and civil rights. During the war and postwar eras, it was clear that the southern bloc, despite its size, was becoming increasingly isolated within the national party. The conditions on the home front during and immediately after World War II precipitated a decade of political turmoil that fundamentally altered the role and responsibilities of the federal government and constituted an important turning point for conservative white southerners within the Democratic Party. Roosevelt had been willing and able to sacrifice support for civil rights in exchange for southern congressional votes during the economic crises of the 1930s; however, the pressure for full production, the accelerated mobility of poor southerners, and the increased political power of African Americans in the North, as well as the unremitting racial violence that marred the war and postwar eras, made the continuation of this compromise increasingly untenable.

Despite the nation's voracious manpower needs, employers—particularly in the South—were reluctant to hire African Americans for fear of challenging segregation. They instead relied on white in-migration.[77] Conscious of their growing political power and the nation's wartime labor shortage, African Americans, led by labor activist A. Philip Randolph, threatened a March on Washington and effectively pressured the president to issue an executive order in June 1941 that forbade employment discrimination in defense industries and established the Fair Employment Practices Committee (FEPC). Although the FEPC's accomplishments could be considered modest at best, for southern lawmakers the agency represented an intrusive precedent into the prerogatives of southern employers. Southern lawmakers feared the inevitability of federal control over labor.[78]

The greatest enemy of the FEPC in Congress was Senator Theodore G. "The Man" Bilbo of Mississippi. Derisively referred to as the "Prince of the Peckerwoods," the five-foot-two Bilbo ascended political office as the champion of the common man. Elected to the US Senate in 1934, Bilbo became one of Roosevelt's more loyal southern New Dealers, giving strong support to relief programs, the Social Security Act, the Wagner Act, and the Fair Labor Standards Act. Yet, like so many liberal southern politicians, Bilbo believed that progress for the working classes could be achieved only by maintaining the color bar. Bilbo became positively apoplectic in his denunciations of the FEPC. His rantings earned him a reputation as the Senate's most vitriolic white supremacist. Bilbo claimed that "every Negro in America who is behind movements of this kind . . . dream[s] of social equality and inter-marriage between whites and blacks."[79] Throughout the FEPC's rocky tenure, southern congresspeople formed the most intractable bloc of opposition.

The pressure tactics used by civil rights leaders that led to the creation of the FEPC illustrated black people's new militancy and assertiveness. During the war, membership in the National Association for the Advancement of Colored People (NAACP) increased tenfold, and the number of chapters tripled. Still, the majority of black southerners did not join the NAACP or any civil rights movement. Even so, the war left few unchanged. If it did not motivate them to join the movement, it at the very least prompted them to aspire to achieve something better for themselves and their families. This change had been especially great for black veterans. Haywood Stephney, a navy veteran from Clarksdale, Mississippi, recalled that not until he served overseas did he begin to understand the damage segregation had done to him. "After seeing what some of the other world was doing then, I realized how far behind I was. As we began to move and stir around and learn other ways then we had a choice—a comparison." With this point of comparison, Stephney realized that once he returned to Clarksdale, it was "going to be difficult to get me back in total darkness." This point was not lost on local white folks, who pointedly reminded black people like Stephney (and themselves, for that matter) that nothing had changed. Dabney Hammer, a highly decorated black veteran, also from Clarksdale, recalled that wartime valor and honor meant nothing to Clarksdale white folks, who went out of their way to remind him that in the Mississippi delta, he was "still a nigger."[80]

The enormous task of mobilizing millions of young men to fight on foreign soil brought forth a confrontation between military necessity and southern racial practices. The arrival of black soldiers on southern military bases set white southerners on edge, and many lodged protests with military and civilian officials. For many white residents, the mere sight of a black man in uniform was cause for concern. Like other white southerners, John H. Bankhead Jr. recognized the war's potential to undermine white supremacy, and he did what he could to defend the color line. In August 1942, Bankhead complained to General George C. Marshall, chief of staff of the US Army, about the quartering of African American troops in southern states. He wrote that white southerners "feel the government is doing a disservice to the war effort by locating Negro troops in the South in immediate contact with white troops at a time when race feeling among the Negroes has been aroused." Bankhead added that if black soldiers must be placed in the South he hoped they would be southern black troops. Marshall disputed Bankhead's claim that recent racial disturbances were caused by black soldiers; rather, "it is understood that harmonious relations between whites and Negroes in the South have been disturbed by what are considered rash actions or remarks on the part of a few members of both races." He dismissed Bankhead's request, stating that "the only sound basis upon which we can proceed in the prosecution of the war is to station our troops in accordance with the dictates of military necessity." Any other considerations "must be secondary to military requirements."[81]

Legislation introduced during the war years compounded the growing social unrest on the home front, further antagonized southern members of Congress, and widened the gap between the South and the Democratic Party. The Soldier Voting Act and an anti–poll tax bill, both introduced in 1942, threatened race relations, voting patterns, and political power in the South more directly than did the FEPC. The anti–poll tax bill was a familiar feature by 1942; once again, southerners defeated the bill. The Soldier Voting Act of 1942 attempted to facilitate voting procedures for members of the armed forces stationed outside their home states. Southern politicians feared that even this slight change would pave the way for the eventual enfranchisement of black voters. Southern Democrats succeeded in attaching an amendment to the bill that would keep the states' election machinery intact, essentially emasculating it.[82] The vote was passed in September of that year, roughly six weeks before Election Day. Senator Bankhead had fought against passage. He viewed the elimination of the poll tax as yet another attempt to "weaken our Southern institutions."[83] Although this legislation had lifted the poll tax, the process of actually receiving and casting a ballot was inefficient and unwieldy; as a result, only a fraction of eligible members of the armed forces had their ballots cast and counted.[84]

The most direct assault on the region's antidemocratic political machinery came from the US Supreme Court in its 1944 decision in the Texas case of *Smith v. Allwright*. The court ruled that the Texas white primary law violated the Fifteenth Amendment and was therefore unconstitutional. While the states of the Upper South acquiesced in the ruling, the decision was a political bombshell in the Deep South. The Mississippi state legislature passed a law requiring voters to swear their opposition to federal antilynching and anti–poll tax legislation and the FEPC. In 1946 the Alabama legislature passed, and white voters approved, the Boswell Amendment to the state constitution, introducing new suffrage standards that required potential voters to "read and write, understand and explain any article of the Constitution of the United States." It also granted local boards the power to administer registration requirements "in as discriminatory a fashion as they saw fit." South Carolina's governor, New Dealer Olin D. Johnston, convened a special session of the state legislature that proceeded to repeal all state primary laws, ostensibly relegating the Democratic Party to the status of a private club with the power to determine membership qualifications. Later that year, Johnston challenged incumbent senator Ellison DuRant "Cotton Ed" Smith. Johnston won in part because he had supported New Deal policies, but he also won because he could no longer be considered soft on white supremacy. His credentials were as strong as the aging Smith's. Even Claude Pepper of Florida, arguably the South's most liberal senator, felt compelled to assure voters of his support for white supremacy.[85]

By 1944, as the number of Americans in the armed forces reached over ten million and the list of casualties and those missing in action lengthened, the issue of soldier voting was paramount. One historian has noted that "not since the Civil War had such a large proportion of young American men been exposed to the probability of death or injury." To deny these soldiers the right to vote through some sort of federal framework by leaving the question of voting to states, Roosevelt argued, would subject them to "unjustifiable discrimination."[86] As more men were inducted into the armed services, pressure mounted on Congress to find a way to facilitate more easily their ability to vote. As one historian has observed, "though it was quite impossible for any member of Congress to oppose, in principle, the idea that citizens who were risking their lives in battle should have the chance to cast a ballot, southern representatives were keenly concerned that an effective federal role of the kind the president was proposing threatened to undermine the restrictions on voting that their states had crafted over many decades."[87] For the state of Alabama, those restrictions had been written into law some forty years earlier by none other than John H. Bankhead Jr. Any attempt to remove voting from state control received his full attention. In his State of the Union message, delivered in January 1944, Roosevelt implored Congress to enact "legislation which would preserve for our soldiers and sailors and marines the fundamental prerogative of citizenship—the right to vote."[88]

The renewed fight over the legislation "pit . . . calls for national unity against other strongly held beliefs and values, most notably inclinations to favor a modest federal role and protect Jim Crow."[89] The 1944 bill was drawn up by the Department of Justice, but a competing states' rights version was sponsored by two Mississippians: Congressman John E. Rankin and Senator James Eastland. From the bill's introduction to its passage, the South's need to preserve Jim

Crow received paramount attention. John H. Bankhead Jr. pulled his weight in the Senate filibuster of the 1944 Soldier Voting Act, which would create a standard federal ballot. Bankhead referred to the bill as "an attempted invasion on my State" and contended that "our colored people are satisfied with the election situation as it now exists." He argued that black citizens would eventually receive the right to vote in the same way that lynching had eventually "disappeared." "As time went on, and Negroes emerged from a state of barbarism and entered into a state of education and civilization, the horrible crime of lynching disappeared from the South almost entirely." He disputed the claim that a poll tax was a burden, arguing that as a result of the wartime economy, black citizens were flush with cash. One merchant told Bankhead that black patrons regularly spent $200–$300 in his store. Although the merchant would "plead with them to buy [war] bonds," these black patrons would want to "spend their money now." But Bankhead also noted that even were black citizens to pay their poll taxes, that would not necessarily make them registered voters, a veiled reference to the multiple obstacles employed by registrars in the state of Alabama. He displayed the paternalistic arrogance of many white elites regarding their knowledge of the political desires of black people: "I am a friend of the Negro in my state, and they know it. . . . I have working for me two domestic servants who are Negroes. They have been in my service approximately 35 and 40 years. They are a man and a woman. They are not married to each other. The woman is my cook. I do not know what I would do without her. She rarely ever misses a day. She is not one of the kind who do not come if it does not suit them. She is raising two children. Everybody in my town knows how highly I regard them. They are Negroes of good character; they are real Christians; they are church attendants; they are good citizens. They feel safe and secure. They are not interested in . . . efforts to reform this country." Should the bill pass, he worried that white people would respond with violence. In particular, he worried that if black citizens in the majority-black counties became registered voters, "the courthouse, as was the case in Reconstruction days, would again be filled with colored county officials, to wait upon our white people, our women and our children." White southerners would not stand for it. "Those who are pressing for the passage of this bill profess to be trying to protect the Negroes. The Negroes do not want them to put their slimy hands on them, and bring them into conflict with the people with whom they have lived in peace and love ever since the days of slavery."[90] Ultimately, an alliance of southern Democrats and Republicans was able to pass a much-diluted bill that minimized federal oversight.[91]

As a recognized leader of the farm bloc, John H. Bankhead Jr. had achieved some measure of national prominence. In 1944, he tested the vice presidential nomination waters but found little support for his candidacy.[92] Certainly he was not the preferred running mate of President Roosevelt, who was running for (and would win) a fourth term in office. At the 1944 convention, Lister Hill nominated Bankhead for the vice presidency, but he received fewer than one hundred votes. On the second ballot, Bankhead and the majority of the Alabama delegation threw their support to Missouri senator Harry S. Truman. Bankhead much preferred Truman over Henry A. Wallace, who he had come to regard as "that dangerous Red."[93] Bankhead played a minimal role in the campaign, only making a few radio speeches, praising the president as "the best friend the farmers ever had in the White House." Although he often differed with the president on agricultural issues, he warned farmers away from voting Republican. "Agriculture will go back to eating at the second table if the Republicans win. So far as I am able to judge, the Republican party is still dominated by rich men who, in turn, are dominated by their hatred of the president." He reminded farmers of the suffering they had faced during the Depression. "The president and the Democratic administration are responsible for the measures that have made agriculture a business instead of a gamble, and a losing gamble at that. . . . The Republicans are wanting the farmers to go back to gambling—to take a chance on Dewey."[94] At one time a supporter of Henry Wallace, Bankhead opposed Wallace's nomination to be secretary of commerce, charging that Wallace "is associated in the public mind with ideas of classes and groups and his expressed views seem to pit the one against the other."[95] The appointment of Wallace and the opposition of conservative Democrats revealed a crack in the party that would continue to grow during the postwar era.

The end of the war brought new challenges. Bankhead and the farm bloc continued to struggle against the OPA, which maintained price controls into the postwar era, ceilings that Bankhead called "ridiculous . . . terrible, terrible."[96] More ominous than the continuation of price controls was the prospect of a permanent FEPC. Southern lawmakers were shocked when Harry S. Truman, ascending to the presidency upon the death of Franklin D. Roosevelt in 1945, called on Congress to make the body permanent. Predictably, southern senators filibustered the effort when a bill to make the FEPC a permanent body reached the floor of the Senate in January 1946. This bill "would have prohibited discrimination based upon race, creed, color, national origin, or ancestry not only by the federal or state governments but also by private employers, with no exemptions for agricultural labor, and by unions." The Senate, led by Richard B. Russell Jr. of Georgia, waged war against the bill. Senator Walter F. George of Georgia cried that the bill represented "the philosophy of totalitarian government, pure and simple." Senator Olin D. Johnston of South Carolina claimed that "FEPC is one of the instruments they want to use to bring about that social equality which leads to miscegenation, mongrelization, intermixing." Bankhead joined the southern chorus, alleging that the bill's supporters were "the Bolshevik crowd, the Communist Crowd."[97] Bankhead insisted that the "South is doing its full part by the Negro" and that the "intelligent Negroes of the South do not want social race equality," which apparently would transpire should a permanent

FEPC be enacted. He also believed that the FEPC would ultimately lead to interracial marriage. Again, he based his arguments on what he believed was his intimate knowledge of black people, whom white southerners "have been helping all the years since slavery was abolished." He warned that should the FEPC become permanent, "Japanese and German workers could oust 'good American citizens'" from employment opportunities.[98] To the senator's claim that African Americans were content with the status quo in the South, Lenora S. Myatt of the Alabama Federation of Negro Women's Club responded that "we don't think Senator Bankhead is very well acquainted with us to say we are content and satisfied with conditions."[99] The FEPC ceased operating on June 30, 1946, when southern congressional representatives succeeded in slashing its funding.

Continuing to fight on behalf of cotton farmers and segregation took its toll on Bankhead. Always a diligent senator, he often worked past midnight, a physical challenge for someone in their seventies. His physician urged him to slow down.[100] To the normal rigors of the job was added the stress of combating an ugly accusation by Washington syndicated columnist Drew Pearson, who in May 1946 alleged that Bankhead, his wife, and his son had been speculating in cotton futures and had profited from the senator's public statements about cotton. Bankhead issued an angry rebuke, stating that he had not owned a pound of cotton while he had been in the Senate, "while he felt 'sure' that his wife had not either."[101] It was a curiously worded denial.

Angered by the Pearson accusation and struggling with the problems of economic reconversion, Bankhead collapsed in a committee room in the Capitol on May 24, 1946. He was initially diagnosed with nervous exhaustion and given a sedative; colleagues reported that he had worked until two o'clock in the morning the night before his attack. Unconscious, he was carried from the building on a stretcher and rushed to the Naval Hospital in Bethesda. Doctors there determined that Bankhead had suffered a stroke. He lay unconscious for two days, regaining consciousness on May 26 and recognizing his grandson, who was a medical student at Johns Hopkins University. His condition improved slightly but remained serious for the next two weeks. He rallied several times, but his condition was further compromised by pneumonia. Senator John Hollis Bankhead Jr. died at 4:10 p.m. on June 12, 1946. He was seventy-three years old. Musa and Walter Will—his wife and son—were by his side.

A special train was dispatched to carry the senator's body and his family back to Jasper. President Truman, "shocked and saddened" by the senator's death, paid his respects to the family on the train before it departed the capital. A congressional delegation of twenty-four members led by Senator Lister Hill accompanied Bankhead's body on this last trip home.

The funeral for John H. Bankhead Jr. was held in Jasper on June 14. Crowds gathered to greet the funeral train. A local Boy Scout troop and a contingent of state highway patrolmen stood for several hours in the soaking rain to direct traffic and to serve as ushers.[102] Mourners—the highborn and the humble—filled the Jasper Methodist Church. Compared to brother Will's funeral, John's service was a simple affair. Flags in the town flew at half-mast, and local farmers paid tribute to "Cotton John." The senator's casket was draped with red and white carnations in the shape of Alabama's state flag.[103] The altar was illuminated by a large white electric cross. Only the gentle whir of fans broke the silence. John Hollis Bankhead Jr. was buried in Oak Hill Cemetery near his brother and parents.

Standing in the rain, one local struggled to put the senator's death into perspective. "We loved his dad right enough and we loved Will—but now that we're losing John it's like losing them all again. This is really the last you see. . . . When we buried the old senator, young Will was already following in his footsteps. That took away the sting a little. Then when we lost Speaker Will, we still had Senator John, so that wasn't quite so bad either. But now, with him gone, well, this time it's the end."

"It's a sad day for Alabama."[104]

Epilogue

With the death of Senator John Hollis Bankhead Jr., history turned a page. President Harry S. Truman recognized as much. In a letter to the senator's widow, Truman wrote, "An era in our congressional life ends with his passing. For three score years . . . the honored name of Bankhead had graced the roll of either House or Senate and sometimes both." He noted that John H. Bankhead Jr. "was the embodiment of the spirit of the Far South. He held firmly to the traditions of the great state which he represented in the national council."[1] Like his father before him, John Jr. helped further the economic interests of the South, making southern economic development a federal priority while using every means at his disposal to thwart federal interference into race relations.

Ironically, President Truman himself posed one of the biggest challenges to the "traditions" to which the Bankheads held fast. Responding to an outbreak of violence against African American veterans and to the growing influence of African American voters in the Democratic Party coalition, Truman appointed a civil rights commission in late 1946 to investigate the state of race relations. He incorporated the committee's recommendations, which included anti–poll tax legislation, antilynching legislation, and a permanent Fair Employment Practices Commission, into an address before Congress in February 1948, becoming the first president since Reconstruction to deliver an address solely devoted to civil rights. In July at the Democratic National Convention, Truman accepted his party's nomination as its presidential candidate and endorsed the civil rights plank in the party platform. This unprecedented act in support of civil rights by a Democrat set off a political revolt across the Deep South. States' rights conservatives denounced Truman's civil rights stance, organized themselves into the States' Rights Democratic Party—popularly known as the Dixiecrat Party—and challenged Truman for the votes of the region's white Democrats.

In the 1948 presidential election, southern politicians in Deep South states found themselves in a quandary, forced to choose between their racial traditions and their political allegiance to the Democratic Party, long the instrument by which white southerners had defended white supremacy. The outcry against the president's civil rights program was long and loud. But in the end, most southern congressional representatives and senators chose to support President Truman, although few campaigned on his behalf. Party patronage was too valuable, and the ability of southern senators to filibuster any civil rights legislation too effective, to encourage more than a handful to cast their lot with the Dixiecrats.[2]

Will Bankhead and John H. Bankhead Jr., of course, did not survive to witness this schism in the Democratic Party's ranks. Loyal party men, they would have likely held their noses and voted for the president. In her memoirs, Tallulah Bankhead claimed that "this revolt of the Dixiecrats would have broken Daddy's heart. Had he and Uncle John been alive it wouldn't have happened."[3] Tallulah herself was a loyal Democrat and a staunch Truman supporter. One local paper criticized Tallulah for her support for the president and his civil rights agenda. "Tallulah has been gone too long and politically she isn't living up to her heritage."[4] Although white Alabamians would continue to claim her as their own, they did so with less enthusiasm.

Seventy-nine-year-old Marie Bankhead Owen threw her lot in with the Dixiecrats. Appointed head of the Women's Division of the States' Rights Democratic Party, Marie traveled the South, addressing groups of white Democratic women on the evils of Truman's civil rights platform.[5] Like many Dixiecrats, Marie sought to tie the pro-segregation fight of white southerners to the recent war against Germany and Japan. For Marie, the president's support of fair employment practices was akin to the "tyranny" Americans fought during the First and Second World Wars.[6] In the end, Truman won an improbable victory over

Figure E.1. Marie Bankhead Owen (*left*) and Tallulah Bankhead, c. 1950s. Courtesy of the Alabama Department of Archives and History.

Republican Thomas E. Dewey. The Dixiecrats captured the Electoral College votes of only four states in the Deep South, including Alabama. Tallulah gleefully accepted Truman's invitation to attend the inauguration, while Marie nursed her political wounds back home in Alabama.

In the 1940s, Tallulah reached the pinnacle of her career. She continued to shine on the stage and followed her success in Alfred Hitchcock's film *Lifeboat* with a nearly two-year run of Noel Coward's play *Private Lives*, the longest run of her career. Still, despite her success in *Lifeboat*, she failed to receive offers to star in quality films. She lost a role in the film version of Tennessee Williams's *The Glass Menagerie* because of her behavior during her screen test. By the late 1940s

Figure E.2. Marie Bankhead Owen at her desk, 1954. Courtesy of the Alabama Department of Archives and History.

Tallulah was drinking heavily, her behavior becoming more outrageous. Studios, cautious enterprises, did not want to take a chance on her. With no good parts forthcoming, Tallulah took a risk in 1950, agreeing to host *The Big Show*, a radio interview show on NBC. Although wracked with anxiety over this new venture, she was a sensation, using her unique vocal talent and outstanding comedic timing to perfection. *The Big Show* was the surprise radio hit of the year. The program ran for two seasons and concluded in April 1952. As she was concluding her radio show, Tallulah published her memoirs, which quickly became a bestseller. She was active in Democratic Party politics throughout the decade, campaigning for Adlai Stevenson's presidential bids in 1952 and 1956. As the entertainment industry continued to evolve, Tallulah proved willing to innovate. Although wary of television, Tallulah made her debut in NBC's *All Star Revue* in fall 1952; she also developed a nightclub act that she performed in Las Vegas and London in the mid-1950s.[7]

Marie remained active into her eighth decade of life, although she cut back considerably on her public events. Still the director of the Alabama Department of Archives and History, she also continued her work on behalf of Confederate veterans and remained active in literary and historical organizations.[8] But personal loss and increasingly poor health forced her to slow down. Marie outlived her siblings and even her son Thomas Jr., who died in December 1948 at the age of fifty-four after what newspapers reported as "a long illness."[9] Marie was hospitalized following a car accident in January 1955 and returned to the hospital after suffering a fall. Recovery was slow; after thirty-five years as its director, she retired from the Department of Archives and History in 1955. She underwent two surgeries in summer 1957; no longer able to live alone, she moved to the Dunn Rest Home in Selma in August 1957. While she was in Selma, the last of her siblings, youngest brother Henry, died in October 1957. Following a twenty-five-year career in the US Army, Henry was appointed consul to the US embassy in Ottawa and served from 1933 to 1948. He retired in 1948 and lived in Miami, but he moved to Jasper in 1957. He was living at Sunset, the home originally purchased by his father in 1910, when he died.[10] Marie's health continued to decline. She slipped into a coma in February 1958 and died on March 1. She was eighty-nine years old.[11]

By the late 1950s, Tallulah herself was increasingly frail. Years of smoking had contributed to her emphysema. She continued to drink, ate poorly, and took heavy narcotics to deal with insomnia. Her behavior became more erratic. She was lonely and increasingly alone. She continued to work even though her health was declining rapidly. The demands of the stage likewise took their toll. Tallulah performed in summer theater and made her last Broadway appearance in 1964 in Tennessee Williams's *The Milk Train Doesn't Stop Here Anymore*. The play closed after five performances. The following year, despite the numerous illnesses that made her a tremendous risk, she accepted a starring role as an unhinged religious zealot in a British horror film entitled *Fanatic*, which was released in the United States as *Die! Die! My Darling*. In 1967, after receiving encouragement from one of her longtime friends from the theater, she accepted the part of the Black Widow in the popular television series *Batman*, guest starring in two episodes. Throughout the decade she appeared on television talk shows including the *Mike Douglas Show*, the *Merv Griffin Show*, and the *Tonight Show*, as well as on the *Smothers Brothers Comedy Hour*.

In late 1968, Tallulah was hospitalized with the flu, which brought on double pneumonia. She had survived bouts of pneumonia in the past, but now her body was simply too weak. Tallulah Bankhead died in New York City on December 12, 1968. Sister Eugenia and her son Billy were at her bedside. Tallulah was sixty-six years old, the same age as her father had been when he died. It is perhaps fitting that even in death, Tallulah remained apart from her family. She was laid to rest in a cemetery on the eastern shore of Maryland, where Eugenia was living. Eugenia died in 1979. She is buried next to her sister.[12]

Jasper, Alabama, is no longer a locus of political power, but the Bankhead presence is still palpable, and the town's claim on the once-powerful family remains a point of pride. Visitors to the beautiful First United Methodist Church, site of the funerals for John Hollis, Will, and John Jr., can marvel at the spectacular stained-glass dome and view the plaque marking the pew where President Franklin D. Roosevelt sat on that sad day of Will's funeral in 1940. Sunset, home to John Hollis Bankhead and John H. Bankhead Jr., remains in private hands, but from the street, passersby can marvel at the stately building and grounds that once housed a political dynasty. The imposing Bankhead gravesite—the final resting place of John Hollis and Tallulah, their children (minus Marie, who is buried near her husband in Montgomery), their children's spouses, and their grandchildren who died before reaching adulthood—constitutes a serene yet formidable landscape of mourning in Oak Hill Cemetery, the Bankheads' collective epitaphs providing a quiet if brief historical narrative. In 2008, a group of Jasper residents purchased and renovated the brick Colonial Revival home once owned by Will Bankhead. It now serves as a house museum, dedicated to preserving the history of the family and of larger Walker County. But even within this museum, the history of the family is incomplete, its connection to the county, state, region, and nation fragmented and vague. As one moves beyond the center of the town, the memory of the Bankheads begins to fade. Families continue to live in the houses that once made up the original Bankhead subsistence homesteads, but the location lacks a historical marker explaining their innovative New Deal origins.

About an hour's drive west from Jasper is the village of Moscow, birthplace of John Hollis, John Jr., Will, and Henry Bankhead. The home built by John Hollis's father, James Greer Bankhead, in the 1850s, still stands. This is the home where John Hollis spent his boyhood, from where he marched off to war that fateful day in 1861, and to where he returned in 1865. Hidden from the highway by trees, the home is accessible by a gravel road. Placed on the Alabama Historical Commission's "Places in Peril" list, the James Greer Bankhead home has fallen into disrepair. Some of the damage—broken windows, graffiti—is the work of vandals. But time and general neglect are the bigger culprits here. Nature is reclaiming the home. A sapling has broken through the front porch,

Figure E.3. Forest Home, the home of James Greer Bankhead, 2019. Photo by author.

while scrubby bushes and vines encroach on the home from all sides. Vulnerable and decrepit, and almost completely obscured from the road, the house shows the ravages of time. It stands in stark contrast to the power and influence of the people who once lived inside its walls.

Notes

Introduction

1. "John Bankhead—1872–1946," *Newsweek*, June 24, 1946, 27.

2. For clarity, the elder John Hollis Bankhead will be referred to as "John Hollis," while his son will be "John Jr."

3. Ira Katznelson, *Fear Itself: The New Deal and the Origins of Our Time* (New York: W. W. Norton, 2013), 16.

Chapter 1

1. James Bankhead, will, 1799, Union County, South Carolina, Probate Court, Will Book A, 102–5, microfilm reel C2381, South Carolina Department of Archives and History, Columbia; George Bankhead and Elizabeth Bankhead to Daniel McMahan, deed, January 1, 1807, Union County, South Carolina, Register of Mesne Conveyances, Deed Book M, 82–83, microfilm reel C2208, South Carolina Department of Archives and History, Columbia.

2. Thomas D. Clark and John D. W. Guice, *The Old Southwest, 1795–1830: Frontiers in Conflict* (Albuquerque: University of New Mexico Press, 1989), 162, 168, 173.

3. James Graham to Thomas Ruffin, November 9, 1817, in *The Papers of Thomas Ruffin*, vol. 1, ed. Joseph Grégoire de Roulhac Hamilton (Raleigh, NC: Edwards and Broughton, 1918), 198.

4. "Petition to the President and Congress by Intruders on Chickasaw Lands," September 5, 1810, in *The Territorial Papers of the United States*, vol. 6, *The Territory of Mississippi, 1809–1817*, ed. and comp. Clarence Edwin Carter (Washington, DC: Government Printing Office, 1938), 106–8.

5. George Bankhead to John Lynn Henderson, deed, November 25, 1816, York County, South Carolina, Register of Mesne Conveyances, Deed Book H, 349–50, microfilm reel C1470, South Carolina Department of Archives and History, Columbia.

6. US Census Bureau, *1820 Census*, Alabama, population, reprinted in *Alabama Historical Quarterly* 6, no. 3 (Fall 1944), 396–415. In his history of Alabama, Thomas McAdory Owen, son-in-law of John Hollis Bankhead, noted that George Bankhead failed to acquire a clear title to the first piece of property he settled and eventually moved to a new tract some thirty miles south near Crew's Depot in Marion County. Owen, *History of Alabama and Dictionary of Alabama Biography*, vol. 3 (Chicago: S. J. Clarke, 1921), 88–92; Albert Burton Moore, *History of Alabama* (University, AL: University Supply Store, 1934), 132–33.

7. Lamar County Heritage Book Committee, *History of Lamar County, Alabama* (Clanton, AL: Heritage, 2000), 2.

8. Slave data listed in US Census Bureau, *1820 Census*, 409; US Census, *1830 Census*, Alabama, population, F-150, roll 4, pp. 169, 339.

9. Joe Acee, *A History of Lamar County, from 1867 to 1972*, rev. ed. (Vernon, AL: Lamar

Democrat, 1972), 172–74; "Bankhead History Entwines Alabama's," *Birmingham News Age-Herald*, September 9, 1936.

10. "Bankhead History Entwines Alabama's," *Birmingham News Age-Herald*, September 9, 1936; *Index to Compiled Service Records of Volunteers Who Served during the Creek War in Organizations from the State of Alabama* (Washington, DC: National Archives and Records Administration, 1957).

11. Acee, *A History of Lamar County*, 174.

12. Acee, 6.

13. Rose Marie Smith, *Lamar County, Alabama: A History to 1900* (Fulton, MS: n.p., 1987), 55–56.

14. James Greer Bankhead's holdings were probably much larger. Most likely he received an inheritance when his father, George, died in 1847. Unfortunately, local records (including wills) for that period were destroyed by fire.

15. US Census Bureau, *1850 Census*, Schedule 4, Productions of Agriculture, Marion County, Alabama, microfilm W9 reel 210.

16. "James Greer Bankhead Home," National Register of Historic Places Inventory Nomination Form, December 12, 1974, folder 32, box SG6874, Public Information Subject File Collection, Alabama Department of Archives and History (hereafter ADAH), Montgomery; also see Marie Bankhead Owen (hereafter MBO) to John Hollis Bankhead Jr. (hereafter JHBjr), April 23, 1941, folder 2, box 1, John Hollis Bankhead Jr. Papers (hereafter JHBjrP), ADAH.

17. US Census Bureau, *1860 Census*, Schedule 4, Productions of Agriculture, Marion County, Alabama, accessed through ancestry.com.

18. Noxubee County Tax Rolls, 1853, box 3448, pp. 53, 62, images 57 and 64; Noxubee County Tax Rolls, 1861, pp. 61, 63, 69; US Census Bureau, *1860 Census*, Slave Schedule, District 2, Noxubee County, Mississippi, p. 19.

19. William Warren Rogers et al., *Alabama: The History of a Deep South State* (Tuscaloosa: University of Alabama Press, 1994), 96.

20. Rogers et al., 170.

21. Rogers et al., 182.

22. Joseph W. Danielson, *War's Desolating Scourge: The Union's Occupation of North Alabama* (Lawrence: University Press of Kansas, 2012), 6.

23. Danielson, 7–8.

24. James M. McPherson, *Battle Cry of Freedom: The Civil War Era* (New York: Oxford University Press, 1988), 318.

25. Rogers et al., *Alabama*, 206.

26. Smith, *Lamar County*, 74, 79.

27. Acee, *A History of Lamar County*, 2.

28. James Greer Family Bible, transcribed, "Bankhead Family Bible" file, Carl Elliot Regional Library, Jasper, AL.

29. ADAH, *Census or Enumeration of Confederate Soldiers Residing in Alabama, 1907–1908* (Montgomery: ADAH, 1908), "John Hollis Bankhead."

30. Rogers et al., *Alabama*, 198.

31. McPherson, *Battle Cry of Freedom*, 332.

32. James Edmond Saunders, *Early Settlers of Alabama*, pt. 1 (Tuscaloosa, AL: M. Milo McEllhiney, 1963), 182.

33. "The Diary of Corporal Westwood Wallace James," *Civil War Illustrated*, October 1978, 35, 37, 39.

34. "The Diary of Corporal Westwood Wallace James," 40.

35. Saunders, *Early Settlers of Alabama*, pt. 1, 193.

36. "Capt. Bankhead and his Confederate War Record," typescript, n.d., folder 1, box 1, John Hollis Bankhead Papers (hereafter JHBP), ADAH.

37. Hugh W. Roberts, "Bankhead, for First Time, Revisits Scenes of Carnage—Senator Sees Battlefield Where 52 Years Ago, Wounded, He Staggered from Scene with Wounded Comrade

on His Back," n.p., May 12, 1915, in William Brockman Bankhead (hereafter WBB) scrapbook, 1916–23, p. 34, box 52, William Brockman Bankhead Papers (hereafter WBBP), ADAH.

38. "Inspection Report," September 14, 1864, and "Inspection Report," August 25, 1864, John H. Bankhead Service Record, Confederate Service Records, ADAH.

39. Major General C. H. Bridges, adjutant general's office, Department of War, "Statement of the Military Service of John H. Bankhead," November 29, 1932, Confederate Service Records, reel 2, ADAH.

40. *Washington Post*, March 6, 1917.

41. Sarah Woolfolk Wiggins, *The Scalawag in Alabama Politics, 1865–1881* (Tuscaloosa: University of Alabama Press, 1977), 7; Henry M. McKiven, "Thomas H. Watts, 1863–1865," in *Alabama Governors: A Political History of the State*, ed. Samuel L. Webb and Margaret E. Armbrester (Tuscaloosa: University of Alabama Press, 2001), 73–76. For a comprehensive examination of Alabama during the Civil War, see Christopher Lyle McIlwain, *Civil War Alabama* (Tuscaloosa: University of Alabama Press, 2016).

42. Rogers et al., *Alabama*, 226.

43. ADAH, *Census or Enumeration of Confederate Soldiers Residing in Alabama, 1907–1908*, "John Hollis Bankhead."

44. MBO to Orline A. Shipman, November 18, 1930, folder 2, box 1, JHBjrP; *Jasper (AL) Mountain Eagle*, June 10, 1908.

Chapter 2

1. Michael W. Fitzgerald, *Reconstruction in Alabama: From Civil War to Redemption in the Cotton South* (Baton Rouge: Louisiana State University Press, 2017), 48–49, 80.

2. *Montgomery Advertiser*, July 26, 1865; Dan T. Carter, *When the War Was Over: The Failure of Self-Reconstruction in the South, 1865–1867* (Baton Rouge: Louisiana State University Press, 1985), 12–15.

3. Jason J. Battles, "Labor, Law, and the Freedmen's Bureau in Alabama, 1865–1867," in *The Yellowhammer War: The Civil War and Reconstruction in Alabama*, ed. Kenneth W. Noe (Tuscaloosa: University of Alabama Press, 2013), 242.

4. Carter, *When the War Was Over*, 16.

5. *Montgomery Advertiser*, July 26, 1865.

6. *Journal of the Session of 1865–66 of the House of Representatives of the State of Alabama* (Montgomery, AL: Reid and Screws, 1866), 14, 15, 19.

7. Carter, *When the War Was Over*, 24.

8. Sarah Woolfolk Wiggins, *The Scalawag in Alabama Politics, 1865–1881* (Tuscaloosa: University of Alabama Press, 1977), 9; Fitzgerald, *Reconstruction in Alabama*, 60.

9. Quoted in Carter, *When the War Was Over*, 24.

10. William Warren Rogers et al., *Alabama: The History of a Deep South State* (Tuscaloosa: University of Alabama Press, 1994), 230.

11. William G. Bankhead, September 9, 1865, Case Files of Applications from Former Confederates for Presidential Pardons, 1865–1867, Records of the Adjutant Generals Office, 1780s–1917, Record Group 94, National Archives and Records Administration, accessed on ancestry.com.

12. Carter, *When the War Was Over*, 27.

13. Sarah Woolfolk Wiggins, "Lewis E. Parsons, June–December 1865," in *Alabama Governors: A Political History of the State*, ed. Samuel L. Webb and Margaret E. Armbrester (Tuscaloosa: University of Alabama Press, 2001), 77; Fitzgerald, *Reconstruction in Alabama*, 63.

14. Albert Burton Moore, *History of Alabama* (University, AL: University Supply Store, 1934), 461.

15. Wiggins, "Lewis E. Parsons," 77.

16. Sarah Woolfolk Wiggins, "Lewis Eliphalet Parsons," *Encyclopedia of Alabama*, updated September 15, 2015, http://encyclopediaofalabama.org.

17. Margaret M. Storey, *Loyalty and Loss: Alabama's Unionists in the Civil War and Reconstruction* (Baton Rouge: Louisiana State University Press, 2004), 174–75.

18. Malcolm Cook McMillan, *Constitutional Development in Alabama, 1798–1901: A Study in Politics, the Negro, and Sectionalism* (Chapel Hill: University of North Carolina Press, 1955), 91; *Montgomery Advertiser*, August 29, 1865.

19. McMillan, *Constitutional Development in Alabama*, 91.

20. Carter, *When the War Was Over*, 56.

21. Storey, *Loyalty and Loss*, 175.

22. McMillan, *Constitutional Development in Alabama*, 92.

23. McMillan, 92.

24. Fitzgerald, *Reconstruction in Alabama*, 71.

25. Storey, *Loyalty and Loss*, 176–77.

26. Quoted in Fitzgerald, *Reconstruction in Alabama*, 73.

27. McMillan, *Constitutional Development in Alabama*, 102.

28. McMillan, 103.

29. McMillan, 97.

30. McMillan, 97.

31. McMillan, 105.

32. McMillan, 109.

33. Reprinted in the *Montgomery Advertiser*, July 26, 1865.

34. *Montgomery Advertiser*, August 5, 1865.

35. See, for example, articles in *Montgomery Advertiser*, August 3 and 4, 1865.

36. *Montgomery Advertiser*, August 3, 1865.

37. *Montgomery Advertiser*, August 3, 1865.

38. Wiggins, *The Scalawag in Alabama Politics*, 11.

39. Wiggins, 16.

40. Wiggins, 14.

41. William Warren Rogers Jr., "Robert M. Patton, December 1865–March 1867," in Webb and Armbrester, *Alabama Governors*, 81.

42. J. Mills Thornton, "Alabama's Presidential Reconstruction Legislature," in *A Political Nation: New Directions in Mid-Nineteenth-Century American Political History*, ed. Gary W. Gallagher and Rachel A. Sheldon (Charlottesville: University of Virginia Press, 2012), 167.

43. Thornton, 169, 168.

44. Wiggins, *The Scalawag in Alabama Politics*, 14.

45. Wiggins, 13–14.

46. Thornton, "Alabama's Presidential Reconstruction Legislature," 174; *Journal of the Session of 1865–66 of the House of Representatives of the State of Alabama*, 85.

47. *Journal of the Session of 1865–66 of the House of Representatives of the State of Alabama*, 98. The text of the law continued: "And they shall be competent to testify only in open court, and only in cases in which freedmen, free negroes and mulattoes are parties, either plaintiff or defendant, and in civil and criminal cases, for injuries in the persons and property of freedmen, free negroes and mulattoes, and in all cases, civil or criminal, in which a freedman, free negro or mulatto is a witness against a white person, or a white person against a freedman, free negro or mulatto, the parties shall be competent witnesses, and neither interest in the question or suit, nor marriage, shall disqualify any witness from testifying in open court."

48. Mary Ellen Curtin, *Black Prisoners and Their World: Alabama, 1865–1900* (Charlottesville: University of Virginia Press, 2000), 45.

49. Rogers et al., *Alabama*, 238.

50. Theodore Brantner Wilson, *The Black Codes of the South* (University: University of Alabama Press, 1965), 76.

51. Thornton, "Alabama's Presidential Reconstruction Legislature," 173–79.

52. Wiggins, *The Scalawag in Alabama Politics*, 18.

53. Wedding photo, box 92, folder 6, JHBP.

54. William Everett Brockman, *The Brockman Scrapbook: Bell, Bledsoe, Brockman, Burrus, Dickson, James, Pedan, Putman, Sims, Tatum, Woolfolk and Related Families* (Minneapolis, MN: Midland National Bank, 1952), 269.

55. John Hollis Bankhead (hereafter JHB) to George W. Dansby, August 16, 1912, folder 2, box 17, JHBP; Mirium Austin Lock to Carter Manasco, February 18, 1938, folder 11, box 3, WBBP; photograph in unidentified news clipping, c. November 1916, WBB scrapbook, box 52, WBBP.

56. Rogers et al., *Alabama*, 241.

57. *Journal of the Session of 1866–67, House of Representatives of the State of Alabama* (Montgomery, AL: Reid and Screws, 1867), 25–26.

58. In a written address to the legislators, Patton laid out his objections. "A careful examination would show that the words, 'nor shall any state deprive any person,' which are contained in the first section, are of vast, if not dangerous import. It would enlarge the judicial powers of the General Government to such gigantic dimensions as would not only overshadow and weaken the authority and influence of the state courts, but might possibly reduce them to a complete nullity." The proposed amendment's second section "would make a radical change in the representative system of the General Government." According to Patton, "The practical effect of this section upon the Southern states would be a loss of nearly half of the representatives to which they are now entitled, if they should not extend the elective franchise to the negroes." He found the third section of the proposed amendment to be even more egregious. "It establishes a test of eligibility for office, both Federal and State, which is not only unnecessarily and unjustly proscriptive, but which might possibly lead to the most ruinous consequences." He saw absolutely no need for another loyalty test. "The officials chosen since the war to conduct the operations of the non-represented States, have had numerous and embarrassing difficulties to contend with. But amidst all their discouraging embarrassments, they have firmly and faithfully discharged their public duties in strict harmony with the Constitution and laws of the United States." For these multiple reasons, Patton concluded, "I am decidedly of the opinion that this amendment should not be ratified." *Journal of the Session of 1866–67, House of Representatives of the State of Alabama*, 33–36.

59. *Journal of the Session of 1866–67, House of Representatives of the State of Alabama*, December 7, 1866, 198–99, 213.

60. Joe Acee, *A History of Lamar County, from 1867 to 1972*, rev. ed. (Vernon, AL: Lamar Democrat, 1972), 2.

61. Rose Marie Smith, *Lamar County, Alabama: A History to 1900* (Fulton, MS: n.p., 1987), 94–95.

62. *Journal of the Session of 1866–1867, of the House of Representatives of the State of Alabama*, 249–320; *Montgomery Advertiser*, January 30, 1867; Smith, *Lamar County*, 99.

63. "Bankhead History Entwines Alabama's," *Birmingham News Age-Herald*, September 6, 1936.

64. William Brockman Bankhead, "The Autobiography of Wm. B. Bankhead," 1895, Washington, DC, folder 4, box 1, WBBP.

65. "Bankhead History Entwines Alabama's," *Birmingham News Age-Herald*, September 6, 1936.

66. Emmet R. Calhoun, "Recollections," unidentified news clipping, n.d., folder 6, box 15, JHBJrP; Jack Brien Key, "John H. Bankhead, Jr.: Creative Conservative" (PhD diss., Johns Hopkins University, 1964), 9.

67. Bankhead, "The Autobiography of Wm. B. Bankhead."

68. Bankhead Campaign Committee, "Honorable John H. Bankhead, His Public Service, Career as a Citizen, and His Platform as a Candidate for the Alternate Nomination to the U.S. Senate, in the State Democratic Primary, August Twenty-Seventh, 1906," July 30, 1906, folder 1, box 1, JHBP.

69. *Vernon (AL) Pioneer*, October 31, 1877. Bankhead lists his occupation as "clerk in a store" in the 1870 federal census. Since the 1877 announcement in the *Vernon Pioneer* is of a new position, it is reasonable to assume that he worked in another retail establishment prior to 1877. Also see Key, "John H. Bankhead, Jr.," 10.

70. *New York Times*, October 30, 1883; *Vernon (AL) Pioneer*, September 5, 1879. In 1880, Bankhead listed his occupation as "commercial traveler." See US Census Bureau, *1880 Census*, Lamar County, Alabama, roll 17, p. 603B.

71. William Brockman Bankhead, "The Autobiography of William B. Bankhead," 1895, Washington, DC, folder 4, box 1, WBBP.

72. *Vernon (AL) Clipper*, December 12, 1879. Cobb, who was deeply entrenched with the industrial and railroad interests in the state, was elected governor in 1878. Robert David Ward, "Rufus W. Cobb," *Encyclopedia of Alabama*, updated November 13, 2016, http://encyclopediaof alabama.org.

73. *Montgomery Advertiser*, November 9, 1866.

74. McMillan, *Constitutional Development in Alabama*, 110.

75. McMillan, 113. Some white men were disfranchised, while others refused to vote as a form of protest.

76. The state Republican Party was formed in June 1867. Wiggins, *The Scalawag in Alabama Politics*, 23, 25.

77. Wiggins, x.

78. Wiggins, 28–29.

79. Rogers et al., *Alabama*, 245.

80. Fitzgerald, *Reconstruction in Alabama*, 170–71.

81. In 1944, Bankhead's son and US senator John H. Bankhead Jr. stated on the floor of the US Senate that his father had joined the Klan during Reconstruction to "protect white supremacy" and to "protect women and children." 90 Cong. Rec. S4304 (1944).

82. Samuel L. Webb, *Two-Party Politics in the One-Party South: Alabama's Hill Country, 1874–1920* (Tuscaloosa: University of Alabama Press, 1997), 32.

83. *Vernon (AL) Clipper*, January 16, 1880; also see MBO to B. B. Box, February 21, 1934, Owen Correspondence, 1920–36, box 13, Marie Bankhead Owen Papers (hereafter MBOP), ADAH. In this letter, Marie dates the family's move to Vernon to 1878 or 1879.

84. Luke Pryor to Rufus W. Cobb, August 30, 1879; W. B. Wood to Rufus W. Cobb, September 8, 1880; "The undersigned citizens of Jefferson County" to Rufus W. Cobb, September 1880; Undersigned Citizens of Fayette County to Rufus W. Cobb, September 11, 1880; S. A. M. Wood to Rufus W. Cobb, September 9, 1880; all in reel 26, Appointment Requests, Rufus Cobb Papers, SG24885, ADAH; and see Elbert L. Watson, "Luke Pryor," *Encyclopedia of Alabama*, updated November 22, 2010, http://encyclopediaofalabama.org.

85. *Vernon (AL) Clipper*, December 17, 1881.

86. Curtin, *Black Prisoners and Their World*, 63; Robert David Ward and William Warren Rogers, *Convicts, Coal, and the Banner Mine Tragedy* (Tuscaloosa: University of Alabama Press, 1987), 27–29; Matthew J. Mancini, *One Dies, Get Another: Convict Leasing in the American South, 1866–1928* (Columbia: University of South Carolina Press, 1996), 99.

87. Curtin, *Black Prisoners and Their World*, 46.

88. Address of Governor, November 12, 1866, *Records of the States of the United States: A Microfilm Collection*, State of Alabama, reel 5; *Journal of the Session of 1866–67, House of Representatives of the State of Alabama*, 17–20 (emphasis added).

89. Mancini, *One Dies, Get Another*, 100–101; Curtin, *Black Prisoners and Their World*, 63.

90. Michael W. Fitzgerald, "William Hugh Smith," in Webb and Armbrester, *Alabama Governors*, 89.

91. Michael W. Fitzgerald, "Robert B. Lindsay," in Webb and Armbrester, *Alabama Governors*, 91–92.

92. William Warren Rogers, "George S. Houston," in Webb and Armbrester, *Alabama*

Governors, 103. Houston appointed a commission that ultimately decided to refinance the debt that saved the state's credit rating. Still, according to historian Mary Ellen Curtin, "Houston's determination to pay off railroad bondholders, coupled with a state constitution that severely limited state taxing authority, placed Alabama in a fiscal squeeze." Curtin, *Black Prisoners and Their World*, 65. Curtin sites section 4536, Penal Code of 1876, which states that the warden of the penitentiary is empowered "to employ or hire out the convicts, to be used without the walls of the penitentiary, either upon public or private work within the state; all contracts of hiring to be approved by the governor; but such hiring shall not be for a longer term than five years."

93. Ward and Rogers, *Convicts, Coal, and the Banner Mine Tragedy*, 31–32; Mancini, *One Dies, Get Another*, 102.

94. Mancini, *One Dies, Get Another*, 102.

95. Curtin, *Black Prisoners and Their World*, 69–70.

96. Ward and Rogers, *Convicts, Coal, and the Banner Mine Tragedy*, 33; *Report of the Joint Committee to Inquire into the Treatment of Convicts Employed in the Mines, and on Convict Farms, and in Any Other Place in the State* (Montgomery, AL: Allred and Beers, 1881), 4.

97. Bankhead, "The Autobiography of Wm. B. Bankhead."

98. Bankhead.

99. "Warden's Report," in *Biennial Report of the Inspectors of the Alabama Penitentiary, from September 30, 1880, to September 30, 1882* (Montgomery, AL: Allred and Beers, 1882), 12; Comer v. Bankhead, Application for Mandamus to Warden of Penitentiary, 70 Ala. 136 (1881); Comer v. Bankhead, Bill in Equity against Warden of State Penitentiary, for Specific Performance of Contract for Hire of Convicts, 70 Ala. 493 (1881); Curtin, *Black Prisoners and Their World*, 83; on the Bankheads' living conditions, see Key, "John H. Bankhead, Jr.," 11.

100. James Sanders Day, *Diamonds in the Rough: A History of Alabama's Cahaba Coal Field* (Tuscaloosa: University of Alabama Press, 2013), 98.

101. *Biennial Report of the Inspectors of the Alabama Penitentiary, from September 30, 1880, to September 30, 1882*, 4, 12.

102. See "Warden's Report," in *Biennial Report*, 14.

103. See "Physician's Report," in *Biennial Report*, 36–38.

104. *Biennial Report of the Inspectors of the Alabama Penitentiary to the Governor, 1884* (Montgomery, AL: W. D. Brown, 1884), 4; JHB to Dr. R. J. Thornton, April 17, 1882, Administrative Correspondence, Outgoing Letters, July 1881–May 1885, Letterpress copybook, Alabama Board of Inspectors of Convicts, SG18154, ADAH.

105. See "Warden's Report," in *Biennial Report of the Inspectors of the Alabama Penitentiary, from September 30, 1880, to September 30, 1882*, 15.

106. "Warden's Report," 15.

107. "Warden's Report," 21, 22.

108. "Warden's Report," 21.

109. Curtin, *Black Prisoners and Their World*, 77–78; Ward and Rogers, *Convicts, Coal, and the Banner Mine Tragedy*, 35–36.

110. *Biennial Report of the Inspectors of the Alabama Penitentiary to the Governor, 1884*, 74.

111. *Biennial Report*, 70.

112. *Biennial Report*, 5, 7.

113. *Biennial Report*, 11.

114. *Biennial Report*, 11.

115. *Biennial Report*, 72.

116. *Biennial Report*, 12.

117. *Biennial Report*, 21.

118. *Biennial Report*, 22.

119. *Biennial Report*, 27.

120. *Biennial Report*, 23.

121. *Biennial Report*, 7.

122. *Biennial Report*, 9.

123. *Biennial Report*, 33, 36, 39.

124. *Fayette (AL) Banner*, January 7, 1904.

125. *First Biennial Report of the Inspectors of Convicts to the Governor, from October 1, 1884, to October 1, 1886* (Montgomery, AL: Barrett, 1886), 3–4.

Chapter 3

1. William Brockman Bankhead, "The Autobiography of Wm. B. Bankhead," 1895, Washington, DC, folder 4, box 1, WBBP.

2. MBO, diary, February 6, 8, and 25, 1893, box 1, MBOP.

3. Herbert Moses Newell Jr. and Jeanie Patterson Newell, *History of Fayette County, Alabama* (Fayette, AL: Newell Offset, 1960), 18.

4. Newell and Newell, 19.

5. The Fayette Male and Female Institute was the county's first public school. It was incorporated in 1884. *Fayette (AL) Sentinel*, October 26, 1894.

6. "J. H. Bankhead," in F. W. Teeple and A. Davis Smith, *Jefferson County and Birmingham, Alabama: Historical and Biographical, 1887* (Birmingham, AL: Teeple and Smith, 1887), 443.

7. Recollections of Leon Dodds, included in Newell and Newell, *History of Fayette County, Alabama*, 22–23; *Fayette (AL) Sentinel*, February 14, 1898. Records in the Fayette County Court of Probate list numerous land purchases by Bankhead and Harkins. See Deed Books, Fayette County, Alabama, vol. 10, p. 425; vol. 13, p. 322; vol. 14, pp. 1, 18, 201, 318.

8. Jack Brien Key, "John H. Bankhead, Jr.: Creative Conservative" (PhD diss., Johns Hopkins University, 1964), 14.

9. J. R. Galloway to JHB, February 26, 1910, folder 13, box 2, JHBP; JHB to J. M. Salter, March 28, 1914, folder 3, box 20, JHBP; C. A. Beasley to C. B. Hyde, September 16, 1918, folder 4, box 25, JHBP.

10. Rebecca Edwards, *Angels in the Machinery: Gender in American Party Politics from the Civil War to the Progressive Era* (New York: Oxford University Press, 1997), 60.

11. Typescript news story, n.d., folder 6, box 4, WBBP.

12. For an excellent analysis of the robust two-party politics of the hill country, see Samuel L. Webb, *Two-Party Politics in the One-Party South: Alabama's Hill Country, 1874–1920* (Tuscaloosa: University of Alabama Press, 1997).

13. *Jasper (AL) Mountain Eagle*, September 29, 1886.

14. Margaret Shirley Koster, "Congressional Career of John Hollis Bankhead" (Master's thesis, University of Alabama, 1931), 2.

15. *Jasper (AL) Mountain Eagle*, November 10, 1886; Handwritten election tallies, Sixth Congressional District, folder 12, Election Files, Secretary of State Records, ADAH; Webb, *Two-Party Politics in the One-Party South*, 72–73.

16. Quoted in John W. Reps, *Washington on View: The Nation's Capital since 1790* (Chapel Hill: University of North Carolina Press, 1991), 188.

17. Quoted in Reps, 196.

18. Receipt, March 4, 1898, box 2, JHBP; Receipt, January 31, 1902, box 2, JHBP.

19. JHB to Charles D. Hilles, December 13, 1911, folder 4, box 15, JHBP; JHB to J. P. Tumulty, October 22, 1913, folder 3, box 19, JHBP; JHB to J. P. Tumulty, December 7, 1915, folder 1, box 22, JHBP.

20. See, for example, *Birmingham Age-Herald*, February 3, 1889.

21. A *Birmingham Age-Herald* article from 1893 notes that on a visit from Washington, Bankhead "took up his old quarters at the Florence." *Birmingham Age-Herald*, March 21, 1893; *Fayette (AL) Sentinel*, November 5, 1897.

22. *Birmingham Age-Herald*, August 1, 1897; Tallulah Bankhead, *Tallulah: My Autobiography* (New York: Harper, 1952), 33.

23. *Birmingham Age-Herald*, January 14, 1892.

24. *Montgomery Journal*, reprinted in *Jasper (AL) Mountain Eagle*, April 23, 1913.

25. "Address of Henry Cabot Lodge," in *John Hollis Bankhead (Late a Senator from Alabama), Memorial Addresses Delivered in the Senate and the House of Representatives of the United States*, 66th Cong., 2nd sess. Proceedings in the Senate, December 9, 1920; Proceedings in the House, January 30, 1921 (Washington, DC: Government Printing Office, 1921), 28.

26. JHB to John B. Gaston, February 12, 1918, folder 4, box 24; J. W. Worthington to JHB, October 13, 1908, folder 10, box 8, JHBP; JHB to Sidney Lucas, November 3, 1908, folder 10, box 8, JHBP.

27. Morton Keller, *Affairs of State: Public Life in Late Nineteenth Century America* (Cambridge, MA: Harvard University Press, 1977), 285–87, 300–304, 522.

28. Evans C. Johnson, *Oscar W. Underwood: A Political Biography* (Tuscaloosa: University of Alabama Press, 1980), 49, 62; *Fayette (AL) Sentinel*, December 10, 1898; *Birmingham Age-Herald*, December 20, 1899.

29. *Jasper (AL) Mountain Eagle*, February 21, 1894; January 13, 1909; *Birmingham Age-Herald*, March 30, 1890; February 26, 1891; March 7, 1891.

30. "Who's Who and Why?," unidentified news clipping, c. 1907, in WBB scrapbook, box 52, WBBP.

31. The Warrior coal field encompassed land in Marion, Fayette, Walker, Jefferson, Tuscaloosa, and Winston Counties.

32. Kenneth D. Willis, *The Harnessing of the Black Warrior River* (Tuscaloosa, AL: City of Tuscaloosa, 1989), 7–10.

33. G. Ward Hubbs, *Tuscaloosan: 200 Years in the Making* (Tuscaloosa: University of Alabama Press, 2019), 76.

34. Samuel P. Hays, *Conservation and the Gospel of Efficiency: The Progressive Conservation Movement, 1890–1910* (1959; repr., Pittsburgh, PA: University of Pittsburgh Press, 1999), 5.

35. Hays, 91. For decades, waterway improvement advocates had made the argument that improved water routes would help regulate railroad rates. See Edward Lawrence Pross, "A History of Rivers and Harbors Appropriation Bills, 1866–1933" (PhD diss., Ohio State University, 1938), 51.

36. Pross, "A History of Rivers and Harbors Appropriation Bills," 84.

37. John H. Bankhead, *Speech of Hon. John H. Bankhead of Alabama, in the House of Representatives, June 13, 1906* (Washington, DC: Government Printing Office, 1906), 2.

38. Bankhead, 3.

39. Pross, "A History of Rivers and Harbors Appropriation Bills," 135.

40. *Birmingham Age-Herald*, August 1, 1897.

41. *Tuscaloosa Times*, March 30, 1892.

42. *Birmingham Age-Herald*, December 31, 1897.

43. Harry Chapin Plummer, "The Black Warrior River Lock and Dam," *Scientific American*, March 7, 1914, 152.

44. *Birmingham News*, news clipping, May 1915, folder 2, box 43, JHBP; *Atlanta Constitution*, May 14, 1915.

45. "The Open Warrior Means Big Future for Tuscaloosa," unidentified news clipping, c. May 15, 1915, WBB scrapbook, box 52, WBBP.

46. Quotation of McDuffie speech included in WBB to MBO, January 16, 1925, folder 3, box 2, WBBP.

47. Bankhead, *Speech of Hon. John H. Bankhead of Alabama, in the House of Representatives*, 2.

48. Bankhead, 3.

49. Charles K. McFarland, "The Federal Government and Water Power, 1901–1913: A Legislative Study in the Nascence of Regulation," *Land Economics* 42, no. 4 (November 1966): 442.

50. "Who's Who and Why," c. 1907, WBB scrapbook, box 52, WBBP.

51. McFarland, "The Federal Government and Water Power," 444.

52. Quoted in McFarland, 450.

53. John H. Bankhead, *Speech of Hon. John H. Bankhead, February 10, 1913* (Washington, DC: Government Printing Office, 1913), 3.

54. Jerome G. Kerwin, *Federal Water-Power Legislation* (New York: Columbia University Press, 1926), 160.

55. McFarland, "The Federal Government and Water Power," 451.

56. Kerwin, *Federal Water-Power Legislation*, 250–63.

57. Joseph A. Fry, *Dixie Looks Abroad: The South and U.S. Foreign Relations, 1789–1973* (Baton Rouge: Louisiana State University Press, 2002), 108–9.

58. Congress voted on April 25, 1898. See 31 Cong. Rec. S4244; *Chicago Daily Tribune*, April 14 and 19, 1898; *Washington Post*, April 26, 1898.

59. *Jasper (AL) Mountain Eagle*, November 2, 1898.

60. *Birmingham News Age-Herald*, December 7, 1930. Ward Seminary would eventually become Ward-Belmont and is today Belmont University.

61. Notation by MBO on back of photograph of Prairie Lawn, in MBO genealogy folder, box 13, MBOP.

62. Mother to WBB, June 29, 1900, folder 1, box 2, WBBP.

63. *Ward Seminary Bulletin, 1885–86*, p. 5, University Archives, Lila D. Bunch Library, Belmont University, Nashville, TN.

64. *Birmingham Age-Herald*, news clipping, n.d., WBB scrapbook, box 75, WPPB; MBO diary, January 2, 1893, box 1, MBOP.

65. *Jasper (AL) Mountain Eagle*, April 19, 1893; James F. Doster, "Thomas McAdory Owen Sr.," in *Keepers of the Past*, ed. Clifford L. Lord (Chapel Hill: University of North Carolina Press, 1965), 97.

66. Thomas McAdory Owen (hereafter TMO) to JHB, December 13, 1892, Letterbook, 1888–97, pp. 218–19, folder 3, box 2, Thomas McAdory Owen Papers (hereafter TMOP), ADAH.

67. MBO diary, January 1 and 4, 1893, box 1, MBOP; *Birmingham Age-Herald*, March 13, 1893.

68. MBO diary, 1893, box 1, MBOP.

69. MBO diary, undated news clipping.

70. MBO diary, January 6, 1893.

71. MBO diary, January 4, 1893.

72. MBO diary, January 6, 1893.

73. MBO diary, January 30, 1893.

74. MBO diary, February 26, 1893.

75. MBO diary, January 24, 1893.

76. MBO diary, February 26, March 8, and April 8, 1893.

77. MBO diary, March 11, 1893.

78. MBO diary, February 16, 1893.

79. MBO diary, January 2, 1893.

80. MBO diary, March 25, 1893.

81. MBO diary, January 21, 1893.

82. MBO diary, February 19, 1893.

83. TMO to JHBjr, February 24, 1893, Letterbook 1888–97, pp. 224–25, folder 3, box 2, TMOP.

84. MBO diary, February 23, 1893, box 1, MBOP.

85. MBO diary, March 2, 1893.

86. MBO diary, March 8, 1893.

87. MBO diary, March 12, 1893.

88. TMO to Mother, May 6, 1893, Letterbook, 1888–97, p. 263, folder 3, box 2, TMOP.

89. MBO diary, March 17, 1893, box 1, MBOP.

90. TMO to Louise Perry, April 8, 1893, Letterbook, 1888–97, p. 257, folder 3, box 2, TMOP; MBO diary, April 12, 1893, box 1, MBOP; *Bessemer (AL) Herald-Journal*, April 13, 1893.

91. MBO diary, April 30, 1893, box 1, MBOP.

92. TMO to Mother, May 6, 1893, Letterbook, 1888–97, p. 262, folder 3, box 2, TMOP.

93. TMO to Captain, August 26, 1893, Letterbook, 1888–97, p. 299, folder 3, box 2, TMOP; TMO to JHB, September 5, 1893, Letterbook, 1888–97, p. 315, folder 3, box 2, TMOP; MBO diary, November 11, 1893, box 1, MBOP; "Thomas McAdory Owen Jr.," in *The Story of Alabama: A History of the State*, by Marie Bankhead Owen, vol. 5, part 2, *Personal and Family History* (New York: Lewis Historical, 1949), 1436.

94. See box 1, TMOP; Doster, "Thomas McAdory Owen Sr.," in Lord, *Keepers of the Past*, 98.

95. See box 1, TMOP, for solicitation letters to various agencies and journals.

96. TMO to Mother, May 6, 1893, Letterbook, 1888–97, p. 263, folder 3, box 2, TMOP.

97. MBO diary, May 7, 1893, box 1, MBOP.

98. TMO to WBB, May 29, 1894, Letterbook, 1893–97, p. 198, folder 3, box 2, TMOP; TMO to WBB, March 6, 1896, Letterbook, 1893–97, p. 390, folder 4, box 2, TMOP.

99. TMO to WBB, May 29, 1894, Letterbook, 1893–97, p. 198, folder 4, box 2, TMOP; TMO to Lewis [*sic*] W. Turpin (in DC), June 15, 1894, Letterbook, 1893–97, p. 208, folder 4, box 2, TMOP.

100. TMO to Father, October 3, 1894, Letterbook, 1893–97, p. 234–35, folder 4, box 2, TMOP.

101. Mama to "My Darling Precious Son," April 12, 1917, WBB scrapbook, box 51, WBBP; *Birmingham Age-Herald*, December 7, 1930.

102. *Boston Globe*, news clipping, c. March 1939, WBB scrapbook, box 69, WBBP.

103. Bankhead, "The Autobiography of Wm. B. Bankhead."

104. "Memorandum for Biographical Sketch of W. B. Bankhead," c. May 1913, folder 7, box 4, WBBP.

105. *Montgomery Advertiser*, January 18, 1942.

106. TMO to WBB, August 30, 1893, Letterbook, 1888–97, folder 3, box 2, TMOP.

107. Key, "John H. Bankhead, Jr.," 19; see also "Radio Speech by John H. Bankhead," November 3, 1930, folder 10, box 3, JHBjrP.

108. *Birmingham Age-Herald*, June 30, 1893; William B. Bankhead, "Impressions of Washington, 1893–94," unpublished manuscript, box 1, WBBP.

109. Bankhead, "The Autobiography of Wm. B. Bankhead."

110. Walker County Heritage Book Committee, *The Heritage of Walker County, Alabama* (Clanton, AL: Heritage, 1999), 14.

111. John Martin Dombhart, *History of Walker County: Its Towns and Its People* (Thornton, AR: Cayce, 1937; repr., Greenville, SC: Southern Historical Press, 2002), 67.

112. *Birmingham Age-Herald*, September 11, 1895.

113. *Montgomery Advertiser*, November 14, 1930. John and Musa became engaged during 1893.

114. *Birmingham Age-Herald*, December 7, 1930.

115. Key, "John H. Bankhead, Jr.," 22.

116. *Jasper (AL) Mountain Eagle*, December 12, 1898.

117. *Birmingham News Age-Herald*, January 6, 1946.

118. *Jasper (AL) Mountain Eagle*, October 17, 1899, May 28, 1903, and March 11, 1903; Charles B. Crow, memo prepared for Associated Press, September 2, 1930, folder 1, box 1, JHBjrP.

119. *Jasper (AL) Mountain Eagle*, October 14, 1896.

120. Bankhead, "The Autobiography of Wm. B. Bankhead."

121. Certification, Thomas E. Goodwin, Clerk of Courts, June 12, 1897, folder 1, box 2, WBBP. This document certifies that Will was admitted to the bar in September 1895; January 7, 1896, WBB Diary, 1896, folder 5, box 1, WBBP.

122. Walter Judson Heacock, "William Brockman Bankhead: A Biography" (PhD diss., University of Wisconsin, 1952), 29.

123. WBB to TMO, October 12, 1897, folder 17, box 1, TMOP.

124. *Birmingham Post*, news clipping, c. 1931, scrapbook 119, box 900, James Thomas Heflin Papers (hereafter JTHP), W. S. Hoole Special Collections Library, University of Alabama,

Tuscaloosa; Heacock, "William Brockman Bankhead," 30; *Jasper (AL) Mountain Eagle*, June 15, 1898.

125. Wayne Flynt, *Alabama in the Twentieth Century* (Tuscaloosa: University of Alabama Press, 2006), 6.

126. William Warren Rogers et al., *Alabama: The History of a Deep South State* (Tuscaloosa: University of Alabama Press, 1994), 290; Sheldon Hackney, *Populism to Progressivism in Alabama* (Princeton, NJ: Princeton University Press, 1969), 5–6.

127. Hackney, *Populism to Progressivism in Alabama*, 13.

128. Webb, *Two-Party Politics in the One-Party South*, 122.

129. Webb, 33.

130. Rogers et al., *Alabama*, 288; Hackney, *Populism to Progressivism in Alabama*, 47.

131. Flynt, *Alabama in the Twentieth Century*, 5.

132. Bankhead, "Impressions of Washington, 1893–1894."

133. Hackney, *Populism to Progressivism in Alabama*, 22.

134. Harvey H. Jackson, "Alabama Bourbons," *Encyclopedia of Alabama*, updated October 17, 2016, http://encyclopediaofalabama.org.

135. Hackney, *Populism to Progressivism in Alabama*, 51–52, 90.

136. Undated news clipping, c. 1890s, WBB scrapbook, box 75, WBBP; unidentified news clipping, March 23, 1892, WBB scrapbook, box 48, WBBP.

137. Koster, "Congressional Career of John Hollis Bankhead," 16; 23 Cong. Rec. H2446 (1892).

138. Unidentified news clipping, March 23, 1892, WBB scrapbook, box 48, WBBP.

139. Webb, *Two-Party Politics in the One-Party South*, 120–25.

140. *Birmingham Age-Herald*, August 7, 1892.

141. *Birmingham Age-Herald*, September 4, 5, 6, 7, 8, and 9, 1894.

142. *Birmingham Age-Herald*, September 11, 1894.

143. *Birmingham Age-Herald*, September 19, 1894; *Jasper (AL) Mountain Eagle*, September 19, 1894.

144. *Birmingham Age-Herald*, September 23, 1894; *Tuscaloosa Times*, November 21, 1894.

145. *Birmingham Age-Herald*, November 22, 1892; *Jasper (AL) Mountain Eagle*, January 17, 1893; Webb, *Two-Party Politics in the One-Party South*, 111.

146. *Jasper (AL) Mountain Eagle*, February 21, 1894.

147. *Birmingham State Herald*, September 2, 1896.

148. *Jasper (AL) Mountain Eagle*, November 11, 1896.

149. "Untitled Agreement," November 16, 1896, folder 1, box 5, JHBP.

150. Webb, *Two-Party Politics in the One-Party South*, 129.

Chapter 4

1. Michael Perman, *Struggle for Mastery: Disfranchisement in the South, 1888–1908* (Chapel Hill: University of North Carolina Press, 2001).

2. *Jasper (AL) Mountain Eagle*, June 7, 1899.

3. ADAH, *Alabama Official and Statistical Register, 1903* (Montgomery, AL: Brown, 1903), 141–42.

4. Wayne Flynt, *Alabama in the Twentieth Century* (Tuscaloosa: University of Alabama Press, 2006), 9.

5. Malcolm Cook McMillan, *Constitutional Development in Alabama, 1798–1901: A Study in Politics, the Negro, and Sectionalism* (Chapel Hill: University of North Carolina Press, 1955), 349.

6. *Tuscaloosa Gazette*, October 10, 1901.

7. Glenn Feldman, *The Disfranchisement Myth: Poor Whites and Suffrage Restriction in Alabama* (Athens: University of Georgia Press, 2004), 34.

8. *Jasper (AL) Mountain Eagle*, July 31, 1901.

9. JHB to I. H. Aiken, n.d., folder 5, box 18, JHBP; J. S. Guyton to JHB, September 27, 1913, folder 2, box 19, JHBP.

10. JHB to Arthur W. Mitchell, February 9, 1914, folder 2, box 20, JHBP.

11. Perman, *Struggle for Mastery*, 193; McMillan, *Constitutional Development in Alabama*, 350–51.

12. Feldman, *The Disfranchisement Myth*, appendix, table 15; ADAH, *Alabama Official and Statistical Register, 1903*, 142.

13. *Jasper (AL) Mountain Eagle*, August 8, 1902, and January 28, 1903.

14. Charles B. Crow, memo prepared for Associated Press, September 2, 1930, folder 1, box 1, JHBjrP; *Jasper (AL) Mountain Eagle*, January 28, 1903.

15. See *Journal of the House of Representatives of the State of Alabama, Session of 1903* (Montgomery, AL: Brown, 1903), 180, 402, 405, 464, 523–64, 2183–84, 2222–27; *Journal of the Senate of Alabama, Session of 1903* (Montgomery, AL: Brown, 1903), 741, 910, 1201.

16. *Jasper (AL) Mountain Eagle*, April 22, 1908.

17. McMillan, *Constitutional Development in Alabama*, 352.

18. Perman, *Struggle for Mastery*, 193–94.

19. Fred Arthur Bailey, "Mildred Lewis Rutherford and the Patrician Cult of the Old South," *Georgia Historical Quarterly* 78, no. 3 (Fall 1994): 515.

20. Bailey, 535.

21. Glenn Robins, "Lost Cause Motherhood: Southern Women Writers," *Louisiana History: The Journal of the Louisiana Historical Association* 44, no. 3 (Summer 2003), 275–76.

22. Robert J. Jakeman, "Marie Bankhead Owen and the Alabama Department of Archives and History, 1920–1955," *Provenance: Journal of the Society of Georgia Archivists* 21, no. 1 (2003): 39.

23. TMO to Sibly King, June 18, 1895, Letterbook, 1888–97, p. 407, folder 3, box 2, TMOP.

24. TMO to JHB, July 1, 1897, folder 17, box 1, TMOP.

25. TMO to Captain, January 3, 1894, Letterbook, 1888–97, pp. 390–93, folder 3, box 2, TMOP.

26. TMO to Mother, May 25, 1895, Letterbook, 1888–97, p. 400, folder 3, box 2, TMOP; TMO to Clay Jones, July 17, 1895, Letterbook, 1888–97, p. 410, folder 3, box 2, TMOP; TMO to Clay Jones, Letterbook, 1888–97, p. 412, folder 3, box 2, TMOP.

27. TMO to Captain, January 3, 1894, Letterbook, 1888–97, p. 390–93, folder 3, box 2, TMOP.

28. TMO to B. C. "Clay" Jones, May 25, 1895, Letterbook, 1888–97, p. 402, folder 3, box 2, TMOP.

29. TMO to Washington Real Estate Company, December 14, 1894, Letterbook, 1893–97, p. 277, folder 4, box 2, TMOP.

30. TMO to Father, October 3, 1894, Letterbook, 1893–97, p. 230, folder 4, box 2, TMOP.

31. See TMO to M. H. Crittenden, September 29, 1894, Letterbook, 1893–97, p. 277, folder 4, box 2, TMOP; TMO to Alabama National Bank, January 2, 1785, Letterbook, 1893–97, p. 290, folder 4, box 2, TMOP; TMO to P. J. McAdory, February 1, 1895, Letterbook, 1893–97, p. 308, folder 4, box 2, TMOP; TMO to C. F. Libbie and Co., November 4, 1895, Letterbook, 1893–97, p. 366, folder 4, box 2, TMOP; TMO to WBB, March 6, 1896, Letterbook, 1893–97, p. 390, folder 4, box 2, TMOP.

32. TMO to Sibly King, June 18, 1895, Letterbook, 1888–97, p. 405, folder 3, box 2, TMOP.

33. TMO to E. H. Owen, June 11, 1895, Letterbook, 1888–97, p. 405, folder 3, box 2, TMOP.

34. Wendell H. Stephenson, "Some Pioneer Alabama Historians: III. Thomas M. Owen," *Alabama Review* 2 (January 1949): 46.

35. ADAH, *Alabama Official and Statistical Register, 1903*, 17.

36. Thomas McAdory Owen Jr., "My Father—Thomas McAdory Owen," handwritten manuscript, n.d., folder 5, box 1, TMOP.

37. TMO to Chap. Cory (in Montgomery), February 17, 1897, Letterbook, 1888–97, p. 445, folder 3, box 2, TMOP.

38. TMO to William Richardson, January 25, 1897, Letterbook, 1888–97, p. 439, folder 3, box 2, TMOP; TMO to Willis C. Clarke, January 25, 1897, Letterbook, 1888–97, p. 440–41, folder 3, box 2, TMOP; TMO to Major John H. Caldwell, February 4, 1897, Letterbook, 1888–97, p. 442, folder 3, box 2, TMOP.

39. TMO to William Richardson, June 2, 1897, Letterbook, 1888–97, p. 494–95, folder 3, box 2, TMOP.

40. TMO to E. W. Barrett, editor of the *Birmingham Age-Herald*, August 10, 1897, Letterbook, 1893–97, p. 484, folder 4, box 2, TMOP.

41. WBB to TMO, October 12, 1897, folder 17, box 1, TMOP.

42. MBO to Mrs. Killingsworth, December 4, 1922, Women's Clubs 1922 file, box 6, MBOP; *Fayette (AL) Sentinel*, February 4, 1898; TMO to JHB, September 26, 1898, folder 17, box 1, TMOP.

43. Biography of Thomas M. Owen, in ADAH, *Alabama Official and Statistical Register, 1903*, 16–17.

44. MBO to Will and Gene, October 26, 1900, personal file, box 1, MBOP. The side effects of calomel could be dangerous, especially for children.

45. Mother to MBO, October 28, 1900, box 1, MBOP.

46. Alabama Historical Society, "Announcement," 1898–99, Alabama Collection, W. S. Hoole Special Collections Library.

47. Alden N. Monroe, "Thomas Owen and the Founding of the Alabama Department of Archives and History," *Provenance: Journal of the Society of Georgia Archivists* 21, no. 1 (January 2003): 31.

48. Thomas C. McCorvey to TMO, January 18, 1898, folder 18, box 1, TMOP.

49. "Act Creating the Alabama History Commission," in *Report of the Alabama History Commission to the Governor of Alabama, December 1, 1900*, ed. Thomas McAdory Owen, vol. 1 (Montgomery, AL: Brown, 1901), 20–21; Alden N. Monroe, "Thomas M. Owen," *Encyclopedia of Alabama*, updated December 10, 2014, http://encyclopediaofalabama.org.

50. W. Fitzhugh Brundage, *The Southern Past: A Clash of Race and Memory* (Cambridge, MA: Belknap Press, 2005), 104.

51. Brundage, 106.

52. Owen, *Report of the Alabama History Commission*, 15.

53. Owen, 296–310.

54. Owen, 36.

55. Owen, 36.

56. Monroe, "Thomas M. Owen."

57. Jakeman, "Marie Bankhead Owen," 36.

58. Jakeman, 37.

59. Stephenson, "Some Pioneer Alabama Historians," 53–55.

60. Monroe, "Thomas Owen and the Founding of the Alabama Department of Archives and History," 22.

61. Thomas McAdory Owen Jr., "My Father—Thomas McAdory Owen," handwritten manuscript, n.d., folder 5, box 1, TMOP.

62. Doster, "Thomas McAdory Owen Sr.," in Lord, *Keepers of the Past*, 104.

63. *Montgomery Advertiser*, July 28, 1901.

64. *Montgomery Advertiser*, August 4, 1901.

65. Stephenson, "Some Pioneer Alabama Historians," 53–55.

66. Monroe, "Thomas Owen and the Founding of the Alabama Department of Archives and History," 34.

67. Jakeman, "Marie Bankhead Owen," 37.

68. Brundage, *The Southern Past*, 117.

69. Stephenson, "Some Pioneer Alabama Historians," 45.

70. John Hollis Bankhead, "The Alabama-Mississippi Boundary," *Transactions of the Alabama Historical Society*, vol. 2, *1897–1898*, ed. Thomas McAdory Owen (Tuscaloosa: Alabama Historical Society, 1898), 90–93.

71. William Robertson Garrett, "The Work of the South in the Building of the United States," in *Transactions of the Alabama Historical Society*, vol. 3, *1898–99*, ed. Thomas McAdory Owen (Tuscaloosa: Alabama Historical Society, 1899), 44–45.

72. William C. Ward, "The Building of the State," in *Transactions of the Alabama Historical Society*, vol. 4, *1899–1903*, ed. Thomas McAdory Owen (Montgomery: Alabama Historical Society, 1904), 64–66.

73. MBO to Montrose Jonas Moses, May 28, 1908, MBO correspondence, 1902–10, box 5, MBOP. This letter is a copy; the original is in the Montrose Jones Moses Papers at Duke University.

74. *Mobile Register*, November 20, 1946.

75. MBO, Talks with Girls, *Montgomery Advertiser*, March 10 and 19, 1911.

76. MBO, Talks with Girls, *Montgomery Advertiser*, March 5, 1911.

77. MBO, Talks with Girls, *Montgomery Advertiser*, March 7, 1911.

78. MBO, Talks with Girls, *Montgomery Advertiser*, March 17, 1911.

79. MBO, Talks with Girls, *Montgomery Advertiser*, July 13, 1911.

80. Karen L. Cox, *Dreaming of Dixie: How the South Was Created in American Popular Culture* (Chapel Hill: University of North Carolina Press, 2011), 3–4.

81. MBO, "The Masked Heart," n.d., unpublished manuscript, box 11, MBOP.

82. MBO, "The Acting Governor," n.d., unpublished manuscript, Alabama Collection, W. S. Hoole Special Collections Library, University of Alabama, Tuscaloosa.

83. Marie Bankhead Owen, *Yvonne of Braithwaite: A Romance of the Mississippi Delta* (Boston: L. C. Page, 1927), 141–42.

84. MBO, "The Acting Governor," 38, 107.

85. Cox, *Dreaming of Dixie*, chapter 5; see also Sarah Gardner, *Reviewing the South: The Literary Marketplace and the Southern Renaissance, 1920–1941* (Cambridge: Cambridge University Press, 2017).

86. Owen, *Yvonne of Braithwaite*, x.

87. Owen, 137.

88. Owen, 138.

89. Owen, 138–39.

90. Owen, 127–28.

91. Owen, 199.

92. Owen, 106.

93. Owen, 109.

94. Owen, 114.

95. G. Ward Hubbs, *Tuscaloosa: 200 Years in the Making* (Tuscaloosa: University of Alabama Press, 2019), 43.

96. Owen, *Yvonne of Braithwaite*, 196.

97. Owen, 202.

98. Owen, 198.

99. Owen, 218.

100. Owen, 222.

101. Walter Judson Heacock, "William Brockman Bankhead: A Biography" (PhD diss., University of Wisconsin, 1952), 30–31; *Huntsville Daily Mercury*, December 6, 1899, and February 6, 1902; *Huntsville Weekly Democrat*, November 21, 1900; *Montgomery Advertiser*, May 11, 1901.

102. Heacock, "William Brockman Bankhead," 32–35; Monroe, "Thomas Owen and the Founding of the Alabama Department of Archives and History," 31.

103. Unidentified news clipping, n.d., WBB scrapbook, box 48, WBBP.

104. "Miss Ada Eugenia Sledge," *Woman's Work*, n.d., WBB scrapbook, box 48, WBBP; Joel Lobenthal, *Tallulah! The Life and Times of a Leading Lady* (New York: HarperCollins, 2004), 5; Tallulah Bankhead, *Tallulah: My Autobiography* (New York: Harper, 1952), 28.

105. Lobenthal, *Tallulah!*, 6.

106. Handwritten note, January 26, 1900, folder 6, box 4, WBBP.

107. Eugenia Sledge to WBB, c. 1899, two letters, folder 1, box 2, WBBP.

108. WBB to Gene, c. 1899, folder 1, box 2, WBBP. Although only a handful of letters between

Will and Gene exist in Bankhead's papers, in one letter he laments, "I have written to you every day, every single day, since I saw you last."

109. Olive Crockett to WBB, April 30, 1937, folder 2, box 3, WBBP.

110. Wedding invitation, folder 1, box 2; Unidentified news clipping, n.d., WBB scrapbook, box 48, WBBP; Lobenthal, *Tallulah!*, 6.

111. Mother to Will and Ada, February 1, 1900, folder 1, box 2, WBBP.

112. Unidentified news clipping, n.d., WBB scrapbook, box 48, WBBP.

113. WBB to TMO, November 22 and 28, 1900, folder 9, box 3, TMOP; MBO to WBB and Gene, c. 1900, folder 9, box 3, WBBP.

114. Torn scrap of letter from Tallulah James Bankhead, n.d., WBB scrapbook, box 52, WBBP.

115. M. A. McAuley to Will and Gene, February 4, 1902, folder 1, box 2, WBBP.

116. WBB, journal entry, February 23, 1921, folder 7, box 1, WBBP.

117. Father to WBB, March 9, 1902, folder 1, box 2, WBBP.

118. Mother to WBB, March 1903, folder 1, box 2, WBBP.

119. Lobenthal, *Tallulah!*, 8.

120. Unidentified news clipping, n.d., WBB scrapbook, box 51, WBBP.

Chapter 5

1. Richard Neil Sheldon, "Richmond Pearson Hobson: The Military Hero as Reformer during the Progressive Era" (PhD diss., University of Arizona, 1970), 72.

2. *Jasper (AL) Mountain Eagle*, December 6, 1904.

3. *Washington Post*, May 19, 1903.

4. Barton Shaw, "The Hobson Craze," *US Naval Institute Proceedings* 102 (February 1976): 54.

5. Sheldon, "Richmond Pearson Hobson," 1–18.

6. Shaw, "The Hobson Craze," 55.

7. Sheldon, "Richmond Pearson Hobson," 19.

8. Jennifer M. Murray, "Richmond Pearson Hobson," *Encyclopedia of Alabama*, updated April 21, 2015, http://encyclopediaofalabama.org; Richard W. Turk, "Richmond Pearson Hobson," *American National Biography Online*, published December 2, 1999, https://anb.org.

9. Thomas McAdory Owen, *History of Alabama and Dictionary of Alabama Biography*, vol. 3 (Chicago: S. J. Clarke, 1921), 821–22.

10. Richmond Pearson Hobson, *The Sinking of the Merrimac: A Personal Narrative of the Adventure in the Harbor of Santiago de Cuba, June 3, 1898, and of the Subsequent Imprisonment of the Survivors* (New York: Century, 1899).

11. Shaw, "The Hobson Craze," 57–58.

12. Henry Austin, *Hobson's Choice: A Poem* (New York: R. F. Fenno, 1898), 11.

13. Sheldon, "Richmond Pearson Hobson," 26.

14. *New York Times*, December 9, 1898.

15. Thomas Adams Upchurch, "John Tyler Morgan," *Encyclopedia of Alabama*, updated May 28, 2014, http://encyclopediaofalabama.org.

16. James M. Hobson to Richmond Pearson Hobson (RPH), March 13, 1900, box 29, congressional file, Richmond P. Hobson Papers (hereafter RPHP), Library of Congress, Washington, DC.

17. Walter E. Pittman Jr., "Navalist and Progressive: The Life of Richmond P. Hobson" (master's thesis, Kansas State University, 1981), 23.

18. Turk, "Richmond Pearson Hobson"; Sheldon, "Richmond Pearson Hobson," 37.

19. Sheldon, "Richmond Pearson Hobson," 40–42.

20. Park Benjamin, "Hobson's Resignation," *Independent*, February 12, 1903, 360.

21. Quoted in Sheldon, "Richmond Pearson Hobson," 43.

22. *Montgomery Advertiser*, March 15, 1903.

23. Sheldon, "Richmond Pearson Hobson," 42.

24. RPH to Grizelda Hull, May 5, 1903, box 29, RPHP.

25. Richmond Pearson Hobson, "Paramount Importance of Immediate Adoption of Progressive Naval Program, January 9, 1904," and "Copy of Letter to Honorable Edmund W. Pettus, Senator from Alabama, December 4, 1904," printed together as a pamphlet, pp. 3, 7, 8; Alabama Pamphlet Collection, folder 40, box 5, ADAH.

26. JHB to TMO, January 16, 1904, folder 2, box 5, JHBP.

27. Sheldon, "Richmond Pearson Hobson," 52.

28. Hobson's request and Bankhead's reply were reprinted side by side. See *Fayette Banner*, February 11, 1904; Bankhead's son-in-law advised Bankhead against debating Hobson. See TMO to JHB, January 14, 1904, folder 2, box 5, JHBP.

29. JHB to TMO, January 16, 1904, folder 2, box 5, JHBP.

30. *Fayette Banner*, February 18, 1904.

31. Sheldon, "Richmond Pearson Hobson," 55–56.

32. *Birmingham Age-Herald*, March 1, 1904.

33. Sheldon, "Richmond Pearson Hobson," 56.

34. *Birmingham Age-Herald*, March 1 and 4, 1904.

35. *Birmingham Age-Herald*, March 1, 1904.

36. Jack Brien Key, "John H. Bankhead, Jr.: Creative Conservative" (PhD diss., Johns Hopkins University, 1964), 25.

37. Kristin L. Hoganson, *Fighting for American Manhood: How Gender Politics Provoked the Spanish-American and Philippine-American Wars* (New Haven, CT: Yale University Press, 1998), 109.

38. *Jasper (AL) Mountain Eagle*, February 20, 1904.

39. "Hobson Bold of the Merrimac," n.d., folder 4, box 5, WBBP. This undated poem was penned on stationery from the US House Committee on Rivers and Harbors. John Hollis Bankhead or perhaps Will Bankhead is the probable author.

40. *Birmingham Age-Herald*, March 2, 1904.

41. *Birmingham Age-Herald*, March 4, 1904; *Montgomery Advertiser*, March 4, 1904.

42. Gail Bederman, *Manliness and Civilization: A Cultural History of Gender and Race in the United States, 1880–1917* (Chicago: University of Chicago Press, 1995), 12.

43. *Montgomery Advertiser*, March 4, 1904.

44. *Jasper (AL) Mountain Eagle*, March 10, 1904.

45. *Birmingham Age-Herald*, March 10, 13, 16, 17, 18, 19, 24, and 26, 1904.

46. *Montgomery Advertiser*, March 14, 1904.

47. Sheldon, "Richmond Pearson Hobson," 65.

48. Sheldon, 71; Certificate of Nomination, April 18, 1904, folder 25, Election Files, Secretary of State Records, ADAH.

49. *Birmingham Age-Herald*, April 15, 1904.

50. Bankhead beat his Republican opponent, S. R. Crumpton, 8,873 votes to 2,718 votes. ADAH, *Alabama Official and Statistical Register, 1907* (Montgomery, AL: Brown, 1907), 236.

51. Pittman, "Navalist and Progressive," 51.

52. RPH to Grizelda Hull, May 28, 1904, box 29, RPHP.

53. RPH to Grizelda Hull, January 10, 1905, box 29, RPHP.

54. RPH to Grizelda Hull, March 28, 1905, box 29, RPHP; *Washington Post*, October 3, 1905.

55. Sheldon Hackney, *Populism to Progressivism in Alabama* (Princeton, NJ: Princeton University Press, 1969), 277.

56. Hackney, 269.

57. Allen W. Jones, "Political Reform and Party Factionalism in the Deep South: Alabama's 'Dead Shoes' Senatorial Primary of 1906," *Alabama Review* 26 (January 1973), 14–15, 17, 19.

58. Joe L. Coker, *Liquor in the Land of the Lost Cause: Southern White Evangelicals and the Prohibition Movement* (Lexington: University Press of Kentucky, 2007), 68; William Warren Rogers et al., *Alabama: The History of a Deep South State* (Tuscaloosa: University of Alabama Press, 1994), 372–73; Sheldon, "Richmond Pearson Hobson," viii.

59. Coker, *Liquor in the Land of the Lost Cause*, 184–85.

60. Quoted in Richard Sheldon, "Richmond Pearson Hobson as a Progressive Reformer," *Alabama Review* 25 (October 1972): 245.

61. Hobson broadsides, c. 1906, box 29, RPHP; RPH to Grizelda Hobson, March 24, 1906, box 29, RPHP.

62. RPH to Grizelda Hobson, January 16, 1906, box 29, RPHP.

63. Jones, "Political Reform and Party Factionalism in the Deep South," 23.

64. Hobson broadsides, c. 1906, box 29, RPHP.

65. Bankhead broadside, c. 1906, box 29, RPHP.

66. RPH to Grizelda Hobson, March 2, 1906, box 29, RPHP.

67. RPH to Grizelda Hobson, February 23, March 1, and April 5, 1906, box 29, RPHP.

68. RPH to Grizelda Hobson, March 11, 1906, box 29, RPHP.

69. RPH to Grizelda Hobson, March 2, 1906, box 29, RPHP.

70. Bankhead broadside, c. 1906, box 29, RPHP.

71. Margaret Shirley Koster, "Congressional Career of John Hollis Bankhead" (master's thesis, University of Alabama, 1931), 76–86.

72. Quoted in Jones, "Political Reform and Party Factionalism in the Deep South," 24.

73. Jones, 26, 27.

74. *Washington Post*, August 31, 1906; *New York Times*, June 16 and 18, 1907; Key, "John H. Bankhead, Jr.," 34–35.

75. *Jasper (AL) Mountain Eagle*, March 15, 1916.

76. News clipping, n.d., WBB scrapbook, box 51, WBBP. For information on Hobson's work with the Anti-Saloon League, see Peter H. Odegard, *Pressure Politics: The Story of the Anti-Saloon League* (New York: Columbia University Press, 1928). According to the author, Hobson collected over $170,000 in speaking fees from that organization between 1914 and 1922.

Chapter 6

1. *Jasper (AL) Mountain Eagle*, June 10, July 15, September 30, and October 5, 1908.

2. Michael Perman, *Pursuit of Unity: A Political History of the American South* (Chapel Hill: University of North Carolina Press, 2009), 213.

3. Thomas L. Karnes, *Asphalt and Politics: A History of the American Highway System* (Jefferson, NC: McFarland, 2009), 6.

4. US Department of Transportation, Federal Highway Administration, *America's Highways, 1776–1976: A History of the Federal-Aid Program* (Washington, DC: Government Printing Office, 1977), 7–12, 16–18.

5. US Department of Transportation, Federal Highway Administration, 19–26, 29–37.

6. US Department of Transportation, Federal Highway Administration, 42–43, 49.

7. Howard Lawrence Preston, *Dirt Roads to Dixie: Accessibility and Modernization in the South, 1885–1935* (Knoxville: University of Tennessee Press, 1991), 13.

8. Office of Public Roads and M. O. Eldridge, *Public Road Mileage, Revenues and Expenditures, in the United States in 1904*, Bulletin 32 (Washington, DC: Government Printing Office, 1907).

9. US Department of Transportation, Federal Highway Administration, *America's Highways, 1776–1976*, 54, 64.

10. US Department of Transportation, Federal Highway Administration, 44.

11. US Department of Transportation, Federal Highway Administration, 75–76; Richard F. Weingroff, "Federal Aid Road Act of 1916: Building the Foundation," *Public Roads* 60, no. 1 (Summer 1996), updated January 31, 2017, http://www.fhwa.dot.gov/publications/publicroads/96summer/p96su2b.cfm.

12. Leonard Calvert Cooke, "The Development of the Road System of Alabama" (master's thesis, University of Alabama, 1935), 146.

13. Cooke, 114, 116, 120; Allen Johnston Going, *Bourbon Democracy in Alabama, 1884–1890*

(Tuscaloosa: University of Alabama Press, 1951), 111; Martin T. Olliff, "Getting Farmers—and Tourists—'Out of the Mud': Alabama's Nineteenth-Century Public Projects and the Federal Road Acts," in *Nation within a Nation: The American South and the Federal Government*, ed. Glenn Feldman (Gainesville: University Press of Florida, 2014), 231–37.

14. Olliff, "Getting Farmers—and Tourists—'Out of the Mud,'" 239–40.

15. Cooke, "The Development of the Road System of Alabama," 144.

16. Logan Waller Page to JHB, January 19, 1912, folder 3, box 32, JHBP; Robert P. Hooper to JHB, March 12, 1912, folder 3, box 32, JHBP; JHB to Robert Hooper, March 14, 1912, folder 3, box 32, JHBP; JHB to Logan Waller Page, April 5, 1912, folder 3, box 32, JHBP.

17. Preston, *Dirt Roads to Dixie*, 35. Bankhead was regularly in demand as a speaker at Good Roads events. See E. D. Tergersen to JHB, November 6, 1913, folder 4, box 19, JHBP; Cecil Beasley to E. D. Tergersen, November 10, 1913, folder 4, box 19, JHBP.

18. JHBjr to JHB, January 28, 1908, folder 1, box 32, JHBP.

19. Charles L. Dearing, *American Highway Policy* (Washington, DC: Brookings Institution, 1941), 46.

20. John H. Bankhead, *Speech of Hon. John H. Bankhead of Alabama, in the House of Representatives, June 13, 1906* (Washington, DC: Government Printing Office, 1906).

21. Karnes, *Asphalt and Politics*, 13; *Christian Science Monitor*, May 20, 1909; Arthur Jackson to JHB, July 4, 1909, folder 7, box 9, JHBP.

22. *Jasper (AL) Mountain Eagle*, August 24, 1910.

23. *Jasper (AL) Mountain Eagle*, August 24, 1910.

24. Bankhead, *Speech of Hon. John H. Bankhead of Alabama, in the House of Representatives*.

25. Report from the Committee on Agriculture and Forestry, "Experiments on Certain Highways," to accompany S6931, March 23, 1910.

26. JHB to George B. Cortelyou, March 23, 1908, folder 1, box 32, JHBP.

27. Tentative program, Good Roads Convention, 1906, folder 5, box 8, JHBP; *Jasper (AL) Mountain Eagle*, August 24, 1910; C. A. Beasley to J. C. Johnson, June 1, 1911, folder 6, box 14, JHBP; JHB to James F. Phillips, April 11, 1912, folder 3, box 32, JHBP; JHB to J. C. Walker, April 12, 1912, folder 3, box 32, JHBP; JHB to A. C. McAnnally, June 8, 1912, folder 5, box 46, JHBP; Arthur C. Jackson to JHB, August 6, 1912, folder 2, box 17, JHBP.

28. US Department of Transportation, Federal Highway Administration, *America's Highways, 1776–1976*, 80; Austin F. MacDonald, *Federal Aid: A Study of the American Subsidy System* (New York: Thomas Y. Crowell, 1928), 87; Paul H. Douglas, "The Development of a System of Federal Grants-in-Aid I," *Political Science Quarterly* 35, no. 2 (June 1920): 263.

29. US Department of Transportation, Federal Highway Administration, *America's Highways, 1776–1976*, 80.

30. Margaret Shirley Koster, "Congressional Career of John Hollis Bankhead" (master's thesis, University of Alabama, 1931), 130.

31. US Department of Transportation, Federal Highway Administration, *America's Highways, 1776–1976*, 87.

32. *Jasper (AL) Mountain Eagle*, January 26, 1916.

33. 53 Cong. Rec. S6426 (1916).

34. 53 Cong. Rec. H1280 (1916). On southern rural opposition to preparedness, see Jeanette Keith, *Rich Man's War, Poor Man's Fight: Race, Class, and Power in the Rural South during the First World War* (Chapel Hill: University of North Carolina Press, 2004), chapter 1.

35. 53 Cong. Rec. H1280 (1916).

36. MacDonald, *Federal Aid*, 11.

37. MacDonald, 91–92, 97; Paul H. Douglas, "The Development of a System of Federal Grants-in-Aid II," *Political Science Quarterly* 35, no. 4 (December 1920), 540–41; US Department of Transportation, Federal Highway Administration, *America's Highways, 1776–1976*, 100.

38. MacDonald, *Federal Aid*, 14–53; John A. Lapp, "Federal Grants in Aid," *American Political Science Review* 10, no. 4 (1916): 739.

39. US Department of Transportation, Federal Highway Administration, *America's Highways, 1776–1976*, 106.

40. "Work of the Bureau of Public Roads for the Last Fiscal Year," *Public Roads*, December 1918, 37.

41. US Department of Transportation, Federal Highway Administration, *America's Highways, 1776–1976*, 90–100, quotation on 93; Douglas, "The Development of a System of Federal Grants-in-Aid I," 269–70.

42. Quoted in US Department of Transportation, Federal Highway Administration, *America's Highways, 1776–1976*, 102.

43. H. L. Bowlby, "Distribution of War Surplus Materials for Road Building," *Public Roads*, April 1920, 27.

44. MacDonald, *Federal Aid*, 5.

45. *Birmingham Age-Herald*, June 27, 1920.

46. Richard F. Weingroff, "Zero Milestone," in *Highway History*, Federal Highway Administration, Department of Transportation, updated June 27, 2017, https://www.fhwa.dot.gov /infrastructure/zero.cfm.

47. Unidentified news clipping, n.d., folder 1, box 3, Charles B. Crow Papers, ADAH.

48. JHBjr to JHB, May 1913, folder 7, box 4, WBBP.

49. Jack Brien Key, "John H. Bankhead, Jr.: Creative Conservative" (PhD diss., Johns Hopkins University, 1964), 30.

50. Key, 25.

51. JHB to JHBjr, February 16, 1907, folder 1, box 2, JHBjrP.

52. JHBjr to TMO, telegram, February 21, 1907, folder 11, box 2, JHBjrP.

53. JHBjr to Oscar Underwood, September 15, 1914, folder 5, box 35, Oscar Wilder Underwood Papers, ADAH.

54. Key, "John H. Bankhead, Jr.," 36.

55. Walter Judson Heacock, "William Brockman Bankhead: A Biography" (PhD diss., University of Wisconsin, 1952), 38.

56. Underwood's decision to have Will place his name in nomination brought intense criticism from Underwood's supporters. See B. T. Selman to O. W. Underwood, June 19, 1912, folder 7, box 30, JHBP; Thomas Hopkins to O. W. Underwood, June 22, 1912, folder 7, box 30, JHBP.

57. *New York Times*, June 28, 1912; *Atlanta Constitution*, June 28, 1912.

58. Arthur S. Link, "The Underwood Presidential Movement of 1912," *Journal of Southern History* 11, no. 2 (May 1945): 230–45; Heacock, "William Brockman Bankhead," 38–44; Key, "John H. Bankhead, Jr.," 39–40.

59. JHBjr to Oscar Underwood, folder 2, box 31, Oscar Wilder Underwood Papers, ADAH.

60. Rebecca Cawood McIntyre, "Zelda Sayre Fitzgerald and Sara Martin Mayfield: 'Alabama Modern,'" in *Alabama Women: Their Lives and Times*, ed. Susan Youngblood Ashmore and Lisa Lindquist Dorr (Athens: University of Georgia Press, 2017), 183–208; Report cards, WBB scrapbook, box 52, WBBP.

61. Mother to MBO, April 13, 1921, box 1, MBOP.

62. Tallulah Bankhead, *Tallulah: My Autobiography* (New York: Harper, 1952), 27.

63. Joel Lobenthal, *Tallulah! The Life and Times of a Leading Lady* (New York: HarperCollins, 2004), 9.

64. Lobenthal, 11.

65. Lobenthal, 12–14; WBB to Louise Lund [sister], May 31, 1913, folder 1, box 2, WBBP.

66. Eugenia Bankhead to WBB, March 10, 1914, folder 1, box 2, WBBP.

67. Richard Sheldon, "Richmond Pearson Hobson as a Progressive Reformer," *Alabama Review* 25 (October 1972): 247–49, 255, quotation on 249; Richmond Pearson Hobson, *Income Tax and the Free List Bill, Speeches of the Honorable Richmond P. Hobson of Alabama in the House of Representatives, July 12, 1909, and April 26, 1911* (Washington, DC: Government Printing Office, 1912).

68. Sheldon, "Richmond Pearson Hobson as a Progressive Reformer," 245, quotation on 254.

69. 43 Cong. Rec. H3400 (1909); *New York Times*, March 15, 1909. On the Brownsville affair, see John D. Weaver, *The Brownsville Raid* (New York: W. W. Norton, 1970); JHB to J. H. Coleman, June 26, 1909, folder 2, box 9, JHBP.

70. 43 Cong. Rec. H3391 (1909).

71. Richmond Pearson Hobson, *The Great Destroyer, Speech of the Honorable Richmond P. Hobson of Alabama in the House of Representatives, February 2, 1911* (Washington, DC: Government Printing Office, 1911).

72. 52 Cong. Rec. H615–16 (1914).

73. *Our Southern Home*, news clipping, December 4, 1912, folder 12, box 4, WBBP.

74. *Birmingham News Age-Herald*, news clipping, January 6, 1946, folder 5, box 16, JHBjrP.

75. *Jasper (AL) Mountain Eagle*, April 23, 1913.

76. *Jasper (AL) Mountain Eagle*, April 23, 1913.

77. News clipping, c. 1914, WBB scrapbook, box 49, WBBP.

78. WBB to Louise Bankhead Perry Lund, May 31, 1913, folder 1, box 2, WBBP.

79. JHBjr. to JHB, c. 1913, folder 16, box 4, WBBP.

80. *Fayette Banner*, news clipping, September 11, 1913, folder 12, box 4, WBBP.

81. Oliver political broadside, n.d., folder 4, box 46, WBBP.

82. Leander Poole to JHB, March 27, 1914, folder 16, box 4, WBBP.

83. WBB to JHB, April 17, 1913, folder 18, box 3, WBBP. See also W. K. Pickens to JHB, April 18, 1913, folder 7, box 4, WBBP; JHB to T. W. Coleman, April 19, 1913, folder 7, box 4, WBBP; WBB to C. A. Beasley, April 21, 1913, folder 7, box 4, WBBP; C. A. Beasely to James H. Oswalt, April 25, 1913, folder 7, box 4, WBBP.

84. JHBjr to JHB, December 13, 1913, folder 11, box 4, WBBP.

85. JHBjr to JHB, November 29, 1913, folder 11, box 4, WBBP.

86. WBB to JHB, May 14, 1913, folder 7, box 4, WBBP; WBB to JHB, June 21, 1913, folder 8, box 4, WBBP; WBB to JHB, June 23, 1913, folder 8, box 4, WBBP; WBB to JHB, August 4, 1913, folder 9, box 4, WBBP.

87. JHB to JHBjr, October 7, 1913, folder 10, box 4, WBBP.

88. WBB to JHB, January 12, 1914, folder 13, box 4, WBBP.

89. JHB to WBB, May 20, 1913, folder 7, box 4, WBBP.

90. JHB to JHBjr, March 21, 1914, folder 16, box 4, WBBP.

91. WBB to "Dear sir," June 23, 1913, folder 8, box 4, WBBP; JHB to "Dear sir," June 26, 1913, folder 8, box 4, WBBP.

92. G. J. Wilson to JHBjr, August 28, 1913, folder 9, box 4, WBBP.

93. JHBjr to JHB, August 21, 1913, folder 9, box 4, WBBP.

94. JHBjr to JHB, August 1913, folder 9, box 4, WBBP.

95. JHB to JHBjr, October 4, 1913, folder 10, box 4, WBBP.

96. Heacock, "William Brockman Bankhead," 48.

97. Evans C. Johnson, "Oscar Underwood and the Hobson Campaign," *Alabama Review* 16 (April 1963): 139.

98. Heacock, "William Brockman Bankhead," 48.

99. See *Jasper (AL) Mountain Eagle*, April 5 and 12, 1916; ADAH, *Alabama Official and Statistical Register, 1915* (Montgomery, AL: Brown, 1915), 412.

100. The population of the existing nine districts was as follows: First, 211,856; Second, 289,770; Third, 249,042; Fourth, 193,958; Fifth, 235,615; Sixth, 240,156; Seventh, 197,409; Eighth, 218,342; Ninth, 301,945. The proposed Tenth District would have had a population of 145,552. *Montgomery Advertiser*, September 26, 1915.

101. Heacock, "William Brockman Bankhead," 50–51; *Montgomery Advertiser*, September 28, 1915.

102. *Jasper (AL) Mountain Eagle*, August 26, 1908, and June 23, 1909.

103. *Chicago Daily News*, news clipping, June 8, 1936, WBB scrapbook, box 50, WBBP; "Will

B. Bankhead Is Married Here," *Birmingham Age-Herald*, n.d., WBB scrapbook, box 52, WBBP; unidentified news clipping, c. 1936, WBB scrapbook, box 62, WBBP.

104. Unidentified news clipping, c. June 1936, WBB scrapbook, box 61, WBBP.

105. Mother to MBO, April 13, 1921, box 1, MBOP.

106. *Birmingham News*, February 22, 1916.

107. Richard Neil Sheldon, "Richmond Pearson Hobson: The Military Hero as Reformer during the Progressive Era" (PhD diss., University of Arizona, 1970), 230. Hobson's salary from the Anti-Saloon League was $525 a week, while, according to Grizelda Hobson, he made a total of $45,000 over the course of his nine years in Congress. Grizelda Hobson to RPH, [February?] 1916, box 30, RPHP; RPH, "Memorandum Brief for the Alabama Campaign Arbitration," November 18, 1916, box 30, RPHP.

108. *Birmingham News*, February 29, 1916.

109. *Jasper (AL) Mountain Eagle*, March 22, 1916.

110. *Jasper (AL) Mountain Eagle*, March 1, 1916.

111. *Jasper (AL) Mountain Eagle*, March 29, 1916.

112. *Birmingham News* reported that Hobson's "most intimate friends" pressured him to enter the race. *Birmingham News*, February 22, 1916.

113. RPH to C. W. Stubblefield, February 23, 1916, box 30, RPHP.

114. Grizelda Hobson to RPH, [March?] 1916, box 30, RPHP.

115. Grizelda Hobson to RPH, [February?] 1916, box 30, RPHP; RPH, "Memorandum Brief for the Alabama Campaign Arbitration," November 18, 1916, box 30, RPHP.

116. *Carbon Hill Journal*, news clipping, n.d., folder 4, box 46, WBBP; *Birmingham News*, March 2, 1916.

117. C. W. Stubblefield to RPH, February 18, 1916, box 30, RPHP; RPH to C. W. Stubblefield, February 23, 1916, box 30, RPHP.

118. RPH to Grizelda Hobson, [March?] 1916, box 30, RPHP.

119. Grizelda Hobson to RPH, [March?] 1916, box 30, RPHP; Grizelda Hobson to RPH, March 18, 1916, box 30, RPHP; Grizelda Hobson to William H. Morgan, April 4, 1916, box 30, RPHP; Grizelda Hobson to E. H. Cherrington, April 17, 1916, box 30, RPHP; RPH to Grizelda Hobson [April?] 1916, box 30, RPHP.

120. *Birmingham News*, March 1, 1916.

121. Heacock, "William Brockman Bankhead," 54; *Jasper (AL) Mountain Eagle*, March 29, 1916; *Birmingham News*, March 1 and 4, 1916.

122. Bankhead, quoted in Heacock, "William Brockman Bankhead," 54.

123. RPH to Grizelda Hobson, [March?] 1916, box 30, RPHP; RPH to Grizelda Hobson, April 1916, box 30, RPHP.

124. Bankhead, quoted in Heacock, "William Brockman Bankhead," 54; *Jasper (AL) Mountain Eagle*, March 16, 22, and 27, 1916.

125. *Birmingham News*, March 8, 1916.

126. WBB to L. B. Musgrove, n.d., folder 4, box 5, WBBP; *Carbon Hill Journal*, news clipping, c. 1916, in folder 4, box 46, WBBP.

127. Quoted in Grizelda Hobson to E. H. Cherrington, April 17, 1916, box 30, RPHP.

128. *Fayette Banner*, news clipping, n.d., WBB scrapbook, box 55, WBBP.

129. Bankhead broadside, WBB scrapbook, box 55, WBBP. Also see open letter from Bankhead to Hobson, *Jasper (AL) Mountain Eagle*, April 12, 1916.

130. Handwritten notes from Hobson campaign speech, n.d., folder 2, box 5, WBBP.

131. Gail Bederman, *Manliness and Civilization: A Cultural History of Gender and Race in the United States, 1880–1917* (Chicago: University of Chicago Press, 1995), 15, 171.

132. Bankhead broadside, WBB scrapbook, box 55, WBBP.

133. Bankhead broadside and unidentified news clipping, n.d., WBB scrapbook, box 55, WBBP; *Jasper (AL) Mountain Eagle*, April 12, 19, and 26, 1916. Once a supporter of women's suffrage, Hobson told an Alabama audience that he had changed his position.

134. *Birmingham News*, May 12, 1916.

135. Heacock, "William Brockman Bankhead," 58; William H. Morgan to Grizelda Hobson, May 15, 1916, box 30, RPHP; ADAH, *Alabama Official and Statistical Register, 1919* (Montgomery, AL: Brown, 1920). The Republican challenger won Winston, Franklin, and Fayette Counties.

136. *Montgomery Advertiser*, May 11, 1916; *Birmingham News*, March 13, 1916.

137. *New York Times*, February 10, 1933.

138. Sheldon, "Richmond Pearson Hobson," 246–48.

139. WBB diary, March 18, 1937, Walker Area Community Foundation, Jasper, AL. Throughout this book, WBB's diary entries for 1937 and 1938 are quoted by permission of the Walker Area Community Foundation.

140. "Elaborate Celebration of Golden Wedding," unidentified news clipping, c. November 1916, WBB scrapbook, box 52, WBBP; Minnie Reynolds Saffold, "Golden Wedding," November 1916, folder 4, box 4, WBBP; Tallulah Bankhead (hereafter TB) to "My dearest grandparents," c. November 1916, folder 2, box 1, Tallulah Bankhead Papers (hereafter TBP), ADAH.

Chapter 7

1. According to the chief assistant librarian at the Library of Congress, there was only one other instance of a father and son serving as members of Congress at the same time. During the Fiftieth Congress, March 4, 1887, to March 3, 1889, Daniel W. Voorhees was a senator from Indiana, while his son Charles S. Voorhees was a delegate from Washington. See A. P. C. Griffin to JHB, December 7, 1916, folder 5, box 22, JHBP; *Louisville Courier Journal*, March 10, 1917.

2. *Washington Post*, March 11, 1917.

3. Joseph A. Fry, *Dixie Looks Abroad: The South and U.S. Foreign Relations, 1789–1973* (Baton Rouge: Louisiana State University Press, 2002), 138–40.

4. Arthur S. Link, "The Cotton Crisis, the South, and Anglo-American Diplomacy, 1914–1915," in *The Higher Realism of Woodrow Wilson*, by Arthur S. Link (Nashville, TN: Vanderbilt University Press, 1971), 309–29.

5. M. Ryan Floyd, "'A Diarrhea of Plans and Constipation of Action': The Influence of Alabama Cotton Farmers, Merchants and Brokers on Anglo-American Diplomacy during the First World War, 1914–1915," in *The American South and the Great War, 1914–1924*, ed. Matthew L. Downs and M. Ryan Floyd (Baton Rouge: Louisiana State University Press, 2018), 13–14.

6. Bruce F. Matthews, "The 1914 Cotton Crisis in Alabama," *Alabama Review* 46 (January 1993): 3–23.

7. Link, "The Cotton Crisis," 309–10.

8. T. J. McConnell to JHB, August 22, 1914, folder 5, box 29, JHBP.

9. Jackson M. Young to JHB, August 27, 1914, folder 5, box 29, JHBP.

10. Matthews, "The 1914 Cotton Crisis in Alabama," 11–15.

11. Matthews, 13–15.

12. JHB to Ballard, September 1, 1914, folder 5, box 29, JHBP; JHB, "Statement to the People of Alabama," October 3, 1914, folder 5, box 29, JHBP.

13. JHB, "Statement to the People of Alabama," October 3, 1914, folder 5, box 29, JHBP.

14. Matthews, "The 1914 Cotton Crisis in Alabama," 18–21; *Jasper (AL) Mountain Eagle*, October 10, 1914; *Tuscaloosa News*, October 20, 1914.

15. *Atlanta Constitution*, October 26, 1914.

16. William J. Cooper Jr., Thomas E. Terrell, and Christopher Childers, *The American South: A History*, vol. 2, *From Reconstruction to the Present*, 5th ed. (New York: Rowman and Littlefield, 2017), 666.

17. Fry, *Dixie Looks Abroad*, 158–59.

18. JHB to W. H. Graves, December 7, 1915, folder 8, box 30, JHBP.

19. JHB to Thomas W. Coleman, January 13, 1915, folder 8, box 30, JHBP.

20. JHB to J. J. Willett, January 31, 1916, folder 8, box 30, JHBP.

21. JHB to W. H. Graves, December 7, 1915, folder 8, box 30, JHBP. See also JHB to Chas.

P. Copeland, January 6, 1918, folder 8, box 30, JHBP; JHB to J. J. Willett, January 31, 1916, folder 8, box 30, JHBP; JHB to Amos L. Griffith, February 2, 1916, folder 8, box 30, JHBP; JHB to Edwin C. Rockwell, April 24, 1916, folder 9, box 30, JHBP.

22. JHB to W. H. Graves, December 7, 1915, folder 8, box 30, JHBP.

23. JHB to Harold H. Himrod, January 25, 1916, folder 8, box 30, JHBP.

24. 53 Cong. Rec. S6376 (1916).

25. JHB to S. S. Swain, April 7, 1917, folder 7, box 22, JHBP; see also JHB to C. W. Sheppard, folder 7, box 22, JHBP.

26. *Time*, November 29, 1937.

27. "Voting Record of Bankhead, William B., 10th Alabama, in the 65th Congress," folder 10, box 22, WBBP.

28. Walter Judson Heacock, "William Brockman Bankhead: A Biography" (PhD diss., University of Wisconsin, 1952), 68.

29. Quoted in Heacock, 69.

30. 55 Cong. Rec. S260 (1917); "Voting Record of Bankhead, William B., 10th Alabama, in the 65th Congress," p. 2, folder 10, box 22, WBBP.

31. WBB diary, April 6, 1937, Walker Area Community Foundation, Jasper, AL.

32. Thomas McAdory Owen Jr., Alabama World War I Service Records, ADAH; Walter Will Bankhead, Alabama World War I Service Records, ADAH.

33. Fry, *Dixie Looks Abroad*, 142–43.

34. JHBjr to WBB, April 20, 1917, folder 6, box 6, WBBP; JHBjr to WBB, April 26, 1917, folder 6, box 6, WBBP.

35. JHB to J. L. Burgess, April 14, 1917, folder 6, box 31, JHBP.

36. JHB to Jno. A. May, April 27, 1917, folder 6, box 31, JHBP.

37. Sydney J. Bowie to WBB, April 20, 1917, folder 6, box 6, WBBP.

38. "Two Congressional Voices: Bankhead's and Huddleston's," unidentified news clipping, n.d., WBB scrapbook, box 51, WBBP; *Mobile Register*, May 4, 1917, WBB scrapbook, box 51, WBBP.

39. 55 Cong. Rec. H1098 (1917).

40. JHBjr to WBB, April 20, 1917, folder 6, box 6, WBBP; JHBjr to WBB, April 26, 1917, folder 6, box 6, WBBP.

41. JHBjr to WBB, April 26, 1917, folder 6, box 6, WBBP.

42. B. G. Farmer to JHB, July 10, 1917, folder 6, box 31, JHBP.

43. JHB to Newton D. Baker, July 16, 1917, folder 6, box 31, JHBP; Newton D. Baker to JHB, July 17, 1917, folder 6, box 31, JHBP.

44. B. C. Bradford to JHB, September 24, 1917, folder 6, box 31, JHBP.

45. Charles B. Storrys to JHB, May 6, 1917, folder 1, box 23, JHBP.

46. JHB to John B. McCain, March 8, 1918, folder 4, box 24, JHBP.

47. Tallulah Bankhead, *Tallulah: My Autobiography* (New York: Harper, 1952), 39–40.

48. Joshua Zeitz, *Flapper: A Madcap Story of Sex, Style, Celebrity, and the Women Who Made America Modern* (New York: Three Rivers Press, 2006), 228.

49. JHB to J. P. Tumulty, December 7, 1915, folder 1, box 22, JHBP; Joel Lobenthal, *Tallulah! The Life and Times of a Leading Lady* (New York: HarperCollins, 2004), 12–15.

50. Lobenthal, *Tallulah!*, 16; TB to JHB, November 22, 1919, folder 5, box 1, TBP.

51. 1st Sgt. T. A. MacDonald to TB, October 30, 1918, folder 2, box 1, TBP.

52. Lobenthal, *Tallulah!*, 17–28; *San Francisco Chronicle*, November 17, 1918.

53. Cooper, Terrell, and Childers, *The American South*, 668.

54. Jack Brien Key, "John H. Bankhead, Jr.: Creative Conservative" (PhD diss., Johns Hopkins University, 1964), 47.

55. JHBjr to JHB, July 12, 1917, folder 3, box 23, JHBP.

56. Key, "John H. Bankhead, Jr.," 51–52.

57. Preston J. Hubbard, *Origins of the TVA: The Muscle Shoals Controversy, 1920–1932* (New York: W. W. Norton, 1968), 1.

58. JHB to J. O. Prude, July 8, 1917, folder 3, box 23, JHBP.

59. Hubbard, *Origins of the TVA*, vii.

60. Matthew L. Downs, *Transforming the South: Federal Development in the Tennessee Valley, 1915–1960* (Baton Rouge: Louisiana State University Press, 2014), 13–14.

61. JHB to J. O. Prude, July 28, 1917, folder 3, box 23, JHBP; also see JHB to J. O. Prude, July 8, 1917, folder 3, box 23, JHBP.

62. Downs, *Transforming the South*, 14–17; JHB and Oscar Underwood to J. W. Worthington, October 1, 1917, folder 24, box 1, JHBP.

63. Hubbard, *Origins of the TVA*, 4; Patricia Bernard Ezzell, "Wilson Dam and Reservoir," *Encyclopedia of Alabama*, updated June 16, 2020, http://encyclopediaofalabama.org.

64. Downs, *Transforming the South*, 17.

65. Key, "John H. Bankhead, Jr.," 49; see JHB to JHBjr, July 20, 1916, folder 5, box 22, JHBP.

66. Dewey W. Grantham Jr., "The Southern Senators and the League of Nations, 1918–1920," *North Carolina Historical Review* 26, no. 2 (April 1949): 190.

67. JHB to John Y. Graham, March 10, 1919, folder 9, box 33, JHBP.

68. JHB to Rev. Henry M. Edmunds, March 29, 1919, folder 9, box 33, JHBP.

69. JHB to G. M. Garth, June 16, 1919, folder 9, box 33, JHBP.

70. Fry, *Dixie Looks Abroad*, 172–73.

71. JHB to Margaret Miller, May 25, 1919, folder 6, box 26, JHBP.

72. Alabama Association Opposed to Woman Suffrage to Alabama Congressional Delegation c/o Senator Bankhead, telegram, December 12, 1917, folder 2, box 24, JHBP.

73. JHB to Julia Jones Lipsomb, September 26, 1917, folder 5, box 23, JHBP; JHB to John L. Burnett, December 10, 1917, folder 2, box 24, JHBP; *Washington Post*, January 11, 1918; 58 Cong. Rec. H94 (1919); 58 Cong. Rec. S635 (1919).

74. Elna C. Green, *Southern Strategies: Southern Women and the Woman Suffrage Question* (Chapel Hill: University of North Carolina Press, 1997), 107–9.

75. Directors Annual Report, 1921–22, p. 14, Administrative Files, Alabama Department of Archives and History Papers (hereafter ADAHP), ADAH.

76. Marie Bankhead Owen, *The Battle of Maubilla. First of a Series of Historical Plays in Commemoration of the Close of a Century of Statehood*, Alabama Centennial Commission (Montgomery, AL: Paragon Press, 1919); Marie Bankhead Owen, *At Old Mobile. Second of a Series of Historical Plays in Commemoration of the Close of a Century of Statehood*, Alabama Centennial Commission (Montgomery, AL: Paragon Press, 1919); Marie Bankhead Owen, *Alabama, or the Making of a State: Wherein Are Presented Some of the More Important Events in Pioneer Life and the Transition from Territory to State. Third of a Series of Historical Plays in Commemoration of the Close of a Century of Statehood*, Alabama Centennial Commission (Montgomery, AL: Paragon Press, 1919); Marie Bankhead Owen, *De Soto and the Indians. First in a Series of Children's Plays in Commemoration of the Close of a Century of Statehood*, Alabama Centennial Commission (Montgomery, AL: Paragon Press, 1919); Marie Bankhead Owen, *How Bienville Saved Mobile. Second in a Series of Children's Plays in Commemoration of the Close of a Century of Statehood*, Alabama Centennial Commission (Montgomery, AL: Paragon Press, 1919); Marie Bankhead Owen, *How Alabama Became a State. Third in a Series of Children's Plays in Commemoration of the Close of a Century of Statehood*, Alabama Centennial Commission (Montgomery, AL: Paragon Press, 1919); MBO to Armand Epiene, January 31, 1914, "1914-Jan–May Clubs" file, box 5, MBOP.

77. Owen, *Alabama, or the Making of a State*, 39.

78. Owen, 32.

79. Robert J. Jakeman, "Marie Bankhead Owen and the Alabama Department of Archives and History, 1920–1955," *Provenance: Journal of the Society of Georgia Archivists* 21, no. 1 (2003): 39.

80. *Jasper (AL) Mountain Eagle*, February 18, 1920.

81. Warren G. Harding to MBO, December 8, 1921, folder 3, box 2, WBBP.

82. WBB diary, January 30, 1921, folder 7, box 1, WBBP.

83. Mama to MBO, September 15, 1921, box 1, MBOP.

84. Mother to WBB, May 16, 1920, box 2, folder 1, WBBP.

85. John Hollis Bankhead, will, August 16, 1919, Probate Court, Walker County, AL.

Chapter 8

1. Robert J. Jakeman, "Marie Bankhead Owen and the Alabama Department of Archives and History, 1920–1955," *Provenance: Journal of the Society of Georgia Archivists* 21, no. 1 (2003): 42.

2. MBO diary, July 5, 1920, box 1, MBOP.

3. MBO diary, July 5, 1920, box 1, MBOP; MBO to Hugh Morrow, February 18, 1931, Board of Trustees Meeting Minutes, 1930–31, Administrative Files, ADAHP.

4. WBB diary, February 19 and 20, 1921, folder 7, box 1, WBBP.

5. See folder 5, box 2, WBBP.

6. Lee N. Allen, "Charles Henderson, 1915–1919," in *Alabama Governors: A Political History of the State*, ed. Samuel L. Webb and Margaret E. Armbrester (Tuscaloosa: University of Alabama Press, 2001), 164.

7. 55 Cong. Rec. H7919 (1917); H.R. 15402, 65th Cong. (1919); H.R. 1204, 66th Cong. (1919); 60 Cong. Rec. H2397–98 (1921); Walter Judson Heacock, "William Brockman Bankhead: A Biography" (PhD diss., University of Wisconsin, 1952), 75–76.

8. 58 Cong. Rec. H6738 (1919).

9. 65 Cong. Rec. H8286 (1924).

10. 75 Cong. Rec. H10590 (1932).

11. Heacock, "William Brockman Bankhead," 79–80.

12. WBB diary, March 9, 1921, p. 68, folder 7, box 1, WBBP.

13. *Time*, November 29, 1937.

14. 67 Cong. Rec. H1781–82 (1926); Heacock, "William Brockman Bankhead," 98.

15. WBB diary, May 4, 1921, folder 7, box 1, WBBP.

16. WBB diary, June 7, 1921, folder 7, box 1, WBBP.

17. Heacock, "William Brockman Bankhead," 95.

18. Heacock, 97; *South Florida Developer*, news clipping, May 9, 1922, folder 1, box 31, WBBP.

19. Heacock, "William Brockman Bankhead," 97; *South Florida Developer*, news clipping, May 9, 1922, folder 1, box 31, WBBP.

20. Heacock, "William Brockman Bankhead," 99–100.

21. Heacock, 93.

22. 60 Cong. Rec. H862 and H864 (1920).

23. WBB diary, February 1, 1921, and undated entry, p. 25, folder 7, box 1, WBBP.

24. Heacock, "William Brockman Bankhead," 86.

25. Jack Brien Key, "John H. Bankhead, Jr.: Creative Conservative" (PhD diss., Johns Hopkins University, 1964), 60–61.

26. Heacock, "William Brockman Bankhead," 94.

27. *Jasper (AL) Mountain Eagle*, October 19, 1921; *Birmingham News*, January 13, 1922.

28. Heacock, "William Brockman Bankhead," 88; *Birmingham News*, February 20, 1922.

29. Heacock, "William Brockman Bankhead," 89.

30. 62 Cong. Rec. H8683–85 (1922).

31. 65 Cong. Rec. H3556–59 (1924).

32. Heacock, "William Brockman Bankhead," 90.

33. Heacock, 90–93.

34. Preston J. Hubbard, *Origins of the TVA: The Muscle Shoals Controversy, 1920–1932* (New York: W. W. Norton, 1968), 236.

35. 74 Cong. Rec. H5570 (1931).

36. *New York Times*, February 22 and 27, March 1 and 3, 1931.

37. WBB diary, January 29, 1921, p. 29, and July 9, 1921, folder 7, box 1, WBBP.

38. Tallulah Bankhead, *Tallulah: My Autobiography* (New York: Harper, 1952), 58.

39. Kathy Peiss, *Cheap Amusements: Working Women and Leisure in Turn-of-the-Century New York* (Philadelphia: Temple University Press, 1986).

40. Lisa Lindquist Dorr, "Fifty Percent Moonshine and Fifty Percent Moonshine: Social Life and College Youth Culture in Alabama, 1913–1933," in *Manners and Southern History*, ed. Ted Ownby (Jackson: University Press of Mississippi, 2011), 46.

41. Joshua Zeitz, *Flapper: A Madcap Story of Sex, Style, Celebrity, and the Women Who Made America Modern* (New York: Three Rivers Press, 2006), 8.

42. Zeitz, 61; Bankhead, *Tallulah*, 58, 110.

43. Rebecca Cawood McIntyre, "Zelda Sayre Fitzgerald and Sara Martin Mayfield: 'Alabama Modern,'" in *Alabama Women: Their Lives and Times*, ed. Susan Youngblood Ashmore and Lisa Lindquist Dorr (Athens: University of Georgia Press, 2017), 192–94.

44. Bankhead, *Tallulah*, 71.

45. Joel Lobenthal, *Tallulah! The Life and Times of a Leading Lady* (New York: HarperCollins, 2004), 32–33, 45–47; *Washington Post*, August 4, 1919; Bankhead, *Tallulah*, 57.

46. Lobenthal, *Tallulah!*, 204; Emily A. Phillips, "'A Bankhead without a Tongue Is No Good to the State of Alabama': Marie Bankhead Owen, Tallulah Bankhead, and Subversions of Normative Gender Conventions," April 2019, pp. 17–18, graduate research seminar, Dr. Margaret Peacock, University of Alabama, unpublished paper in author's possession, used by permission; *Atlanta Constitution*, November 24, 1918.

47. Bankhead, *Tallulah*, 213.

48. Lobenthal, *Tallulah!*, 30–31, 43–46.

49. Lobenthal, *Tallulah!*, 53–55; Bankhead, *Tallulah*, 110–14.

50. Mother to MBO, April 13, 1921, box 1, MBOP.

51. WBB to TB, November 23, 1919, folder 5, box 1, TBP.

52. *Washington Post*, August 16, 1920, box 31, WBBP; *Evening Star* (Washington, DC), August 21, 1920, box 31, WBBP; *Sunday American* (Atlanta), March 13, 1932, box 31, WBBP; *Birmingham News Herald*, February 2, 1942, box 31, WBBP; WBB diary, January 24, 1921, folder 7, box 1, WBBP.

53. WBB diary, January 29, 1921, folder 7, box 1, WBBP.

54. Unidentified news clipping, c. 1933, folder 1, Bankhead Family Photographs Collection, ADAH.

55. Key, "John H. Bankhead, Jr.," 61.

56. WBB diary, February 6, 1921, folder 7, box 1, WBBP.

57. Jakeman, "Marie Bankhead Owen," 43.

58. Quotations in Key, "John H. Bankhead, Jr.," 57–58; Board of Trustees Meeting Minutes, 1930–31, Administrative Files, ADAHP.

59. Annual Report of the Director, p. 15, Board of Trustees Meeting Minutes, 1920–21, Administrative Files, ADAHP.

60. Annual Report of the Director, Board of Trustees Meeting Minutes, 1919–20, 1920–21, 1921–22, 1923–24, 1926–27, 1927–28, 1929–30, Administrative Files, ADAHP.

61. See Annual Report of the Director for years 1920–28, Board of Trustees Meeting Minutes, Administrative Files, ADAHP.

62. Heacock, "William Brockman Bankhead," 112.

63. Key, "John H. Bankhead, Jr.," 58–59.

64. Annual Report of the Director, Board of Trustees Meeting Minutes, 1929–30, Administrative Files, ADAHP.

65. Heacock, "William Brockman Bankhead," 63.

66. William Warren Rogers et al., *Alabama: The History of a Deep South State* (Tuscaloosa: University of Alabama Press, 1994), 411.

67. Rogers et al., 430–31.

68. Rogers et al., 431–32.

69. Virginia Van der Veer Hamilton, *Hugo Black: The Alabama Years* (Baton Rouge: Louisiana State University Press, 1972), 117.

70. Key, "John H. Bankhead, Jr.," 64.

71. Michael Breedlove, "Thomas E. Kilby, 1919–1923," in Webb and Armbrester, *Alabama Governors*, 168.

72. Key, "John H. Bankhead, Jr.," 65–66; *Birmingham News*, April 28, 1926.

73. Key, "John H. Bankhead, Jr.," 66; JHBjr to WBB, January 16, 1926, JHBjrP.

74. Hamilton, *Hugo Black*, 32–38.

75. Hamilton, 59–62.

76. Hamilton, 91.

77. Key, "John H. Bankhead, Jr.," 66; JHBjr to WBB, April 21, 1926, JHBjrP.

78. Steve Suitts, "Hugo L. Black," *Encyclopedia of Alabama*, updated January 31, 2017, http://encyclopediaofalabama.org.

79. Hamilton, *Hugo Black*, 76, 83.

80. Glenn Feldman, *Politics, Society, and the Klan in Alabama, 1915–1949* (Tuscaloosa: University of Alabama Press, 1999), 81.

81. Key, "John H. Bankhead, Jr.," 67; WBB to JHB, March 9, 1926, JHBjrP; JHB to WBB, January 16, 1926, JHBjrP.

82. Key, "John H. Bankhead, Jr.," 67.

83. Key, 68–69.

84. JHBjr to WBB, March 19, 1926, folder 11, box 5, WBBP.

85. Samuel L. Webb, "Hugo Black, Bibb Graves, and the Ku Klux Klan: A Revisionist View of the 1926 Alabama Democratic Primary," *Alabama Review* 57 (October 2004): 256–57.

86. Key, "John H. Bankhead, Jr.," 69; *Montgomery Advertiser*, August 11, 1926.

87. WBB to Kenneth Romney, August 18, 1926, folder 12, box 5, WBBP.

88. Wayne Flynt, "Bibb Graves, 1927–1931, 1935–1939," in Webb and Armbrester, *Alabama Governors*, 174–76.

89. Webb, "Hugo Black, Bibb Graves, and the Ku Klux Klan," 273.

90. Key, "John H. Bankhead, Jr.," 71.

91. Feldman, *Politics, Society, and the Klan in Alabama*, 92.

92. Hamilton, *Hugo Black*, 146–47.

93. Hamilton, 148.

94. Key, "John H. Bankhead, Jr.," 72; *Montgomery Advertiser*, October 27, 1927.

95. Heacock, "William Brockman Bankhead," 122.

96. *New York Times*, October 30, 1930.

97. Hamilton, *Hugo Black*, 151.

98. Hamilton, 152.

99. James Thomas Heflin (hereafter JTH) to William A. Gunter, April 30, 1928, scrapbook 114, box 898, JTHP.

100. Hamilton, *Hugo Black*, 167.

101. Hamilton, 156; S. W. Williamson to WBB, October 14, 1928, WBBP.

102. Heacock, "William Brockman Bankhead," 124.

103. Key, "John H. Bankhead, Jr.," 73; Walter Will Bankhead to MBO, July 24 and August 10, 1928, in MBOP.

104. Hugh D. Reagan, "Race as a Factor in the Presidential Election of 1928 in Alabama," *Alabama Review* 19 (January 1966): 5–19.

105. *Alabama Christian Advocate*, November 1, 1928, quoted in Reagan, 9.

106. *Montgomery Advertiser*, news clipping, October 30, 1928, scrapbook 114, box 898, JTHP.

107. Hamilton, *Hugo Black*, 182; Wayne Flynt, *Alabama in the Twentieth Century* (Tuscaloosa: University of Alabama Press, 2006), 46.

108. Heacock, "William Brockman Bankhead," 125.

109. *Birmingham News*, news clipping, June 1, 1929, scrapbook 1929–30, box 20, JHBjrP.

110. *Andalusia Star*, news clipping, April 18, 1930, scrapbook 1929–30, box 20, JHBjrP.

111. John McDuffie to L. J. Bugg, Monroeville, June 7, 1929, folder 26, box 1, John D. McDuffie Papers, W. S. Hoole Special Collections Library, University of Alabama, Tuscaloosa.

112. Heacock, "William Brockman Bankhead," 125–26; WBB to Miles Allgood, September 26, 1929, folder 13, box 6, WBBP; Miles Allgood to WBB, October 1, 1929, folder 13, box 6, WBBP.

113. Hamilton, *Hugo Black*, 181–82; George Huddleston to WBB, October 4, 1929, folder 13, box 6, WBBP.

114. *Atlanta Constitution*, October 20, 1929, scrapbook 1929–30, box 20, JHBjrP.

115. *Jefferson Countian*, news clipping, November 21, 1929, scrapbook 1929–30, box 20, JHBjrP; WBB to Ben F. Ray, November 15, 1929, folder 13, box 6, WBBP; WBB to Jouett Shouse, October 8, 1929, folder 13, box 6, WBBP; WBB to George Huddleston, October 1, 1929, folder 13, box 6, WBBP; Huddleston to WBB, October 4, 1929, folder 13, box 6, WBBP.

116. Quoted in "Punishing Hoovercrats in Alabama," *Literary Digest*, January 4, 1930, 9.

117. JTH to Carter H. Rice, March 11, 1930, scrapbook 114, box 898, JTHP.

118. Hamilton, *Hugo Black*, 185.

Chapter 9

1. Virginia Van der Veer Hamilton, *Lister Hill: Statesman from the South* (Chapel Hill: University of North Carolina Press, 1987), 60.

2. Hamilton, 62.

3. See letters in folder 53, box 72, Lister Hill Papers, W. S. Hoole Special Collections Library, University of Alabama, Tuscaloosa.

4. John McDuffie to Jesse B. Hearin, Montgomery Chamber of Commerce, January 2, 1930, folder 26, box 1, John D. McDuffie Papers.

5. Jack Brien Key, "John H. Bankhead, Jr.: Creative Conservative" (PhD diss., Johns Hopkins University, 1964), 82; JHBjr to WBB, January 23, 1930, WBBP; see also *Montgomery Advertiser*, February 25, 1930.

6. JHBjr to John McDuffie, April 23, 1930, folder 31, box 1, John D. McDuffie Papers.

7. John McDuffie to JHBjr, April 26, 1930, folder 27, box 1, John D. McDuffie Papers.

8. JHBjr to WBB, March 24, 1930, WBBP; Key, "John H. Bankhead, Jr.," 83.

9. Key, "John H. Bankhead, Jr.," 83–84.

10. Unidentified news clipping, May 1, 1930, WBB scrapbook, box 56, WBBP.

11. Glenn T. Harper, "'Cotton Tom' Heflin and the Election of 1930: The Price of Party Disloyalty," *Historian* 30, no. 3 (May 1968): 398.

12. Harper; Glenn Feldman, *Politics, Society, and the Klan in Alabama, 1915–1949* (Tuscaloosa: University of Alabama Press, 1999), 200.

13. John T. Adams to JTH, August 26, 1930, folder 65, box 830, JTHP; E. A. Phillips to JTH, August 6, 1930, folder 65, box 830, JTHP.

14. Feldman, *Politics, Society, and the Klan in Alabama*, 202.

15. JTH to editor, *Birmingham News*, August 18, 1930, folder 65, box 830, JTHP.

16. Harper, "'Cotton Tom' Heflin and the Election of 1930," 400; *New York Times*, August 22, 1930.

17. JHBjr, transcript of radio speech, November 3, 1930, folder 10, box 3, JHBjrP.

18. Harper, "'Cotton Tom' Heflin and the Election of 1930," 405.

19. Quoted in Walter Judson Heacock, "William Brockman Bankhead: A Biography" (PhD diss., University of Wisconsin, 1952), 139; *Montgomery Advertiser*, October 5, 1930.

20. "Do You Know," campaign circular, Woman's Democratic Campaign Committee, folder 10, box 3, JHBjrP.

21. John H. Bankhead Jr., speech, c. 1930, folder 2, box 13, JHBjrP.

22. T. M. Watlington to JHBjr, October 25, 1930, folder 2, box 3, JHBjrP.

23. Wayne Flynt, *Alabama in the Twentieth Century* (Tuscaloosa: University of Alabama Press, 2006), 134–35.

24. *Marion Times*, news clipping, November 6, 1930, scrapbook, box 20, JHBjrP. Heflin won

Chambers, Chilton, Clay, Coosa, DeKalb, Escambia, Henry, Shelby, St. Clair, and Winston Counties.

25. Virginia Van der Veer Hamilton, *Hugo Black: The Alabama Years* (Baton Rouge: Louisiana State University Press, 1972), 189.

26. Hamilton, 189; *Birmingham News*, November 3 and 8, 1930.

27. JTH to Edward I. Broom, January 20, 1931, folder 70, box 831, JTHP.

28. Horace C. Wilkinson to JTH, July 25, 1931, folder 76, box 832, JTHP.

29. JTH to C. Needham Avery, November 21, 1930, folder 68, box 831, JTHP.

30. Frank Hilburn to JTH, November 4, 1930, folder 68, box 831, JTHP.

31. J. S. Daw to JTH, November 20, 1930, folder 68, box 831, JTHP.

32. S. J. Martin to JTH, November 14, 1930, folder 68, box 831, JTHP.

33. JHBjr to Gerald P. Nye, January 31, 1931, folder 14, box 6, JHBjrP; see also JHBjr to WBB, January 26, 1931, folder 14, box 6, JHBjrP; WBB to JHBjr, January 28, 1931, folder 14, box 6, JHBjrP.

34. 74 Cong. Rec. S5945–46 (1931).

35. 74 Cong. Rec. S6462–63 (1931).

36. *Birmingham News*, news clipping, c. March 1931, folder 72, box 832, JTHP; *Gadsden Times*, news clipping, March 25, 1931, scrapbook 130, box 916, JTHP.

37. *Senator from Alabama: In re the Contest of J. Thomas Heflin v. John H. Bankhead for a Seat in the United States Senate from the State of Alabama, before the Subcommittee of the Committee on Privileges and Elections; Briefs and Arguments of Counsel* (Washington, DC: Government Printing Office, 1931), 2–3.

38. *Senator from Alabama*, 69.

39. Key, "John H. Bankhead, Jr.," 92; *Senator from Alabama*, 139–50, 162.

40. *Washington Daily News*, news clipping, June 22, 1931, scrapbook, box 22, JHBjrP.

41. *Birmingham News*, May 10, 1931.

42. *Birmingham Post*, May 14, 1931.

43. *Birmingham News*, May 25, 1931; Key, "John H. Bankhead, Jr.," 92–93.

44. *Birmingham Age-Herald*, news clipping, May 25, 1931, scrapbook 130, box 916, JTHP.

45. JHBjr journal, December 7, 1931, Walker Area Community Foundation, Jasper, AL, used by permission; *Tuscaloosa News*, December 7, 1931.

46. JTH to Daniel O. Hastings, January 28, 1932, folder 80, box 832, JTHP.

47. *Miami Herald*, news clipping, January 6, 1932, scrapbook 130, box 916, JTHP; *Birmingham Post*, February 10, 1932.

48. *Alabama Journal*, March 7, 1932.

49. WBB to Sam J. Sanders, March 19, 1932, folder 1, box 7, WBBP.

50. *Birmingham News*, news clipping, April 26, 1932, scrapbook 130, box 916, JTHP.

51. 75 Cong. Rec. S8924 (1932).

52. 75 Cong. Rec. S8925 (1932).

53. 75 Cong. Rec. S8942 (1932).

54. *Tuscaloosa News*, April 26, 1932.

55. *Time*, news clipping, May 9, 1932, scrapbook 130, box 916, JTHP.

56. *Birmingham Age-Herald*, April 28, 1932.

57. 75 Cong. Rec. S9021 (1932).

58. 75 Cong. Rec. S9022 (1932).

59. 75 Cong. Rec. S9024 (1932).

60. *Washington Herald*, news clipping, April 29, 1932, scrapbook, box 22, JHBjrP; Hamilton, *Hugo Black*, 203.

61. *Tuscaloosa News*, April 28, 1932.

Chapter 10

1. WBB to JHBjr, January 26, 1931, box 6, folder 14, JHBjrP; *Akron Beacon Journal*, news clipping, January 22, 1931, folder 3, box 31, WBBP.

2. *New York World-Telegram*, February 3, 1932, folder 4, box 31, WBBP.

3. WBB to Arthur Lund, May 25, 1932, folder 10, box 3, WBBP.

4. WBB to F. H. LaGuardia, January 26, 1934, folder 8, box 7, WBBP.

5. WBB to Maude Hogden, May 7, 1934, folder 11, box 7, WBBP.

6. WBB to Thomas Owen Jr., August 10, 1936, folder 13, box 3, WBBP; Thomas Owen Jr. to WBB, December 2, 1938, folder 13, box 3, WBBP; WBB to Thomas Owen Jr., February 21, 1940, folder 13, box 3, WBBP.

7. Nora Martin to WBB, April 3, 1930, folder 12, box 3, WBBP.

8. Advertisement, unidentified clipping, WBB scrapbook, box 56, WBBP.

9. WBB to John J. Raskob, May 27, 1929, folder 13, box 6, WBBP.

10. MBO to JHBjr, November 13, 1931, Board of Trustees Meeting Minutes, 1930–31, Administrative Files, ADAHP; MBO to Hugh Morrow, November 18, 1931, Board of Trustees Meeting Minutes, 1930–31, Administrative Files, ADAHP.

11. MBO to Tallulah Bankhead, May 2, 1931, folder 8, box 1, MBOP.

12. MBO to WBB, May 16, 1937, folder 10, box 2, WBBP; *Wetumpka Herald*, March 6, 1958.

13. Quoted in Joel Lobenthal, *Tallulah! The Life and Times of a Leading Lady* (New York: HarperCollins, 2004), 171.

14. Lobenthal, 105.

15. Tallulah Bankhead, *Tallulah: My Autobiography* (New York: Harper, 1952), 174.

16. Lobenthal, *Tallulah!*, 116.

17. Bankhead, *Tallulah*, 140.

18. Bankhead, 137, 170–71, 189–90.

19. MBO to TB, January 22, 1931, box 3, MBOP.

20. MBO to TB, May 2, 1931, folder 8, box 1, TBP.

21. MBO to Janice O'Connell, January 30 and August 12, 1931, folder 20, Administrative Files, ADAHP; Norton Parker to MBO, February 20, 1933, folder 20, Administrative Files, ADAHP.

22. Lobenthal, *Tallulah!*, 202.

23. WBB to Sam Rayburn, October 21, 1930, folder 5, box 7, WBBP.

24. *Birmingham News*, news clipping, November 27, 1932, folder 4, box 31, WBBP.

25. Walter Judson Heacock, "William Brockman Bankhead: A Biography" (PhD diss., University of Wisconsin, 1952), 164; *New York Times*, August 26, 1934.

26. 75 Cong. Rec. H239 (1931).

27. Heacock, "William Brockman Bankhead," 243, 248.

28. 75 Cong. Rec. H243–49 (1931).

29. *Washington Herald*, quoted in Heacock, "William Brockman Bankhead," 165.

30. *Montgomery Advertiser*, August 26, 1931.

31. Speech transcript, "Senator Bankhead's Authorship of the Bankhead Cotton Control Act," January 1, 1944, folder 1, box 1, JHBjrP.

32. Jack Brien Key, "John H. Bankhead, Jr.: Creative Conservative" (PhD diss., Johns Hopkins University, 1964), 97–99.

33. Gilbert C. Fite, "Voluntary Attempts to Reduce Cotton Acreage in the South, 1914–1933," *Journal of Southern History* 14, no. 4 (November 1948): 481.

34. Pete Daniel, *Breaking the Land: The Transformation of Cotton, Tobacco, and Rice Cultures since 1880* (Urbana: University of Illinois Press, 1985), 18.

35. Fite, "Voluntary Attempts to Reduce Cotton Acreage in the South."

36. Seymour Melman, "An Industrial Revolution in the Cotton South," *Economic History Review* 2, no. 1 (1949): 61–62.

37. Gilbert C. Fite, *American Agriculture and Farm Policy since 1900* (New York: Macmillan, 1964), 10.

38. R. Douglas Hurt, *Problems of Plenty: The American Farmer in the Twentieth Century* (Chicago: Ivan R. Dee, 2002), 43.

39. Hurt, 47–48; Fite, *American Agriculture and Farm Policy since 1900*, 3.

40. Key, "John H. Bankhead, Jr.," 97–98.

41. Fite, *American Agriculture and Farm Policy since 1900*, 13.

42. 75 Cong. Rec. H9761 (1932).

43. Heacock, "William Brockman Bankhead," 169.

44. 75 Cong. Rec. H12189–90 (1932).

45. Heacock, "William Brockman Bankhead," 169; *New York Times*, July 12, 1932.

46. 75 Cong. Rec. H11926–31 (1932).

47. Evans C. Johnson, "John H. Bankhead 2d: Advocate of Cotton," *Alabama Review* 41 (January 1988): 33–34.

48. Key, "John H. Bankhead, Jr.," 95; Franklin Roosevelt to WBB, November 7, 1931, WBB scrapbook, box 56, WBBP.

49. WBB to Richard M. Kleberg, October 25, 1932, folder 5, box 7, WBBP; George H. Combs to WBB, October 16, 1932, folder 5, box 7, WBBP; Key, "John H. Bankhead, Jr.," 110.

50. WBB to Sam Rayburn, October 29, 1932, folder 5, box 7, WBBP.

51. *Birmingham News*, news clippings, November 28 and December 19, 1932, folder 4, box 31, WBBP.

52. Key, "John H. Bankhead, Jr.," 114.

53. *Birmingham News*, news clipping, December 7, 1932, folder 4, box 31, WBBP.

54. Key, "John H. Bankhead, Jr.," 115; 76 Cong. Rec. S108 (1932); 76 Cong. Rec. S725–32 (1932).

55. Edward L. Schapsmeier and Frederick H. Schapsmeier, "Farm Policy from FDR to Eisenhower: Southern Democrats and the Politics of Agriculture," *Agricultural History* 53, no. 1 (January 1979): 356.

56. Schapsmeier and Schapsmeier, 353.

57. Fite, *American Agriculture and Farm Policy since 1900*, 18.

58. Transcript, "America's Farm Problems," *American Forum of the Air*, Station WOL, Washington, DC, May 1, 1939, pp. 9–10, folder 2, box 13, JHBjrP; Rupert B. Vance, "Human Factors in the South's Agricultural Readjustment," *Law and Contemporary Problems* 1, no. 3 (June 1934): 260.

59. Heacock, "William Brockman Bankhead," 176; 76 Cong. Rec. H1341 (1933).

60. Lobenthal, *Tallulah!*, 219; WBB to TB, March 24, 1933, TBP.

61. Eugenia Bankhead Hoyt to WBB, February 9, 1933, folder 10, box 2, WBBP.

62. *New York Times*, April 12, 1933.

63. *Washington Post*, April 12, 1933.

64. Arthur G. Lund to WBB, April 11, 1933, folder 3, box 2, WBBP.

65. Heacock, "William Brockman Bankhead," 187; *New York Times*, April 12, 1933; *Jasper (AL) Mountain Eagle*, April 12, 1933.

66. Eugenia Bankhead Hoyt to WBB, April 13, 1933, folder 10, box 2, WBBP.

67. Heacock, "William Brockman Bankhead," 187; unidentified news clipping, c. May 1933, WBB scrapbook, box 56, WBBP.

68. *New York World-Telegram*, news clipping, June 21, 1934, WBB scrapbook, box 56, WBBP.

69. Key, "John H. Bankhead, Jr.," 119.

70. Gilbert C. Fite, "Farmer Opinion and the Agricultural Adjustment Act, 1933," *Mississippi Valley Historical Review* 48, no. 4 (March 1962): 656–73; *Jasper Advertiser*, June 20, 1933, WBB scrapbook, box 56, WBBP.

71. Fite, *American Agriculture and Farm Policy since 1900*, 15.

72. Henry I. Richards, *Cotton under the Agricultural Adjustment Act: Developments up to July 1934* (Washington, DC: Brookings Institution, 1934), 79.

73. *Birmingham Age-Herald*, news clipping, March 21, 1933, folder 5, box 31, WBBP.

74. Johnson, "John H. Bankhead 2d," 34–35.

75. Vance, "Human Factors in the South's Agricultural Readjustment," 259; Richards, *Cotton under the Agricultural Adjustment Act*, 35.

76. Chester D. Davis, *One Year of the AAA: The Record Reviewed* (Washington, DC: US Department of Agriculture, 1934), 2.

77. Davis, 4, 8.

78. Hurt, *Problems of Plenty*, 78.

79. Key, "John H. Bankhead, Jr.," 147.

80. Johnson, "John H. Bankhead 2d," 35.

81. Quoted in Key, "John H. Bankhead, Jr.," 148.

82. *New York Times*, February 8, 1934; *London Times*, news clipping, February 8, 1934, box 50, WBBP; *Washington Post*, news clipping, January 26, 1934, WBB scrapbook, box 50, WBBP. Rupert B. Vance asserts that the act was endorsed by over 75 percent of farmers questioned. See Vance, "Human Factors in the South's Agricultural Readjustment," 259.

83. "The Bankhead Act," *Saturday Evening Post*, news clipping, May 26, 1934, WBB scrapbook, box 50, WBBP; see also Vance, "Human Factors in the South's Agricultural Readjustment," 259.

84. *New York World-Telegram*, June 21, 1934, WBB scrapbook, box 56, WBBP.

85. "Progress Made by Major Legislation from March 29 to April 28, 1934," *Congressional Digest*, May 1934, 153.

86. *New York World-Telegram*, June 21, 1934, WBB scrapbook, box 56, WBBP.

87. *Washington Daily News*, April 2, 1934, WBB scrapbook, box 57, WBBP.

88. *New York World-Telegram*, June 21, 1934, WBB scrapbook, box 56, WBBP; unidentified news clipping, March 6, 1934, WBB scrapbook, box 57, WBBP.

89. *Saturday Evening Post*, "The Temptation to Use Force," August 31, 1937, 22.

90. Vance, "Human Factors in the South's Agricultural Readjustment," 261.

91. *New York Times*, news clipping, September 23, 1934, WBB scrapbook, box 50, WBBP.

92. US Department of Agriculture, Agricultural Adjustment Administration, Division of Information, State Summary Series, Alabama #1, "Agricultural Improvement in Alabama, 1932–1935," May 1, 1936, pp. 1, 2, 4, folder 1, box 8, JHBjrP.

93. Paul S. Haley to WBB, March 3, 1937, folder 4, box 2, WBBP.

94. Charles Kenneth Roberts, *The Farm Security Administration and Rural Rehabilitation in the South* (Knoxville: University of Tennessee Press, 2015), 11–12.

95. Gilbert C. Fite, *Cotton Fields No More: Southern Agriculture, 1865–1980* (Lexington: University Press of Kentucky, 1984), 143.

96. Howard Kester, *Revolt among the Sharecroppers* (1936; repr., Knoxville: University of Tennessee Press, 1997), 26.

97. Kester, 27.

98. Roberts, *The Farm Security Administration and Rural Rehabilitation in the South*, 158.

99. *Montgomery Advertiser*, news clipping, March 9, 1933, folder 5, box 31, WBBP.

100. John H. Bankhead, "Back to the Farm," June 10, 1932, in *Speeches of Hon. John H. Bankhead of Alabama in the Senate of the United States* (Washington, DC: Government Printing Office, 1934), 7–8.

101. Quoted in Roberts, *The Farm Security Administration and Rural Rehabilitation in the South*, xvii.

102. *New York Times*, March 5, 1933.

103. Roberts, *The Farm Security Administration and Rural Rehabilitation in the South*, xxvi; Mississippi State Planning Commission, "Farm Tenancy in Mississippi," March 1937, p. 24, folder 8, box 19, WBBP.

104. Roberts, *The Farm Security Administration and Rural Rehabilitation in the South*, 6, 8, 15.

105. Roberts, 34; "A Bill to provide for the redistribution of the overbalance of population in industrial centers by aiding in the purchase of subsistence farms, and for other purposes," H.R. 4234, 73rd Cong. (1933), folder 7, box 39, WBBP.

106. *An Act to Encourage National Industrial Recovery, to Foster Fair Competition, and to Provide for the Construction of Certain Useful Public Works, and for other Purposes (H.R. 5755)*, Public Law No. 67 (Washington, DC: Government Printing Office, 1933), 12.

107. Untitled speech, n.d., folder 2, box 13, JHBjrP.

108. JHBjr to Charles E. Pynchon, July 26, 1934, folder 5, box 4, JHBjrP.

109. JHBjr to Hugh MacRae, February 14, 1935, folder 6, box 4, JHBjrP.

110. JHBjr to Rex Tugwell, November 11, 1935, folder 6, box 4, JHBjrP.

111. For an excellent discussion of this and other rural rehabilitation programs undertaken during the New Deal, see Roberts, *The Farm Security Administration and Rural Rehabilitation in the South*, chapter 8.

112. WBB to Sarah B. Mustard, November 19, 1935, folder 4, box 20, WBBP.

113. WBB to resettlement director, January 30, 1936, folder 4, box 20, WBBP; WBB to J. W. Cornelius, April 14, 1936, folder 4, box 20, WBBP.

114. Steve Wilson to WBB, August 13, 1936, folder 4, box 20, WBBP; WBB to John Beecher, September 22, 1936, folder 4, box 20, WBBP; WBB to John Beecher, September 26, 1936, folder 4, box 20, WBBP; Albert C. Hester to WBB, September 25, 1936, folder 4, box 20, WBBP; WBB to John Beecher, September 28, 1936, folder 4, box 20, WBBP.

115. MBO to JHBjr, August 31, 1933, folder 12, Administrative Files, ADAHP.

116. MBO to JHBjr, November 1, 1933, folder 12, Administrative Files, ADAHP; JHBjr to MBO, c. November 1933, folder 12, Administrative Files, ADAHP; MBO to JHBjr, January 8, 1934, folder 12, Administrative Files, ADAHP; MBO to president, Alabama Utilities Company, January 11, 1934, folder 12, Administrative Files, ADAHP; MBO to Southern Natural Gas Corp., January 16, 1934, folder 12, Administrative Files, ADAHP.

117. Mrs. H. N. McLean to JHBjr, May 19, 1937, folder 2, box 5, JHBjrP.

118. Roberts, *The Farm Security Administration and Rural Rehabilitation in the South*, 176.

119. *New York Times*, August 20, 22, and 26, 1934; see also letters in folder 3, box 8, WBBP.

120. WBB to Sam Rayburn, September 11, 1934, folder 7, box 5, WBBP.

121. E. E. Cox to WBB, November 14, 1934, folder 3, box 8, WBBP.

122. *New York Times*, December 12, 1934.

123. Unidentified news clipping, c. December 1934, WBB scrapbook, box 59, WBBP.

124. *New York Times*, December 23 and 30, 1934.

125. Ray Tucker, "A Master for the House," *Collier's*, January 5, 1935, 22, 49.

126. *New York Times*, January 3, 1935; Heacock, "William Brockman Bankhead," 201; *Birmingham Age-Herald*, January 3, 1935, WBB scrapbook, box 59, WBBP.

127. *New York Times*, January 27, 1935; *Birmingham News*, September 15, 1940.

128. "The Congress," *Time*, January 14, 1935, 12–13.

129. Heacock, "William Brockman Bankhead," 203–4; "The Washington Sideshow," news clipping, n.d.; unidentified news clipping, WBB scrapbook, box 59, WBBP; WBB to JHBjr, June 13, 1935, folder 3, box 2, WBBP; WBB to T. Jeff Bailey, February 20, 1935, folder 6, box 8, WBBP; Lobenthal, *Tallulah!*, 239.

130. WBB to JHBjr, June 13, 1935, folder 3, box 2, WBBP.

131. WBB to George W. Calver, June 13 and July 2, 1935, folder 2, box 3, WBBP.

132. WBB to James Knox Julian, August 27, 1935, folder 12, box 2, WBBP.

133. Heacock, "William Brockman Bankhead," 204–5.

134. *New York Times*, December 24, 1935.

Chapter 11

1. WBB to Eugenia Bankhead Hoyt, April 22, 1936, folder 10, box 2, WBBP.

2. *New York Times*, December 24, 1935.

3. William E. Leuchtenburg, *Franklin D. Roosevelt and the New Deal, 1932–1940* (New York: Harper and Row, 1963), 170.

4. *New York Times*, January 7, 1936; 80 Cong. Rec. H1499 (1936).

5. Department of Agriculture, Economic Research Service, "History of Agricultural Price-Support and Adjustment Programs, 1933–1984," *Agriculture Information Bulletin*, no. 485 (December 1984): 10.

6. Walter Judson Heacock, "William Brockman Bankhead: A Biography" (PhD diss., University of Wisconsin, 1952), 207. See also *Time*, December 23, 1935, January 13 and 20, 1936, and February 10, 1936.

7. Leuchtenburg, *Franklin D. Roosevelt and the New Deal*, 172.

8. "New Speaker," *Literary Digest*, clipping, n.d., WBB scrapbook, box 61, WBBP; *Evening Star*, June 4, 1936; 80 Cong. Rec. H9016 (1936).

9. *Birmingham Age-Herald*, June 6 and 9, 1936.

10. Telegram, Tallulah Bankhead to WBB, June 4, 1936, WBB scrapbook, box 61, WBBP.

11. This was one of Bankhead's favorite stories, and it appears in feature articles about the Speaker throughout his career. See *Birmingham Age-Herald*, September 17, 1940.

12. WBB diary, January 25, 1937, Walker Area Community Foundation, Jasper, AL.

13. "Master" to Zip, December 25, 1936, WBB scrapbook, box 63, WBBP.

14. *Birmingham Age-Herald*, c. 1936, WBB scrapbook, box 61, WBBP.

15. *Birmingham Age-Herald*, c. 1936, WBB scrapbook, box 61, WBBP.

16. WBB diary, March 15, 1937, Walker Area Community Foundation, Jasper, AL.

17. *Life*, December 28, 1936, 9–11; Eugenia Bankhead Hoyt to WBB, February 13, 1937, folder 10, box 2, WBBP.

18. "Southern Lady Makes Good in a Complicated Role," *Democratic Digest*, July 1937, 19; *Washington Post*, March 21, 1940.

19. Unidentified news clipping, c. June 1936, box 61, WBBP.

20. Unidentified news clipping, c. June 1936, box 61, WBBP; "Southern Lady Makes Good in a Complicated Role," 19.

21. WBB diary, February 1, 1937, Walker Area Community Foundation, Jasper, AL.

22. WBB diary, March 1, 1938.

23. WBB diary, January 19, 1938; *Montgomery Advertiser*, July 7, 1940.

24. *Time*, September 23, 1940, 17.

25. Charles Kenneth Roberts, *The Farm Security Administration and Rural Rehabilitation in the South* (Knoxville: University of Tennessee Press, 2015), xxii, quotation on xxiii.

26. Roberts, 51.

27. Rupert B. Vance, "Human Factors in the South's Agricultural Readjustment," *Law and Contemporary Problems* 1, no. 3 (June 1934): 273.

28. Vance, 274.

29. Howard Kester, *Revolt among the Sharecroppers* (1936; repr., Knoxville: University of Tennessee Press, 1997), 17.

30. Vance, "Human Factors in the South's Agricultural Readjustment," 268.

31. Vance, 269.

32. Vance, 270.

33. *New York Times*, December 5, 1933.

34. W. W. Alexander, "Farm Tenancy," paper read at National Planning Conference, June 3, 1937, p. 9, folder 8, box 19, WBBP.

35. Roberts, *The Farm Security Administration and Rural Rehabilitation in the South*, 55.

36. *New York Times*, April 14, 1935.

37. Tore C. Olsson, *Agrarian Crossings: Reformers and the Remaking of the US and Mexican Countryside* (Princeton, NJ: Princeton University Press, 2017), 51.

38. *New York Times*, April 14, 1935.

39. Vance, "Human Factors in the South's Agricultural Readjustment," 273.

40. *To Create the Farm Tenant Homes Corporation: Hearing before a Subcommittee of the Committee on Agriculture and Forestry, United States Senate*, 74th Cong., 1st sess., March 5, 1935 (Washington, DC: Government Printing Office, 1935).

41. Testimony of Henry A. Wallace, in *To Create the Farm Tenant Homes Corporation*, 7; Testimony of L. C. Gray, in *To Create the Farm Tenant Homes Corporation*, 18; S. H. Hobbs Jr. to JHBjr, March 2, 1935, in *To Create the Farm Tenant Homes Corporation*, 75.

42. Testimony of Henry A. Wallace, in *To Create the Farm Tenant Homes Corporation*, 7.

43. Testimony of Henry A. Wallace, 8, 10.

44. Testimony of L. C. Gray, in *To Create the Farm Tenant Homes Corporation*, 17.

45. Testimony of Lawrence Westbrook, in *To Create the Farm Tenant Homes Corporation*, 42.

46. Frank Fitts to JHBjr, March 1, 1935, in *To Create the Farm Tenant Homes Corporation*, 73.

47. Clarence Poe to JHBjr, March 5, 1935, in *To Create the Farm Tenant Homes Corporation*, 74.

48. JHBjr, "Bankhead Tenant Aid Bill Explained," unidentified news clipping, c. 1936, WBB scrapbook, box 57, WBBP.

49. Olsson, *Agrarian Crossings*, 52.

50. "The Nation-Wide Problem of Farm Tenancy," *Congressional Digest*, February 1937, 37; John H. Bankhead Jr., "Will Government Aid for Small Farm Purchasers Solve the Tenancy Problem?" *Congressional Digest*, February 1937, 49–50.

51. *Birmingham News*, February 10, 1936.

52. WBB to TB, March 11, 1940, folder 7, box 12, WBBP; TB to WBB, March 20, 1940, folder 7, box 12, WBBP; TB to organizers of National Sharecroppers Week, March 20, 1940, folder 7, box 12, WBBP.

53. Testimony of Henry Wallace, in *To Create the Farm Tenant Homes Corporation*, 7.

54. "Share-Croppers: Whites and Negroes, under Same Roof and Union, Ask for Action and Get It," *Newsweek*, June 13, 1936, 7–8.

55. JHBjr to James E. Chappell of the *Birmingham News*, November 30, 1936, folder 1, box 5, JHBjrP.

56. "The Nation-Wide Problem of Farm Tenancy," 37; JHBjr, "Will Government Aid for Small Farm Purchasers Solve the Tenancy Problem?"

57. WBB to JHBjr, May 23, 1936, folder 4, box 2, WBBP.

58. *Philadelphia Record*, news clipping, September 27, 1936, scrapbook, box 23, JHBjrP.

59. WBB to James Knox Julian, February 27, 1936, folder 12, box 2, WBBP; WBB to Eugenia Bankhead Hoyt, April 22, 1936, folder 10, box 2, WBBP.

60. WBB to JHBjr, May 23, 1936, folder 4, box 2, WBBP.

61. Charles B. Crow to E. F. Creekmore, October 13, 1936, folder 2, box 1, Charles B. Crow Papers.

62. WBB to James Knox Julian, November 10, 1936, folder 12, box 2, WBBP.

63. J. E. Chappell to Charles B. Crow, September 9, 1936, folder 2, box 1, Charles B. Crow Papers; Charles B. Crow to E. F. Creekmore, October 13, 1936, folder 2, box 1, Charles B. Crow Papers; Charles B. Crow to E. F. Creekmore, December 7, 1936, folder 2, box 1, Charles B. Crow Papers.

64. WBB to JHBjr, [October?] 23, 1936, folder 4, box 2, WBBP.

65. WBB to Eugenia Bankhead Hoyt, April 22, 1936, folder 10, box 2, WBBP.

66. *New York Times*, September 13, 1933.

67. Eugenia Bankhead Hoyt to WBB, February 9 and undated, 1933, folder 10, box 2, WBBP; Eugenia Bankhead Hoyt to WBB, March 21 and July 9, 1935, folder 10, box 2, WBBP; Eugenia Bankhead Hoyt to WBB, December 13, 1936, folder 10, box 2, WBBP; Eugenia Bankhead Hoyt to WBB, January 20, 1937, folder 10, box 2, WBBP; WBB to Eugenia Bankhead Hoyt, April 22, 1936, folder 10, box 2, WBBP.

68. Tallulah Bankhead, *Tallulah: My Autobiography* (New York: Harper, 1952), 212.

69. *Los Angeles Times*, September 15, 1933.

70. Quoted in Joel Lobenthal, *Tallulah! The Life and Times of a Leading Lady* (New York: HarperCollins, 2004), 224.

71. *Atlanta Constitution*, November 4, 1933; *Los Angeles Times*, November 4, 1933.

72. Bankhead, *Tallulah*, 213; Lobenthal, *Tallulah!*, 225; *Jasper (AL) Mountain Eagle*, December 27, 1933, and January 3, 1934.

73. WBB to James Knox Julian, February 27, 1936, folder 12, box 2, WBBP.

74. WBB to James Knox Julian, June 16, 1936, folder 12, box 2, WBBP.

75. WBB to James Knox Julian, September 2 and 24 and November 10, 1936, folder 12, box 2, WBBP.

76. Leuchtenburg, *Franklin D. Roosevelt and the New Deal*, 188.

77. *Jasper (AL) Mountain Eagle*, November 25, 1936; Heacock, "William Brockman Bankhead," 219–20; unidentified news clipping, n.d., WBB scrapbook, box 61, WBBP.

78. WBB diary, January 26, 1937, Walker Area Community Foundation, Jasper, AL.

79. *New York Times Magazine*, February 14, 1937, WBB scrapbook, box 63, WBBP.

80. *New York Times*, December 16, 1936.

81. Frank Miller Smith, "The Greatest Show on Earth," c. December 1936, WBB scrapbook, box 63, WBBP.

82. *New York Times*, January 16, 1937.

83. Unidentified news clipping, January 5, 1937, WBB scrapbook, box 63, WBBP.

84. Report of the Director, Board of Trustees Meeting Minutes, 1931–34, Administrative Files, ADAHP.

85. Report of the Director, Board of Trustees Meeting Minutes, 1929–30, Administrative Files, ADAHP.

86. Quoted in William Warren Rogers et al., *Alabama: The History of a Deep South State* (Tuscaloosa: University of Alabama Press, 1994), 479.

87. Robert J. Jakeman, "Marie Bankhead Owen and the Alabama Department of Archives and History, 1920–1955," *Provenance: Journal of the Society of Georgia Archivists* 21, no. 1 (2003): 36–65.

88. Jakeman, 38.

89. Report of the Director, Board of Trustees Meeting Minutes, 1931–34, Administrative Files, ADAHP; Marie Bankhead Owen, *Alabama: An Economic and Political History of the State*, illus. Nathan Glick (Montgomery, AL: Dixie Book, 1937); Walter M. Jackson and Marie Bankhead Owen, *History of Alabama for Junior High Schools* (Montgomery, AL: Dixie Book, 1938); Marie Bankhead Owen, *From Campfire to Cahaba* (Montgomery, AL: Dixie Book, 1936); Marie Bankhead Owen and Mary Edward Mitchell, *Our Home Land* (Montgomery, AL: Dixie Book, 1936). The junior high school textbook was used by students in Tuscaloosa.

90. Owen, *Alabama*, 271.

91. Owen, 266. For slavery's continuing profitability, see Walter Johnson, *Soul by Soul: Life inside the Antebellum Slave Market* (Cambridge, MA: Harvard University Press, 1999); Edward E. Baptist, *The Half Has Never Been Told: Slavery and the Making of American Capitalism* (New York: Basic Books, 2014).

92. Owen, *Alabama*, 271–72; Jackson and Owen, *History of Alabama for Junior High Schools*, 100.

93. MBO to M. E. Laul, *Southern Radio News*, January 28, 1938, folder 21, Administrative Files, ADAHP.

94. Jackson and Owen, *History of Alabama for Junior High Schools*, 101.

95. MBO to Mollie Jones, May 20, 1936, box 6, United Daughters of the Confederacy (UDC) Historian 1936 folder, MBO-UDC Papers, ADAH.

96. "Report of Division Historian," c. 1937, box 6, UDC Historian 1936 folder, MBO-UDC Papers.

97. MBO to Wilmer L. Hall, May 19, 1938, folder 23, Administrative Files, ADAHP.

98. MBO to "The Press of Alabama," February 11, 1937, folder 16, Administrative Files, ADAHP.

99. *Atlanta Constitution*, April 26, 1939; *New York Times*, May 21, 1939.

100. MBO to TB, May 20, 1931, folder 8, box 1, TBP.

101. MBO to TB, April 1, 1924, folder 7, box 1, TBP.

102. WBB to TB, August 13, 1932, folder 8, box 1, TBP; Lobenthal, *Tallulah!*, 194.

103. Lobenthal, *Tallulah!*, 206.

104. MBO to TB, August 6, 1932, folder 8, box 1, TBP.

105. TB to MBO, August 11, 1932, folder 8, box 1, TBP.

106. WBB to TB, August 13, 1932, folder 8, box 1, TBP.

107. MBO to WBB, August 6, 1932, folder 1, box 3, TBP; WBB to MBO, August 25, 1932, folder 1, box 3, TBP; MBO to Charlie Pell, August 27, 1932, folder 1, box 3, TBP; MBO to W. W. Brandon, August 22, 1932, folder 1, box 3, TBP.

108. Susan J. Douglas and Andrea McDonnell, *Celebrity: A History of Fame* (New York: New York University Press, 2019), 99.

109. Franklin D. Roosevelt to Henry A. Wallace, November 16, 1936, in National Resources Committee, Special Committee on Farm Tenancy, *Farm Tenancy: Report of the President's Committee* (Washington, DC: Government Printing Office, 1937), 25, 28.

110. "Recommendations Regarding Tenancy Legislation Submitted to the Special Committee on Farm Tenancy by the Southern Policy Association," December 14, 1936, p. 5, folder 7, box 19, WBBP.

111. *Atlanta Constitution*, December 15, 1936.

112. "President Roosevelt Urges Farm Tenancy Legislation," *Congressional Digest*, February 1937, 45.

113. President's message to Congress, February 16, 1937, in National Resources Committee, *Farm Tenancy*, 25–26.

114. National Resources Committee, 4.

115. National Resources Committee, 6–7.

116. National Resources Committee, 24.

117. National Resources Committee, 11–15.

118. Charles S. Leyden to Charles B. Crow, January 14, 1937, box 1, folder 3, Crow Papers.

119. JHBjr to Charles B. Crow, January 18, 1937, box 1, folder 3, Charles B. Crow Papers.

120. Charles Whelan to Charles B. Crow, March 25, 1937, box 1, folder 3, Charles B. Crow Papers; JHBjr to Charles B. Crow, March 28, 1937, box 1, folder 3, Charles B. Crow Papers; WBB diary, January 27, 1937, Walker Area Community Foundation, Jasper, AL.

121. Roberts, *The Farm Security Administration and Rural Rehabilitation in the South*, 66–67.

122. Roberts, 67.

123. J. L. Edwards to JHBjr, December 3, 1936, folder 1, box 5, JHBjrP; JHBjr to J. L. Edwards, December 8, 1936, folder 1, box 5, JHBjrP.

124. Robert Shogan, *Backlash: The Killing of the New Deal* (Chicago: Ivan R. Dee, 2006), 49.

125. *New York Times*, January 28, 1937, WBB Scrapbook, Speakership, p. 84, box 63, WBBP.

126. WBB diary, January 27 and 29, 1937, Walker Area Community Foundation, Jasper, AL.

127. Shogan, *Backlash*, 137.

128. Shogan, 138.

129. Shogan, 153.

130. WBB diary, March 15, 1937, Walker Area Community Foundation, Jasper, AL.

131. WBB diary, February 5, 1937.

132. *New York Times*, February 6, 1937.

133. WBB diary, February 5, 1937.

134. *New York Times*, February 6, 1937; Shogun, *Backlash*, 84.

135. Quoted in Shogan, *Backlash*, 121.

136. WBB diary, February 5, 1937, Walker Area Community Foundation, Jasper, AL.

137. Shogan, *Backlash*, 123.

138. Shogan, 83.

139. WBB to JHBjr, February 9, 1937, folder 4, box 2, WBBP.

140. Quoted in Leuchtenburg, *Franklin D. Roosevelt and the New Deal*, 234.

141. WBB diary, February 8, 1937, Walker Area Community Foundation, Jasper, AL.

142. WBB to JHBjr, February 16, 1937, folder 4, box 2, WBBP.

143. WBB to JHBjr, March 5, 1937, folder 4, box 2, WBBP.

144. WBB diary, March 25, 1937, Walker Area Community Foundation, Jasper, AL.

145. WBB diary, March 2, 1937.

146. WBB diary, March 2, 1937.

147. *New York Times*, June 15, 1937.

148. WBB diary, April 14, 1937, Walker Area Community Foundation, Jasper, AL.

149. WBB diary, news clipping, c. April 1937.

150. WBB to JHBjr, May 20, 1937, folder 4, box 2, WBBP.

151. Shogan, *Backlash*, 211–13.

152. WBB diary, June 10, 1937, Walker Area Community Foundation, Jasper, AL.

153. WBB diary, July 8, 1937.

154. WBB diary, July 15, 1937.

155. WBB diary, July 15, 1937.

156. Shogan, *Backlash*, 213–19.

157. WBB diary, June 10, 1937, Walker Area Community Foundation, Jasper, AL.

158. Lawrence Westbrook, "Will Government Aid for Small Farm Purchases Solve the Tenancy Problem?," *Congressional Digest*, February 1937, 63.

159. "The Nation-Wide Problem of Farm Tenancy," 38.

160. W. W. Alexander, "Farm Tenancy," paper read at National Planning Conference, June 3, 1937, p. 10, folder 8, box 19, WBBP.

161. WBB to JHBjr, May 20, 1937, folder 4, box 2, WBBP.

162. 81 Cong. Rec. H6453 (1937).

163. *New York Times*, June 10, 1937.

164. Jack Brien Key, "John H. Bankhead, Jr.: Creative Conservative" (PhD diss., Johns Hopkins University, 1964), 212.

165. *Montgomery Advertiser*, July 26, 1937.

166. Roberts, *The Farm Security Administration and Rural Rehabilitation in the South*, 68.

167. Olsson, *Agrarian Crossings*, 41.

168. Olsson, 43.

169. Roberts, *The Farm Security Administration and Rural Rehabilitation in the South*, 68.

170. Roberts, 74.

171. Roberts, 110–11.

172. *Washington Daily News*, February 8, 1938, scrapbook, box 23, JHBjrP; *Montgomery Advertiser*, August 23, 1938; *Newsweek*, February 14, 1938, 16; *Birmingham News*, February 17, 1940.

173. Roberts, *The Farm Security Administration and Rural Rehabilitation in the South*, 112–13, 127.

174. Roberts, 109.

175. Roberts, 84–85.

176. "Borrowers under Terms of Bankhead-Jones Farm Tenant Act," n.d., folder 2, box 8, JHBjrP.

177. WBB diary, March 1, 1938, Walker Area Community Foundation, Jasper, AL.

178. WBB diary, November 22, 1937.

179. WBB to JHBjr, August 11, 1937, folder 4, box 2, WBBP; see also WBB diary, August 3, 1937.

180. *Time*, November 29, 1937, 20.

181. WBB diary, November 22, 1937, Walker Area Community Foundation, Jasper, AL.

182. News clipping, n.d., WBB scrapbook, box 63, WBBP.

183. News clipping, c. November 1937, WBB scrapbook, box 63, WBBP.

184. Quoted in Heacock, "William Brockman Bankhead," 236.

185. *Washington Post*, December 14, 1937.

186. *Atlanta Constitution*, December 18, 1937; WBB diary, January 19, 1938, Walker Area Community Foundation, Jasper, AL.

187. William Mitch to WBB, December 20, 1937, WBBP.

188. Leuchtenburg, *Franklin D. Roosevelt and the New Deal*, 251.

189. Heacock, "William Brockman Bankhead," 237.

190. Howard D. Samuel, "Troubled Passage: The Labor Movement and the Fair Labor Standards Act," *Monthly Labor Review*, December 2000, 32–37, https://www.bls.gov/opub/mlr /2000/12/art3full.pdf.

191. *Birmingham News*, June 18, 1938.

Chapter 12

1. Robert Shogan, *Backlash: The Killing of the New Deal* (Chicago: Ivan R. Dee, 2006), 233.

2. Sam Rayburn to WBB, August 15, 1938, folder 7, box 16, WBBP.

3. Sam Rayburn to WBB, September 1938, folder 7, box 16, WBBP; WBB to Sam Rayburn, September 19, 1938, folder 7, box 16, WBBP.

4. William E. Leuchtenburg, *Franklin D. Roosevelt and the New Deal, 1932–1940* (New York: Harper and Row, 1963), 271.

5. Joseph A. Fry, *Dixie Looks Abroad: The South and U.S. Foreign Relations, 1789–1973* (Baton Rouge: Louisiana State University Press, 2002), 198–99.

6. WBB diary, March 15, 1937, Walker Area Community Foundation, Jasper, AL.

7. *New York Times*, January 8, 1938.

8. 83 Cong. Rec. H277 (1938), copy in box 39, WBBP.

9. *Birmingham Age-Herald*, news clipping, n.d., WBB scrapbook, box 65, WBBP; Fry, *Dixie Looks Abroad*, 200.

10. *London Times*, January 11, 1938.

11. JHBjr to MBO, April 20, 1939, MBOP.

12. 84 Cong. Rec. H8509–10 (1939); *New York Times*, July 1, 1939.

13. *New York Times*, May 22, 1939; unidentified news clipping, May 22, 1939, folder 7, box 31, WBBP.

14. *New York Times*, July 1, 1939.

15. *Montgomery Advertiser*, September 5, 1939; *Mobile Times*, September 15, 1939.

16. Quoted in Jack Brien Key, "John H. Bankhead, Jr.: Creative Conservative" (PhD diss., Johns Hopkins University, 1964), 238.

17. Cordell Hull to WBB, November 3, 1939, folder 4, box 12, WBBP.

18. Key, "John H. Bankhead, Jr.," 217.

19. Key, 238.

20. Eleanor Roosevelt, "My Day," January 10, 1938, *Eleanor Roosevelt Papers Digital Edition*, last modified June 9, 2017, https://www2.gwu.edu/~erpapers/myday/displaydoc.cfm?_y =1938&_f=md054847.

21. *Birmingham News*, December 9, 1939.

22. *Baltimore Sun*, May 29, 1940.

23. Susan Dunn, *1940: FDR, Willkie, Lindbergh, Hitler: The Election amid the Storm* (New Haven, CT: Yale University Press, 2013), 167–69.

24. Quotations in Dunn, 171.

25. Eugenia Bankhead Hoyt to TB, April 1, 1937, folder 10, box 2, WBBP.

26. Tallulah Bankhead, *Tallulah: My Autobiography* (New York: Harper, 1952), 230.

27. Bankhead, 232.

28. Quoted in Joel Lobenthal, *Tallulah! The Life and Times of a Leading Lady* (New York: HarperCollins, 2004), 248.

29. Bankhead, *Tallulah*, 233.

30. *New York Times*, September 2, 1937.

31. *Baltimore Sun*, November 21, 1937.

32. *Chicago Daily Tribune*, November 21, 1937.

33. Bankhead, *Tallulah*, 226–27.

34. Lobenthal, *Tallulah!*, 327.

35. Bankhead, *Tallulah*, 235–36.

36. Bankhead, 237.

37. Bankhead, 240–41.

38. Charles B. Crow to Grover C. Hall, October 15, 1937, folder 3, box 1, Charles B. Crow Papers.

39. *Boston Globe*, c. March 1939, WBB scrapbook, box 65, WBBP.

40. WBB diary, March 2, 1937, Walker Area Community Foundation, Jasper, AL.

41. *Birmingham News*, June 18, 1938.

42. Walter Judson Heacock, "William Brockman Bankhead: A Biography" (PhD diss., University of Wisconsin, 1952), 261, 263; *Washington Post*, September 28, 1938.

43. Lister Hill to WBB, August 14, 1930, folder 3, box 17, WBBP.

44. WBB to MBO, September 1, 1938, folder 1, box 17, WBBP.

45. Tom Owen Jr. to WBB, October 4, 1938, folder 13, box 3, WBBP.

46. "Bankhead Birthday," *Newsweek*, April 24, 1939, 16.

47. WBB, statement to Alabama state legislature, August 23, 1939, folder 3, box 17, WBBP.

48. Heacock, "William Brockman Bankhead," 265.

49. *Montgomery Advertiser*, April 7, 1940.

50. *Alabama Journal*, April 30, 1940.

51. "Bankhead for President Fund," box 2, WBBP.

52. J. Thomas Heflin to WBB, January 8, 1940, folder 5, box 17, WBBP.

53. *New York Times*, May 8, 1940.

54. Heacock, "William Brockman Bankhead," 268–69.

55. *Birmingham News*, February 25, 1940.

56. *New York Times*, July 15, 1940.

57. John Dingell to Lister Hill, July 9, 1940, folder 19, box 17, WBBP.

58. *Montgomery Advertiser*, March 14, 1940, folder 11, box 31, WBBP.

59. *Alabama Journal*, April 2, 1940; WBB to JHBjr, May 21, 1940, folder 7, box 17, WBBP.

60. WBB to JHBjr, May 21, 1940, folder 4, box 2, WBBP.

61. Heacock, "William Brockman Bankhead," 270.

62. *Montgomery Advertiser*, May 24, 1940.

63. *Birmingham News*, June 23, 1940.

64. Key, "John H. Bankhead, Jr.," 244; JHBjr to WBB, July 8, 1940, folder 4, box 2, WBBP.

65. Dunn, *1940*, 131–32.

66. JHBjr to WBB, June 27, 1940, folder 4, box 2, WBBP.

67. WBB to JHBjr, July 3, 1940, folder 4, box 2, WBBP.

68. WBB to JHBjr, July 3, 1940, folder 4, box 2, WBBP.

69. WBB to JHBjr, July 5, 1940, folder 9, box 30, WBBP.

70. *Birmingham News*, July 15, 1940.

71. JHBjr to WBB, July 6, 1940, folder 9, box 17, WBBP.

72. Dunn, *1940*, 134.

73. *New York Times*, July 17, 1940.

74. *Christian Science Monitor*, July 18, 1940.

75. *New York Times*, July 15, 1940.

76. *New York Times*, July 16 and 17, 1940.

77. *Christian Science Monitor*, July 16, 1940.

78. *Baltimore Sun*, July 16, 1940.

79. Dunn, *1940*, 134.

80. *New York Times*, July 16, 1940.

81. *New York Times*, July 16, 1940.

82. MBO to WBB, July 19, 1940, box 3, MBOP.

83. *Los Angeles Times*, July 16, 1940.

84. *New York Times*, July 17, 1940.

85. Dunn, *1940*, 136.

86. *Christian Science Monitor*, July 16, 1940.

87. *Los Angeles Times*, July 16, 1940.

88. *Baltimore Sun*, July 17, 1940.

89. *Christian Science Monitor*, July 17, 1940.

90. Dunn, *1940*, 138.

91. *Baltimore Sun*, July 17, 1940.

92. *New York Times*, July 17, 1940.

93. *Christian Science Monitor*, July 18, 1940.

94. MBO to WBB, July 19, 1940, box, MBOP; WBB to MBOP, July 23, 1940, box 3, MBOP.

95. *Christian Science Monitor*, July 18, 1940.

96. For an excellent account of the convention, see Dunn, *1940*, 134–42.

97. Dunn, 143.

98. *Birmingham News*, July 21, 1940.

99. *Los Angeles Times*, July 19, 1940.

100. *Atlanta Constitution*, July 19, 1940.

101. *Washington Post*, July 19, 1940.

102. *New York Times*, July 19, 1940.

103. *Los Angeles Times*, July 19, 1940.

104. *Birmingham News*, July 19, 1940.

105. *Atlanta Constitution*, July 19, 1940.

106. *Baltimore Sun*, July 19, 1940.

107. Key, "John H. Bankhead, Jr.," 245.

108. Henry A. Wallace to JHBjr, August 7, 1940, folder 13, box 17, WBBP.

109. *Birmingham News*, July 19, 1940.

110. Dunn, *1940*, 130.

111. Editorial, *Alabama: News Magazine of the Deep South*, September 23, 1940, 1.

112. *Tuscaloosa News*, July 20, 1940.

113. S. W. Williams to WBB, July 30, 1940, folder 13, box 17, WBBP.

114. Carrie Long Worthington to WBB, July 20, 1940, folder 11, box 17, WBBP.

115. WBB to Bessie O. Chenowith, July 27, 1940, folder 11, box 17, WBBP.

116. *Anniston (AL) Star*, September 16, 1940.

117. *Birmingham News*, August 9, 1940.

118. MBO to WBB, July 19, 1940, box 3, MBOP.

119. MBO to WBB, July 19, 1940, box 3, MBOP.

120. WBB to MBO, July 23, 1940, box 3, MBOP.

121. *National Record*, September 21, 1940, WBB scrapbook, box 71, WBBP.

122. *Birmingham Post*, July 19, 1940.

123. Quoted in Dunn, *1940*, 174.

124. Dunn, 175.

125. J. Garry Clifford and Samuel R. Spencer Jr., *The First Peacetime Draft* (Lawrence: University of Kansas Press, 1986), 208.

126. *Los Angeles Times*, September 6, 1940.

127. *Washington Post*, September 8, 1940.

128. Nora Sweeney to WBB, July 30, 1940, folder 6, box 18, WBBP.

129. D. P. Knapp to WBB, August 2, 1940, folder 6, box 18, WBBP.

130. Frank Dixon to WBB, August 5, 1940, folder 7, box 18, WBBP.

131. William J. Calvert Jr. to WBB, August 7, 1940, folder 7, box 18, WBBP; WBB to William J. Calvert Jr., August 12, 1940, folder 7, box 18, WBBP.

132. Clifford and Spencer, *The First Peacetime Draft*, 213.

133. *Alabama Journal* (Montgomery), September 12, 1940.

134. *Birmingham News*, September 19, 1940.

135. *Birmingham News*, September 10, 1940.

136. *Birmingham Post*, September 11, 1940.

137. *Birmingham News*, September 12, 1940.

138. *Birmingham News*, September 14, 1940.

139. *Montgomery Advertiser*, September 15, 1940.

140. *Birmingham Post*, September 16, 1940.

141. *Birmingham Age-Herald*, September 16, 1940.

142. *Birmingham Post*, September 16, 1940.

143. *Washington News*, September 17, 1940, folder 17, box 32, WBBP.

144. *Bangkok Chronicle*, September 17, 1940, folder 14, box 31, WBBP.

145. *Birmingham News*, September 18, 1940; *Birmingham Age-Herald*, September 18, 1940.

146. *University of Alabama Alumni News* (Tuscaloosa), October 1940, 14; *Decatur (AL) Daily*, September 17, 1940, folder 14, box 31, WBBP; *Birmingham Post*, September 18, 1940.

147. *Birmingham Post*, September 18, 1940.

Chapter 13

1. J. D. Ratcliff, "Revolution in Cotton," *Collier's*, July 21, 1945, 24.

2. *Birmingham News*, May 9, 1941; Jack Brien Key, "John H. Bankhead, Jr.: Creative Conservative" (PhD diss., Johns Hopkins University, 1964), 249.

3. Key, "John H. Bankhead, Jr.," 258.

4. *Montgomery Advertiser*, October 31, 1941.

5. *Birmingham News*, news clipping, n.d., folder 5, box 15, JHBjrP.

6. 87 Cong. Rec. S9506 (1941).

7. *Birmingham News*, January 12 and February 8, 1941.

8. *Birmingham News*, May 25, 1941.

9. Gilbert C. Fite, *Cotton Fields No More: Southern Agriculture, 1865–1980* (Lexington: University Press of Kentucky, 1984), 158, 163–64.

10. Key, "John H. Bankhead, Jr.," 240.

11. Key, 248.

12. Fite, *Cotton Fields No More*, 164.

13. Meg Jacobs, "'How about Some Meat?': The Office of Price Administration, Consumption Politics, and State Building from the Bottom Up, 1941–46," *Journal of American History* 84, no. 3 (December 1997): 913, 915, 918.

14. Key, "John H. Bankhead, Jr.," 259.

15. *Washington Post*, April 3, 1941.

16. Key, "John H. Bankhead, Jr.," 262.

17. Key, 263.

18. Meg Jacobs, *Pocketbook Politics: Economic Citizenship in Twentieth-Century America* (Princeton, NJ: Princeton University Press, 2005), 5.

19. 87 Cong. Rec. S3607 (1941); *Commodity Loans and Marketing Quotas, Hearings before the Committee on Agriculture and Forestry, United States Senate*, 77th Cong., 1st sess. (Washington, DC: Government Printing Office, 1941), 130.

20. *New York Times*, March 16, 1941.

21. 87 Cong. Rec. S4020–23 (1941); *Washington Post*, May 14, 1941; *Chicago Tribune*, May 12, 1941; *Atlanta Constitution*, February 22 and May 12, 1941; *Washington Post*, March 29, 1941.

22. *Washington Post*, May 17, 1941; *New York Times*, May 27, 1941; *Baltimore Sun*, May 27, 1941.

23. Key, "John H. Bankhead, Jr.," 252.

24. Senate Committee on Banking and Currency, *Hearings on HR 5990, Emergency Price Control Act* (Washington, DC: Government Printing Office, 1941); *Christian Science Monitor*, January 3, 1942.

25. R. Douglas Hurt, *Problems of Plenty: The American Farmer in the Twentieth Century* (Chicago: Ivan R. Dee, 2002), 98.

26. John H. Bankhead, "The Price Control Bill," *Montgomery Advertiser*, January 25, 1942.

27. *Chicago Tribune*, January 10, 1942; *Washington Post*, January 10, 1942.

28. *Washington Post*, January 10, 1942.

29. *Atlanta Daily World*, January 14, 1942; *Wall Street Journal*, January 31, 1942.

30. Key, "John H. Bankhead, Jr.," 275–76; Hurt, *Problems of Plenty*, 100.

31. *Birmingham News*, January 14, 1942.

32. *Birmingham News*, April 18, 1943.

33. John Mark Hansen, *Gaining Access: Congress and the Farm Lobby, 1919–1981* (Chicago: University of Chicago Press, 1991), 95.

34. Ira Katznelson, *Fear Itself: The New Deal and the Origins of Our Time* (New York: W. W. Norton, 2013), 216.

35. Key, "John H. Bankhead, Jr.," 277.

36. Charles Kenneth Roberts, *The Farm Security Administration and Rural Rehabilitation in the South* (Knoxville: University of Tennessee Press, 2015), 195–200.

37. MBO to JHBjr, November 30, 1943, box 3, MBOP; JHBjr to MBO, December 17, 1943, box 3, MBOP.

38. *New York Times*, October 17, 1943; *Washington Post*, February 12, 1944.

39. *Atlanta Constitution*, December 10, 1943.

40. *Washington Post*, January 20, 1944.

41. *Washington Post*, November 2, 1943.

42. *Washington Post*, April 7, 1943.

43. Joel Lobenthal, *Tallulah! The Life and Times of a Leading Lady* (New York: HarperCollins, 2004), 331–41.

44. Tallulah Bankhead, *Tallulah: My Autobiography* (New York: Harper, 1952), 250.

45. Bankhead, 249.

46. Bankhead, 258.

47. Lobenthal, *Tallulah!*, 342–59.

48. Bankhead, *Tallulah*, 270–74.

49. Lobenthal, *Tallulah!*, 355–62.

50. Bankhead, *Tallulah*, 269.

51. Lobenthal, *Tallulah!*, 366–67.

52. J. Mitchell Morse, "Revolution in Cotton," *New Republic*, August 19, 1946, 192–94; Ratcliff, "Revolution in Cotton," 24.

53. Hurt, *Problems of Plenty*, 68; see also Morse, "Revolution in Cotton," 192.

54. Fite, *Cotton Fields No More*, 161.

55. Charles D. Chamberlain, *Victory at Home: Manpower and Race in the American South during World War II* (Athens: University of Georgia Press, 2003), 13.

56. Chamberlain, 71, 75; *Washington Post*, January 22, 1943.

57. Chamberlain, *Victory at Home*, 70.

58. Chamberlain, 80.

59. *Baltimore Sun*, February 10, 1943.

60. 89 Cong. Rec. S262–66 (1943); *New York Times*, January 28, 1943.

61. John Hollis Bankhead Jr., "Farming to Win the War," address, Orangeburg, SC, December 2, 1942, folder 3, box 13, JHBjrP.

62. *Washington Post*, February 21, 1943.

63. *Christian Science Monitor*, March 5, 1943.

64. *New York Times*, February 22, 1943.

65. *Washington Post*, March 3, 1943.

66. *New York Times*, February 4 and 19, 1943.

67. Key, "John H. Bankhead, Jr.," 284–85; *Baltimore Sun*, March 1, 1943

68. *Alabama Journal*, March 17, 1943; *Baltimore Sun*, March 18, 1943.

69. *Chicago Defender*, April 10, 1943.

70. *Washington Post*, March 7, 1943.

71. *Christian Science Monitor*, April 21, 1943.

72. Fite, *Cotton Fields No More*, 169; Chamberlain, *Victory at Home*, 16.

73. "Senator Bankhead's Views," *Birmingham News*, September 25, 1942.

74. Fite, *Cotton Fields No More*, 150.

75. Fite, 153–56, 164, 174.

76. Chamberlain, *Victory at Home*, 43.

77. Chamberlain, 34.

78. Chamberlain, 30.

79. Quoted in Louis Ruchames, *Race, Jobs, and Politics: The Story of FEPC* (New York: Columbia University Press, 1953), 94.

80. Quoted in Neil R. McMillen, "How Mississippi's Black Veterans Remember World War II," in *Remaking Dixie: The Impact of World War II on the American South*, ed. Neil R. McMillen (Jackson: University Press of Mississippi, 1997), 102–3.

81. *Birmingham News*, August 13, 1942.

82. Katznelson, *Fear Itself*, 195–226.

83. *Montgomery Advertiser*, September 2, 1942.

84. Katznelson, *Fear Itself*, 197.

85. Kari Frederickson, *The Dixiecrat Revolt and the End of the Solid South, 1932–1968* (Chapel Hill: University of North Carolina, 2001), 39–41.

86. Katznelson, *Fear Itself*, 197.

87. Katznelson, 196.

88. Katznelson, 196.

89. Katznelson, 202.

90. 90 Cong. Rec. S4301–5 (1944).

91. Katznelson, *Fear Itself*, 222.

92. Key, "John H. Bankhead, Jr.," 301.

93. JHBjr to Oscar Johnson, July 26, 1944, JHBjrP.

94. *Birmingham News*, November 1, 1944.

95. Quoted in Key, "John H. Bankhead, Jr.," 307.

96. *Washington Post*, January 15, 1946.

97. Katznelson, *Fear Itself*, 190.

98. *Mobile Register*, January 25, 1946; 92 Cong. Rec. S1153 (1946).

99. *Birmingham News*, February 27, 1946.

100. *Birmingham News*, June 13, 1946.

101. *Washington Post*, May 21, 1946.

102. *Birmingham Post*, June 15, 1946.

103. *Birmingham Age-Herald*, June 13, 1946; *Birmingham News*, June 13, 1946; *Atlanta Constitution*, June 13, 1946; *New York Times*, June 13, 1946.

104. *Birmingham Post*, June 15, 1946.

Epilogue

1. *Gadsden (AL) Times*, June 13, 1946.

2. For a history of the Dixiecrat movement, see Kari Frederickson, *The Dixiecrat Revolt and the End of the Solid South, 1932–1968* (Chapel Hill: University of North Carolina, 2001).

3. Tallulah Bankhead, *Tallulah: My Autobiography* (New York: Harper, 1952), 282.

4. *Talladega (AL) Daily Home*, October 22, 1948.

5. *Dothan (AL) Eagle*, August 18, 1948.

6. *Decatur (AL) Daily*, October 8, 1948.

7. Joel Lobenthal, *Tallulah! The Life and Times of a Leading Lady* (New York: HarperCollins, 2004), 412–68.

8. *Anniston (AL) Star*, September 28, 1948; *Wetumpka (AL) Herald*, October 7, 1954; *Wetumpka (AL) Herald*, February 19, 1948; *Greenville (AL) Advocate*, May 26, 1955.

9. *New York Times*, December 7, 1948.

10. *Jasper (AL) Mountain Eagle*, October 31, 1957.

11. *Selma (AL) Times-Journal*, August 14, 1957; *New York Times*, March 2, 1958; *Wetumpka (AL) Herald*, March 1, 1958.

12. Lobenthal, *Tallulah!*, 497–534; *New York Times*, March 16, 1979.

Bibliography

Primary Sources

Manuscripts
Alabama Department of Archives and History (ADAH), Montgomery
Administrative Files, Alabama Department of Archives and History Papers (ADAHP).
Alabama Board of Inspectors of Convicts.
Alabama Pamphlet Collection.
Alabama World War I Service Records.
Bankhead, John Hollis. Papers (JHBP).
Bankhead, John Hollis, Jr. Papers (JHBjrP).
Bankhead, Tallulah. Papers (TBP).
Bankhead, William Brockman. Papers (WBBP).
Bankhead Family Photographs Collection.
Cobb, Rufus. Papers, Administrative Files.
Confederate Regiment History Files, Sixteenth Infantry Regiment.
Confederate Service Records.
Crow, Charles B. Papers.
Owen, Marie Bankhead. Papers (MBOP).
Owen, Marie Bankhead, and United Daughters of the Confederacy. Papers (MBO-UDC).
Owen, Thomas McAdory. Papers (TMOP).
Public Information Subject File Collection.
Secretary of State Records.
State Democratic Executive Committee. Papers.
Underwood, Oscar Wilder. Papers.

Carl Elliott Regional Library, Jasper, Alabama
James Greer Bankhead Family Bible. Transcribed. "Bankhead Family Bible" file.

Library of Congress, Washington, DC
Hobson, Richmond P. Papers (RPHP).

Lila D. Bunch Library, Belmont University, Nashville, Tennessee
Ward Seminary Bulletin.

National Archives and Records Administration, College Park, Maryland
Case Files of Applications from Former Confederates for Presidential Pardons, 1865–1867; Records of the Adjutant Generals Office, 1780s–1917; Record Group 94.

W. S. Hoole Special Collections Library, University of Alabama, Tuscaloosa
Alabama Collection.
Heflin, James Thomas. Papers (JTHP).
Hill, Lister. Papers.
McDuffie, John D. Papers.

Walker Area Community Foundation, Jasper, Alabama
Bankhead, John H. Jr. Diary.
Bankhead, William Brockman. Diary.
Bankhead House and Heritage Center Collection.

Public Records
Fayette County, Alabama, Probate Court
Deed Books. Volumes 10, 13, and 14.

Noxubee County, Mississippi
Tax Rolls. 1853. Accessed through ancestry.com.
Tax Rolls. 1861. Accessed through ancestry.com.

South Carolina Department of Archives and History, Columbia
Bankhead, George, and Elizabeth Bankhead, to Daniel McMahan. Deed. January 1, 1807.
    Union County, South Carolina, Register of Mesne Conveyances, Deed Book M, 82–83. Mi-
    crofilm reel C2208.
Bankhead, George, to John Lynn Henderson. Deed. November 25, 1816. York County, South
    Carolina, Register of Mesne Conveyances, Deed Book H, 349–50. Microfilm reel C1470.
Bankhead, James. Will. 1799. Union County, South Carolina, Probate Court, Will Book A,
    102–5. Microfilm reel C2381.

Walker County, Alabama, Probate Court
Bankhead, John Hollis. Will.

Government Documents
*An Act to Encourage National Industrial Recovery, to Foster Fair Competition, and to Provide for the
    Construction of Certain Useful Public Works, and for other Purposes (H.R. 5755).* Public Law No.
    67. Washington, DC: Government Printing Office, 1933.
Alabama Department of Archives and History. *Alabama Official and Statistical Register, 1903.*
    Montgomery, AL: Brown, 1903.
———. *Alabama Official and Statistical Register, 1907.* Montgomery, AL: Brown, 1907.
———. *Alabama Official and Statistical Register, 1915.* Montgomery, AL: Brown, 1915.
———. *Alabama Official and Statistical Register, 1919.* Montgomery, AL: Brown, 1920.
———. *Census or Enumeration of Confederate Soldiers Residing in Alabama, 1907–1908.* Mont-
    gomery: Alabama Department of Archives and History.
Bankhead, John H. *Speeches of Hon. John H. Bankhead of Alabama in the Senate of the United
    States.* Washington, DC: Government Printing Office, 1934.
———. *Speech of Hon. John H. Bankhead, February 10, 1913.* Washington, DC: Government
    Printing Office, 1913.
———. *Speech of Hon. John H. Bankhead of Alabama, in the House of Representatives, June 13, 1906.*
    Washington, DC: Government Printing Office, 1906.
*Biennial Report of the Inspectors of the Alabama Penitentiary, from September 30, 1880, to September
    30, 1882.* Montgomery, AL: Allred and Beers, 1882.
Biennial Report of the Inspectors of the Alabama Penitentiary to the Governor, 1884. Montgomery,
    AL: W. D. Brown, 1884.
Commodity Loans and Marketing Quotas, Hearings before the Committee on Agriculture and Forestry,

United States Senate. 77th Cong., 1st sess. Washington, DC: Government Printing Office, 1941.

Compiled Service Records of Volunteers Who Served during the Creek War in Organizations from the State of Alabama. Washington, DC: National Archives and Records Administration, 1957.

Congressional Record. Vol. 19 (50th Cong., 1st sess.)–Vol. 92 (79th Cong., 2nd sess.).

Department of Agriculture, Economic Research Service. "History of Agricultural Price-Support and Adjustment Programs, 1933–1984." *Agriculture Information Bulletin*, no. 485 (December 1984).

Department of Agriculture, Office of Public Roads and Rural Engineering. *Public Roads*, 1918–20.

Dimitri, Carolyn, Anne Effland, and Neilson Conklin. *The 20th Century Transformation of U.S. Agriculture and Farm Policy.* Economic Information Bulletin 3. Washington, DC: US Department of Agriculture, Economic Research Service, 2005.

First Biennial Report of the Inspectors of Convicts to the Governor, from October 1, 1884, to October 1, 1886. Montgomery, AL: Barrett, 1886.

Hobson, Richmond Pearson. *The Great Destroyer, Speech of the Honorable Richmond P. Hobson of Alabama in the House of Representatives, February 2, 1911.* Washington, DC: Government Printing Office, 1911.

———. *Income Tax and the Free List Bill, Speeches of the Honorable Richmond P. Hobson of Alabama in the House of Representatives, July 12, 1909, and April 26, 1911.* Washington, DC: Government Printing Office, 1912.

John Hollis Bankhead (Late a Senator from Alabama), Memorial Addresses Delivered in the Senate and the House of Representatives of the United States. 66th Cong., 2nd sess. Proceedings in the Senate, December 9, 1920; Proceedings in the House, January 30, 1921. Washington, DC: Government Printing Office, 1921.

Journal of the House of Representatives of the State of Alabama, Session of 1903. Montgomery, AL: Brown, 1903.

Journal of the Senate of Alabama, Session of 1903. Montgomery, AL: Brown, 1903.

Journal of the Session of 1865–66 of the House of Representatives of the State of Alabama. Montgomery, AL: Reid and Screws, 1866.

Journal of the Session of 1866–67, House of Representatives of the State of Alabama. Montgomery, AL: Reid and Screws, 1867.

National Resources Committee, Special Committee on Farm Tenancy. *Farm Tenancy: Report of the President's Committee.* Washington, DC: Government Printing Office, 1937.

Office of Public Roads, and M. O. Eldridge. *Public Road Mileage, Revenues and Expenditures, in the United States in 1904.* Bulletin 32. Washington, DC: Government Printing Office, 1907.

Owen, Thomas McAdory, ed. *Report of the Alabama History Commission to the Governor of Alabama, December 1, 1900.* Vol. 1. Montgomery, AL: Brown, 1901.

Records of the States of the United States of America: A Microfilm Collection. State of Alabama, Reel 5.

Report of the Joint Committee to Inquire into the Treatment of Convicts Employed in the Mines, and on Convict Farms, and in Any Other Place in the State. Montgomery, AL: Allred and Beers, 1881.

Senate Committee on Banking and Currency. *Hearings on HR 5990, Emergency Price Control Act.* Washington, DC: Government Printing Office, 1941.

Senator from Alabama: In re the Contest of J. Thomas Heflin v. John H. Bankhead for a Seat in the United States Senate from the State of Alabama, before the Subcommittee of the Committee on Privileges and Elections; Briefs and Arguments of Counsel. Washington, DC: Government Printing Office, 1931.

To Create the Farm Tenant Homes Corporation: Hearing before a Subcommittee of the Committee on Agriculture and Forestry, United States Senate. 74th Cong., 1st sess., March 5, 1935. Washington, DC: Government Printing Office, 1935.

US Census Bureau. *1820 Census.* Alabama, population. Published in *Alabama Historical Quarterly* 6, no. 3 (Fall 1944).

———. *1830 Census.* Alabama, population.

———. *1850 Census*. Schedule 4, Productions of Agriculture, Marion County, Alabama.

———. *1860 Census*. Schedule 4, Productions of Agriculture, Marion County, Alabama.

———. *1860 Census*. Slave Schedule, District 2, Noxubee County, Mississippi.

———. *1880 Census*. Lamar County, Alabama.

Books

Barefield, Marilyn Davis. *Old Huntsville Land Office Records and Military Warrants, 1810–1854*. Greenville, SC: Southern Historical Press, 1985.

Carter, Clarence Edwin, ed. and comp. *The Territorial Papers of the United States*. Vol. 6, *The Territory of Mississippi, 1809–1817*. Washington, DC: Government Printing Office, 1938.

Hamilton, Joseph Grégoire de Roulhac, ed. *The Papers of Thomas Ruffin*. Vol. 1. Raleigh, NC: Edwards and Broughton, 1918.

Index to Compiled Service Records of Volunteers Who Served during the Creek War in Organizations from the State of Alabama. Washington, DC: National Archives and Records Administration, 1957.

Moore, Mary Daniel [Mrs. John Trotwood], comp. *Records of Commissions of Officers in the Tennessee Militia, 1796–1815*. Baltimore, MD: Genealogical, 1977.

Saunders, James Edmond. *Early Settlers of Alabama*. Pt. 1. Tuscaloosa, AL: M. Milo McElhiney, 1963.

Newspapers

Alabama Journal (Montgomery).

Anniston (AL) Star.

Atlanta Constitution.

Atlanta Daily World.

Baltimore Sun.

Bessemer (AL) Herald-Journal.

Birmingham Age-Herald.

Birmingham News.

Birmingham News Age-Herald.

Birmingham Post.

Chicago Defender.

Chicago Tribune.

Christian Science Monitor.

Decatur (AL) Daily.

Dothan (AL) Eagle.

Evening Star (Washington, DC).

Fayette (AL) Banner.

Fayette (AL) Sentinel.

Fayette (AL) Tribune.

Gadsden (AL) Times.

Greenville (AL) Advocate.

Huntsville Daily Mercury.

Huntsville Weekly Democrat.

Jasper (AL) Mountain Eagle.

Lamar News (Vernon, AL).

London Times.

Los Angeles Times.

Mobile Register.

Mobile Times.

Montgomery Advertiser.

New York Times.

Selma (AL) Times-Journal.

Sunday American (Atlanta).

Talladega (AL) Daily Home.

Tuscaloosa Gazette.

Tuscaloosa News.

Tuscaloosa Times.

University of Alabama Alumni News (Tuscaloosa).

Vernon (AL) Clipper.

Vernon (AL) Pioneer.

Wall Street Journal.

Washington Post.

Wetumpka (AL) Herald.

Contemporary Articles

Alabama: News Magazine of the Deep South. Editorial. September 23, 1940, 1.

Bankhead, John H., Jr. "Will Government Aid for Small Farm Purchasers Solve the Tenancy Problem?" *Congressional Digest*, February 1937, 49–50.

Benjamin, Park. "Hobson's Resignation." *Independent*, February 12, 1903, 359–60.

Clark, Stetson. "Whooping Up Muscle Shoals." *Nation* 137 (August 2, 1933): 124–26.

Congressional Digest. "The Nation-Wide Problem of Farm Tenancy." February 1937, 37–38.

———. "President Roosevelt Urges Farm Tenancy Legislation." February 1937, 45.

———. "Progress Made by Major Legislation from March 29 to April 28, 1934." May 1934, 153.

———. "Should Uncle Sam Operate Muscle Shoals?" May 1930, 129–60.

Democratic Digest. "Southern Lady Makes Good in a Complicated Role." July 1937, 19.

Durand, Walter. "The Need for Public Yardsticks: Muscle Shoals, Boulder Canyon, California, St. Lawrence." *New Republic*, May 16, 1926, 30–32.

Gilfond, Duff. "The Muscle Shoals Lobby: How the Cyanamid Company Has Hoodwinked Farmers." *New Republic*, April 16, 1930, 234–36.

Hall, Gladys. "Has Hollywood Cold-Shouldered Tallulah?" *Motion Picture Magazine*, September 1932, 47, 86–87.

James, Westwood Wallace. "The Diary of Corporal Westwood Wallace James." *Civil War Illustrated*. October 1978.

Literary Digest. "Punishing Hoovercrats in Alabama." January 4, 1930, 9.

Morse, J. Mitchell. "Revolution in Cotton." *New Republic*, August 19, 1946, 192–94.

New Republic. "The Choice at Muscle Shoals." January 21, 1925, 215–17.

Newsweek. "Bankhead Birthday." April 24, 1939, 16.

———. "John Bankhead—1872–1946." June 24, 1946, 27.

———. "Share-Croppers: Whites and Negroes, under Same Roof and Union, Ask for Action and Get It." June 13, 1936, 7–8.

Plummer, Harry Chapin. "The Black Warrior River Lock and Dam." *Scientific American*, March 7, 1914, 152–53.

Ratcliff, J. D. "Revolution in Cotton." *Collier's*, July 21, 1945, 24, 40–41.

Saturday Evening Post. "The Temptation to Use Force." August 31, 1937, 22.

Time. "The Congress." January 14, 1935, 12–13.

Tucker, Ray. "A Master for the House." *Collier's*, January 5, 1935, 22, 49.

Tugwell, Rexford G. "Will Government Aid for Small Farm Purchases Solve the Tenancy Problem?" *Congressional Digest*, February 1937, 58.

Westbrook, Lawrence. "Will Government Aid for Small Farm Purchases Solve the Tenancy Problem?" *Congressional Digest*, February 1937, 63.

Plays

Owen, Marie Bankhead. *Alabama, or the Making of a State: Wherein Are Presented Some of the More Important Events in Pioneer Life and the Transition from Territory to State. Third of a Series of Historical Plays in Commemoration of the Close of a Century of Statehood.* Alabama Centennial Commission. Montgomery, AL: Paragon Press, 1919.

———. *At Old Mobile. Second of a Series of Historical Plays in Commemoration of the Close of a Century of Statehood.* Alabama Centennial Commission. Montgomery, AL: Paragon Press, 1919.

———. *The Battle of Maubilla. First of a Series of Historical Plays in Commemoration of the Close of a Century of Statehood.* Alabama Centennial Commission. Montgomery, AL: Paragon Press, 1919.

———. *De Soto and the Indians. First in a Series of Children's Plays in Commemoration of the Close of a Century of Statehood.* Alabama Centennial Commission. Montgomery, AL: Paragon Press, 1919.

———. *How Alabama Became a State. Third in a Series of Children's Plays in Commemoration of the Close of a Century of Statehood.* Alabama Centennial Commission. Montgomery, AL: Paragon Press, 1919.

———. *How Bienville Saved Mobile. Second in a Series of Children's Plays in Commemoration of the Close of a Century of Statehood.* Alabama Centennial Commission. Montgomery, AL: Paragon Press, 1919.

SECONDARY SOURCES

Books

Acee, Joe. *A History of Lamar County, from 1867 to 1972.* Rev. ed. Vernon, AL: Lamar Democrat, 1972.

Ashmore, Susan Youngblood, and Lisa Lindquist Dorr, eds. *Alabama Women: Their Lives and Times.* Athens: University of Georgia Press, 2017.

Austin, Henry. *Hobson's Choice: A Poem.* New York: R. F. Fenno, 1898.

Bankhead, Tallulah. *Tallulah: My Autobiography.* New York: Harper, 1952.

Baptist, Edward E. *The Half Has Never Been Told: Slavery and the Making of American Capitalism.* New York: Basic Books, 2014.

Bederman, Gail. *Manliness and Civilization: A Cultural History of Gender and Race in the United States, 1880–1917.* Chicago: University of Chicago Press, 1995.

Bridges, Edwin C. *Alabama: The Making of an American State.* Tuscaloosa: University of Alabama Press, 2016.

Brockman, William Everett. *The Brockman Scrapbook: Bell, Bledsoe, Brockman, Burrus, Dickson, James, Pedan, Putman, Sims, Tatum, Woolfolk and Related Families.* Minneapolis, MN: Midland National Bank, 1952.

Brundage, W. Fitzhugh. *The Southern Past: A Clash of Race and Memory.* Cambridge, MA: Belknap Press, 2005.

Carter, Dan T. *When the War Was Over: The Failure of Self-Reconstruction in the South, 1865–1867.* Baton Rouge: Louisiana State University Press, 1985.

Chamberlain, Charles D. *Victory at Home: Manpower and Race in the American South during World War II.* Athens: University of Georgia Press, 2003.

Clark, Thomas D., and John D. W. Guice. *The Old Southwest, 1795–1830: Frontiers in Conflict.* Albuquerque: University of New Mexico Press, 1989.

Clifford, J. Garry, and Samuel R. Spencer Jr. *The First Peacetime Draft.* Lawrence: University of Kansas Press, 1986.

Coker, Joe L. *Liquor in the Land of the Lost Cause: Southern White Evangelicals and the Prohibition Movement.* Lexington: University Press of Kentucky, 2007.

Cooper, William J., Jr., Thomas E. Terrell, and Christopher Childers. *The American South: A History.* Vol. 2, *From Reconstruction to the Present.* 5th ed. New York: Rowman and Littlefield, 2017.

Cox, Karen L. *Dreaming of Dixie: How the South Was Created in American Popular Culture.* Chapel Hill: University of North Carolina Press, 2011.

Curtin, Mary Ellen. *Black Prisoners and Their World: Alabama, 1865–1900.* Charlottesville: University of Virginia Press, 2000.

Daniel, Pete. *Breaking the Land: The Transformation of Cotton, Tobacco, and Rice Cultures since 1880.* Urbana: University of Illinois Press, 1985.

Danielson, Joseph W. *War's Desolating Scourge: The Union's Occupation of North Alabama.* Lawrence: University Press of Kansas, 2012.

Davis, Chester D. *One Year of the AAA: The Record Reviewed.* Washington, DC: US Department of Agriculture, 1934.

Day, James Sanders. *Diamonds in the Rough: A History of Alabama's Cahaba Coal Field.* Tuscaloosa: University of Alabama Press, 2013.

Dearing, Charles L. *American Highway Policy.* Washington, DC: Brookings Institution, 1941.

Dick, Everett. *The Dixie Frontier: A Social History.* 1948. Reprinted. Norman: University of Oklahoma Press, 1993.

Dombhart, John Martin. *History of Walker County: Its Towns and Its People.* Thornton, AR: Cayce, 1937. Reprinted. Greenville, SC: Southern Historical Press, 2002.

Douglas, Susan J., and Andrea McConnell. *Celebrity: A History of Fame.* New York: New York University Press, 2019.

Downs, Matthew L. *Transforming the South: Federal Development in the Tennessee Valley, 1915–1960.* Baton Rouge: Louisiana State University Press, 2014.

Downs, Matthew L., and M. Ryan Floyd, eds. *The American South and the Great War, 1914–1924.* Baton Rouge: Louisiana State University Press, 2018.

Dunn, Susan. *1940: FDR, Willkie, Lindbergh, Hitler: The Election amid the Storm.* New Haven, CT: Yale University Press, 2013.

Edgar, Walter B. *South Carolina: A History.* Columbia: University of South Carolina Press, 1998.

Edwards, Rebecca. *Angels in the Machinery: Gender in American Party Politics from the Civil War to the Progressive Era.* New York: Oxford University Press, 1997.

Fayette County Heritage Book Committee. *The Heritage of Fayette County, Alabama.* Clanton, AL: Walsworth, 1999.

Fayette County Historical Society. *Looking Back: Fayette County, Alabama, 1824–1974.* Fayette, AL: Fayette County Historical Society, 1974.

———. *150 Yesteryears: Fayette County, Alabama.* Vol. 2. Fayette, AL: Fayette County Historical Society, 1971.

Feldman, Glenn. *The Disfranchisement Myth: Poor Whites and Suffrage Restriction in Alabama.* Athens: University of Georgia Press, 2004.

———, ed. *Nation within a Nation: The American South and the Federal Government.* Gainesville: University Press of Florida, 2014.

———. *Politics, Society, and the Klan in Alabama, 1915–1949.* Tuscaloosa: University of Alabama Press, 1999.

Fite, Gilbert C. *American Agriculture and Farm Policy since 1900.* New York: Macmillan, 1964.

———. *Cotton Fields No More: Southern Agriculture, 1865–1980.* Lexington: University Press of Kentucky, 1984.

Fitzgerald, Michael W. *Reconstruction in Alabama: From Civil War to Redemption in the Cotton South.* Baton Rouge: Louisiana State University Press, 2017.

Flynt, Wayne. *Alabama in the Twentieth Century.* Tuscaloosa: University of Alabama Press, 2006.

Frederickson, Kari. *The Dixiecrat Revolt and the End of the Solid South, 1932–1968.* Chapel Hill: University of North Carolina Press, 2001.

Fry, Joseph A. *Dixie Looks Abroad: The South and U.S. Foreign Relations, 1789–1973.* Baton Rouge: Louisiana State University Press, 2002.

Gallagher, Gary W., and Rachel A. Sheldon, eds. *A Political Nation: New Directions in Mid-Nineteenth-Century American Political History.* Charlottesville: University of Virginia Press, 2012.

Gardner, Sarah. *Reviewing the South: The Literary Marketplace and the Southern Renaissance, 1920–1941.* Cambridge: Cambridge University Press, 2017.

Going, Allen Johnston. *Bourbon Democracy in Alabama, 1884–1890*. Tuscaloosa: University of Alabama Press, 1951.

Green, Elna C. *Southern Strategies: Southern Women and the Woman Suffrage Question*. Chapel Hill: University of North Carolina Press, 1997.

Hackney, Sheldon. *Populism to Progressivism in Alabama*. Princeton, NJ: Princeton University Press, 1969.

Hamilton, Virginia Van der Veer. *Hugo Black: The Alabama Years*. Baton Rouge: Louisiana State University Press, 1972.

———. *Lister Hill: Statesman from the South*. Chapel Hill: University of North Carolina Press, 1987.

Hansen, John Mark. *Gaining Access: Congress and the Farm Lobby, 1919–1981*. Chicago: University of Chicago Press, 1991.

Hays, Samuel P. *Conservation and the Gospel of Efficiency: The Progressive Conservation Movement, 1890–1910*. 1959. Reprinted. Pittsburgh, PA: University of Pittsburgh Press, 1999.

Hobson, Richmond Pearson. *The Sinking of the Merrimac: A Personal Narrative of the Adventure in the Harbor of Santiago de Cuba, June 3, 1898, and of the Subsequent Imprisonment of the Survivors*. New York: Century, 1899.

Hoganson, Kristin L. *Fighting for American Manhood: How Gender Politics Provoked the Spanish-American and Philippine-American Wars*. New Haven, CT: Yale University Press, 1998.

Holley, I. B., Jr. *The Highway Revolution, 1895–1925*. Durham, NC: Carolina Academic Press, 2008.

Hubbard, Preston J. *Origins of the TVA: The Muscle Shoals Controversy, 1920–1932*. New York: W. W. Norton, 1968.

Hubbs, G. Ward. *Tuscaloosa: 200 Years in the Making*. Tuscaloosa: University of Alabama Press, 2019.

Hurt, R. Douglas. *Problems of Plenty: The American Farmer in the Twentieth Century*. Chicago: Ivan R. Dee, 2002.

Ingram, Tammy. *Dixie Highway: Road Building and the Making of the Modern South, 1900–1930*. Chapel Hill: University of North Carolina Press, 2014.

Jackson, Walter M., and Marie Bankhead Owen. *History of Alabama for Junior High Schools*. Montgomery, AL: Dixie Book, 1938.

Jacobs, Meg. *Pocketbook Politics: Economic Citizenship in Twentieth-Century America*. Princeton, NJ: Princeton University Press, 2005.

Johnson, Evans C. *Oscar W. Underwood: A Political Biography*. Tuscaloosa: University of Alabama Press, 1980.

Johnson, Walter. *Soul by Soul: Life inside the Antebellum Slave Market*. Cambridge, MA: Harvard University Press, 1999.

Karnes, Thomas L. *Asphalt and Politics: A History of the American Highway System*. Jefferson, NC: McFarland, 2009.

Katznelson, Ira. *Fear Itself: The New Deal and the Origins of Our Time*. New York: W. W. Norton, 2013.

Keith, Jeanette. *Rich Man's War, Poor Man's Fight: Race, Class, and Power in the Rural South during the First World War*. Chapel Hill: University of North Carolina Press, 2004.

Keller, Morton. *Affairs of State: Public Life in Late Nineteenth Century America*. Cambridge, MA: Harvard University Press, 1977.

Kerwin, Jerome G. *Federal Water-Power Legislation*. New York: Columbia University Press, 1926.

Kester, Howard. *Revolt among the Sharecroppers*. 1936. Reprinted. Knoxville: University of Tennessee Press, 1997.

Lamar County Heritage Book Committee. *History of Lamar County, Alabama*. Clanton, AL: Heritage, 2000.

Lesseig, Corey T. *Automobility: Social Changes in the American South, 1909–1939*. New York: Routledge, 2009.

Leuchtenburg, William E. *Franklin D. Roosevelt and the New Deal, 1932–1940.* New York: Harper and Row, 1963.

Lewis, Herbert James. *Clearing the Thickets: A History of Antebellum Alabama.* New Orleans: Quid Pro Books, 2013.

Link, Arthur S. *The Higher Realism of Woodrow Wilson and Other Essays.* Nashville, TN: Vanderbilt University Press, 1971.

Lobenthal, Joel. *Tallulah! The Life and Times of a Leading Lady.* New York: HarperCollins, 2004.

Lord, Clifford L., ed. *Keepers of the Past.* Chapel Hill: University of North Carolina Press, 1965.

MacDonald, Austin F. *Federal Aid: A Study of the American Subsidy System.* New York: Thomas Y. Crowell, 1928.

Mackrell, Judith. *Flappers: Six Women of a Dangerous Generation.* New York: Farrar, Straus and Giroux, 2013.

Mancini, Matthew J. *One Dies, Get Another: Convict Leasing in the American South, 1866–1928.* Columbia: University of South Carolina Press, 1996.

McIlwain, Christopher Lyle. *Civil War Alabama.* Tuscaloosa: University of Alabama Press, 2016.

McMillan, Malcolm Cook. *Constitutional Development in Alabama, 1798–1901: A Study in Politics, the Negro, and Sectionalism.* Chapel Hill: University of North Carolina Press, 1955.

McMillen, Neil R., ed. *Remaking Dixie: The Impact of World War II on the American South.* Jackson: University Press of Mississippi, 1997.

McPherson, James M. *Battle Cry of Freedom: The Civil War Era.* New York: Oxford University Press, 1988.

Moore, Albert Burton. *History of Alabama.* University, AL: University Supply Store, 1934.

Newell, Herbert Moses, Jr., and Jeanie Patterson Newell. *History of Fayette County, Alabama.* Fayette, AL: Newell Offset, 1960.

Noe, Kenneth W., ed. *The Yellowhammer War: The Civil War and Reconstruction in Alabama.* Tuscaloosa: University of Alabama Press, 2013.

Odegard, Peter H. *Pressure Politics: The Story of the Anti-Saloon League.* New York: Columbia University Press, 1928.

Olsson, Tore C. *Agrarian Crossings: Reformers and the Remaking of the US and Mexican Countryside.* Princeton, NJ: Princeton University Press, 2017.

Owen, Marie Bankhead. *Alabama: An Economic and Political History of the State.* Illustrated by Nathan Glick. Montgomery, AL: Dixie Book, 1937.

———. *From Campfire to Cahaba.* Montgomery, AL: Dixie Book, 1936.

———. *The Story of Alabama: A History of the State.* New York: Lewis Historical, 1949.

———. *Yvonne of Braithwaite: A Romance of the Mississippi Delta.* Boston: L. C. Page, 1927.

Owen, Marie Bankhead, and Mary Edward Mitchell. *Our Home Land.* Illustrations by Nathan Glick. Montgomery, AL: Dixie Book, 1936.

Owen, Thomas McAdory. *History of Alabama and Dictionary of Alabama Biography.* 4 vols. Chicago: S. J. Clarke, 1921.

Ownby, Ted, ed. *Manners and Southern History.* Jackson: University Press of Mississippi, 2011.

Peiss, Kathy. *Cheap Amusements: Working Women and Leisure in Turn-of-the-Century New York.* Philadelphia: Temple University Press, 1986.

Peiss, Kathy, and Christina Simmons, eds. *Passion and Power: Sexuality in History.* Philadelphia: Temple University Press, 1989.

Perman, Michael. *Pursuit of Unity: A Political History of the American South.* Chapel Hill: University of North Carolina Press, 2009.

———. *Struggle for Mastery: Disfranchisement in the South, 1888–1908.* Chapel Hill: University of North Carolina Press, 2001.

Preston, Howard Lawrence. *Dirt Roads to Dixie: Accessibility and Modernization in the South, 1885–1935.* Knoxville: University of Tennessee Press, 1991.

Reps, John W. *Washington on View: The Nation's Capital since 1790.* Chapel Hill: University of North Carolina Press, 1991.

Richards, Henry I. *Cotton under the Agricultural Adjustment Act: Developments up to July 1934.* Washington, DC: Brookings Institution, 1934.

Roberts, Charles Kenneth. *The Farm Security Administration and Rural Rehabilitation in the South.* Knoxville: University of Tennessee Press, 2015.

Rogers, William Warren, Robert David Ward, Leah Rawls Atkins, and Wayne Flynt. *Alabama: The History of a Deep South State.* Tuscaloosa: University of Alabama Press, 1994.

Rogers, William Warren, Jr. *Confederate Home Front: Montgomery during the Civil War.* Tuscaloosa: University of Alabama Press, 1999.

Rohrbough, Malcolm J. *Trans-Appalachian Frontier: People, Societies, and Institutions, 1775–1850.* Bloomington: Indiana University Press, 2008.

Rosenfeld, Harvey. *Richmond Pearson Hobson: Naval Hero from Magnolia Grove.* Las Cruces, NM: Yucca Tree Press, 2000.

Ruchames, Louis. *Race, Jobs, and Politics: The Story of FEPC.* New York: Columbia University Press, 1953.

Seely, Bruce E. *Building the American Highway System: Engineers as Policy Makers.* Philadelphia: Temple University Press, 1987.

Shogan, Robert. *Backlash: The Killing of the New Deal.* Chicago: Ivan R. Dee, 2006.

Smith, Rose Marie. *Lamar County, Alabama: A History to 1900.* Fulton, MS: n.p., 1987.

Storey, Margaret M. *Loyalty and Loss: Alabama's Unionists in the Civil War and Reconstruction.* Baton Rouge: Louisiana State University Press, 2004.

Teeple, F. W., and A. Davis Smith. *Jefferson County and Birmingham, Alabama: Historical and Biographical, 1887.* Birmingham, AL: Teeple and Smith, 1887.

US Department of Transportation, Federal Highway Administration. *America's Highways, 1776–1976: A History of the Federal-Aid Program.* Washington, DC: Government Printing Office, 1977.

Walker County Heritage Book Committee. *The Heritage of Walker County, Alabama.* Clanton, AL: Heritage, 1999.

Ward, Robert David, and William Warren Rogers. *Convicts, Coal, and the Banner Mine Tragedy.* Tuscaloosa: University of Alabama Press, 1987.

Weaver, John D. *The Brownsville Raid.* New York: W. W. Norton, 1970.

Webb, Samuel L. *Two-Party Politics in the One-Party South: Alabama's Hill Country, 1874–1920.* Tuscaloosa: University of Alabama Press, 1997.

Webb, Samuel L., and Margaret E. Armbrester, eds. *Alabama Governors: A Political History of the State.* Tuscaloosa: University of Alabama Press, 2001.

Wiggins, Sarah Woolfolk. *The Scalawag in Alabama Politics, 1865–1881.* Tuscaloosa: University of Alabama Press, 1977.

Willis, Kenneth D. *The Harnessing of the Black Warrior River.* Tuscaloosa, AL: City of Tuscaloosa, 1989.

Wilson, Theodore Brantner. *The Black Codes of the South.* University: University of Alabama Press, 1965.

Zeitz, Joshua. *Flapper: A Madcap Story of Sex, Style, Celebrity, and the Women Who Made America Modern.* New York: Three Rivers Press, 2006.

Articles

Bailey, Fred Arthur. "Mildred Lewis Rutherford and the Patrician Cult of the Old South." *Georgia Historical Quarterly* 78, no. 3 (Fall 1994): 509–35.

Bankhead, John Hollis. "The Alabama-Mississippi Boundary." In *Transactions of the Alabama Historical Society,* vol. 2, *1897–1898,* edited by Thomas McAdory Owen, 90–93. Tuscaloosa: Alabama Historical Society, 1898.

Bernstein, Barton J. "Clash of Interests: The Postwar Battle between the Office of Price Administration and the Department of Agriculture." *Agricultural History* 41, no. 1 (January 1967): 45–58.

Danbom, David B. "Rural Education Reform and the Country Life Movement." *Agricultural History* 53, no. 2 (April 1979): 462–74.

Davis, R. O. E. "Muscle Shoals, Nitrogen and Farm Fertilizers." *Annals of the American Academy of Political and Social Science* 135 (January 1928): 157–65.

Douglas, Paul H. "The Development of a System of Federal Grants-in-Aid I." *Political Science Quarterly* 35, no. 2 (June 1920): 255–71.

———. "The Development of a System of Federal Grants-in-Aid II." *Political Science Quarterly* 35, no. 4 (December 1920): 522–44.

Fite, Gilbert C. "Farmer Opinion and the Agricultural Adjustment Act, 1933." *Mississippi Valley Historical Review* 48, no. 4 (March 1962): 656–73.

———. "Voluntary Attempts to Reduce Cotton Acreage in the South, 1914–1933." *Journal of Southern History* 14, no. 4 (November 1948): 481–99.

Garrett, William Robertson. "The Work of the South in the Building of the United States." In *Transactions of the Alabama Historical Society*, vol. 3, *1898–99*, edited by Thomas McAdory Owen, 27–45. Tuscaloosa: Alabama Historical Society, 1899.

Grantham, Dewey W., Jr. "The Southern Senators and the League of Nations, 1918–1920." *North Carolina Historical Review* 26, no. 2 (April 1949): 187–205.

Harper, Glenn T. "'Cotton Tom' Heflin and the Election of 1930: The Price of Party Disloyalty." *Historian* 30, no. 3 (May 1968): 389–411.

Jacobs, Meg. "'How about Some Meat?': The Office of Price Administration, Consumption Politics, and State Building from the Bottom Up, 1941–46." *Journal of American History* 84, no. 3 (December 1997): 910–41.

Jakeman, Robert J. "Marie Bankhead Owen and the Alabama Department of Archives and History, 1920–1955." *Provenance: Journal of the Society of Georgia Archivists* 21, no. 1 (2003): 36–65.

Johnson, Evans C. "John H. Bankhead 2d: Advocate of Cotton." *Alabama Review* 41 (January 1988): 30–58.

———. "Oscar Underwood and the Hobson Campaign." *Alabama Review* 16 (April 1963): 125–40.

Jones, Allen W. "Political Reform and Party Factionalism in the Deep South: Alabama's 'Dead Shoes' Senatorial Primary of 1906." *Alabama Review* 26 (January 1973): 3–32.

Lapp, John A. "Federal Grants in Aid." *American Political Science Review* 10, no. 4 (1916): 738–43.

Link, Arthur S. "The Underwood Presidential Movement of 1912." *Journal of Southern History* 11, no. 2 (May 1945): 230–45.

Matthews, Bruce F. "The 1914 Cotton Crisis in Alabama." *Alabama Review* 46 (January 1993): 3–23.

McFarland, Charles K. "The Federal Government and Water Power, 1901–1913: A Legislative Study in the Nascence of Regulation." *Land Economics* 42, no. 4 (November 1966): 441–52.

Melman, Seymour. "An Industrial Revolution in the Cotton South." *Economic History Review* 2, no. 1 (1949): 59–72.

Monroe, Alden N. "Thomas Owen and the Founding of the Alabama Department of Archives and History." *Provenance: Journal of the Society of Georgia Archivists* 21, no. 1 (January 2003): 22–35.

Pisani, Donald J. "Water Planning in the Progressive Era: The Inland Waterways Commission Reconsidered." *Journal of Policy History* 18, no. 4 (November 2006): 389–418.

Reagan, Hugh D. "Race as a Factor in the Presidential Election of 1928 in Alabama." *Alabama Review* 19 (January 1966): 5–19.

Robins, Glenn. "Lost Cause Motherhood: Southern Women Writers." *Louisiana History: The Journal of the Louisiana Historical Association* 44, no. 3 (Summer 2003): 275–300.

Schapsmeier, Edward L., and Frederick H. Schapsmeier. "Farm Policy from FDR to Eisenhower: Southern Democrats and the Politics of Agriculture." *Agricultural History* 53, no. 1 (January 1979): 352–71.

Shaw, Barton. "The Hobson Craze." *US Naval Institute Proceedings* 102 (February 1976): 54–60.

Sheldon, Richard. "Richmond Pearson Hobson as a Progressive Reformer." *Alabama Review* 25 (October 1972): 243–61.

Stephenson, Wendell H. "Some Pioneer Alabama Historians: III. Thomas M. Owen." *Alabama Review* 2 (January 1949): 45–62.

Vance, Rupert B. "Human Factors in the South's Agricultural Readjustment." *Law and Contemporary Problems* 1, no. 3 (June 1934): 259–74.

Ward, William C. "The Building of the State." In *Transactions of the Alabama Historical Society*, vol. 4, *1899–1903*, edited by Thomas McAdory Owen, 64–66. Montgomery: Alabama Historical Society, 1904.

Webb, Samuel L. "Hugo Black, Bibb Graves, and the Ku Klux Klan: A Revisionist View of the 1926 Alabama Democratic Primary." *Alabama Review* 57 (October 2004): 243–73.

Dissertations and Theses

Cooke, Leonard Calvert. "The Development of the Road System of Alabama." Master's thesis, University of Alabama, 1935.

Hackett, Berkeley North. "Walker County, Alabama, 1850 to 1950: A Migration Study." Master's thesis, University of Alabama, 1974.

Hamner, Ned. "The Congressional Career of John Hollis Bankhead, Jr." Master's thesis, University of Alabama, 1951.

Heacock, Walter Judson. "William Brockman Bankhead: A Biography." PhD diss., University of Wisconsin, 1952.

Hunt, Robert Eno. "Organizing a New South: Education Reformers in Antebellum Alabama, 1840–1860." PhD diss., University of Missouri, 1988.

Key, Jack Brien. "John H. Bankhead, Jr.: Creative Conservative." PhD diss., Johns Hopkins University, 1964.

Koster, Margaret Shirley. "Congressional Career of John Hollis Bankhead." Master's thesis, University of Alabama, 1931.

Pittman, Walter E., Jr. "Navalist and Progressive: The Life of Richmond P. Hobson." Master's thesis, Kansas State University, 1981.

Pross, Edward Lawrence. "A History of Rivers and Harbors Appropriation Bills, 1866–1933." PhD diss., Ohio State University, 1938.

Sheldon, Richard Neil. "Richmond Pearson Hobson: The Military Hero as Reformer during the Progressive Era." PhD diss., University of Arizona, 1970.

Electronic Sources

Encyclopedia of Alabama. *http://encyclopediaofalabama.org*

Braund, Kathryn. "Creek War of 1813–1814." Updated January 30, 2017.

Ezzell, Patricia Bernard. "Wilson Dam and Reservoir." Updated June 16, 2020.

Jackson, Harvey H. "Alabama Bourbons." Updated October 17, 2016.

Monroe, Alden N. "Thomas M. Owen." Updated December 10, 2014.

Murray, Jennifer M. "Richmond Pearson Hobson." Updated April 21, 2015.

Suitts, Steve. "Hugo L. Black." Updated January 31, 2017.

Upchurch, Thomas Adams. "John Tyler Morgan." Updated May 28, 2014.

Ward, Robert David. "Rufus W. Cobb." Updated November 13, 2016.

Watson, Elbert L. "Luke Pryor." Updated November 22, 2010.

Wiggins, Sarah Woolfolk. "Lewis Eliphalet Parsons." Updated September 15, 2015.

Other Electronic Sources

Roosevelt, Eleanor. "My Day." January 10, 1938. *Eleanor Roosevelt Papers Digital Edition*. Last modified June 9, 2017. https://www2.gwu.edu/~erpapers/myday/displaydoc.cfm?_y=1938&_f=md054847.

Samuel, Howard D. "Troubled Passage: The Labor Movement and the Fair Labor Standards Act." *Monthly Labor Review*, December 2000, 32–37. https://www.bls.gov/opub/mlr/2000/12/art3full.pdf.

Turk, Richard W. "Richmond Pearson Hobson." *American National Biography Online.* Published December 2, 1999. https://anb.org.

Weingroff, Richard F. "Federal Aid Road Act of 1916: Building the Foundation." *Public Roads* 60, no. 1 (Summer 1996). Updated January 31, 2017. http://www.fhwa.dot.gov/publications/publicroads/96summer/p96su2b.cfm.

———. "Zero Milestone." *Highway History.* Federal Highway Administration, Department of Transportation. Updated June 27, 2017. https://www.fhwa.dot.gov/infrastructure/zero.cfm.

Unpublished Text

Phillips, Emily A. "'A Bankhead without a Tongue Is No Good to the State of Alabama': Marie Bankhead Owen, Tallulah Bankhead, and Subversions of Normative Gender Conventions." April 2019. Graduate research seminar, Dr. Margaret Peacock, University of Alabama. Unpublished paper in author's possession. Used by permission.

Index

Page numbers in italics refer to figures.